Multi-Story Air-Supported and Fluid-Inflated Building Structures

Concepts, Design Principles, and Prototypes

Jens Pohl

Professor of Architecture (Emeritus)
California Polytechnic State University
San Luis Obispo, California

Published by: Jens G. Pohl
ISBN 978-0-9755698-8-7

Second Edition - July 2014

Copyright © 2014 Jens G. Pohl
All rights reserved.
ISBN 978-0-9755698-8-7

Table of Contents

Chapter 1: Historical Roots 15
    1.1   Heavyweight Construction as an Architectural Paradigm 19
    1.2   Structural Efficiency Principles 20
    1.3   Hydraulics and Pneumatics 21

Chapter 2: Slender Column Challenges 27
    2.1   The Buckling Phenomenon 28
    2.2   The Original Concept 29
    2.3   A Logical Explanation 30
    2.4   An Exhilarating Idea 32
    2.5   Structural Flexible Membrane Columns 32
           2.5.1   The Experimental Investigation 34
           2.5.2   Analysis of Experimental Results 37
           2.5.3   Theoretical Analysis 40
           2.5.4   Comparison of Theoretical and Empirical Results 43

Chapter 3: Multi-Story Air-Supported Buildings 47
    3.1   A Multi-Story Building as a Pressurized Column 49
    3.2   Physiological Aspects 52
    3.3   Membrane Materials 53
           3.3.1   Tensile Strength 53
           3.3.2   Weatherability 54
           3.3.3   Fire Resistance 54
    3.4   Pressure-Utilization Efficiency 55
    3.5   Fire Protection 57
    3.6   Building Services 58
           3.6.1   Thermal Insulation 59
           3.6.2   Water Supply and Sanitary Fittings 61
    3.7   Cable-Networks 63
    3.8   General Safety Considerations 66
    3.9   Erection and Construction Considerations 68
    3.10 Comparative Cost Projections 75

Chapter 4: Bracing of Multi-Story Air-Supported Buildings 81

   4.1   Wind Forces 81

   4.2   Restoring Force Due to Internal Pressure 83

   4.3   External Stabilizing Tension Net 88

   4.4   Shear Walls and Stabilizing System 90

   4.5   Summary of Structural Design Procedures 91

        4.5.1   Multi-Story Air-Supported Buildings without Cable-Networks ... 91

        4.5.2   Multi-Story Air-Supported Buildings with Cable-Networks 92

        4.5.3   Reexamination of the Principal Design Equations 94

        4.5.4   Typical Multi-Story Air-Supported Office Building Structure 97

        4.5.5   Typical Multi-Story Air-Supported Tower Structure 100

        4.5.6   Comparison of Office Building and Tower Structure 104

Chapter 5: Two Prototype Multi-Story Air-Supported Buildings 107

   5.1   Single-Skin with Cable-Network Prototype 107

        5.1.1   Site Selection 107

        5.1.2   Design 108

        5.1.3   Construction Details 111

        5.1.4   Construction Planning 113

        5.1.5   The Construction Phase 116

        5.1.6   Operation and Erection Test 117

   5.2   Multi-Cellular Multi-Enclosure Prototype 118

        5.2.1   Design 119

        5.2.2   Construction Details 121

        5.2.3   Construction Phase 122

        5.2.4   Operation and Performance 124

Chapter 6: Multi-Story Air-Supported and Fluid-Inflated Building Types 127

   6.1   Principal Building Types 128

        6.1.1   The Pressurization Medium 131

        6.1.2   Column Height and Slenderness Ratio 133

   6.2   A Prototype Fluid-Inflated Experimental Building 135

   6.3   Further Structure-Environment Interface Possibilities 139

        6.3.1   Heat Pipe Technology 140

        6.3.2   The Collector-Storage Interface 142

        6.3.3   Air-Inflated Concentrating Solar Collectors 142

   6.4   A Multi-Story Pneumatic Greenhouse 144

	6.4.1	Project Objectives	145
	6.4.2	Structural Considerations	145
	6.4.3	Selection of Material	146
	6.4.4	General Design Considerations	147
	6.4.5	The Floor System	148
	6.4.6	The Access System	150
	6.4.7	The Prototype Model	151
	6.4.8	Structural Stability of the Model	156
	6.4.9	Non-Structural Feasibility Considerations	156

Chapter 7: Air-Supported and Fluid-Inflated Rigid Membrane Structures 159

7.1	Pressurized Rigid Membrane Structures	160
7.2	Feasibility of Rigid Membrane Building Structures	163
7.3	Previous Work in Historical Context	164
	7.3.1 Early Experimental Observations	164
	7.3.2 The Small Deflection Theory	165
	7.3.3 The Large Deflection Theory	166
	7.3.4 Design Formulas Based on Empirical Results	170
	7.3.5 The Plastic Buckling Theory	172
	7.3.6 Pressurized Monocoque Cylinders	173
	7.3.7 Conclusions and Terms of Reference	176
7.4	An Additional Experimental Investigation	178
	7.4.1 Design of the Test Cylinders	178
	7.4.2 The Test Procedure	181
	7.4.3 Analysis of the Experimental Results	182
	7.4.4 Conclusions and Design Implications	187
7.5	Potential Rigid Membrane Building Applications	192
	7.5.1 Multi-Story Air-Supported Rigid Membrane Buildings	194
	7.5.2 Fluid-Inflated Rigid Membrane Columns	197
	7.5.3 Example of a Fluid-Inflated Column	198
	7.5.4 Structural Design Procedure for Fluid-Inflated Columns	200
	Case 1 and Example 1	201
	Case 2 and Example 2	203
	Case 3 and Example 3	206
	Case 4 and Example 4	209
7.6	Summary of Rigid Membrane Analysis Proposals	213

Chapter 8: Pressurized Cable Floor and Roof Systems 219

8.1 Circular Pneumatic Cable Floors 219
- 8.1.1 Construction and Safety Considerations 224
- 8.1.2 Cables and Connections 229
- 8.1.3 Design Process for Circular Pneumatic Cable Floors 233
- 8.1.4 Example Design of Two Pneumatic Cable Floors 236
  - Example 1 (150 FT diameter floor) 236
  - Example 2 (300 FT diameter floor) 241
  - Comparison of Examples 1 and 2 244

8.2 Circular Pneumatic Cable Roofs 245
- 8.2.1 Example Design of Two Pneumatic Cable Roofs 246
  - Example 1 (200 FT diameter roof) 246
  - Example 2 (400 FT diameter roof) 250
  - Comparison of Examples 1 and 2 253

8.3 Rectangular Fluid-Inflated Cable Floors 254
- 8.3.1 Constructional Aspects of Fluid-Inflated Cable Floors 258
- 8.3.2 Design Process for Fluid-Inflated Cable Floors 259
- 8.3.3 Example Design of Two Fluid-Inflated Cable Floors 264
  - Example 1 (100 FT span rectangular floor) 264
  - Example 2 (200 FT span rectangular floor) 270
  - Comparison of Examples 1 and 2 277

8.4 Comparison of Pneumatic and Fluid-Inflated Cable Floors 280

References and Bibliography 283

Appendix A: Single-Story Air-Supported and Air-Inflated Structures 299
- A-1 Air-Building Types 302
- A-2 Intrinsic Structural Morphology 305
- A-3 Comparison of Air-Building Types 307
- A-4 Air-Building Technology 311
  - A-4.1 Basic Shapes 312
  - A-4.2 Access and Exit Facilities 314
  - A-4.3 Physical Dimensions and Stresses 314
  - A-4.4 Lighting, Thermal Insulation, and Ventilation 318
  - A-4.5 Wind Loads 320
- A-5 Tension Cables and Nets 322
- A-6 Soap Bubbles 325
- A-7 Mathematical Analysis 327

A-8   Anchorage Forces and Methods 328
A-9   Ancillary Plant 331
A-10 Membrane Materials 332
    A-10.1 Fire Hazard 334
    A-10.2 Fabrication 334
A-11 Geometry of Single-Story Air-Buildings 335
    A-11.1 Full Profile and Low Profile Domes 336
        A-11.1.1 Design of Low Profile Dome 338
            Panel width for given material roll width 339
            Quantity of membrane material required 341
            Membrane weight 341
            Membrane stress without external cables 341
            Membrane stress with external cables 342
            Cable stress (dome) 343
            Anchorage forces 344
        A-11.1.2 Design of Full Profile Dome 345
            Panel width for given material roll width 346
            Quantity of membrane material required 346
            Membrane weight 347
            Membrane stress without external cables 347
            Anchorage forces 347
    A-11.2 Full Profile and Low Profile Elongated Air-Buildings 347
        A-11.2.1 Design of Low Profile Elongated Air-Building 348
            Panel width for given material roll width 350
            Quantity of membrane material required 351
            Membrane weight 352
            Membrane stress without external cables 352
            Membrane stress with external cables 353
            Cable stress barrel vault 353
            Membrane and cable stress (dome ends) 354
            Anchorage forces 356
        A-11.2.2 Design of Full Profile Elongated Air-Building 357
            Panel width for given material roll width 358
            Quantity of membrane material required 359
            Membrane weight 359
            Membrane stress without external cables 359
            Membrane stress with external cables 359
            Cable stress (barrel vault) 360
            Membrane and cable stress (dome ends) 361
            Anchorage forces 363

Appendix B: Pneumatic-Within-Pneumatic Dwellings **365**

    B-1   The Pneumatic-Within-Pneumatic Approach 366

    B-2   The Conceptual Design 367

            B-2.1   Structural Considerations 368

            B-2.2   Thermal Considerations 375

            B-2.3   Architectural Planning 377

    B-3   Postscript 382

Definition of Mathematical Symbols **383**

Keyword Index **395**

Preface to the Second Edition

What is new in this 2nd Edition? Since the first publication of this book on multi-story pneumatic and fluid-inflated building structures in 2013 the author has continued research into extensions of the same principles to large span floors and roofs. Whereas the initial focus was on lightweight vertical structures such as air-supported multi-story buildings with flexible plastic membrane enclosures and pressurized thin-walled columns with rigid metal walls, the new research has centered on lightweight horizontal structures. Chapter 7, which previously included an introductory section on pneumatic cable floors, has been divided into two chapters. Chapter 7 now deals exclusively with vertical rigid membrane air-supported and fluid-inflated building structures. The previous Section 7.6 dealing with pneumatic cable floor systems has been expanded into Chapter 8. Due to the comprehensiveness of the new research Chapter 8 has grown in size beyond Chapter 7.

Original Preface. This book is about a very different kind of architecture than the buildings we see around us at the beginning of the 21st Century. The buildings we work in or call our homes are typically constructed of timber, masonry, reinforced concrete, or steel and in many cases combinations of these traditional construction materials. The notion that weight and rigidity are associated with strength and safety is deeply entrenched in our understanding of the built environment in which we are firmly *situated*.

Added to this is our human aversion to change. Our cognitive system is based on experience. We collect this experience throughout our life and feel most confident and comfortable with what we already know. It is therefore quite natural for us to form an attachment to the past, including the vernacular that we grew up in. Our taste in architecture is molded from our earliest childhood experiences and only slightly modified as it is passed from generation to generation. In this way, new architectural styles are seldom major deviations from the past but rather extensions and refinements of existing perceptions and practices. Even though technology in many fields, particular in the information sharing and processing domain, has seen revolutionary advances this has not led to any major changes in the design and construction of buildings.

Buildings today are still largely static structures with little thought given to useful lifespan, structural efficiency and mechanical economy, environmental impact, and material consumption. The constraints that govern building design are not severe. They are based on the duration and cost of construction, the availability of materials and labor, resale value based largely on adherence to existing aesthetic norms, building regulations enforced by local government agencies, and only recently the need for energy conservation. Such constraints do not call for radical solutions. In fact, quite the opposite is true. The dominance of cost considerations tends to encourage conformance to existing practices and aesthetic values. A much more severe constraint such as a minimum weight or sealed environment criterion would call for radically different building design solutions.

Considering this societal context it is no wonder that when the well known aeronautical engineer, Frederick Lanchester, was invited to address the annual meeting of the Manchester Society of Engineers in England in 1932 his presentation was met with surprise, disbelief and skepticism. He proposed a building supported wholly by air. Even though he presented the concept of an air-supported structure with a great deal of logic, detailed design suggestions, and was even able to point to actual modular field hospital implementations during World War I, there was many a learned engineer in the audience who thought that the elderly presenter was no longer in full command of his faculties. The proposal was simply too far removed from the reality of existing building construction practices. Faced with the severe constraints of a mobile field hospital unit that was of minimum weight, could be rapidly manufactured in quantity, was able to be erected by a small team in less than an hour, could be easily packaged and transported to any site, and was relatively inexpensive, Lanchester's brilliant engineering mind had conceived a novel solution. A solution that met all design criteria, but was so far removed from the prevailing architecture and engineering paradigm that it was unacceptable and perhaps incomprehensible to many members of that community.

Midway through his undergraduate architectural studies at the University of Melbourne in Australia the author became intrigued by what appeared to be an inefficiency of compression members (i.e., columns) in building structures. In his structural mechanics courses he discovered the well known fact that all but the shortest columns tend to deflect laterally under vertical loading. Structural engineers had been well aware of this phenomenon, commonly referred to as *overall buckling*, for more than two centuries. To compensate for this structural behavior the column must be either braced at intermediate points or engineers must follow the more common practice of increasing the thickness of the column shaft. This latter remedy did not appeal to the uncompromising purist principles of a budding young architect. On further exploration the author found to his chagrin that even in the story-height columns of two and three-story buildings over 30% of the thickness of the column shaft was necessary to overcome the inherent buckling problem. To the author this appeared to be an unacceptable structural inefficiency for two reasons. First, since the behavior of such columns under axial vertical loads is as much a stability failure as a material failure, it did not seem possible to design a structure that could fully utilize the compressive strength of the column material. Second, the more slender the column the more severe the tendency to buckle, thereby setting a limit on the potential elegance of vertical structural members.

Through somewhat faulty initial reasoning the author conceived an idea of how the tendency for slender columns to buckle under axial loads could be counteracted. This idea led to the exploration of a novel approach to the structural support of multi-story buildings, namely *fluid-supported* construction that forms the subject of this book. The author postulated that maintaining tension throughout the shaft of a slender column should mitigate the tendency of that column to buckle. It should be possible to create such a tension state by selecting a circular column cross-section, in the form of a hollow pipe, and filling the inside of the column with a liquid or gas (i.e., a fluid) under pressure. To ensure that any axial compressive load imposed on the upper end of the column would not be transmitted to the circular column wall, the author designed an elaborate piston mechanism at that end. In this way the compression load acting downward would be resisted directly by the internal column pressure acting upward. To the surprise of his professors the author was able to demonstrate with a scale model that a very slender[1] hollow, circular column pressurized internally to over 2,000 pounds per square inch of water pressure could resist an axial load that was twice as high as that predicted theoretically. However, the explanation of this result was quite different from the initial reasoning of the author. Even though the column wall might be under tension, the fluid inside the column will itself act as a column and since it is contained by the solid column wall the net effect will still be a buckling of the column as a whole. The reason why the load-bearing capacity of the column with the internal fluid pressure is significantly

---

[1] The slenderness ratio of the first experimental column tested by the author exceeded 200.

greater than an identical empty column will be explained in the chapter on Slender Pressurized Columns.

The author realized that even if the load-bearing capacity of slender columns could be doubled with internal pressure, such columns would still have only very limited value and probably no application in building construction. One day, while agonizing over this dilemma, an inspiration suddenly came to the author: Could an entire multi-story building be considered as a column? To the author this was an electrifying idea that marked the beginning of several years of intensive research into fluid-supported systems of building construction. In particular, it opened up a whole range of structural solutions involving thin-walled cylindrical shells, which are also subjected to instability failure due to a different kind of buckling. In such structures the external wall is very thin in comparison with the diameter of the column. Consider for example a 10-story circular building of 80 feet diameter, with an external wall that is made of a thin material capable of resisting tension but not compression. If the air inside the building were to be pressurized then it should be possible to suspend the floors of the building from the roof, which would be supported by the air pressure. The thin building envelope would be acting in tension to contain the air pressure. The failure mechanism of such a thin-walled cylindrical shell structure is due to crinkling or *local buckling* of the thin membrane enclosure. This failure mechanism is well known to mechanical engineers in the design of pressure vessels.

As is the nature of research, an inspiration may after further scrutiny not lead to the hoped for solution. However, it may well open up related areas of research that eventually lead to solutions that are far superior to the potential promise of the initial idea. In this particular case the concept of a slender pressurized column, while certainly interesting from a theoretical point of view, did not hold out much promise for practical application in the construction of buildings. On the other hand, the notions of an entire building supported by an elevated internal air pressure or a building supported by one or more large-diameter, pressurized, thin-walled columns could be a more attractive proposition. Particularly in situations where either weight constraints or the need for an artificially maintained atmosphere are dominant design criteria, fluid-supported structures may offer the only viable solution. Certainly, such situations exist in both extraterrestrial and under-water environments. In the case of building structures in space both the need for an artificially maintained atmosphere and the enormous cost associated with the transportation of material to the building site, are very favorable to a fluid-supported construction solution. In the case of under-water construction there is less concern about material weight, but the same need for maintaining an artificial atmosphere. In both cases the ability to utilize the artificial atmosphere that is essential for the preservation of life also as a principal structural element of the habitat is surely a decided advantage.

This book explores a wide range of fluid-supported building structures, based on the research performed by the author during doctoral studies at the University of Sydney in Australia and subsequent work with several large scale experimental structures at the University of New South Wales in Australia and the California Polytechnic State University (Cal Poly, San Luis Obispo) in the United States (U.S.). Most of this work was performed in the late 1960s and early 1970s.

The reader may well ask: What is the relevance of the subject of fluid-supported construction today, if the initial discoveries and research work in this field occurred more than 40 years ago? Even the increasing concern about embedded energy in construction materials will not in the foreseeable future lead to the adoption of minimum weight design criteria for buildings. However, the prospects for applying fluid-supported principles for the design of extraterrestrial structures are not only promising but in fact essential. In this case, where the cost of transporting every pound of material weight into space is prohibitively expensive, structural efficiency and minimum weight criteria are an essential requirement. In addition, the ability to combine the life support system with the structural functions by making additional use of the artificial atmosphere that must be provided in any habitable extraterrestrial building for structural support purposes is surely a significant advantage.

Even though air-supported multi-story structures cannot be considered more than a curiosity for Earth-based applications at this time, they are discussed in this book in all seriousness with a particular focus on construction methods, pressurization facilities, fire protection, and safeguards to prevent structural failure during occupancy. In addition, several chapters are devoted to the exploration of terrestrial building applications that are feasible and practical at this time. Among these are: self-inflatable, fully air-supported greenhouse units that can be packaged and dropped by parachute into remote regions; low cost, air-inflated, concentrating solar collectors; multi-level air-supported dwellings; and, buildings in which fluid-supported columns serve the triple functions of structural support, solar heat storage, and heat distribution in an environmentally and structurally integrated system.

Finally, the purpose of this book is to show that there are many possibilities for alternative approaches to building construction that are ready for application in situations where the constraints are much more severe than is currently the case on Earth. It provided an opportunity for the author to revisit a subject that he pursued with a great deal of passion and enjoyment during the earliest stages of his professional career. Hopefully, the reader will derive some pleasure and creative stimulation from sharing in this discourse on multi-story air-supported and fluid-inflated building structures.

All of the structures discussed are essentially classified as cylindrical shells with internal fluid pressure, acting either as vertical columns or horizontal struts. Chapters 2, 3, 4 and 5 are focused on flexible membrane shells with and without an external cable-network for reinforcement purposes. In such pressurized structures the combination of a cable-network made of steel surrounding a flexible membrane made of a synthetic material such as plastic is particularly well matched. Due to its much lower modulus of elasticity the membrane bulges out between cables thereby greatly reducing the stresses experienced by the membrane, since these stresses are a function of the radius of curvature of the membrane.

Chapter 7 deals exclusively with rigid membrane shells that lack the ductility of flexible membrane materials and are therefore subject to a different failure mode under axial load. Prediction of the critical stress that causes local buckling failure of these cylindrical shells has been a focus of theoretical and empirical research for the past century. While their structural behavior is now well understood, the influence of unavoidable initial geometric and material imperfections in the rigid membrane does not allow an accurate theoretical failure load prediction.

Chapter 6 groups fluid-supported building structures into multi-story air-supported buildings in which the habitable building environment is pressurized and fluid-inflated columns that can serve as the vertical support structure of a multi-story building in which the habitable spaces remain at ambient atmospheric pressure. This chapter also discusses the possibility of combining the structural support system of the latter type of building with its environmental control system. A two-story prototype building in which a rigid membrane central column supports floors suspended from roof level and serves as a heat store for air-inflated concentrating solar collectors is discussed in some detail.

Appendices A and B deal exclusively with single-story air-supported buildings that have been in common use for mostly large-span applications since the 1940s. Those sections are included for the sake of completeness, since these more common air-buildings are part of the field of fluid-supported structures. However, in Section A-11 of Appendix A the geometry and step-by-step design of both high profile and low profile air-supported domes and barrel vaults with quarter-spherical ends are treated in detail.

Jens Pohl, *May 2014*

Chapter 1
Historical Roots

The title of this introductory chapter is somewhat of a misnomer. It might suggest that the concepts and principles related to air-supported and fluid-inflated building structures that are described in this book arose directly from the initial interest and practical implementation of air-building technology that climaxed in the middle of the 20th Century. For a period of some 20 years extending from about 1955 to 1975, single-story air-supported buildings were seen as offering a low cost solution for large area buildings such as warehouses, exhibition halls and sports stadiums. In some cases such as exhibition halls and swimming pool covers the design criteria included the need for mobility, however, in virtually all cases these buildings were considered to be a temporary solution. In fact, the author was only vaguely aware of this kind of lightweight building structure when the first thoughts of utilizing internal fluid pressure as a structural element crossed his mind.

During the final two years of his undergraduate architectural studies the author had often pondered with some degree of discontent about an apparent lack of innovation in the construction of buildings. Certainly in comparison with many other technologies it seemed that there had been very little fundamental change in systems and methods of building construction for the past several decades. Since innovation usually follows a perceived need or threat, one could argue that throughout recorded history there has not been any extraordinary pressure exerted on building technology and therefore there has been little incentive to innovate. Certainly there has been no driving force comparable to the threat of nuclear weapons that led to the accelerated development of nuclear physics during the later part of World War II.

Historical evidence gleaned from archeological excavations suggests that the earliest materials used by man for works of construction were earth, stone and timber. Of these, only earth in the form of baked bricks and stone may be considered as relatively durable materials, virtually unaffected by natural precipitation. The significant lack of tensile strength of stone (i.e., a mere 50 to 100 pounds per square inch (psi) in tension compared to 20,000 to 50,000 psi in compression) forced mankind at a very early stage in technical development to accept massive compression construction as the most useful structural system. Wood fibers and reeds with a potential tensile capacity of a few thousand pounds per square inch could not be accepted as reliable structural components due to their scarcity in many regions and due to the acute danger of destruction by fire and lack of resistance to insects (e.g., termites) and decay. Therefore, in view of the superior compressive strength of available materials it is not surprising to find that man readily accepted the principles of what might be referred to as massive compression construction.

However, there remained the problem of spanning horizontal distances. Only very short stone lintels and no real stone beams were possible, due to the significant role that tensile strength plays in such components. Where possible this inadequacy was overcome temporarily by the use of timber beams and later, more permanently by the development of more sophisticated horizontal compression structures such as the arch, vault and dome. Heralded as major technological advances in building construction technology by most historians, they pale in comparison with what has been achieved in the last half of the 20th Century in the fields of aviation, computer technology and communication systems.

Additional innovation had to wait for the discovery of new materials. Gradually man developed the ability to separate metals from ore, although at first in fairly small quantities and only sufficient for jewelry, weapons, tools, and fastening devices. Until the end of the 17th century, iron for example, had never been used as a principal structural material (Pannell 1964).

In the 1850s, with the discovery of steel and its economical production by means of the Bessemer process, entirely new structural possibilities emerged. In one giant stride the tension gap had been breached with a material capable of developing a tensile strength more than equal to its compressive capability. Although not fully understood at the time, the foundations of tensile construction had been laid. In fact, however, the original system of compression construction was not significantly changed and the new material was mostly heralded in terms of durability, fire-resistance and greater compressive strength.

Figure 1.1: The Brooklyn Bridge designed by John Roebling and constructed by his son Washington Roebling was completed in 1883. [New York Post, June 30, 2008[1]]

From this point onward a rapid increase in the tension capacity of steel alloys ensued. World War I one saw the development of aircraft steel with a tensile strength of up to 120,000 psi. A few years later chrome-nickel steel with an ultimate tensile strength of over 300,000 psi was found to have numerous uses in connection with the advent of jet-travel. After World War II a great deal of research was directed to the development of high strength crystals and plastic fibers. It was shown that tensile strengths in the vicinity of 5,000,000 psi are theoretically possible although not practical at that time. However, even if they do become practical and economical through mass production, they are unlikely to find much utilization in the existing paradigm of building construction.

---

[1] http://www.nypost.com/seven/07302008/news/regionalnews/crisis_puts_ny_in_sell_hell_122211.htm

Use of the new-found tensile capability of materials was first made, in the engineering field, by the development of suspension bridges. In 1814 Telford (Pannell 1964) designed a suspension bridge of 1000 feet across the Mersey River at Runcorn (U.K.). While this project was not executed it did nevertheless serve as a forerunner to the highly successful Menai suspension bridge (Straits of Menai, U.K.) completed in 1826 (Smiles 1966). This was followed by the development of wire-cables, a process normally credited to Roebling (Fuller 1968, Pannell 1964), and the advent of continuous suspension that remained unchanged in principle for many years to come. Roebling's greatest achievement was undoubtedly the Brooklyn Bridge connecting the New York City boroughs of Manhattan and Brooklyn in the U.S. (Pannell 1964), which was suspended over a distance of more than 1500 feet and completed toward the end of the 19th Century (Figure 1.1). The Brooklyn Bridge was the first of a whole series of wire-cable suspension bridges, the construction of which has continued to the present day.

Figure 1.2: The Dorton Arena in Raleigh, South Carolina, designed by Matthew Nowicki as a saddle-shaped tensile cable structure, was completed in 1952. [Petroski H., Pushing the Limits[2]]

The adoption of similar tension systems in building construction has been much more gradual and less popular. Probably the first suspended cable roofs appeared in Russia in the 1890s, designed by the Russian engineer Shookhov (Bethlehem Steel 1967). These examples included pavilions for the Nijny-Novgorod Industrial Fair and workshops for the Bary Boilerworks in Moscow, roofed over by a network suspension system with a maximum span of around 220 feet. There followed a period of singular inactivity until Nowicki's design for the Raleigh Arena in North Carolina (U.S.) was adopted in 1954 (Hottinger 1962). Since then a modest number of cable-network roof structures have been erected in the U.S., Europe and Russia, notable exponents being Otto in Germany (Otto 1961), Le Ricolais in France and the U.S. (Le Ricolais 1962), Jawerth in Sweden (Hottinger 1962, Bethlehem Steel 1967), Liudkovsky in Russia (Bethlehem Steel 1967), and others (Figures 1.2, 1.3 and 1.4).

---

[2] Petroski H., Pushing the Limits: New Adventures in Engineering; http://www.ralphmag.org/DN/engineering.html

Figure 1.3: Dulles International Airport designed by Eero Saarinen was completed in 1965[3].

Figure 1.4: Arizona Veterans Memorial Coliseum in Phoenix, Arizona designed by T. Y. Lin International[4] as a hyperbolic paraboloid cable-network, was completed in 1965.

During the late 1920s the first proposals were made to incorporate tension systems in multi-story construction. These involved the introduction of suspended floors in tall buildings, utilizing cables or hangers normally anchored to the foundations for pre-stressing purposes. A multi-story

---

[3] Image released into the public domain by its author, JetBlastBWI, under the English Wikipedia project.

[4] http://www.arcaro.org/tension/album/arizona.htm ; T. Y. Lin International , Album of Space Structures.

suspension system consists basically of a hanging skeleton composed primarily of vertical tension members that are suspended from the top of a massive central compression core. Projects of this type include the designs of the 4D Tower Garage in 1927 by Buckminster Fuller, the Moscow Lenin Library in 1927 by Leonidow, a Buenos Aires office building in 1938 by Williams, a Chicago office building in 1948 by Goldsmith, the Rotterdam Observation Tower in 1957 by Broek and Bakema, the Beach Hotel in 1961 by Otto, the BMW Tower in Munich by Schwarzer, and others (Roland 1963), but relatively few of these have been actually constructed. A notable exception was the construction of the BMW Office Building in Munich, Germany, which was completed in 1972 and consists of four circular modules of 22 suspended floors representing a four-cylinder engine.

1.1 Heavyweight Construction as an Architectural Paradigm

It would be appropriate to analyze some of the fundamental tendencies embodied in the foregoing discussion. There is no doubt that the radical increase in the tensile strength of construction materials, together with the scarcity of skilled labor in the technically more advanced countries has had at least some influence on the design of large building structures. However, the impact has been spasmodic with a focus on architectural design uniqueness and nowhere near as significant as in the fields of aeronautical and mechanical engineering.

In defense it must be stated that the building industry has clearly neither experienced the same design incentives nor been subjected to the weight penalties that have been imposed on other industries, such as the transportation industry. For example, in aircraft design structural dead-weight is at a premium, thus forcing the designer to optimize the strength-weight ratio of the supporting structure. At the beginning of the 21st Century with the increasing cost and politically constrained availability of oil, even the structural weight of automobiles, railcars and all kinds of large and small water vessels has become a major design concern.

In the case of a multi-story building, on the other hand, weight is considered to be a significant design criterion only in as far as this will affect the design of members that transfer this load to the foundations. It is not uncommon to come across architecture and construction publications in which it is stated with at least a certain degree of implied pride that thousands of tons of steel have been or will be used in the construction of a particular building. Furthermore, it is still common practice to use relatively heavy materials (e.g., bricks and pre-cast concrete panels) for non-structural purposes in tall buildings. Why should such an obvious anomaly exist in an otherwise highly technical and economy conscious society? The author ventures to suggest the following answers. First, it is human nature to consider a heavy item to be a strong item. Therefore, a majority of persons involved in the building industry, including building owners, intuitively consider a heavy structure to be a safe and reliable structure. Second, there is the serious problem of fire-protection that is commonly solved by the addition of a fairly thick layer (i.e., 2 to 3 inches) of concrete, thereby giving each structural component a specific fire-rating. The weight added by the concrete at between 100 and 140 pounds per cubic foot of material certainly does not provide an incentive for the application of minimum weight design criteria. Third, there still exists even among some architects the misconception that a heavy material such as concrete is also a good thermal insulator. That it simply takes longer for the heat to flow through from one surface to the other, because the heavier material is capable of absorbing more heat, is not intuitively obvious[5]. Once this initial time lag has been passed the heat flow is relatively uninhibited.

---

[5] The heat capacity of a material is a product of the weight and specific heat of the material (Pohl 2007, 65-83).

However, finally there exists another significant factor. The principles of the compression system of building construction mitigate against structural economy in terms of weight reduction.

Compression failures normally occur due to instability, especially when we try to reduce the overall massiveness of the structural system. Steel has a comparatively high compressive strength yet long before a yield point is reached a slender column will deflect beyond acceptable safety limits due to *buckling*. After the load has been removed the member will return to its original shape without any resultant material damage. This inherent instability behavior that even moderately slender compression members are subject to has historically impeded the application of a minimum weight design criterion in multi-story building design. The accepted remedy has been to increase the cross-sectional thickness of the member beyond the purely compressive requirements to overcome the buckling tendency. Needless to say, if material strength is only of minor consequence to the overall stability of a structural system, why bother with high quality materials, exact methods of calculation, and minimization of structural weight. It would appear that our structural heritage in building construction is at least one factor in our willingness to continue to accept sub-optimally designed building structures.

For high strength materials to be effectively used in building structures a fairly substantial reorientation of the building industry as a whole will be necessary. Experience has shown that such a paradigm shift can occur on an evolutionary timescale over long periods of time, in which case it is typically discerned from historical analysis often long after it has occurred. These are the kind of changes in the design and construction of buildings that our world has experienced in the past. However, it can also occur on a revolutionary timescale over a relatively short period of time as we are currently experiencing in the information technology field. In the latter case we are faced by new threats such as fierce economic competition, diminishing energy resources, uneven distribution of food supplies, and terrorism that are all driving a paradigm shift in communication and information management technology. Only to survive those kinds of threats to our economic and physical welfare, do we appear to be grudgingly willing to change our ways. No such forces have so far in human history been imposed on the built environment.

1.2 Structural Efficiency Principles

The first instance of external forces causing a paradigm shift in the construction principles of human shelters will occur in extraterrestrial structures. Currently, space exploration is still a modestly funded research activity that is driven more by human curiosity and scientific interest than dire need. This may well change in future generations and concurrently lead to a greater desire to apply the experience gained from designing structures under more highly constrained criteria on Earth as well. Extraterrestrial construction factors such as the minimization of the weight of material that has to be transported to the building site in space, the need for an artificial atmosphere inside the building or building complex, complete self-sufficiency of the built environment, shielding from radiation, and so on, are all radical design criteria that have so far been relegated to a very small number of esoteric research projects on Earth.

As a starting point under the far less constrained environmental conditions on Earth much could be achieved by the application of more rigorous scientific principles to the assessment of such design criteria as factor of safety, live-loads, building life-span, and overall structural economy. The basis of such an approach has been prepared in advance by aeronautical engineers over the past 50 years. In particular, the author would like to draw attention to two engineering principles that are fundamental to the concept and design criteria of air-supported and fluid-inflated building construction systems.

Minimal Structure: A minimal structure can be defined as a structure that utilizes a minimum of material, thereby leading to a high degree of mechanical efficiency (Howard 1966). The definition implies: that any load imposed on one section of the structure is immediately distributed equally to all parts of the structure; that the kind of stress experienced by the structure is one, which if increased, would finally cause material failure (as distinct from stability failure); and that the material has a high strength to weight ratio for the type of stress it will experience in the structure.

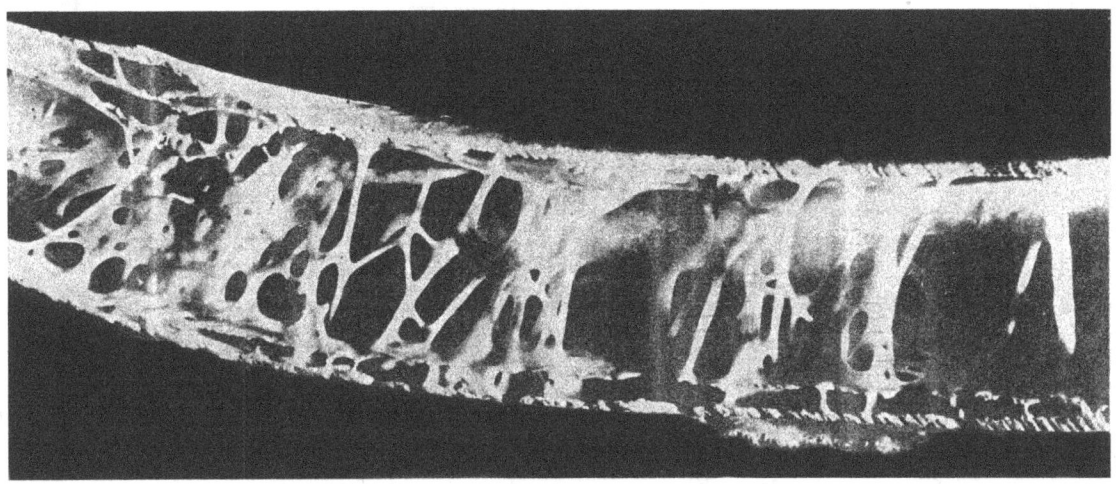

Figure 1.5: Human first metatarsal bone
[Thompson D. W., On Growth and Form, Cambridge University Press, London, UK, 1942]

Nature produces structures that appear to at least approximate to this concept of efficiency. As shown in Figure 1.5, in animals the skeleton is progressively shaped by the forces that act upon individual bones during their growth period (Thompson 1942), while in plants the cellulose fibers are arranged according to functional necessity. Both Buckminster Fuller (Fuller 1968) and Otto (Otto and Trostel 1962) have pointed out the significant role played by hydraulics in botanical and biological structures, where nature has utilized the non-compressibility of liquids as one of its principal structural principles. Examples are found not only in the branches of trees and slender vine stems, but also in organic containers where skin membranes are stressed by internal blood and tissue pressure.

Mechanical Economy: As the primary characteristic of a minimal structure, mechanical economy implies both an economy of means by relating structural design to the general intellectual principle of maximum result for least effort (Siegel 1962) and also financial economy because it may be very time consuming and thus expensive to reduce the material content to a minimum (Howard 1966).

1.3 Hydraulics and Pneumatics

The inherent mechanical economy of hydraulics and pneumatics has been apparent to mankind as far back as the Greek and Roman ages. The primary factors that contribute to this mechanical economy may be summarized as follows: fluids transmit imposed forces equally in all directions and this transfer is almost instantaneous; fluid containers experience tensile stresses only, since a direct compression load imposed on the fluid is transformed into a pressure that must be resisted by the container in tension; and, the vertical load-bearing capacity of a closed fluid container is governed by the relative areas on which pressure and load are imposed.

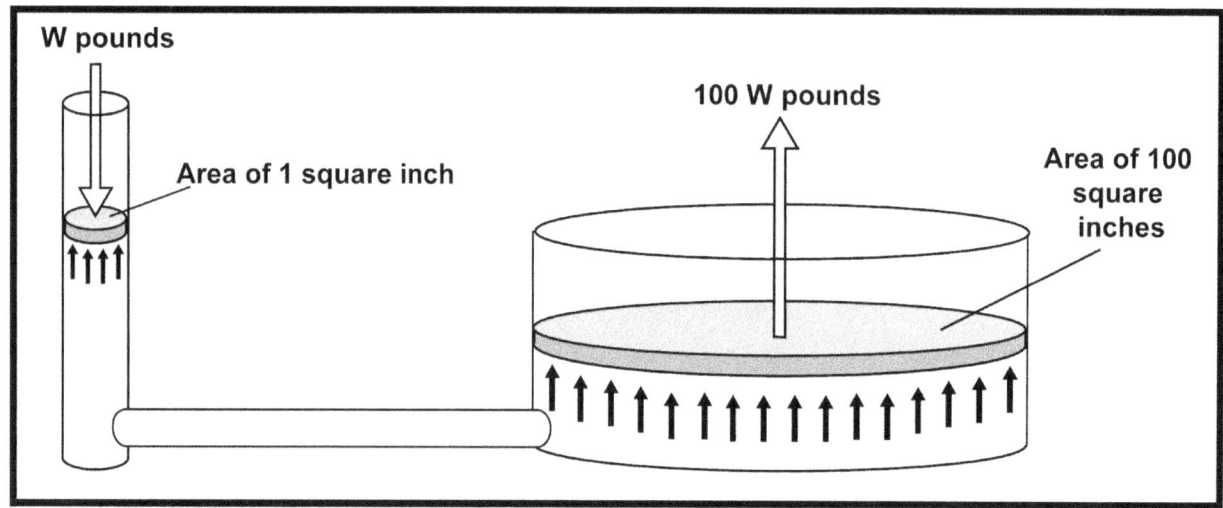

Figure 1.6: Mechanical advantage of a hydraulic system[6].

The latter factor implies the existence of a potential pressure to load-bearing capacity advantage. Certainly the concept of a hydraulic advantage has been long recognized and applied with great success (Figure 1.6). In postulating the possibility of applying either hydraulics or pneumatics to building structures it is of interest to note that magnification of scale appears to be a favorable proposition. While hydraulic and pneumatic pressures are typically rated in pounds of load on the fluid *per square inch* of area (psi), building loads are measured in pounds of load *per square foot* of area (psf). For example, a relatively small fluid pressure of 1 to 10 psi equates to a potential load-bearing capacity in a building structure of 144 to 1,440 psf.

The sail, which is basically a membrane stretched by aerodynamic pressure differences, is probably the oldest form of pneumatic structure devised by man (Otto and Stromeyer 1961). Over centuries the shape and position of the sail has been perfected in respect to its specific function and required flexibility. However, the balloon also must be considered as a prototype pneumatic structure with a long history (Davy 1950). In 1783 the Montgolfier brothers constructed a hot-air balloon with a volume of some 23,000 cubic feet, which ascended to a height of about 6,000 feet. At the time the true explanation of the hot-air balloon's ability to rise was not known. It was instead credited to the presence of an unknown gas often described as Montgolfier's Gas. This misconception persisted until the French physicist De Saussure (Davy 1950) discovered the rarefaction of air as its temperature rises toward the end of the 18th Century.

---

[6] According to Pascal's Law an increase in pressure at any point in a confined liquid produces an equal increase in pressure at any other point in the container. The W pound load acting on a piston of 1 square inch area in the small container causes a pressure of 100W pound in lifting a piston of 100 square inches area in the larger container.

Balls, tires, rubber dinghies, air-cushions, inflatable furniture, pressure vessels as well as high pressure gas storage tanks (i.e., gasometers) all illustrate further developments of these beginnings. Today they form part of the product line of not just one industry, but a considerable number of diverse groups with little, if any, sharing of engineering design and manufacturing knowledge. For example, the problems encountered during the design and manufacture of car tires, rubber dinghies and air-supported buildings may be similar in several respects and yet these problems are being solved by engineers of quite different disciplines, normally without the slightest interaction.

In the building construction field, the first attempt at the design of a pneumatic building in the form of an air-supported roof is attributed to the English aeronautical engineer Frederick Lanchester (Kingsford 1960, Lanchester 1938). During World War I, in response to the urgent need for temporary buildings and shelters for a multitude of purposes, he prepared a model of a field hospital covered by an air-supported roof membrane. This first known proposal for a single-story air-supported building resembled a cylindrical shell with hemispherical ends, anchored to the ground and inflated internally at a small pressure. In 1917 Lanchester was awarded two patents incorporating the principles of this scheme, however, the signing of the Armistice Agreement prevented the field hospital project from being implemented. It was not until the early 1920s that this innovative building construction concept resurfaced in the form of an exhibition building (Figures 1.7) comprising substantially built masonry walls roofed over by an air-supported canvas dome. The dome was restrained by a system of primary cables. A similar scheme was prepared a year later by Lanchester's brother, a Fellow of the Royal Institute of British Architects (Figure 1.8).

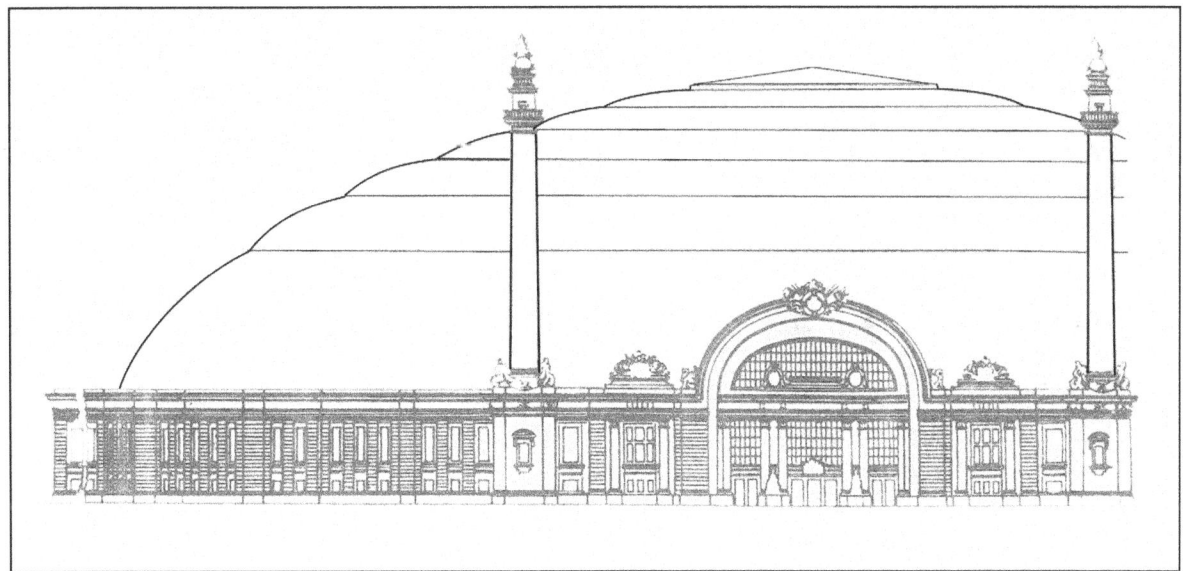

Figure 1.7: Lanchester's concept of an air-supported roof for an exhibition building[7].

In November of 1938 Lanchester accepted an invitation to present the second annual lecture to the Manchester Association of Engineers (Lanchester 1938). The title of the lecture *Span*, while not really in the field of aeronautical engineering, allowed Lanchester to introduce his own highly

---

[7] Design prepared together with his brother (Henry V. Lanchester) who was an architect. The building was over 1,000 FT in diameter and utilized cables to reinforce the air-supported membrane and define the structural form.

creative thoughts to the field of architectural engineering. After a preliminary analysis of the suspension and cantilever systems of construction by a method of mechanical equivalence, he finally introduced his audience to the concept of an "... air-borne span". In his own words:

> "... it must have been some years before the War of 1914 that an idea came to me, one which seemed at the time to be no more than an inventor's dream. With an indulgent smile I dismissed it from my mind. The idea, to put it tersely, was an inflated roof."

To illustrate this structural principle he had constructed a model and produced drawings of an exhibition building. Basically, a masonry surround roofed by means of an air-supported canvas dome restrained by exterior cables (Figure 1.9). He proposed that the pressure within the dome be sustained by the action of wind through cowlings or by air-blowers (Lanchester 1938). Lanchester did not see any of his projects executed.

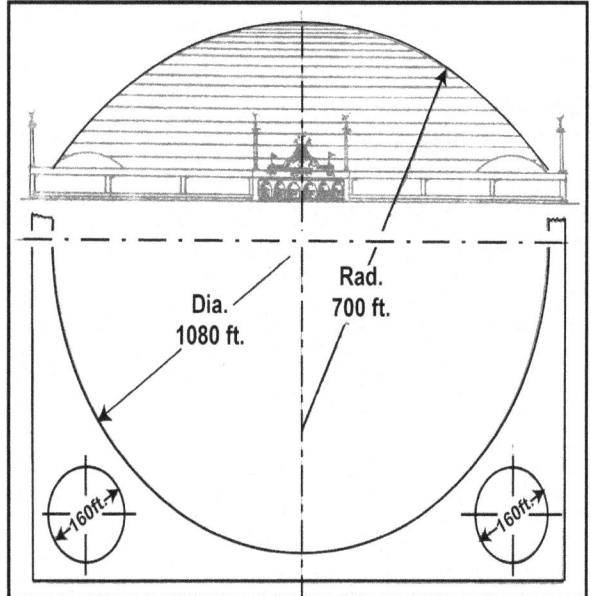 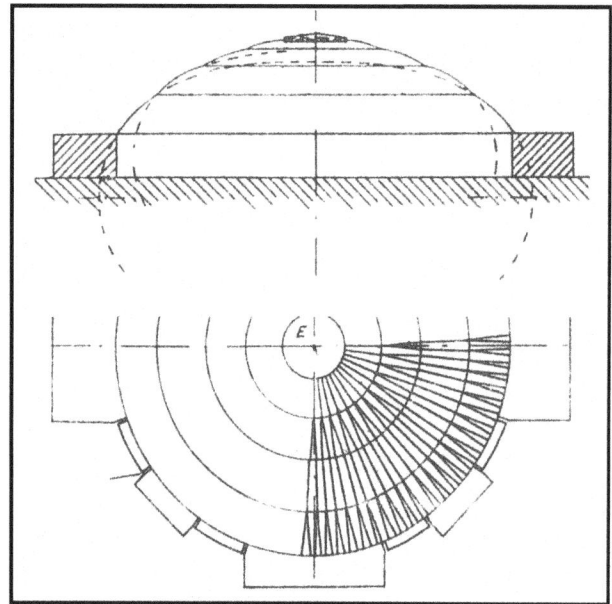

Figure 1.8: Design by Lanchester's brother   Figure 1.9: Lanchester's original drawings

During the 1930s in the U.S. Stevens (Otto and Trostel 1962) tried to force along the development of air-supported structures. However, the practical solution belonged to Walter Bird, who built a number of air-supported halls after World War II. In 1946, when the air-building development began to accelerate, Bird was a young engineer, employed at the Cornell Aeronautical Laboratory (U.S.), a non-profit independent research adjunct of Cornell University (Allison 1959). With research funds provided by the U.S. Air Force, a task group under Bird's direction designed, built, and successfully tested a prototype air-building for the weather protection of large radar antennas planned for the Arctic. By 1954 there were hundreds of these bubble-shaped plastic structures scattered across the U.S. and Canada (Allison 1959).

A number of coincident developments had taken place to make air-supported buildings a practical proposition, namely: the development of plastic materials capable of withstanding severe weather exposure and solar radiation; the chemical industry succeeded in developing synthetic materials with more advantageous strength-weight ratios than aluminum and steel; and, the invention of sealing systems stable under severe wind loads (in excess of 100 mph). As the practicality of air-supported buildings became apparent, a number of companies such as Birdair, U.S. Rubber

Company, Irwin, and Texair in the U.S., Schjedahl in Sweden, and Krupp and Stromeyer in Germany, were formed and began to design, manufacture and promote air-supported structures throughout the world.

Concurrently with this wave of interest in single-story air-supported building structures, a systematic and highly innovative investigation into pneumatic structures as a form-giving element in building design was conducted by Frei Otto in conjunction with the Washington University of St. Louis, Yale University and the Hochschule für Gestaltung at Ulm (Germany) in the period 1958 to 1961, and from 1962 onward at the Entwicklungsstätte für den Leichtbau (Berlin, Germany) under the sponsorship of Stromeyer and Company. This research group has at various times included Koch (U.S.), Miles (U.S.), Trostel (Germany), and others (Otto and Stromeyer 1961, Otto and Trostel 1962).

Despite this initial enthusiasm only a relatively small number of air-supported halls were erected during the 1960s mainly for sport, convention, exhibition, and military purposes, mostly in the U.S. and Europe. The construction of the Fuji Group Pavilion at the EXPO'70 World Fair in Osaka, Japan (Dent 1971) and the Second International Symposium on Pneumatic Structures organized by the International Association for Shell and Spatial Structures (IASS) in Delft, Netherlands in September 1972 (IASS 1972) marked the culmination of this relatively widespread interest in air-buildings. The proceedings of the Delft Symposium list, apart from air-building fabric suppliers, over 200 firms actively engaged in the manufacture and construction of air-supported structures. Thereafter, toward the mid and late 1970s references to air-supported structures became less frequent and finally quite rare as virtually all of the larger commercial companies that had initially embraced this promising new market quickly phased out their fledgling air-building departments.

Although, as stated earlier, the multi-story air-supported and fluid-inflated building system concepts and principles that form the focus of this book are not directly based on the technical foundations of single-story air-supported structures they are certainly related to each other within the same family of lightweight structures. It would therefore seem to be somewhat of an omission not to at least provide an overview of the history, structural principles, and constructional aspects of single-story air-buildings for the sake of completeness. The author's solution to this quandary has been the inclusion of Appendix A, which summarizes the evolution and practical implementation of single-story air-supported building structures.

Chapter 2
Slender Column Challenges

It may indeed seem strange that the application of pneumatic construction to multi-story structures did not develop directly from the single-story air-supported buildings described in Appendix A. Although proposals incorporating two or three floor levels in inflated spheres have been made in the past, these proposals cannot be credited with forming the beginnings of multi-story air-supported construction. They may be more appropriately viewed as a sophisticated form of the single-skin air-building type. An exception may be the tension structure research that Engineering Professor Robert Le Ricolais (1894-1977) performed with graduate students in the Institute of Architectural Research at the University of Pennsylvania in the late 1950s (Le Ricolais 1962). The *Cosmorama* model depicted in Figure 2.1 suggests a multi-story structure with what appear to be suspended floors and a very elegantly configured external membrane envelope. Whether the internal space enclosed by the envelope was intended to be pressurized for purposes of supporting the roof and floors is not clear. However, even though Le Ricolais' proposal may have been treated more as a theoretical exercise than a practical building proposal, the structure would certainly be feasible as a multi-story air-supported building.

Figure 2.1: Model of a multi-level tension structure proposed by Le Ricolais in 1960

In 1966, during a research program[1] dealing with the structural aspects of pressurized, cylindrical columns, the author was struck by an idea from which developed during the following two years a completely new system of multi-story construction. The idea itself and its logical basis are briefly described in this chapter.

---

[1] The research was conducted by the author in the Department of Architectural Science at the University of Sydney and subsequently in the School of Building at the University of New South Wales (Sydney, Australia) during the period 1966 to 1972.

2.1 The Buckling Phenomenon

For some years prior to 1966, the author had been thinking about tension structures in general and, in particular, the fundamental structural inefficiency of slender compression members. It is well known that a slender column will ultimately collapse due to buckling, which is considered to be a stability failure. In fact, as long as the elastic limit of the material is not exceeded, the buckled column will return to its original position without any resultant material damage after the superimposed load has been removed. Although it is true that slender columns are normally avoided in building construction, being replaced by frames consisting of shorter struts, this in itself could be considered as a validation of the inherent inefficiency of structural compression members. The author therefore gave considerable thought to the question of achieving economies in compression members.

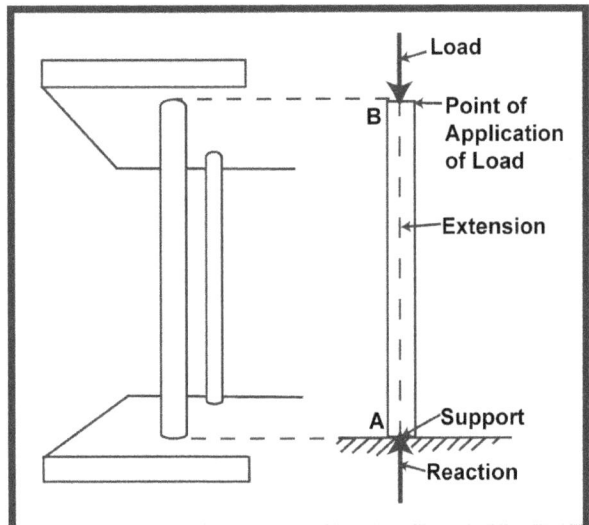
Figure 2.2: Compression member components

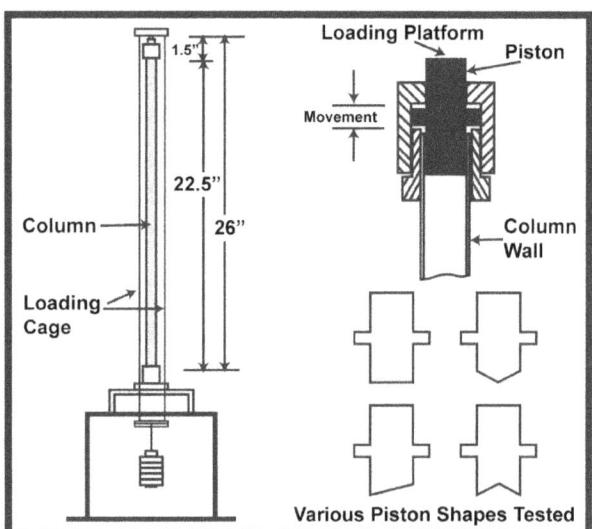
Figure 2.3: Piston-column test apparatus

After weeks of an unsuccessful search for a hypothesis that might conceivably lead toward this aim, the author decided to analyze the problem on the basis of definitions developed from first principles (Pohl 1966).

1. As shown in Figure 2.2, a compression member may be defined as the extension between the point of application of a load at point *A* and the support at point *B*, the load being directed toward the support. Having thus divided a compression member into three parts it will be possible to consider each section separately and ascertain whether or not economies can be achieved.

2. At point *B* both the eccentricity of the applied load and the fixing conditions of the extension are critical. However, if the load is assumed to be both axial and concentric for a given end-fixing condition, then no further economies can be reasonably expected to arise out of any other factor.

3. At point *A* the inclination of the support, the fixing conditions, and the effective bearing area of the extension are also critical. Again, on the assumption of perfect bearing conditions no further economies can be expected.

This leaves only the *extension* between points *A* and *B* for further consideration. The *extension* must be composed of a material capable of transmitting forces induced by the load imposed at *B* down to the support at *A*. Experience has shown that materials such as steel, concrete, and timber that are commonly used for this purpose will buckle in much the same manner. Individual differences are determined only by the cross-sectional shape of the member and the modulus of elasticity of the material, and not at all by the strength of the material.

2.2 The Original Concept

The author then posed the following question to himself: Can any useful purpose be served by substituting a liquid or gas for the normal solid *extension* between points A and B? Certain aspects of such a pressurized system immediately came to mind. First, fluids do not resist a shearing force. When they flow a finite shear is produced by a zero stress and hence we may conclude that their shear modulus is zero. Second, fluids under pressure will induce only tensile stresses in their container. Third, fluids such as air and water are readily available at negligible cost.

A subsequent model analysis dealing with the load-bearing capacity of open-ended, slender, pressurized, cylindrical columns did indicate that economies could be achieved by a pressurized system under certain circumstances (Cowan and Pohl 1967). The apparatus consisted of an aluminum tubular test column (½ inch diameter and 20 gauge (0.036 inch) wall thickness) fitted with a piston at the uppermost end, as shown in Figure 2.3. The piston, which was restrained from unlimited vertical movement by means of a cap fitted to the upper end of the column, enabled the load to be physically separated from the column shaft. The author felt that this elaborate arrangement was necessary to provide a direct platform supported by fluid pressure for the point of application of the load, without any transfer of compressive forces to the cylindrical column shell.

The column was tested in free-standing mode to eliminate the possible influence of end-fixing conditions at the point of application of the load. As shown in Figure 2.3, the load was applied below the bottom of the column through a loading cage that was balanced on a ball-bearing located in the center of the piston. First, the column was tested without internal pressure and was found to be capable of supporting a maximum load of just under 55 LB before buckling. This was in conformity with the calculated maximum load of the column according to the well-known Euler formula (equation 2.1).

maximum load (W) $= (\pi^2 E I) / (H_E)^2$ .... (2.1)

where: W = buckling load of the column (LB)

E = modulus of elasticity of the column material (psi)

I = moment of inertia of the column cross-section (IN^4)

H_E = effective height of the column, which is twice the actual height for a free-standing column (IN)

Then the column was pressurized incrementally with oil to a maximum pressure of 4,000 psi. For a column slenderness ratio[2] of 290 and an internal liquid pressure (oil) of 1,500 psi buckling was

---

[2] Slenderness Ratio is defined as the effective height of a column divided by the Radius of Gyration. The effective height of a free-standing column is twice its actual height.

first observed at a load that was 75% greater than the load predicted by the Euler formula (equation 2.1). At higher internal pressures the buckling load increased further but not in a linear manner. Based on these exploratory test results the following preliminary conclusions were drawn:

- The pressurization of slender tubular columns of circular cross-section increases the load-bearing capacity of such columns.

- The contribution of internal pressure to the load-bearing capacity of slender columns appears to be indirect (i.e., a secondary effect) for two reasons. First, because of the relatively high pressure required to produce a relatively modest increase in load-bearing capacity. Second, because large increases in internal pressure produce disproportional smaller increases in load-bearing capacity.

Nevertheless, in consideration of the Euler formula (equation 2.1) it was perplexing that internal pressure would have any impact at all on the buckling load of slender hollow columns. Was it possible that the separation of the axial load from the column wall by the piston device at the load-bearing end of the column maintained the column wall in a state of tension under internal pressure, and that this tension state diminishes the tendency of the column to buckle?

2.3 A Logical Explanation

With an initial inability to find a logical explanation for the increased load-bearing capacity of pressurized slender columns the author embarked on a related set of experiments with a different type of column. It occurred to the author that while a flexible plastic tube made of a very thin membrane material (20 mil or $1/50^{th}$ of an inch in thickness) such as the transparent material commonly used for a zip-lock lunch bag could easily support a load in tension, it could not even support its own weight in compression (Figure 2.4). However, if the membrane tube is sealed at both ends with two wooden disks of the same diameter as the plastic tube and pressurized internally then it becomes a useful compression member (Figure 2.5).

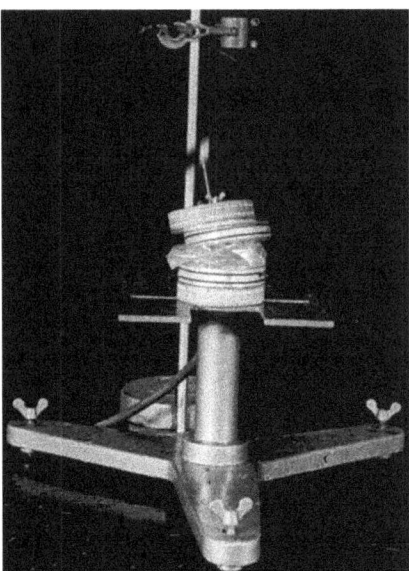 

Figure 2.4: Unpressurized flexible tube   Figure 2.5: Pressurized flexible tube

In the pressurized state the load is supported directly by the internal pressure. However, unless the column is very short there is still a buckling tendency if the load is increased beyond a certain point. At that critical point an increase in internal pressure will tend to straighten the column again. Clearly, the additional internal pressure is producing a secondary effect that is directed against the bending of the column shaft rather than the support of the axial load. While these experiments were convincing evidence that internal fluid pressure in a slender column can increase the load-bearing capacity of such columns, the final explanation of this secondary effect came to the author from another direction.

The Bourdon pressure gauge is based on the principle that a bent hollow tube will tend to straighten if subjected to internal liquid pressure. Typically such a pressure gauge is made of a brass tube that is sealed at both ends and bent into a horseshoe shape, with the two ends a few inches apart. The addition of an inlet for the pressurized liquid that is to be measured and a dial for recording the pressure measurement completes the principal components of the pressure gauge assembly. The distance between the ends of the horseshoe tube is so sensitive to pressure changes inside the tube that it can be calibrated. As long as the tube material is not stressed beyond its elastic limit the relationship of the distance between the tube ends and the internal liquid pressure is repeatable with a high degree of accuracy.

The explanation of the Bourdon pressure gauge principle is quite simple. Before the tube is bent into a horseshoe its cross-sectional profile is circular. During bending the circular profile is distorted into an elliptical profile. When the bent tube is subjected to internal pressure the forces in the fluid are transmitted equally in all directions. The optimum form of a tube for resisting such fluid forces is cylindrical. Therefore, increasing internal pressure will tend to force the elliptical cross-sectional profile to return to its original circular profile. Since the ends of the tube are unrestrained they will move further apart as the tube tries to straighten. Theoretically, if the pressure continues to increase the tube will eventually become perfectly straight with a circular cross-sectional profile.

How does this explanation relate to the author's experimental observation that slender hollow columns of circular cross-section are able to carry axial loads that exceed the buckling load predicted by the Euler formula (equation 2.1), if they are pressurized internally? The Euler formula is based on a limit theorem. It assumes quite correctly that the largest axial load that an unpressurized column of any cross-sectional profile is able to carry is the load at which the column starts to buckle. At that point even a miniscule bending of a free-standing column will produce an eccentricity at the point of application of the load. This induces a bending moment in addition to the axial load. Therefore, the effective load at the point of buckling is greater than the axial load that produced the buckling. Accordingly, the largest load that the slender column can carry is the buckling load. A secondary effect of the buckling action is that the cross-sectional profile of the column will tend to change from a circle to an ellipse. Now, when the column is pressurized internally the pressure acting equally in all directions will try to force the column to maintain its original circular cross-sectional profile.

The experimental behavior observed by the author in his experiments with internally pressurized slender columns are therefore quite correct. Also, the fact that relatively high pressures were required and that the required pressure was not in linear proportion to the load-bearing capacity of the column is logical. The internal pressure creates a force that has the primary effect of resisting the elliptical deformation of the cylindrical column acting as a container. The straightening of the column is a secondary or indirect effect because a perfect circular cross-section will also require a straight column. In other words, pressurized slender columns can support a post-buckling load that is greater than the initial buckling load. Euler's formula does not address the post-buckling behavior of slender columns because it applies to unpressurized columns only. Its assumption that the largest load that can be carried by an unpressurized slender column is the load at which the column starts to buckle is absolutely correct. However, this limitation does not apply to pressurized slender columns.

At the same time, the author was quite incorrect in the initial assumption that slender columns subjected to internal pressure would need to be fitted with pistons to ensure that the axial load does not bear directly on the column wall. Whether or not the column wall is in tension or compression has no bearing on the nature or extent of the secondary force that is generated indirectly by the action of the internal pressure on the column wall.

2.4 An Exhilarating Idea

Following the explanation of the post-buckling behavior of pressurized slender columns the author conducted a more comprehensive experimental study of the load-bearing capacity of flexible plastic tubes under internal pressure. The results of this investigation will be presented in some detail in the concluding section of this Chapter. For these columns, in the slenderness ratio range of 9 to 72, it was found that under low internal pressure local buckling (i.e., settlement of the load due to insufficient internal pressure) takes place and under higher internal pressures (i.e., up to 10 psig) the tendency of overall buckling is significantly increased.

While considering the potential application of these pneumatic tubes in construction, it suddenly occurred to the author that such a large diameter tube could in the inflated state represent an entire multi-story building with floors suspended internally from the roof. Immediately, comparisons came to mind with existing structures such gasometers, hydraulic jacks, pressure vessels, and rocket fuselages, all of which seemed at first sight to incorporate similar principles.

During subsequent months apparently insurmountable problems such as how to ensure that an adequate internal pressure would be maintained at all times, what the physiological effect of a pressurized environment would be on the building occupants, how to deal with the fire hazard, and so on, were identified and analyzed. On a balancing scale with the obvious advantages pertaining to a tension structure (i.e., full utilization of material strength, potential speed of erection, lightness) the safety issues were found to be surmountable. The details of the analysis of each of these issues, the proposed solutions, the construction of two prototype buildings, and exploration of alternative structural configurations in which the internal building environment is not pressurized, form the contents of the following chapters. In sum total these studies suggest that fluid-supported buildings do constitute a feasible system of multi-story building construction if the design constraints are sufficiently severe. While this is the case today in respect to extraterrestrial buildings, it may also become relevant to buildings on planet Earth in the future under sustainability constraints such as minimum site disturbance, embodied energy, closed-loop material considerations, and recycling.

2.5 Structural Flexible Membrane Columns

Although a cylindrical form may evolve when a floating soap bubble is contacted by a horizontal surface at the apex, a cylinder cannot be regarded as a minimal surface. The classical definition of

Plateau's problem (i.e., to find the surface of the smallest area bounded by a given closed contour in space) does not apply to closed structures that derive their stability from internal fluid pressure (Courant and Robbins 1961). Euler showed that all minimal surfaces must be saddle-shaped and that the mean curvature at every point must be zero. Therefore, the hemispherical, floating soap bubble does not qualify in this category and, consequently, it is quite erroneous to describe all soap films as minimal surfaces. However, if one dips any closed contour made of wire into soap solution, then on withdrawal a film of minimal surface will span the contour (Steinhaus 1960). More importantly both the sphere and cylinder are stable forms under the action of internal pressure. In fact, very slender, pressurized, flexible tubular membranes will automatically assume a cylindrical form even if the restraining ends are non-circular.

Let us consider a flexible, plastic membrane tube sealed at both ends as shown in Figure 2.4, earlier in the Chapter. Although this tube has no load-bearing capacity in the deflated state, it becomes a stable compression member when subjected to a proportionate internal air pressure (Figure 2.5). While a rigid membrane column made of thin tinplate would retain its shape even in the absence of internal pressure, the flexible membrane column depends upon fluid pressure for its shape, resistance to bending, local buckling, and torsion. For short columns this resistance is likely to be a function of the internal pressure and the physical characteristics of the membrane material.

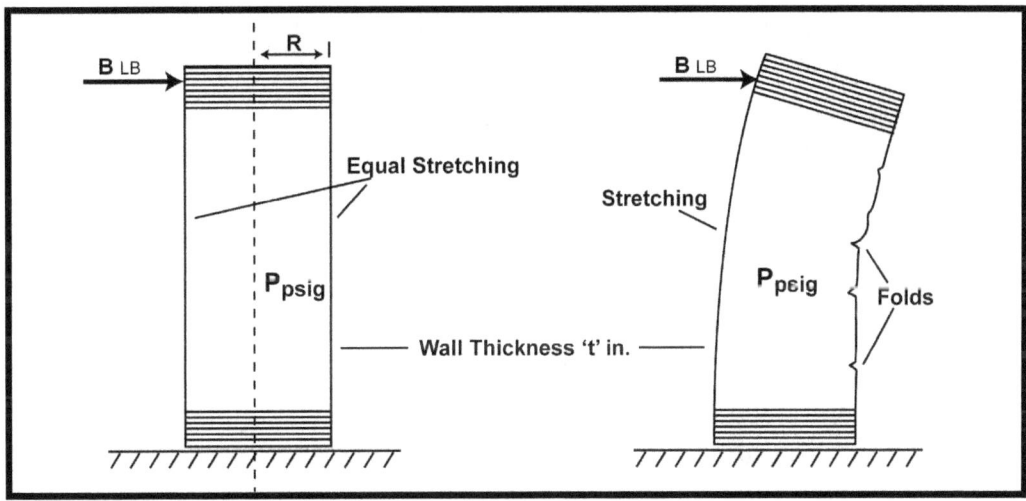

Figure 2.6: Bending mechanism under horizontal load

When pressurized, flexible membrane columns are displaced by a horizontal force acting at the free end (Figure 2.6) the fibers on one side of the column are stretched, while on the opposite side a corresponding unloading action takes place. Folds can occur only, after the tensile stress due to internal pressure can no longer absorb the compressive stresses induced by the lateral force. However, as soon as folds appear the load-bearing capacity of the membrane column decreases rapidly. This sudden lack of stability is due to two reasons. First, the stability of the pressurized membrane column is dependent on the presence of tensile stresses throughout the membrane. Second, the displacement of the column at the free end will produce a moment that effectively increases the total load imposed on the column.

With the anticipated application of pressurized, flexible membrane columns to multi-story building construction, it becomes important to ascertain not only the failure mechanism but also the pressure-utilization ability of such columns under axial load. Therefore, the author undertook an experimental study in an attempt to derive a practical procedure for the structural design of free-standing, pressurized, flexible membrane columns under axial load. From the outset it was envisioned that the load-bearing capacity of these membrane columns would be basically a function of the internal pressure, the wall-thickness of the membrane, the modulus of elasticity of the membrane material, and the slenderness ratio of the column. While the existing theories covering orthodox compression members approximate the proportionate interaction of material failure and lateral instability for specific ranges of slenderness ratios, it seemed probable to the author that in the case of pressurized, membrane columns a single theory would also not suffice for the full range of slenderness ratios. Therefore, on the assumption that for various practical reasons the number of floors in multi-story air-supported buildings would likely be constrained to less than 20, the range of slenderness ratios of the tested columns and the range of internal pressures was correspondingly limited.

2.5.1 The Experimental Investigation

The experimental investigation was limited to a slenderness range of 9 to 72 on the assumption that the most effective application of these pneumatic compression members would be in the short to medium column range. Also, the internal pressure was applied in eight equal increments within a range that would be appropriate for the support of suspended floors within an actual building. The test plan was based on the following parameters:

Column dimensions: A column diameter range of 3.9, 3.2, 2.4, and 1.9 IN was tested at 3 IN height increments from 6 to 24 IN. Therefore, a total of 28 combinations of height and diameter were investigated.

Slenderness Ratios: The following slenderness ratios[3] applied to the 28 column sizes that were tested: 72, 63, 55, 54, 49, 48, 45, 42, 41, 38, 36 (twice), 35, 33, 30, 28 (twice), 27, 24 (twice), 21, 19, 18 (twice), 14 (twice), 12, and 9.

Internal pressures: A simple mercury U-tube manometer graduated in *cm* was used to measure the internal column pressure.

$$1 \text{ } cm \text{ of mercury} = 13.6 \text{ gm cm}^{-2} \text{ or } 0.193 \text{ psig pressure}$$

Readings were taken in 2 *cm* (i.e., 0.386 psig) mercury pressure increments from 0.39 to 3.09 psig (i.e., 0.39, 0.77, 1.16, 1.54, 1.93, 2.32, 2.70, and 3.09 psig).

Membrane material: The nylon film used was manufactured from Nylon Polymer Type 6, with small quantities of stabilizers and lubricants added to facilitate processing. The following material constants, excluding Poisson's Ratio, were supplied by the manufacturer and verified experimentally (Pohl 1970, Appendix 1B):

$$\begin{aligned}
\text{Modulus of Elasticity} &= 5.5 \times 10^4 \text{ psi} \\
\text{Poisson's Ratio (longitudinal)} &= 0.2 \\
\text{ultimate tensile strength (longitudinal)} &= 7,500 \text{ psi} \\
\text{ultimate tensile strength (transverse)} &= 7,500 \text{ psi}
\end{aligned}$$

---

[3] Throughout Chapters 2, 3, 4, and 5 the effective height (H_E) is assumed to be twice the actual height (H) of a free-standing air-supported building or air-inflated column (i.e., $H_E = 2H$), for purposes of slenderness ratio calculations.

membrane thickness = 0.002 IN
yield tensile strength (longitudinal) = 2,400 psi
yield tensile strength (transverse) = 2,400 psi

Loading condition: Due to the difficulty of visually establishing critical buckling loads on the basis of the assumed *zero-stress criterion*[4], an arbitrary critical deflection for the determination of failure loads was adopted throughout the experimental investigation.

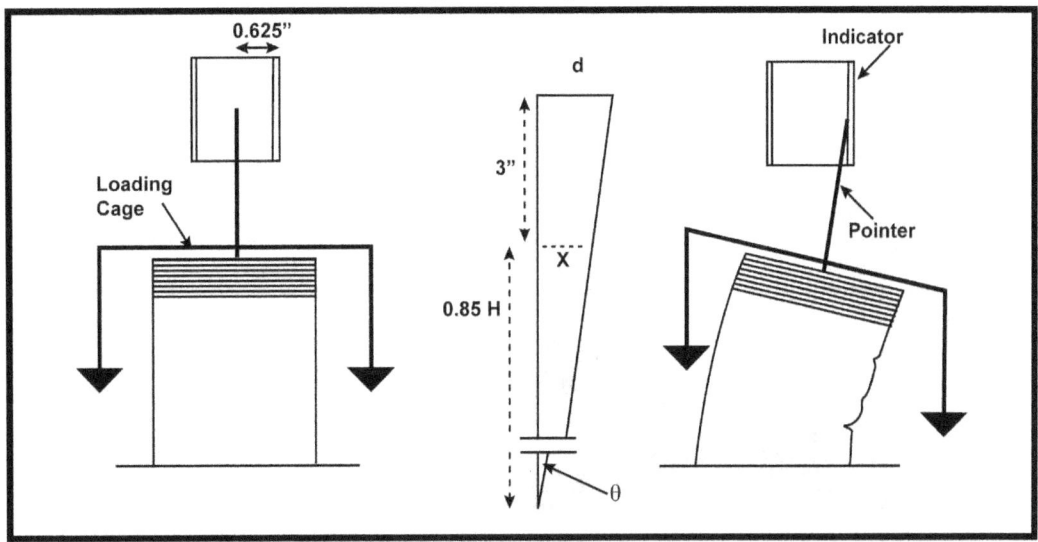

Figure 2.7: Loading procedure showing the assumed eccentricity

A nail (i.e., 3 inch long) fixed in the center of each column-head disc served as a deflection indicator within the confines of a 1.25 inch diameter ring tube (Figure 2.7). For each internal pressure any particular test column was considered to have failed under the imposed eccentric (i.e., eccentricity of 0.625 inch) load, whenever the deflection indicator contacted the inside surface of the tube. Since this critical deflection was measured at a point 3 in. above the column head and test columns varied in height from 6 to 24 inches, a correction factor was required to enable the effective eccentricity (X inch) of the superimposed load to be determined for each column height. In Figure 2.7 it can be seen that the deflected shape of the column is not linear and therefore the tangent of the deflected centerline will meet the undeflected centerline (i.e., the original position of the column) at some point above the base of the column. When looking closely at the difference between Figures 2.8 (left side) and 2.8 (right side), it can be seen that when the imposed load exceeds the buckling load of the pressurized column a hinge forms at the base of the column (Figure 2.8 (b)). For experimental purposes it was assumed that in the case of short columns the distance from this hinge to the upper free end of the column is approximately 0.85 times the actual height of the column (H inches). Therefore, by applying the method of *Similar Triangles*:

$$X = 0.85\,[\,d\,H\,/\,(0.85\,H + 3)\,]$$

Since *d* was fixed at *0.625 inches* throughout the sequence of tests:

---

[4] Short to medium height (i.e., slenderness ratio of 30 or less) pressurized membrane columns are stable under load as long as all sections of the membrane are under tensile stress. The test column in Figure 2.8 (right side) shows crinkling of the membrane on the left side due to a *zero stress* condition on that side of the column.

$$X = 0.625\,H / (H + 3.5)$$

The above equation allowed the calculation of the effective eccentricity for each column:

For test column height	6 IN	eccentricity	=	0.39 IN
For test column height	9 IN	eccentricity	=	0.45 IN
"	12 IN	"	=	0.48 IN
"	15 IN	"	=	0.51 IN
"	18 IN	"	=	0.52 IN
"	21 IN	"	=	0.54 IN
"	24 IN	"	=	0.55 IN

End-Fixing Conditions: All columns were tested under free-standing conditions, with the column base built-in and the uppermost end unrestrained. At the beginning of each test run the column was leveled by means of a three-screw adjustment at the base of the tripod test stand.

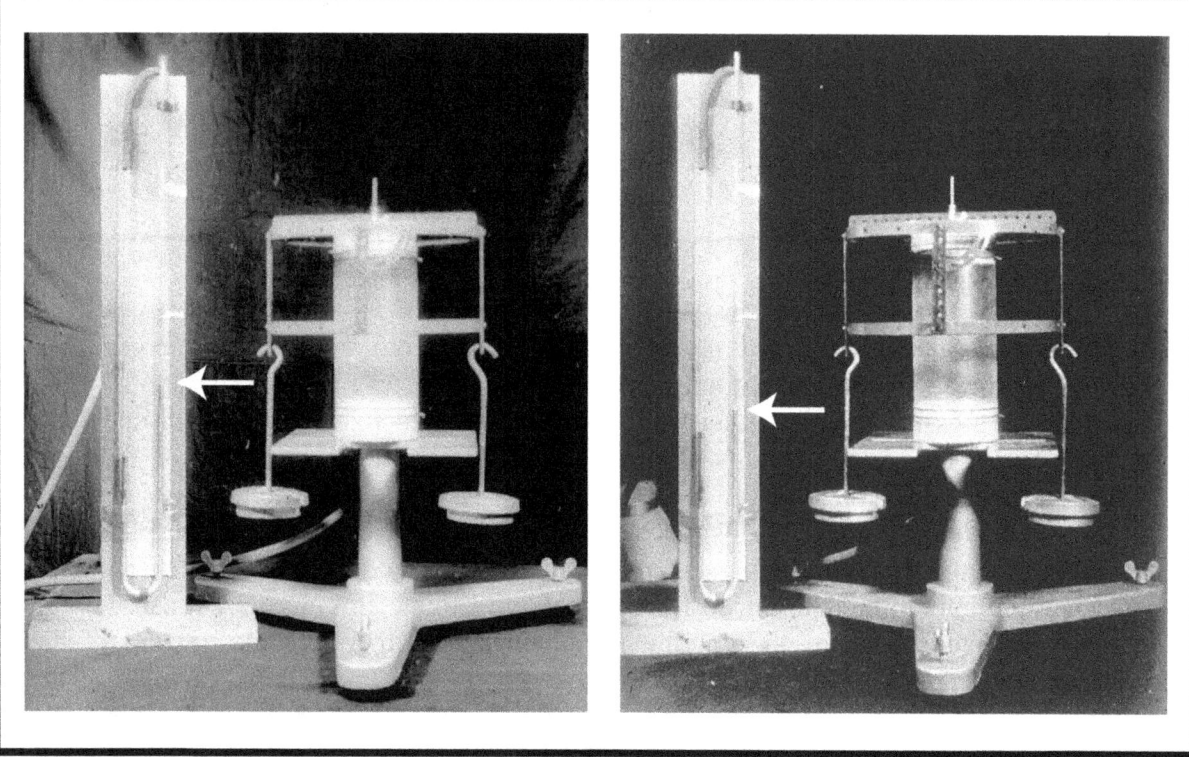

Figure 2.8: Induced *zero stress condition* through reduction of internal pressure

Miscellaneous Considerations: Care was taken to avoid exposure of columns to direct sunlight immediately before and during test runs. Furthermore, a constant time sequence was observed (i.e., 30 seconds per measurement) to discount as far as practicable the influence of the characteristic *creep* behavior of the plastic membrane material.

A total of 1792 measurements were recorded; namely, five different column diameters were tested at seven heights, while each column of a given height was loaded to failure at eight incremental internal pressures. Due to redundancies (i.e., columns of different heights and diameters sharing the same slenderness ratio) these measurements yielded 204 distinct results.

2.5.2 Analysis of Experimental Results

The experimental results were tabulated in a manner that allowed graphs to be plotted with the load per unit area L at 0.625 IN deflection and equivalent eccentricity X, on the vertical axis, and the internal pressure P *psig* acting on unit area on the horizontal axis. Results at three different heights for one typical test column are shown in Table 2.1 and plotted in Figure 2.9 together with the other four heights that were tested for this column.[5]

Table 2.1: Sample experimental results for a typical test column at three heights

(Test column parameters: diameter = 3.9 IN   column head area = 12.0 SQIN)

Height (IN)	Pressure (psig)	Average Load (LB)	Average Load (psi)
24	0.39	2.9	0.24
	0.77	5.2	0.43
	1.16	7.0	0.58
	1.54	8.2	0.68
	1.93	8.2	0.68
	2.32	8.2	0.68
	2.70	8.2	0.68
	3.09	8.2	0.68
15	0.39	3.9	0.32
	0.77	7.4	0.61
	1.16	10.8	0.90
	1.54	12.8	1.07
	1.93	14.3	1.19
	2.32	15.2	1.27
	2.70	15.2	1.27
	3.09	15.2	1.27
6	0.39	3.9	0.32
	0.77	9.1	0.76
	1.16	12.9	1.08
	1.54	16.8	1.32
	1.93	19.8	1.65
	2.32	23.2	1.93
	2.70	26.5	2.20
	3.09	29.3	2.45

The load-pressure curves shown in Figure 2.9 are typical of the results obtained for all of the test columns. They fall into three general graph forms depending on the slenderness ratio of the test columns. Curve type A is close to linear, curve type B is in the form of a polynomial, and curve type C is a combination of a polynomial curve (at low pressures) and a horizontal straight line (at higher pressures with no increase in load-bearing capacity).

Curve A: For test columns with slenderness ratios of 9, 12, 14, 14, 18, and 18.

---

[5] For the complete set of test results see Pohl (1970, Appendix 2B).

Curve B: For test columns with slenderness ratios of 19, 21, 24, 24, 27, 28, 30, 35, and 36.

Curve C: For test columns with slenderness ratios of 28, 33, 36, 38, 41, 42, 45, 48, 49, 54, 55, 63, and 72.

The experimental evidence supported the existence of an approximately linear relationship between the internal pressure and the load-bearing capacity for very small slenderness ratios. While it is true, that no column with a slenderness ratio below 9 was tested and that the measured load-pressure relationship for columns with slenderness ratios below 19 was only approximately linear, there seems to be sufficient evidence to suggest, that at least in the low pressure range (i.e., below 5 psig) this linear load-pressure relationship will hold for a slenderness ratio of 15 and below.

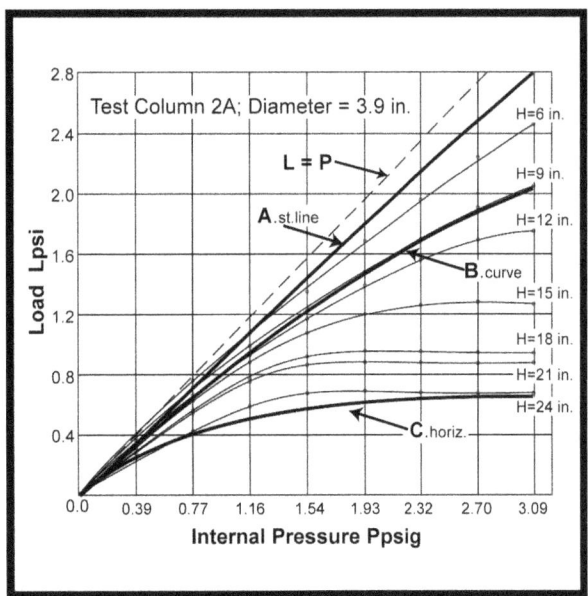 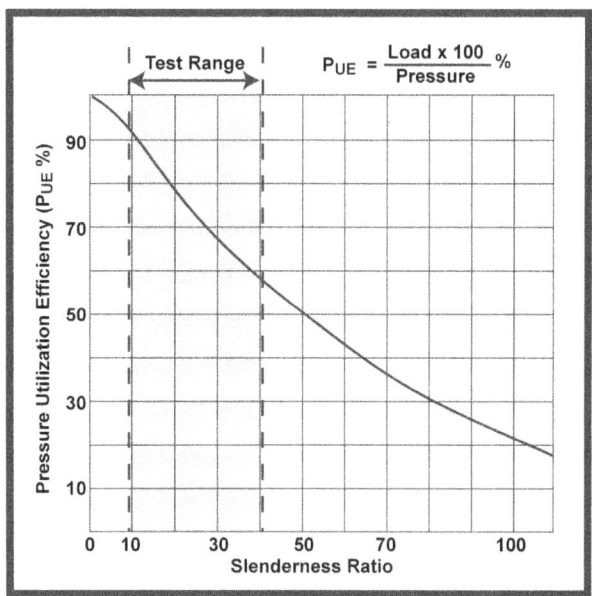

Figure 2.9: Load-pressure relationship for a typical test column

Figure 2.10: Hypothetical general curve form for pressurized membrane columns

Closer inspection of curve type C could suggest that curve types A, B and C may in fact represent sections of the hypothetical general curve, shown in Figure 2.10 as a function of pressure-utilization efficiency and slenderness ratio. It is interesting to note that this postulated curve is similar to the recommended relationship of allowable compression stress and slenderness ratio that was proposed by the West Coast Lumberman's Association in the U.S. in the late 1950s for timber columns (WCLA 1958)[6].

Curve types A and B were explored in more detail by plotting the polynomial relationship $L=aP^n$ logarithmically as $log(L) = n[log(P)]+log(a)$. Applying the statistical method of *Least Squares*

---

[6] However, in the case of internally pressurized membrane columns there is the additional possibility that the relationship between pressure and load is non-linear for different pressures and may in itself be independent of the slenderness ratio. This possibility has not been investigated by the author on the assumption that if it were found to be valid it would be of negligible consequence in the range of internal pressures and structural configurations envisioned for practical building applications.

(Devore 1987, 456), values *a* and *n* were obtained for each test column (Pohl 1970, Appendix 3B). It was found that for slenderness ratios below 30 the value of *n* approximates to unity (i.e., *1*), while the value of *a* was found to vary with the slenderness ratio of the column (Pohl 1970, Appendix 4B). Based on these experimental results the author recommends the following pressure-utilization efficiency factors for pressurized, flexible membrane columns as a function of slenderness ratio:

$$\begin{aligned} &\textbf{slenderness ratio range 10 to 15:} \quad k = 0.85 \\ &\textbf{slenderness ratio range 16 to 20:} \quad k = 0.80 \\ &\textbf{slenderness ratio range 21 to 25:} \quad k = 0.75 \\ &\textbf{slenderness ratio range 26 to 30:} \quad k = 0.70 \end{aligned} \quad (2.2)$$

The pressure-utilization factor *k* above is proposed as a practical guide for the determination of approximate design values. It is derived as follows:

$$L = a(P^n) \quad \text{(based on actual experimental results)}$$
$$L = k(P^{1.0}) \quad \text{(based on interpretation of experimental data)}$$
$$\text{thus:} \quad L = a(P^n) = kP$$
$$k = a(P^n)/P \quad \text{(where } k \text{ is the pressure-utilization factor)}$$

The above relationship allowed the calculation of individual values of *k* based on the average values of *a* and *n* obtained empirically[7]. As a further test of the assumed linearity of the pressure-load relationship of short membrane columns, the Sampling Theory of Regression was applied to the experimental column range conforming to curve types A and B (Pohl 1970, Appendix 4B). It was confirmed that the hypothesis $n = 1.0$ (i.e., $L = aP$) held in all cases for a slenderness ratio range of 10 to 50 within greater than 99.5% confidence limits. This result would be expected, when it is considered that the lowest value of the Coefficient of Correlation was determined to be 0.9938 for a test column of height 15 IN and slenderness ratio 45.

At the time that the experimental analysis of pressurized membrane columns was performed it was considered of interest by the author to compare the recommended pressure-utilization factors (*k*) with the allowable compressive strength of normal steel columns. By reference to structural steel tables for columns[8] it is a simple matter to determine the compressive strength utilization factors (*S*) for gross steel sections under axial load. In Table 2.2, the strength utilization factors (*S*) for steel are based on the permissible working stresses at specific slenderness ratios expressed as a fraction of the allowable working stress at zero slenderness ratio.

Table 2.2: Comparison of load factors for pressurized membrane and steel columns

Slenderness Ratio	Membrane Columns	Steel Columns	Difference
15	k = 0.85	S = 0.92	8.2%
20	k = 0.80	S = 0.89	11.3%

---

[7] Recommendations of the pressure-utilization factor (*k*) in equations 2.2 were based on an internal pressure of 3 psig.

[8] Since the experimental analysis was performed at the University of Sydney, the Australian structural steel code tables applicable in 1969 were used.

25	k = 0.75	S = 0.86	11.5%
30	k = 0.70	S = 0.84	20.0%

It can be seen in Table 2.2 that for slenderness ratios below 20 the pressure-utilization of a membrane column is within 11% of the compressive strength utilization of an orthodox steel column. However, the stability of a pressurized membrane column tends to decrease more rapidly than the stability of a steel column as the slenderness ratio increases. On the other hand, the amount of material required for a membrane column is less than $1/200^{th}$ of that used in a solid steel column of the same slenderness ratio.

2.5.3 Theoretical Analysis

The theoretical approach described in this section for the determination of the load-bearing capacity of a pressurized, flexible membrane column is based on two assumptions. First, it is assumed that the load is applied with an initial eccentricity and, second, that the failure mechanism of the columns is subject to the *zero-stress criterion*, defined previously (see Section 2.5.1).

The first of these assumptions may be justified on the basis of the well-known empirical approach to column design. Most practical columns lie between two extremes, namely Euler buckling limited to very slender columns and the direct compression failure of very short columns. Considerable efforts have been made in the past to obtain a reasonably simple design formula that would apply to columns of any length (Higdon et al. 1967). However, in view of the uncertainty of many of the factors involved, which lend themselves only to statistical or empirical analysis, most columns are designed by means of either one of a number of empirical formulae or a modified form of the Euler formula. Nevertheless even in the development of an empirical formula it is helpful to begin with some rational mathematical expression. Since it is likely that any practical building application of a pressurized membrane column will incorporate slight imperfections, it has been considered reasonable to take these factors into account by assuming that the load is applied eccentrically.

The adoption of a *zero-stress criterion* enables us to equate the vertical tensile stress due to internal pressure with the compressive stresses due to axial load plus a moment induced by deflection. Based on the author's experimental observations the *zero-stress criterion* is justified on the basis that first stage failure of a membrane column will occur at the instant when the tensile stress due to pressure is completely negated by the dual action of axial compression and deflection moment, on one side of the column perimeter. This implies that a pressurized, flexible membrane column will become unstable not when there is an unequal stress distribution present in the membrane, but as soon as any part of the membrane experiences no stress at all in the longitudinal (i.e., vertical) direction.

For eccentrically loaded columns (eccentricity e IN) of short to medium height the maximum deflection (d IN) at the free end (Pohl 1970, Appendix 8B) is given by:

maximum deflection (d) $= W e H^2 / (2 E I_m)$ .... (2.3)

   where: W = vertical load imposed on column (LB)
            H = column height (IN)
            E = modulus of elasticity of membrane material (psi)

I_m = moment of inertia of membrane (IN⁴)

In reference to Figure 2.11, the basic expression applicable to the *zero-stress criterion* of a pressurized, flexible membrane column subjected to an eccentric load *W* lb may be written as:

total vertical tension = total vertical compression

$$P R / (2 t) = W / A_m + W (e + d) / Z_m \quad \text{.................................. (2.4)}$$

where: P = internal pressure (psig)
R = column radius (IN)
t = membrane material thickness (IN)
A_m = cross-sectional area of membrane (IN²)
Z_m = modulus of section of membrane (IN³)

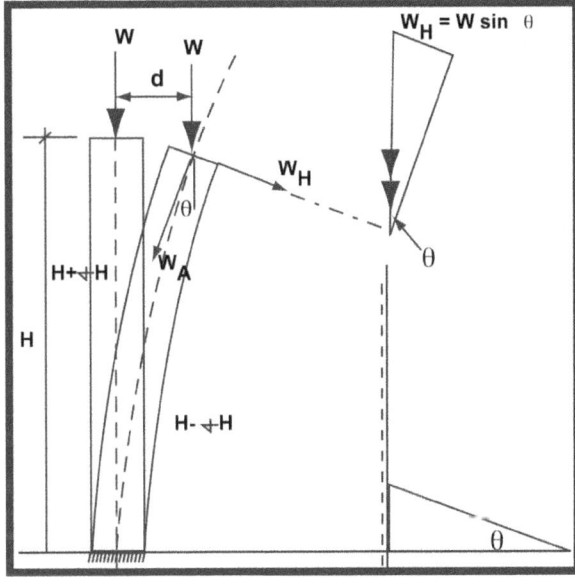

Figure 2.11: Pressurized membrane column under axial load

Figure 2.12: Theoretically derived equations for pressurized membrane columns

$$W = \frac{EI_m(2e+R)}{2eH^2}\left[\left[1 + \frac{4eH^2P}{Et(2e+R)^2}\right]^{1/2} - 1\right] \text{ (LB)} \ldots (2.6)$$

$$L = \frac{EI_m(2e+R)}{2eAH^2}\left[\left[1 + \frac{4eH^2P}{Et(2e+R)^2}\right]^{1/2} - 1\right] \text{ (psi)} \ldots (2.7)$$

$$P = \frac{2Wt}{R}\left[\frac{1}{A_m} + \frac{e}{Z_m} + \frac{WeH^2}{2EI_mZ_m}\right] \text{ (psi)} \ldots (2.8)$$

By substituting for *d* of equation (2.3) in equation (2.4) we are able to obtain an expression for the critical load *W* that will just cause instability of the membrane column, as follows:

$$P R / (2 t) = (W / A_m) + (W / Z_m) + (W^2 e H^2) / (2 E I_m Z_m)$$

This expression may be rewritten as a quadratic equation of the type $ax^2 + bx + c = 0$:

$$[(e H^2) / (2 E I_m Z_m)] W^2 + [(1 / A_m) + (e / Z_m)] W - [(P R) / (2 t)] = 0 \quad \text{............. (2.5)}$$

The solution of this quadric equation may be simplified by substituting the following expressions for I_m, Z_m, and A_m in terms of the column radius (*R*) and the membrane material thickness (*t*):

$$I_m = \pi R^3 t; \quad Z_m = \pi R^2 t; \quad A_m = 2 \pi R t$$

According to Pohl (1970, Appendix 9B) the solution of quadratic equation (2.5) is given by:

$$W = E I_m ((2 e) + R) / (2 e H^2) [(1 + (4 e H^2 P) / (E t ((2 e) + R)^2))^{0.5} - 1] \text{ (LB) .... (2.6)}$$

The vertical load per unit cross-sectional area of the column head ($L = W / A$) is given by:

$$L = E\,I_m\,((2e)+R)\,/\,(2\,e\,A\,H^2)\,[(1+(4\,e\,H^2\,P)\,/\,(E\,t\,((2e)+R)^2))^{0.5}-1] \text{ (psi)} \quad\quad (2.7)$$

The internal pressure (P) required to support a vertical load (W) is obtained by making P the subject of equation (2.4), as follows:

$$P = (2\,W\,t\,/\,R)\,[(1\,/\,A_m) + (e\,/\,Z_m) + ((W\,e\,H^2)\,/\,(2\,E\,I_m\,Z_m))] \text{ (psig)} \quad\quad (2.8)$$

These equations are shown Figure 2.12 in a more easily understandable format with the principal terms grouped.

As a precursor to the application of a pressurized flexible membrane column as the primary structure of a multi-story building, which is the primary subject matter of this book and will be discussed in much greater detail in subsequent chapters, it is of interest to briefly explore the internal pressure requirements that are predicted by equation 2.8 based on the following hypothetical parameters:

building shape: circular floor plan with floors suspended from roof level
building diameter: 60 FT
building height: 110 ft (including airlock entrance at ground level)
story-height: 10 FT
number of floors: 9 air-supported floors plus roof
building load: 140 psf (100 psf live-load and 40 psf dead-load)
membrane thickness: 1/16 IN (0.0625 IN)
modulus (E): 500,000 psi

In terms of the variables contained in equation 2.8 these hypothetical building parameters translate into the following values:

radius (R): 360 IN
height (H): 1,080 IN
total load (W): 3,562,529 LB
membrane thickness (t): 0.0625 IN

With a height to diameter ratio of 1.5 and *slenderness ratio* of 8.5, the hypothetical building is equivalent to a short column[9]. The loading eccentricity (e) for a short column can be determined as a function of the radius or the height of the column. In the past there has been some debate on this issue (Higdon et al. 1967, Timoshenko and MacCullough 1949). It seems reasonable that in the case of short membrane columns (i.e., *slenderness ratios* up to 30) there may be more merit in choosing the column radius as the criterion[10]. In the case at hand, selecting a ratio of R/50 will produce an initial load eccentricity (e) of 7.2 IN, which is equivalent to H/150. Therefore:

Eccentricity (e): 7.2 IN

By substituting these parameters for the principal variables in equation 2.8 we can calculate the

---

[9] Slenderness Ratio (SR) = $H_E / (I_m/A_m)^{0.5}$ and since $H_E=2H$ and $I_m=\pi R^3 t$ and $A_m=2\pi R t$, then SR = $2H / (R^2/2)^{0.5}$.

[10] However, later in Chapter 4 (Section 4.5.3) the question of what the loading eccentricity of a multi-story air-supported building should be based on is revisited. It is argued that the slenderness ratio of the building, rather than either the radius or the height of the building, provides a more appropriate basis. In this case the slenderness ratio is 8.5 and the eccentricity suggested in Section 4.5.3 is twice the slenderness ratio (i.e., 17 IN), which is a much more conservative eccentricity.

required internal building pressure to be 9.26 psig, with a resultant pressure-utilization factor (k) of 94.5%[11]. This result appears to be in alignment with the empirically based k values proposed earlier in this Chapter for pressurized, flexible membrane columns (i.e., equations 2.2). In equation 2.2 the k factor suggested for a slenderness ratio range of 10 to 15 is 85%. Considering that the slenderness ratio of the hypothetical building is 8.5 and that the calculated internal pressure does not include a factor of safety, a k factor of *0.945* would appear to be quite appropriate.

To contain this pressure the building membrane would need to have a design strength of at least 3,334 LB/IN, which is far in excess of the tensile strength capabilities of available flexible membrane materials. Therefore, an exterior cable-network would be required to relieve the membrane stresses. Since such a network would be composed of steel cables and steel has a much higher modulus of elasticity than plastic, the membrane would bulge out between the cables thereby transferring most of the stresses to the network[12]. The combination of pressurized flexible membrane columns with cable-networks is discussed in Chapters 3 and 4.

2.5.4 Comparison of Theoretical and Empirical Results

It is apparent that for small slenderness ratios equation 2.7 predicts a very high pressure-utilization efficiency for membrane columns, which is in general agreement with the experimental data obtained for slenderness ratios below 30 (Pohl 1970, Appendix 12B). This correlation is confirmed in Figure 2.13, which shows the ratio of experimental to theoretical load plotted against the internal pressure. Unavoidable experimental inaccuracies due to inadequate pressure control and loading procedure, are probably responsible for the consistently smaller values predicted by equation 2.7 in the very low pressure range (Figure 2.13).

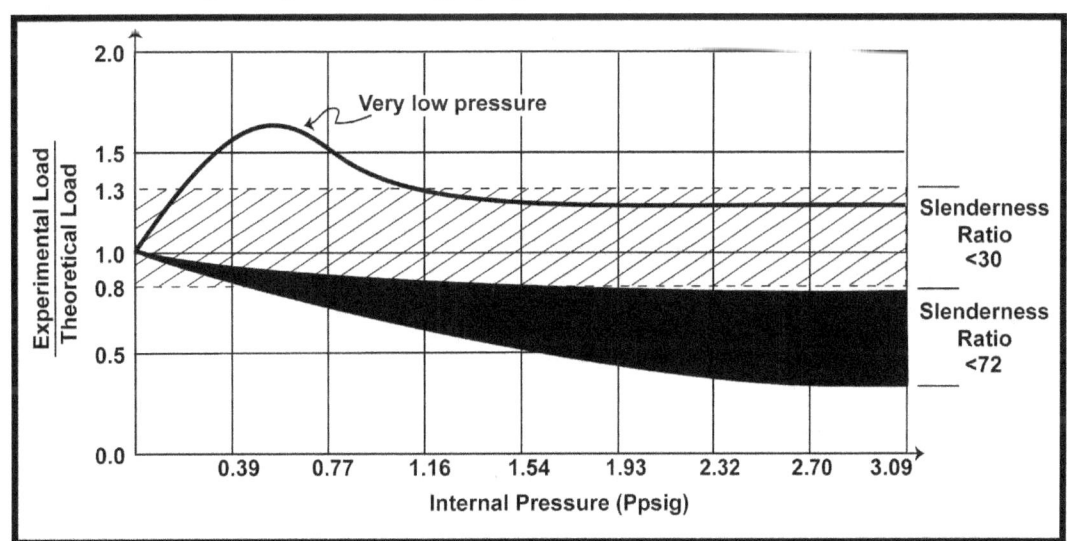

Figure 2.13: Ratio of experimental load to theoretical load (equation 2.7).

---

[11] An internal pressure of 9.26 psig acting on the roof of the building (407,150 SQIN or 2,827 SQFT) would produce an upward force of 3,770,209 LB on the underside of the roof. Since the total floor and roof load of the building is 3,562,529 LB the pressure-utilization factor is 94.5%.

[12] The stresses in the membrane are a function of the radius of curvature of the membrane. Bulging out between cables reduces the radius of curvature and therefore also reduces proportionally the stress in the membrane.

However, for the practical applications of membrane columns we are concerned with a pressure range that would normally exclude pressures below 1 psig. Thus the apparent deviation of equation 2.7 from the experimental results in the very low pressure region (i.e., 0.3 to 0.6 psig.) is not critical to the design of multi-story, pressurized membrane buildings.

There remains at least one further test before equation 2.6 can be accepted with some confidence as a practical design equation for the prescribed slenderness ratio range of 1 to 30. In view of observations made during the experimental investigation and subsequent theoretical speculation, there seems little doubt that if the assumed eccentricity tends to zero then the *pressure-utilization efficiency* of a short membrane column should tend to 100%. This was verified by calculating equation 2.7 for the *3.9 IN* diameter test column[13] shown in Table 2.1 (Section 2.5.2) at a height of *6 IN*, which is equivalent to a *slenderness ratio* of *8.7* and an internal pressure of *3 psig*. By comparison, the slenderness ratio of the hypothetical nine-story building considered earlier in this section was *8.5* and therefore the verification is in the slenderness range of a potential multi-story air-supported building structure. The last figure in parentheses on each line below is the *pressure-utilization ratio* expressed as a percentage of the internal pressure[14].

if eccentricity (e) = 1.0000 IN then load-bearing capacity = 1.3980 psi *(46.6%)*
if eccentricity (e) = 0.1000 IN then load-bearing capacity = 2.6655 psi *(88.8%)*
if eccentricity (e) = 0.0100 IN then load-bearing capacity = 2.9620 psi *(98.7%)*
if eccentricity (e) = 0.0010 IN then load-bearing capacity = 2.9962 psi *(99.9%)*
if eccentricity (e) = 0.0001 IN then load-bearing capacity = 2.9990 psi *(100.0%)*

The same test column at a height of *20 IN* would have a *slenderness ratio* of *29*, which is approximately equivalent to a height to diameter *(H/D)* ratio of *5* as opposed to *1.5* in the case of the *6 IN* high column. For this taller column, which is close to the upper limit of the *slenderness ratio* range suggested in equations 2.2 (Section 2.5.2), equation 2.7 provides the following results for decreasing eccentricities (e):

if eccentricity (e) = 1.0000 IN then load-bearing capacity = 1.0046 psi *(33.5%)*
if eccentricity (e) = 0.1000 IN then load-bearing capacity = 2.2729 psi *(75.8%)*
if eccentricity (e) = 0.0100 IN then load-bearing capacity = 2.8905 psi *(96.3%)*
if eccentricity (e) = 0.0010 IN then load-bearing capacity = 2.9884 psi *(99.6%)*
if eccentricity (e) = 0.0001 IN then load-bearing capacity = 2.9989 psi *(100.0%)*

Clearly, for *slenderness ratios* of below *30*, equation 2.7 predicts a vertical load-bearing capacity (L *psi*) that approaches the internal pressure (P *psig*) as the load eccentricity (e) approaches zero (i.e., as the eccentricity approaches zero the *pressure-utilization ratio* approaches 100%). The question then arises whether this holds true for any internal pressure or just a range of pressures? This question was explored by the author for pressurized, flexible membrane columns with *slenderness ratios* below *30* (Pohl 1970, Appendix 13B). The results of this investigation are shown in Figure 2.14, where the load-bearing capacity per unit area (L *psi*) predicted by equation 2.7 has been plotted against the internal pressure (P *psig*) within the relevant slenderness ratio range. As expected the relationship is not linear, with the vertical load-bearing capacity reducing disproportionally with higher internal pressures.

---

[13] The parameters of the column membrane are: thickness = 0.002 IN; and, Modulus of Elasticity = 55,000 psi.

[14] Pressure-utilization ratio = [internal pressure (P *psig*) / load-bearing capacity (L *psi*)] x 100.

However, for practical multi-story building applications in which the building environment is pressurized the acceptable pressure range is limited. Foremost among the limiting factors is the physiological impact of a hyperbaric environment on the building occupants, which is discussed in Chapter 3. It seems likely that a practical upper boundary of one atmosphere above ambient atmospheric pressure (i.e., 14.5 psig) would not normally be exceeded for such buildings constructed on Earth. In the case of extraterrestrial shelters constructed on planets with no atmosphere the internal building pressure could be higher, but is unlikely to exceed *30 psig* (i.e., two atmospheres). On the other hand, from a structural point of view much higher pressures may be considered in conjunction with high pressure framework structures in which the building environment is not pressurized. Such multi-story fluid-inflated structures featuring one or more pressurized columns are discussed in Chapters 6 and 7.

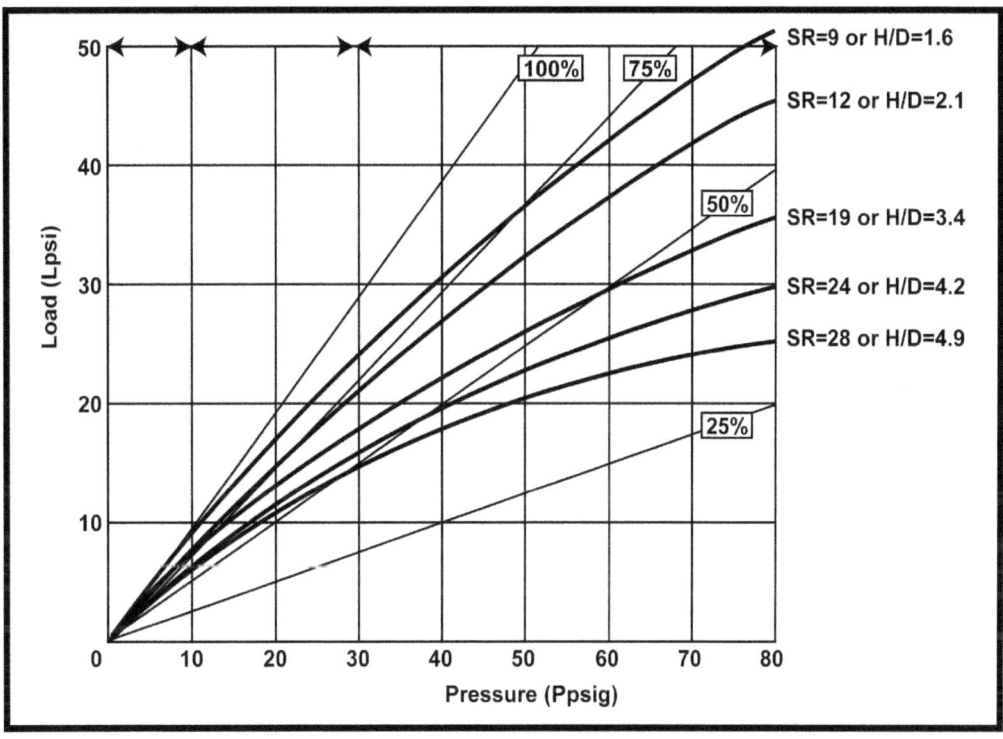

Figure 2.14: Relationship between vertical load-bearing capacity and internal pressure

Chapter 3
Multi-Story Air-Supported Buildings

The experiments relating to the load-bearing capacity of pressurized, flexible, membrane columns described in Chapter 2 were conducted by the author as a means of assessing the ability of such columns to act as multi-story structures. In fact, the transition of membrane column to multi-story building is a relatively simple one, requiring little imagination beyond initial recognition of the fact that all thin-walled pressurized cylinders are potentially stable building structures.

Virtually all persons have had occasion to benefit from simple hydraulic mechanisms such as the bicycle pump, car jack, vehicular suspension system, and certain types of elevators. Yet, the possibility of utilizing a similar hydraulic system for the structural support of a multi-story building appears to have been overlooked. This is particularly surprising when considering that the even more ambitious concept of a vast air-supported roof, serving as a mega structure to cover an area of several square miles, has been considered at least in theory for several years (see Appendix A, Section A-5, Figure A-22). At the same time, the ability of powerful air-jets to render a heavy object practically weightless is a principle that has been used extensively in the industrial field as a means of simplifying the precise positioning of heavy and cumbersome machinery.

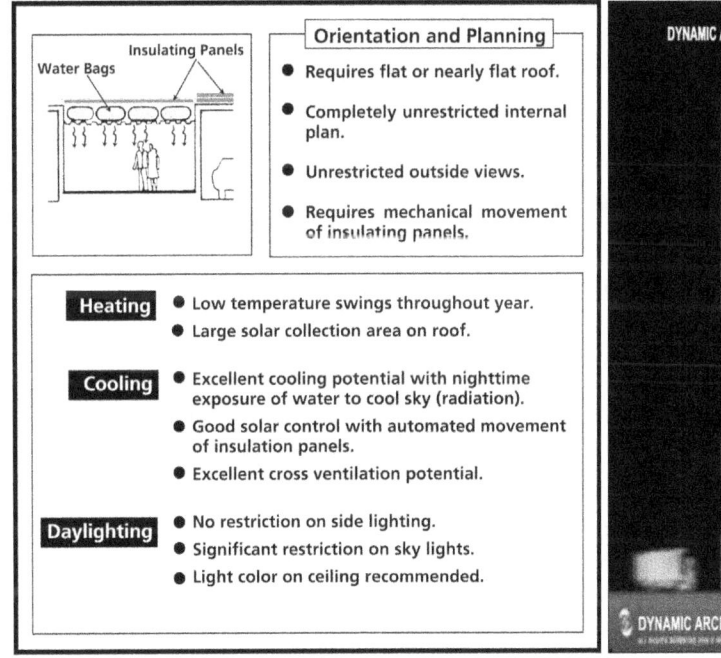

Figure 3.1: The SkyTherm™ passive solar building system invented by Harold Hay

Figure 3.2: The Da Vinci Rotating Tower proposed by architect David Fisher in Dubai

Unlike automobiles, the popular view of buildings as largely static structures is still prevalent. Even slight deviations from this view such as the ingenious *roof pond* or SkyTherm™ system invented by Harold Hay as a passive solar design solution has not fared well (Hay 1973). It utilizes the solar pond principle to collect solar heat during winter days and radiate heat to the colder night sky in summer. The solar pond, a fairly shallow pool of water contained in one or more plastic bags, is located at roof level and serves as both a solar collector and a heat storage facility[1]. Movable insulation panels are activated by differential thermostats to cover the solar ponds during times when neither heating nor cooling of the water is required. At other times the roof ponds remain exposed to the sun so that they can collect heat. During a typical winter day-night cycle the insulation panels will automatically slide over the roof ponds in the late afternoon (or during cloudy daytime periods) to minimize the loss of heat from the water during the cold night. Then, when the sun rises in the morning and there is sufficient radiation to collect heat the panels slide to one side of the roof (normally over the garage area) to allow the water to collect solar energy. During the summer the day-night cycle is simply reversed. The insulation panels automatically slide over the roof ponds during the day to avoid overheating under intense solar radiation, and slide away from the roof ponds after sunset to facilitate the cooling of the water through nighttime radiation to the relatively cool sky. At sunrise the same cycle is repeated with the insulation panels again automatically sliding over the water bags.

The SkyTherm™ system overcomes virtually all of the overheating and temperature swings that characterize most of the alternative passive solar design approaches. Its relatively low acceptance to date is not due to any lack of solar performance, but related to an entirely different set of problems. The maintenance requirements related to the need for movable insulation panels and the ultra violet radiation degradation of the clear plastic bags that are required to contain the water on the roof have proven to be strong deterrents within the context of current building practices.

An even more ambitious innovation in multi-story building design has been proposed by the Italian architect David Fisher (Fisher 2010a, 2010b). His Da Vinci Rotating Tower (Figure 3.2) proposed for construction in Dubai in the United Arab Emirates is designed to allow each floor to rotate independently at a maximum rate of 20 feet per minute, with a full rotation taking 90 minutes. The tower, which is 1,378 feet high, will have 80 floors of 40 prefabricated hotel, residential and office units on each floor. Each unit will be factory produced complete with plumbing, electrical systems, bathrooms, kitchen, and all finishes customized to the specification of the owner. After they have been transported to the site the units are hooked together mechanically and hoisted up the central concrete core of the building.

Fitted with solar panels on the roof and top of each floor, as well as horizontal wind turbines between the rotating floors, it is claimed by the designer that the building will produce about five times as much electricity as is needed for its own operation. The design clearly foreshadows several of the building construction features that are rapidly becoming desirable with the increasing interest in ecological design principles and sustainable architecture (Pohl 2010, 293-331). Foremost among those features are the energy generation capabilities of the building, a 30% reduction in the on-site construction time, the deconstruction and recycling potential of a building in which 90% of the components are prefabricated, and the increased quality and control that can be applied in an off-site, factory-based, manufacturing environment.

Yet, even these small but promising beginnings are being met with a great deal of skepticism by the owners and occupants of buildings. Resistance to change, which is a core characteristic of human behavior, appears to manifest itself in particular in our architectural tastes and preferences. To treat a building as a dynamic system based on mechanical principles as proposed in the design of the Da Vinci Rotating Tower by architect David Fisher or hydraulic principles as proposed by

---

[1] Water at any depth acts as a *black body*, which by definition absorbs all incident radiation (Pohl 2010, 22-24).

the author for multi-story air-supported buildings, is still clearly contrary to the general public notion of a building. The advantages that could accrue with the full utilization of mechanical and hydraulic building systems will not be appreciated until the construction industry is impacted by much more severe constraints. Such constraints already exist in the case of extraterrestrial structures that will be required to support any prolonged habitation on the Moon or Mars, and are beginning to emerge for ecological reasons with the growing world-wide concern about the serious consequences of global warming.

3.1 A Multi-Story Building as a Pressurized Column

While the initial notion that a pressurized membrane column could serve as the principal structure of a multi-story building was the product of an inspirational thought, the implementation of this notion into a practical design solution is largely based on technical concepts and principles that have been well established in other fields for some time. In other words, while the necessary implementation principles may be foreign to building design and construction, they are technically well grounded in a long history of practical experience.

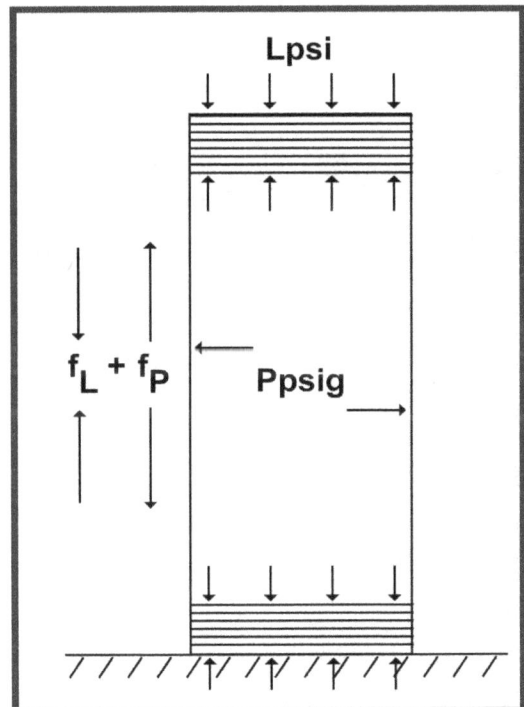

Figure 3.3: Forces acting on a short pressurized, flexible membrane column

Figure 3.4: Working model of an 8-story air-supported structure

By increasing the internal pressure of a short membrane column (Figure 3.3) beyond 1 psig we are able to enter the realm of multi-story air-supported construction (Pohl 1967). In the structural design of buildings we measure loads in terms of pounds per square foot (psf) rather than pounds per square inch (psi). This difference in scale becomes a decided advantage in the case of multi-story air-supported buildings for the simple reason that:

$$1 \text{ psig of internal pressure} = 144 \text{ psf of potential load-bearing capacity}$$

Vertical building loads are of two kinds: dead-loads that account for all permanent vertical loads such as the self-weight of the structure itself, external walls, permanent internal walls, and some of the building services, particularly if these include heavy components (e.g., boilers, packaged and built-up air-conditioning units); and, live-loads that account for people, furniture, and any other temporary and potentially unpredictable vertical loads. For commercial high-rise buildings, codes typically stipulate a live-load of *100 psf*, while the dead-load for such multi-story buildings normally equates to around *40* to *50 psf*[2]. Therefore, if the normal floor load considered in the design of multi-story buildings is in the vicinity of *140* to *150 psf*, then it would appear plausible that for every one pound per square inch of internal air pressure above external atmospheric pressure (*1 psig*) one floor of a multi-story structure can be supported.

The floors would need to be suspended from the roof by internal hangers or cables. This allows multi-story air-supported construction to also take advantage of some of the well established economies of a suspension system, such as concentration of compression forces within a single pneumatic column and the ability to vary the length of the hangers without increasing their cross-sectional area (Roland 1963). Furthermore, it is possible to attach the hanging skeleton to the foundations, resulting in the equivalent of a prestressed space-net. Such a prestressed configuration is well suited to a multi-story tension structure for at least two reasons. First, it maintains its form and stress distribution regardless of the loading condition and second, it has the ability to develop high strength while being relatively insensitive to wind, earthquake forces, and uneven foundation settlement.

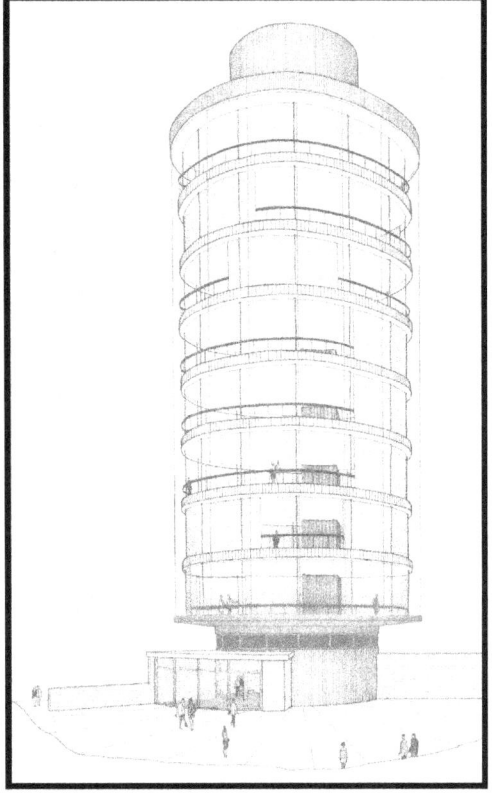

Figure 3.5: Conceptual drawing of a multi-story air-supported building

Figure 3.6: Glass skyscraper project designed by Mies van der Rohe (1921)

---

[2] For example, a *4 IN* thick reinforced concrete floor slab weighs about *48 psf*.

A primitive working model of an eight-story, pressurized, flexible membrane structure is shown in Figure 3.4. The model was constructed to a scale of 1:50. The architect's rendering of a full-size multi-story air-supported building (Figure 3.5) does not differ markedly from the prototype working model. At the time the model was constructed and the architectural rendering was drawn the author could not help but notice the striking similarity between the rendering of the multi-story air-supported building shown in Figure 3.5 and the project for a glass skyscraper designed by Mies van der Rohe in 1921, shown in Figure 3.6 (Drexler 1960, 14). Although the building enclosure in this project is not structural, Mies van der Rohe's proposal for a facade treatment that is utterly devoid of ornamentation and shadow molding is strikingly similar in character to both the working model (Figure 3.4) and the architect's rendering of an actual building (Figure 3.5).

While the potential application of multi-level air-supported buildings to the architectural field may seem very promising at first sight, there are nevertheless a number of limiting factors that require careful consideration. These include:

- The potential physiological affects of a hyperbaric building environment on the occupants of the building.

- The availability of membrane materials with the required tensile strength (including tear resistance), thermal properties, and serviceable life-span.

- The ability to implement fire protection measures that will shield the building envelope (i.e., the external membrane) from the radiant heat produced by an internal or external fire.

- General safety in respect to maintaining the structural integrity of the building under emergency conditions such as pressurization equipment failure, puncture of the external membrane, earthquakes, extreme wind forces, and minor local explosions within the building.

- The mechanical requirements and possible physiological problems associated with entry and exit from a pressurized environment.

- The measures that have to be taken to ensure the proper functioning of the hydrological building services, in particular sewage.

- The formulation of a construction sequence that will devise a method for raising the roof of the building under internal pressure, hoisting the floors while maintaining the integrity of the air-supported structure, and differentiate between the construction tasks that can be performed inside the pressurized building environment and those that must be completed before the external membrane is in place and the building is pressurized.

At least some of these issues would appear to pose insurmountable problems. However, as will be seen in subsequent sections the issues that would appear to be most serious, such as the physiological impact of a hyperbaric environment on the building occupants, maintaining the integrity of the structure under emergency conditions, and fire protection, have surprisingly promising solutions.

3.2 Physiological Aspects

The physiology of long term exposure to a hyperbaric environment is by no means an unknown subject. A long history of experimental investigations and experience with deep sea diving and the construction of caissons for bridges has shown that there are essentially two potential human health risk factors that must be considered.

1. Long term effects in respect to the incidence of compressed-air illnesses, bends syndrome, and oxygen-poisoning, at low pressures.

2. Short term effects on persons working in a compressed-air environment, involving the measurement of physiological strain with one of the available indices (MacPherson 1965).

Decompression sickness is an illness that may occur in persons who return to normal atmospheric pressure after exposure to high pressure. The basic pathological process in decompression sickness is the formation of gas bubbles in both intravascular and extravascular body tissues (Dewey 1962, Lanthier 1964, Taunton et al. 1970, Flook 1987). In the compressed-air environment any such bubbles formed, will consist mainly of nitrogen with a small addition of carbon dioxide. In keeping with the laws of partial pressures, the proportion of a given gas that will dissolve in a liquid is determined by the percentage of that gas in the total mixture and by the pressure to which the mixture as a whole is subjected. If the pressure of the mixture is increased there will be a pressure gradient forcing each gas into solution in proportion to its partial pressure, until equilibrium is reached between the tensions of the dissolved and undissolved portions of the gas.

While some degree of microscopic bubble formation will probably occur whenever the partial pressure of nitrogen in the tissue exceeds that in the surrounding air, it is clearly stated in the medical literature that symptom producing bubble formation (i.e., decompression sickness) will not occur until the tissue partial pressure of the nitrogen is more than twice that in the surrounding atmosphere[3]. In the case where this 2:1 threshold pressure-gradient is exceeded, the extent of symptom producing bubble formation will be in proportion to the magnitude of the partial pressure gradient.

The physiological aspects that are most pertinent to the feasibility of multi-story air-supported buildings may be summarized as follows:

a) The degree of compression and the rate of decompression are the primary variables that determine whether or not decompression sickness will be the result of a return to normal atmospheric pressure. The duration of exposure to hyperbaric conditions appears to be of less significance.

b) Decompression sickness will not occur after exposure to pressures below two atmospheres absolute, regardless of duration.

c) While the author was unable to find any published results of specific experiments designed to establish the long term interrelated aspects of life in a hyperbaric environment and decompression effects, there do not appear to be any a priori

---

[3] The percent of a particular gas in the total volume of gas containing two or more gases is its partial pressure. As the concentration of the particular gas increases, so does its partial pressure. However, the sum of all partial pressures of the gases in the total volume of gas is equal to 100% of the pressure in the entire volume of gas.

reasons for predicting a negative result. A great deal is known about life at high altitude but far less about the chronic effects of increased atmospheric pressure. Mirror image predictions are unlikely to apply because the capability of the human adaptation mechanism is relatively unknown for hyperbaric environments.

d) Symptom producing nitrogen bubble formation in the blood stream will not occur unless a threshold pressure-gradient of 2:1 is exceeded. This means that if the building environment is pressurized to less than two atmospheres absolute (i.e. approximately 14 psig) then long term physiological effects are unlikely to occur even if this change of pressure is produced instantaneously.

Since the rates of compression and decompression are the primary variables that determine the occurrence of decompression sickness, it would appear that higher environmental pressures and therefore taller buildings are feasible, provided the rate of change from one pressure to the other is sufficiently slow. Nevertheless, present practical considerations of multi-story air-supported buildings have been purposely limited to structures involving pressures below 14 psig, with a maximum of 10 to 12 floors.

3.3 Membrane Materials

One of the most distinguishing characteristics of multi-story air-supported buildings is undoubtedly that structure and enclosure are synonymous. Furthermore, the structural enclosure experiences tensile stresses only and derives its stiffness directly from the fluid pressure that it contains. Both of these structural conditions are favorable for the selection of a plastic material. Plastic membranes are easily reinforced, joined, and modified with plasticizers, fillers, and pigments. They are typically classified into thermoplastic and thermosetting groups. The former soften when heated and harden if subsequently cooled and this cycle can be repeated. Thermosetting plastics first soften when heated, but after they have been cured a tough material results that cannot be softened by re-heating. The membrane enclosures of multi-story air-supported buildings will be of the thermoplastic type, most likely laminated with a woven nylon scrim for added tensile strength and tear resistance.

The safety of a multi-story air-supported building depends largely on the satisfactory performance of two structural elements namely, the internal air-pressure and the membrane envelope. Since both are dependent on maintaining the integrity of the building, the satisfactory performance of the membrane material is critical in respect to: tensile strength and tear-resistance; life-span and weatherability; fire resistance; and, thermal insulation or reflectivity.

3.3.1 Tensile Strength

The procedure for determining the circumferential or hoop stress in the membrane of a multi-story air-supported building is identical to equations A-2 and A-4 used in Appendix A (Section A-4.3) for determining the circumferential stress (f_c) in the membrane of a single-story cylindrical air-building with quarter spherical ends, namely for an internal pressure of P *psig* and building radius of R *IN*:

$$f_c = [\,P\,R\,] \quad \text{LB/IN} \quad \text{..................................... A-2}$$

$$f_c = [\,P\,R\,]\,/\,t \quad \text{psi} \quad \text{..................................... A-4}$$

The difference between the two equations is that equation A-2 determines the circumferential stress per linear inch of membrane material (i.e., f_c LB/IN), while equation A-4 determines the stress in pounds per square inch (f_c psi) by dividing equation A-2 by the thickness of the membrane material.

Applying equation A-2 to a multi-story air-supported building of *100 FT* diameter with an internal pressure of *14 psig*, the maximum tensile stress in the membrane is determined to be 8,400 LB/IN. Assuming the membrane thickness to be *24 mil*[4], the yield strength may be calculated with equation A-4 as *350,000 psi*, and this would require the membrane material to have an ultimate strength in tension of over *500,000 psi*. This exceeds the tensile strength of available plastic membrane materials by a considerable margin. The ultimate strength of plastic membrane materials used for single-story air-buildings does not normally exceed *300 LB/IN*. This includes laminates and reinforced plastics containing glass fiber combined with a liquid resin, which is converted to a solid by catalysts and hardeners. While such glass-reinforced plastics can have an ultimate tensile strength of over *200,000 psi* they are likely to be too expensive.

However, as discussed previously (Chapter 2, Section 2.5.3), a much more feasible solution for multi-story air-supported buildings is to employ an external cable-network to resist most of the hoop stress. The required membrane strength is then simply a function of the spacing of the cables. Since the cable material is likely to be steel, with a much higher modulus of elasticity then plastic, the membrane will bulge out between cables resulting in a significant reduction of the effective radius of curvature of the membrane. In combination with such an external cable-network, nylon scrim-based plastic laminates capable of developing a yield strength of *500 LB/IN* should be adequate and readily available from normal commercial sources.

3.3.2 Weatherability

A satisfactory approach to the problem of weather-resistance has been to surface the plastic base-material with a thin film of a weather-resistant material. For this purpose both polyvinyl chloride (PVC) and polyvinyl fluoride (PVF) have been found satisfactory for outdoor exposure in excess of 10 years (Makowski 1964, Everard 1965). A competent review of aspects relating to the weather resistance of plastics has been undertaken by Lever and Rhys (1962) who divided the optical properties involved into separate groups, namely, color, haze, surface irregularities and glossiness, bleeding of color, light transmission, scattering and reflectance.

3.3.3 Fire Resistance

The heat resistance of a thermosetting plastic is generally better than that of a thermoplastic material. The maximum service temperature of some prominent plastics are given by Nix and van Aardt (1964, 7). Improvements on low service temperatures may be achieved by using fillers such as mica. However, some plastics exist that show a relatively high resistance to heat. For example, the thermal degradation of Teflon starts at the relatively high temperature of 840° F. In the early 1960s the Du Pont Company announced the discovery of a synthetic resin (aromatic imide) with a heat resistance comparable to that of mild steel (Heine 1963, 26). Generally, the cost of such heat-resistant plastics have been considered prohibitive for building construction purposes.

---

[4] Since one *mil* is equal to one thousands of an inch, *24 mil* is approximately equal to *1/42 IN* thickness.

The measures that can be taken to improve the fire resistance of flexible plastic membrane materials during their manufacture are likely to be marginal and not adequate for the fire protection of multi-story air-supported buildings. Therefore, the design of these buildings will need to include measures for shielding the membrane from heat radiation in the case of a fire. Such design measures will be discussed later in this Chapter (Section 3.5).

3.4 Pressure-Utilization Efficiency

In Chapter 2 we compared the vertical load-bearing capacity predicted by equation 2.6 with experimental test results and found a fairly good correlation for slenderness ratios below *30* and internal pressures above *1 psig*. It will be of interest to apply equation 2.8, which predicts the internal pressure required to support a given load, to a range of multi-story air-supported buildings. This will require the upward scaling of the diameter and height dimensions of the pressurized, flexible membrane columns that were considered during the empirical analysis, as well as the assumption of typical building floor loads and membrane parameters. The following fixed parameters are assumed:

number of floors = 8 (plus roof)
story height = 12 FT
live-load = 100 psf
dead-load = 40 psf
membrane thickness = 20 mil (0.02 IN)
membrane Modulus of Elasticity = 500,000 psi

Based on these fixed parameters the height of the building is *108 FT* measured from the lowest suspended floor to the roof. The load on the roof is assumed to be the same as the floor loads that are suspended from the roof. By varying the diameter of the building from *20 FT* to *150 FT* it is possible to explore the internal pressure requirements predicted by equation 2.8 for a slenderness ratio range of *30.5* to *4.1* (Table 3.1). The range of building diameters has been chosen to facilitate comparison with the *k factors* that were derived from the empirical study of pressurized, flexible membrane columns (i.e., equations 2.2). It is unlikely that an eight-story air-supported building would have a diameter of less than *50 FT*, unless it is a special purpose building such as a storage or vertical farming facility utilizing hydroponic and/or aeroponic technologies (Despommier 2009).

It must be pointed out that the internal pressure calculated on the basis of equation 2.8 does not take into account horizontal forces due to wind loads, but only vertical live and dead-loads. Wind loads may be resisted by increasing the internal pressure or by wrapping an exterior network of diagonal cables around the membrane. These alternatives are discussed in Chapter 4.

Also, the tensile stresses calculated for the membrane are far in excess of the strength properties of currently available plastic materials that are affordable for multi-story air-supported buildings constructed on Earth. In the case of extraterrestrial structures the cost of transporting building materials into space may well allow consideration of lightweight, high strength materials that would be considered prohibitively expensive for terrestrial application. However, this problem is easily solved by means of horizontal steel cables around the perimeter of the building, evenly spaced from the bottom to the top of the pressurized building cylinder. Since the modulus of elasticity of steel is by an order of magnitude greater than that of plastic, the membrane will bulge out between the cables. This will effectively reduce the radius of curvature of the membrane, thereby transferring most of the circumferential stress due to the internal pressure to the cables (see Section 3.7).

Table 3.1: Pressure-utilization efficiencies predicted by equation 2.8 for multi-story buildings

Building Diameter	Slenderness Ratio	Building Load	Internal Pressure	Membrane Tension	Pressure Efficiency	k Factor
20 FT	30.5	395,840 LB	11.24 psig	1,349 LB/IN	0.78	0.70
30 FT	20.4	890,641 LB	10.53 psig	1,895 LB/IN	0.83	0.75
40 FT	15.3	1,583,361 LB	10.17 psig	2,441 LB/IN	0.86	0.80
50 FT	12.2	2,474,002 LB	9.96 psig	2,988 LB/IN	0.88	0.85
60 FT	10.2	3,562,563 LB	9.81 psig	3,532 LB/IN	0.89	0.85
70 FT	8.7	4,849,045 LB	9.71 psig	4,078 LB/IN	0.90	-----
80 FT	7.6	6,333,446 LB	9.64 psig	4,627 LB/IN	0.91	-----
90 FT	6.8	8,015,767 LB	9.58 psig	5,173 LB/IN	0.91	-----
100 FT	6.1	9,896,009 LB	9.53 psig	5,718 LB/IN	0.92	-----
110 FT	5.6	11,974,171 LB	9.49 psig	6,263 LB/IN	0.92	-----
120 FT	5.1	14,250,253 LB	9.46 psig	6,811 LB/IN	0.93	-----
130 FT	4.7	16,724,254 LB	9.43 psig	7,355 LB/IN	0.93	-----
140 FT	4.4	19,396,178 LB	9.41 psig	7,904 LB/IN	0.93	-----
150 FT	4.1	22,266,022 LB	9.39 psig	8,451 LB/IN	0.93	-----

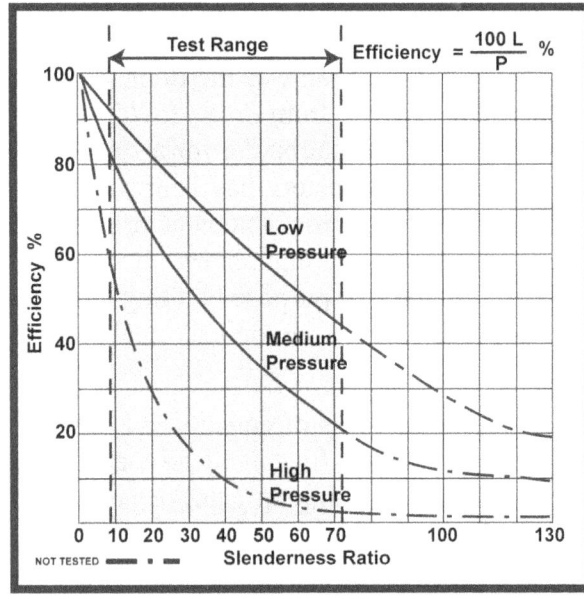
Figure 3.7: Pressure-utilization efficiency by slenderness ratio

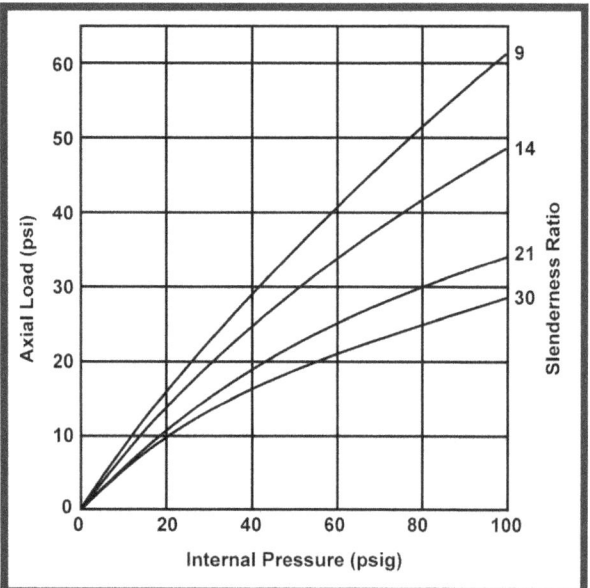
Figure 3.8: Pressure-utilization efficiency by internal pressure

Another structural issue that was briefly mentioned in Chapter 2 is that the pressure-utilization efficiency of membrane columns may be influenced by the degree of pressurization. In Section

2.5.4 the lack of agreement between the loads predicted by equation 2.6 and the experimental values obtained for very low pressures (i.e., 0.3 to 0.6 psig) shown in Figure 2.13 was assigned to experimental inaccuracies. An alternative equally plausible explanation of this incongruence is that the load-bearing capacity of membrane columns is dependent (even if only to a minor degree) on the magnitude of the internal pressure. A graphical representation of such a relationship is shown hypothetically in Figure 3.7, where curves represented by full lines are based on experimental data obtained by the author (Pohl 1966) and broken lines are hypothetical extrapolations.

Plotting the maximum vertical loads predicted by equation 2.6 for a wide range of pressures (i.e., 1 to 100 psig), as shown in Figure 3.8, suggests that this equation does take such a relationship into account (Pohl 1970, Appendix 13B). In fact, closer inspection of equation 2.7 clearly indicates that the load-bearing capacity per unit area of short membrane columns not only varies inversely as the square of the height, but also more indirectly as the square root of the internal pressure.

However, neither the lack of correlation with experimental results at very low internal pressures nor the experimentally unverified predictions at slenderness ratios above 30 should be of concern for practical multi-story air-supported building applications. Normal building loads will require at least 1 psig of internal pressure for the support of each floor and the adoption of a 15 psig pressure limit due to physiological reasons will keep the slenderness ratio of such buildings well below 20 for practical building height to diameter ratios. For example, a 14-story building with a floor diameter of 60 FT (any smaller diameter would surely be impractical from a space planning point of view) and even a fairly exorbitant story height of 14 FT would have a slenderness ratio of only 18.5 (i.e., $H_E \times 2^{0.5} / R = [2 \times 14 \times 14 \times 1.4142] / 30 = 18.48$).

Finally, it must be mentioned that the design pressure which is obtained on the basis of equation 2.8 does include a safety factor by virtue of the building loads prescribed by relevant authorities. Since the floors are suspended unequal live-load distribution on any floor, which is an important factor of safety consideration in orthodox frame construction, is of very minor (if any) consideration due to the vertical continuity provided by the hangers.

3.5 Fire Protection

In the context of presently accepted standards of fire-resistance multi-story air-supported buildings will present problems that may well seem insurmountable at first sight. Building authorities will be reluctant to change existing regulations to accommodate the significantly different fire protection problems associated with a pressurized membrane building. Therefore, to come to terms with this aspect of multi-story air-supported buildings, it will be necessary to re-evaluate fundamental concepts on the basis of relating fire-hazard to the complete structure. We start with the prudent and well established assumption that economic risk should be relegated to secondary importance in relation to the danger to human life. The following guiding principles are proposed:

Principle 1: Minimization of the building's fire-load in relationship to structure, cladding, and contents. It seems plausible that the effective fire-load of a building can be reduced by providing separate fire-rated storage units for areas containing a high density of combustibles (Pohl 1968). In isolating combustible content in high density units it should be possible to reduce the potential fire-hazard of the non-combustible structure and concentrate treatment to smaller areas more effectively.

Principle 2: The installation of effective fire services in the form of detectors, shielding systems, and deluge sprinklers, which will allow sufficient time for mass evacuation before catastrophic structural failure takes place. It will be desirable to plan evacuation in two stages: first, to a fire-rated shelter at basement level within the building confines; and, second, from this shelter to the exterior.

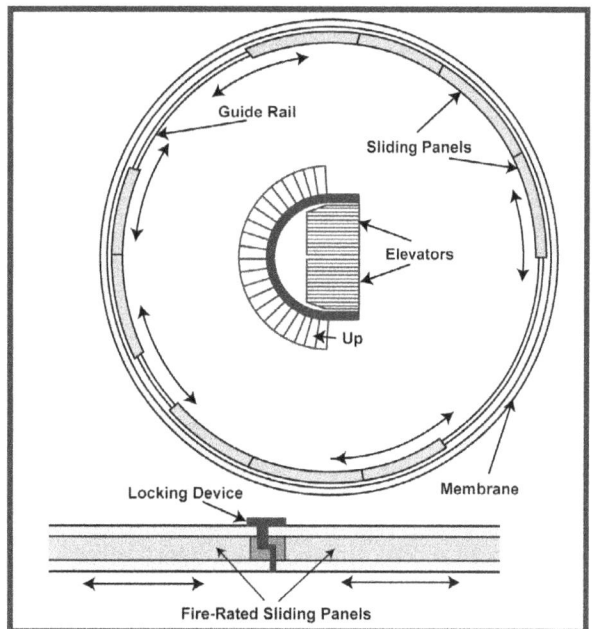
Figure 3.9: Fire-rated perimeter screens

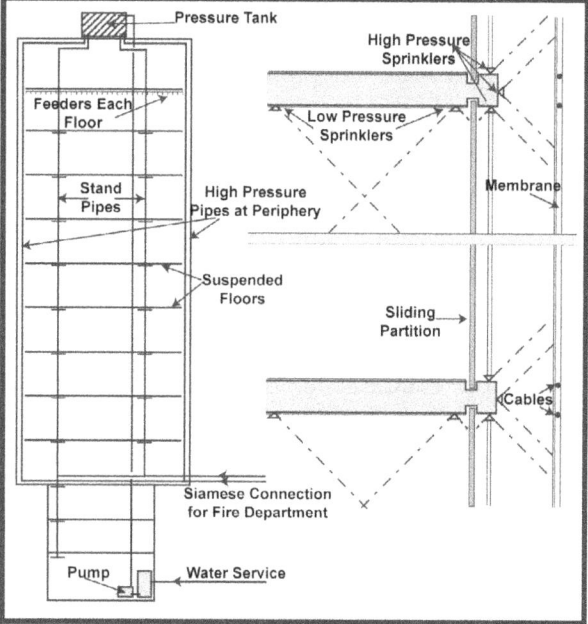
Figure 3.10: Fire protection installation

Measures must be applied to shield the membrane envelope from radiation and thermally insulate the suspension cable system. In the first case, it is proposed to provide automatically controlled reflective, sliding screens around the perimeter of each floor (Figure 3.9). In the case of a fire occurring at any point within the building, these screens will slide between the fire and the membrane acting as shields against radiation, heat transfer, and flame penetration. At the same time, deluge type sprinklers will spray water against the membrane and the external side of the screens (Figure 3.10). The screens themselves will need to be designed to the requirements of applicable building code fire-rating standards for structural members. It is suggested that with these measures in combination with mass evacuation provisions it should be possible to achieve an acceptable degree of fire-protection for multi-story air-supported buildings.

3.6 Building Services

Apart from fire protection, there are several other non-structural characteristics that distinguish a multi-story air-supported building from its conventional counterparts. For a start, not only does the ambient internal air pressure need to be maintained, but it also needs to be controlled within fairly strict limits. This certainly precludes the provision of any openings that are operable by the occupants. In other words, the interior of a multi-story air-supported building will by necessity be a sealed environment. Even though the external membrane envelope may have transparent sections, in the common nomenclature of orthodox building construction it will be classified as a windowless building. The basic requirements for such buildings were already a subject of interest and research some 50 years ago (Roubal et al. 1963, BRS 1965).

1. The minimum air volume per occupant in an airtight building should be 90 CF and the minimum floor area should be 65 SF.

2. The amount of fresh air drawn by the air-conditioning equipment must not be less than 10% of the total changed air volume.

3. A supplementary air-conditioning and ventilating system should be added to the main system as a safety measure for maintaining an uninterrupted circulation of clean air.

4. Ceilings and walls should be insulated to prevent condensation. This should be aided by suitably directed air-currents.

5. Air-conditioning and other plants must operate at the lowest possible noise level. All mechanical equipment should be sound and vibration insulated from the building structure at the base.

In the specific case of multi-story air-supported buildings the concept of a sealed, pressurized environment introduces a stringent requirement for conditioning the air and, above all, maintaining the internal pressure. The range of pressure indicated, 0-14 psig, is well below the usual range of reciprocating compressors but above that of centrifugal blowers. The most appropriate method of achieving pressures toward the upper end of this range would probably be with a rotary vane compressor, which could conveniently be directly coupled to a high-speed motor or to a turbine. The output of the compressor would be at an elevated temperature so that additional cooling would be necessary in summer. The winter requirement would depend upon the rates of air exchange and heat exchange between the building and the outside air.

3.6.1 Thermal Insulation

Since the building is sealed against air exchange with the atmosphere and the membrane is envisaged as a thin and partly transparent envelope, considerable transfer of heat by conduction and radiation can be expected. Therefore, an air-conditioning system will be required that provides enough make-up air to supply oxygen to the occupants and controls the temperature and humidity within a comfortable range. The make-up air will replace air lost through controlled leakages such as the entrance air-lock. However, the total make-up air should be greater than these losses so that an additional self-balancing air escape can be provided to control the internal pressure and allow any excess air to escape. This will also take care of the relatively small changes in air pressure that may occur due to diurnal temperature changes.

The total heat gain due to exposure to direct solar radiation is likely to be much higher than for a conventional building, for several reasons.

- There is no optimum orientation for a circular building.

- There is no provision for sunshading in an air-supported building that is enclosed by a continuous membrane envelope. However, the external cable-network that will be required to reduce the tensile forces in the membrane may also provide convenient support for external sunshading devices. In addition, a degree of thermal control may be achieved through the division of the membrane into reflecting, translucent, and transparent sections.
- Without sunshading devices or membrane reflection, the transmission of heat by radiation and conduction through a thin membrane will approach that of glass in a conventional building.

The maximum solar radiation falling on a cylindrical surface occurs when the sun's altitude is in the range of 30 to 40 degrees[5]. This maximum corresponds to about 4 pm on a summer afternoon. Depending on the type of climate the air temperature in the shade may also be close to its maximum at that time. It should be noted that this situation may occur even in midwinter, so that on a sunny winter day considerable cooling may be required.

Let us assume a multi-story air-supported building that is 60 FT in diameter and 120 FT high, with a design temperature difference of 20°F between inside and outside and a thermal resistance (R value) of only 1 for the membrane. This will be compared with a conventional square building of similar area, having windows occupying 25% of the external wall area and using typical R values for the walls and roof. Approximate heat gain values are shown in Table 3.2 below.

Table 3.2: Summer heat gain comparison of air-supported and conventional buildings

Building Component	Membrane Building	Conventional Building
Wall conductivity	500,000 BTU/hr	237,000 BTU/hr
Wall direct radiation	1,060,000 BTU/hr	324,000 BTU/hr
Wall diffuse radiation	340,000 BTU/hr	110,000 BTU/hr
Roof conductivity	22,000 BTU/hr	22,000 BTU/hr
Totals:	1,922,000 BTU/hr	693,000 BTU/hr

Thus the heat gain for this membrane building at the worst time is about three times that of a conventional building. However, the radiant heat gain through the membrane can be substantially reduced by coating all but the vision strips with an opaque, reflecting surface such as a metallic coating. Using a reflectivity to solar radiation of 0.80 over three quarters of the surface reduces the total external heat load of the membrane building to about twice that of a comparable conventional building.

In the above example an air-supply at the rate of six air changes per hour at atmospheric pressure (i.e., three air changes per hour at two atmospheres) would permit a heat exchange of 700,000 BTU/hour with a temperature difference of 20°F between inlet and outlet. For the peak cooling condition, it would be necessary to either increase the air supply to about 12 changes per hour at 1 atmosphere, or to use secondary cooling such as chilled water fan-coil units within the building. If

---

[5] The intensity of radiation normal to the sun's rays falls off as the altitude decreases. This falling off is much more rapid at altitudes below about 30 degrees. The sun strikes a maximum projected area of the cylindrical surface when the altitude is zero

additional air-handling is used it should be carried out in a high-pressure circuit, with the acceptable minimum of make-up air, since the energy required to pressurize the make-up air to the required internal building pressure would otherwise add greatly to the energy needed for cooling the building.

Although the thermal performance of the pneumatic membrane building in its simple form is substantially inferior to that of a conventional building, improvements are certainly feasible. Apart from the addition of reflective coatings to large sections of the membrane, it should be possible to add flexible insulation material to the opaque sections of the membrane and provide external sunshading devices. For example, horizontal sunshading louvers could be hung from the top bearing floor (i.e., roof) on the external side of the membrane and attached at intermediate points to the existing cable-network. Under these circumstances the portion of the heat load that is produced by solar radiation impinging directly on the building enclosure could be substantially reduced as a function of the vertical spacing and horizontal projection of the louvers.

From the point of view of heat load, air supply and access, a multi-story air-supported structural solution has particular merit where the number of occupants is small and the anticipated lifespan of the building is relatively short (e.g., less than 15 years). In the case of a building housing mainly equipment or materials, the delay of ingress and egress through the airlock, the problems of fire escape, the need for fresh air supply and the desirability of transparent areas in the membrane are all reduced.

3.6.2 Water Supply and Sanitary Fittings

The effect of a hyperbaric building environment on the design and installation of sanitary fittings has received no consideration in the past. The pressure inside single-level air-buildings is obviously too small to have any effect on sanitary installations, and in the case of high pressure caissons the maximum allowable exposure times are severely limited by the applicable codes for physiological reasons. Therefore, the problems posed in this area by multi-story air-supported buildings are without precedent and may in the future lead to new waste removal systems and equipment. It is not the intention of the author to deal with the design of sanitary plumbing suitable for a hyperbaric environment, but merely to set out the special conditions encountered in these buildings and suggest tentative methods of catering for these in the light of presently available sanitary systems.

Sanitary fixtures are appliances (e.g., basins, water closets, showers, and so on) installed in a building for the purpose of receiving and passing graywater[6] and blackwater[7]. They are presently designed to prevent gases that may arise from decomposed organic matter from infiltrating into the building. The fixtures are connected ultimately to a public drainage system, while the passage of gases into the building is prevented by means of a water seal, normally incorporated directly in the fixture.

First, let us consider the question of water supply for a multi-story air-supported building with an internal design pressure of up to 15 psig. A considerable amount of boosting will be required to

---

[6] Graywater is defined as water from showers, bathtubs, kitchen and bathroom sinks, hot tub and drinking fountain drains, and washing machines.

[7] Blackwater is defined as water containing human excreta, such as wastewater from toilets.

overcome this environmental pressure for the purpose of feeding mains water into storage tanks at the roof or basement level. If the pressure in the mains is 50 psig then an increase of 30% in pump capacity will be required in comparison with an orthodox building. The accompanying increase in cost is likely to be quite small, if not negligible.

Unfortunately, the problem of waste disposal will present greater complications. Under present conditions no local government authority is likely to tolerate the discharge of excremental matter into a public sewerage system at 15 psig pressure. To overcome this restriction one of the following procedures could be adopted with a minimum of alteration to accepted plumbing practice:

- A. Unpressurized service areas could be provided within the multi-story air-supported building. While this would require individual airlocks at each floor level, existing fixtures and reticulation may be used without modification.

- B. Possibly a simpler method would be to provide air-lock mechanisms within waste pipes. In this case the function of the water seal is preserved and the waste will reach the sewer after passing through one or more stages of decompression. This method can be further improved by combining a number of similar waste pipes at a central decompression unit. It seems highly probable that these waste pipes would require artificial ventilation at 15 psig pressure, in conjunction with the central air-conditioning system.

To summarize, a hyperbaric building environment of less than 15 psig should have little impact on water supply, apart from the necessity of providing pumps of approximately one third greater capacity than in an orthodox building. The rate at which the water must be boosted will exceed the limit of draw permitted by the local water utility. Although water utilities are willing to accept a considerable drop in mains pressure for emergency purposes, near negative pressures can of course not be tolerated. Therefore, even purely from the point of view of fire services the multi-story air-supported building will require considerable tank storage. Low level storage is likely to be preferable, with the actual volume being determined by agreement with the fire department and water utility. Since there is a need for storage at low level it will be worthwhile to make it adequate and minimize that at high level in the building, thereby reducing the weight to be carried by the internal pressure of the building.

The disposal of wastes in multi-story air-supported buildings does present more severe problems, due to the existence of a pressure differential between the external atmosphere and the building environment. For a water seal to be preserved within individual fixtures, it is necessary for the air pressure acting on the two exposed surfaces of the seal to be the same. For this reason, if existing installations are to be used with a minimum of modification, the pressure within the plumbing system may be either atmospheric or identical to, the building environment. Depending on the solution adopted, airlocks will be required between the service area (on each floor) and the remainder of the building or within the waste pipes themselves. The latter approach in which the airlocks are centralized within the waste pipes is likely to be preferable in respect to cost and convenience.

Lessons can be drawn from extraterrestrial research, in particular investigations dealing with the design of lunar bases that commenced as far back as the 1950s (Gaume 1958, Szilard 1959) and accelerated during the period that achieved the first landing on the moon on 20 July, 1969.

3.7 Cable-Networks

It was mentioned previously that for most air-supported membrane buildings it will be advisable to resist the circumferential stress due to internal pressure by means of a cable-network, while the membrane serves simply as a non-porous envelope. Under these circumstances the required tensile strength of the membrane material is substantially lowered, allowing the use of a much wider range of plastic materials than would have been possible if the membrane were required to resist the entire circumferential tension.

The typical cable-network arrangement shown in Figure 3.11 can be used to derive an approximate design formula for the cable-network and the membrane envelope. The analysis employed is very much a simplification, relying for its general validity on the following assumptions:

Assumption 1: The elastic membrane will bulge out between cables and therefore the reactions at each bulge are those of the cables. In this respect the modulus of elasticity of the membrane material should preferably be lower than that of the cable material. In actual practice, it is quite likely that this condition will be satisfied by a factor of at least 10 when steel cables are used in combination with a plastic membrane.

Assumption 2: The cables are free to slide over each other at joints.

Assumption 3: The cables in each direction will carry equal loads. If there are k cables altogether then there will be $k/2$ cables in each direction inclined at an angle of θ degrees to the vertical axis.

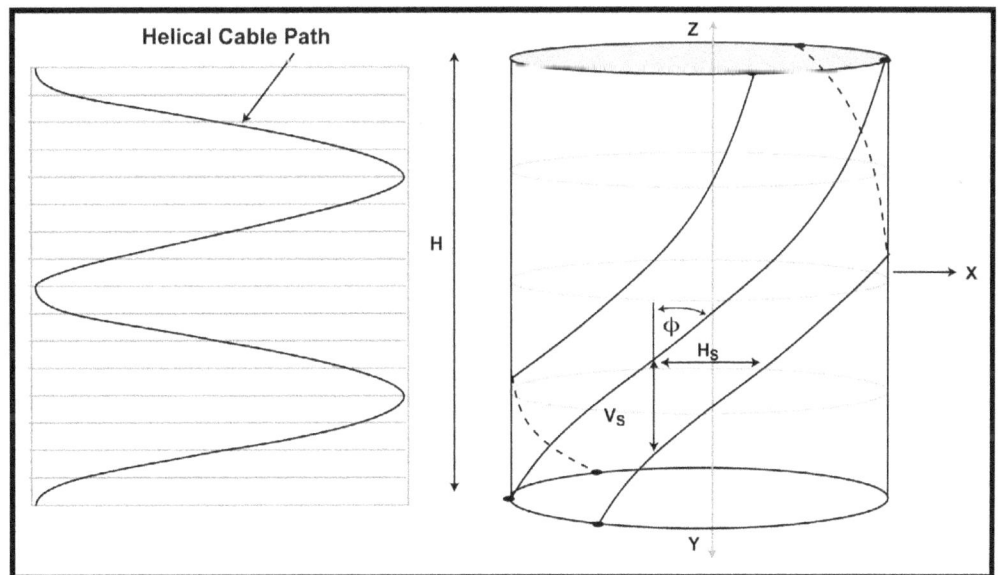

Figure 3.11: A cable-network as the primary structural element of a multi-story air-supported building

There remains the question of the actual shape assumed by a typical cable. When a plane cuts a cylinder at some angle less than 90 degrees and greater than zero degrees to the horizontal, then the resultant section is an ellipse (Gerard 1967, 2083). However, the path traced out on the curved cylindrical surface by a cable significantly deviates from an ellipse at the ends (i.e., at the fixing points of each cable). In that region the tangent of an ellipse will tend toward zero. However, it would appear quite clearly in Figure 3.4 that this condition does not hold for the cable-network[8] under consideration. It is more likely that the cable configuration is helical and that the cable curve is identified as the locus of a point whose angular movement is in constant ratio to its movement to the longitudinal axis of a *right* cylinder[9]. The resultant curve is shown in Figure 3.11 as a cylindrical helix, whose pitch is defined as the distance moved forward for 360° of angular motion (Davies 1967, 94-5).

Let us consider a flexible membrane tube subjected to an internal pressure (P psig) and contained by circumferential, diagonal cables in two directions. If there are a total of k cables, then there will be $k/2$ cables in each direction inclined at θ to the vertical axis. In reference to Figure 3.11 and the previous assumptions, cable tensions are determined for two critical loading conditions as follows.

Spacing of cables (H_S) in the horizontal direction is given by:

$$H_S = 2 \pi R / (k/2) = 4 \pi R / k \quad \text{(FT)} \quad \text{.. 3.1}$$

Similarly, spacing of cables (V_S) in the vertical direction is given by:

$$V_S = 2 \pi R \cot \theta / (k/2) = 4 \pi R \cot \theta / k \quad \text{(FT)} \quad \text{........................ 3.2}$$

Consideration of equilibrium conditions for a vertical section yields:

$$P H / (2 R) = 2 (H / V_S) T_{CAH}$$

$$T_{CAH} = 4 P \pi R^2 \cot \theta / k \quad \text{(LB)} \quad \text{..................... 3.3}$$

Consideration of equilibrium conditions for a horizontal section yields:

$$P \pi R^2 - W = k T_{CAV}$$

$$T_{CAV} = (P \pi R^2 - W) / k \quad \text{(LB)} \quad \text{..................... 3.4}$$

Where T_{CAH} and T_{CAV} are the horizontal and vertical components of the cable tension (T_{CA}), respectively.

The cable-network will assume a cylindrical form for a specific angle θ, where the numerical value of θ is constant for all load conditions as long as the diameter of the cylindrical building is the same at all levels. However, it is necessary to design multi-story, air-supported buildings with an external cable-network for two critical loading conditions.

Loading Condition 1 (W = 0): When the external load (W LB) is zero all of the longitudinal and circumferential forces due to internal pressure will be resisted by the diagonal cables. The membrane will act purely as a non-porous container bulging out between intersecting cables and may therefore be designed on the assumption that its

---

[8] The possibility that a portion of the ellipse could serve as an approximation for the actual cable path was investigated by the author, but the expression derived for the corresponding cable tension is not used in the design approach for multi-story air-supported buildings with external cable-networks presented in this and the following chapter. Instead a helical cable path was chosen as a more appropriate alternative.

[9] A *right* cylinder is a cylinder that has its top and bottom circular bases vertically aligned (i.e., the bases are of equal diameter and the upper base is directly above the lower base).

radius of curvature will not exceed the maximum mesh size (R_M) of the constraining cable-network[10].

$$R_M = 2\pi R / (k/2) = 4\pi R / k$$

Therefore, the stress in the membrane (f_M) is given by:

$$\mathbf{f_M = PR_M = 4\pi PR/k \text{ (LB/IN)}} \quad \dots\dots\dots\dots\dots\dots 3.5$$

Similarly, the required membrane thickness (t) is given by the expression:

$$\mathbf{t = 4\pi PR/(k f_M) \text{ (IN)}} \quad \dots\dots\dots\dots\dots\dots 3.6$$

where f_M LB/IN is the allowable working stress in tension of the membrane material.

For the same loading condition (i.e., $W = 0$) the angle of inclination (θ) of each cable to the vertical axis is obtained by equating T_{CAV} and T_{CAH}:

$$T_{CA} \cos\theta = P\pi R^2/k \quad \text{and} \quad T_{CA}\sin\theta = (4P\pi R^2 \cot\theta)/k$$
$$T_{CA}\sin\theta = P\pi R^2 \tan\theta/k = (4P\pi R^2 \cot\theta)/k$$
$$\tan\theta = 2$$
$$\theta = 63°26' \quad \dots\dots\dots\dots\dots\dots\dots\dots\dots\dots 3.7$$

In this case the cable tension (T_{CA}) is given by either T_{CAV} or T_{CAH}, as follows:

$$\mathbf{T_{CA}\sin\theta = P\pi R^2/(k\cos\theta) = T_{CAV}/\cos\theta = T_{CAH}/\sin\theta \text{ (LB)}} \dots\dots 3.8$$

Loading Condition 2 ($W = W_{ULT}$): If the external load (W LB) is increased to the point where the internal pressure (P psig) acting on the cross-sectional column area (A SI) is no longer capable of resisting this superimposed load (i.e., W becomes the ultimate load), then the tension in the diagonal cables will tend to zero and all of the circumferential force due to internal pressure will be resisted by the membrane. For reasons of safety it will therefore be necessary to provide multi-story, air-supported cable-network buildings with circumferential (i.e., horizontal) cables in addition to the diagonal cable-network. Diagonal cables in preference to vertical cables are justified on the basis of wind bracing requirements discussed in Chapter 4). The total circumferential forces (H_F) to be resisted by the horizontal cables under the condition $W = W_{ULT}$ and $T_{CA} = 0$ is given by:

$$H_F = PRH$$

for *n* horizontal cables the tension T_H in each cable is given by the expression:

$$\mathbf{T_H = PRH/n \text{ (LB)}} \quad \dots\dots\dots\dots\dots\dots 3.9$$

Equations 3.5 to 3.9 enable us to calculate the membrane stress, and tensile forces in the diagonal and circumferential cables, respectively. However, to complete the design of multi-story, air-supported cable-network buildings it will be necessary to consider the influence of the diagonal cable-network on the pressure-utilization efficiency of the structure as a whole. It is intended to use the vertical component of the tensile capacity of the cables as the sole means of stabilizing the pneumatic structure in its capacity as a load-bearing, free-standing column. Therefore, equations

---

[10] The maximum radius of curvature of the membrane will also depend on its modulus of elasticity. The required elongation for the membrane to stretch from R to R_M is approximately 5%.

2.6 and 2.7 derived previously in Chapter 2 for pressurized flexible membrane columns can now be rewritten in terms of an exterior cable-network. The total cross-sectional area (A_E) of the cable-network inclined at θ degrees to the vertical building axis is given by:

$$A_E = k\, A_{CA} / \cos\theta \quad (SI)$$

If this area (A_E) is spread equally around the circumference of the building (i.e., the membrane), then the effective thickness (t_{CA}) is:

$$t_{CA} = k\, r^2 / (2\, R \cos\theta) \quad (IN)$$

Substituting in equation 2.7 for E_{CA}, I_{CA} and t_{CA} we obtain the following expression for the load-bearing capacity per unit area ($L\ psi$) of multi-story, air-supported cable-network buildings:

$$L = (E_{CA}\, I_{CA}\, ((2e) + R) / (2eAH^2))\, [((1 + 8eH^2\, P\, R \cos\theta)^{0.5} - 1) / (k\, E_{CA}\, r^2\, (2e + R)^2)] \ldots\ 3.10$$

Similarly, the required internal pressure ($P\ psig$) for a given load ($W\ LB$) is given by:

$$P = (k\, W\, r^2 / (R^2 \cos\theta))\, [(\cos\theta / (k\, A_{CA})) + (e / Z_{CA}) + (We\, H^2 / (2\, E_{CA}\, I_{CA}\, Z_{CA}))] \ldots\ 3.11$$

To complete this analysis it should be mentioned that the expression derived in Chapter 4 (Section 4.2) for the excess pressure ($P_E\ psig$) required to stabilize a multi-story, air-supported cable-network building under the action of horizontal wind loads:

$$P_E = D_H\, H\, t / (R\, Z) \quad (psig) \ldots\ 4.10$$

may be rewritten in terms of an external cable-network as follows:

$$t_{CA} = k\, r^2 / (2\, R \cos\theta)$$

$$Z_{CA} = k\, R\, A_{CA} / (2 \cos\theta)$$

$$P_E = D_H\, H / (\pi\, R^3) \quad (psig) \ldots\ 3.12$$

The above equation enables us to determine the internal pressure (over and above the design pressure calculated to support vertical loads) required to stabilize a multi-story, air-supported cable-network building under a horizontal force (D_H).

3.8 General Safety Considerations

From the point of view of safety the structural stability of a multi-story air-supported building is heavily dependent upon:

A. The satisfactory performance of the pressurization equipment in being capable of sustaining an increased air-input under emergency conditions.

B. The ability of the building membrane to resist tearing, after local punctures have occurred.

In view of the critical requirement of reliability the design of the mechanical equipment will present problems not usually encountered in building construction. The provision of standby plant and probably alternative energy sources will be necessary. It may be pointed out that single-engine aircraft and helicopters are accepted as a reasonable risk, being solely dependent on a single power unit. A better analogy for the air-supported building under consideration would be the multiple-engine airliner, which is capable of operating with part of its power system out of action. Strict maintenance and inspection programs similar to those applied to commercial aviation will need to be applied by building authorities to the pressurization equipment of a multi-story air-supported building.

Special consideration will also need to be given to the performance of the building membrane. The type of currently available plastic material that will satisfy the performance requirements related to tensile strength and weatherability is a nylon scrim base laminate coated with a polyvinyl chloride (PVC) or polyvinyl fluoride (PVF) film externally and a polyurethane film internally. The nylon scrim has the ability to localize rupture by developing a fairly high tear-resistance. If the building membrane is punctured by accident or as an indirect result of civil disturbance or as the direct outcome of an act of terrorism (e.g., bullets and larger projectiles) and this perforation remains localized due to the tear-resistance of the membrane material, then the continuing stability of the building will be purely a question of pressurized air-input. The design of the mechanical equipment can therefore be dealt with statistically, namely: What is the probability of failure in relationship to the effective size of a puncture that may occur during the lifespan of the building?

While such a calculated risk has become acceptable in commercial aviation it is unlikely to be acceptable in the near future in buildings, which are occupied for much longer periods. Total collapse of a multi-story air-supported building is no more acceptable than the total collapse of any orthodox building structure. The integrity of the pneumatic structure must be maintained for a sufficient period of time following a disastrous event to allow the building to be evacuated. This will require the provision of an emergency pressurized shelter immediately below the building, to avoid the inevitable time delays associated with the airlock entrance to the building on the ground floor.

In addition, the fire-rated perimeter sliding panels that were suggested in Section 3.5 for shielding the membrane from the heat radiation of an internal fire may be assigned a secondary structural function under emergency conditions. If, for whatever reasons, the internal building pressure falls below a specified level these shields would be automatically activated to slide into predetermined positions around the perimeter of each floor. Considering that the occupancy live-load assumed during the design of the building is likely to be much greater than the actual live-load at any time during the lifespan of the building and that the perimeter panels are optimally located to support the floor above, the proposed additional structural function assigned to these panels can be easily accommodated.

The proposed safety provisions for a multi-story air-supported building subjected to a loss of internal pressure due to equipment failure or catastrophic air leakage can be summarized in stages, as follows:

Stage 1: As the internal air pressure falls below a *first alert* level the normal air-outlet is automatically shut off and standby pressurization equipment is automatically activated.

Stage 2: If the internal air pressure continues to fall below a *second alert* level the perimeter panels are automatically activated to slide into predetermined positions on each floor. In addition an alarm is automatically sounded to initiate evacuation of the building occupants to the pressurized emergency shelter in the basement of the building.

Stage 3: Should the internal air pressure remain below the *second alert* level evacuation from the emergency shelter to the external environment will be initiated concurrently through several airlocks located around the perimeter of the shelter.

It should be noted that a multi-story, air-supported cable-network building is ideally suited for resisting earthquake loads. First, it is a very flexible building with few rigid structural joints. The building is essentially a cylindrical container with the internal air-pressure providing stability. Second, the external cable-network is optimally located at the furthest distance from the neutral axis at the center of the building. Therefore, the building acting as a column has the largest possible moment of inertia. Third, the external cables wrapped around the pressurized membrane container serve as an excellent bracing mechanism. They are oriented in three directions (i.e., at an angle of *63° 26'* (see equation 3.7) on either side of the vertical and horizontally at an angle of *90°* to the vertical). The bracing provided by the cable-network in combination with the membrane provides a degree of ductile stability that is not achievable with orthodox steel or reinforced structural frames.

3.9 Erection and Construction Considerations

Multi-story air-supported buildings of the type described here will require new procedures for erection, new sequences of assembly, and different allocations of construction manpower. The suspension scheme depends upon a framework of trusses or a beam system at roof level, with main supporting fixtures around the outside perimeter and a smaller number around the inner perimeter of the underside of the air-supported roof slab. From these the floors are suspended by means of high-tensile steel rods. The rods are not continuous but in approximately story-height sections that are connected vertically by means of turnbuckles. The secondary role of the turnbuckles is to provide a convenient mechanism for adjusting the story-height and for leveling each individual floor horizontally.

Experience with the construction of a two-story prototype air-supported building (see Chapter 5) suggests that the joints for the suspension rods should be about one foot below the underside of each floor. Longer rods would make it difficult to thread the rods through the prepositioned gusset plates located on the upper and lower surface of each floor during the erection of the building. A *100 FT* diameter building would likely require in the order of 16 suspension rods equidistantly spaced around the outside perimeter of each floor and probably no more than four around the inner perimeter[11]. Based on normal building loads of *100 psf* live-load and *60 psf* dead-load (i.e., a relatively lightweight prestressed post-tensioned concrete slab and a very lightweight building envelope) each suspension rod would carry a load of around *70,000 LB*. Assuming a steel design stress of *50,000 psi*, the rod diameter would be less than *1½ IN*.

Once the roof has been lifted into its final position it will block the hoisting of the floors, since the diameter of the roof is larger by two feet than the floors that will be suspended from it. For this reason four equidistantly spaced open vertical pipes will need to be embedded in the roof near its outer perimeter. The diameter of these four pipes must be large enough (e.g., *2 IN* diameter) to allow the four crane cables to pass freely through the roof as the floors are being hoisted one-by-one. Before the lifting of each floor the internal air pressure in the building must be increased proportionally to allow for the weight of the floor that is next in sequence to be hoisted. After all of the floors have been lifted into their final positions the crane cables can be withdrawn to allow

---

[11] This assumes that the floor is annular in shape with a central hole of about 20 FT diameter to allow for a winding staircase around an elevator shaft.

the pipes to be capped at both ends, so that the building is airtight. The internal air pressure in the building is then adjusted to its final design level.

The first floor to basement levels will be of normal compression construction with circular, prestressed, post-tensioned concrete perimeter walls enclosing all pressurized areas. The entrance to the building at ground level will require an airlock. This should be as unobtrusive as possible so that persons entering the building will be largely unaware that they are entering a pressurized environment. Ideally, the airlock entrance would be designed so that the change from external atmospheric pressure to the internal hyperbaric pressure is not abrupt. This can be accomplished architecturally through the provision of several contiguous spaces performing, unbeknownst to the entering or exiting person, as a multi-stage airlock. However, in addition to the main building entrance, provision will need to be made for an emergence airlock facility that will expedite the mass exit of the building occupants from the basement evacuation shelter to the outside in case of a fire or other structural emergency.

The construction of a typical 10-story air-supported cable-network building will involve about two dozen major tasks that are postulated in Figure 3.12 to proceed in a sequence that will allow some tasks to be performed in parallel.

Task 1: Site preparation and excavation to the footing level of the basement.

Task 2: Erection of standard compression structure to first floor level including main airlock entrance to the building on the ground floor, an emergence shelter with separate airlock facilities for mass evacuation in case of a structural emergency, and mechanical equipment spaces, both below ground level. The diameter of the first floor to be identical to the diameter of the roof (i.e., at least two feet larger in diameter than the suspended building floors).

Task 3: Fabrication of the membrane that will serve as the external building envelope (off-site).

Task 4: Fabrication of the external diagonal and horizontal cables sheathed in flexible plastic sleeves to minimize potential abrasion between the cables and the membrane (off-site).

Task 5: Fabrication of the floor suspension fittings consisting of high tensile steel rods with threaded ends, turnbuckles, and mild steel gusset plates for attachment points on each floor (off-site).

Task 6: Installation of air pressurization equipment in the basement mechanical spaces.

Task 7: Fabrication of the roof trusses from which the building floors will be suspended (off-site). The roof will be at least two feet larger in diameter than the building floors.

Task 8: Pouring of prestressed post-tensioned concrete floors one above the other on top of the ground floor compression structure. The floors are annular in shape with four equidistant perimeter hoisting attachments and all gusset plates at suspension points cast in place.

Task 9: Post-tensioning and preparation of the floors for hoisting in lift-slab fashion, following an adequate curing period.

Task 10: Assembly of the roof trusses on top of the uppermost lift-slab floor, with four crane hook attachments on the upper surface of trusses in preparation for later hoisting of the roof.

Task 11: Construction of air-tight roof layer securely attached to underside of trusses and water-tight roof surface attached to upper surface of trusses. Includes preparation of the perimeter surfaces of the roof and the first floor (compression structure) for later attachment of the building envelope.

Task 12: Draping of the building envelope over the roof and floors, including attachment of the membrane at the perimeter of both the roof and first floor (compression structure) to achieve airtight seals.

Task 13: Assembly of a four-tower portal crane, capable of moving 90° on circular rail tracks (at ground level) around the circular building footprint. The tower cranes are equal-distance spaced around the perimeter of the building and connected at a height of about 120 FT across the top of the building by a portal framework of trusses. Preparation of the four lifting cables and attachments for later hoisting of the roof and suspended floors.

Task 14: Initial hoisting of the roof (with attached building envelope) to a level of approximately two feet above the uppermost lift-slab floor.

Task 15: Hoisting of roof to full height utilizing the crane only. Concurrently, the internal air pressure should be raised slightly and only sufficiently to maintain the cylindrical form of the building envelope in preparation for the attachment of the external cable-network..

Task 16: Attachment of the external diagonal cables around the building envelope at predefined angles and in opposing directions on either side of the vertical axis.

Task 17: Attachment of the external horizontal cables around the building envelope at the required vertical spacing.

Task 18: Attachment of suspension rods to the underside of the roof ready for the suspension of the top floor after hoisting. The crane cables that were used to lift the roof into position are removed from their attachments and threaded through four pipes embedded in the roof ready for attachment to the top floor that will be hoisted next. The internal air pressure in the building is increased in proportion to the weight of the floor that is intended to be hoisted next.

Task 19: Lifting of each floor one-by-one. Once the floor is in place the suspension rods/hangers are attached (i.e., threaded through the gusset plates at the points of attachment). Turnbuckles, located about one to two feet below the underside of the floor above, are used to connect the suspension rod sections and to level each floor.

Task 20: Construction of internal staircases, service ducts, and perimeter fire-rated (sliding) screens.

Task 21: Adjustment of all external cables to final positions.

Task 22: Capping of the four pipes in the roof that were required for the hoisting of the floors, with airtight covers at both ends and adjustment of the internal air pressure to the final building occupancy level.

Task 23: Completion of all electrical, plumbing, mechanical, and waste management work.

Task 24: Installation of elevators.

Task 25: Completion of final finishes.

Task 26: Final inspection and pressurization system shakedown tests in preparation for building occupancy.

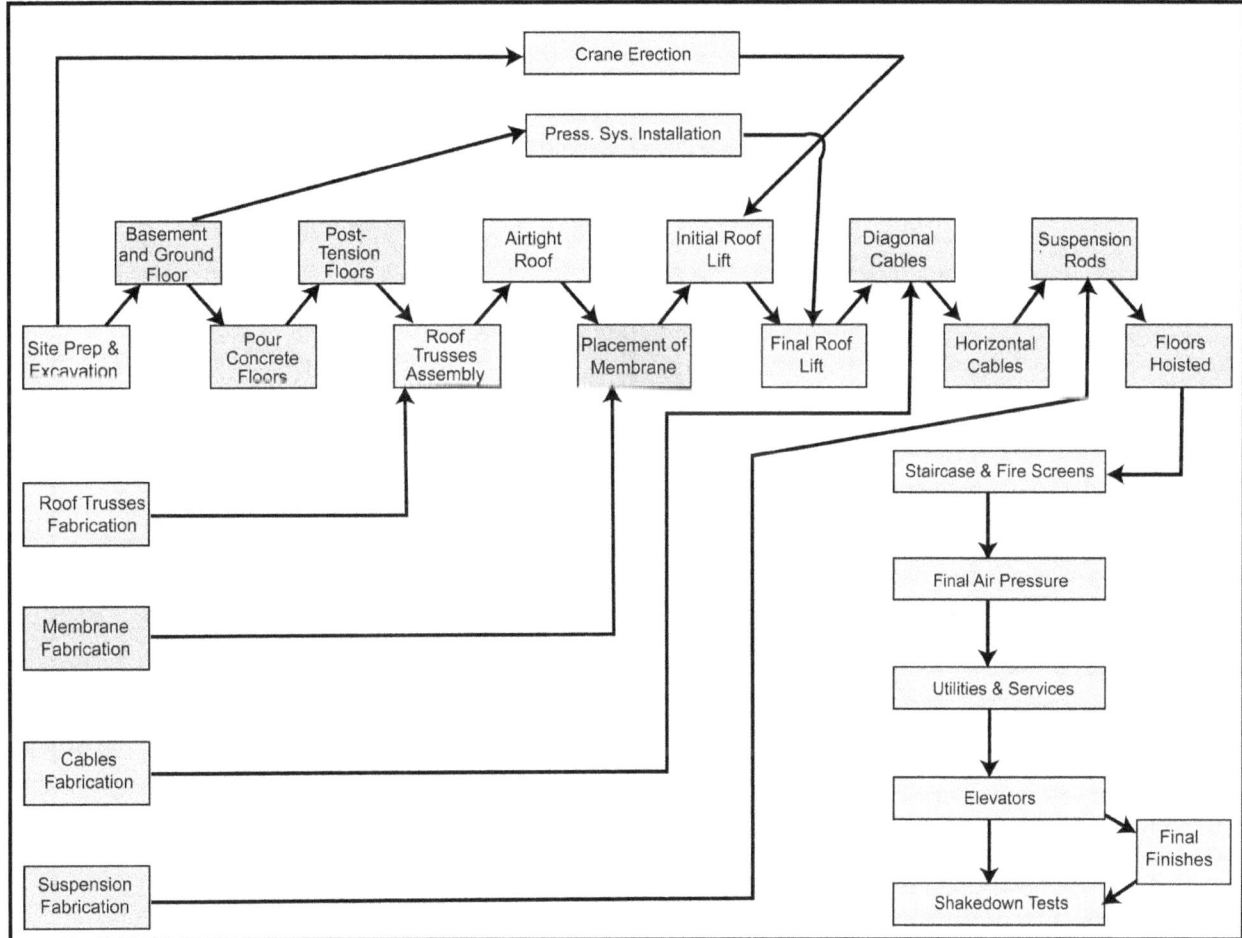

Figure 3.12: Construction sequence of multi-story air-supported cable-network buildings

The construction of a multi-story air-supported building of the type described above certainly has some features that involve task sequences requiring careful planning and preparation, critical timing, and skills that are new to the building construction domain. However, similar critical task sequences have become fairly common in the construction of civil engineering works, in particular suspension bridges where careful planning, accuracy and timing are of paramount importance.

What in particular sets multi-story air-supported buildings apart from orthodox multi-story building construction is the reliance on internal air pressure as a principal structural component. The maintenance of the air pressure depends on the integrity of a relatively thin and fragile external plastic membrane that must be carefully protected during the erection process. The fact that this membrane is in one piece, brought onto the site as an open-ended cylinder that may be up to *120 FT* long and *314 FT* wide (i.e., double folded) for a *100 FT* diameter building, and has to be fixed in position before the roof and floors of the building have been hoisted into position, is certainly not a trivial undertaking. The membrane has to be literally threaded over the roof and floors when these are still stacked in lift-slab fashion one on top of the other on the upper platform of the basement-ground floor compression structure that also serves as the first floor of the building. Even if the membrane weighs less than *½ LB per square foot*, the total weight of the membrane for a 12-story building of *100 FT* diameter would be almost *20,000 LB* (or nine tons). Therefore, the assistance of a crane will be required to accomplish this rather exacting construction task.

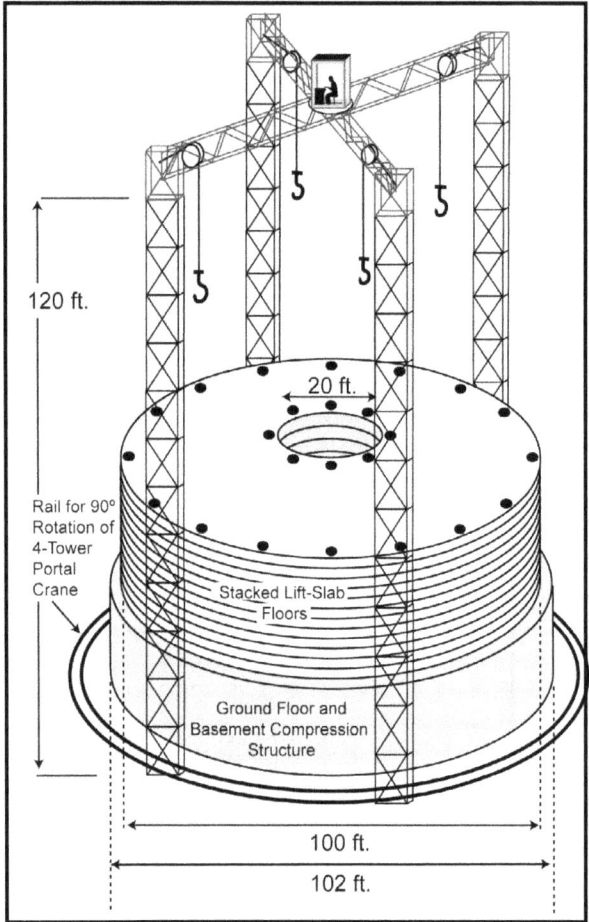

Figure 3.13: Portal crane assembly for the erection sequence

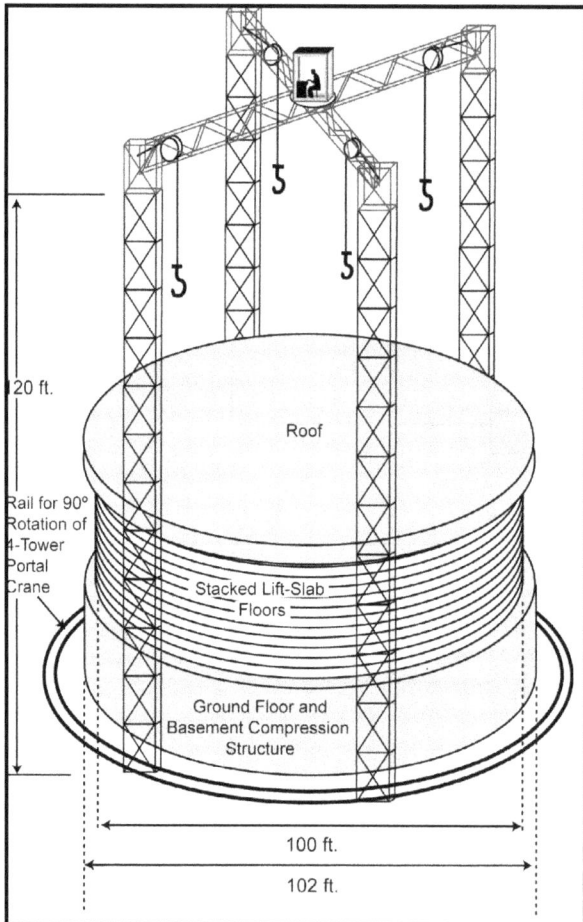

Figure 3.14: Erection stage prior to hoisting of roof and floors

Since a crane will be required for several other major construction tasks, such as hoisting of the roof and floors, the configuration of the crane assembly warrants further consideration. It is suggested that the crane assembly consist of four towers positioned at equal spacing around the perimeter of the building on rails. As shown in Figure 3.13, the crane towers are connected by trusses across the top of the building and are able to swivel in unison 90° around the central vertical axis of the building. In this way the crane assembly provides a framework with four lifting points above the roof and at the required distance from the center of the building. This allows the roof to be lifted to its final height by attachment of the four crane cables to the outside perimeter in 3, 6, 9, and 12 o'clock positions. While the roof is being lifted the air pressure inside the membrane envelope will need to be just sufficiently raised to stiffen the membrane as a cylinder. An internal air pressure of no more than a ¼ *psig* will be sufficient to produce a taut building envelope without creating unnecessary material stress in the membrane. The function of the internal air pressure during this stage of the construction process is to maintain the cylindrical form of the building envelope for the attachment of the external cable-network, and to allow construction personnel to enter the building through the ground floor compression structure and prepare the floors for hoisting.

The attachment of the external cable-network should proceed in the following order. First, the diagonal cables should be placed into position in both directions at the optimum angle according to equation 3.7. This is followed by the attachment of the horizontal cables, which can be tied to the intersections of diagonal cables at reasonable intervals to hold them in place. Only after the cable-network has been fully installed should the internal air pressure be raised incrementally to first support the roof and then the suspended floors as they are sequentially hoisted into position.

However, the hoisting of the floors is complicated by two factors. First, the floors are inside the sealed building envelope and therefore cannot be attached to the crane cables from outside the membrane as was possible in the case of the roof. Second, the roof overlaps the floors because its diameter is at least 2 FT larger than the diameter of the floors. The best solution to this problem that the author can propose is to embed four open-ended vertical pipes of *2 to 3 IN* diameter in the roof structure directly above the lifting points of the floors. This will allow the crane cables to reach inside the pressurized membrane tube, where they can be readily attached to the perimeter of the next floor to be hoisted by construction personnel. Before the floor is lifted by the crane assembly, the air pressure inside the membrane is increased to allow for the additional dead-load of the floor. Once in position the suspension rods from the floor above are threaded through the gusset plates of the attachment points of the floor being hoisted and locked into position. The same process is followed for the hoisting of the successively lower floors. At the first floor level the suspension rods are anchored and slightly prestressed to overcome any differential changes in suspension rod lengths due to unequal live-load distribution or thermal expansion during the occupancy of the building.

The draping of the relatively fragile plastic building envelope around the roof and floor plates, while these are stacked in lift-slab fashion on top of the ground floor compression structure (i.e., Task 12), is perhaps the most exacting task during the construction sequence (Figure 3.14). There are several complicating factors that raise technical questions:

1. Even though the membrane material per unit area is very light, since it has to be in one piece the complete membrane tube for a realistic building will weigh several tons (e.g., almost 10 tons for a 12-story building with 100 FT diameter floors). How can this

relatively heavy and fragile building component be handled and moved into position on the construction site?

2. The membrane cannot be easily attached to one or more cranes because the stress level at the point of attachment could exceed the strength of material. For example, if the full weight of the membrane is lifted concurrently at four equidistant points then the load at each pick-up point could exceed *5,000 LB*. How should the membrane be configured (i.e., folded) while it is moved onto the site? How can the membrane be lifted by crane(s) so that it does not tear? What kind of lifting equipment will be required to maneuver the membrane into position over the stacked floors and roof?

3. The membrane is a fairly tight fit around the roof and the first floor (i.e., the top level of the ground floor compression structure). It will be extremely difficult, if not impossible, to drape the membrane over the roof if it is in the shape of a cylinder that is just slightly larger in diameter (i.e., 1 or 2 inches) than the diameter of the roof. Even if physically possible it is likely that the membrane would be damaged, or at least severely tarnished, during such an intricate operation. Would it be possible to manufacture the membrane as a single flat sheet, which is provided with a vertical joint that can be connected to form a cylinder after the membrane has been draped around the roof and first floor?

4. As an alternatively course of action consideration could be given to moving the membrane into position around the stacked floors before the roof is constructed. Could the membrane be adequately protected so that it would not be damaged or tarnished during the construction of the roof?

It would appear most convenient to move the membrane on-site horizontally rolled-up in the shape of an annulus. This will allow slings to be wrapped around the annulus at four equidistantly spaced positions, to serve as crane pick-up points. At least two mobile cranes would be used for the on-site movement of the annulus.

In respect to the factors listed above it would appear that there are at least two alternative approaches for placing the building envelope in position. The first approach would apply if the membrane cylinder is delivered onto the site in its final form as a cylinder without a vertical joint. Under these circumstances it will be necessary to drape the membrane over the stacked-up floors before the roof is constructed (Task 10). Since the diameter of the lift-slab floors is *2 FT* smaller than the diameter of the building envelope, the membrane should slide over the floors with some room to spare, even when horizontally rolled-up in the shape of an annulus. Two mobile cranes would lift up the membrane at two opposite pick-up points and move it to the building so that it is suspended several feet above the uppermost lift-slab floor. Two additional mobile cranes would then move into position on the periphery of the building and pick up the remaining two slings between the two cranes that brought the membrane to the building. With some manual help from workmen standing on top of the stacked-up floors it should be possible to gently lower the membrane onto the edge of the first floor (i.e., the top of the ground floor compression structure). This would be followed by the construction of the roof on top of the uppermost lift-slab floor, the threading of the membrane around the external perimeter of the roof, and the fixing of the top of the membrane to form an airtight seal around the roof.

The second approach is in the view of the author only possible if the membrane is delivered onto the site as a single sheet with a vertical joint that allows the membrane to be converted into a cylinder on-site by closing a zipper fixed along the length of the vertical joint. In this case the roof can be constructed on top of the uppermost lift-slab floor before the membrane is positioned around the building. Three mobile cranes would be used to lift up the membrane at three contiguous pick-up points and move it to the building, so that it is suspended several feet above the uppermost lift-slab floor. A fourth mobile crane would then move into position and lift the membrane at the remaining pick-up point to the same height as the other three pick-up points. With the manual assistance of several workmen standing on top of the roof the top of the membrane can now be fixed in place around the external perimeter of the roof. Toward the conclusion of this task the vertical zipped joint should be closed from the top, but only three or four feet downward. The fixing of the membrane at the bottom around the perimeter of the first floor (i.e., the top of the ground floor compression structure) and the closing of the zipped vertical joint to the bottom of the membrane should wait until the four-tower portal crane has been erected (Task 13).

In the case of either approach the four mobile cranes can be removed from the site after the membrane enclosure has been fixed around the external perimeter of the roof. The roof can then be lifted by the portal crane as described in Tasks 14 and 15, followed by the fixing of the bottom of the membrane to the first floor (i.e., the top of the ground floor compression structure) as described in the second part of Task 12. Clearly, the sequence of operations suggested in either of the two alternative approaches will require a great deal of planning and utmost care during execution. The complexity of the tasks involved would be greatly reduced if the membrane could be assembled in multiple sections that are incrementally joined together during erection to form the building enclosure. However, this would likely require portable on-site joining facilities for plastic membrane materials that may be beyond the limits of currently available technology.

3.10 Comparative Cost Projections

Any attempt to predict with accuracy the cost of construction of what would be the first full-size multi-story air-supported building is fraught with danger. The construction or manufacture of any first-of-its-kind artifact must be viewed as being experimental and will often involve costly errors in judgment that are relatively easily corrected in later editions of the same artifact. This is the reason for the well established process in industrial engineering that transitions an idea through the successive stages of Proof-of-Concept, Prototype, and Initial Operating Capability (IOC) for limited field testing to Final Operating Capability (FOC). Based on the experience gained during the early transitional stages significant cost reductions are likely to accrue by the time the FOC stage is reached. Nevertheless, there is a justified need to project even at the earliest Proof-of-Concept stage how the methods and costs associated with the construction of a multi-story air-supported building will compare with orthodox construction practices and costs.

Replacement of the metal and glass curtain wall or precast concrete elements of the external envelope of a traditional multi-story building with a continuous plastic membrane that is reinforced by an external cable-network should reduce the need for on-site labor. Also, the suspended floor system above the first floor level should realize economies by realigning the work of skilled labor for greater efficiency. The construction process, by virtue of a higher content of prefabricated components and the ability to mechanize on-site erection operations, has the potential for lowering erection time with subsequent savings in labor costs and investment losses.

A variety of advanced technologies that have been successful in other industrial domains can be utilized. In addition to the industrial techniques that are readily applied to the construction of the membrane, the cable-network, and the floor suspension system, the erection of a multi-story air-supported building will be able to employ proven techniques for lifting heavy loads that have been successfully applied in building construction (e.g., lift-slab construction) and other civil engineering works. However, the problems that will be encountered during the on-site movement and attachment of the membrane must not be underestimated. The length of the discussion in Section 3.9 relating to this particular portion of the construction sequence is evidence of a high degree of complexity and the need for careful timing.

From a general point of view the economical aspects of air-supported buildings are influenced by a set of parameters that are new to the domain of multi-story building design and construction. Chief among these are the following:

1. Full realization of material strength due to the conversion of axial load forces into tensile stresses. In this regard air-supported structures will invite the use of high-strength materials, leading to the application of more accurate and critical structural design methodologies.

2. With the efficient use of materials in tension, minimum-weight design criteria become relevant as a means of optimizing the strength-weight ratio of the structure.

3. Building structure and enclosure must be considered one entity. Since the enclosure is continuous, problems associated with joint sealants, drainage, expansion, and moving parts are eliminated. However, the membrane enclosure also introduces a new set of problems related to material lifespan (e.g., ultraviolet light degradation), thermal insulation and fire protection.

4. The structural integrity of the building is entirely dependent on two factors, namely: the control and continuous presence of an internal air pressure that is sufficient to support the roof and suspended floor loads; and, the air tightness of the building enclosure.

5. A rather complex on-site erection process that requires the building enclosure to be essentially wrapped around the roof and floors in one or a small number of very large pieces, without damaging the relatively fragile plastic membrane.

6. The requirement of a fairly elaborate portal crane assembly for lifting the roof and floors, before the air inside the building can be pressurized to function as the principal structural support element.

7. A fairly elaborate electronic monitoring and control system that is required to ensure the structural integrity of the building in case of puncture of the membrane enclosure or fire. The safety of the building occupants is dependent on the proper functioning of these controls to an extent that is common practice in air transportation, but has hitherto not been associated with buildings.

In estimating the construction costs of a building during the advanced concept development stage of the design process it is common practice to adopt an elemental cost estimating approach that divides the building into major components (Mooney 1983, 30-42). Data based on recent industry experience with the particular building type under consideration allows the proportional cost of each component to be defined as a percentage of the total building cost. Table 3.3 utilizes this cost estimating approach to project the increase or decrease in costs for a multi-story air-supported building in comparison with an orthodox building (i.e., reinforced concrete or steel frame) of identical dimensions.

Table 3.3: Comparative analysis of air-supported and orthodox construction costs

Building Component	Orthodox Construction Proportional Cost	Air-Supported Construction Adjustment Factor
Site Improvements	0.8%	1.0 (or 0%)
Foundations	1.5%	0.9 (or − 10%)
Floors Below Grade	1.7%	1.1 (or + 10%)
Floors Above Grade	0.6%	1.2 (or + 20%)
Superstructure	**16.0%**	**0.3 (or − 70%)**
Roofing	0.8%	1.2 (or + 20%)
Exterior Walls	**15.0%**	**0.3 (or − 70%)**
Internal Partitions	16.1%	1.0 (or 0%)
Wall Finishes	3.1%	0.8 (or -20%)
Floor Finishes	1.7%	1.0 (or 0%)
Ceiling Finishes	2.2%	1.0 (or 0%)
Elevators	0.8%	1.0 (or 0%)
Specialties	0.5%	1.0 (or 0%)
Fixed Equipment	0.4%	1.0 (or 0%)
HVAC	**18.0%**	**1.4 (or + 40%)**
Plumbing	6.6%	1.1 (or +10%)
Electrical	11.6%	1.1 (or +10%)
General Conditions	2.6%	1.0 (or 0%)
	100%	

As highlighted in Table 3.3, the principal construction cost differences between a 12-story building of orthodox construction (i.e., reinforced concrete or steel frame) and an air-supported building of the same dimensions are projected for three components.

Superstructure: A 70% reduction in cost is projected since the air-supported building does not require columns and only minimal internal bracing around the central core. The floor suspension system is required to resist only tensile forces and bracing is provided by the external cable-network, which is in an optimum location to perform this structural function[12]. Again, the external cables are subjected only to tensile forces allowing the full tensile strength of the cable material to be exploited.

---

[12] The cable-network is located furthest away from the neutral axis of the building, giving it the largest moment of inertia that is achievable within the footprint of the building.

External Walls: While the continuous membrane of the building enclosure poses some erection problems, its material and fabrication costs will be a fraction of the equivalent costs of a metal and glass curtain wall or a precast concrete façade with windows. Even taking into account that the plastic membrane may have to be replaced periodically during the lifespan of the building a 70% reduction in cost should be achievable[13].

HVAC: The requirement of air pressurization and standby equipment suggests a substantial (40%) additional cost for the air-supported building. This is perhaps a conservative estimate because much of the cost of an air-conditioning system is associated with the heating, cooling, and distribution (i.e., ductwork) facilities that do not have to be duplicated in the standby equipment. Only the pressurization facilities and fans need to be duplicated in the standby plant.

More minor cost differences are expected to apply to the following components:

Foundations: The air-supported building is much lighter than a multi-story building of orthodox construction in respect to the self-weight of the structure and external walls (i.e., dead-loads). Therefore, at least a 10% reduction in the cost of footings should be achievable.

Floors Below Grade: A 10% increase in cost is projected due to the requirements of a basement capable of serving as an emergency mass evacuation space. This space needs to be pressurized and requires at least two exits with airlock facilities.

Floors Above Grade: The suggested 20% increase in costs is projected to allow for prestressed post-tensioned floors and the special fittings that will be required to attach the floors to the suspension system.

Roofing: The roof will need to support the full load of 11 suspended floors. It is expected to be designed as a series of steel trusses radiating from the center. However, the trusses will not be subjected to cantilever action since the underside of the roof rests on a cushion of air distributed evenly over its entire surface. Therefore, a 20% increase in cost should be considered a conservative projection.

Wall Finishes: The projected 20% reduction in cost accounts for the fact that no external wall finishes are required.

Plumbing: A 20% increase in cost is projected to allow for the boosting of mains water and the provision of centralized or distributed decompression units for waste disposal. Admittedly, this estimate may be on the optimistic side considering the potential problems associated with the waste disposal problem.

Electrical: A 10% increase in cost is projected to allow for the additional control systems that are required for the operation and monitoring of the airlocks and the internal air pressure within the building, as well as the movement of the sliding fire-rated panels around the perimeter of each floor.

All of these cost projections are based on the construction of a first-of-its-kind prototype building and do not make allowance for any cost reductions that are likely to accrue as experience is

---

[13] It should be possible to replace the membrane enclosure from the interior while the building remains under internal air pressure.

progressively gained with the construction of multiple instances of this building type. In particular the emergence of commercial HVAC, plumbing and electronic (i.e., controls) products that are customized for multi-story air-supported buildings may reduce the cost of those building components by 10% to 20%. In addition, apart from these direct savings, it would not be unreasonable to expect commensurate indirect savings in respect to on-site labor and erection time.

Based on the adjustment factors listed in Table 3.3, the expected cost of a prototype *100 FT* diameter, circular, 12-story (i.e., 11 suspended floors) air-supported building with a total floor area of approximately *94,000 SF* is calculated in Table 3.4 to be 12% less than a building of the same dimensions utilizing an orthodox compression structure. The comparison is based on a 2010 construction cost of (U.S.) $300 per square foot of floor area.

Table 3.4: Comparative construction costs of air-supported and orthodox buildings

Building Component	Orthodox Construction		Air-Supported Construction		
	$/SF	Cost	Adj. Factor	$/SF	Cost
Site Improvements	$2.40	$226,195	1.0	$2.40	$226,195
Foundations	$4.50	$424,116	0.9	$4.05	$381,704
Floors Below Grade	$5.10	$480,665	1.1	$5.61	$528,731
Floors Above Grade	$1.80	$169,646	1.2	$2.16	$203,576
Superstructure	$48.00	$4,523,904	0.3	$14.40	$1,357,171
Roofing	$2.40	$226,195	1.2	$2.88	$271,434
Exterior Walls	$45.00	$4,241,160	0.3	$13.50	$1,272,348
Internal Partitions	$48.30	$4,552,178	1.0	$48.30	$4,552,178
Wall Finishes	$9.30	$876,506	0.8	$7.44	$701,205
Floor Finishes	$5.10	$480,665	1.0	$5.10	$480,665
Ceiling Finishes	$6.60	$622,037	1.0	$6.60	$622,037
Elevators	$2.40	$226,195	1.0	$2.40	$226,195
Specialties	$1.50	$141,372	1.0	$1.50	$141,372
Fixed Equipment	$1.20	$113,098	1.0	$1.20	$113,098
HVAC	$54.00	$5,089,392	1.4	$75.60	$7,125,149
Plumbing	$19.80	$1,866,110	1.2	$23.76	$2,239,332
Electrical	$34.80	$3,279,830	1.1	$38.28	$3,607,813
General Conditions	$7.80	$735,134	1.0	$7.80	$735,134
Totals:	**$300.00**	**$28,274,400**	**0.877**	**$262.98**	**$24,785,339**

The dependence of a multi-story air-supported building on internal air pressure for its structural integrity, the necessary provision of airlocks for access and egress, and the requirement of all building services to operate within a hyperbaric environment, adds a set of design criteria that are significantly more exacting than are normally encountered in orthodox construction. It may therefore be appropriate to define more precisely certain parameters that are currently only vaguely considered in the design of buildings. Such parameters include lifespan, structural minimum weight design principles, deconstructability and recycling, and factor of safety determination based on load-factor principles (Schriever 1960).

Chapter 4
Bracing of Multi-Story Air-Supported Buildings

Apart from the normal vertical loads due to material weight and occupancy that the multi-story air-supported building will support by means of internal pressure, consideration must be given to lateral loads. As mentioned previously in Chapter 3 (see Section 3.7) the multi-story air-supported building, acting as a cylindrical column that is subjected to internal pressure, can resist horizontal forces if the internal pressure is adequately increased. However, the existence of an external cable-network for purposes of reinforcing the membrane would suggest that these steel cables could also be employed to resist wind loads. This was foreseen by their two-directional diagonal configuration.

4.1 Wind Forces

The total force due to wind pressure acting on a building involves two main components, namely the horizontal *drag* component and the vertical *lift* component (Blanjean 1961).

$$\text{drag } (D_H) = C_H A_{VP} q \quad (\text{LB}) \quad \quad 4.1$$

$$\text{lift } (U_V) = C_V A_{HP} q \quad (\text{LB}) \quad \quad 4.2$$

where: C_H = total aerodynamic (drag) coefficient
C_V = overall aerodynamic coefficient in vertical direction
A_{VP} = projected area on vertical plane (SF)
A_{HP} = projected area on horizontal plane (SF)
q = $V^2 / 400$ (psf), - pressure as a function of wind speed (mph)

In order to be able to determine the *drag* and *lift* coefficients for cylindrical buildings of the type discussed here, we may refer to experiments carried out by a Belgian Commission and contained in a report by Blanjean (1961) as follows:

$$C_H = 0.60 \text{ and } C_V = 0.75$$

According to this report the total *lift* force (U_V) should be applied upstream at a distance of one third of the radius along the vertical axis of the building (Figure 4.1).

$$\text{drag } (D_H) = 0.0015 \, V^2 \, A_{VP} \quad (\text{LB}) \quad \quad 4.3$$

$$\text{lift } (U_V) = 0.0019 \, V^2 \, A_{HP} \quad (\text{LB}) \quad \quad 4.4$$

For a cylindrical building of height *H* FT and diameter *D* FT equations 4.3 and 4.4 may be rewritten in terms of the actual building dimensions, as follows:

$$\text{drag } (D_H) = 0.0015 \, V^2 \, D \, H \quad (\text{LB}) \quad \quad 4.5$$

$$\text{lift } (U_V) = 0.0015 \, V^2 \, D^2 \quad (\text{LB}) \quad \quad 4.6$$

Applying equations 4.5 and 4.6 to the multi-story, air-supported building design discussed in Chapter 3 (i.e., 12-story with 11 suspended floors, *10 FT* story height, and *102 FT* diameter) and assuming a gale force wind speed of 130 mph the corresponding horizontal *drag* (D_H) and vertical *lift* (U_V) forces are calculated to be:

$$drag\ (D_H) = 0.0015 \times 130 \times 130 \times 102 \times 120$$
$$= \mathbf{310{,}284\ LB}$$
$$lift\ (U_V) = 0.0015 \times 130 \times 130 \times 102 \times 102$$
$$= \mathbf{263{,}741\ LB}[1]$$

Methods of bracing employed in multi-story buildings of orthodox construction would normally not apply in the case of an air-supported building. While shear walls and rigid service cores may be used to advantage in a reinforced concrete or steel framed structure, they would constitute a disproportionate and unnecessary material load in an air-supported membrane building. The following two lightweight methods of bracing that take advantage of the intrinsic features of pneumatic construction are attractive alternatives:

a) The use of excess internal pressure as a means of stabilizing the air-supported structure when exposed to lateral loads (i.e. wind loads). This alternative will be discussed in more detail in the following section (Section 4.2, see also Chapter 3, Section 3.7).

b) The assignment of a secondary bracing function to the external cable-network as a stabilizing system under wind forces, which is discussed later in Section 4.3.

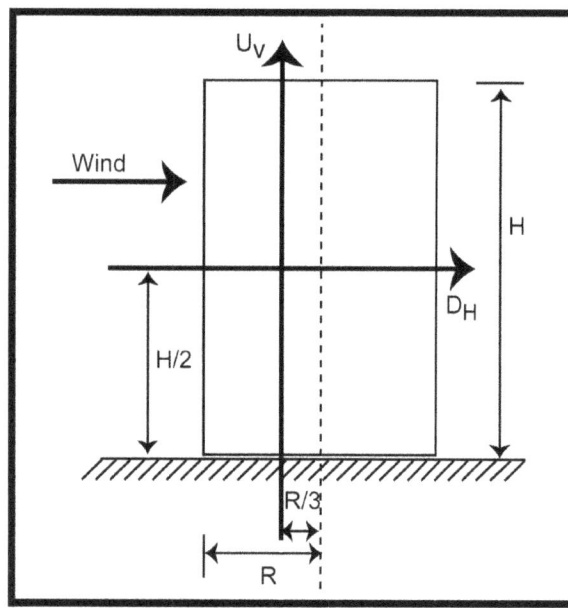

Figure 4.1: Resultant wind *drag* and *lift* forces

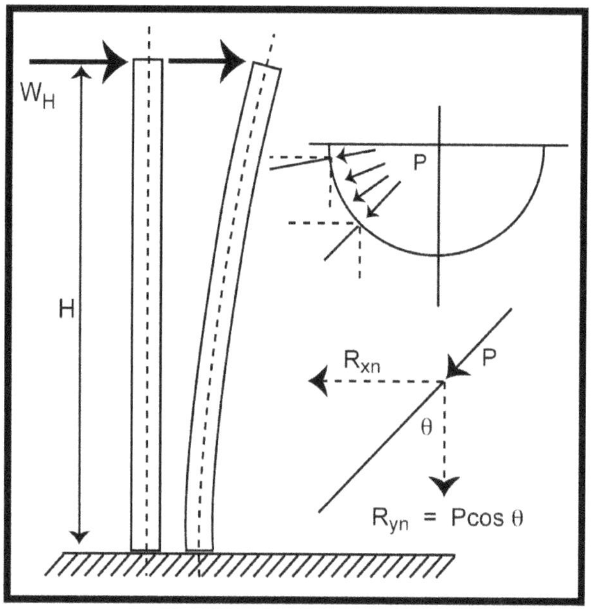

Figure 4.2: Membrane column under lateral load

---

[1] Is it justified to consider the decrease in the effective building load that must be supported by the internal (building) air pressure, under wind conditions? While this vertical lift force (U_V) due to wind would allow a slight reduction in the internal (building) air pressure, there would be little advantage in implementing such a fine grained pressure regulation mechanism. In the example at hand, let us assume a dead-load of 40 LB per square foot of floor (and roof) area. Therefore, for the 12 story building with 100 FT diameter floors and 102 FT diameter roof, subjected to a storm with 130 mph winds, the total dead-load carried by the internal air pressure is just under 3.8 million LB. In this rather extreme case the vertical lift force is less than 7% of the building dead-load.

In addition, under severe wind conditions, the sliding fire-protection panels around the perimeter of each floor[2] could be designed to provide a secondary bracing function. Previously it was suggested that these panels could be assigned an emergency structural function under catastrophic failure conditions (i.e., internal air pressure failure). It would therefore not be unreasonable to extend this emergency structural role for the support of axial vertical loads, also to horizontal wind loads.

4.2 Restoring Force Due to Internal Pressure

While the existence of a restoring force due to internal air pressure in short and medium length membrane columns is easily demonstrated in practice, the theoretical explanation of this phenomenon is nevertheless more complicated.

Under the action of a horizontal force (W_H LB) the typical deflection mechanism is shown in Figure 4.2. It is erroneous to assume that the internal pressure P psig will tend to straighten the column when deflected by a horizontal force by acting on the increased area of the convex side. By reference to Figures 4.3 and 4.4 it can be shown that the apparent restoring force induced by the action of the internal pressure (P psig) on the increased area of the convex side is neutralized by the horizontal component of (P_H psig) of the pressure acting on the inclined column head surface. As shown in Figure 4.4, the cross-sectional area of the convex side on which the restoring force will act is semi-circular. The pressure (P psig) acting normal to the membrane surface can be resolved into forces R_{yn} and R_{xn} of which the latter will cancel out with a symmetrical counterpart, so that only R_{yn} can be considered as a potential restoring force.

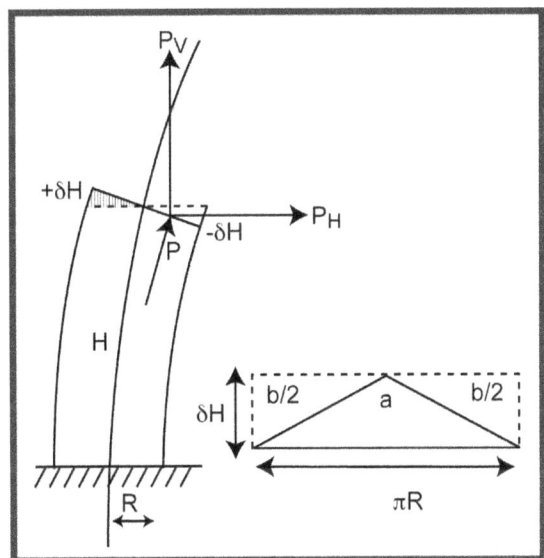
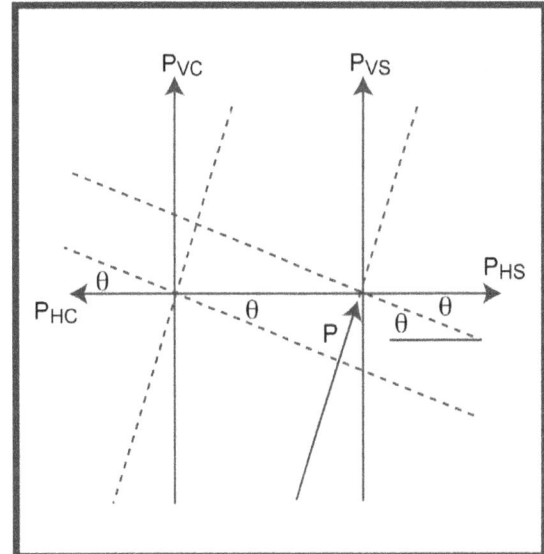

Figure 4.3: Deflected pressurized column   Figure 4.4: Geometrical relationships

On the convex side:

$$\text{increased area (a)} \;=\; (\pi R \, \delta H)/2 \quad \text{(SI)}$$

---

[2] As discussed earlier these panels are activated by heat sensors to automatically slide between the fire and the membrane, thereby shielding the membrane from heat radiation and compartmentalizing the floor.

On the concave side:

$$\text{decreased area (b)} = (\pi R \delta H)/2 \quad (SI)$$

The total effective area is $(a + b)$ square inches (SI) and the restoring force (P_{HC} LB) is equal to:

$$P_{HC} = \pi R \delta H P \cos\theta \quad \quad \quad \quad 4.7$$

At the same time the horizontal component of the internal pressure (P_{HS}) acting on the inclined column head surface (in the opposite direction to P_{HC}) is given by:

$$P_{HS} = \pi R^2 P \sin\theta \quad \quad \quad \quad 4.8$$

However, it can be shown for equation 4.7 that $\delta H = R\theta$ (Pohl 1970, Appendix 7B (b)) and therefore by substitution equation 4.7 becomes:

$$P_{HC} = \pi R^2 P \theta \cos\theta$$

For small deflections θ is small and therefore tends to $\tan\theta$. Thus:

$$P_{HC} = \pi R^2 P \tan\theta \cos\theta = \pi R^2 P \sin\theta = P_{HS}$$

A more appropriate approach is to consider the stress conditions on the tension and compression sides of the membrane wall when the air-supported building is subjected to a horizontal wind force (D_H LB) as shown in Figure 4.5.

On the tension side of the column:

stress due to internal pressure (f_I) = $P R / (2 t)$ (tension)

stress due to horizontal force (F_H) = $D_H H / (2 Z)$ (tension)

On the compression side of the column:

stress due to internal pressure (f_I) = $P R / (2 t)$ (tension)

stress due to horizontal force (F_H) = $D_H H / (2 Z)$ (compression)

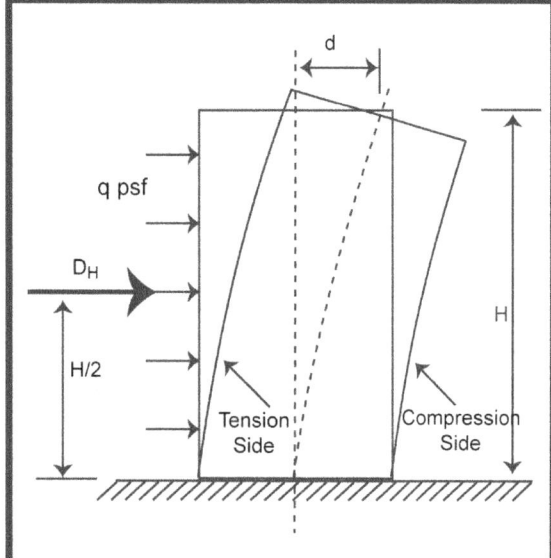
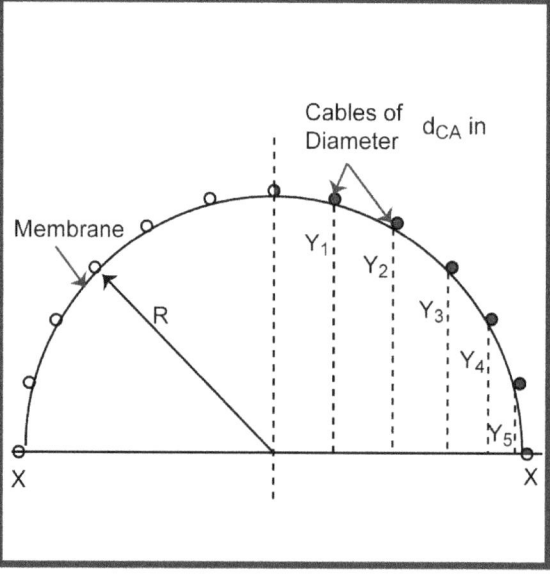

Figure 4.5: Deflection of pressurized membrane column under internal lateral load

Figure 4.6: Symmetrical vertical (diagonal) cable distribution

Although a deflection (d IN) may occur by elastic deflection, this deflection becomes critical only when the stress on the compression side of the column is zero (i.e., when the *zero stress criterion* applies). Therefore, we may equate the tensile stress due to internal pressure with the compressive stress due to the applied horizontal force on the compression side of the column:

$$D_H H / (2Z) = PR / (2t)$$

$$\mathbf{D_H = PRZ/(Ht)} \text{ (LB)} \quad \ldots\ldots\ldots\ldots\ldots \quad 4.9$$

Equation 4.9 may be transformed to give the excess internal pressure (P_E *psig*) required to resist an evenly distributed horizontal load of D_H LB:

$$\mathbf{P_E = D_H H t / (RZ)} \text{ (psig)} \quad \ldots\ldots\ldots\ldots \quad 4.10$$

At the same time any elementary textbook (Axelrad 1965, Benham 1965) dealing with the theory of structures will derive the following expression for the deflection (d IN) at the free end of a column subjected to a horizontal load (i.e., cantilever action):

$$d = D_H H^3 / (8EI) \text{ (IN)}$$

On substituting for D_H in the above equation, we obtain an expression for the deflection (d) in terms of the physical properties of a pressurized membrane column:

$$\mathbf{d = P_E R Z H^2 / (8 E I t)} \text{ (IN)} \quad \ldots\ldots\ldots\ldots \quad 4.11$$

As an example, let us consider a membrane column of *1.95* IN radius, *12* IN height and *0.002* IN membrane thickness, pressurized internally to *1.93 psig*. The Modulus of Section (Z)[3] for this column is calculated to be *0.024* IN³. Applying equation 4.9 we are able to calculate the maximum horizontal force (D_H) that can be resisted by this membrane column before folds will appear in the membrane on the compression side of the column:

$$D_H = PRZ/(Ht) = \underline{\mathbf{3.76 \text{ LB}}}$$

With equation 4.11 we are also able to determine the deflection (d) that this force will produce at the free end of the column:

$$d = P_E R Z H^2 / (8EIt) = \underline{\mathbf{0.314 \text{ IN}}}$$

It should be noted that where axial and horizontal (or eccentric) loads occur at the same time the term P in equation 4.9 must be replaced by P_E, which is defined as the excess internal building pressure (i.e., over and above the pressure required to safely support the vertical compression load) required to resist horizontal loads.

For a more practical example let us revisit the multi-story air-supported building considered in Chapter 3 (Section 3.4) with the following parameters:

number of floors =	8 (plus roof)
story height =	12 FT
live-load =	100 psf
dead-load =	40 psf
membrane thickness =	0.1 IN
membrane Modulus of Elasticity =	500,000 psi

---

[3] $Z = (\pi R^2 t) = (3.1416 \times 1.95 \times 1.95 \times 0.002) = 0.024$ (IN³)

In Table 3.1 (Chapter 3, Section 3.4) for a *50 FT* floor diameter the required internal pressure to support the axial building loads (*P psig*) was calculated with equation 2.8 (Chapter 2, Section 2.5.3 and Figure 2.12) to be *9.96 psig*. For a *90 mph* wind velocity the drag force D_H can be calculated with equation 4.5[4] to be *65,610 LB* (with eight suspended floors, a *12 FT* floor to floor height and allowing for a ground floor that is not suspended, the total height of the building is *108 FT*). If this horizontal force is to be resisted purely by excess internal pressure then the excess pressure (P_E *psig*) is given by equation 4.10:

$$P_E = D_H H t / (R Z) = \mathbf{1.0\ psig}$$

Therefore, the total internal pressure required to support both the vertical and horizontal loads of this building will be *11 psig* (i.e., 9.96 + 1.0 = 10.96). At the same time the deflection (*d*) at the top of the building due to the action of the horizontal wind force is given by equation 4.11:

$$d = P_E R Z H^2 / (8 E I t) = \mathbf{0.42\ IN}$$

This is equivalent to a deflection to height ratio of over 1 in 3,000 that far exceeds the structural deflection limits normally imposed on orthodox reinforced concrete or steel frames. It may be of interest to determine the internal pressure (P_E *psig*) required for a deflection to height ratio of 1 in 500 (i.e., 2.59 IN). Transposing equation 4.11 the required internal pressure may be calculated as follows:

$$P_E = 8 d E I t / (P_E R Z H^2)$$

$$P_E = \mathbf{0.62\ psig}$$

Even though the multi-story air-supported structural system emerges from these calculation with stability characteristics that are far superior to orthodox multi-story building frames it should not be necessarily bound by the same rigidity requirements. Reinforced concrete and steel frames, which depend for their strength on rigidity and continuity, must be severely restricted in regard to deflection. However, the air-supported building is essentially a fluid container that derives its rigidity from internal air pressure contained by a flexible membrane shell. From a structural point of view the membrane shell represents a highly ductile structure that is not subject to the kind of local failure that can occur at the joints of a reinforced concrete or steel frame under severe stress conditions.

It is therefore suggested that permissible deflection limits for multi-story air-supported buildings may and should be governed by factors that are not directly based on structural considerations, but are instead related to the influence of the deformation of the external shell on the internal non-structural elements of the building. In particular, such factors will include the safety and convenience of the building occupants and the degree to which movement can be accommodated by the building services (i.e., pipes, ducts, elevators, and furnishings). It is of interest to note that according to equation 4.11 increasing the internal pressure (P_E *psig*) beyond the value derived in equation 4.10 for resisting a given horizontal load will not decrease but actually increase the overall deflection of the building. This serves as a reminder that deflection is a stability rather than material strength issue. As might be expected, closer examination of equation 4.11 shows that the overall building deflection is sensitive to the building diameter[5], the thickness of the membrane (*t*), and the modulus of elasticity of the membrane material (*E*). Clearly, placing a

---

[4] $D_H = (0.0015 \times 90 \times 90 \times 50 \times 12 \times (8 + 1)) = 65,610$ (LB).

[5] Increasing the building diameter will increase the moment of inertia (*I*).

network of steel cables around the plastic building envelope will greatly reduce the overall deflection of the air-supported building[6].

However, before proceeding with an analysis of the impact of an external cable-network on the overall deflection of multi-story air-supported buildings under wind loads we need to consider another potential structural factor that is applicable to the membrane, namely the stress condition in the membrane under axial force and shear. Although both the longitudinal and circumferential stresses in the membrane due to internal pressure are tensile, it may nevertheless be possible that the principal maximum or minimum stress is compression. As shown in Figure 4.7, a small element removed from the membrane of a pressurized column subjected to wind forces (D_H), internal pressure (P) and vertical compression load (W), will be subjected to normal stresses (S_x and S_y as well as a shear stress S_{xy}.

$$S_x = P R / t \text{ (psi)} \quad \text{................................} \quad 4.12$$

$$S_y = P R / (2 t) - W / (2 \pi R t) \text{ (psi)} \quad \text{................} \quad 4.13$$

$$S_{xy} = 2 a H / (144 \pi t) \text{ (psi)} \quad \text{...........................} \quad 4.14$$

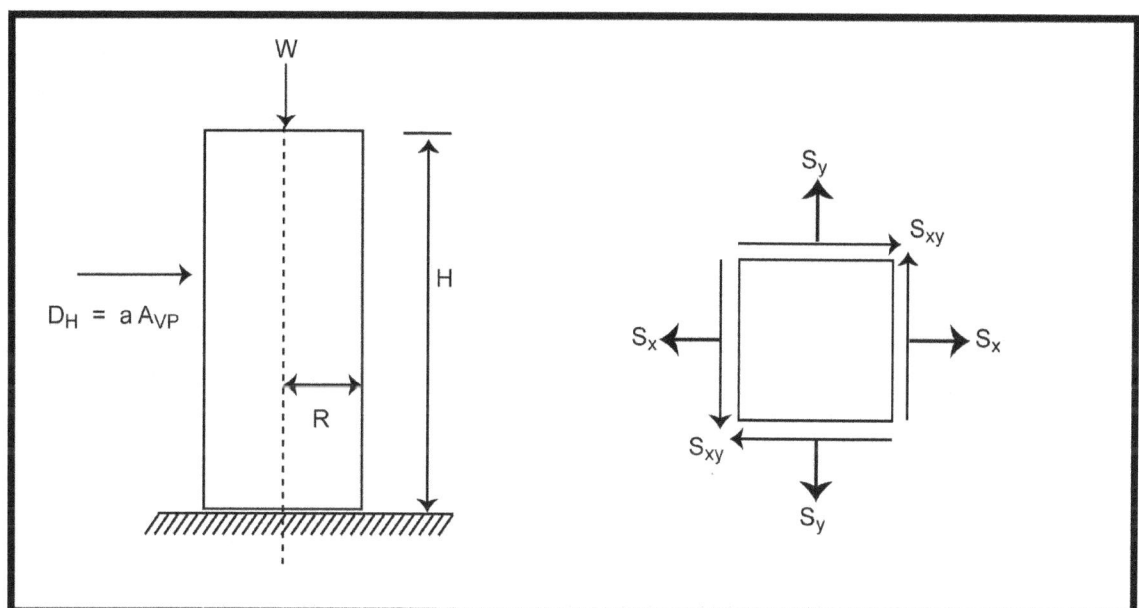

Figure 4.7: Pressurized membrane column under combined axial and horizontal loads

Let us revisit the two extreme critical loading conditions considered previously in Chapter 3 (Section 3.7); namely: when the vertical compression load is *zero* and S_y is a maximum; and, at ultimate load when the longitudinal tensile stress due to internal pressure is completely negated by the compressive stress due to the vertical load (i.e., $S_y = 0$)

Loading Condition 1 (W_{zero} and $S_y=PR/(2t)$): In this case the principal maximum and minimum stresses are given by (Nash 1957, 257):

$$S_{max} = (1/2)(S_x + S_y) + [(1/4)(S_x + S_y)^2 + S_{xy}^2]^{0.5}$$

$$S_{min} = (1/2)(S_x + S_y) - [(1/4)(S_x + S_y)^2 + S_{xy}^2]^{0.5}$$

---

[6] The modulus of elasticity of steel is approximately 30,000,000 psi, which is in the order of 60 times greater than the modulus of elasticity of the plastic membrane material used in the example.

$$\tan 2\theta = -2(S_{xy}) / (S_x - S_y)$$

Loading Condition 2 (W_{max} and $S_y=0$): Here we are only concerned with one normal stress and a shear stress. Therefore the principal maximum and minimum stresses are given by:

$$S_{max} = (1/2)(S_x) + [(1/4)(S_x)^2 + S_{xy}^2]^{0.5}$$

$$S_{min} = (1/2)(S_x) - [(1/4)(S_x)^2 + S_{xy}^2]^{0.5}$$

$$\tan 2\theta = -2(S_{xy}) / (S_x)$$

In terms of the typical example of an eight-story, air-supported building discussed earlier (i.e., *R=25 FT; H=108 FT; W_{max}=2,474,010 LB; t=0.1 IN; P_{total}=11 psig* (i.e., 9.96 + 1.0 = 10.96; and, *V=130 mph* (wind speed)) the relevant stresses are determined according to equations 4.12, 4.13 and 4.14 to be:

$$S_x = 33,000 \text{ psi}$$
$$S_y = 13,125 \text{ psi}$$
$$S_{xy} = 1,614 \text{ psi}$$

The relevant principal maximum and minimum stresses that will occur at specific angles (i.e., angles between the *X* axis and the planes on which the principal stresses occur) are given in Table 4.1.

Table 4.1: Principal maximum and minimum stresses

Loading Condition	Principal Stresses		Angle θ
	MAX (psi)	MIN (psi)	(to nearest degree)
Loading Condition 1 [W = 0 and S_y = PR/(2t)]	46,185 (tension)	56 (compression)	85° and 175°
Loading Condition 2 [W_{max} and S_y = 0]	33,079 (tension)	79 (compression)	87° and 177°

It is clear from Table 4.1 that under the extreme loading conditions chosen for this example a very small compressive stress may in fact occur. Although it is unlikely that *loading condition 1* will ever occur there is no doubt that *loading condition 2* will occur under ultimate failure conditions. However, the smallest value below which S_y must not fall so that the minimum principal stress is always tensile is very small indeed (Pohl 1970, 186).

4.3 External Stabilizing Tension Net

An external tension net in direct contact with the building membrane will have the dual advantage of strengthening the membrane envelope as well as stabilizing the building laterally. While the strengthening function has been discussed in Chapter 3 (Section 3.7), we will now consider the stabilizing function. In reference to Figure 4.3, the action of a wind force (D_H) will produce a stress f_{CA} in a stabilizing network of cables[7].

$$f_{CA} = D_H H / (2 Z_{CA}) \text{ (psi)}$$

However, since the cables are inclined at an angle θ to the vertical axis, the modulus of section (Z_{CA}) is approximately equal to:

$$Z_{CA} = \pi R^2 t_{CA}$$
$$\text{where:} \quad t_{CA} = k A_{CA} / (2 \pi R \cos\theta)$$

Therefore, the force (F LB) in each cable on one side of the building is given by:

$$F = D_H H \cos\theta / (k R) \text{ (LB)}$$

If the allowable working strength in tension of the cable material is f_{CA} *psi*, then the required cable radius r IN is given by:

$$r = (F / (\pi f_{CA}))^{0.5} \text{ (IN)} \quad\quad\quad 4.15$$

In the case of the previous example, designing for a wind force D_H of *65,610 LB* (i.e., *90 mph wind speed*) and assuming 32 cables with an allowable design stress (f_{CA}) of *30,000 psi* inclined at the optimum angle (θ) of *63° 26'* to the vertical building axis, we obtain the following cable radius (r IN) if the height (H) and radius (R) of the building are *108 FT* and *50 FT*, respectively:

$$F = (65610 \times 108 \times 12 \times 0.4473) / (32 \times 50 \times 12)$$
$$F = \mathbf{\underline{1,981 \text{ LB}}}$$
$$r = (1981 / (\pi \times 30000))^{0.5}$$
$$r = \mathbf{\underline{0.145 \text{ IN}}}$$

It will therefore be necessary to use 32 cables of *0.29 IN* diameter, if the allowable working stress of the cable material is *30,000 psi*.

The deflection (d IN) that will occur at the top of the building when the entire wind load (D_H) is resisted by the cable-network is given by the expression:

$$d = D_H H^3 / (8 E_{CA} I_{CA})$$

Again, since the cables are inclined at an angle θ to the vertical axis, the moment of inertia (I_{CA}) is approximately equal to:

$$I_{CA} = \pi R^3 t_{CA}$$
$$\text{where:} \quad t_{CA} = k A_{CA} / (2 \pi R \cos\theta)$$

Therefore, the deflection (d IN) may be obtained from the expression:

$$d = D_H H^3 \cos\theta / (4 k R^2 E_{CA} A_{CA}) \text{ (IN)} \quad\quad 4.16$$

Substituting for D_H, H, R, E_{CA}, A_{CA}, and θ in equation 4.16, we obtain:

$$d = \mathbf{\underline{1.1 \text{ IN}}}$$

---

[7] As discussed earlier in Chapters 3 (Section 3.7), the cables are inclined in opposing directions to the vertical axis of the building at an optimum angle of 63°26' on either side of the vertical axis. The tensile stress in the horizontal cables is simply a function of the hoop stress imposed on the membrane container by the internal pressure. The function of the horizontal cables is to maintain the cylindrical shape of the membrane.

This is equivalent to a deflection to height ratio of 1 in 1178. While this ratio is considerably smaller than the 1:3000 ratio that was calculated in Section 4.2 for stabilizing the building under the same *90 mph* wind forces with additional internal air pressure (i.e., in the absence of an external cable-network), the 1:1200 ratio is still more than satisfactory from a structural point of view.

4.4 Shear Walls and Stabilizing Systems

In the design of orthodox, framed, multi-story buildings it is often considered practical to provide bracing by means of shear walls. A careful analysis will show that every building inherently contains a number of bracing or stiffening elements. While staircase walls, service cores and elevator shafts form vertical shear walls, reinforced concrete floors provide rigid, horizontal platforms. In this manner a structure with considerable overall rigidity is obtained at little extra cost (Joedicke 1962). Shear walls may therefore be defined as a structural system providing stability against lateral building loads that derives its stiffness from its inherent structural form (Frischmann and Prabhu 1967). Most commonly, such a system will incorporate either plane walls, sections of curved walls, closed hoops, rectangular boxes as in service cores, or a combination of these within an integrated building structure.

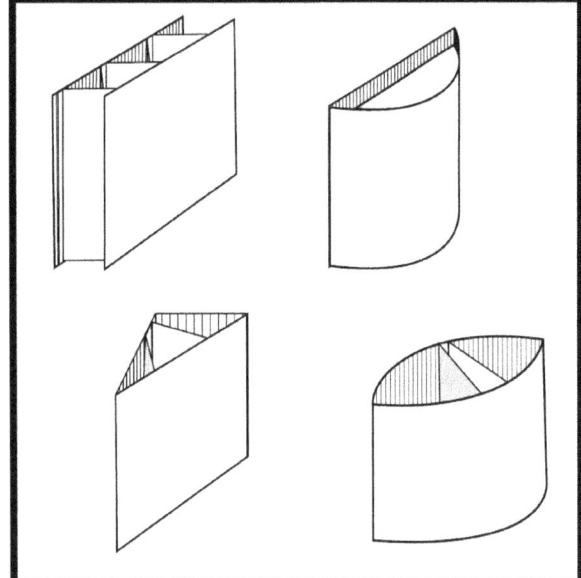
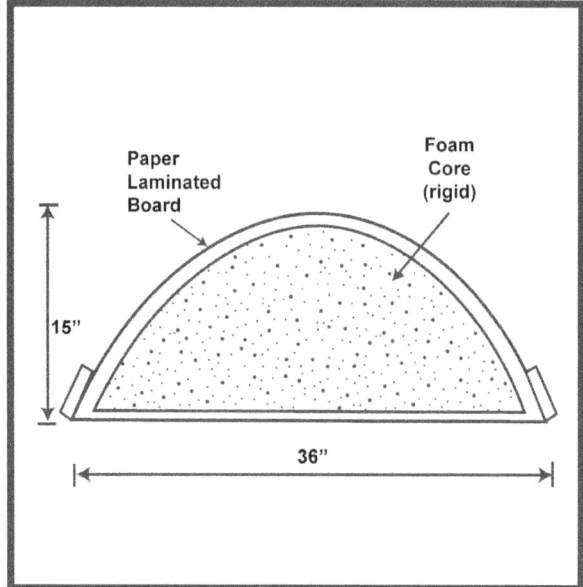

Figure 4.8: Folded plate panels   Figure 4.9: Foam plastic laminated panels

Although the internal planning of multi-story air-supported buildings will be based on the same design criteria (i.e., flexibility of sub-divisions, grouping of services into ducts, and so on) used extensively in multi-story buildings of orthodox construction, there nevertheless exists one major difference. In multi-story air-supported buildings weight is at a premium, since the internal air pressure that supports the building loads is limited for both physiological (see Chapter 3, Section 3.2) and physical reasons. The physiological limit is based on the desirability of not exceeding a two-to-one pressure gradient between the internal building pressure and the external environmental pressure. Therefore, the lighter the building loads the greater the number of floors that can be supported by an internal air pressure that does not exceed one atmosphere above the ambient atmospheric pressure (i.e., approximately 14 psig). The physical limit is related to the allowable strength in tension of the membrane material or the exterior cable-network that are required to contain the building pressure.

If shear planes are to be used, then these must derive their rigidity not from mass but surface configuration, lamination or stiffeners. At first sight there seem to be at least two possibilities of achieving light weight shear panels (University of Michigan 1965).

- Folded plate construction, where the required stiffness is obtained from the surface configuration of each panel (Figure 4.8).

- Laminated sandwich panels using foam plastics as a core material. The later separates the outer structural skins and serves only to resist buckling of the skins. An additional material must be introduced between the skins to resist shear, otherwise shear creep of the core material may produce unacceptable deflections (Figure 4.9).

There remains the possibility of utilizing the internal floor suspension system as a means of providing rigidity in a pneumatic structure. Diagonal tension cables strung between floors around the periphery of the building could provide a light-weight bracing system.

Buildings with suspended floors that have been constructed in the past (e.g., El Pilar Apartment Building in Montevideo, 1960, B.P. Petrol Headquarters in Antwerpen, 1961) consist essentially of a cantilever construction fixed to a central core from which hangers are suspended. These hangers are utilized for supporting the floor system only. For largely economical reasons the entire wind load is resisted by shear cores. Due to the fact that the cores act as a compression structure it is worthwhile to provide a massive structure preloaded by the total floor load. In multi-story air-supported buildings, where such heavy central cores have been replaced by a relatively small evenly distributed environmental pressure, the utilization of the suspended skeleton as bracing must be given serious consideration. Whether this is best achieved by a system of diagonal cables or a rigid cage from which floors are suspended can be resolved only after a considerable amount of practical experience has been gained with this type of construction.

4.5 Summary of Structural Design Procedures

Discussions in the previous chapter and this chapter suggest that there are basically two types of multi-story air-supported building structures; namely, those in which the membrane acts as the primary structural element and those in which the structural role has been transferred to an external cable-network. The design steps and formulas proposed by the author for each of these structural cases are summarized below.

4.5.1 Multi-Story Air-Supported Buildings without Cable-Networks

The design formulas listed below will apply to buildings with a slenderness ratio of less than *30* and variables in the following units of measurement: load eccentricity (e *IN*); building radius (R *IN*); building height (H *IN*); membrane thickness (t *IN*); modulus of elasticity of membrane material (E *psi*); total building load (W *LB*); and, internal air pressure (P *psig*).

Step 1: Determine the slenderness ratio (*SR*) to ensure that it is below *30*.

$$SR = H_E / (I_m / A_m)^{0.5} = 2H / (R^2 / 2)^{0.5}$$

since: $H_E = 2H$; $I_m = \pi R^3 t$; $A_m = 2\pi R t$

Step 2: Determine the required internal air pressure (*P psig*) to support the total vertical live and dead-loads.

$$P = (2\,W\,t\,/\,R)\,[(1/A_m) + (e/Z_m) + ((W\,e\,H^2)/(2\,E\,I_m\,Z_m))] \quad (psig) \quad \dots\dots\dots\dots (2.8)$$

where: $A_m = 2\pi R t$; $Z_m = \pi R^2 t$; $I_m = \pi R^3 t$; $e = R/50$

Step 3: Calculate the wind drag force (D_H *LB*) for a wind speed of *V mph*.

$$D_H = C_H\,A_{VP}\,q = 1.04 \times 10^{-5}\,(R\,H\,V^2) \quad LB$$

since: $C_H = 0.60$; $A_{VP} = RH/144$; $q = V^2/400$

Step 4: Calculate the excess internal pressure (P_E *psig*) required to resist the wind drag force.

$$P_E = D_H\,H\,t\,/\,(R\,Z_m) \quad (psig) \quad \dots\dots\dots\dots\dots\dots\dots\dots\dots\dots\dots\dots\dots\dots\dots\dots (4.10)$$

where: $D_H = C_H\,A_{VP}\,q$; $C_H = 0.60$; $A_{VP} = RH/144$; $q = V^2/400$; $Z_m = \pi R^2 t$

Step 5: Check membrane thickness (*t IN*) required to contain the total internal pressure ($P+P_E$ *psig*) by comparing the circumferential membrane stress (f_c *psi*) with the allowable working stress of the material:

$$f_c = (P + P_E)\,R\,/\,t \quad (psi)$$

Step 6: Calculate the deflection (*d IN*) at the top of the building due to the wind drag force.

$$d = P_E\,R\,Z_m\,H^2\,/\,(8\,E\,I_m\,t) \quad (IN) \quad \dots\dots\dots\dots\dots\dots\dots\dots\dots\dots\dots\dots\dots\dots (4.11)$$

where: $Z_m = \pi R^2 t$; $I_m = \pi R^3 t$

4.5.2 Multi-Story Air-Supported Buildings with Cable-Networks

The design formulas listed below will apply to buildings with a slenderness ratio of less than *30* and variables in the following units of measurement: load eccentricity (*e IN*); building radius (*R IN*); building height (*H IN*); number of diagonal cables (*k*); modulus of elasticity of cable material (E_{CA} *psi*); radius of each individual diagonal cable (*r IN*); total building load (*W LB*); and, internal air pressure (*P psig*).

Step 1: Determine the slenderness ratio (*SR*) to ensure that it is below *30*.

$$SR = H_E / (I_m / A_m)^{0.5} = 2H / (R^2 / 2)^{0.5}$$

since: $H_E = 2H$; $I_m = \pi R^3 t$; $A_m = 2\pi R t$

Step 2: The optimum angle of the diagonal cables on either side of the vertical axis of the building is independent of the radius (*R FT*), the height (*H FT*) and the internal air pressure (*P psig*) of the building.

$$\theta = 63°\,26'\ \text{(and }\cos\theta = 0.4473\text{)}$$

Step 3: Determine the required internal air pressure (P *psig*) to support the total vertical live and dead-loads (W *LB*).

$$\mathbf{P = (kWr^2 / (R^2 \cos\theta)) [(\cos\theta / (kA_{CA})) + (e/Z_{CA}) + (WeH^2 / (2\, E_{CA} I_{CA} Z_{CA}))]}\ \text{(psig)} \quad\ldots\ (3.11)$$

where: $A_{CA} = \pi r^2$; $t_{CA} = kr^2/(2R\cos\theta)$; $Z_{CA} = \pi R^2 t_{CA}$; $I_{CA} = \pi R^3 t_{CA}$; $e = R/50$

Step 4: Calculate the tension (T_{CA} *LB*) in each diagonal cable due to the design pressure (P *psig*).

$$T_{CA} = \pi P R^2 / (k\cos\theta)\ \text{(LB)}$$

Step 5: Calculate the tension (T_H *LB*) in each of *n* horizontal cables.

$$T_H = P R H / n\ \text{(LB)}$$

therefore, the number of horizontal cables (*n*) with an allowable working tension ($T_{H(allow)}$ *LB*) is given by:

$$n = P R H / T_{H(allow)}$$

Step 6: Determine the required membrane thickness (t *IN*) for the allowable membrane stress ($f_{m(allow)}$ *psi*).

$$t = 4\pi P R / (k\, f_{m(allow)})\ \text{(IN)}$$

Step 7: Calculate the wind drag force (D_H *LB*) for a wind speed of V *mph*.

$$D_H = C_H A_{VP}\, q = 2.08 \times 10^{-5} (R H V^2)\ \text{LB}$$

since: $C_H = 0.60$; $A_{VP} = 2RH/144$; $q = V^2/400$

Step 8: Calculate the excess internal pressure (P_E *psig*) required to resist the wind drag force.

$$\mathbf{P_E = D_H H\, t_{CA} / (R\, Z_{CA})}\ \text{(psig)} \quad\ldots\ldots\ldots\ (4.10)$$

where: $D_H = C_H A_{VP} q$; $C_H = 0.60$; $A_{VP} = 2RH/144$; $q = V^2/400$; $Z_{CA} = \pi R^2 t_{CA}$; $t_{CA} = k r^2/(2R\cos\theta)$

Step 9: Calculate the tension ($T_{CA(total\text{-}P)}$ *LB*) in each diagonal cable due to the total internal pressure ($P + P_E$ *psig*).

$$T_{CA(total\text{-}P)} = \pi (P + P_E) R^2 / (k\cos\theta)\ \text{(LB)}$$

Step 10: Calculate the tension ($T_{H(total\text{-}P)}$ *LB*) in each of *n* horizontal cables due to the total internal pressure ($P + P_E$ *psig*).

$$T_{H(total\text{-}P)} = (P + P_E) R H / n\ \text{(LB)}$$

therefore, the number of horizontal cables (*n*) with an allowable working tension ($T_{H(allow)}$ *LB*) is given by:

$$n = (P + P_E) R H / T_{H(allow)}$$

Step 11: Check membrane thickness (*t IN*) required to contain the total internal pressure ($P+P_E$ psig) by comparing the circumferential membrane stress (f_c psi) with the allowable working stress of the material:

$$f_c = 4\pi (P + P_E) R / (k\, t) \text{ (psi)}$$

Step 12: Calculate the deflection (*d IN*) at the top of the building due to the wind drag force.

$$\mathbf{d = P_E\, R\, Z_{CA}\, H^2 / (\,8\, E_{CA}\, I_{CA}\, t_{CA}\,)} \text{ (IN)} \quad\quad\quad (4.11)$$

where: $Z_{CA} = \pi R^2 t_{CA}$; $I_{CA} = \pi R^3 t_{CA}$; $t_{CA} = kr^2/(2R\cos\theta)$

Step 13: Calculate both the force (*F LB*) in the diagonal cables on one side of the building when the wind drag force (D_H *LB*) is resisted by the cable-network and the radius (*r IN*) of each cable.

$$F = D_H\, H\, \cos\theta / (k\, R) \text{ (LB)}$$

$$\mathbf{r = (F / (\pi\, f_{CA}))^{0.5}} \text{ (IN)} \quad\quad\quad (4.15)$$

where: f_{CA} (psi) is the allowable working strength in tension of the cable material

Step 14: Calculate the deflection (*d IN*) at the top of the building when the wind drag force is resisted by the cable-network.

$$\mathbf{d = D_H\, H^3 \cos\theta / (4\, k\, R^2\, E_{CA}\, A_{CA})} \text{ (IN)} \quad\quad\quad (4.16)$$

where: $D_H = C_H A_{VP}\, q$; $C_H = 0.60$; $A_{VP} = 2RH/144$; $q = V^2/400$; $A_{CA} = \pi r^2$

4.5.3 Reexamination of the Principal Design Equations

It is of interest to reexamine the two principal design equations, namely: equation 2.8 for calculating the required internal air pressure for buildings without an external cable-network; and, equation 3.11 for buildings with an external cable-network. The objective of such an investigation is to determine whether it may be possible to simplify these equations by eliminating one or more of the terms *A*, *B*, *C*, or *D* as shown below.

$$P = (2\, W\, t_m / R) [(1/A_m) + A + B] \text{ (psig)} \quad\quad\quad (2.8)$$

where: $A = (e / Z_m)$; $B = (W\, e\, H^2) / (2\, E_m\, I_m\, Z_m)$ and $X = (1 / A_m)$

$$P = (k\, W\, r^2 / (R^2 \cos\theta))\, [(\cos\theta / (k\, A_{CA})) + C + D] \text{ (psig)} \quad\quad\quad (3.11)$$

where: $C = (e / Z_{CA})$; $D = (W\, e\, H^2) / (2\, E_{CA}\, I_{CA}\, Z_{CA})$ and $Y = (\cos\theta / (k\, A_{CA}))$

If all or some of the terms *A*, *B*, *C*, or *D* are very small in comparison with the corresponding term *X* in equation 2.8 or *Y* in equation 3.11 then equations 2.8 and 3.11 could be significantly simplified by neglecting one or more of the *A*, *B* or *C*, *D* terms in the design calculations.

It is interesting to note that *A*, *B*, *C*, and *D* are the only terms that include the assumed initial load eccentricity (*e*). Therefore, elimination of both terms from the corresponding equation would suggest that at least within a certain range of slenderness ratios the pressure-utilization efficiency of a multi-story air-supported building is only minimally impacted by the assumed eccentricity of the applied vertical building loads. The reader will recall that the arguments presented in Section 2.5.1 for assuming an initial loading eccentricity are based on considerations related to the experimental investigation of pressurized membrane columns. In Section 2.5.3 it was further argued that within the range of slenderness ratios applicable to practical multi-story air-supported buildings[8] the loading eccentricity could be related to the building diameter (i.e., building radius (R) in inches divided by 50). Table 4.2 lists the values of the terms A and B in equation 2.8, and C and D in equation 3.11 for a range of practical building diameter to height ratios. For convenience not the actual values of these terms but their proportional contributions to the term X in equation 2.8 or Y in equation 3.11 are given as percentages.

Table 4.2: Proportional contributions of the terms A and B to X (equation 2.8) and terms C and D to Y (equation 3.11) for 9 floors (plus roof), 10 FT story-height, and vertical load eccentricity as function of building diameter (radius/50).

Diameter (FT)	Height (FT)	Slend. Ratio	e = R/50 (IN)	Air Pressure (psig)	Equation 2.8			Equation 3.11		
					X	A	B	Y	C	D
40	100	15.0	4.8	9.9	0.005	4.0%	0.46%	0.022	4.0%	0.13%
60	100	10.0	7.2	10.2	0.004	4.0%	0.31%	0.010	4.0%	0.06%
80	100	8.0	9.6	10.4	0.003	4.0%	0.24%	0.005	4.0%	0.03%
100	100	6.0	12.0	10.5	0.002	4.0%	0.19%	0.003	4.0%	0.02%
140	100	5.0	16.8	10.6	0.002	4.0%	0.14%	0.002	4.0%	0.01%
180	100	4.0	21.6	10.6	0.001	4.0%	0.11%	0.001	4.0%	0.01%

It can be seen that neither of the terms A and B in equation 2.8 nor the terms C and D in equation 3.11 have a significant impact on terms X and Y, respectively. While the impact of A and C is an order of magnitude greater than B and D, it is still only 4%. However, it may be argued that the assumed eccentricity of the vertical building loads should be a function of the slenderness ratio rather than the building diameter, since the slenderness ratio is based on the building height to diameter ratio.

Table 4.3: Proportional contributions of the terms A and B to X (equation 2.8) and terms C and D to Y (equation 3.11) for 9 floors (plus roof), 10 FT story-height, and vertical load eccentricity as a multiple (x) of the slenderness ratio (SR).

Diameter (FT)	Height (FT)	Slend. Ratio	e = x(SR) (IN)	Air Pressure (psig)	Equation 2.8			Equation 3.11		
					X	A	B	Y	C	D
100	100	6.0	6.0 ($x = 1$)	10.3	0.002	2.0%	0.10%	0.019	2.0%	0.01%
100	100	6.0	12.0 ($x = 2$)	10.5	0.002	4.0%	0.19%	0.003	4.0%	0.02%
100	100	6.0	18.0 ($x = 3$)	10.7	0.002	6.0%	0.29%	0.003	6.0%	0.03%
100	100	6.0	24.0 ($x = 4$)	10.9	0.002	8.0%	0.39%	0.003	8.0%	0.04%
100	100	6.0	30.0 ($x = 5$)	11.1	0.002	10.0%	0.48%	0.003	10.0%	0.05%
100	100	6.0	36.0 ($x = 6$)	11.3	0.002	12.0%	0.58%	0.003	12.0%	0.06%
100	100	6.0	48.0 ($x = 8$)	11.7	0.002	16.0%	0.77%	0.003	16.0%	0.07%
100	100	6.0	60.0 ($x = 10$)	12.1	0.002	20.0%	0.96%	0.003	20.0%	0.09%
100	100	6.0	96.0 ($x = 16$)	13.3	0.002	32.0%	1.54%	0.002	32.0%	0.12%

---

[8] Under typical vertical building loads the number of floors would normally not exceed 10 (i.e., 9 suspended floors plus roof) if a maximum 2:1 pressure gradient between the internal building pressure and the external atmospheric pressure is adhered to on physiological grounds (building occupants) and a minimum floor diameter of 40 FT is assumed due to practical considerations. The corresponding slenderness ratio of a building with these dimensions is 15, if we assume a story-height of 10 FT.

To explore this argument further Table 4.3 provides the *A-B to X* and *C-D to Y* relationships for a typical air-supported building with assumed loading eccentricities that are multiples of the slenderness ratio. As would be expected the proportional contributions of *A* to *X* and *C* to *Y* increase linearly with increases in the assumed eccentricity of the vertical building loads. In the case where the eccentricity is more than five times the slenderness ratio, the contributions of *A* to *X* and *C* to *Y* become significant at the 10% level. However, even when the contributions of *A* and *C* are at the 10% level the contributions of *B* and *D* are still less than 0.5% and 0.05%, respectively. It can therefore be concluded that terms *B* and *D* in equations 2.8 and 3.11 can be safely omitted in the design of multi-story air-supported buildings for typical commercial occupancies (e.g., offices and retail) where the building diameter is likely to be at least 60 ft.

$$P = (2 W t_m / R) [(1 / A_m) + (e / Z_m)] \text{ (psig)} \quad \text{(2.8a)}$$

$$P = (k W r^2 / (R^2 \cos\theta)) [(\cos\theta / (k A_{CA})) + (e / Z_{CA})] \text{ (psig)} \quad \text{(3.11a)}$$

Nevertheless, it may be useful to determine under what circumstances terms *B* and *D* do become significant in equations 2.8 and 3.11, respectively. Inspection of Tables 4.2 and 4.3 indicates that the contributions of terms *B* and *D* to *X* and *Y* tend to increase with higher slenderness ratios (first line of Table 4.2) and greater loading eccentricities (last line of Table 4.3). The question then becomes, what would be considered a reasonable loading eccentricity? In Table 4.3 the loading eccentricities are assumed as multiples of the slenderness ratio range from R/100 (where *R* is the building radius), when the eccentricity is equal to the slenderness ratio, to R/6.25, when the eccentricity is equal to 16 times the slenderness ratio.

It is of interest to note that term *D* in equation 3.11 is much less sensitive to the loading eccentricity (*e*) then term *B* in equation 2.8. In fact, the value of *B* is consistently about 10 times the value of *D*, increasing slightly beyond a factor of 10 as the assumed eccentricity is increased. This should not come as a surprise when we consider that equation 3.11 applies to multi-story air-supported buildings in which the principal structural component is a cable-network surrounding the membrane envelope, while in equation 2.8 the principal structural component is the membrane envelope itself. The fundamental difference between the two building types is related to material properties, namely the modulus of elasticity (*E*). The modulus of elasticity of steel (i.e., E_{CA} of the steel cables) is between 10 to 15 times higher than the modulus of elasticity of plastic (i.e., E_m of the membrane envelope). Since *E* is a first order divisor in terms *B* and *D* the order of magnitude difference in the values of these terms is to be expected. As can be seen in Table 4.4, even in the extreme case when the assumed eccentricity is equal to the radius (*R*) of the building, term *D* in equation 3.11 contributes less than 1% to term *Y*.

Table 4.4: Extreme cases of the proportional contributions of the terms *A* and *B* to *X* (equation 2.8) and terms *C* and *D* to *Y* (equation 3.11) for 9 floors (plus roof), 10 FT story-height, and vertical load eccentricity as a multiple (*x*) of the slenderness ratio (SR).

Diameter (FT)	Height (FT)	Slend. Ratio	e = x(SR) (IN)	Air Pressure (psig)	Equation 2.8			Equation 3.11		
					X	A	B	Y	C	D
100	100	6.0	120 (x = 20)	14	0.002	40%	2%	0.002	40%	0.14%
100	100	6.0	150 (x = 25)	15	0.002	50%	2%	0.002	50%	0.16%
100	100	6.0	300 (x = 50)	21	0.002	100%	5%	0.001	100%	0.22%
100	100	6.0	600 (x = 100)	31	0.002	200%	10%	0.001	200%	0.28%

We can therefore conclude that for all practical multi-story air-supported building applications[9], in which the principal structural component is an external cable-network, the omission of term D in equation 3.11a is permissible without jeopardizing the safety of the building.

Next, we will explore the impact of higher slenderness ratios on the contributions of terms B and D on X and Y in equations 2.8 and 3.11, respectively. A reasonable loading eccentricity would appear to be twice the slenderness ratio, which is still an order of magnitude greater than the R/50 value discussed previously in regard to empirical results (Section 2.5.1) and standard structural engineering practices (Section 2.5.3). In reference to Table 4.5, the equivalent ratios are R/7.1, R/6.0, R/5.2, R/4.6, and R/4.1 as the story-height increases in 2 FT increments from 12 to 20 FT.

Table 4.5: Extreme cases of the proportional contributions of the terms A and B to X (equation 2.8) and terms C and D to Y (equation 3.11) for 9 floors (plus roof), 10 to 20 FT story-height (increasing in increments of 2 FT), and vertical load eccentricity of twice the slenderness ratio (SR).

Diameter (FT)	Height (FT)	Slend. Ratio	$e = x$(SR) (IN)	Air Pressure (psig)	Equation 2.8			Equation 3.11		
					X	A	B	Y	C	D
40	120	17	34 (x = 2)	12.2	0.005	28%	5%	0.016	28%	1.0%
40	140	20	40 (x = 2)	12.8	0.005	33%	7%	0.015	33%	1.5%
40	160	23	46 (x = 2)	13.4	0.005	38%	11%	0.015	38%	2.1%
40	180	26	52 (x = 2)	13.9	0.005	43%	16%	0.014	43%	2.9%
40	200	29	58 (x = 2)	14.4	0.005	48%	22%	0.013	48%	3.8%

It can be seen in Table 4.5 that even with a slenderness ratio of 29 (equivalent to a building height to diameter ratio of 5:1) the contribution of term D to Y is less than 4% when a cable-network serves as the principal structural component. We can therefore conclude that also in the case of special purpose air-supported structures (e.g., a multi-story greenhouse or storage facility) that are more slender than buildings for normal occupancies, equation 3.11a is a satisfactory alternative to equation 3.11.

It should be noted that the same does not necessarily apply to multi-story air-supported structures without a cable-network in which a plastic membrane serves as the sole structural component. In those cases, as can be seen in Tables 4.4 and 4.5 the contribution of term B to X can be significant. Therefore, equation 2.8a should be applied only after careful consideration of the dimensions and purpose of the particular structure. However, it is acknowledged that multi-story air-supported buildings without exterior cable-networks serving as the principal structural component would be very rare because of the limited tensile strength properties of plastic membrane materials.

4.5.4 Typical Multi-Story Air-Supported Office Building Structure

The structural design results for a typical multi-story air-supported building with a cable-network surrounding the plastic building envelope and serving as the principal structural component are

---

[9] This includes air-inflated columns supporting a building structure in which the occupied spaces are not pressurized.

shown below. The building has a height and diameter of *100 FT*, giving it a height to diameter ratio of *1*. As explained previously in Chapter 3 (Section 3.9), to facilitate the erection of the building envelope during construction the diameter of the nine suspended floors is *98 FT* to provide a *1 FT* wide gap between the perimeter of each floor and the building envelope. Based on discussions relating to an appropriate vertical loading eccentricity (*e*) in the previous section (Section 4.5.3), the eccentricity is assumed to be twice the slenderness ration (*SR*) or *12 IN* from the central axis of the building. Since the building is intended for an office occupancy normal building loads applicable to public buildings have been assumed (i.e., *100 LB/SF* live-load and *50 LB/SF* dead-load). Finally, horizontal wind loads have been based on a maximum wind speed of *110 mph*.

(1) Assumed Design Data:

modulus of elasticity of membrane material	=	2,000,000 psi
modulus of elasticity of cable material	=	29,000,000 psi
design strength of membrane material	=	15,000 psi
design strength of cable material	=	60,000 psi
building form constant for wind drag forces	=	0.60
optimum angle (to vertical) for diagonal cables	=	63 deg 26 min
approximate spacing of diagonal cables	=	4 FT
approximate spacing of horizontal cables	=	2 FT

(2) Entered Design Data:

building diameter	=	100 FT
floor diameter	=	98 FT
number of air-supported floors	=	10 (including roof)
building height	=	100 FT (with ground floor)
membrane thickness	=	0.125 IN
live-load	=	100 LB
dead-load	=	50 LB
wind speed	=	110 mph

(3) Derived Design Data:

total building load	=	11,361,089 LB
building slenderness ratio (SR)	=	5.7
assumed vertical loading eccentricity	=	11.4 IN (twice SR)
building height to radius ratio	=	2.0

(4) Calculated Cross-Sectional Membrane Properties:

cross-sectional membrane area	=	471.2 IN^2
membrane thickness around perimeter	=	0.125 IN
section modulus of membrane	=	141,372 IN^3
moment of inertia of membrane	=	84,822,936 IN^4

(5) Calculated Internal Air-Pressure Based on Membrane (only):

internal design air pressure (no wind and membrane only) = 10.47 psig (efficiency = 0.96)

(6) Calculated Preliminary Diagonal Cable Size and Spacing:

tension in diagonal cables due to air pressure	=	101,904 LB
number of diagonal cables	=	79

spacing of diagonal cables = 3 FT 11.72 IN
diameter of diagonal cables = 1.47 IN

(7) Calculated Preliminary Cross-Sectional Cable Properties:
cross-sectional cable area = 134.2 IN^2
equivalent cable thickness around perimeter = 0.080 IN
section modulus of cables = 89,989 IN^3
moment of inertia of cables = 53,993,392 IN^4

(8) Calculated Internal Air-Pressure Based on Diagonal Cables:
internal design air pressure (cables) = 10.45 psig (efficiency = 0.96)

(9) Calculated Wind Force Results Based on Cable-Network:
additional air pressure to resist wind force = 0.32 psig
deflection due to wind force = 0.03 IN
tension in diagonal cables due to wind force = 4,595 LB

(10) Calculated Final Diagonal Cable Size at Original Spacing:
tension in diagonal cables due to air pressure = 106,252 LB
number of diagonal cables = 79
spacing of diagonal cables = 3 FT 11.72 IN
diameter of diagonal cables = 1.50 IN

(11) Calculated Final Cross-Sectional Cable Properties:
final cross-sectional cable area = 139.9 IN^2
equivalent cable thickness around perimeter = 0.083 IN
final section modulus of cables = 93,828 IN^3
final moment of inertia of cables = 56,296,960 IN^4

(12) Final Internal Air-Pressure Based on Diagonal Cables:
final internal design air pressure (cables) = 10.45 psig (efficiency = 0.96)

(13) Final Wind Force Results Based on Cable-Network:
final air pressure to resist wind force = 0.32 psig
final deflection due to wind force = 0.02 IN
tension in diagonal cables due to wind force = 4,595 LB

(14) Final Combined Vertical plus Wind Loads Pressure:
final combined air pressure (wind plus vertical load) = 10.77 psig (efficiency = 0.93)

(15) Calculated Final Revised Cable Size at Original Spacing:
tension in diagonal cables due to air pressure = 110,847 LB
number of diagonal cables = 79
spacing of diagonal cables = 3 FT 11.72 IN
diameter of diagonal cables = 1.53 IN

(16) Calculated Horizontal Cable Size and Spacing:
tension in horizontal cables due to pressure = 158,256 LB
number of horizontal cables = 49
spacing of horizontal cables = 2 FT 0.49 IN

diameter of horizontal cables = 1.83 IN

(17) Calculated Building Envelope and Cable-Network Weights:

total weight of building envelope and cable-network = 267,495 LB (7% of dead-load)
weight of plastic membrane = 22,907 LB
weight of 79 diagonal steel cables = 106,426 LB
weight of 49 horizontal steel cables = 138,162 LB

(18) Calculated Length of Each Cable and Total Length:

length of each diagonal cable = 224 FT
total length of diagonal cables = 17,662 FT
length of each horizontal cable = 314 FT
total length of horizontal cables = 15,394 FT

4.5.5 Typical Multi-Story Air-Supported Tower Structure

More slender air-supported column structures than those considered in the previous two sections of this Chapter (Sections 4.5.3 and 4.5.4) may be called for in other building applications such as portable observation towers, temporary air traffic control towers, grain silos, and vertical greenhouses. These structures may have height to diameter ratios that greatly exceed the *2:1* ratio (i.e., slenderness ratio of 6) that is likely to apply to a multi-story office building of the type designed in the previous section (Section 4.5.4).

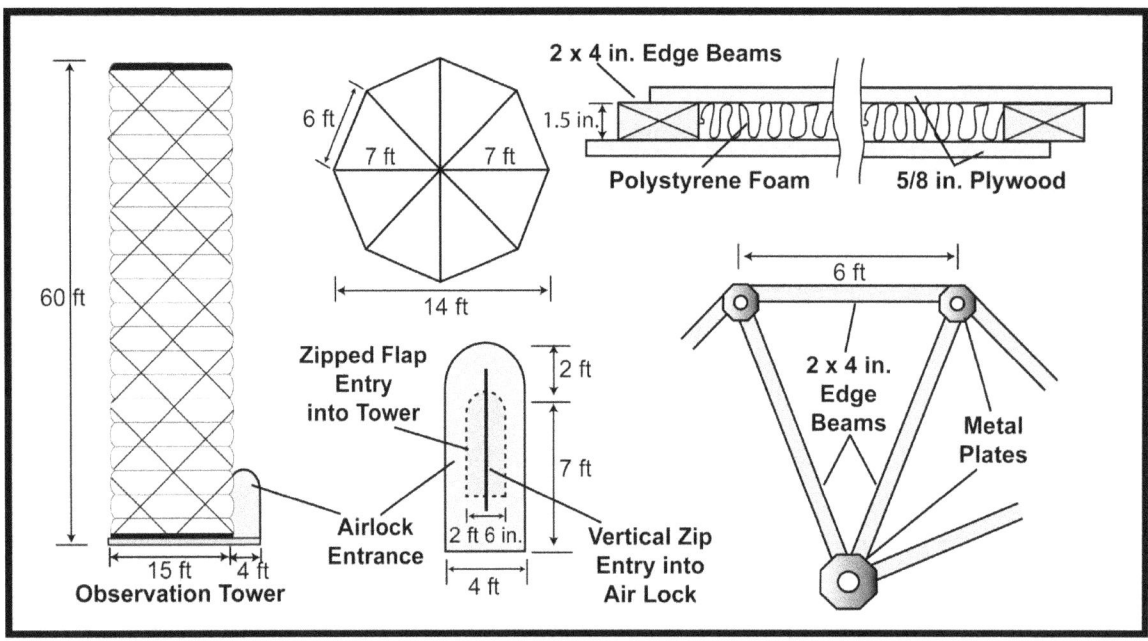

Figure 4.10: A typical more slender, air-supported, temporary observation tower structure.

For example, let us consider a portable structure that could be used as a temporary air traffic control tower or fire watch tower. As shown in Figure 4.10, the proposed structure has a diameter of *15 FT* and is *60 FT* high. One floor is suspended 8 FT below the air-supported roof and a second floor functions as an elevator platform to shuttle the occupants to and from the airlock entrance to their workstations on the suspended floor. Designed to move from approximately *1 FT* above ground level to a height of around *45 FT* (i.e., *7 FT* below the suspended floor from where a ladder allows the occupants to reach their workstations), the elevator platform may be motorized or alternatively could be manually raised and lowered with a system of pulleys.

A *4 FT* diameter inflatable flexible membrane cylinder with a hemispherical roof and a timber floor serves as a simple airlock that is attached to the membrane envelope of the tower. It is fitted with a vertical zipper that extends from *1 FT* above ground level to a height of *6 FT*. The zipper is located on the far side of the airlock (i.e., at a point that is furthest from the envelope of the tower) and can be opened from both the outside and the inside. Another slightly more elaborate zipped flap *2 FT* above the elevator platform (when it is in its ground floor position), *2 FT 6 IN* wide and *5 FT* high is located at the point where the airlock cylinder is joined to the tower envelope. The zipper to open this flap is also double-sided. With both the tower and the airlock initially in an inflated state and both zippers closed, a person entering the tower would proceed in the following sequence: open the airlock zipper and step into the airlock (this will of course temporarily deflate the airlock but should not pose a problem because of the very light hemispherical membrane roof of the airlock); close the airlock zipper; open the zipper in the tower envelope, which will re-inflate the airlock; step onto the elevator platform inside the tower; and, close the zipper in the tower envelope (Figure 4.11). The last action will leave the airlock in an inflated state ready for the next entry or exit. The exit procedure is essentially the same but in reverse order.

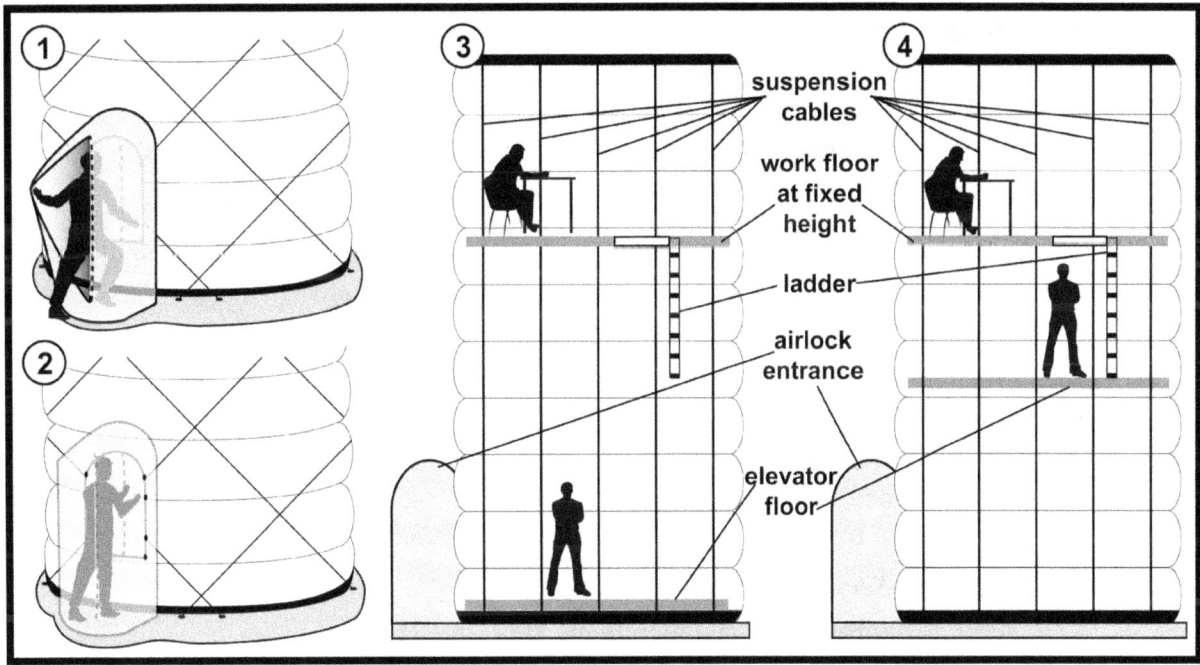

Figure 4.11: Observation tower entry and exit sequence

With a height of *60 FT* and a diameter of *15 FT* the structure has a height to diameter ratio of *4*. As explained previously in Chapter 3 (Section 3.9), to facilitate the erection of the building envelope during construction the diameter of the suspended floor and the elevator platform should be slightly smaller to provide a gap between their perimeters and the tower envelope. In this case, due to the relatively small tower diameter a *6 IN* gap should provide sufficient clearance. Similar to the office building example described in the previous section, a vertical load eccentricity (*e*) of twice the slenderness ratio (*SR*) is assumed. Therefore, with a slenderness ratio of *22.6*[10], the vertical load eccentricity (*e*) is *45.2 IN* measured from the central axis of the tower. Since the tower is intended to accommodate no more than three persons (two persons under normal circumstances) a live-load of only *10 psf* would seem reasonable (i.e., assuming a *1000 LB* load for three persons the distributed load would be *5.7 psf*). Both the suspended floor and the elevator platform are each assumed to be constructed of eight triangular sandwich panels as shown in Figure 4.10, with an estimated weight of *250 LB* per panel (including steel connectors) or *2000 LB* per floor (i.e., a distributed load of *11.3 psf*). Therefore a dead-load of *15 psf* will be conservatively assumed. Finally, since the tower may well be exposed to high winds a maximum wind speed of *110 mph* will be assumed.

(1) Assumed Design Data:

modulus of elasticity of membrane material =	500,000 psi
modulus of elasticity of cable material =	29,000,000 psi
design strength of membrane material =	4,800 psi (300 LB/IN)
design strength of cable material =	40,000 psi
building form constant for wind drag forces =	0.60
optimum angle (to vertical) for diagonal cables =	63 deg 26 min
approximate spacing of diagonal cables =	4 FT
approximate spacing of horizontal cables =	3 FT

(2) Entered Design Data:

building diameter =	15 FT
floor diameter =	14 FT
number of air-supported floors =	3 (including roof)
building height =	60 FT
membrane thickness =	0.0625 IN
live-load =	10 LB
dead-load =	15 LB
wind speed =	110 mph

(3) Derived Design Data:

total building load =	12,115 LB
building slenderness ratio (SR) =	22.6
assumed vertical loading eccentricity =	45.2 IN (twice SR)
building height to radius ratio =	8.0

(4) Calculated Cross-Sectional Membrane Properties:

cross-sectional membrane area =	35.3 IN^2
membrane thickness around perimeter =	0.0625 IN
section modulus of membrane =	1590.4 IN^3
moment of inertia of membrane =	143138.7 IN^4

(5) Calculated Internal Air-Pressure Based on Membrane (only):

internal design air pressure (no wind and membrane only) = 0.98 psig (efficiency = 0.48)

---

[10] If the tower height (H) is 720 IN and the tower radius (R) is 90 IN then the Slenderness Ratio (SR) is given by:
SR = (2 H / (R^2 / 2)$^{0.5}$) = ((2 x 720) / (90 x 90 /2)$^{0.5}$) = (1440 / (4050)$^{0.5}$) = (1440 / 63.64) = 22.6 .

(6) Calculated Preliminary Diagonal Cable Size and Spacing:

    tension in diagonal cables due to air pressure = 1,481 LB
    number of diagonal cables = 12
    spacing of diagonal cables = 3 FT 11.12 IN
    diameter of diagonal cables = 0.22 IN

(7) Calculated Preliminary Cross-Sectional Cable Properties:

    cross-sectional cable area = 0.4 IN^2
    equivalent cable thickness around perimeter = 0.002 IN
    section modulus of cables = 44.7 IN^3
    moment of inertia of cables = 4023.1 IN^4

(8) Calculated Internal Air-Pressure Based on Diagonal Cables:

    internal design air pressure (cables) = 0.98 psig (efficiency = 0.49)

(9) Calculated Wind Force Results Based on Cable-Network:

    additional air pressure to resist wind force = 5.14 psig
    deflection due to wind force = 6.53 IN
    tension in diagonal cables due to wind force = 10,890 LB

(10) Calculated Final Diagonal Cable Size at Original Spacing:

    tension in diagonal cables due to air pressure = 12,354 LB
    number of diagonal cables = 12
    spacing of diagonal cables = 3 FT 11.12 IN
    diameter of diagonal cables = 0.63 IN

(11) Calculated Final Cross-Sectional Cable Properties:

    final cross-sectional cable area = 3.7 IN^2
    equivalent cable thickness around perimeter = 0.015 IN
    final section modulus of cables = 372.8 IN^3
    final moment of inertia of cables = 33556.1 IN^4

(12) Final Internal Air-Pressure Based on Diagonal Cables:

    final internal design air pressure (cables) = 0.96 psig (efficiency = 0.49)

(13) Final Wind Force Results Based on Cable-Network:

    final air pressure to resist wind force = 5.14 psig
    final deflection due to wind force = 0.78 IN
    tension in diagonal cables due to wind force = 10,890 LB

(14) Final Combined Vertical plus Wind Loads Pressure:

    final combined air pressure (wind plus vertical load) = 6.10 psig (efficiency = 0.08)

(15) Calculated Final Revised Cable Size at Original Spacing:

    tension in diagonal cables due to air pressure = 23,244 LB
    number of diagonal cables = 12
    spacing of diagonal cables = 3 FT 11.12 IN
    diameter of diagonal cables = 0.86 IN

(16) Calculated Horizontal Cable Size and Spacing:
    tension in horizontal cables due to pressure = 20,803 LB
         number of horizontal cables = 19
        spacing of horizontal cables = 3 FT 1.89 IN
        diameter of horizontal cables = 0.81 IN

(17) Calculated Building Envelope and Cable-Network Weights:
  total weight of building envelope and cable-network = 4,307 LB (59% of dead-load)
           weight of plastic membrane = 1,031 LB
       weight of 12 diagonal steel cables = 1,692 LB
      weight of 19 horizontal steel cables = 1,585 LB

(18) Calculated Length of Each Cable and Total Length:
         length of each diagonal cable = 134.1 FT
        total length of diagonal cables = 1609.7 FT
       length of each horizontal cable = 47.1 FT
      total length of horizontal cables = 895.4 FT

4.5.6 Comparison of Office Building and Tower Structure

A side-by-side comparison of the structural design values determined for the typical 10-story air-supported office building designed in Section 4.5.4 and the much more slender air-supported observation tower designed in Section 4.5.5, is shown in Table 4.6. In both cases the vertical loading eccentricity, measured from the central vertical axis of the structure is assumed to be twice the slenderness ratio. The assumed dead-loads and live-loads are considerably different for the two buildings. While these load differences are certainly significant, they are in alignment with the divergent purposes (i.e., occupancies) of the two structures and should not unduly distort the structural comparison of the two buildings.

Table 4.6: Comparison of squat and slender air-supported structures

Structural Parameter	Unit	Office Building	Observation Tower
building height (with air-lock)	FT	100	60
building diameter	FT	100	15
internal floor diameter	FT	98	14
area of each floor	SF	7,543	154
area of air-supported roof	SF	7,854	177
height to diameter ratio (H/D)	--	1	4
height to radius ratio (H/R)	--	2	8
slenderness ratio	--	5.7	22.6
wind speed	mph	110	110
air pressure (vertical load)	psig	10.45 (0.96)	0.96 (0.49)
air pressure (wind load)	psig	0.32	5.14
combined internal air pressure	psig	10.77 (0.93)	6.10 (0.08)

deflection (combined loads)	IN	0.02	0.78

As expected the pressure-utilization efficiency[11] of the air-supported structure decreases rapidly with increasing slenderness ratio. Closer inspection of Table 4.6 shows that a four-fold increase in slenderness ratio (i.e., from 5.7 to 22.6) results in a two-fold decrease in efficiency for vertical loads alone and an eleven-fold decrease in efficiency if wind forces are considered as well. In fact, for the tower structure the internal air pressure required to resist *110 mph* wind loads is more than five times the air pressure required to resist vertical loads. This is markedly different from the squat office building where resistance to the same *110 mph* wind force requires only a 3% increase in internal air pressure. The deflection experienced by the tower structure (*0.78 IN*) when subjected to a horizontal wind force of this magnitude is 39 times the deflection experienced by the office building (*0.02 IN*).

Earlier in this Chapter (Section 4.5.3) we discussed the possible simplification of design equation 3.11 for multi-story air-supported buildings with external cable-networks, by omission of terms C and D. As shown in Table 4.7, there is no doubt that term D can be omitted in both cases. Even for the observation tower with a height to diameter ratio of *4* and equivalent slenderness ratio of more than *20*, the *0.33%* influence of the term D on the term Y is not significant. It can be shown that for any practical air-supported, or even air-inflated[12], structural building application term D will never exceed the *1%* influence level.

Table 4.7: Comparison of the proportional contributions of the terms C and D to Y in equation 3.11 for the squat office building and the more slender observation tower.

Building Type	Diameter (FT)	Height (FT)	Slenderness Ratio (SR)	e = 2(SR) (IN)	Air Pressure (psig)	Equation 3.11		
						Y	C	D
Office Bdg.	100	100	5.7	11.4	10.77	0.003	4%	0.02%
Obs. Tower	15	60	22.6	45.2	6.10	0.121	102%	0.33%

However, at a level of *102%* term C does have a very significant influence on term Y in the case of the observation tower and therefore must not be omitted from equation 3.11. This is consistent with the conclusion reached previously in Section 4.5.3 that while term D can be safely omitted in the design of any practical air-supported or air-inflated building structure, term C should be retained in all cases.

---

[11] Pressure-utilization efficiency is defined as the ratio of the total vertical building load divided by the product of the internal air pressure and the roof area, expressed as a percentage (Chapters 2 (2.5.2) and Chapter 3 (3.4)).

[12] As opposed to an air-supported application in which the occupants of the building are exposed to the internal pressure, an example of an air-inflated application would be a building structure consisting of one or more pressurized (i.e., inflated) columns.

Chapter 5
Two Prototype Multi-Story Air-Supported Buildings

Consistent with the author's initial conception of a pressurized structural system for multi-story buildings that was triggered more by the observation of practical inflated artifacts (e.g., balloons, tires, pumps) rather than theoretical considerations, the desire to build a large-scale prototype was very strong from the beginning. The first opportunity came in 1970 in Sydney, Australia, followed by a second opportunity when the author immigrated with his family to the U.S. in 1972 (Pohl and Montero 1973).

5.1 Single-Skin with Cable-Network Prototype

It is only natural that the single-skin air-supported building type should have been selected to form the basis of the first large-scale prototype building. Apart from offering the greatest structural efficiency, this building type also embodies the most severe architectural, constructional, and environmental challenges to the designer. During January 1968 the author began formulating plans for the construction of a large-scale, single-skin air-supported building to serve as an experimental structure for investigating the operational requirements of a building environment pressurized for structural support purposes.

In the ensuing years considerable efforts were made to generate interest and obtain financial sponsorship from the Australian plastics industry for the construction and testing of a small number of prototype fluid-supported buildings. Despite the potential promotional and market development value of these early proposals the plastics industry did not respond positively. Similarly, while the proposals generated some interest in the Australian construction industry, this interest did not materialize into any serious commitment to support the construction of a prototype building. Therefore, the author pursued the alternative path of a university research project. Accordingly, the construction of the first multi-story air-supported building was undertaken as an educational project by a senior class of undergraduate construction engineering students.

In April 1970 decisive steps were taken by the author to accomplish the design, construction, and in-service operation of a three-story fully air-supported prototype building as an undergraduate student project in the School of Building at the University of New South Wales, Sydney, Australia. At the outset of the project it was resolved that the building should be designed, documented, and constructed by the students as an integrated project in their construction, architectural structures, building science, estimating, and operational planning classes. Due to the eventual generosity of the New South Wales construction industry, the majority of materials were donated and delivered to the site before the commencement of the construction phase. A petty cash fund of $3,000 (Australia 1970) was established by the School of Building for miscellaneous material expenses and equipment hiring charges.

5.1.1 Site Selection

The Experimental Research Laboratory of the School of Building was located in a converted bus maintenance building within walking distance of the campus. For a number of reasons it was decided that the proposed air-supported building should be constructed inside the laboratory building. First, an existing movable 12 ton electric beam-crane could be utilized as a convenient safety device and construction aid. However, the beam-crane was no longer operational as a lifting device. In view of the participation of students and the experimental nature of the structure, much thought was given at the formulation stage of the project to the provision of a standby secondary structural support system. Second, the research area incorporated a well-equipped workshop under the control of a full-time laboratory technician. Tools and expert assistance would be available to the students throughout the construction stage. Third, the research building floor featured a number of *5 FT* deep maintenance trenches, one of which could conveniently serve as the airlock entrance to the building.

A suitable space *25 FT* by *25 FT* with a maximum usable height (to the underside of the beam-crane) of *21 FT* and a *5 FT* deep by *4 FT* wide maintenance trench running centrally across the floor area was selected.

5.1.2 Design

The dimensions of the building were primarily governed by the height restriction of the site and the strength of available membrane materials. The students insisted that the building should incorporate at least two fully air-supported floors suspended from roof level. To save on height, the floor-to-floor spacing was reduced to a minimum dimension of *7 FT* for the two suspended floors, while the spacing between the ground and first floors was limited to *1 FT 6 IN*. It was argued that from a structural point of view the building would demonstrate the ability of the internal air pressure to support at least two floors of a multi-story structure while leaving the ground floor with insufficient head room to function as a usable building space. This sacrifice was considered to be small in relation to the general structural concept of the building. To conserve further building height, the airlock entrance was sunk into the existing maintenance trench. As shown in Figure 5.1, the overall height of the building from the bottom of the trench (serving as the airlock floor) to the top of the roof was just over *24 FT*.

Since the stresses in the membrane enclosure of a single-skin air-supported building are directly proportional to the diameter, the horizontal dimensions of the proposed building were primarily governed by the strength characteristics of available plastic membrane materials. It was considered desirable for the membrane enclosure to be transparent, thereby permitting a clear view into and out of the building. At the same time, it was necessary for the material to be relatively inexpensive, readily available, and amenable to heat sealing as a jointing method. A transparent *20 mil* PVC film was finally selected partly because of its low cost and good transparency and partly due to the offer of a private company to fabricate the main building and airlock membranes free of charge. Tests conducted on the PVC material yielded the following results:

working stress at 20% (approx.) elongation = 11.5 LB/IN
ultimate stress at 400% (approx.) elongation = 36.5 LB/IN

Since these test results indicated that even under moderate tensile stress the membrane would experience substantial elongation, it was resolved to incorporate a number of horizontal cables in the exterior cable-network[1]. In this manner, the circumferential expansion of the envelope could be controlled at the environmental pressure required to maintain stability of the building structure. The airlock was designed simply as a *4 FT* diameter cylinder featuring a built-in timber floor and a *7 FT* long vertical zipper to serve as a convenient entrance and exit mechanism.

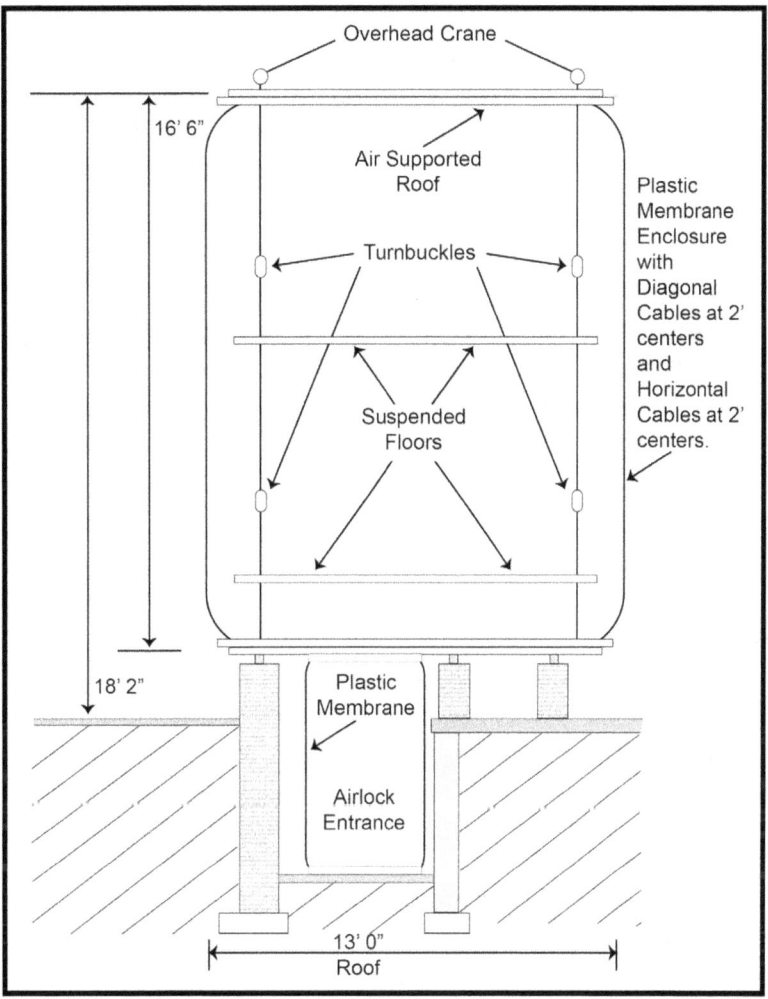

Figure 5.1: Sectional view of first prototype

Early, during the design stage of the project one of the students was assigned to investigate pressurization requirements and implications on the design and construction of the building. Two alternative approaches for controlling the environment of the main building and the airlock were investigated. The two chambers could be pressurized separately or jointly. In view of the large difference in volume (25 to 1) between the main chamber *2,260 CF* and the airlock chamber *88 CF*, as well as considering the simplicity of providing a connecting adjustable valve between the two chambers, it was resolved to pressurize the airlock by leaking air from the main building. Since the building would normally be operating at an environmental pressure greater than the minimum pressure required for structural purposes, it was felt that the sudden reduction in

---

[1] The need to incorporate horizontal cables was discovered in the construction of this prototype. During the initial pressurization the membrane ballooned out horizontally despite the presence of diagonal vertical cables. This led to the realization that horizontal cables would be required in all multi-story air-supported buildings.

pressure experienced by the main chamber during the inflation of the airlock entrance would be negligible.

A number of additional design factors related to the air-supported nature of the building structure were identified:

1. In view of the difficulty of eliminating all air leakages in the main building chamber the pressurization unit would need to operate at all times but at different rates. For example, during the inflation of the airlock the demand for air supply would be much greater than at other times. The following performance parameters were established for the selection of the pressurization equipment:

    1.1 A pressure range of between *8-14 IN* water gauge (i.e., 0.3 to 0.5 psig) would be required for the operation of the building.[2]

    1.2 The pressurization equipment would be required to operate at variable speeds to allow for an air leakage rate of between *10-50 CF/min* per minute. It was acknowledged that in the case of a direct current (DC) electric motor variations in speed could be achieved by means of a manually operated rheostat.

    1.3 The pressurization equipment would need to be capable of continuous operation over periods of at least *6-8 hours*. It was assumed that in between demonstrations and tests the building would be deflated and remain suspended by the safety cables attached to the overhead beam crane.

    Considerable difficulties were experienced later during the search for a suitable pressurization unit. While it was generally agreed that a Roots blower[3] by virtue of its efficient operation over the required pressure range would provide the most economical solution, no such unit could be found within the time constraints of the project. Eventually a discarded axial-fan blower (Spencer Turbine Company) driven by a *3/4 horsepower* (Black & Decker) continuous duty electric DC motor was discovered in the Aeronautical Engineering School and generously donated to the project. Although limited to a maximum air volume capacity of around *20 CF/min* at a static pressure of *10 IN* water gauge, this unit performed well during the early operation of the building. It was finally relegated to a standby role after a larger axial-fan unit was obtained.

2. The opening between the airlock entrance and the main building would need to be designed in a manner that would not allow the trap door to be opened before pressure equalization between the two chambers had been completed during entry and exit operations. Industry standard design practices applicable to pressure chamber doors would need to be studied and incorporated in the final construction details.

---

[2] The final design pressure, being dependent on the weight of the building, could not be calculated before the completion of most of the construction details pertaining to the floors, roof, and suspension system.

[3] Roots blowers are positive displacement lobe pumps that operate by pumping fluids with a pair of meshing lobes. The fluid is trapped in pockets surrounding the lobes and carried from the intake side to the exhaust. They are typically used in applications where a large volume of air must be moved across a relatively small pressure differential.

3. Separate means of measuring the pressure in the main building chamber and the airlock would have to be provided.

4. During the development of construction details particular care would need to be taken to ensure the elimination of air leakage through the construction joints of the roof and ground floor and the point of attachment of the exterior building membrane.

5. For safety reasons, a pressure release valve should be provided in the main building chamber (possibly at roof level) to avoid rupture of the membrane due to over-pressurization.

While the natural shape of a single-skin air-supported building is cylindrical, the apparent need for a circular roof and floor was viewed with some concern. The only readily available material suitable for the construction of the roof and floor was standard structural grade timber and pressed core-board. The requirement of circular floors would have resulted in considerable material wastage and fabrication problems. As a compromise solution, an octagonal shape was adopted on the assumption that this would have a minimal effect on the final cylindrical shape of the membrane enclosure.

5.1.3 Construction Details

Having finalized the overall dimensions of the building, attention was next focused on the construction stage and in particular the development of suitable construction details for the floors, roof, footings, main membrane and airlock attachments, suspension hangers, and the pressure control system. It became immediately apparent that the two suspended floors, roof and ground floor provided an excellent opportunity for prefabrication (Figures 5.2 and 5.3). Apart from savings in construction time, the adoption of a systematic fabrication method would broaden the proposed educational experience for the participating students.

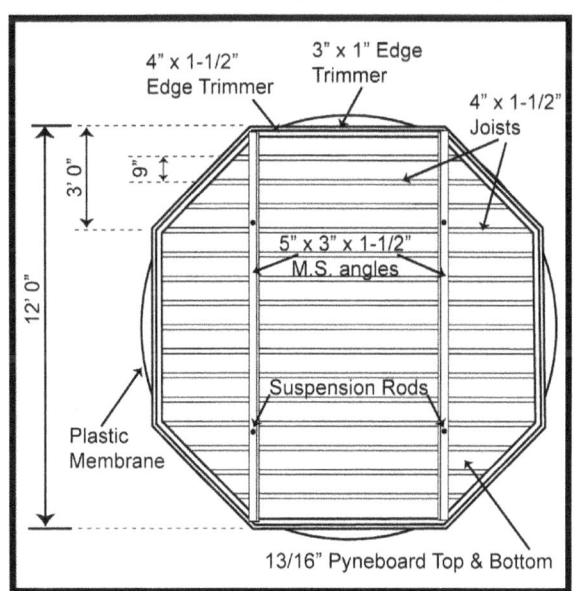
Figure 5.2: Structural roof plan

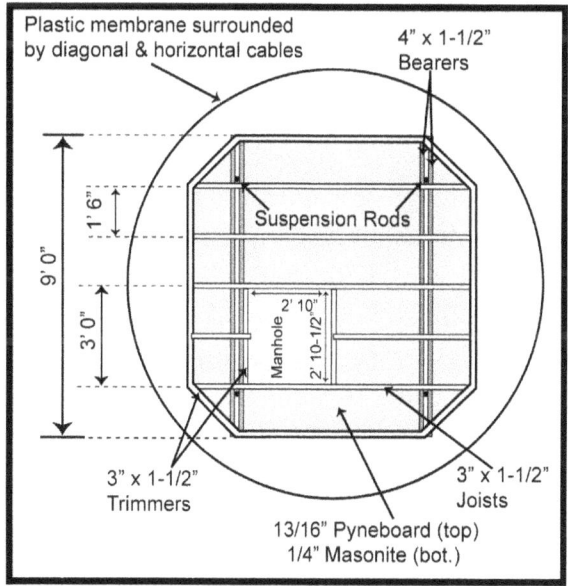
Figure 5.3: Typical structural floor plan

To prevent abrasion between the suspended floors and the exterior building membrane and at the same time simulate as closely as possible a real-world building situation, the size of the intermediate floors was reduced to *9 FT* by *9 FT* leaving a clear air space between the perimeter of each floor and the plastic membrane. The reader will recall that in Chapter 5 the need for a clear air space between the perimeter of each suspended floor and the membrane envelope is discussed in respect to erection and fire protection requirements.

As shown in Figure 5.3, each suspended floor consisted of seven *3 IN* by *1.5 IN* joists sandwiched between *13/16 IN* structural grade particle board and *1/4 IN* low density composite board. The floors were to be supported by two sets of double bearers (*4 IN* by *1.5 IN*) at *6 FT* spacing, while each set of bearers was planned to be suspended from roof level by two suspension rods at *6 FT* centers.

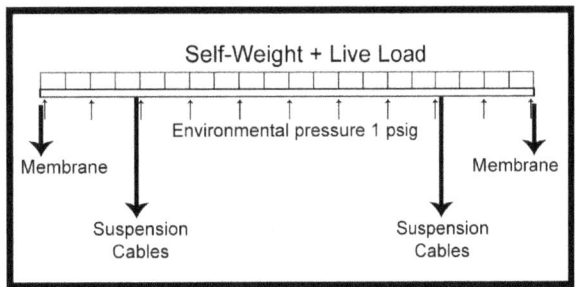

Figure 5.4: Forces if building is inflated

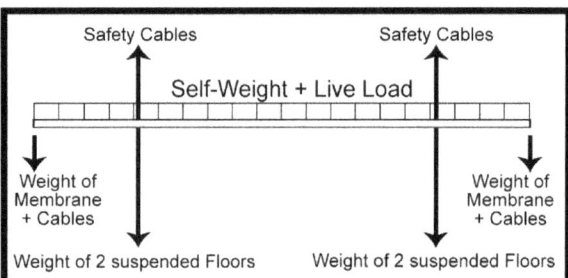

Figure 5.5: Forces if building is deflated

The roof and ground floor presented an unusual structural problem. Apart from the action of much higher loads, it was necessary to consider two distinct loading situations. Under maximum internal pressure[4] the roof plate would be subjected to a uniformly distributed upward force of *144 psf* to be resisted by the four suspension cables at *6 FT* centers, as well as the membrane and cables attached around the perimeter (Figure 5.4). During the construction stage and at other times when the building might be deflated, the roof would be required to support up to 10 persons while suspended from the overhead beam-crane (Figure 5.5). It was necessary to increase the size of the joists to *4 IN* by *1.5 IN* and reduce the spacing to *9 IN*, as well as provide *13/16 IN* structural grade particle board top and bottom, In addition, *5 IN* by *3 IN* by *1/4 IN* mild steel angles were required to serve as bearers to resist the relatively large loads due to pressurization. To minimize air leakage through construction joints and nail holes, it was resolved to place a thin *10 mil* polyethylene membrane between the joists and the upper and lower particle board sheets of the roof and ground floor, respectively.

It was proposed that the two intermediate floors be suspended from roof level by cables fixed at each level to *7/8 IN* diameter mild steel round rods bolted to roof and floor plates. Adjustments in floor levels could be made by the manual operation of turnbuckles located at a convenient height above each floor surface.

Considerable time was devoted to the development of a suitable construction detail for fixing the plastic membrane enclosure to the roof and ground floor perimeters. After evaluating a number of alternative proposals, it was decided to: cut a V-shaped groove into the perimeter fascia board as shown in Figure 5.6; nail a *3/16 IN* diameter fully insulated electric cord into the acute angle of the V-groove to provide a suitable seating for the membrane; drape the membrane over the floor (or

---

[4] The building was designed to sustain a maximum environmental pressure of *28 IN* water gauge (i.e., 1 psig).

roof); and, tie a *5/16 IN* diameter nylon cord around the perimeter to force the membrane into the V-groove. Next, the free end of the membrane would be returned over the nylon cord to form a loop and strapped into position by means of a continuous *½ IN* steel packaging strip. Finally, it was proposed to fix a *3 IN* by *1 IN* trimmer over the membrane loop around the perimeter. The trimmer was to be screwed down at *9 IN* centers. Since the nylon rope with the membrane looped around it was designed to protrude approximately *⅛ IN* beyond the V-shaped recess, it would be possible to apply considerable tension to the membrane loop. As an additional advantage, the trimmer could be retightened at regular intervals during the life-span of the building.

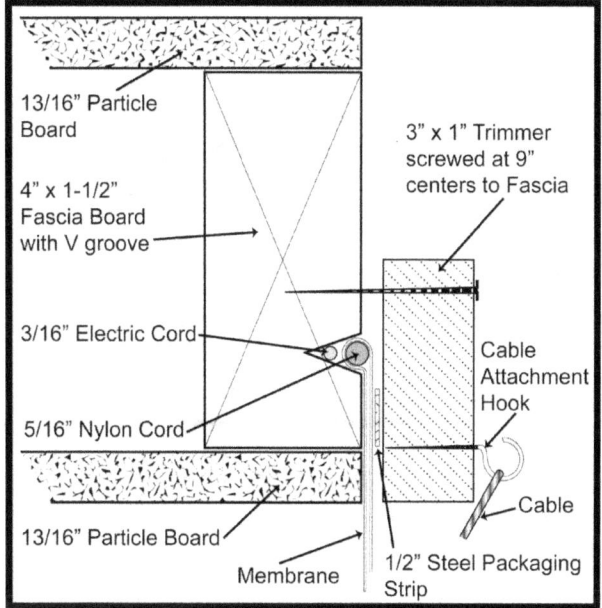   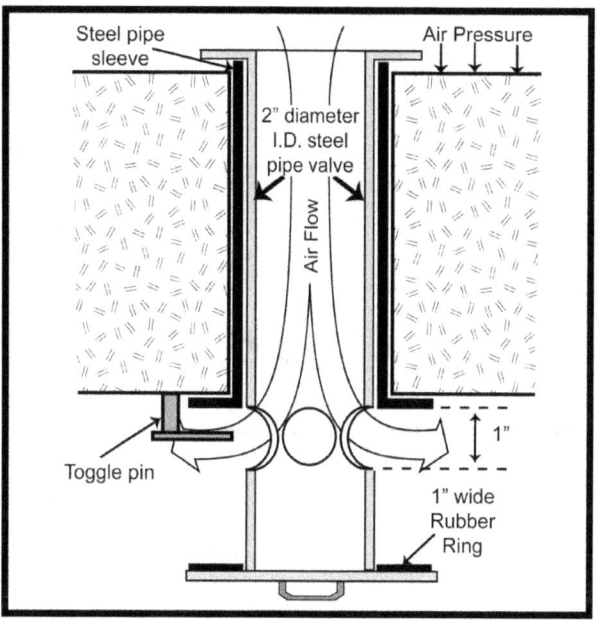

Figure 5.6: Membrane attachment detail   Figure 5.7: Airlock pressure control detail

It was proposed that the manhole entrance located in the ground floor between the airlock and the main building chamber be provided with a rebated timber trap door complete with rubber lining strips for sealing purposes. By virtue of the air pressure acting downward it would therefore be almost impossible for the trap door to be opened from either side whenever the pressure in the main chamber exceeds the pressure in the airlock chamber. For purposes of equalizing the pressure in these two chambers during entry and exit operations, a special valve was designed (Figure 5.7) to be located in the trap door. The valve consisted of a *2 IN* diameter steel pipe capped at one end and provided with a number of *1IN* diameter holes in a band close to the sealed end. By moving the pipe a few inches up or down, the valve could be closed or opened as required. In case of excess pressure a weighted safety valve was allowed for at roof level, while two simple U-tube manometers sufficed to monitor the pressures in the main building and the airlock entrance.

5.1.4 Construction Planning

Considerable efforts were made to plan in advance the sequence of operations to be followed during the construction stage of the building. Detailed time and cost estimates were prepared by the students in their regular classes. Allowances were made for the relative inexperience of the work force, although most of the students could count on at least six months of intermittent site experience. While time estimates of construction operations prepared by the students were often considered to be somewhat optimistic by more experienced staff advisers, it must be admitted in retrospect that most student estimates were very close to the mark. There is no doubt that the students benefited greatly from the detailed analysis of the construction project required for the development of accurate estimates and a meaningful precedence diagram. As shown in Figure 5.8, it was agreed that the construction phase should begin concurrently with the fabrication and assembly of the lifting gear and the construction of the substructure. This was to be followed by the prefabrication of the roof and floors ready for the commencement of the erection stage.

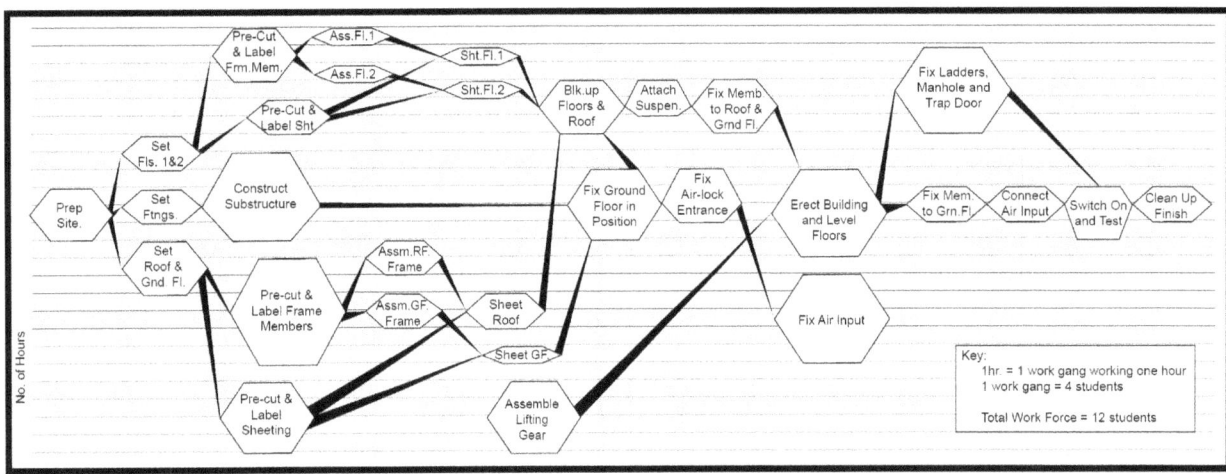

Figure 5.8: Construction sequence of first prototype

Three alternative erection procedures were considered in detail.

> ***Erection Alternative (1):*** To raise the roof by internal pressure with a mobile crane functioning solely as a lateral stabilizer. With the roof in place, the external cable-network could be fixed in position, the internal pressure raised, and the floors hoisted up internally by using cables.
>
> ***Erection Alternative (2):*** To manually hoist the roof with the intermediate floors attached into position in one lifting operation from the overhead beam-crane using chain blocks (since the beam-crane was no longer operable as a lifting device). Subsequently it would be necessary to use a movable scaffold platform to fix the membrane into position at roof level.
>
> ***Erection Alternative (3):*** To rent a mobile crane and hoist the roof with intermediate floors attached into position in one lifting operation. Subsequently, as in alternative (2) it would be necessary to use a movable scaffold platform to fix the membrane into position at roof level.

The final decision made during a site conference one day before the erection operation was scheduled to take place, was to use alternative (3). Paramount importance was placed on safety considerations and lack of confidence in the ability of the membrane envelope to sustain (without cable reinforcement) the initial pressure required to lift the roof plate. In view of the structural rigidity required, the weight of the roof plate increased to approximately *1,420 LB* compared with *560 LB* for each of the suspended floors. Allowing for the weight of the membrane and suspension system an initial pressure of around *4 IN* water gauge, producing a material stress of *10 LB/IN*, would have been required to lift the roof under air pressure (alternative (1)). The adoption of alternative (3) was accompanied by one major disadvantage in comparison with alternative (1). A mobile scaffold supporting a working platform *18 FT* above ground floor level would be required for the attachment of the plastic membrane and the network to the suspended roof plate. As it turned out later during the construction phase, the erection of the scaffold tower was accomplished in less than two hours by four students.

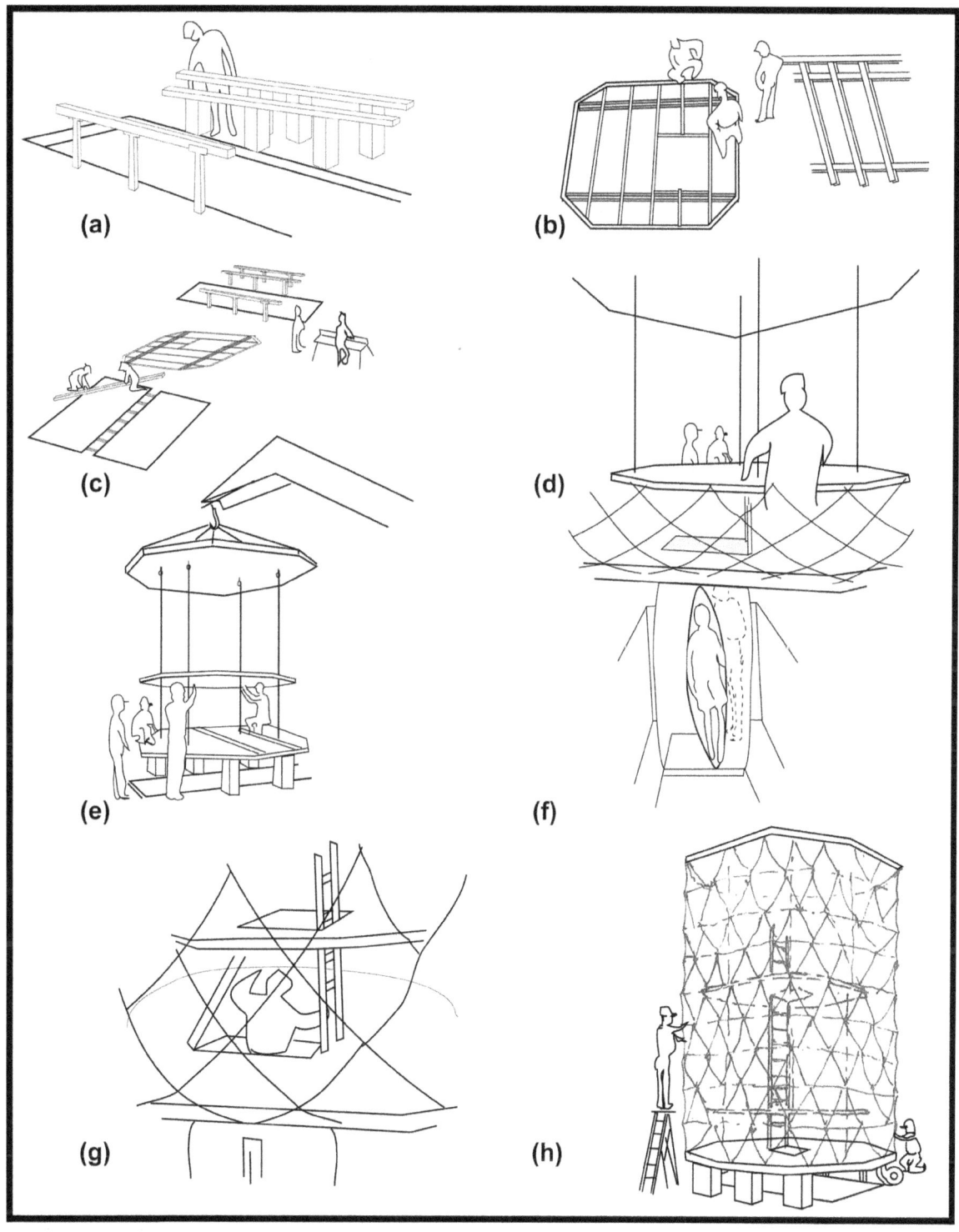

Figure 5.9: Principal construction stages of the first prototype building

5.1.5 The Construction Phase

Prior to the commencement of the construction phase the students were divided into work gangs and a foreman was elected. The seven construction days that were estimated to be required for the completion of the project were spread over seven weeks with site work to proceed on every Tuesday morning. This allowed ample time for the solution of unforeseen problems and the rescheduling of activities, the delivery of additional materials, and the collection of tools. It soon became apparent that the staggered arrangement of the construction days had a profound influence on the educational benefits enjoyed by the students. Between workdays all of the students were involved in, at times, heated discussions dealing with the organizational and practical aspects of the construction phase.

The various construction stages shown in Figure 5.9 proceeded on schedule up to and including the attachment of the membrane. The particle and composite board surfaces of the roof and floors were first glued and then nailed to the joists. Finally, the intermediate floors and roof were stacked on the ground floor with *2 FT* high blocks in between to enable the suspension attachments to be fitted. The entire hoisting operation was accomplished in 90 minutes using a hired 4 ton mobile crane. With the roof and intermediate floors safely suspended from the overhead beam-crane the plastic enclosure was lifted up by ropes, attached at four points near the upper edge of the membrane, and tied with a *5/16 IN* diameter nylon cord as planned. To enable the perfect positioning (i.e., leveling) of the membrane, a line was drawn around the circumference at both ends indicating the positions of the lower edge of the roof and the upper edge of the ground floor respectively.

Unfortunately, no donation was obtained for the exterior cable-network material. Every effort was made to purchase a plastic coated steel cable, which would prevent abrasion between itself and the membrane. It was absolutely necessary to use a metal cable with a much higher modulus of elasticity than the PVC membrane to achieve the required stress transfer from the membrane to the cable-network. (As shown in Figure 5.10, it is essential that the membrane bulges out between the cables thereby reducing the radius of curvature and stress in the membrane.) No cable material to this specification could be located in the Sydney area at a cost compatible with the budget available for the building project. There was no choice but to separately purchase steel cable and plastic tubing to be threaded on site. It required close to 20 man hours to cover the required *1,200 FT* of cable with the plastic tubing. Not only was this task very tedious and frustrating, but it was unforeseen and added close to two workdays to the construction schedule.

Initial pressurization of the main building chamber clearly demonstrated the need for horizontal cables in addition to the diagonal cable-network. Without horizontal cables the PVC membrane expanded in diameter in direct proportion to increases in internal pressure until the ground floor started to lift off the footings. Horizontal cables were immediately added at *4 FT* centers between roof and ground floor, but to no avail. The spacing was too great, allowing the membrane to bulge out between the horizontal cable rings to such a degree that the ground floor again lifted off the footings. To add to the problem one of the horizontal cables broke during a trial pressurization run. Fortunately, the fast reflexes of the fan operator and the sudden increase in volume of the main chamber saved the membrane from rupture. Following this near disaster the spacing of the horizontal cables was reduced to *2 FT* and the splices of the existing and new cables were carefully checked. Finally, on the ninth construction day, to the great delight of all concerned, the roof with the two suspended floors attached became air-supported for the first time (Figure 5.10). As expected, the safety cables linking the roof to the overhead beam-crane slackened as the roof rose by some *2 IN* under the upward force of the internal pressure. This upward movement had been allowed for in the adjustment of the suspension system between the lower intermediate floor and the ground floor.

Figure 5.10: The inflated (fully air-supported) first prototype building

5.1.6 Operation and Erection Test

During the following four weeks some 200 persons enjoyed the experience of walking on air. The following simple operational procedure was followed for entering and exiting the building:

Entering the Building: The entry procedure consisted of the following steps: open the vertical zipper of the airlock cylinder and step into the airlock; close the zipper; open the pressure equalization valve by rotating and pulling it downward; wait for the pressure in the airlock to equalize with the pressure in the main building chamber (about 2 min); open the trap door and climb the ladder onto the first floor of the building; close the trap door; and, close the equalization valve by pulling it upward.

Exiting the Building: The exit procedure required the following sequence of actions to be performed: open the equalization valve by rotating and pushing it downward; wait for the pressures in the airlock and main chamber to equalize; open the trap door and descend the ladder into the airlock; close the trap door and push the equalization valve upward; open the airlock zipper and step out of the airlock; and, close the zipper.

It was noted that during the pressurization of the airlock chamber the pressure in the main building chamber fell quickly by *2* to *2.5 IN* water gauge. During normal operation the building was maintained at a minimum internal pressure of *12 IN* water gauge, providing an upward force of approximately *6,400 LB* at roof level. Allowing for five occupants (i.e., at *180 LB* each) and a loss in pressure of *3 IN* water gauge during entering, a safety margin of *2 IN* water gauge pressure or an upward force of *1,000 LB* remained to ensure the stability of the building at all times.

After the completion of the student project there remained the question whether or not it would have been possible to erect the building by first raising the roof plate under pressure and then hoisting up the suspended floors internally one by one (i.e., erection alternative (1)). Accordingly, in early 1973 another group of students under the guidance of three students from the former construction team decided to test the feasibility of this proposed erection procedure. Masonry blocks were positioned in various locations on the ground floor to enable the first suspended floor to be lowered without damaging the attached turnbuckles. Similar masonry blocks were positioned on the first and second suspended floors. All cable intersections of the exterior cable-network were laced to ensure the correct positioning of the cables during deflation and subsequent inflation of the main building chamber.

Four guy ropes were attached to the roof plate to enable the building to be held in a fairly vertical position during deflation and inflation. Next the main chamber was inflated and the safety cables to the overhead beam-crane detached. The building was now ready for the deflation test to commence. The environmental pressure was reduced until the roof started to descend. As expected, considerable force was required to be exerted by the students handling the guy ropes to maintain the building in a reasonably vertical position. The roof plate and suspended floors were allowed to descend to about half height before the building was re-inflated. During inflation the roof and attached floors were lifted by the air pressure to their final position without any adverse effect on the membrane enclosure. Throughout the test the building behaved in the predicted manner indicating the feasibility of the proposed erection procedure.

5.2 Multi-Cellular Multi-Enclosure Prototype

The design and construction of the second prototype multi-story air-supported building was undertaken by undergraduate students in the School of Architecture and Environmental Design at the California Polytechnic State University, San Luis Obispo, California in 1973. The design concept developed by graduate student James Montero, who led the student group, involved a combination of separately and jointly pressurized spaces acting as a conglomerate of cells. This type of structure falls under the category of multi-cellular, multi-enclosure, air-supported buildings. Multi-cellular indicates the existence of two or more sealed and therefore separately pressurized compartments, while multi-enclosure refers to the ability of one continuous membrane to enclose any number of individually defined but jointly pressurized spaces.

5.2.1 Design

The basis of this student project was James Montero's Master degree thesis research (Montero 1973). He saw the need for exploring air-supported building forms compatible with the allocation and function of spaces enclosed by a common membrane envelope. It was his contention that while most existing commercially available single-story air-supported buildings are either dome shaped or semi-cylindrical with quarter spherical or rectangular ends, these standard shapes are hardly conducive to the architectural planning of multiple internal building spaces. Particularly in the case of smaller buildings, such as homes, the provision of partitions and support services poses problems that had been largely ignored by the air-building industry at that time (i.e., 1960-70s). From the manufacturer's point of view any deviation from the standard shapes was likely to involve time-consuming geometrical analyses, as well as intricate patterns leading to more complicated jointing operations.

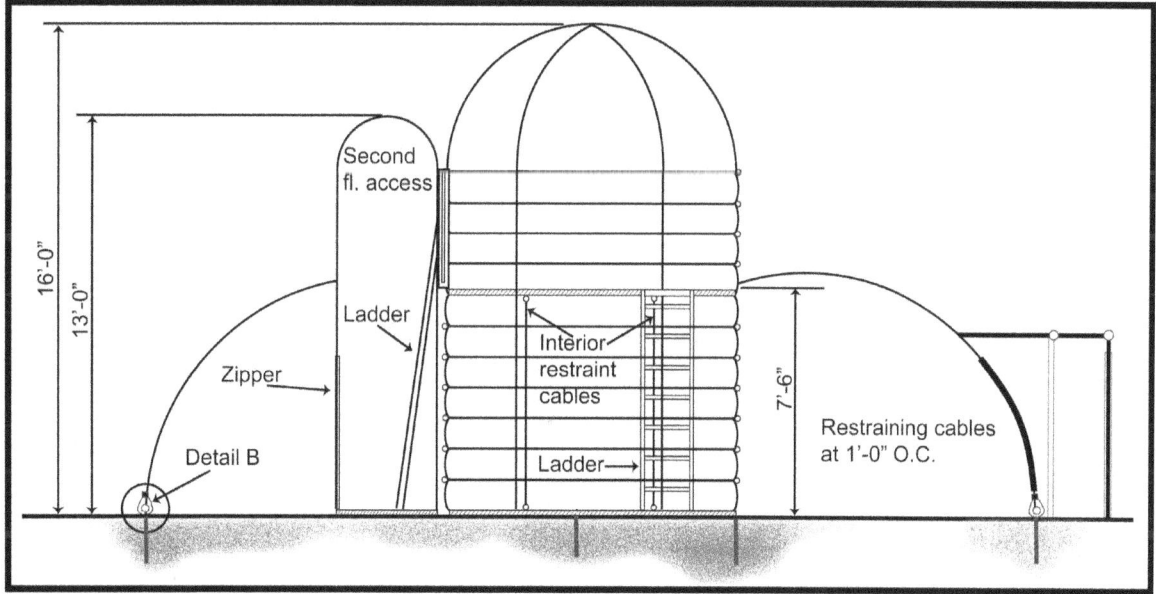

Figure 5.11: Sectional view of the second prototype building

The final design adopted for construction (Figures 5.11 and 5.12) consisted of a central two-story cylindrical cell surrounded by four single-story multi-enclosure domes. The dimensions of the two-story cell were *10 FT* diameter by *16 FT* height. Contrary to the first prototype building constructed in Sydney, Australia, the air-supported floor was attached directly to the membrane enclosure at the first floor level. In this manner floor loads were designed to be supported by the plastic membrane, which in turn was supported by the interior air pressure acting on the underside of the dome-shaped roof cap. The four peripheral domes were *16 FT* in diameter, interconnected and pressurized indirectly through air-release valves located in the cylindrical wall of the two-story core.

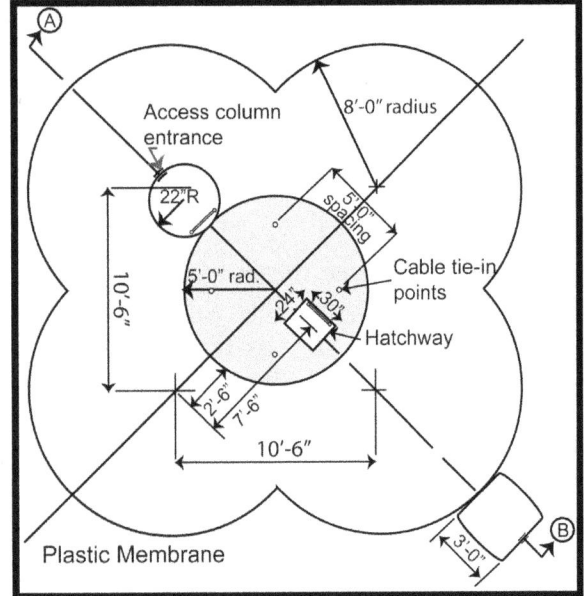 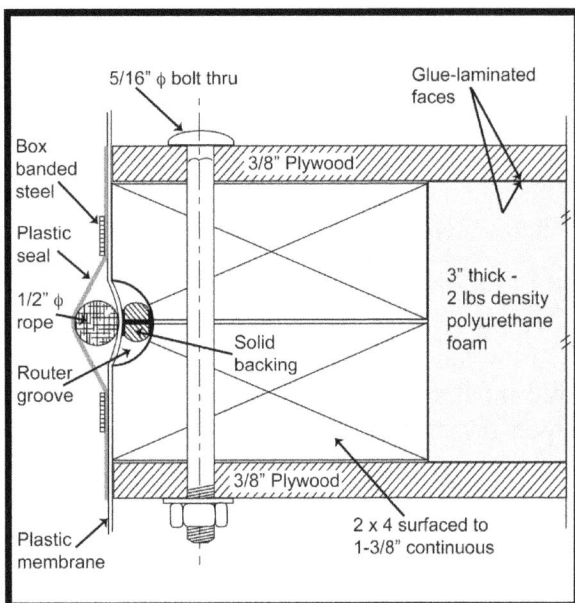

Figure 5.12: Floor plan of the second prototype   Figure 5.13: Membrane attachment detail

In view of the desirability of a transparent enclosure glass-clear, partially ultra-violet stabilized PVC with a thickness of *20 mil* was selected as the membrane material. A further important factor in this selection was the availability of an operational heat sealer that could be used for the jointing of PVC films. While the construction of the building was funded by a $1,000 (U.S. 1973) student grant from the National Science Foundation, this sum was only adequate for the purchase of materials and did not include labor costs for the fabrication of the membrane enclosure. It was therefore resolved that the fabrication of the membrane using the available heat sealer should form part of the construction process.

Estimates of the final weight of the air-supported floor including occupants indicated that an environmental pressure of around *5 IN* water gauge would be required for the two-story core chamber, while *1 IN* water gauge would suffice for the surrounding domes. An exterior cable-network consisting of concentric horizontal and radial vertical cables was incorporated in the design of the two-story core, to account for the higher air pressure.

Much consideration was given to alternative methods for providing access to the core chamber. The solution adopted for the first prototype building could not be applied in this case since the building was to be sited on a grassed area in which no excavation was permitted. It was finally decided to provide a *3 FT 8 IN* diameter vertical airlock tube adjacent to the central chamber, allowing direct access to the first floor level. However, the type of opening that could be employed between the airlock and the high pressure chamber remained a major source of concern for some time. Experience with the first prototype building suggested that some form of stiffening would be required around the penetrated area of the core membrane. At the same time due to the circumferential stresses in the membrane a vertical zipper was likely to be unsatisfactory. The final solution consisted of a rectangular steel frame attached to the exterior cable-network and taped to the perimeter of a *2 FT* square opening in the membrane. A *3 FT* square plastic flap attached at the top edge to the inside surface of the membrane served as a self-sealing door. The bottom edge of the flap was stiffened by means of a steel rod with a radius of curvature similar to that of the membrane enclosure. This simple device performed most efficiently during the operation of the building and suggested that the extra expense of providing more elaborate structurally self-supporting entrance systems of the type used in the first building may not be warranted.

Since the building was to be sited in the open, there was no opportunity for the provision of overhead safety ropes in case of sudden collapse. A self-supporting steel frame to be positioned inside the core chamber between the ground and first floors was proposed as an alternative solution. The frame was designed so that it could be used as a support platform during erection and yet permit the first floor to lift off and remain air-supported some *9 IN* above the frame during normal building operations. Threaded through the tubular columns of the frame were four cables acting as ties between the ground and first floors. These cables were designed to act as intermediate supports for the first floor plate whenever it was required to close the trap door and support the floor by air pressure acting on its underside. In other words, the first floor could be air-supported in two ways. First, with the trap door open, the supporting force would be provided by the membrane enclosure due to the environmental pressure acting on the dome roof of the chamber; - the normal mode of operation. Second, with the trap door closed and the environmental pressure in the ground floor compartment greater than in the first floor compartment, the supporting force would be provided by the greater environmental air pressure acting on the underside of the first floor plate.

5.2.2 Construction Details

Several alternative methods of constructing the air-supported first floor plate were investigated, namely: timber framing with plywood skins; timber framing with steel reinforcement; and, polyurethane foam core with plywood skins. While the latter offered by far the lightest structural solution, it was initially viewed with skepticism due to the absence of an accurate theoretical method of structural analysis. Accordingly, a *1 FT* wide by *8 FT* long test section was constructed for full scale load tests. The test section consisted of a *3 IN* thick polyurethane (*2 LB* density) foam core sandwiched between two *⅜ IN* thick plywood sheets glued at the interfaces. Subsequent load tests demonstrated the inherent strength of this type of laminated construction. Shear failure of the foam core occurred at a maximum uniformly distributed load of *800 LB* (i.e., *100 LB/FT*). Before the foam failed, a maximum deflection of *2 IN* was recorded at mid-span. In view of this excellent test result the same construction was adopted for the building floor with the addition of blocking pieces at *2 FT* centers.

The membrane enclosure was designed to be prefabricated in eight sections, namely: the central cylinder; the central dome cap; the airlock cylinder; the airlock dome cap; and, the four peripheral domes. While the patterns for the central chamber and airlock entrance were determined by the application of simple spherical geometry, the interface between the peripheral domes and the cylindrical core chamber required a much more complex geometrical analysis. One of the students with a sound background in mathematics volunteered to investigate this problem and finally developed a small computer program that provided a good estimate of the required shape. In view of the difficulties that would be encountered in heat sealing the resultant multi-curved seam, it was decided to tape the peripheral domes to the central cylinder. In the case of the dome sections, temporary timber moulds were constructed to serve as a firm base during the jointing operation.

As shown in Figure 5.13, the construction detail of the attachment of the central cylinder membrane to the ground and first floors did not differ in any significant respect from the detail adopted for the first prototype building (Figure 5.6). However, while the latter was erected on brick piers and steel pipe footings, the second prototype building was designed to rest directly on a level surface. It was, therefore, proposed to anchor the central chamber by means of pipe stakes sliding through a series of eyebolts screwed into the curved edge of the ground floor. At the same time, it was decided to seam a *1 IN* diameter steel pipe that could be anchored to the ground with pegs, into the hem of the four peripheral domes.

5.2.3 Construction Phase

The construction phase of the multi-cellular, multi-enclosure building began with the grouping of the 20 students into work gangs delegated with the responsibility of executing the separate phases of the project. As shown in Figure 5.14, the construction of the building was planned over a period of 21 working days. The bar chart identifies the number of students involved (vertical axis) in each sequence and the time allotted to complete each operation. The structure was prefabricated in five general sections, namely: the two floors of the central chamber; the peripheral domes; the central chamber envelope and cable-network; the airlock chamber; and, the entrance to the building. Again the search for a suitable inflation unit required more time than anticipated at the planning stage. Finally, two axial fan units were connected in series with a centrifugal fan to produce the required environmental pressure of *5 IN* water gauge for the two-story central chamber.

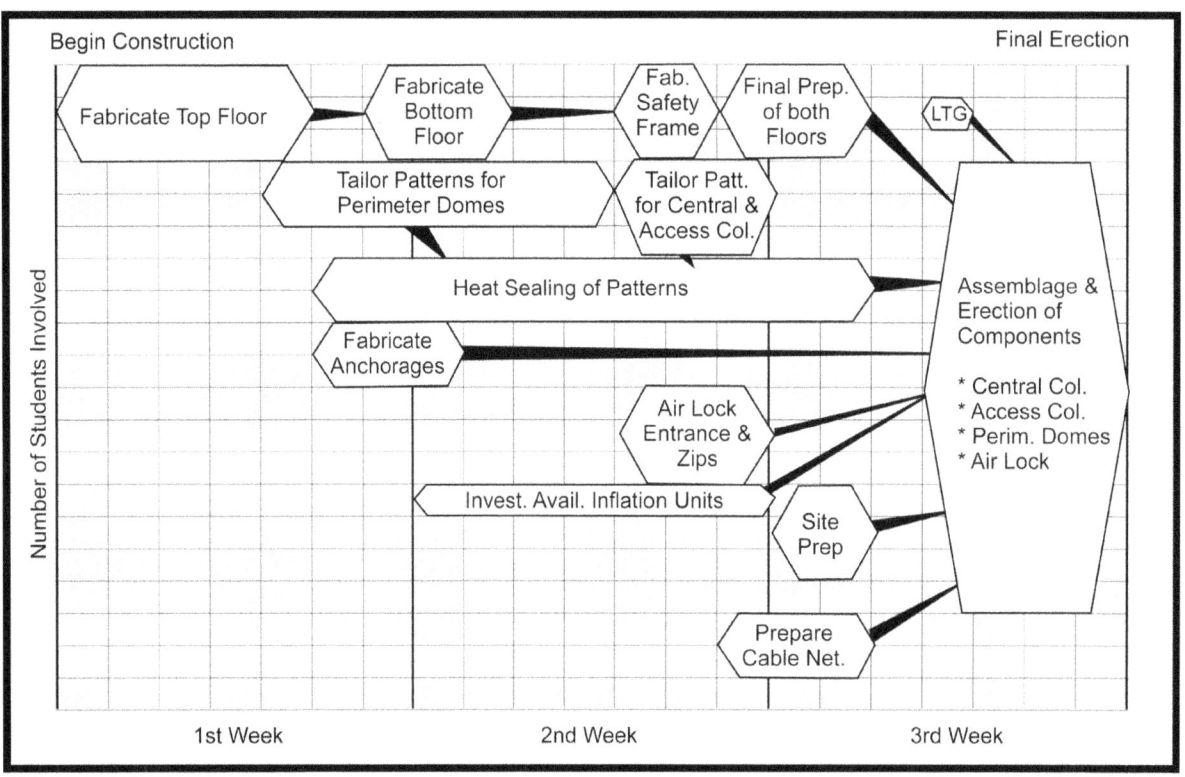

Figure 5.14: Construction sequence of second prototype building

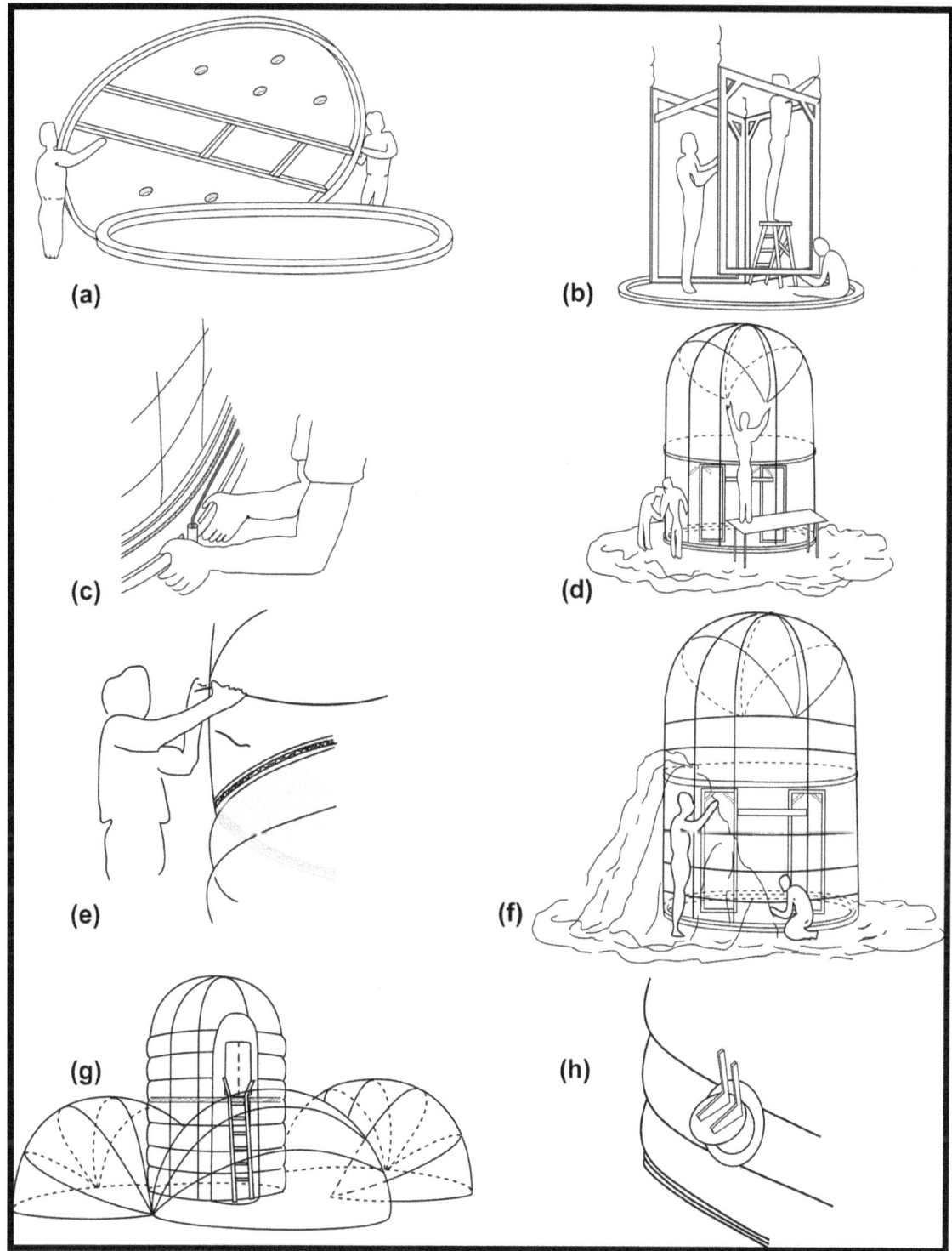

Figure 5.15: Principal construction stages of the second prototype building

The sequence of operations employed for the assembly of the prefabricated components is shown in Figure 5.15. The location of the central cylinder and domes was set out with a white marking agent. After the ground floor had been set in place with the safety frame securely fastened, the first floor plate was lifted onto the frame and the interior cables attached. Next, the membrane cylinder was draped over both floors and fixed into position. This enabled the central chamber to be temporarily inflated so that the exterior network of plastic coated cables could be positioned. Finally, the membrane interface between the peripheral domes and the central cylinder was completed using a lacing technique in addition to the tape joint originally planned (Figure 5.15).

Full inflation of the structure required the operation of all three fan units at maximum power for six minutes. Subsequently, the environmental pressures of the central and peripheral chambers were monitored by two U-tube manometers and controlled by regulating the speed of the centrifugal fan unit. After an initial running-in period, no difficulties were encountered in the regulation of the pressure in the peripheral domes by adjustment of the air-release valves located in the membrane enclosure of the central high pressure chamber.

While 600 person-hours were required for the construction of the building, the material cost totaled $656 (U.S. 1973). It may be of interest to note that on the basis of a more suitable inflation unit such as a Roots blower the daily operating costs of the building structure were calculated as $1.20 (U.S. 1973) for a total floor area of close to *750 SF*.

5.2.4 Operation and Performance

The building remained open for public display over a period of 10 days. During this time, at least 500 persons entered the peripheral chamber of the building while some 80 students and campus visitors were sufficiently interested to climb through the airlock cylinder onto the air-supported first floor level of the central chamber. The peripheral area of the building was connected to the outside by a short airlock tunnel fitted with a simple zipped door at each end. Once inside the building, the following procedure was followed in entering or departing from the central two-story chamber:

> ***Entering the Building:*** The entry procedure consisted of the following steps: open the vertical zipper of the airlock cylinder and step into the airlock; close the zipper; ascend the ladder and slide the plastic flap sealing the entrance of the first floor compartment slightly to one side, thereby allowing the air pressure on either side to equalize; fold the flap back and climb onto the air-supported first floor; and, then close the flap.
>
> ***Exiting the Building:*** The exit procedure required the following sequence of actions to be performed: slide the entrance flap slightly across the opening in the membrane enclosure, thereby allowing the air pressure on either side to equalize; fold the flap back and step onto the ladder in the airlock cylinder; close the flap and descend the ladder; open the zipper and step out of the building; and, close the zipper.

Observation of the environmental properties of the building continued under a variety of conditions of occupancy during the entire period of public display. Some 50 persons noted their reactions after experiencing the air-supported building environment. Their conclusions may be summarized as follows:

- The transparency and extremely low thermal resistivity of the PVC membrane resulted in high heat gains during daylight hours and correspondingly high heat losses during the night. For example, during the morning hours of 8:00 to 10:00 am, while the external air temperature in the shade did not exceed 58°F the building temperature rose to 75°F. By noon on the same day the indoor temperature had risen 22°F above the outdoor temperature of 73°F. At night the indoor temperature quickly fell to the same level as the outdoor temperature.

- There was no noticeable effect of the hyperbaric environment (i.e., *1 IN* water gauge) on entering the peripheral dome area. However, on entering the vertical airlock cylinder some persons experienced a slight pop within the middle ear. While no official complaints were recorded, it might be suggested that more care should have been taken in the design of the building to control the rate of compression and decompression in the airlock chamber. In view of the satisfactory performance of the airlock system in the first prototype building, which required a much higher environmental pressure (i.e., *10 IN* water gauge), it was assumed that the rate of pressurization in the second prototype building could be virtually instantaneous.

Figure 5.16: The inflated (fully air-supported) second prototype building

- The acoustical environment of the building was clearly dictated by the curved form of the perimeter domes and central cylinder. In the inflated state, the impervious membrane acted as an acoustically hard (reflecting) surface. At the center of each dome there was a distinct concentration of sound leading to echoes. Upon moving slightly out of the center, the echo disappeared. Similar effects could be experienced in the central chamber, particularly at first floor level.

Structurally, the second prototype building performed extremely well in resisting wind gusts of up to *40 mph* that occurred on one occasion during the public display period. From the architectural point of view the building was designed to combine a number of separately defined spaces.

Although the peripheral domes were structurally one space, they appeared to the internal viewer to possess individual qualities. At the same time the central chamber became the focal point of the building with the first floor area offering the greatest degree of privacy.

In all, the results were most heartening and suggested that the multi-cellular, multi-enclosure, air-supported building type should warrant further experimental studies in the near future.

Chapter 6
Multi-Story Air-Supported and Fluid-Inflated Building Types

Objection to a pressurized building environment does not necessarily rule out pneumatic construction systems. In Figures 6.1 and 6.2 are shown two systems that do not require pressurization of the building environment. In the air-inflated annular building structure (Figure 6.1) a ring of air-inflated cells surrounds the perimeter of the building. Acting as pressurized columns this annulus is capable of supporting a roof from which a number of floors can be suspended. This is essentially a double skin system carrying with it the advantage of superior thermal insulation and the disadvantage of reduced structural efficiency.

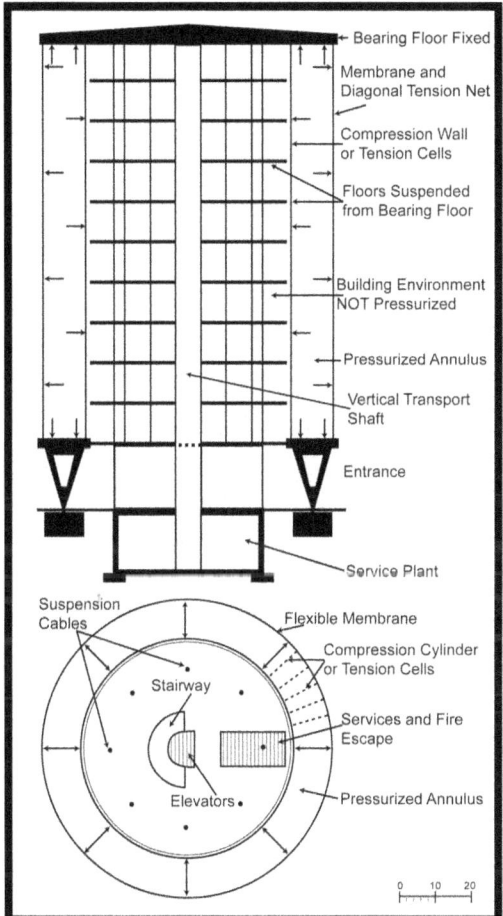
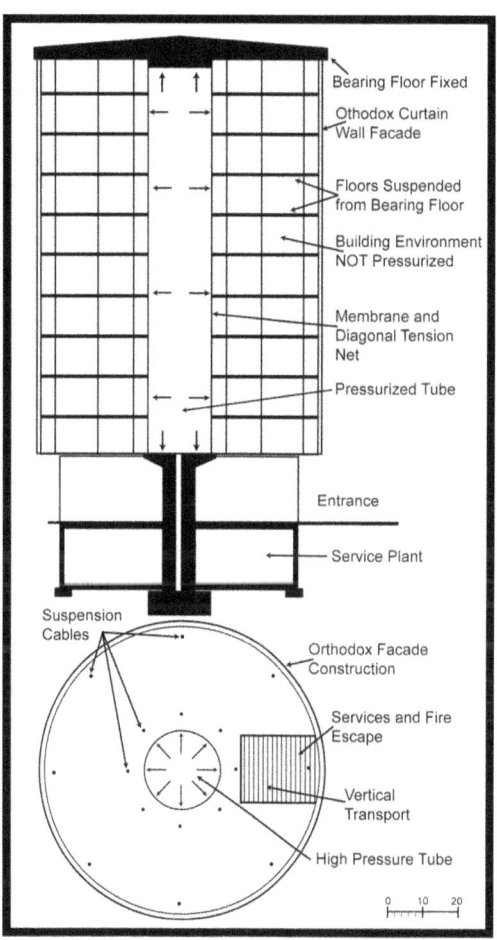

Figure 6.1: Air-inflated cellular annulus   Figure 6.2: Air-inflated central column

Normally, in this type of building the cross-sectional area of the annulus would be equal to the area of a single suspended floor, so that our assumptions relating to the pressure-utilization efficiency of multi-story air-supported buildings may still apply to some degree. However, this is not the case when a column pressurized with any fluid (e.g., air or water) or fluid-like substance (e.g., sand) is situated at the center of the building and annular floors are suspended from a cantilever beam system (Figure 6.2). Here we may expect a pressure-utilization efficiency of below 50%. Thus a column of diameter D_C *FT* with a slenderness ratio of less than *60* and pressurized to *100 psig* may be capable of supporting 10 floors of $2D_C$ *FT* diameter. While the structural efficiency that is fundamental to the fully pressurized, air-supported building is sacrificed in a high-pressure column, the latter may nevertheless provide a convenient compromise solution due to its less extreme deviation from orthodox building construction practices. Since the occupied internal spaces of the building are not pressurized there is no need for an airlock entrance nor are the building occupants exposed to a hyperbaric environment.

6.1 Principal Building Types

In more general terms the following seven types of multi-story air-supported and fluid-pressurized building types can be identified (Figure 6.3), namely: single-skin with cable-network; double-skin cellular; single-skin compartmentalized; multi-cellular multi-enclosure; single-skin rigid membrane; double-skin rigid-flexible membrane; and, high pressure central core.

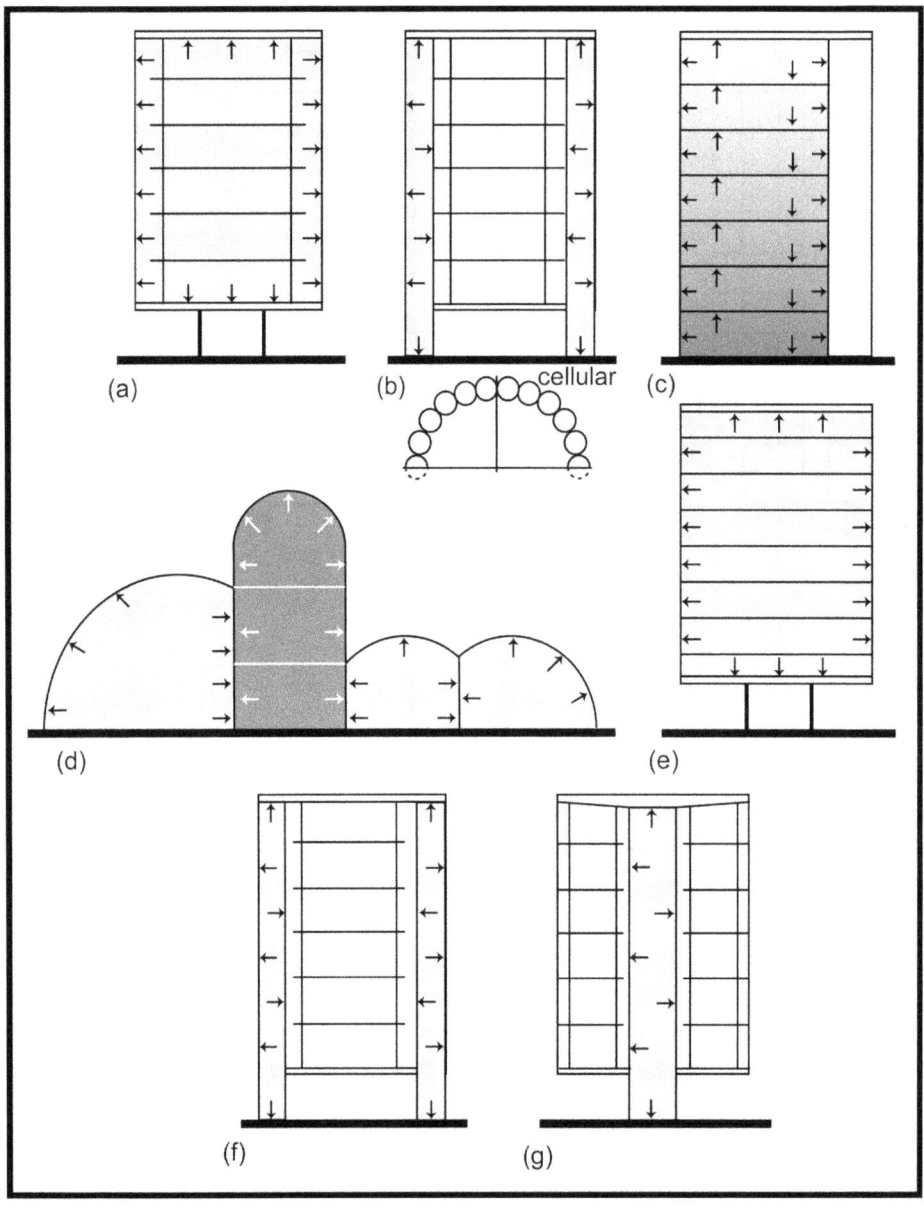

Figure 6.3: Multi-story air-supported and fluid-pressurized structural configurations

Single-Skin with Cable-Network: This is structurally the most efficient fluid-supported building type and the primary focus of this book. In principle it may be described as consisting of a pressurized building environment that is contained by an external flexible plastic membrane acting concurrently as structure and enclosure. For purposes of wind bracing and reinforcement of the plastic skin, a cable-network surrounds the membrane enclosure (Figure 6.3 (a)). The environmental pressure produces an upward supporting force on the underside of the roof plate from which the building floors are suspended by means of tension hangers or cables. An internal air pressure of approximately *1 psig* above the ambient atmospheric pressure is required for each air-supported building floor. Accordingly, a 10-story building will require an internal, environmental air pressure of around *10 psig*. Access to the single-skin cable-network building is gained by means of an airlock entrance normally located at ground floor level.

Double-Skin Cellular: In this configuration structural support is provided by a continuous multi-cellular annulus around the perimeter of the building. Floors are suspended from a truss system at roof level that in turn is supported by the pressurized multi-cellular building enclosure (Figure 6.3 (b) and Figure 6.1). Once the cells have been inflated the pressurization equipment will not be required again unless a leakage develops. Wind bracing may be provided by an external cable-network or an internal bracing system. In this type of fluid-pressurized building structure the required cell pressure is dependent on the ratio of the floor area to the combined cross-sectional area of the cells. Since the cellular annulus is pressurized independently of the building environment, higher pressures and therefore taller buildings are possible. As mentioned previously, while sacrificing structural efficiency the cellular configuration provides the designer with opportunities for achieving superior thermal control and a higher factor of safety that might be more acceptable for terrestrial buildings.

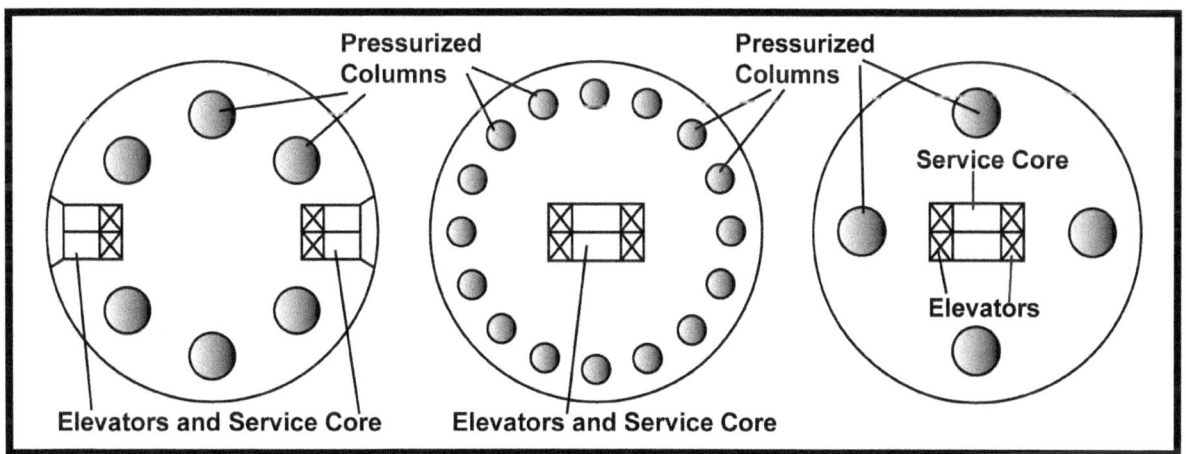

Figure 6.4: Typical floor layouts of the double-skin cellular air-inflated building type

The three alternative design configurations of the double-skin cellular building type shown in Figure 6.4 vary only in respect to the size and location of the structural cells (i.e., the pressurized columns) and the placement of the service core in the layout of each floor. As discussed previously the cross-sectional area of each structural cell is dependent on the number of cells, the total vertical building load (i.e., live-loads and dead-loads), the internal pressure, and the tensile strength characteristics of the cell wall material. The smaller the combined cross-sectional area of the cells in proportion to the area of one floor, the higher the internal cell pressure will need to be. This suggests that in most cases a rigid cell wall material such as metal or a filament-wound composite is likely to be preferred. In this case the structural design of each cell will be governed by thin-walled monocoque cylinder design principles, which are discussed in Chapter 7.

Single-Skin Compartmentalized: In this air-supported building type separately pressurized, compartmentalized floors are stacked vertically on top of each other (Figure 6.3 (c)). This requires airlocks to be integrated into each floor plan since the internal pressure of each floor compartment will increase proportionally for the lower floors. While this building type is still classified as an air-supported (as opposed to air-inflated) building, the underlying structural concept differs markedly from the standard multi-story air-supported single-skin building with either a flexible (Figure 6.3 (a)) or rigid (Figure 6.3 (e)) enclosure. Since the compartments are stacked vertically on a floor-to-floor basis, the required environmental pressure may be reduced incrementally from ground floor to roof level. Although the airlock requirement for each floor may prove expensive, cost savings will accrue in the construction of the floors themselves. For design purposes, the upward reaction due to pressure acting on the underside of each floor is required to be equal to the sum of the self-weight and superimposed live loads of each floor. Since the floors are literally floating on the supporting air pressure they will experience maximum loads only when no live loads are acting. This leads to some interesting structural possibilities. First, the normal load-balancing principles commonly used in the design of post-tensioned prestressed concrete floor slabs may be applied to counteract the self-weight of the slab during construction. After construction the internal pressure of the compartment immediately below the slab will support the floor uniformly over its entire underside like an air-mattress. This means that both the dead and live loads are supported by the air pressure without the bending forces that a horizontal member would normally be subjected to coming into consideration. Instead, since the internal air pressure of the compartment has to be sufficient to support maximum live loads the floor plate will be subject to reverse loading and tend to dish upward like the top plate of a pressure vessel. These dishing forces can be counteracted by vertical ties between the top and bottom slabs within each floor compartment.

Multi-Cellular Multi-Enclosure: As shown in Figure 6.3 (d), this air-supported building type consists of a combination of separately pressurized compartments (i.e., multi-cellular) and individually defined but jointly pressurized spaces (i.e., multi-enclosure). It is described in some detail in the previous chapter (Chapter 5), as a prototype air-supported building that was constructed as an architecture graduate student project at Cal Poly, San Luis Obispo, California. Individual design configurations may include combinations of multi-story and single-story air-supported sections, both requiring a hyperbaric building environment.

Single-Skin Rigid Membrane: The building environment is pressurized and contained by a rigid metal or filament-wound composite membrane envelope acting as a short monocoque cylindrical shell under internal pressure, axial compression (i.e., vertical building loads) and lateral wind loads (Figure 6.3 (e)). The required pressure of the internal building environment is dependent not only on the building loads but also on the thickness of the membrane enclosure. In single-skin rigid membrane buildings floors may be suspended from trusses at roof level or attached directly to the membrane envelope, thereby contributing to the overall stiffness and continuity of the air-supported structure.

Double Rigid-Flexible Cylinders: The internal building environment, which is at normal atmospheric pressure, is surrounded by two concentric cylinders adequately pressurized to support a suspended floor system at roof level (Figure 6.3 (f)). The internal rigid cylinder is required to resist horizontal air pressure in compression, while the external flexible membrane container is subjected to tension only. The pressurized annulus may be divided into separate cells or compartments for increased safety.

High Pressure Central Core: In this fluid-inflated building type a high pressure fluid column acts as the supporting element of a hinged beam or truss system at roof level from which a number of annular floors are suspended (Figures 6.2 and 6.3 (g)). Depending on the proportional relationship between the total cross-sectional column area and the typical floor area, columns in the height to diameter ratio range of 4:1 to 8:1 are normally pressurized to around 100 psig. The internal pressure has the function of resisting local buckling in the rigid metal or filament-wound composite column wall.

Instead of a single central column with a relatively large cross-sectional area, a cluster of more slender columns can be considered as an alternative structural solution. If these columns are tied together throughout their height then the structural efficiency of the cluster may approximate that of a single column, but is unlikely to exceed it. However, the structural design of a tightly bound group of pressurized columns is complex and outside the scope of the experimental analysis performed by the author in support of the design equations for air-supported buildings proposed in Chapters 2 and 4. In either case, water rather than air is suggested as the pressure medium in view of its incompressibility.

6.1.1 The Pressurization Medium

Unlike pneumatic multi-story buildings in which only air can serve as both the principal structural component and the essential life-preserving internal environment, pressurization media other than air can be considered for the fluid-inflated building types shown in Figures 6.3 (b), (f) and (g). For these building types the choice of a suitable pressurization material is governed by a number of structural, constructional and thermal factors.

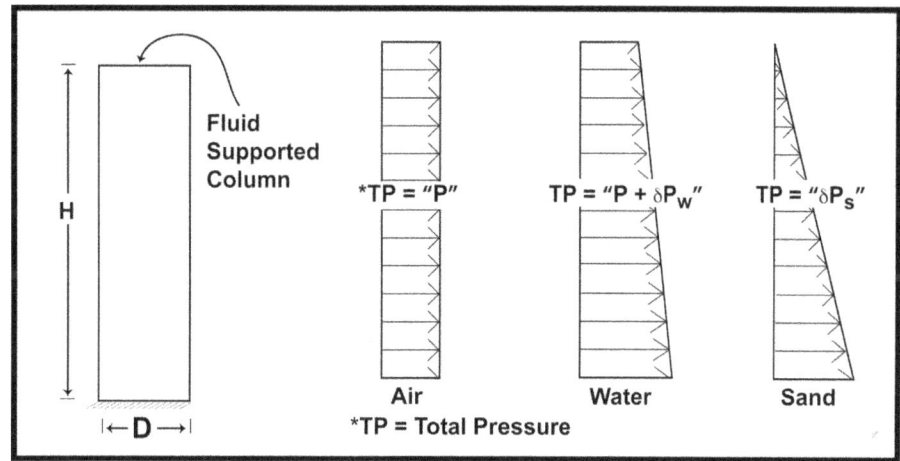

Figure 6.5: Air, water, and sand pressurization media

From a structural point of view it is desirable but not essential that the pressurization medium should be of light weight so that the static pressure generated within the column due to the self-weight of the material is a minimum. This criterion is satisfied by gases such as air, but not by liquids and granular substances such as water and sand. In the case of water, the static pressure gradient due to self-weight acting normal to the column shell is almost *0.5 psig* per foot of column height (Figure 6.5).

The presence of this static pressure gradient can increase the circumferential stress in the column wall by an appreciable amount within the lower half of the column wall, depending on the height of the column. Sand with a self-weight of *95 CF* and a coefficient of friction of around *0.4* will produce a static pressure gradient of approximately *0.2 psig*. Due to the fact that air has negligible self-weight it would appear to be a good candidate for the pressurization medium of fluid-inflated columns. However, air suffers from at least one serious disadvantage. By virtue of its compressibility air will produce a potentially dangerous explosive force under ultimate load conditions of the column. For this reason it is standard industrial practice to test all pressure vessels with water prior to implementation. In view of safety considerations, it is therefore suggested that the use of air as the pressurization medium in high pressure columns be reserved for special circumstances.

Water and sand present some constructional problems that require careful consideration. First, there is the existence of the static pressure difference of approximately *5 psig* for water and some *2 psig* in the case of sand for every *10 FT* of column height that may require circumferential strengthening of the lower section of the column wall. Second, to contain water adequately the column must be absolutely leak-proof and corrosion resistant. In the case of a factory produced column lined with a suitable sealing compound, which may also provide the required corrosion resistance, it should be possible to achieve adequate waterproofness. For an on-site welded column it is suggested that a watertight plastic bag, substantially larger than the internal volume of the column, be placed inside the column. As long as the bag is oversized and is placed correctly inside the column it will act purely as a liner and will not experience any significant tensile stresses. It is important that the bag should be tested for airtightness prior to insertion.

Since water is incompressible the slightest change in volume of the column due to thermal expansion or changes in building loads could result in a significant reduction in pressure. It is therefore desirable, from the point of view of pressure control, to place a small air cushion into the column between the liner and the top seal of the column. The height of the air cushion need not exceed *6 IN*, but it should be contained in an airtight bag of adequate strength to resist twice the axial load supported by the column. In this way, small changes in column volume are accommodated by corresponding changes in volume of the air cushion, allowing the water pressure to be regulated by means of a standard hand pump.

If sand is selected as the pressurization medium, special precautions must be taken to ensure that the building loads are supported directly by the sand and not the column wall. By virtue of the frictional forces between adjacent grains, sand has a limited shear resistance, so that only approximately one-third of the vertical compression force is transmitted in a horizontal direction to the column shell. Although this very much limits the ability to pressurize the column, it does not impair the overall load-bearing capacity of sand columns. Provided the building loads are supported directly by the sand and the enclosing column shell is capable of sustaining the circumferential stress produced by the limited horizontal transfer of load within the sand, the sand column will be stable[1]. There is therefore a fundamental difference between the structural

---

[1] The fact that the internal pressure at the top of the column is zero is immaterial to the structural stability of the column, provided all of the vertical loads are carried by the sand.

functions of fluid pressurization media, such as air and water, and a granular substance like sand. In the case of fluids, the internal pressure increases the resistance of the column wall against local instability, and this is necessary since the building loads are supported directly by the column wall. However, when sand is used the building loads are supported directly by the sand and the column wall acts purely as a container, designed to resist the hoop stresses produced by the limited horizontal pressure transferred through the sand. Accordingly, it is feasible to utilize materials such as gravel and rock salt with superior heat storage properties, where the pressurization medium also serves a secondary environmental control function (see Section 6.3). The direct transfer of the building loads to the granular material may be achieved in a variety of ways such as an air-inflated tire, wafer bag or piston floating on the sand. In the latter case it is advisable to attach three or more vertical piles to the underside of the piston, equal in length to the diameter of the column, to ensure equal settlement and provide firm anchorage for the loaded piston.

From a constructional point of view sand has one decided advantage over water; - it does not require a leak-proof column. Furthermore, experience with one prototype building has shown that the cost of sand to fill a column *4 FT 8 IN* diameter and *23 FT 6 IN* high may be as much as 20% less than the cost of a plastic-liner bag that would be required in the case of water. However, the labor resources and effort involved in filling the same column with sand were significant.

Finally, from a thermal point of view, in consideration of the secondary function of the pressurization medium as a heat store, we are primarily concerned with the ability of the material to absorb heat. The quantity of heat that can be stored in any substance is given by the product of the specific heat and density of the substance and the temperature difference between the heat to be stored and the storage material. In Table 6.1 we see that of the materials under consideration water has by far the greatest heat storage potential. Rock salt is listed since it has found application in solar heat storage units and there appear to be no reasons, other than perhaps cost and corrosion characteristics, to exclude it from consideration as an alternative pressurization material to sand.

Table 6.1: Heat storage capacity of candidate pressurization materials

Material	Specific Heat	Density	Heat Storage Capacity
Air	0.24 BTU/LB-°F	0.075 LB/CF	0.02 BTU/CF-°F
Rock Salt	0.22 BTU/LB-°F	136.0 LB/CF	29.9 BTU/CF-°F
Sand	0.19 BTU/LB-°F	94.6 LB/CF	18.0 BTU/CF-°F
Water	1.00 BTU/LB-°F	62.4 LB/CF	62.4 BTU/CF-°F

6.1.2 Column Height and Slenderness Ratio

While internal pressure will increase the load-bearing capacity of fluid-supported columns to any height that is relevant to the construction of buildings, there is likely to be an optimum height to diameter ratio. Apart from the height and diameter of the column the primary parameters involved in such a determination are the thickness, weight, tensile strength, and cost of the column wall material, as well as the cost of the pressurization material. Secondary factors include the value of the space taken up by the cross-sectional area of the column at each floor level and ease of construction. In this regard the term *value* should be interpreted in the more general sense that considers not only construction costs but also real estate factors such as rentability and occupancy.

The structural tests of pressurized flexible membrane columns conducted by the author and described in Chapter 2 were limited to a slenderness ratio range of 9 to 72, where the effective height of each column (H_E) was assumed to be twice the actual height (i.e., $2H$). The results of those tests indicated that for slenderness ratios above 30 the relationship between load-bearing capacity and internal pressure becomes increasingly non-linear with increasing internal pressure. Consequently, the practical application of these results was limited to slenderness ratio range of 1 to 30 for both the recommended pressure-utilization efficiency factors (equations 2.2) and the theoretically derived design equations (equations 2.6 through 2.8).

The conversion of slenderness ratio (*SR*) to an equivalent height (*H*) to diameter (*D*) ratio can be calculated based on the following relationships:

$$SR = H_E / (I / A_W)^{0.5}; \quad I = \pi R^3 t; \quad \text{and} \quad A_W = 2 \pi R t$$

where: H_E = effective height (assumed to be twice the actual height (H) for a free-standing column)
I = moment of inertia
R = radius of column (i.e., D/2)
A_W = cross-sectional area of column wall
t = thickness of column wall

therefore: $SR = (2H) / [(\pi R^3 t) / (2 \pi R t)]^{0.5}$

$$\mathbf{SR = (2H) / [R^2 / 2]^{0.5}} \quad \text{...} \quad (6.1)$$

Substituting in equation 6.1 for a slenderness ratio (SR) of *30* we obtain an equivalent height to radius ratio of approximately 10, as follows:

$$30 = (2H) / [R^2 / 2]^{0.5}$$
$$30 [R^2 / 2]^{0.5} = (2H)$$
$$900 [R^2 / 2] = (4 H^2)$$
$$112.5 R^2 = H^2$$
$$H / R = 10.6 \text{ and } \mathbf{H / D = 5.3}$$

Accordingly for a 10-story building with an actual height (*H*) of around *100 FT* the column diameter would be in the vicinity of *19 FT*. While greater height to diameter ratios are certainly feasible they lead to disproportionally lower pressure-utilization efficiencies. It should be noted, however, that the pressure-utilization efficiencies that led to the 1 to 30 slenderness ratio range assumed in this section are based on a structural model analysis that was confined to flexible membrane columns. The structural behavior of rigid membrane columns under internal pressure differs markedly from their flexible membrane counterparts in several respects. First, the lack of ductility of the rigid membrane leads to stress concentrations in the column wall that are significantly influenced by geometrical imperfections that are unavoidable in the initial state of the cylindrical column wall. Second, the rigid cylindrical wall itself has considerable load-bearing capacity without any internal pressure. In the case of a flexible membrane the entire load-bearing capacity is derived from the internal pressure, while the membrane performs the sole function of a container.

Since it is likely that pressurized columns with rigid cylindrical walls will be preferred for most building applications in which the habitable building environment is not pressurized, this topic is treated in some depth in the next chapter. In the analysis of such cylindrical shells it is common practice to consider the effective height (H_E) to be equal to the actual height (H) and to measure slenderness as the relationship of height to diameter expressed as a height to radius (H/R) ratio. However, for the sake of consistency with Chapters 2 to 5, the reader may assume that the calculation of any slenderness ratios referred to throughout this book, including Chapters 6 and 7, is based on an effective height that is twice the actual height (i.e., $H_E = 2H$) for free-standing columns.

While the structural analysis and design of air-supported and fluid-inflated structures composed of rigid membrane walls (e.g., sheet metal) is treated in Chapter 7, an introduction to this topic from an architectural design point of view is provided in the following section. However, the structural design of the fluid-inflated rigid membrane column that supports the prototype building described in Section 6.2 is deferred to Section 7.5.3 in Chapter 7.

6.2 A Prototype Fluid-Inflated Experimental Building

An interesting concept for combining the structural support system of a building with the storage requirements of a typical active solar heating system was investigated during the mid 1970s in a full-size test building constructed by students in the College of Architecture and Environmental Design at the California Polytechnic State University (Cal Poly), San Luis Obispo, California.

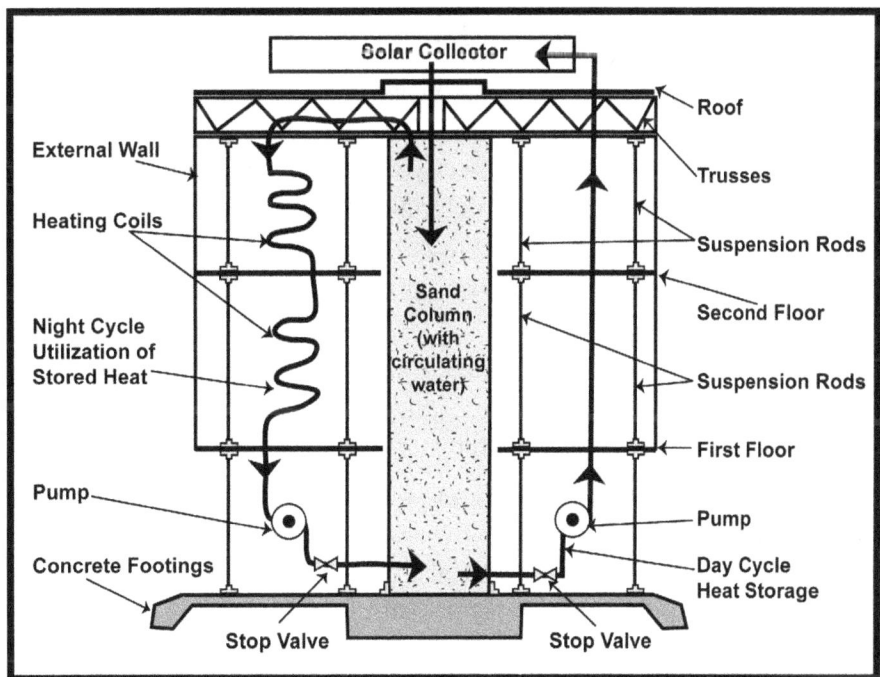

Figure 6.6: Schematic design diagram of the sand-column building

The building incorporated a fluid-supported core; - consisting of a central *5 FT* diameter column fabricated from *18 gauge* galvanized steel sheeting and filled with a mixture of sand and water. It was the dual function of the sand-water mixture to support the building loads and act as a convenient heat store for solar energy collected at roof level (Figure 6.6).

The original concept called for the design of a three-story residential building. To qualify as a student project the building was required to be designed, documented and constructed by students with the majority of materials donated by industry. As a regular part of their construction laboratory class a group of 17 students commenced to identify and interrelate in the form of a flow diagram the various tasks to be accomplished under each of four categories; namely, fund raising, design, management, and construction. It soon became apparent that the students were generally much more interested in proving the validity of the structural concept (of which some were doubtful) than the environmental control aspect of the project. Accordingly, the construction of the building was divided into two phases to be accomplished, if necessary, by different student groups. It was resolved that the first phase should incorporate the fabrication of all of the structural components and the erection and completion of the building shell, while the construction and installation of the environmental control system including the solar collectors was designated for the second phase. The design of the building was undertaken by four groups of students on a competitive basis in accordance with the following general design criteria:

1. The building should be of adequate size to accommodate a family of two adults and two children by providing the following minimum facilities:

    1.1 Living and dining area of 320 SF.
    1.2 Food preparation area (kitchen) of 140 SF.
    1.3 Two bathrooms of at least 40 SF each.
    1.4 Three sleeping areas (bedrooms) of 180 SF each.
    1.5 Laundry of 80 SF.
    1.6 Single car garage or carport of 240 SF.

2. The structural support system should consist of one or more fluid-inflated rigid membrane columns.

3. The building should incorporate at least two levels to demonstrate the multi-story characteristics of the fluid-inflated structural system.

4. The heating system for the building should obtain at least 70% of its energy from solar radiation and utilize the pressurization material in the supporting structure as a heat store.

5. The construction concept should be of a simple and inexpensive nature, permit a high degree of prefabrication, and generally take into consideration the limited capabilities of a relatively unskilled student work force.

The final design submissions were reviewed by a student-faculty committee, which rated the three-story building shown in Figures 6.7, 6.8, 6.9 and 6.10 as the most practical proposal that met all of the criteria. The design called for a central *6 FT* diameter water-inflated column provided with a series of sixteen radial open-web steel joists at the upper end, from which two floors were suspended by means of ¾ IN steel rods. The central column was fabricated from *1/16 IN (0.0625 IN)* galvanized steel sheeting sealed at both ends with ¼ IN thick steel plates and welded at all joints. A *5 FT 10 IN* diameter reinforced concrete pedestal served as a base on which the column was to be erected and bolted into position. The water in the column was to be pressurized to *15 psig* by means of a conventional hydraulic pump.

Careful consideration was given to the question of safety, particularly since this building would constitute the first attempt at the construction of a full-sized fluid-inflated high pressure central core building (Pohl and Montero 1973). Since the prototype building was to be sited in the open there would be no opportunity to ensure the safety of the structural support system by means of emergency roof support cables attached to an overhead crane, which had been the safety mechanism of choice in the case of the prototype multi-story air-supported building constructed a few years previously in Sydney, Australia (see Chapter 5, Section 5.1). The central column was therefore designed to be just capable of supporting the total building load (i.e., dead-load and live-load) without the presence of internal pressure. It was the function of the internal pressure to increase the load-bearing capacity of the column to twice the total building load, thereby providing an acceptable factor of safety. The structural design of the column with water as the pressurization medium is described in Chapter 7 (Section 7.5.2).

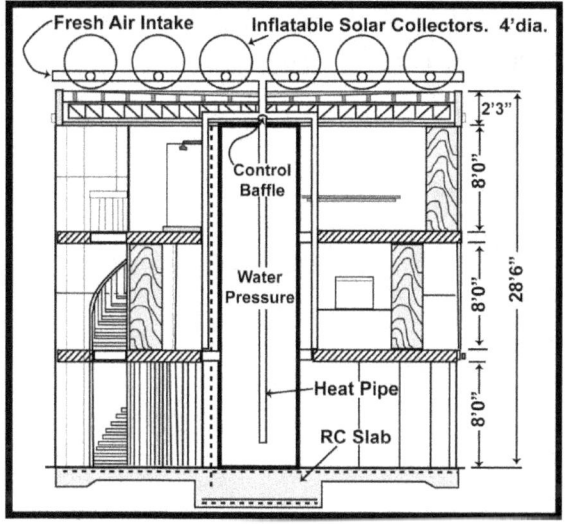

Figure 6.7: Original design concept of three-story house

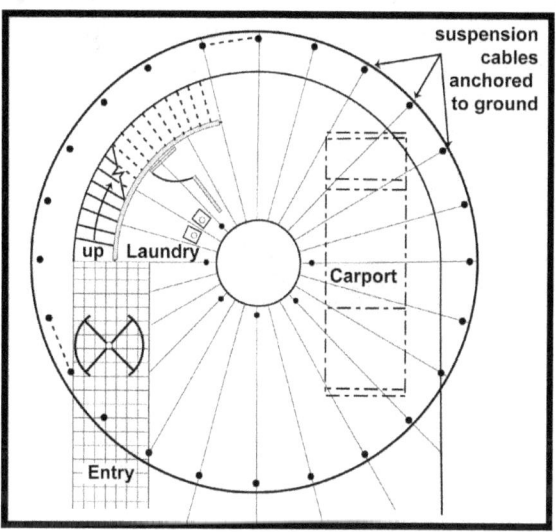

Figure 6.8: Plan of ground floor entrance, laundry, and carport

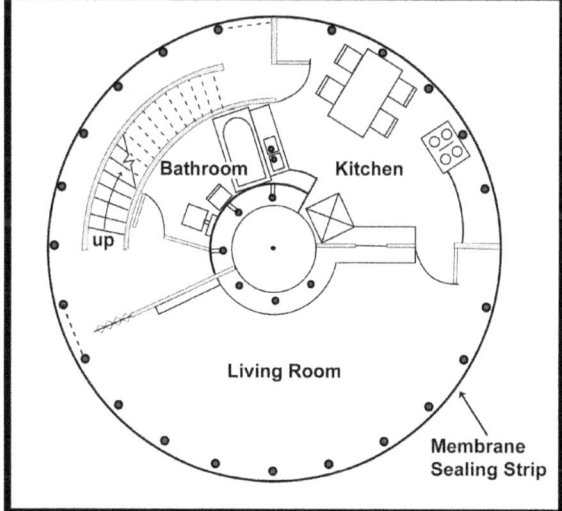

Figure 6.9: First floor plan

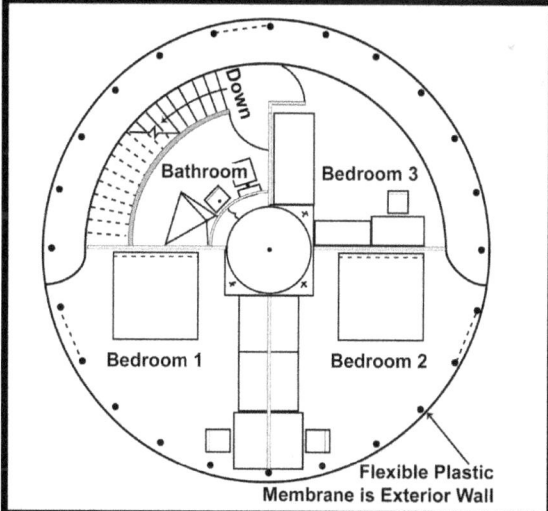

Figure 6.10: Second floor plan

In view of the undesirability of attaching floors directly to the thin column wall, the building was designed to incorporate a suspension system consisting of a framework of open-web steel joists welded to the upper end of the central column, with main supporting fixtures at distances of *1 FT* and *12 FT 6 IN* from the column wall. The suspension hangers were to be carried through to the reinforced concrete slab at the base of the building and prestressed to approximately *100 LB* to provide for thermal expansion and unequal live load distribution. Each floor was designed to be prefabricated in eight identical sandwich panel sections.

Approximately 70% of the space and water heating requirements of the building were calculated to be supplied by 11 inflatable concentrating solar collectors utilizing air as the heat collecting medium and the water inside the column for heat storage purposes. The solar heat was intended to be transferred to the water by means of a centrally located heat pipe whenever the amount of heat collected exceeded that required for immediate usage. A simple thermostatically activated baffle would suffice to control the rate of air flow within the building and across the heat pipe. A small electric booster heater was provided as a temporary supplementary heat source.

Figure 6.11: Fluid-column building under Construction

Figure 6.12: The finished fluid-column building

Several decisions to deviate from the original design had to be made prior and during construction due to resource limitations and practical considerations. Unfortunately, two attempts to render the column waterproof by inserting a plastic bag inside the column failed. Each time the plastic bag developed a leak either before or during the filling operation. Therefore, it was decided to substitute sand for water as the pressurizing medium. Although sand is not commonly described as a fluid, it does display a number of fluid properties as discussed previously in this chapter

(Section 6.1.1). When a bucket of dry sand is poured onto the ground, it forms a heap with sides sloping at an angle of approximately *45°*, governed by the friction between individual sand grains. This indicates that sand has limited shear strength and therefore transmits a proportion of superimposed vertical loads sideways. Accordingly, the sand in the building column produces pressure on the inside surface of the column wall, thereby resisting the formation of local buckles (i.e., wrinkles or folds) in the column wall. In addition, the sand has the ability to directly support the vertical load of the building as long as it is contained by the column wall.

The column wall was welded at all joints and sealed top and bottom with circular mild steel plates (i.e., *0.25 IN* thick). At roof level, eight open-web steel joists (i.e., trusses) were welded to the top column plate. The trusses were fabricated from mild steel angles (i.e., *2 IN* by *3 IN* by *0.25 IN* thick) that cantilevered approximately *10 FT* out from the central column.

The suspended floors were approximately *24 FT* in diameter and of octagonal shape. Each floor consisted of eight wedge-shaped prefabricated panels constructed with *1.75 IN* thick rigid polystyrene foam sheets sandwiched (i.e., glued) between two layers of *3/8 IN* plywood sheets. Each floor panel was provided with a frame of standard *2 IN* by *4 IN* timber beams laid flat around the perimeter. Individual panels were joined by gluing together overlapping plywood skins. The final panel thickness was *2.25 IN*. The floors were suspended from roof level by means of *16* mild steel suspension rods, attached to the radial roof trusses and prestressed to the footings by means of turnbuckles. The rods were of *5/8 IN* diameter (Figure 6.11).

The solar collector consisted simply of a *1,300 FT* long, *3/4 IN* diameter, black polyethylene hose laid onto the roof surface in the form of a spiral and glazed over with a single layer of translucent Tedlar coated panels. With an estimated efficiency of *35%*, the *330 SF* solar collector area was capable of providing *100%* of the space heating requirements in January, while the central sand-column had a heat storage capacity of five days.

The principal advantages of this type of fluid-supported building are related to the ability to integrate the structural and environmental functions into one efficient component, thereby obviating the need to accommodate a separate, large heat storage unit. Moreover, the structural efficiency of the fluid-supported column itself can lead to additional cost savings, particularly on sloping sites (Figure 6.12).

6.3 Further Structure-Environment Interface Possibilities

The initial proposal for the fluid-supported central column building described in Section 6.2 above was considerably more ambitious. Not only was it intended to utilize water as the pressurization and heat storage medium, but consideration was also given to the application of heat pipes as the heat transfer mechanism and air-inflated tubes with concentrating capabilities for the collection of solar heat. While the implementation of these concepts was considered to be too difficult at the time and beyond the scope of a student project, they are certainly worthy of further discussion.

Commercially available solar heating systems for residential buildings normally limit the size of the heat storage unit as a means of reducing overall system costs. This necessitates the addition of an auxiliary heat source to the system, so that under peak load or extensively cloudy conditions the solar system may be supplemented or replaced by the auxiliary heat source. The combination of solar collectors with auxiliary heating, cooling and storage systems is a major undertaking.

Using conventional heat transfer techniques, a multi-story building would require a network of pipes and a pumping system. A pumped system will consume energy and can be the source of problems such as leaks and pump failures. Ideally, one should use a passive system that can offer high reliability and consumes no energy. Initially, this would appear to be an objective that cannot be met in reality. However, a heat pipe system combined with solar collectors, as well as energy storage and auxiliary heating and cooling could conceivably meet such an objective (Pohl and Basiulis 1976).

6.3.1 Heat Pipe Technology

The thermal characteristics of heat pipes have been under investigation for many years, but it is only recently that they have been fully explored for practical applications such as temperature control, cooling, and heat recovery (Grover et al 1990). The basic heat pipe is a closed container consisting of a capillary wick structure and a small amount of vaporizable fluid (Figure 6.13). The heat pipe employs a boiling-condensing cycle with the capillary wick pumping the condensate to the evaporator. The vapor pressure drop between the evaporator and the condenser is very small and, therefore, the boiling-condensing cycle is essentially an isothermal process. In fact, it is very similar to an old-fashioned steam radiator, except that it is self-contained.

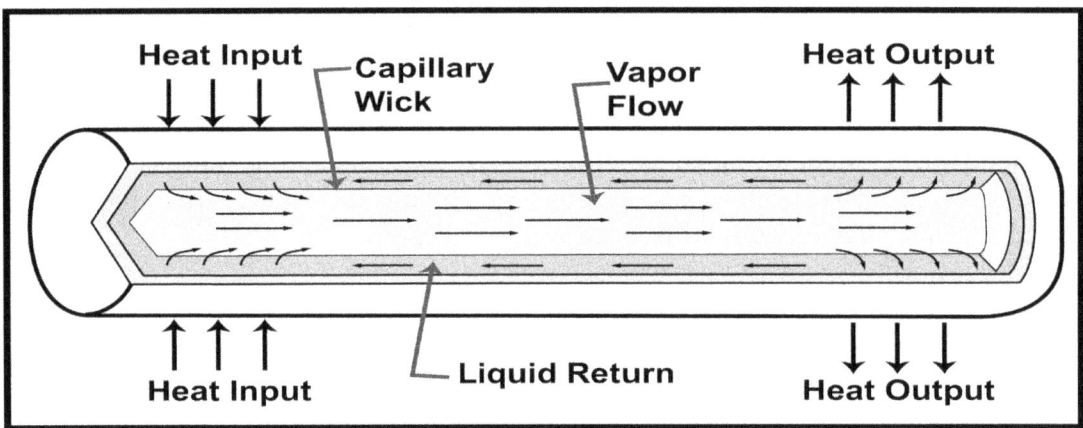

Figure 6.13: The basic heat pipe mechanism

The temperature losses between the heat source and the heat sink can be made very small by proper design. The analysis of the heat pipe begins with a pressure drop balance that allows the heat pipe parameters to be calculated as follows (Kemme 1969):

$$\partial P_c = \partial P_v + \partial P_l + \partial P_g$$

where: ∂P_c = capillary pumping head
∂P_v = pressure drop in the vapor
∂P_l = pressure drop in the liquid
∂P_g = gravity head

Although heat pipes behave like a \]-system of very high conductance and have no moving parts, they possess heat transfer limitations imposed by the principles of hydrodynamics. Basic limitations are sonic, entrainment, wicking, and boiling. These limits are important for heat pipe design, since once these limits are exceeded heat pipes will cease to operate.

The operating temperature of a heat pipe is dictated by the selection of its working fluid. Good working fluids should possess the following characteristics: high latent heat of vaporization; high surface tension; and, low viscosity. In addition, the fluid must be compatible with the heat pipe envelope material and the capillary wick. Wick structures can be constructed from porous materials such as screen, cloth, felt, and sintered powder or, alternatively, they can be fabricated as grooves, threads, arteries, or combinations of these. Heat pipe envelopes must transfer heat and may sometimes have to support high internal pressure. Therefore, the envelope material is selected on the basis of high thermal conductivity, strength, and compatibility with the working fluid (Basiulis and Hummel 1972).

Performance tests have shown that heat pipes designed and fabricated from appropriate materials are quite reliable (Basiulis and Prager 1975). A life-span of 170,000 hours (i.e., 20 years) of continuous operation is not an unreasonable expectation as long as compatible materials are selected, proper manufacturing techniques are used, and suitable heat pipe envelope materials appropriate to the operating environment are chosen. For particular applications, heat pipes can be designed and manufactured in virtually any shape or size, as cylinders, plates, or even flexible structures. In actual applications, they can be bare or finned in order to accommodate higher heat fluxes requiring larger heat transfer areas[2].

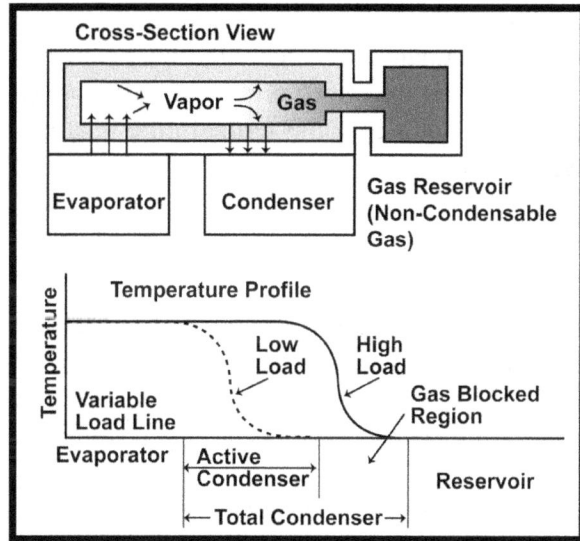

Figure 6.14: Schematic representation of a constant temperature heat pipe

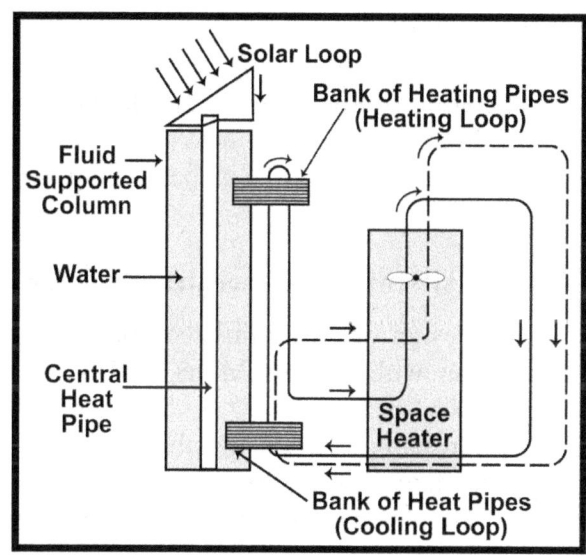

Figure 6.15: Combined cycle heat pipe energy storage system

The fluid inside a heat pipe may be combined with inert gas to give the heat pipe unique characteristics. For example, when combined with a large inert gas reservoir a heat pipe can be used as an efficient temperature control device. In such constant temperature gas-controlled heat pipes the thermal conductance of the heat pipe is automatically and precisely varied by the blocking action of the non-condensable gas in the condenser section (Harbough and Eastman 1970). By regulating the pressure of the inert gas reservoir the operating temperature of the heat pipe can be controlled. The non-condensable gas moves in and out of the reservoir in relationship to the heat load, thereby varying the heat rejection zone and maintaining the heated zone at a

---

[2] No matter how good a conductor the heat pipe is, sufficient heat transfer area is required to transfer the heat in and out of the pipe.

constant temperature. This technique, which is shown schematically in Figure 6.14, may be applied effectively in a variety of climate control applications including a combined cycle energy conservation system utilizing fluid-supported columns for heat storage purposes.

6.3.2 The Collector-Storage Interface

Thermal energy from solar collectors may be pumped into a fluid-supported column. A conventional interface system would normally provide for the introduction of the heated medium at the bottom of the column, requiring high pressure lines with their associated potential problems. Heat pipes, however, since they are self-contained, are independent of the pressurized medium in the fluid-supported column. In other words, heat can be introduced directly into the fluid column through a centrally located heat pipe. Conversely, heat may be recovered from the fluid-supported column by pumping water or blowing air over a bank of heat pipes thermally coupled with the fluid column.

In the combined cycle climate control system for a multi-story building shown in Figure 6.15, heat from solar collectors is stored in the fluid-supported column. When heat for space heating purposes is required in the building a circulating air system will remove heat from the fluid-supported column. The same system will provide cooling when the temperature within the living area increases due to the heat generated by the building occupants, utilities, appliances, or other heat generating equipment (i.e., circulating air will remove heat and store it in the fluid-supported column). More sophisticated heat pipe systems could utilize such constant temperature heat pipes to absorb or reject heat at the ambient temperature without any external controls.

6.3.3 Air-Inflated Concentrating Solar Collectors

A simple design of an air-inflated concentrating solar collector was proposed by the author in collaboration with Charles Miller in 1975 and subsequently developed into a patent that was granted to Cal Tech in 1977 (U.S. Patent 4,046,462). The cylindrical collector consists of an exterior transparent plastic membrane, lined over a portion of its surface with an aluminized highly reflective film (Figure 6.16).

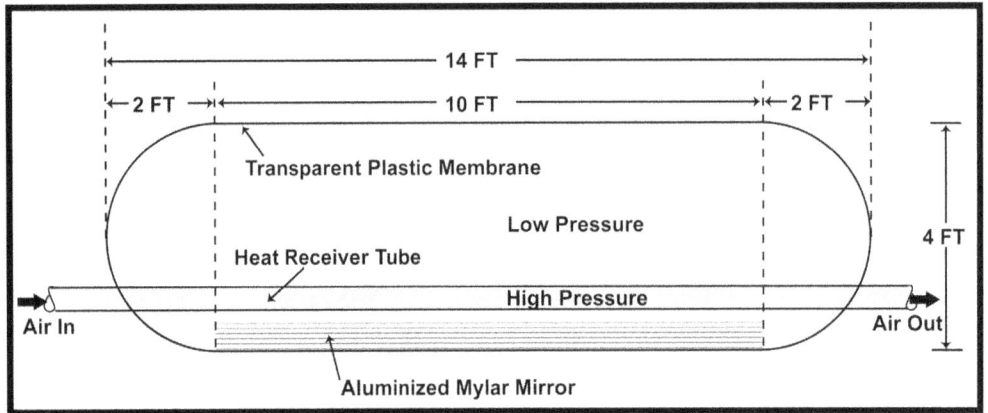

Figure 6.16: Longitudinal view of an air-inflated concentrating solar collector

A slight internal air pressure maintains the cylindrical form of the collector, while a small diameter opaque (i.e., black) plastic tube serves as the receptor for the solar radiation that is focused onto it by the curved reflecting portion of the larger diameter plastic membrane container. Circulating air, maintained at a higher pressure, serves both as a heat collecting medium and as a structural stabilizer of the small diameter tube. In this way the tube is able to span as an air-inflated beam between the two hemispherical ends of the larger diameter membrane container.

In this type of concentrating collector it is the function of the outer membrane to provide the equivalent of single glazing and to focus the solar radiation incident in the region of the aluminized film acting as a curved mirror onto the internal tube. Both the outer membrane and the internal tube are dependent for their structural stability and cylindrical form on the maintenance of internal pressures in the vicinity of *⅓ IN* and *14 IN* water gauge, respectively. The resulting collector incorporates a concentration ratio of approximately *3:1* despite the inferiority of a cylindrical, as opposed to parabolic, mirror shape. Transparent polyvinyl chloride (PVC) or similar material (*0.002 IN* thick) is recommended for the outer membrane, while an opaque plastic membrane material capable of resisting temperatures above 220°F, such as silicon resin impregnated glass cloth with a black finish, may be used for the small diameter internal heat receiver tube.

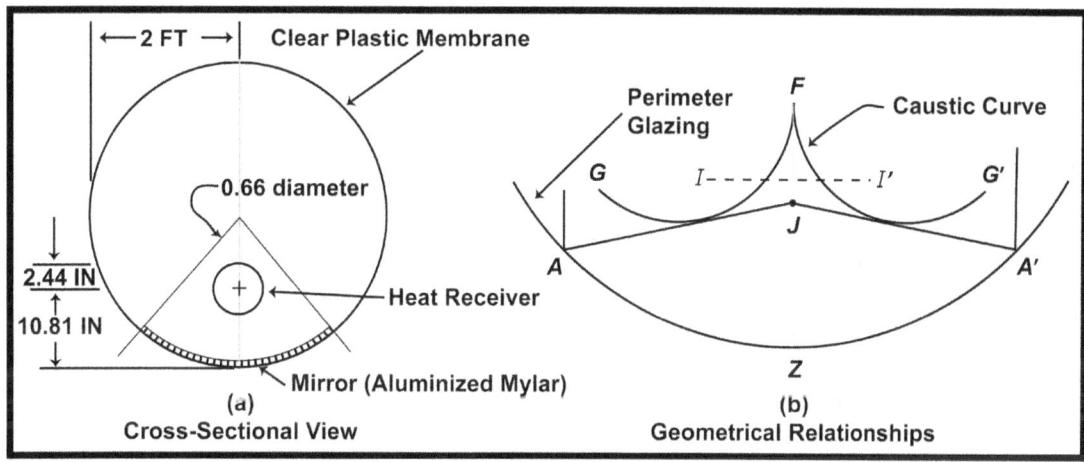

Figure 6.17: Cross-sectional view of an air-inflated concentrating solar collector

The term *caustic* applies to the region of a concave cylindrical reflecting surface (i.e., mirror) where parallel rays of light, in this case solar radiation, come to different foci. The rays from the sun are considered to be parallel because of the distance between the sun and the earth. As shown in Figure 6.18, the further these rays are removed from the principal axis of the circular mirror the closer the focus is to the mirror.

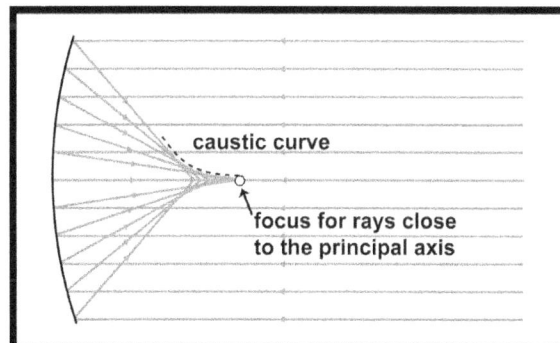 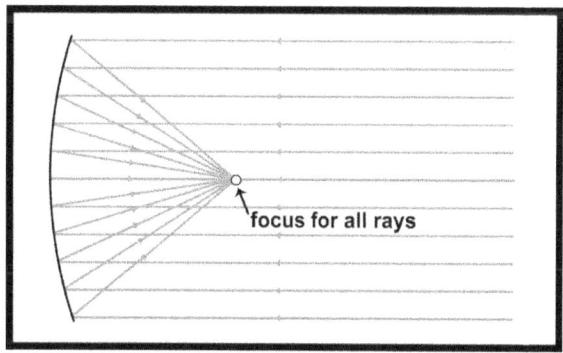

Figure 6.18: Multiple foci for circular mirror   Figure 6.19: Single focus for parabolic mirror

In the case of a concave parabolic mirror any of the rays parallel to the principal axis, regardless of how far they are removed from the axis, are reflected to a common focus (Figure 6.19). The absence of a single focus in the inflated solar collector is not necessarily a disadvantage, since the target of the reflected radiation is a tube rather than a single line. The optimization of the diameter of the tube for a particular combination of environmental and operational conditions is a complex undertaking. The variables involved include: the diameter of the external cylinder expressed as the radius of curvature of the reflecting surface; the ratio of reflecting to transparent portions of the external cylinder expressed in terms of the area covered by the reflecting surface; the pressure required for structural integrity and flow rate of the air in the inner target tube; the distance of the target tube from the center of the external cylinder; the required temperature of the heat absorbing medium (i.e., air) in the target tube; and, the desired efficiency of the collector.

Since this type of collector incorporates no rigid components it is extremely lightweight (i.e., typically weighing less than *5 LB/SF*) and portable. The angle of acceptance of the curved aluminized mirror and the diameter and location of the inner tube are all derived directly from the position of the sun and the geometry of the caustic curve (i.e., *G-F-G'* shown in Figure 6.17 (b)). Tests performed with a *4 FT* diameter and *10 FT* effective length prototype collector indicate that an efficiency in excess of 35% (i.e., based on total radiation) at 200°F may be readily achieved. These predictions are dependent on fabrication tolerances and accurate alignment of the pressurized receiver tube. In addition, there is some uncertainty relating to the reliability in respect to smoothness and reflectivity of the aluminized mirror over the life-span of the collector.

6.4 A Multi-Story Pneumatic Greenhouse

In 1975 the author explored the application of a combination of air-inflated and air-supported structural concepts to the design of a lightweight multi-story greenhouse. This investigation resulted in the construction of a five-story prototype. The structure was fabricated from clear polyethylene film and consisted of an inflated cellular floor system, a pressurized central access column, and an air-supported external envelope. The prototype model demonstrated the structural feasibility of employing similar full-size units as low-cost, high-density, super-light greenhouses that could be employed as market gardening units in urban areas or dropped from aircraft as compact, self-inflating, packages into environmentally hostile regions.

The investigation was at least partly motivated by the prospect that increases in population and a general shortage of fuel will in the not too distant future create a need for low-cost, high-productivity greenhouse structures in market gardens located in or near urban areas. The advantages of producing food in proximity to where it can be consumed rather than transporting it over large distances from rural farms to urban areas have received an increasing amount of attention in recent years (Despommier 2010, Lim and Lui 2010, Bailey 1915). Apart from reducing transportation costs and fuel consumption, such advantages include the ability to recycle graywater, minimize spoilage and the need for refrigeration, while producing multiple harvests per year. Needless to say there are of course also obstacles to the realization of vertical farming. Somewhat surprisingly, chief among these is the difficulty of providing the natural sunlight that is required for optimum growth conditions in sufficient quantities. Tall buildings are typically designed as free-standing columns with compact floor plans for structural reasons. Therefore, the external wall to floor area ratio tends to be small by necessity[3].

Greenhouses are commonly used in market gardens to provide a controlled plant growth environment. They consist basically of an external envelope capable of transmitting solar radiation into the interior, but unable to retransmit this electromagnetic radiation to the outside once it has been absorbed and reradiated by the various materials inside the greenhouse. During the absorption and reradiation process the wavelength of the electromagnetic radiation changes and, by virtue of its selective transmission properties, the external envelope acts as a heat trap. Typically, the material used for greenhouses is glass supported by steel or timber frames, although in recent years air-supported structures consisting of a transparent plastic film supported by a small environmental air pressure have found limited acceptance.

The majority of orthodox glass-framed structures and all air-supported greenhouses are single-story buildings with a very favorable wall-roof surface to covered area ratio in the vicinity of 2:1 (i.e., contrary to their multi-story counterparts). The cost of these single-story structures is relatively small and smallest for the air-supported version. However, with the rising cost of energy the continuous overhead of the blower to maintain the structural integrity of the air-building has become a non-trivial maintenance cost consideration.

6.4.1 Project Objectives

The principal objective of this research project was to explore the structural feasibility of a multi-story, pneumatic greenhouse through the construction of a quarter full-size working model. With minimum self-weight as a major design criterion the avoidance of rigid components and reliance to the extent possible on pneumatic structural principles appeared to be a necessity. In addition, there was an expectation that the prototype would provide some indication of feasibility in respect to the fabrication and erection process of a full-size, multi-story, pneumatic greenhouse structure.

6.4.2 Structural Considerations

From the outset of this research project it was assumed that a system of construction based on pneumatic principles would provide the most economical structural solution for a multi-story greenhouse building, based on the following design criteria:

1. An extremely lightweight structure for ease of transportation, erection, and deflation.
2. Maximum daylight penetration into the building.
3. Adequate structural stability under vertical building loads and horizontal wind loads.
4. Structure to lend itself to prefabrication in large components using techniques available to small plastics manufacturers and fabricators.
5. Simple and fast erection (and demounting) procedures, requiring no skilled labor.
6. Cost competitive with existing single-story, glass and plastic (rigid) framed greenhouse structures.

---

[3] The ideal building footprint from a structural point of view is circular or square. In either case the ratio of external wall area to floor area becomes geometrically smaller as the diameter or width of the building increases. For example, for a circular building of *10 FT* diameter the floor area to perimeter ratio is 5:1, while for a *100 FT* diameter building the ratio is 50:1.

During the earliest selection stages of a suitable pneumatic system it was recognized that a combination of structural systems would be necessary to satisfy these design criteria. Clearly, the advantages of structural efficiency and minimum weight favored a single-skin solution. However, while a single-skin air-supported structure appeared to be most appropriate for both the external enclosure of the greenhouse building and the airlock access facility, it would not be appropriate for the horizontal floors or shelves required to support the plants that would be grown without soil utilizing hydroponic or aeroponic technology (Raviv and Lieth 2008, Van Patten 2012). The horizontal components would need to be based on a double-skin air-inflated structural solution.

6.4.3 Selection of Material

Even today with the availability of a wide range of rigid and flexible plastics, glass remains a widely used roof and wall cladding material for greenhouses. Apart from its favorable light transmission properties and resistance to ultra-violate radiation degradation, glass has the ability to act as a heat-trap. However, glass has a limited structural capability, is a relatively expensive material prone to breakage, and requires fairly elaborate and therefore somewhat expensive frame fittings.

One of the first plastic materials to be applied in horticulture as an alternative to glass was polyethylene (or polythene). Although polyethylene films thinner than *0.001 IN* can be manufactured, thicker films in the vicinity of *0.005 IN* to *0.010 IN* are now in general use. Polyethylene film is a translucent flexible material with an ultimate tensile strength of about *10 LB/IN* to *50 LB/IN* depending on thickness. A low modulus of elasticity of around *20,000 psi* creates some structural problems in as much as the material is subject to considerable elongation under load. It was acknowledged that if used as the principal component of a multi-story air-supported structure relatively thicker films or, alternatively, an exterior cable-network might be required for reinforcement purposes.

The light transmission properties of polyethylene film are at least equal to those of 24 oz. horticultural glass. Over 90% of the visible spectrum (i.e., 350 to 750 millimicron) is transmitted by polyethylene. In addition, transmissions in the infra-red and ultra-violet regions are superior to glass. Unfortunately, polyethylene and in fact all clear plastic films are subject to degradation by the ultra-violet component of sunlight. This characteristic has a profound influence on the life-span of the film, necessitating replacement every two to three years depending on the precise chemical composition of the plastic material.

Polycarbonate sheeting is more rigid than polyethylene film and has become a highly competitive alternative in recent years due to its durability, light transmission, and ease of transport. It is strong with a relatively high impact value, shatterproof, hail proof, has a good load bearing capacity, is less flammable, and not as rigid as glass. However, polycarbonate sheets have a relatively high coefficient of thermal expansion requiring special installation considerations.

Besides polyethylene, polyvinyl chloride (PVC) and fiberglass, nylon or polyester reinforced plastics have been applied in horticulture. While these materials are more expensive than polyethylene, they have superior strength characteristics. PVC, in particular, has been successfully applied in the construction of air-buildings for a number of years. In respect to light transmission there is little difference between PVC and polyethylene, although the former is somewhat less transparent to long wave heat radiation thereby leading to a slightly stronger greenhouse effect. In addition, the life-span of stabilized (against ultra-violet degradation) clear PVC normally exceeds that of polyethylene by a factor of between *1.5* and *2.5*.

In the case of the proposed air-supported greenhouse, due to the need for a flexible membrane material, both polyethylene and PVC have the appropriate properties. Either of these plastic films could have been selected for the construction of the prototype multi-story pneumatic greenhouse. Both materials are readily joined by simple heat-sealing methods and therefore even in respect to fabrication they remained equal candidates. However, *0.006 IN* thick and *12 FT* wide polyethylene film was finally chosen on a cost basis, since the superior strength properties of PVC would not have been utilized in a scale model subject to a very much reduced internal pressure.

6.4.4 General Design Considerations

Before the design and construction of the proposed quarter full-size working model could be undertaken, it was necessary to establish in general terms the governing design parameters of a typical full-size multi-story pneumatic greenhouse. In single-skin multi-story air-supported buildings the required environmental pressure is directly proportional to the total vertical building load. At the same time, the stress in the enclosing plastic membrane is a function of both the environmental pressure and the diameter of the building. Accordingly, the optimum number of floors to be supported by the structure is almost entirely governed by the floor load per unit area and the allowable working stress in tension of the building envelope.

Based on a deductive process the design of the full-size multi-story air-supported greenhouse commences with the assumption of a minimum *5 FT* floor to floor height to provide for adequate access to each floor by a person in a stooped or kneeling position. It might be argued that a high density production unit of the type described here would be highly mechanized and require access by personnel only during seeding, harvesting and at predetermined time intervals for inspection purposes. Allowing for a maximum solar radiation incidence angle of 35° over at least 90% of each floor surface and an average floor thickness of *1 FT* a building diameter of approximately *16 FT* is obtained.

The strongest clear, ultra-violet stabilized membrane that was commercially available at the time the prototype was constructed (1974) was *0.020 IN* thick PVC with a working strength in tension of around *10 LB/IN* to *15 LB/IN*. Although the ultimate strength of this material is over *50 LB/IN* the elongation at rupture will normally exceed *300%*. Accordingly, the spacing of the reinforcing exterior cable-network for a full-size building will need to be sufficiently close (i.e., between *1 FT* and *2 FT*) to keep the stress in the membrane envelope within acceptable limits. Experience with the two previous prototype multi-story air-supported buildings described in Chapter 5 indicated that for the type of building application under consideration a suitable cable spacing would allow a stress ratio of approximately *7:1* between the steel cables and the plastic membrane.

To estimate the required internal environmental pressure based on a building diameter of *16 FT* it is convenient to assume a hypothetical envelope equal in strength to the combined action of the plastic membrane and steel cable-network. Providing for a plastic material with a conservative working strength of *10 LB/IN* and a stress ratio between the membrane and the cable-network of *7:1*, we arrive at a hypothetical envelope strength of *70 LB/IN*. The interaction between material stress, internal environmental pressure, and diameter for all single-skin multi-story air-supported buildings is given by the simple relationship:

$$\text{membrane stress (psi)} = \text{pressure (psig)} \times \text{building radius (IN)}$$

Therefore, for a building radius of *8 FT* (or *96 IN*) and an allowable material stress (i.e., hypothetical envelope) of *70 LB/IN*, we obtain a maximum environmental pressure (*P psig*) of:

$$P = (70/96) = \mathbf{0.73\ psig}\ (\text{or 20.4 IN Water Gauge})$$

In the case of multi-story air-supported buildings with a height to diameter ratio of 2:1 (slenderness ratio of 11.3), overall buckling of the building acting as a column is insignificant in relationship to local buckling of the membrane enclosure. Accordingly, on a conservative basis, a pressure-utilization efficiency of 95% may be assumed, allowing calculation of the allowable vertical building load per square foot (psf) of cross-sectional building area, as follows:

$$\text{allowable vertical load (W)} = \text{pressure (psig)} \times \text{efficiency} \times 144\ (\text{psf})$$
$$W = 0.73 \times 0.95 \times 144 = \mathbf{100\ psf}$$

In view of the lightweight nature of the materials involved, it is convenient to combine the weight of the plastic enclosure, exterior cable-network and hydroponic (or aeroponic) cultivation equipment with the expected dead and live floor loads in a single vertical load per square foot of floor area value. Assuming an inflatable floor system with an extremely small self-weight (i.e., less than *2 psf*) and making a conservative allowance for the weight of the cultivation equipment, a total design load of 20 per square foot of floor area was adopted. Based on this estimate, the maximum number of floors that can be supported by an environmental pressure of 0.73 psig (or 20.4 IN Water Gauge) is found to be:

$$\text{total number of floors (X)} = \text{total load capacity} / \text{load per square foot of floor area}$$
$$X = 100/20 = \mathbf{5\ floors}$$

6.4.5 The Floor System

The requirement of an extremely lightweight structure according to the first and primary design criterion led to the investigation of various air-inflated floor system configurations. Two systems in particular appeared to warrant detailed study:

Alternative A: Pressurized cylindrical beams fabricated from plastic membrane.

Alternative B: Double-skin cushion subdivided into pressurized cells.

While pressurized components provide potentially the lightest horizontal structural system, they are subject to fairly large deflections at mid-span (Figure 6.20). The deflection can be reduced to some extent by increasing the air pressure in the beam. However, for every beam a point is reached where further increases in pressure have a disproportionately small effect on the central deflection. Beyond this point, only increases in diameter or decreases in span will reduce the deflection.

In the greenhouse structure under consideration the allowable thickness of the floor system is somewhat restricted for at least two reasons. Thicker floors will lead to taller buildings subject to higher environmental pressures and larger material stresses, as well as increased material quantities. It was therefore resolved that regardless of the type of inflated floor system finally selected, vertical support would be provided not only at the perimeter of each floor but also at the center of the building.

Alternative (A) would have required radially distributed rows of *9 IN* to *12 IN* diameter beams pressurized to approximately *1.5 psig* (or *42 IN* Water Gauge) under an allowable deflection of around *2 IN* (Figure 6.20). Alternatively, the beams might be rearranged into parallel rows with some members unable to take advantage of the vertical support at the center of the building. The major disadvantage of Alternative (A) in either configuration is the problem of attachment to the building enclosure at the perimeter and the requirement of a further layer of material to provide a waterproof floor surface capable of accommodating the liquid nature of the plant cultivation facilities.

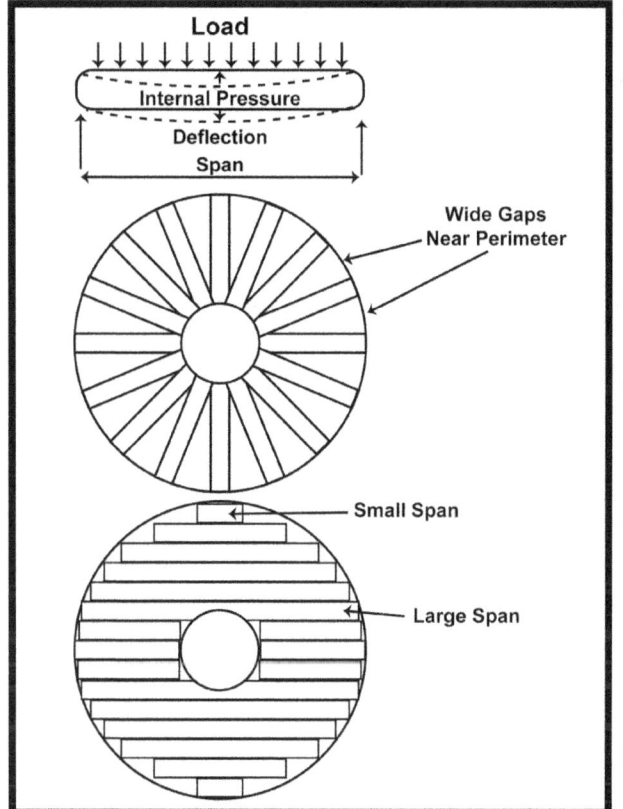

Figure 6.20: Pressurized beams floor system (Alternative A)

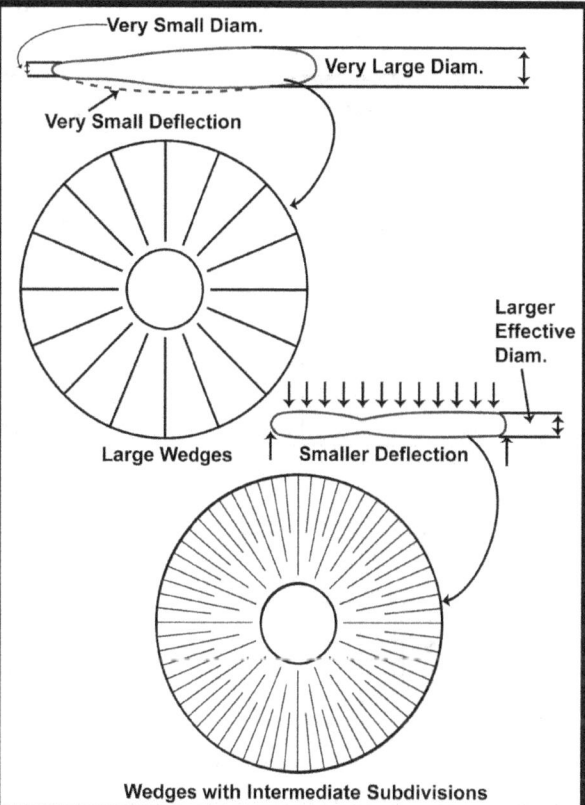

Figure 6.21: Cellular cushion floor system (Alternative B)

Exploration of Alternative (B) focused on the design of a pressurized cell pattern capable of sustaining a uniformly distributed load of 20 LB/SF within reasonable deflection limits (i.e., *1/50th* of span or approximately *2 IN* for an *8 FT* span). A concentric ring pattern was considered to be unsatisfactory, not only due to fabrication complications, but also due to an expectation of excessive deflection. The support conditions were seen to be unfavorable since the rings would span in a direction at right angles to the principal support axis.

The radial subdivision of the floor into wedges (Figure 6.21 upper diagram) proved to be a more promising approach. However, while the pressurized wedges are aligned with the support axis, variations in the effective diameter of each wedge are excessively large. To overcome this problem it was decided to subdivide the wedges in a staggered pattern with the number of cells increasing toward the perimeter of the floor (Figure 6.21 lower diagram). In this manner variations in the effective diameter of each wedge are readily controlled.

A detailed investigation of variations in the relationship between span, internal pressure, wedge width, and the number and lengths of subdivisions within each wedge was considered to be beyond the scope of the research project. Such an investigation would have entailed an extensive structural model analysis involving the construction and testing of a number of large scale working models. Accordingly, the wedge pattern with subdivisions was adopted as the most suitable configuration. Based on experience with pressurized beams and a modest degree of structural intuition the final design of a full-size greenhouse shown in Figure 6.22 was adopted to form the basis of the working model. While the required inflation pressure of this floor system cannot be determined accurately prior to a structural model analysis, it is estimated to be in the range of 2 psig to 4 psig.

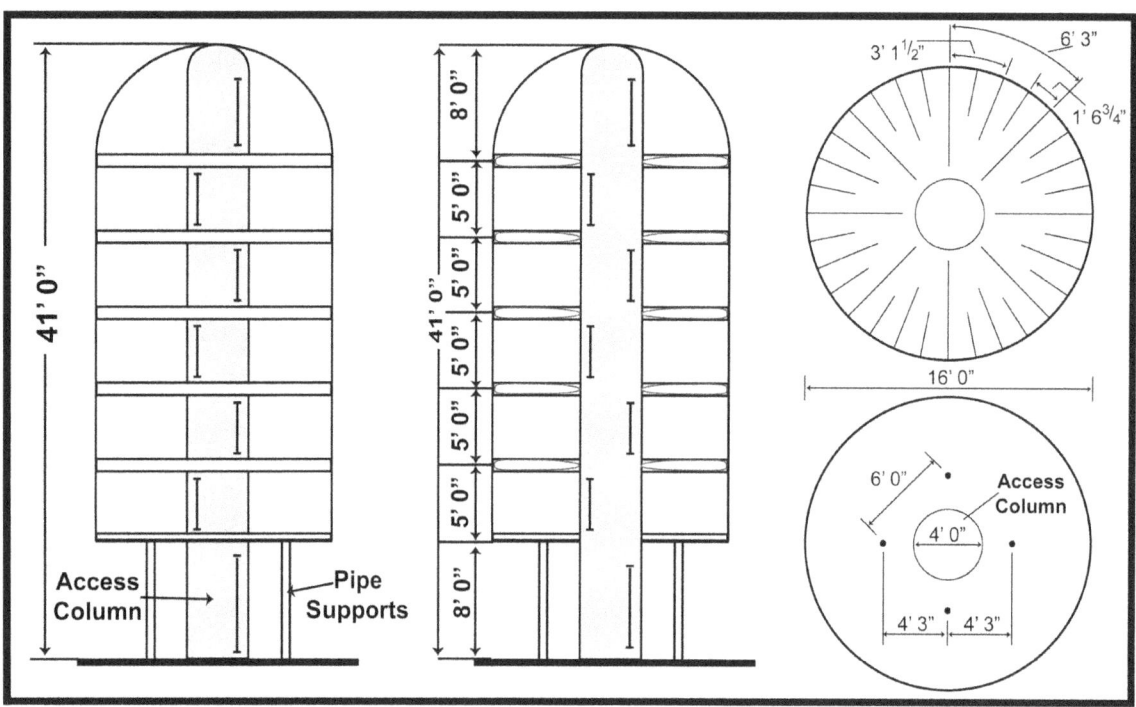

Figure 6.22: The proposed design of a full-size pneumatic greenhouse

6.4.6 The Access System

Persons entering or leaving a multi-story air-supported building incorporating a hyperbaric environment are required to pass through an airlock chamber. In the greenhouse structure under consideration an opportunity presented itself to combine the additional floor support at the center of the building with the required access system to each floor level. It was therefore resolved to provide in the center of the building a *4 FT* diameter pressurized column with simple zipped openings leading to each floor compartment (Figure 6.22).

At ground floor level the central column could be accessed by means of an inflated tunnel, or alternatively the building could be raised off the ground and a solid self-supporting entrance provided below the column. In either case the pressure inside the central column is required to be considerably greater than in the main building chamber. On the assumption that the column should be capable of supporting one-sixteenth of the total building load, based on relative areas, we obtain:

$$\text{total load (w)} = (\text{\# of floors} \times \text{floor area} \times \text{floor load}) / 16 + \text{self-weight (LB)}$$
$$w = (5 \times 200 \times 20) / 16 + 50 \text{ (LB)}$$
$$w = \mathbf{1{,}300 \text{ LB}}$$

At the same time the cross-sectional area of the access column is given by:

$$\text{column area (a)} = \pi r^2 \text{ (SF)}$$
$$a = \mathbf{12.5 \text{ SF}}$$

Allowing for a pressure-utilization factor of approximately 0.70 for a height to diameter ratio of 10:1 (slenderness ratio of 29, since in this case the column is not free-standing but braced at intermediate points by the floors and therefore the effective height is assumed to be the actual height), the required internal pressure of the access column is calculated to be:

$$\text{pressure (p)} = (\text{load} / (\text{area} \times \text{efficiency factor})) + \text{environmental pressure}^4 \text{ (psig)}$$
$$p = (1300 / (12.5 \times 0.70 \times 144)) + 0.73 \text{ (psig)}$$
$$p = 1.03 + 0.73 = \mathbf{1.76 \text{ psig}} \text{ (or 49.3 IN Water Gauge)}$$

Accordingly the tensile stress in the column membrane material is given by[5]:

$$\text{material stress (f)} = \text{pressure} \times \text{column radius (LB/IN)}$$
$$f = 1.03 \times 2 \times 12 = \mathbf{24.7 \text{ LB/IN}}$$

Since the central column need not be transparent (or even translucent) a reinforced plastic material such as polyester or nylon-reinforced PVC with an ultimate tensile strength of around *100 LB/IN* may be used.

6.4.7 The Prototype Model

The principal constraining factors governing the design of the working model were the restricted financial resources and the limitations of an existing heat-sealing device to be used during the fabrication stage. The project budget did not permit the fabrication of any section or component of the model to be subcontracted to an outside commercial organization. Accordingly, the success of this project depended to a large extent on a homemade high-frequency heat-sealer utilizing two hot-wire elements of variable length and incorporating an automatic timing device. Although the performance of this unit met the expectations of its designer in most respects, it did not produce seams equal in quality to those produced by an equivalent commercial unit. Despite careful calibration prior to each heat-sealing operation and the progressively improving skill of the operators, approximately every third seam proved to be defective and was required to be repeated. Unfortunately, this led to a certain amount of material wastage and a considerable amount of extra labor. There is no doubt that these problems would not occur in the case of a full-size building constructed by a commercial fabrication company.

---

[4] Since the access column is located inside the main greenhouse the environmental pressure of *0.73 psig* must be added to the internal pressure of the access column.

[5] For purposes of material stress calculations only the difference in pressure between the central access column and the main greenhouse chamber is taken into consideration.

Design of the model: Although the model was designed to simulate as closely as possible the full-size building, a complete quarter full-size duplication could not be achieved. While the differences between the model and the full-size building are not critical they are noteworthy of mention:

1. A truly scaled model would have required an increase in internal pressure in proportion to the scaled dimensions of the model, if the material stresses in the full-size building were to be accurately reproduced. Accordingly, the environmental pressure in the main chamber of the model would have had to be increased to approximately *3 psig*, while the pressure in the central column would have had to be just over *7 psig*. A pressurization unit capable of supplying the required quantity of air at these pressures was not available. To overcome this problem, the exterior cable-network was omitted, thus increasing the stresses in the polyethylene membrane to an acceptable level under a much lower and therefore manageable internal pressure.

   Since the same solution could not be adopted in the case of the central column, the reinforced plastic film called for in the design of the full-size building was replaced with a polyethylene membrane of much reduced strength. While it is readily admitted that this solution was by no means ideal, it was considered reasonable under the circumstances.

2. Using the existing heat-sealer it was not possible to render the floor sections completely air-proof. For this reason, each of the five floors required a continuous supply of air during the operation of the model. In the case of a full-size building it is anticipated with some certainty that the floor system would not require a continuous source of air after inflation.

3. Mainly for convenience of erection and transportation the main air-supported chamber of the model was raised *2 FT* off the ground and attached to a *¾ IN* thick, circular particle board platform supported by a *1 FT* diameter steel drum at the center. This ensured direct access to all air inlet ducts and allowed the model to be erected on virtually any type of foundation (i.e., the drum could be easily leveled).

The joining of the floors to the membrane enclosure and central column presented an unforeseen problem. It had been intended to heat-seal each floor to plastic flaps attached around the inside perimeter of the enclosure and the outside wall of the central column. Due to difficulties with the heat-sealer, the design had to be changed. It was finally resolved to use standard press-stud fasteners to attach the floor to the supporting membranes (Figure 6.23). Eleven fasteners were distributed around the outside and four around the inside floor perimeters. The fasteners very much simplified the erection process and should certainly come under serious consideration for use in a full-size building.

Two standard domestic vacuum cleaners (connected in reverse) and one small axial fan (⅛ Horse Power) were available for purposes of inflation. It was resolved that the axial fan be connected to the main building chamber (requiring the lowest pressure) to produce an environmental pressure of around *0.036 psig* (or *1 IN* Water Gauge). The more powerful vacuum cleaner was used to inflate the floors (i.e., *½ psig* or *14 IN* Water Gauge) through five separate ducts and the remaining vacuum cleaner was connected to the central access column. This allowed the central column, by virtue of its small volume, to be pressurized to *0.22 psig* (or *6 IN* Water Gauge). The completed model is shown in Figure 6.24.

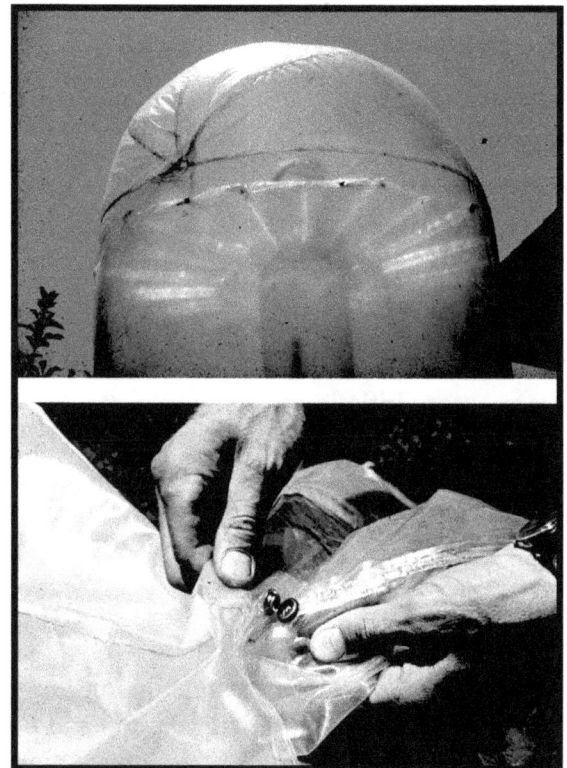

Figure 6.23: Attachment of floors to external enclosure and internal access column

Figure 6.24: The completed quarter scale working model

Construction of the model: The model was prefabricated in four sections, namely, the membrane enclosure, the floors, the central access column, and the self-supporting base. Both the membrane enclosure and the central column were fabricated as cylinders with one vertical joint, capped by domes consisting of four panels joined together and attached to the respective cylinders. A *1 IN* wide heat-sealed lap joint was used for all seams.

The fabrication of the floor system proved to be considerably more complicated. A rectangular sheet measuring approximately *68 IN* by *136 IN* was folded double and a circle of diameter larger than the final inflated diameter of the floor was drawn on the uppermost surface using a marking pen. Next the circular area was divided into radial sections to produce ten equal wedges. Each wedge was then divided into two equal parts from the floor perimeter to a point halfway between the perimeter and the center of the sheet. Finally, a second circle of diameter slightly larger than the central column was drawn around the center point of the sheet.

The external and internal diameters of the floor pattern were required to be larger than the dimensions of the pressurized floor to allow for cramping and bulging of the cells after inflation. These differences in diameter between the pattern and the final floor may be estimated from the geometry of the floor before and after inflation. On the assumption that the cellular floor will become approximately circular on full inflation, the final circumference of the floor is given by:

$$\pi D_P = n(d_P + s) \text{ (IN)}$$

where: D_P = diameter of inflated floor (IN)

n = number of cells (wedges) at perimeter
d_P = diameter of inflated cell (wedge) at perimeter (IN)
s = width of seam between cells (wedges) at perimeter (IN)

We therefore obtain the following expression for the diameter (d_P) of a typical inflated cell at the perimeter of the floor:

$$\mathbf{d_P \ = \ (\pi \, D_P \,) \, / \, n \ - \ s \quad (IN)} \quad \text{................................} \quad 6.2$$

However, the sum of half the circumference of all cells (wedges) at the perimeter plus the seam width between the cells is equal to the perimeter of the floor before inflation:

$$\pi \, D_U \ = \ n \, [\, (\, \pi \, d_P \,) \, / \, 2 \ + \ s] \quad (IN)$$

where: D_U = diameter of floor before inflation (IN)

Accordingly, the required diameter of the floor pattern before inflation is given by:

$$\mathbf{D_U \ = \ (\, n \, / \, \pi \,) \, [\, (\, \pi \, d_P \,) \, / \, 2 \ + \ s] \quad (IN)} \quad \text{..................................} \quad 6.3$$

Applying equations 6.2 and 6.3 to the model dimensions of D_P (48 IN), n (20), and s (0.5 IN) we obtain:

from equation 6.2: d_P = 7.0 IN
from equation 6.3: D_U = 73.5 IN

However, it is now necessary to apply a correction to these values, since the calculations assume a circular cell cross-section at the perimeter of the floor. In fact, at the perimeter the top and bottom surfaces of the floor are heat-sealed together thereby reducing the cells to zero diameter. Experiments with a number of test floors indicated that the values for d_p and D_U derived from equations 6.2 and 6.3 should be reduced by approximately 15%.

adjusted depth of floor after inflation = **6.0 IN**
adjusted diameter of floor before inflation = **62.5 IN**

The required diameter of the inside circle cannot be calculated in this manner since the radial cell seams terminate at some distance (i.e., *3 IN* for main seams and *8 IN* for intermediate seams) from the inner circle seam. This is necessary to ensure the simultaneous inflation of all cells using only one air inlet per floor. Again, based on previous experiments with several test floors an estimate of the diameter of the inside circle before inflation may be obtained by increasing the diameter after inflation by 15%.

adjusted diameter of inside circle before inflation = **14.0 IN**

After the floor patterns were marked and cut according to these dimensions, the seams were heat-sealed and a *½ IN* diameter brass air inlet was attached to one of the cells near the perimeter. Unfortunately, considerable difficulties were encountered during the heat-sealing process requiring three of the floors to be remade, due to excessive air leakage.

The base of the model consisted of two parts, a *4 FT* diameter *¾ IN* thick particle board plate supported by a *1 FT* diameter *1 FT 6 IN* high steel drum. The edge of the plate was lined with standard two-strand electrical cord to provide a groove suitable for fixing the membrane enclosure of the main model chamber. It was proposed that during erection the membrane would be draped over the edge of the plate and tied securely into the perimeter groove by means of a single-strand wire. Apart from supporting the particle board plate, the drum served as a convenient entry point for the various air supply ducts.

Erection of the model: Unfortunately, even a quarter full-size model is not sufficiently large to allow access by a person. Therefore, the model could not be used to simulate the erection procedure of a full-size multi-story air-supported greenhouse.

The erection of a full-size building would commence with the assembly of the ground floor platform, whether this be raised off the ground and supported by a central airlock entrance or simply a prefabricated slab on grade[6]. This would be followed by the attachment of the central access column to the ground floor platform and inflation of each of the floors. With the inflated floors stacked vertically on the platform (i.e., threaded on the deflated central column) the central column may be inflated to approximately 10% of its final design pressure. Next, the membrane enclosure would be lifted onto the uppermost floor and threaded over the floors one by one, allowing each floor to be fixed to the membrane enclosure at the correct height. After the membrane has been fixed (and sealed) around the perimeter of the ground floor platform, the central column and main building chamber may be simultaneously inflated to their respective final design pressures. During the inflation of the main chamber, the floors being attached to the enclosure would be slowly lifted into position. Thereafter, it would be possible for one or more persons to enter the central column, climb up to each floor level and fix the inner circle of each floor to the central column wall. Finally, ducts conveniently attached to the underside of each floor (and the dome roof of the main building chamber) could be activated, and the required hydroponic facilities and plants brought into the building.

Figure 6.25: The central access column with the five attached floors

In the case of the model, erection also commenced with the attachment of the ground floor platform to the upper rim of the supporting steel drum. Next the central column was attached to the platform and inflated to approximately 50% of the final pressure. This allowed each floor to be threaded onto the column (lying on its side) and fixed to the column wall (Figure 6.25), using four press-stud fasteners per floor. Tubes of correct length were attached to the air inlet fittings allowing each floor to be inflated and the membrane enclosure to be draped over the central column and floors. During this process each floor was attached to the enclosure, which was finally

---

[6] In this case an airlock tunnel would be fitted to the central column before stacking of the floors and fitted to the membrane enclosure before the latter is attached (i.e., sealed) to the ground floor platform, ready for inflation.

sealed around the perimeter of the ground floor platform. The simultaneous inflation of the central access column and the main chamber completed the erection of the model (Figure 6.24).

6.4.8 Structural Stability of the Model

Three separate components contribute to the structural stability of the pneumatic greenhouse, namely: the air-supported membrane enclosure; the air-inflated central access column: and, the air-inflated floors. Although the floors of the model could not be loaded (due to lack of access), it was possible to simulate a quasi-loaded condition by reducing the air pressures within the main greenhouse chamber, the central access column, and floors themselves proportionally. During such tests the model retained its stability and performed generally in agreement with theoretical predictions. However, it was noted that there was a tendency for the floors to assume a humped shape under fully pressurized but unloaded conditions.

Typically, the deflection at the inner circle occurred downward resulting in an additional vertical load on the central access column. It was therefore necessary to manually stretch the central column during the erection of the model, until at least three of the suspended floors had assumed a horizontal shape. Subsequently, the fully pressurized column was capable of resisting the downward deflections of the unloaded floors and sustaining a completely extended vertical position throughout the operation of the model. This structural characteristic of the floor system suggested a minor change in the design of a full-size building. Instead of allowing the central access column to finish just above the level of the uppermost floor, it should be extended up to the peak of the domed roof of the main greenhouse chamber and attached at that point. In this way the inflated main chamber will ensure a fully extended vertical access column at all times.

A typical floor was tested outside the model, while supported both around the outside perimeter and the inner circle. Under an inflation pressure of *0.5 psig* (*14 IN* Water Gauge) the floor was capable of supporting a dead-load of *3.5 LB/SF*, with a maximum deflection of no more than ½ *IN* (Figure 6.26).

Figure 6.26: Testing of the inflated floor system under a makeshift distributed dead-load

6.4.9 Non-Structural Feasibility Considerations

While there appears to be no doubt that multi-story pneumatic greenhouses are structurally feasible, it remains to consider their practical feasibility from a greenhouse management point of view in terms of initial construction costs, plant growth environment, cultivation management, and harvesting.

From the point of view of construction costs the multi-story pneumatic greenhouse has much to commend it. First, it lends itself to factory mass-production using automated (and computer controlled) equipment, including large heat-sealing presses for the fabrication of the air-inflated floors. Second, it is extremely light and readily packaged into small volume containers. Third, it is structurally efficient by virtue of its ability to convert vertical loads into tensile material stresses and by utilizing the building enclosure as the principal structural component. An estimate of the construction costs of a full-size multi-story pneumatic greenhouse (Figure 6.22) can be at least initially based on predicted material, fabrication, and erection costs not using mass-production techniques. However, in view of the innovative nature of the structure and the complete lack of previous experience such an estimate can at best be accepted only as a guide for comparison with orthodox greenhouse structures. In 1974, when the prototype study was conducted, the construction cost of a pneumatic greenhouse of the dimensions shown in Figure 6.22 was estimated to be about (U.S.)$4,000 as shown in Table 6.2 (Pohl and Montero 1975).

Table 6.2: Construction cost estimate of pneumatic greenhouse (1974 (U.S.)$)

Cost Item	Description	$ (U.S. 1974)
Site preparation	leveling, excavation, and concrete footings for pipe supports	80
Substructure	ground floor timber platform, 4 steel pipe supports, bracing, and airlock entrance	220
Membrane enclosure	clear plastic film (0.020 IN), fabrication (heat-sealing), floor attachment, and external cable-network	740
Central access column	reinforced plastic film (0.020 IN), fabrication, zippers, and provision for floor attachment	180
Inflated floors (5)	reinforced plastic film (0.020 IN), fabrication, and provision for attachment to main chamber enclosure and central access column	2,500
Fans (2)	fans and air ducts	160
Erection labor	two person days (i.e., 2 unskilled laborers for 1 day)	80
	Total:	**$3,960**

Based on the following unit costs: Clear plastic film   0.16 per SQFT
Reinforced plastic film   0.20 per SQFT
Fabrication costs   20.00 per hour
Laborer wages   5.00 per hour
[Other materials (medium quality) at September 1974 $(U.S.) prices.]

If each floor has a usable area of *188 SF* (Figure 6.22), then with five suspended floors and the non-suspended ground floor the total covered usable area is *1,128 SF*. Accordingly, based on 1974 U.S. fabrication and construction rates the cost of the multi-story pneumatic greenhouse is estimated to be *$3.52 per SF* of usable covered area. This estimate compared very favorable with the 1974 U.S. cost of orthodox glass or plastic (rigid) framed greenhouses that ranged from *$5.00* to *$6.00 per SF* of usable covered area.

While the multi-story pneumatic greenhouse takes advantage of the benefits that have been postulated for vertical farms in urban areas (Despommier 2009), it is also subject to potential problems related to the management of the cultivation process in an environment that is subject to access constraints. The impact of the necessary operational changes to traditional greenhouse management practices cannot be predicted from a structural model analysis. Further studies need to be undertaken to address themselves to the following topics:

- Installation, operation and maintenance of the hydroponic (or aeroponic) plant and equipment that is the essential component of the cultivation environment.

- The ability to maintain at minimum operating costs, a controlled environment conducive to accelerated plant growth in a full-size structure.

- The impact on present-day greenhouse management practices of this type of greenhouse structure. This must include an evaluation of operational changes based on practical experience with at least one full-size structure.

- Optimization of the air-inflated floor system with respect to structural stability, and suitability for crop and equipment support. Customized hydroponic (or aeroponic) plant is likely to be a necessity.

- Fabrication requirements and cost reduction opportunities for large-scale mass production.

In summary, it would appear that the continued investigation of this type of low cost structure for high-productivity, vertical farming applications in densely populated areas is warranted.

Chapter 7
Air-Supported and Fluid-Inflated Rigid Membrane Structures

Exploration of the applications of fluid-supported construction to multi-story buildings would be incomplete without an investigation into the suitability of rigid membrane structures as distinct from the flexible membrane-cable-network buildings discussed previously in Chapters 3 and 4. During the late 1960s and early 1970s when the author first explored the structural behavior of pressurized, flexible membrane columns there was no existing test data to draw upon[1]. However, the situation is quite the reverse in the case of rigid membrane structures. The stability of thin-walled, monocoque and reinforced, circular cylinders is a subject that has received considerable attention during the past 100 years from aeronautical and mechanical engineers.

Circular cylindrical shells have been used extensively in many major industries such as chemical, petroleum, electrical, and nuclear energy. They are also widely applied as one of the principal structural components in submarines, aircraft, guided missiles, and rockets. During the 1950s the increased use of pure monocoque construction in aircraft and missile structures forced a closer inspection of the stability analysis of unstiffened circular cylinders with and without the action of internal fluid pressure.

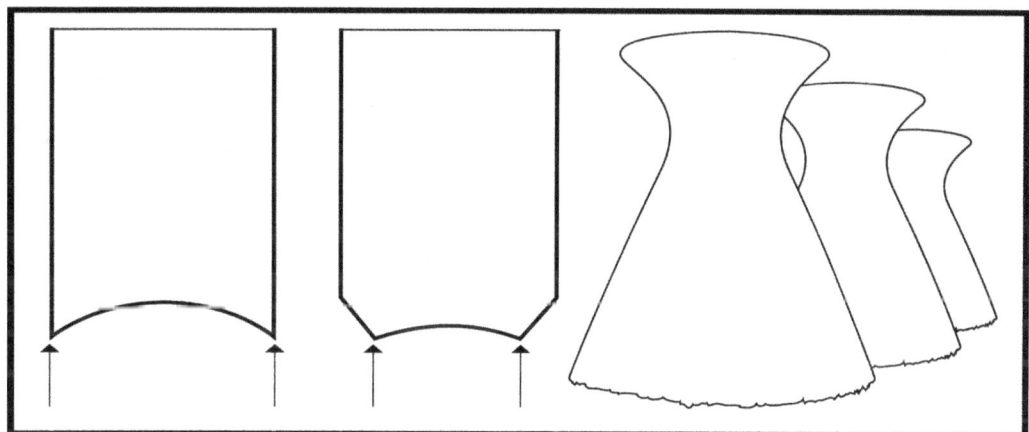

Figure 7.1: Common concrete shell container forms

So far there has been little interest shown in the application of similar structural systems to the field of building construction. Shell-shaped containers (Figure 7.1) have been constructed of reinforced and prestressed concrete on the assumption that the restrictions of the classical small deflection membrane theory are satisfied (Angerer 1961, 63). Although concrete is neither a flexible film nor of negligible self-weight and generally incompatible with the requirements of a membrane material, it has nevertheless been favored for a number of years as a most economical substitute. By satisfying a number of special conditions (e.g., continuous curvature, very thin shell in relationship to span, and evenly distributed loading) the shell designer is able to correlate in principle the structural behavior of a concrete shell with the postulates of a theory more applicable to thin plastic or metal sheets. In addition, designers typically choose shapes in which

---

[1] This is essentially still the case today in 2014. The use of fluid-inflated components in building structures, let alone fully air-supported multi-story buildings, is unlikely to be acceptable for the foreseeable future. However, the same does not apply to extraterrestrial structures that are subject to severely hostile environmental conditions and critical material transportation constraints.

the approximated membrane condition is disturbed as little as possible and in which, therefore, additional bending stresses are avoided. However, in cylindrical shells such as those shown in Figures 7.2 and 7.3 a disturbance of the classical membrane condition is always produced to varying degrees by the interaction of three elements:

- The extension (i.e., expansion) of the cylinder surface.
- The extension of the end surfaces (i.e., roof and container floor).
- The extension or contraction of the supporting ring or end-beam.

The architect or structural engineer will then endeavor to produce the optimum shape that will minimize the unfavorable interaction of these elements.

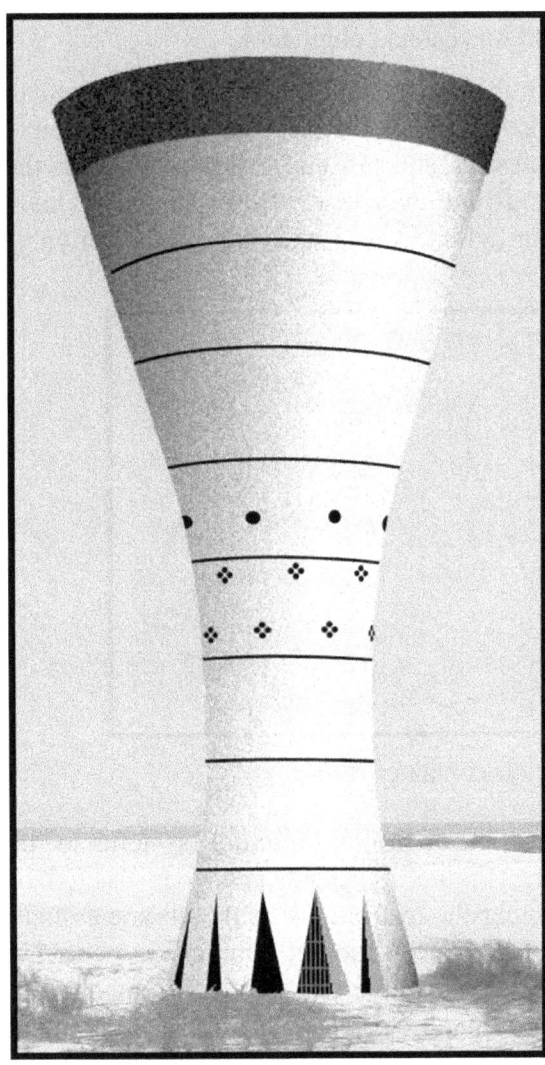
Figure 7.2: Cylindrical shell container

Figure 7.3: Shell with vertical ribs

7.1 Pressurized Rigid Membrane Structures

A reasonably comprehensive review of the possible application of pressurized rigid membrane structures in buildings will require consideration of at least four distinct structural types that may be either fluid-supported or fluid-inflated.

Type 1: Multi-story, air-supported, rigid membrane buildings in which structure and enclosure are synonymous (see Chapter 6, Figure 6.3 (a), (b) and (f)).

Type 2: Pressurized columns (i.e., fluid-inflated) of medium height serving as structural components within the framework of a building structure.

Type 3: Metal structures fabricated from flat sheets, sealed in a fluid-tight manner and inflated under internal pressure to a desired form (Rawlings 1967, 44).

Type 4: Rigidized membrane and expandable self-rigidizing honeycomb structures that have been developed for extraterrestrial applications in space research programs (Forbes 1962; Forbes and Vasiloff 1963, 507).

Although the emphasis in this chapter is focused on rigid membrane air-supported buildings and fluid-inflated columns of medium height, structure types 3 and 4 will be briefly described for the sake of completeness.

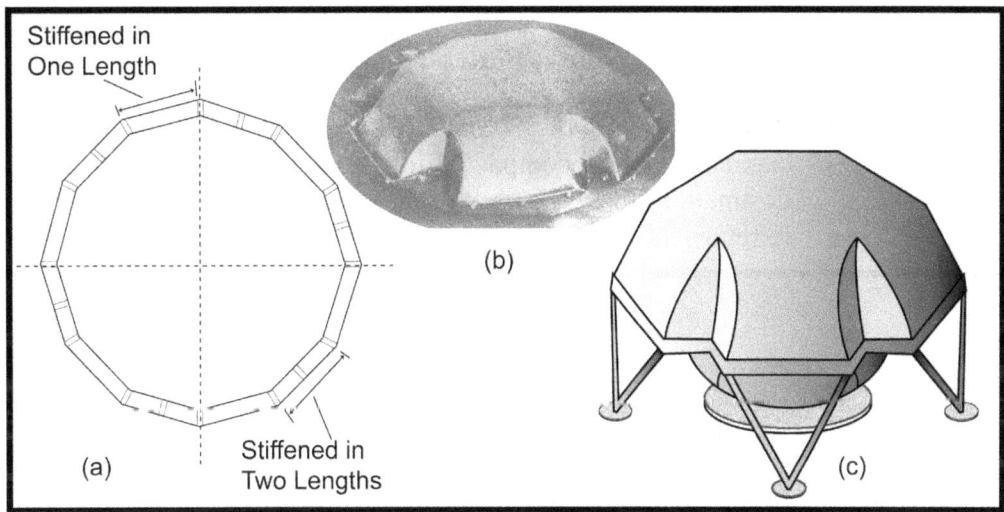

Figure 7.4: Dodecagon metal sheet with stiffened edges

The fabrication of ductile materials by deep pressing has been a well recognized procedure in production engineering for many years. In the 1960s some interesting research was conducted to explore the feasibility of applying this process for forming large scale metal structures. In the experimental work described by Rawlings (1967), no moulds are considered and the material is allowed to develop a surface configuration compatible with the internally applied pressure and the stresses arising within the metal sheet. The final form of the structure may be modified to some extent by the end-fixing conditions of the metal sheets. As shown in Figure 7.4 (a), a regular dodecagon with every alternate edge stiffened in one length and the remaining edges stiffened in two lengths will after pressurization to the developable limit[2] assume a useful container form as indicated in Figure 7.4 (b). However, further pressurization will result in substantial plastic straining of the material with subsequent increases in volume and slight changes in the configuration of folds (Figure 7.4 (c)).

---

[2] Developable limit is loosely defined as the stress level in a material (e.g., thin metal sheeting in this case) before significant plastic strain occurs.

While such structures would no doubt be suited to a number of storage applications (i.e., water, grain, etc.), there nevertheless remains the problem of producing the required fabrication conditions necessary for the production of large-scale structures. However, while pressures in the vicinity of 100 psig may be required to deform an experimental model beyond the developable limit, one would expect much lower pressures to achieve this result in the case of full-scale structures[3].

Around the same period there was some interest in expandable, rigidized plastic membranes involving vapor catalysis, yield metallic foils, plasticizer boil-off, and cross linking by solar radiation (Forbes 1962). Of these, vapor catalysis and yield metallic foils appeared to be the most likely techniques for extraterrestrial applications.

> *Vapor Catalysis:* Membranes of partially reacted polymers are fabricated into the desired structural form and packaged for transport (Forbes 1962). At the destination a catalyst is vaporized, which will inflate the structure and also complete the cross linking of the polymer until it is completely rigidized. This sequence is shown in Figure 7.5 (a) and (b) for the fabrication of a gelatin dome (Monsanto 1962).
>
> *Yield Metallic Foils:* A structure may be fabricated from lightweight metallic sheets capable of being compacted into a small package. At the final destination this package will be inflated to a pressure sufficient to return the collapsed structure back to its original shape.

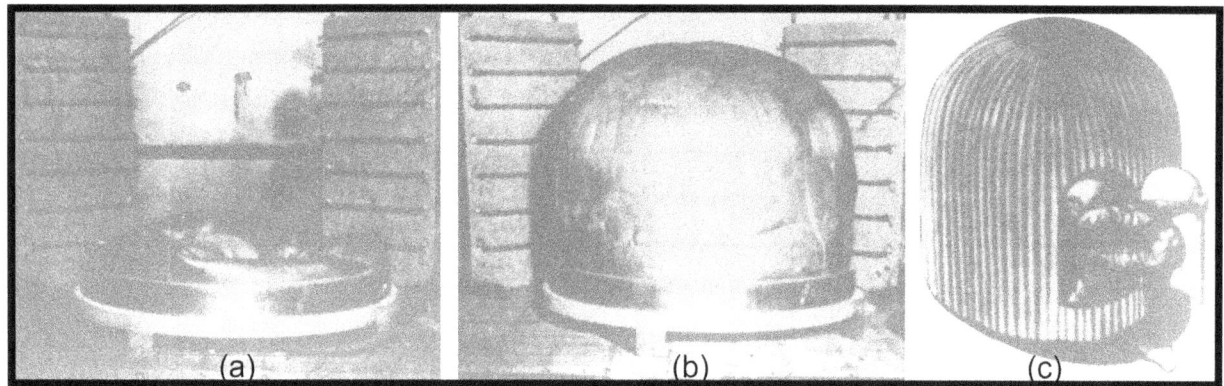

Figure 7.5: Typical vapor catalysis and self-rigidized honeycomb structures

A self-rigidizing technique employing honeycomb was proposed by Forbes and others (1962, 1963). As shown in Figure 7.5 (c), this concept is based on the fabrication of structures from expandable honeycomb, which after expansion is rigidized to provide the structural properties of rigid conventional honeycomb. The core is fabricated from metallic foil with flexible unattached foil skins that are attached after expansion by an automatic adhesion process.

These novel structural solutions were proposed for extraterrestrial shelters, which are required to be not only exceptionally light but also extremely compact during transportation. However, where internal pressurization is part of the solution it is used solely for fabrication purposes and

---

[3] The stresses generated by internal pressure in a container are directly proportional to the internal diameter of the container (i.e., the radius of curvature of the container wall); - the larger the diameter, the larger the stresses.

does not address the ambient atmospheric pressure needs of the final structure for human habitation purposes. In this respect a fluid-supported structure would provide not only structural stability but also a habitable shelter if air is chosen as the pressurization medium.

7.2 Feasibility of Rigid Membrane Building Structures

Whereas in Chapters 2 to 5 the focus has been on multi-story air-supported structures in which the building envelope consists of a flexible membrane with or without an exterior cable-network, the subject matter of Chapter 7 is rigid membrane structures. In particular, we will explore the potential use of thin-walled, unreinforced, cylindrical shells as the structural enclosure of multi-story air-supported buildings. The use of fluid-inflated, thin-walled, cylindrical columns as primary structural components of buildings, such as the *Sand-Column Building* described in Chapter 6 (Section 6.2), will also be discussed in some detail.

It would appear that substitution of a rigid membrane for a flexible membrane serving as the building enclosure may not only extend the scope of multi-story pneumatic construction but also provide the following economies for certain applications:

1. It is possible to utilize rigid membrane materials such as sheet metal with far superior tensile strength properties. The tensile strength of steel, in the elastic range, is of an order of magnitude greater than the tensile strength of a commonly available plastic membrane material such as PVC (i.e., at least 20,000 psi for tinplate as compared to less than 2,000 psi for a transparent flexible plastic material).

2. In the case of virtually all multi-story air-supported buildings utilizing flexible membrane envelopes it will be necessary to resist the circumferential stress due to internal pressure by means of an exterior cable-network; - while the flexible membrane serves solely as a fluid-tight container. A rigid membrane material will allow the designer to replace the combined functions of envelope and cable-network with a single envelope (see Chapter 6, Figure 6.3 (e)).

3. Some of the fluid-inflated building types discussed in Chapter 6 (e.g., Figures 6.1 and 6.3 (f)) require an inner skin that needs to resist external pressure. Only a rigid membrane is capable of resisting an externally imposed load. Also, the normal choice for buildings supported by fluid-inflated columns such as several of the building types discussed in Chapter 6 (e.g., Figures 6.2 and 6.3 (b) and (g)) and, in particular, the *sand-column building* described in Section 6.2, would be a rigid membrane.

From a structural theory point of view the application of rigid membrane construction to multi-story air-supported buildings is basically concerned with thin-walled, cylindrical shells under the action of internal or external pressure in combination with axial compression loads. Based on practical considerations the height to diameter range of such multi-story air-supported cylinders is unlikely to extend beyond 3:1[4]. Therefore, the experimental investigation of the critical buckling stresses in internally pressurized rigid building enclosures under axial compression, described

---

[4] Where *height* is the actual height of the cylinder (i.e., the air-supported portion of the building) as opposed to the effective height, which would be twice the actual height in the case of a free-standing column. This is considered reasonable since local buckling of the column wall rather than overall buckling is the failure mode of short to medium height, internally pressurized columns.

later in this chapter, is limited to this range. However, for fluid-inflated columns the height to diameter ratio range may extend to 10:1, which is equivalent to a very long cylinder.

7.3 Previous Work in Historical Context

The behavior of a thin-walled (monocoque) cylinder under axial compression with or without the action of internal fluid pressure has received a great deal of attention in past years from aeronautical and mechanical engineers. Much of this work was driven by the need for reliable design data in support of advances in aircraft, missiles, and rockets for space travel. Although the structural behavior of monocoque cylinders constitutes a fundamental case, it became a subject of considerable controversy (Donnell and Wan 1950). Indeed, even today designers are forced to accept the validity of semi-empirical design curves and empirical design formulas on par with the structural engineering approach to the design of columns in orthodox building construction.

While this chapter is primarily concerned with the load-bearing capacity of pressurized cylinders, it is nevertheless relevant to briefly summarize early work dealing with unpressurized cylinders. The pressurized and unpressurized cases are inseparable for two reasons:

1. Similar factors appear to govern the critical buckling stress in each case.

2. The principal reason for pressurizing cylinders that are subjected to an axial compression load is to increase the load-bearing capacity; - i.e., to increase the critical buckling stress of the cylinder.

The first attempts to provide a solution for the local buckling stability of thin-walled cylindrical shells and curved plates were made almost simultaneously in Britain (Southwell 1914, Dean 1925, Robertson 1928), Germany (Lorenz 1908 and 1911, Flügge 1934), and the U.S. (Timoshenko 1936). This work was performed mostly prior to 1940 and centered on the development of the classical small deflection theory (see Section 7.3.2).

7.3.1 Early Experimental Observations

Early experimental work aimed at demonstrating the failure mechanism of unpressurized, thin-walled cylinders subjected to axial compression published by several researchers (Lundquist 1933, Wilson and Newmark 1933, Kanemitsu and Nojima 1939) may be summarized as follows:

- If the axial compressive stress is sufficiently large the cylinder will buckle into many comparatively small waves.

- Buckling occurs quite suddenly, almost explosively, and usually covers only a section of the cylinder wall (Donnell and Wan 1950, Jones 1966).

- The number of waves around the circumference of the cylinder is approximately 10, regardless of diameter. Furthermore, the wave shape ratio (i.e., the ratio of circumferential wavelength to axial wavelength) is always close to unity with an average value of 0.75.

In the case where a similar cylinder is additionally subjected to internal pressure the following buckling mechanism has been observed (Tsai-Chen 1967, Jones 1966, Harris et al. 1957):

- Failure is preceded by the formation of diamond shaped buckles whose wave height decreases as the internal pressure increases (Fung and Sechler 1957).
- The occurrence of these symmetrical buckles is not synonymous with the ultimate collapse load of the cylinder.
- Once a specimen is close to the critical stress, a buckle can be easily induced by the application of a slight external point-load to the cylinder wall (Harris et al. 1957).

7.3.2 The Small Deflection Theory

The classical theory for the case of thin-walled cylinders subjected to axial compression developed by Lorenz (1908, 1911), Southwell (1914), Timoshenko (1910, 1936), Robertson (1928), Flügge (1934) and others is based on the small deflection shell theory, which assumes perfect elasticity and a perfect initial shape. The value predicted by the small deflection theory for the critical buckling stress (f_x psi) of a thin-walled cylinder of moderate length with simply supported edges is given by:

$$f_x = E\,t / (R\,(3\,(1 - u^2))\,)^{0.5} \; \text{psi}$$

where: E = modulus of elasticity of the material (psi)
t = cylinder wall thickness (IN)
R = radius of cylinder (IN)
u = Poisson's ratio

If we assume a Poisson's ratio (u) of *0.316*, then:

$$f_x = 0.608\,(E\,t / R)\; \text{psi} \quad\quad\quad 7.1$$

Experiments by Donnell (1934), Lundquist (1933), Wilson and Newmark (1933), Ballerstedt and Wagner (1936) and others (Lorenz 1908, Flügge 1934, Kanemitsu and Nojima 1939) have shown that the actual critical stress is much lower than that predicted by equation 7.1. Von Karman, Tsien and Dunn (1939, 1940) have discussed in detail the apparent short-comings of the small deflection theory. Except in the case of short cylinders, experiments usually give values for the critical buckling stress that are only one third to one fifth of the theoretical predictions. Moreover, the observed buckling pattern is different from that predicted by the theory (Van Karman and Tsien 1941, Batdorf et al. 1947). It is also apparent that the attempted explanations of this significant discrepancy advanced by Donnell (1934) and Flügge (1934), based on consideration of edge support conditions and initial deviations from a perfect cylindrical shape, are not satisfactory (Van Karman and Tsien 1939, Van Karman et al. 1940, Ballerstedt and Wagner 1936).

In these theoretical treatments of the buckling of cylindrical shells three simultaneous partial differential equations have been used to express the relationship among the components of the shell's median surface, namely surface displacement in the axial, circumferential and radial directions. However, no general agreement was reached on the precise nature of these equations (Batdorf 1947) leading to the general contention that the buckling behavior of curved shells cannot be explained by means of the small deflection theory (Donnell 1934, Van Karman and Tsien 1941).

7.3.3 The Large Deflection Theory

Donnell's 1934 definitive publication dealt in principle with the effect of initial deviations from perfect shape on the critical buckling stress of thin-walled cylinders. He pointed out that the differences in the various sets of equations in use at that time arose from the inclusion or selective omission of a number of relatively insignificant terms. Consequently, he proposed the use of three simpler equations in which only the first order terms are retained, and justified this proposal with the contention that for thin-walled cylinders, where the square of the number of circumferential waves is much greater than unity, the omitted terms are of no consequence. Further to this, Donnell (1934) was able to combine these three simplified equations into a single eighth-order partial differential equation in which the effects of the displacements in the axial and circumferential directions are taken into account. Omission of the higher-order terms, as well as the requirement of an integral number of circumferential waves, enabled Donnell to introduce new parameters that combined the geometrical properties of the cylinder and the material properties in such a way that a single curve sufficed to represent the result (Batdorf 1947).

$$k_x = (f_x t H^2) / (D \pi^2) \quad \text{.............................. dimensionless parameter (1)}$$

$$Z = (H^2 / (R t))(1 - u^2)^{0.5} \quad \text{....................... dimensionless parameter (2)}$$

These two parameters have been used with minor variations by Kromm (1939), Legget (1942), and Redshaw (1938). At the same time according to Batdorf (1947) Donnell's single equation is given by:

$$D(O)^8 w + [((E t) / R^2)(\partial^4 w / \partial x^4)] + [P(O)^4]$$
$$+ t(O)^4 [f_x (\partial^2 w / \partial x^2) + (2 f)(\partial^2 w / \partial x \partial y) + f_y (\partial^2 w / \partial y^2) + (f_y / R)] \quad \text{.......... 7.2}$$

where: $D = (E t^3) / (12 (1 - u^2))$ is the flexural stiffness per unit length
- $(O)^8$ = operator $[(\partial^2 / \partial x^2) + (\partial^2 / \partial y^2)]^4$
- $(O)^4$ = operator $[(\partial^2 / \partial x^2) + (\partial^2 / \partial y^2)]^2$
- E = modulus of elasticity
- t = thickness of cylindrical shell (wall)
- f = applied shear stress
- f_x = applied axial stress
- f_y = applied circumferential stress
- w = displacement in radial direction of point on shell median surface
- P = lateral pressure applied externally to shell (wall) only

When only axial stress (i.e., vertical loading) is present equation 7.2 may be rewritten as follows:

$$D(O)^8 w + [((E t) / R^2)(\partial^4 w / \partial x^4)] + [(f_x t (O)^4)(\partial^2 w / \partial x^2)] = 0 \quad \text{....................... 7.3}$$

Again with the proper substitutions and dividing by *D* the following equation is obtained:

$$(O)^8 w + ((12 Z^2) / H^4)(\partial^4 w / \partial x^4) + ((k_x \pi^2) / H^2)(O)^4 (\partial^2 w / \partial x^2) = 0 \quad \text{................. 7.4}$$

where the curvature parameter (*Z*) is given by:

$$Z = (H^2 / (R t))(1 - u^2)^{0.5}$$

and the axial compressive stress coefficient (k_x) is given by:

$$k_x = (f_x t H^2)/(D \pi^2)$$

where H is the actual length (i.e., height) of the cylinder.

Combination of equation 7.4 with the deflection equation for simple support, below:

$$w = w_o \sin(\pi y / \lambda) \sin(m \pi x / H)$$

where: x = axial coordinate
y = circumferential coordinate
m = an integer
λ = half wavelength of buckles measured in circumferential direction

will yield the following equation for the compressive stress coefficient (k_x) with $\beta = H/\lambda$:

$$k_x = ((m^2 + \beta^2)/m^2) + (12 Z^2 m^2)/(\pi^4 (m^2 + \beta^2)^2) \quad \dots \quad 7.5$$

The critical value of the axial compressive stress coefficient (k_x) for a given value of Z may be found by minimizing k_x with respect to the parameter $(m^2 + \beta^2)^2/m^2$. Without any restrictions being placed on the value of this parameter, the minimum value of k_x is found to be:

$$\mathbf{k_x = 0.702\, Z} \quad \dots \quad 7.6$$

This value of k_x has some similarity with the results generally given for the buckling of long cylinders (Batdorf 1947). As shown in Figure 7.6, for any value of R/t some values of Z always exist above which H/R is so large that the cylinder fails as an Euler column (i.e., overall buckling) rather than by local buckling of the cylinder wall.

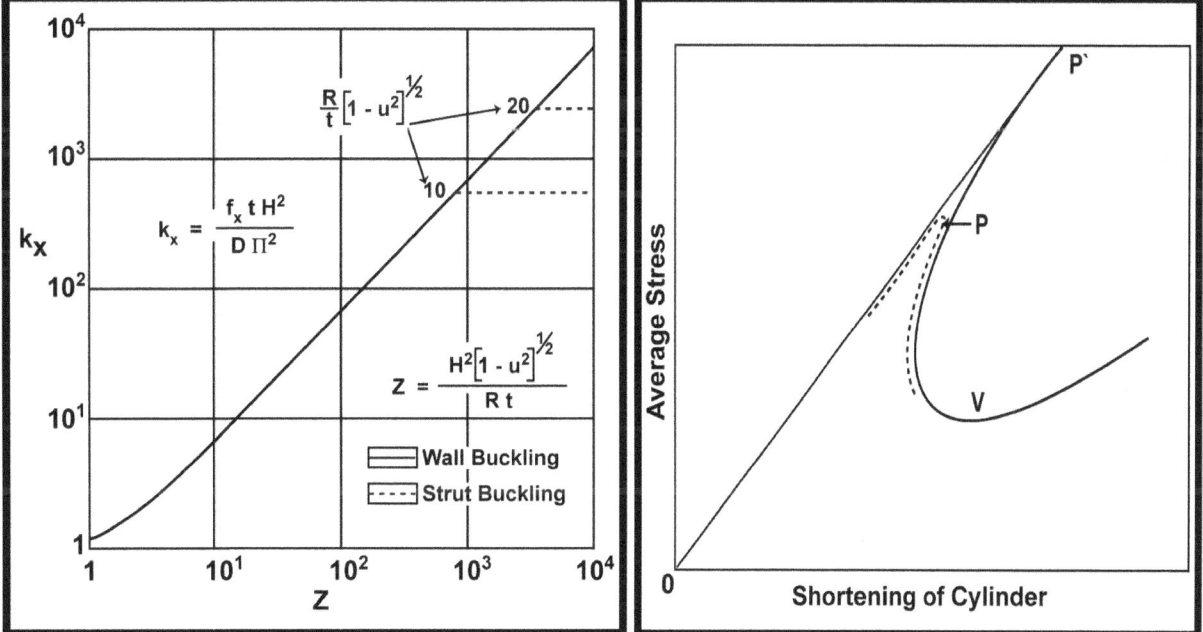

Figure 7.6: Critical axial stress coefficient (according to Batdorf)

Figure 7.7: Relationship of stress to shortening (according to Von Karman and Tsien)

In a 1950 publication, Donnell and Wan acknowledged that in this over simplified approach, in which the energy is minimized for only one parameter and several other concessions are made to reduce the mathematical difficulties, the final result is unsatisfactory. Nevertheless, this approach to estimating the critical stress in cylindrical shells has proved to be useful.

In 1941, Von Karman and Tsien made an important contribution by combining the principles of the large deflection theory[5] with the *Durchschlag* phenomenon[6] (Marguerre 1938, Jones 1966). They assumed a deflection shape of the type:

$$w = (a\,t)\,[(\cos(m\,n\,x/R)\cos(n\,y/R)) \\ + b\cos(2\,m\,n\,x/R) \\ + c\cos(2\,n\,y/R) \\ + d \quad\quad\quad\quad\quad\quad\quad\quad\quad\quad\quad\quad\quad\quad\quad\quad\quad\quad\quad 7.7$$

where: m = the wave shape factor
         n = number of circumferential waves
         x = coordinate in axial direction
         y = coordinate in circumferential direction
   a, b, c, d = other parameters

In equation 7.7 the parameter *d* defines a uniform inward displacement caused by circumferential shortening due to finite deflections. Since *d* is eliminated in the process of differentiation, it need not be considered further. The remaining parameters *a*, *b*, *c*, *m*, and *n* must be either assumed or determined, so as to minimize the energy. Von Karman and Tsien assumed *c* to be equal to *b* and minimized the energy for two of the remaining parameters *a* and *b* (Kanemitsu and Nojima 1939). They then proceeded to find the relationship between the average stress (*f*) and the unit shortening of the cylinder (*e*) for various assumed values of *m* and *n*. These relationships turned out to be of the type shown in Figure 7.7, where *P'* is comparable with the Small Deflection Theory (Lorenz 1908, Southwell 1914, Timoshenko 1914, Robertson 1928) that assumes elastic conditions and perfect initial shape of the cylindrical wall.

Donnell and Wan (1950) pointed out the considerable difference between this result and current observations of columns. These observations tended to indicate a horizontal (or rising) curve after buckling, instead of the steep drop off shown in Figure 7.7. As a plausible explanation Von Karman and Tsien (1941) postulated that there are equilibrium positions of the buckled shape that involve a much lower load than that predicted by the small deflection theory. They therefore concluded that even slight imperfections in the cylindrical shell (wall) are sufficient to significantly lower the buckling load. Based on this conclusion, Von Karman and Tsien suggested that a more accurate solution of the differential equation of equilibrium would be desirable to substantiate the large deflection theory. They further suggested that subject to the work of Kappus (1939) and the current state of research into non-linear elasticity, particular attention be paid to the calculation of the elastic energy stored in the shell.

Based on the same approach a theory for the buckling stresses of perfect cylinders was proposed by Tsien (1942). He found the critical buckling stress of thin-walled cylinders axially loaded with ideal hydraulic testing machines, or dead weight, to be given by:

$$f_x = 0.238\,(E\,t/R)$$

---

[5] Derivation of an expression for the total energy of the system taking into account the stresses in the median surface.

[6] Durchschlag refers to the explosive local buckling failure of the cylinder wall under axial compression.

Extensions of the basic work of Von Karman and Tsien were subsequently published by Legget and Jones (1942), Michielsen (1948), Kempner (1953), and Yochimura (1951) among others. Legget and Jones assumed perfect elasticity, an initial shape, and the constants c and b to be equal. They succeeded in minimizing the energy for all four of the parameters and obtained one curve (i.e., the full line in Figure 7.7). The significance of this approach is that the equation of distortion assumed by the middle surface is only an approximate solution, so that the equation of equilibrium for motion normal to the middle surface is not exactly satisfied. Accordingly, the authors concluded that in addition to the uniformly distributed end load, constraining forces would have to be applied to the curved surface of the cylinder in order to maintain the assumed form of distortion.

Further refinements of this approach were advanced by Donnell and Wan (1950), who also pointed out the following apparent shortcomings of the large deflection theory, relating to the manner in which it was being applied at that time:

- The approach merely answers in general terms why the discrepancy between the small deflection theory and experiments exists, without providing a reliable design methodology.

- In reference to Figure 7.7 the authors questioned the conclusion that the low point at V obviously represents a stable condition and that the resistance at this point should be used as a safe value. According to Legget and Jones (1942) this safe value could be assumed to be approximately one-third of the classical buckling resistance. In this respect Donnell and Wan argued that for very large values of R/t this resistance is not at all conservative, while for small values of R/t it would lead to rather wasteful designs. In this context it should be mentioned that Von Karman and Tsien (1941) had already pointed out that the form of the large deflection theory that they used was only a second approximation and could therefore be quite inaccurate in the case of the relatively large deflections occurring at V; - suggesting that this whole region in Figure 7.7 is in doubt.

- The authors finally suggested that the only hope of finding the actual reduction in resistance at V would be to attempt a quantitative study of the following factors that were likely contributors to this reduction:

    (a) Initial deviations from perfect shape.
    (b) Initial stresses.
    (c) Deviations from ideal elastic behavior.
    (d) Accidental lateral loadings.

Subsequently Donnell and Wan (1950) proposed a modified large deflection theory that included the effects of irregularities and accounted for the plastic behavior of the shell. Using the equation derived by Von Karman and Tsien (equation 7.7) for the deflection under load as a starting point, Donnell and Wan assumed that the amplitude $a_o t$ of the initial equivalent geometric deviation is related to other properties in a manner analogous to that assumed for the analysis of columns.

$$w_o = (a_o t) \sin(\pi x / l)$$
$$a_o = (l^2 / t)(U / \pi^2)$$

where: U = uneveness coefficient
1_x = half the wave length of w_o and w in the axial direction (l for columns)
1_y = half the wave length of w_o and w in the circumferential direction

The authors further suggested that if there were no preferred directions in the cylinder wall it would be reasonable to replace l^2 with $l_x l_y$. This gives the following expression for the amplitude of the cylinder deviation:

$$a_o = ((U/\pi^2) l_x l_y) / t^2$$

However, most thin-walled cylinders in practice (i.e., for tests and real world applications) are fabricated by bending flat sheets into a cylinder shape, which tends to flatten out waves that are long in the circumferential direction. To allow for this Donnell and Wan proposed the following relationship:

$$a_o = ((U/\pi^2) l_x^{1+q} l_y^{1-q}) / t^2 \quad \text{...............} 7.8$$

Taking into account that l_s should obviously not have a negative exponent, the numerical value of q was fixed at 0.5 (i.e., half way between zero and unity). The expression for the initial deviation could then be written as:

$$w_o = [(a_o t)(\cos(m n x / R) \cos(n y / R))]$$
$$+ b \cos(2 m n x / R)$$
$$+ c \cos(2 n y / R)$$
$$+ d \quad \text{...............} 7.7a$$

Substituting for q in equation 7.8, a_o is then given by:

$$a_o = (U R^2) / (m^{1.5} n^2 t^2) \quad \text{...............} 7.8a$$

It was then considered reasonable to assume that the value of the unevenness coefficient (U), defined in equation 7.8a for an average cylinder formed from metal sheet, would be of the same order of magnitude as the corresponding value for metal columns, since the process and errors of manufacture are similar. The results obtained by Donnell and Wan (1950) are in reasonable correlation with experimental results, when the initial eccentricities are known. Their results also suggest the dependence of the critical stress coefficient (k_x) on the R/t value, since initial imperfections in a monocoque cylinder are likely to be greater when the R/t value is large (Harris et al. 1957).

From a general point of view the various forms of the large deflection theory fail to adequately describe the buckling behavior of real world thin-walled cylinders in at least two respects:

1. They are formulated for long cylinders only and, therefore, seriously underestimate the critical buckling stress for very short cylinders.

2. Even in the case of long cylinders the experimental determination of the coefficient C in the general buckling formula (equation 7.9 below) has resulted in substantial experimental scatter.

$$f_x = C(E t / R) \quad \text{...............} 7.9$$

7.3.4 Design Formulas Based on Empirical Results

In the absence of a unique and satisfactory theoretical explanation for the critical buckling stress of thin-walled cylinders, a number of researchers including Lundquist (1933), Wilson and Newmark (1933), Ballerstedt and Wagner (1936), Batdorf et al. (1947), and Kusmiss (1958) have proposed empirical design formulas based in the first instance on available test data. The formula proposed by Ballerstedt and Wagner in 1936 takes into account the length of the cylinder, as follows:

$$f_x / E = (3.3 (t/H)^2) + (0.2 (t/R)) \quad \text{...............................} 7.10$$

where: f_x = critical buckling stress
E = modulus of elasticity
t = wall thickness of the cylindrical shell
H = actual height of cylinder
R = cross-sectional radius of cylinder

In 1939, Kanemitsu and Nojima considered the majority of available test data and modified equation 7.10 to bring it into better agreement with experiments; - within the range of *H/R* greater than *0.1* but less than *1.5* and *R/t* greater than *500* but less than *3000*:

$$f_x / E = (0.16 (t/H)^{1.3}) + (9 (t/R)^{1.6}) \quad \text{..........................} 7.11$$

While equation 7.11 (plotted in Figure 7.8) is in better agreement with experimental results than equation 7.10, it must be regarded as being purely empirical if only by virtue of the odd exponents.

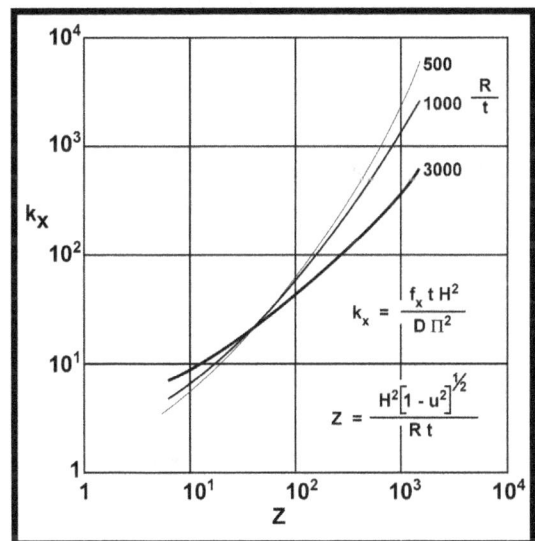
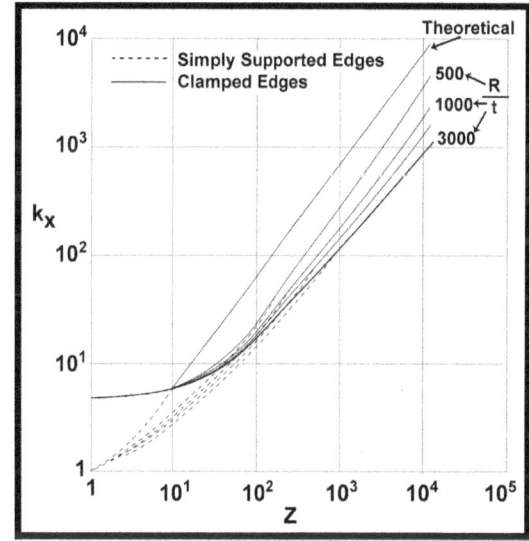

Figure 7.8: Empirical buckling formula (according to Kanemitsu and Nojima)

Figure 7.9: Critical axial stress coefficient (according to Batdorf et al.)

For the purpose of extending the range of validity of the empirical results existing at that time Batdorf et al. (1947) plotted the test data in terms of the two principal parameters of the thin-walled cylinder theory prevailing at that time.

$$k_x = (f_x t H^2) / (D \pi^2) \quad \text{..} 7.12$$

$$Z = (H^2 / (R t))(1 - u^2)^{0.5} \quad \text{..} 7.13$$

where: $D = (E t^3) / (12 (1 - u^2))$

The authors presented a number of curves for individual *R/t* ratios on the assumption that for long cylinders this ratio is a reasonable indicator of the initial imperfections of the cylinder. For the critical stresses of long cylinders these curves were based on experimental data, while theoretical results were used to supplement the test data for the purpose of ascertaining the critical stress of very short cylinders (Figure 7.9). The authors (Batdorf et al. 1947) stated the following conclusions:

- For long cylinders the buckling stress is considerably below that predicted by theory, the degree of discrepancy depending on the *R/t* ratio in each case.

- For very short cylinders the values of the critical stresses approach those for flat plates. In these cases the agreement between theoretical and experimental results is known to be good.

- As shown in Figure 7.9, for large values of *Z* the curves for k_x become straight lines given by the formula:

$$k_x = 1.15 (C Z) \quad \quad \quad \quad \quad \quad \quad \quad \quad \quad \quad \quad \quad \quad \quad \quad 7.14$$

In equation 7.14 the value of *C* depends on the ratio *R/t*, as shown in Figure 7.10. Batdorf proposed the use of equation 7.14 whenever the length of cylinder is greater than *0.75 R*.

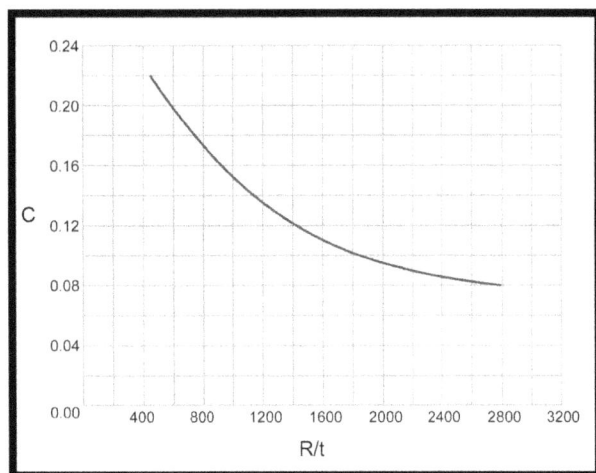
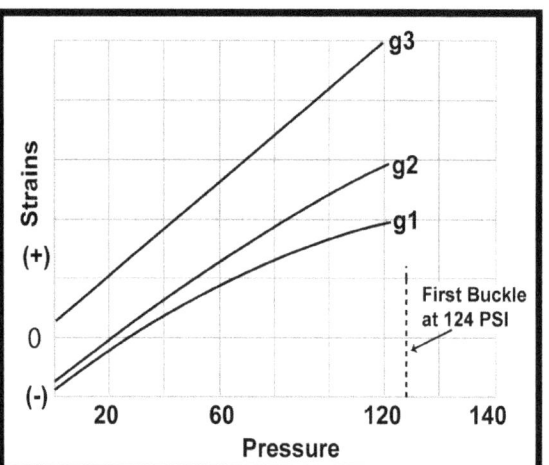

Figure 7.10: Relationship between *C* and *R/t* (according to Batdorf et al.)

Figure 7.11: Pressure strain curves (according to Fung and Sechler)

7.3.5 The Plastic Buckling Theory

The earliest developments in the plastic buckling of plates and shells are well documented by Timoshenko and Gere (1961) and it is not intended to reiterate their summary here. Over a 10-year period from 1938 to 1949 Bijlaard (1938, 1947, 1949) published a series of theoretical generalizations of Engesser's (1898) tangent modulus theory for the plastic buckling of plates and shells. He concluded that for the case of a cylindrical shell under axial compression the circumferential (i.e., diamond shaped) wave mode of buckling requires a higher load than the axisymmetrical mode, and that loads predicted by a deformation theory of plasticity agreed fairly well with experiments.

In 1956 Gerard conducted a much broader study on this subject and reached essentially the same conclusions (Allinikov 1960). A few years later Lee (1962) attempted to bring the predictions of an incremental theory, which assumed that incremental stress-strain relations are essential for an accurate description of irreversible plastic behavior, into closer agreement with test results (Batterman 1965). He considered the effects of initial imperfections on the loading process and the non-linear relationship between strain and displacement. It is somewhat unfortunate that Lee assumed a circumferential wave mode of initial imperfections, although the majority of his test specimen buckled in an axisymmetrical mode.

Although available evidence (Drucker and Onat 1954, Batterman 1965) pointed to the validity of adopting an incremental theory, predictions of buckling stresses using this theory often bear little resemblance to the buckling stresses observed during experiments. On the other hand, the predictions made by a deformation theory are generally good. This apparent paradoxical situation was examined by Onat and Drucker (1953), who demonstrated that this discrepancy could be due to very small and therefore unavoidable, initial imperfections in the shape of the shell. Accordingly, the authors explained that observed plastic buckling loads are maximum loads corresponding to some geometrical imperfection or dynamic disturbance during testing. Obviously, the classical condition of neutral equilibrium of the idealized perfect system under constant load defines a different critical load. Drucker (1954, 1960) claimed that the relevance of the latter to the observed buckling load is not always apparent.

In his 1965 paper dealing with trends in the theoretical analysis of the buckling of shells Batterman suggested that classical stability concepts are more useful in predicting the buckling loads under axial compression of thick-walled cylinders (i.e., R/t less than *60*). He agreed that for thin-walled cylinders it is necessary to include initial imperfections in the analysis and employ Shanley's (1947) method of considering the growth of deflection disturbances along the loading path until a maximum load is reached.

7.3.6 Pressurized Monocoque Cylinders

Some of the earliest work concerning the effect of internal pressure on the critical buckling stress of thin-walled cylinders under axial compression was performed by Prescott (1946) in 1924, who proposed the dimensionless parameter:

$$P' = (P/E)(R/t)^2 \quad \text{...} 7.15$$

Equation 7.15 indicates a parabolic increase in the critical buckling stress. Conversely, the results of an extensive study published by Flügge (1932), based on the small deflection theory current at that time, indicated a negligible effect of the internal pressure on the buckling load. Subsequently, based on the obvious contradictions of experimental results with Flügge's (1932) conclusions, Lo et al. (1951) developed a large deflection theory using the methods of Von Karman and Tsien (1941) to show that the buckling load increases with increasing values of *P'* to an upper limit of *P'=0.169* and then remains constant for values of *P'* greater than *0.169*. It was found that this theoretical stress for large values of *P'* is the classical buckling load of the small deflection theory (Fung and Sechler 1957). While experimental values were again found to be lower than those predicted by the theory, these discrepancies were contended to be the result of initial imperfections of the cylinder wall.

It has been observed by all experimenters in this field that diamond shaped buckling patterns are typical for compressive buckling in monocoque (i.e., unstiffened) cylinders. However, internal pressure will change this buckling pattern by decreasing the axial and circumferential wavelengths, not necessarily in the same proportion. The diamonds at low internal pressure are found to be approximately square, while those at higher internal pressure are significantly elongated sometimes with a wave length in the circumferential direction ten times longer than a wave in the axial direction. Fung and Sechler (1957) observed that the ring shaped buckles that occur at high internal pressures generally resemble the sinusoidal waves assumed in the classical small deflection theory. The typical load-strain curves derived by these authors are shown in Figure 7.11. It can be clearly seen that in places on the cylinder wall far away from the diamond buckles the load-strain relationship remains nearly linear at the critical stage and in the post-buckling range.

$$P' = (P/E)(R/t)^2 \quad \text{...7.15}$$

$$f_x' = (f_x/E)(R/t) \quad \text{...7.16}$$

In terms of a critical load P_{cr} the dimensionless stress parameter f_x' may be expressed as follows:

$$f_x' = (P_{cr})/(2\pi E t^2) \quad \text{...7.16a}$$

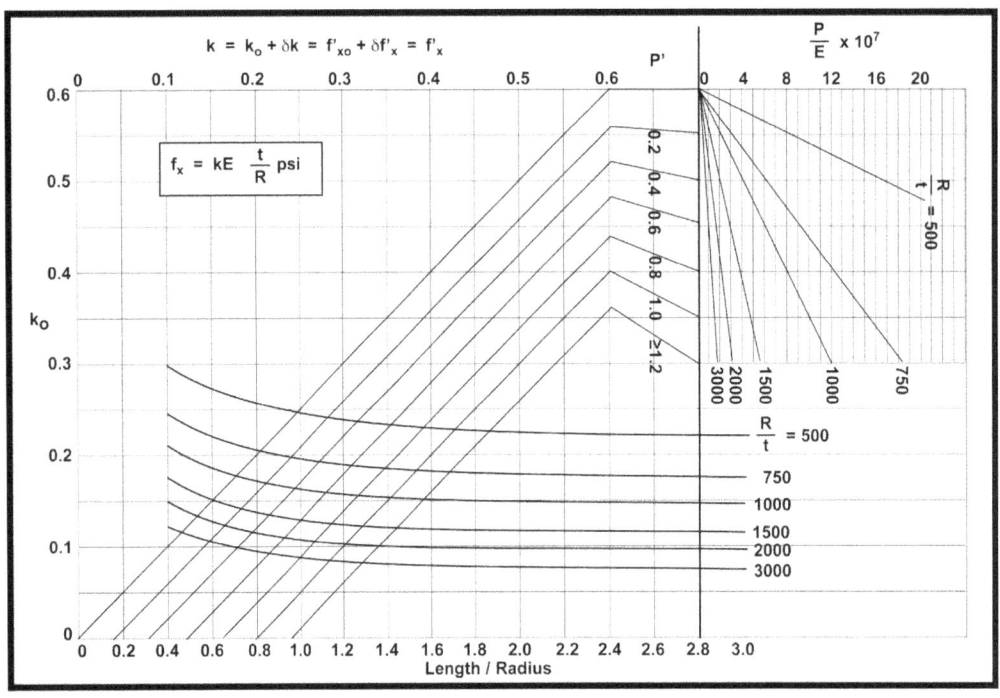

Figure 7.12: Nomogram for the determination of the buckling stress of thin-walled cylinders (according to Fung and Sechler)

Equations 7.15 and 7.16 are identical with the two dimensionless parameters introduced by Lo et al. (1951). Subsequent to their investigation Fung and Sechler (1957) proposed the following design method for thin-walled cylinders subjected to both internal pressure and axial load (Figure 7.12):

1. Determination of the critical buckling coefficient (k_o) for zero internal pressure using Kanemitsu and Nojima's (1939) modification of Ballerstedt and Wagner's (1936) empirical equation.

$$k_o = (R/t)[(0.16(t/H)^{1.3}) + (9(t/R)^{1.6})] \quad \quad \quad 7.17$$

2. For values of *P'=0 to 1.20* a linear increase in *∂k'* (i.e., *∂k'= k'-k_o'*) from zero at *P'=1.20* was recommended.

3. For all values of *P'* greater than *1.20* Fung and Sechler suggested the use of *∂k'=0.229*.

Two examples of the utilization of the Fung and Sechler's nomogram (Figure 7.12) for the design of pressurized thin-walled cylinders under axial compression follow below.

Example 1: Consider a monocoque cylindrical section that has the following dimensions and properties:

    R = 36 IN   H = 72 IN
    t = 0.03125 IN (or 1/32 IN)   E = 10,000,000 psi
    P = 10 psig   hoop stress = 11,520 psi
thus: R/t = 1,152   H/R = 2.0   P/E = 10×10^{-7}

Entering the right hand portion of the nomogram (Figure 7.12) with *P/E=0.0000010* and dropping to the *R/t=1152* line we obtain *P'=1.15*. This value is transferred to the left hand side of the curve. Then going from *H/R=2.0* vertically to the *R/t=1152* curve we intersect the *P'=1.15* line horizontally at a value of *k=0.365*. If so desired the value of k_o can also be found from the extreme left hand scale that gives $k_o=0.145$, indicating that *∂k* due to internal pressure is equal to *0.22*. The critical axial buckling stress is therefore given by:

$$f_x = (0.365 \times 10000000 \times 1 / 1152) = \textbf{3,168 psi}$$

Example 2: Consider another unstiffened cylindrical section of the following dimensions and properties:

    R = 24 IN   H = 60 IN
    t = 0.01563 IN (or 1/64 IN)   E = 30,000,000 psi
    P = 20 psig   hoop stress = 30,710 psi
thus: R/t = 1,536   H/R = 2.5   P/E = 6×10^{-7}

From the right hand portion of the nomogram (Figure 7.12) we see that the intersection of the *R/t=1536* line with the *P/E=0.0000006* line will occur at a value of *P'* greater than *1.20*. Therefore, the *P'=1.20* is used to complete the solution. Going from *H/R=2.5* to *R/t=1536*, then horizontally to *P'=1.20* we find that $k_o=1.12$ and *k=0.36* giving a value of *∂k=0.24* due to internal pressure. The critical design buckling stress is therefore given by:

$$f_x = (0.36 \times 30000000 \times 1 / 1536) = \textbf{7,029 psi}$$

In 1957 Harris et al. recommended a statistical probability approach, leading to a semi-empirical procedure that enables the determination of the critical buckling stress based on knowledge of the cylinder geometry alone. On the assumption that the load at which buckling of a thin-walled monocoque cylinder occurs may be considered as ultimate (i.e., since no further load-carrying capacity remains) the authors developed 90% probability curves. This concept places the onus on the designer to decide what probability is appropriate based on the intrinsic design criteria of a particular structure.

7.3.7 Conclusions and Terms of Reference

It is apparent that the compressive buckling behavior of unpressurized monocoque cylinders may be considered in four groups based on the relative slenderness (i.e., height to radius relationship) of any specific cylindrical shell. According to Batterman (1965) and others the effective height to be considered in this context is the physical height of the cylinder.

Short Cylinders tend to follow the pattern of flat plate columns, where buckling occurs in a sinusoidal wave form. The theoretical value of the buckling coefficient (k_x) is given as a function of the geometric parameter (Z). Theoretically, the short cylinder range will occur at $Z=0$, in which case for simply supported end conditions $k_x=1.12$ approximately and for fixed end conditions $k_x=4.12$ approximately.

Transition Cylinders tend to behave somewhere between the short and long cylinder ranges depending on length and end fixing conditions.

Long Cylinders buckle into the characteristic diamond pattern and the critical buckling stress is generally independent of both the length of the cylinder and the end fixing conditions. Minimizing equation 7.5 in respect to the parameter $(m^2 + \beta^2)^2/m^2$ reduces the buckling coefficient (k_x) to:

$$k_x = 0.702\, Z \quad\quad\quad\quad\quad 7.6$$

Toward the lower limit of the long cylinder range (and within the transition cylinder range) the buckling coefficient (k_x) for simply supported end conditions can be determined by substituting the limiting values of $\beta=0$ and $m=1$ into equation 7.5, to yield:

$$k_x = 1 + 0.123\, Z^2 \quad\quad\quad\quad\quad 7.6a$$

Very Long Cylinders buckle by overall column instability without local buckling of the cylinder wall.

The fact that the buckling of a cylinder under axial compression, lateral hydrostatic pressure, and torsion involves substantially the same parameters is not a coincidence but a direct result of the underlying differential equation (equation 7.3). This equation implies that when the requirement of an integer number of circumferential waves is deleted the six variables H (actual length of cylinder), R (radius of cylinder), t (wall thickness), E (modulus of elasticity), u (Poisson's ratio), and f_x (compressive stress) may be combined into two non-dimensional parameters, namely: k_x describing the stress condition; and, Z describing the geometry.

$$k_x = (f_x\, t\, H^2)/(D\, \pi^2) \quad\quad\quad\quad\quad 7.12$$

$$Z = (H^2/(R\, t))(1 - u^2)^{0.5} \quad\quad\quad\quad\quad 7.13$$

The critical stress of an unpressurized cylinder may therefore be represented by a single curve relating these two non-dimensional parameters, provided that the number of circumferential waves may be regarded as continuously variable (Batdorf 1947). As shown in Figure 7.13, this restriction becomes significant for very large values of Z (i.e., long cylinders) in which the curve may split into a number of curves for cylinders of different values of R/t. According to Batdorf (1947), if the small correction due to Poisson's ratio (u) is neglected then a direct physical significance can be assigned to Z when it is of small magnitude (i.e., in the case of short cylinders).

$$Z = (H^2)/(8Rt)$$

Batdorf (1947) also proposed the following equations for the buckling coefficients in the axial and circumferential directions, applicable to long cylinders within the limits stated:

$$k_x = 0.072\,Z \quad\ldots\ldots\ldots\text{ for } Z > 3 \text{ and } Z < (6R^2)(1-u^2)/t^2$$

$$k_y = 1.04\,Z^{0.5} \quad\ldots\ldots\ldots\text{ for } Z > 100 \text{ and } Z < (5R^2)(1-u^2)/t^2$$

As discussed previously, experimental investigations by Prescott (1924), Lo et al. (1951), Fisher (1965), and others have shown that the critical buckling stress of thin-walled cylinders is significantly increased by internal pressure. Subsequent theoretical studies by Lo et al. (1951) and Tsai-Chen (1967) determined that the effect of internal pressure on the buckling of cylindrical shells under axial compression depends on the dimensionless parameters:

$$P' = (P/E)/(R/t)^2 \quad\ldots\ldots\ldots\ldots\ldots\ldots\ldots\ldots\ldots\ldots\ldots\ldots\ldots\ldots\ldots\ldots 7.15$$

$$f_x' = (f_x/E)(R/t) \quad\ldots\ldots\ldots\ldots\ldots\ldots\ldots\ldots\ldots\ldots\ldots\ldots\ldots\ldots\ldots\ldots 7.16$$

This determination was further extended by Lo et al. (1951) with the finding that the buckling coefficient (k_x) increases from the Tsien (1942) value of $k_x=0.375$ at zero pressure to $k_x=0.605$ at $P'=0.169$. The relevant large deflection curve is shown in Figure 7.13 (Harris et al. 1957). It is apparent that similar to the situation with unpressurized cylinders, substantial discrepancies also exist between theory and experiment for pressurized cylinders. For example, in the region of maximum critical stress the experimental value of the buckling coefficient (k_x) varies from $k_x=0.3$ to $k_x=0.585$, while theory predicts $k_x=0.605$.

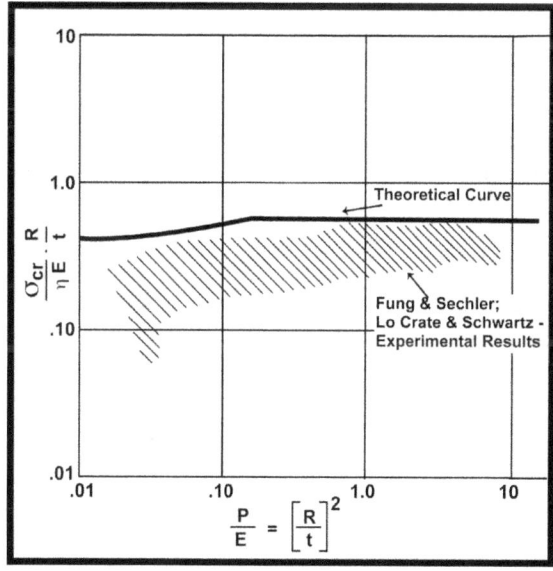

Figure 7.13: Large Deflection Theory curve (according to Harris et al. 1957)

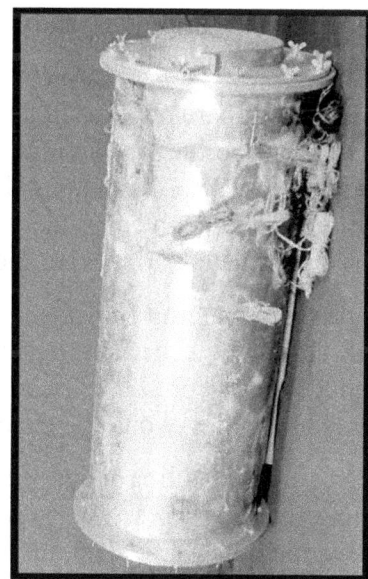

Figure 7.14: Test cylinder with strain gauges (according to Pohl 1970)

Plastic buckling theories relating to thin-walled cylinders may be categorized into three fundamental groups, namely: incremental theories (Handelman et al. 1947, Drucker 1951); slip theories (Batdorf and Budiansky 1949, Lin 1954); and, deformation theories (Hencky 1925, Nadai 1950, Handelman and Warner 1954). It has been shown by Handelman and Warner (1954) that the incremental theories and the deformation theories agree precisely for proportional loading. On the other hand, the results predicted by these two theories for the inelastic buckling of plates and shells differ considerably (Lee 1962).

The available experimental results (Stowell 1948, Bijlaard 1949) seem to agree best with the deformation theories. Yet the deformation theories do not satisfy the conditions of continuity of all components of stress and displacement on the boundary between the elastic and the plastic regions (Handelman and Prager 1949). Nevertheless, according to Budiansky (1959) and Lee (1962) this objection does not rule out the application of the deformation theories to the plastic buckling of cylindrical shells under axial compression. In an analytical and experimental study published by Lee in 1962 the author concluded that the plastic stress-strain relationship given by the deformation theories leads to a fairly accurate prediction of the buckling strength, but fails to provide a correct description of post-buckling behavior.

7.4 An Additional Experimental Investigation

In 1968-9 the author conducted a limited experimental investigation into the buckling of thin-walled cylindrical shells with and without internal pressure (Pohl 1970 Section C). These explorations were based on the following terms of reference:

A. To ascertain the degree of reduction of compressive stresses in loaded cylinders during and after pressurization.

B. To establish the ultimate compressive loads of thin-walled cylinders for a limited range of internal pressures, and compare these values with stress contours obtained in non-destruction tests.

To allow for the comparison of ultimate loads, stress contours based on strain gauge readings were drawn to describe the stress conditions found in the curved walls of thin-walled cylinders under the combined action of an external axial compression load and internal pressure. In view of the dual nature of the problem under investigation (i.e., determination of stress patterns and comparison with ultimate loads) experiments on test cylinders were performed in two stages.

Stage 1: Stress patterns prevalent in the curved surface of monocoque cylinders were measured (utilizing electric strain gauges) under the action of axial compression load, with and without internal pressure. Load increments were generally well below the ultimate load at which buckling would be expected to occur.

Stage 2: Critical buckling loads were obtained for monocoque cylinders held at various constant internal pressures. Two types of test specimen were tested to destruction, but no strain measurements were taken during these ultimate load tests.

7.4.1 Design of the Test Cylinders

The test cylinders were manufactured from tin plate with a high yield point (i.e., 58,000 psi.) so that no plasticity corrections would be required for those measurements that led to the development of stress contour maps.

Test Specimen Type 1: Cylinders were of *9.48 IN* internal diameter, made of *0.01 IN* thick *MRT 5 CA* grade tin plate in heights of *9.0 IN*, *18.0 IN*, *30.0 IN* and *48.0 IN*. The cylinders were manufactured by soft soldering in the longitudinal direction, with one joint per cylinder. As shown in Figure 7.14, the two ends were attached to rings that provided a seal for the fluid under pressure but did not form part of the loading system. Instead, the load was transmitted to the cylinder by means of a loading cage resting on a ball-bearing. End assemblies could be removed from one cylinder and reused in subsequent tests (Figures 7.15 and 7.16) even if such tests involved ultimate loads.

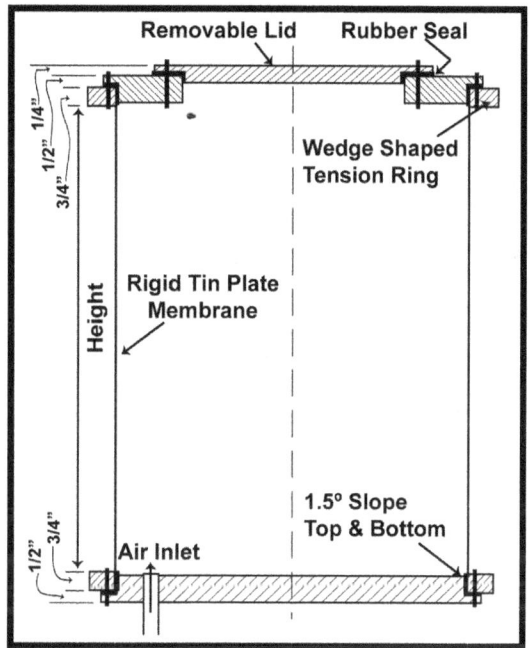 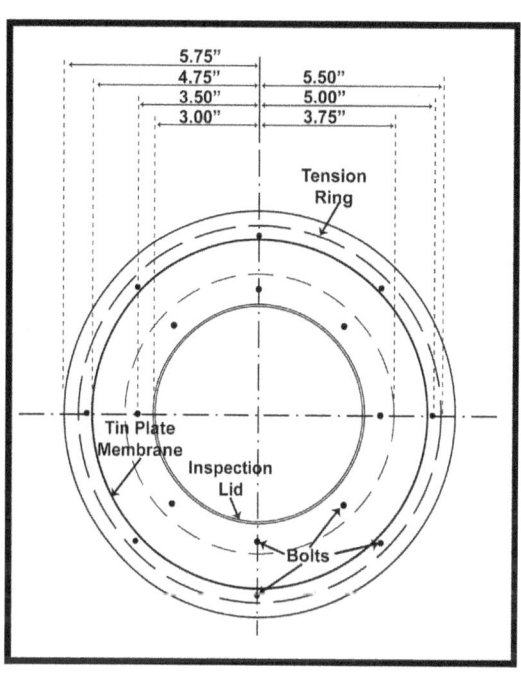

Figure 7.15: Test specimen type 1 section   Figure 7.16: Test specimen 1 top seal

Specimen dimensions and material constants were calculated to be:

external column diameter =	9.50 IN
internal column diameter =	9.48 IN
column circumference =	10.21 IN
cylinder wall thickness (mean) =	0.01 IN
cross-sectional wall material area =	0.24 SI
internal column area =	70.65 SI
height to diameter ratio of 9 IN high column =	0.95 (approx. 1)
height to diameter ratio of 18 IN high column =	1.89 (approx. 2)
height to diameter ratio of 30 IN high column =	3.16 (approx. 3)
height to diameter ratio of 48 IN high column =	5.05 (approx. 5)
moment of inertia =	2.69 IN^4
radius of gyration =	3.36 IN
modulus of section =	0.57 IN^3
material (tin plate) yield stress =	58,000 psi

material (tin plate) ultimate stress = 63,400 psi
modulus of elasticity = 28,100,000 psi
Poisson's ratio = 0.316

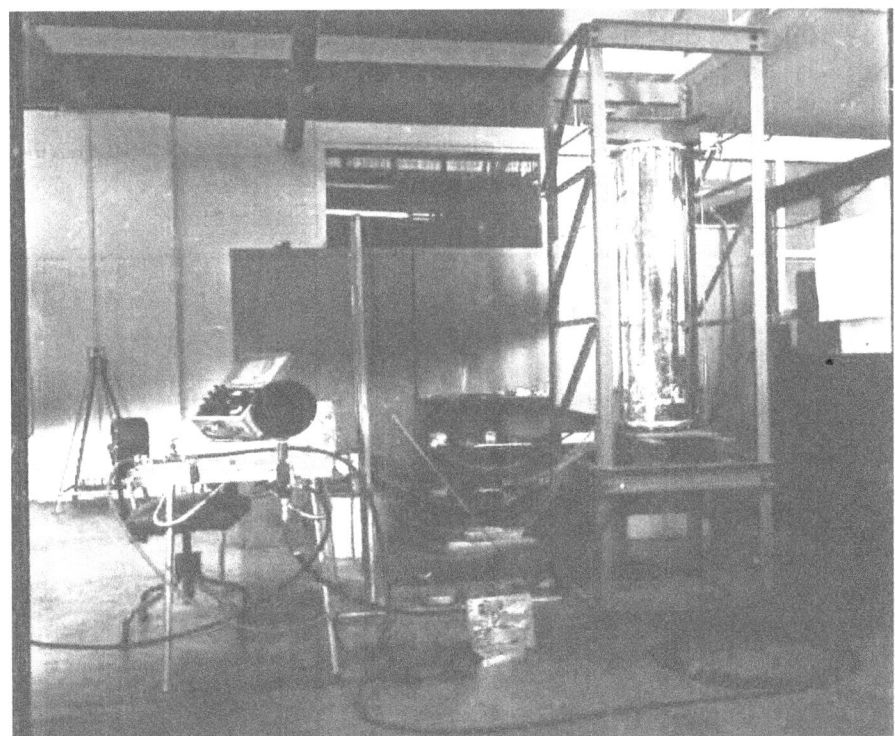

Figure 7.17: Test rig for test specimen type 1

Test Specimen Type 2: Cylinders were of *3.23 IN* internal diameter, *6.75 IN* in height, and made from *0.01 IN* thick *MRT 5 CA* grade tin plate. Commercially available tins were fitted with a pressure inlet device that could be recovered after tests to destruction. Specimen dimensions and material constants were calculated to be:

external column diameter = 3.25 IN
internal column diameter = 3.23 IN
column circumference = 29.83 IN
cylinder wall thickness (mean) = 0.01 IN
cross-sectional wall material area = 0.10 SI
internal column area = 8.20 SI
height to diameter ratio of 6.8 IN high column = 2.09 (approx. 2)
moment of inertia = 1.13 IN^4
radius of gyration = 1.15 IN
modulus of section = 0.08 IN^3
material (tin plate) yield stress = 58,000 psi
material (tin plate) ultimate stress = 63,400 psi
modulus of elasticity = 28,100,000 psi
Poisson's ratio = 0.316

Cylinders were tested as free-standing columns by means of axial dead-loads, utilizing a loading cage and hydraulic ram. The position of a typical test specimen type 1 column in the test stand is shown in Figure 7.17. Each of the cylinders was rigidly bolted to the testing platform at the lower end and separated from the loading cage (i.e., loading beam) at the upper end by means of a ball-bearing.

Pressure and manometer leads were placed in the lower end plate of each cylinder, thus allowing pressurization by compressed air. During tests the internal pressure was measured by a mercury manometer and the compression load was measured by a pressure gauge attached to the hydraulic jack assembly. The strains were recorded with standard strain gauge equipment on a *Philips IM 2124* strain bridge.

In view of the theoretical discussion presented by Batdorf (1947) it appears that the effect on the buckling stresses of boundary conditions is unimportant if warping normal to the curved edges of the cylinder is prevented. Accordingly, with bulkheads in place the circumferential displacement for both ends of the test cylinders was zero, while the cylinders were free to warp in the axial direction. The end-fixing conditions of the cylindrical surface could then be described as being simply supported.

7.4.2 The Test Procedure

A total of 11 unpressurized and 20 pressurized cylinders were tested to destruction, while stress contours were drawn for 4 cylinders of varying heights under a number of external and internal loading conditions.

Ultimate load tests:
- 5 cols. test specimen type 1   height = 18 IN   pressure = 0 psig
- 2 cols. test specimen type 1   height = 18 IN   pressure = 5 psig
- 2 cols. test specimen type 1   height = 18 IN   pressure = 10 psig
- 2 cols. test specimen type 1   height = 18 IN   pressure = 15 psig
- 2 cols. test specimen type 1   height = 18 IN   pressure = 20 psig
- 6 cols. test specimen type 2   height = 6.8 IN pressure = 0 psig
- 6 cols. test specimen type 2   height = 6.8 IN pressure = 50 psig
- 6 cols. test specimen type 2   height = 6.8 IN pressure = 100 psig

In these tests, columns were firstly pressurized and then the axial compression load applied at a steady (continuously increasing) rate until failure occurred. Buckling was always observed to be instantaneous (explosive) in general agreement with the Durchschlag (snap-through) buckling phenomenon (Jones 1966).

Stress measurements:
- test specimen type 1   height = 9 IN   pressure = 0 to 18 psig
- test specimen type 1   height = 18 IN   pressure = 0 to 18 psig
- test specimen type 1   height = 30 IN   pressure = 0 to 18 psig
- test specimen type 1   height = 48 IN   pressure = 0 to 18 psig

Axial compression loads were applied in *180 LB* increments to a maximum of *1260 LB*, with strain readings taken after each incremental loading at eight points on the same level in the longitudinal and circumferential directions. The maximum axial load of *1260 LB* was retained while the column specimen was pressurized internally in *3 psig* increments to *18 psig*. Strain measurements were again recorded at each of these stages and subsequently during deflation and incremental release of the compression load. This process was repeated for a single strain-gauge rosette in turn at each level. In this way good overall accuracy was achieved, with strain gauges often returning to within 5 micro-strains of the original zero reading after 13 separate loading stages (Pohl 1970 Appendix 1C.).

During these tests deflections were measured in two 90° directions at the free end of each column. Since the deflections were always found to be less than *0.05 IN* it was concluded that the primary failure mechanism of these cylinders would have been local buckling (i.e., Durchschlag) rather than Euler buckling[7]. This observation further suggested that multi-story, air-supported, rigid membrane buildings will also be subject to local buckling failure rather than overall buckling[8]. However, this may not necessarily apply to fluid-inflated structural members such as thin-walled rigid membrane columns for which the height to diameter could exceed 10:1.

7.4.3 Analysis of the Experimental Results

Typical stress contours obtained for test specimen type 1 are shown in Figure 7.18 for the first level of strain gauges. These stress contour graphs were plotted in accordance with biaxial strain readings converted to single stress values on the basis of the following biaxial strain relationships (Hartog 1939, Pohl 1970 Appendix 2C):

$$\text{circumferential stress} = E \, (\, \varepsilon_l + (u)\varepsilon_c \,) \quad \text{...7.18}$$

$$\text{longitudinal stress} = E \, (\, \varepsilon_l + (u)\varepsilon_c \,) \, / \, (\, 1 - u^2 \,) \quad \text{.............................7.19}$$

These calculations were subsequently repeated to produce similar stress contour graphs for an eccentric load (i.e., *0.5 IN* eccentricity) under otherwise identical loading conditions (Figure 7.19). The strain gauge rosettes were attached at least *4.5 IN* (i.e., one cylinder radius) distant from the cylinder ends. In this manner stress concentrations due to edge restraint were avoided[9].

Although the difference between the highest and lowest stresses encountered in any one column (Tables 7.1 and 7.2) is not significantly affected by a load eccentricity of *0.5 IN*, when we inspect the stress levels under maximum compression load in Figures 7.18 and 7.19 (full line) there is an apparent tendency for stress concentrations to be slightly emphasized when the test specimen is subjected to an eccentric compression load (e.g., compare strain gauge V_6 in Figures 7.18 and 7.19). However, as soon as the columns are pressurized internally quite irregular stress patterns appear. While there are considerable stress concentrations present in all columns at this stage, these seem to be generally independent of the initial stress pattern that developed under the action of compression only. Indeed, in certain areas the compressive stress increased during

---

[7] The largest height to diameter ratio of any of the tested cylinders was 5 (i.e., H/D ~ 5:1).

[8] In these buildings in which the internal environment is pressurized, the physiological pressure limit of around *14.5 psig* limits the building height to about *150 FT* (i.e., *12* stories at *12 FT* story height). Accordingly, the height to diameter ratio of these buildings is unlikely to exceed 5:1.

[9] Comparison of strain readings taken at this level and a second level (i.e., *10.5 IN* from the end) indicated that there were no significant differences in strain readings between these two levels. It was therefore concluded that if stress concentrations occurred during any of the loading sequences, then these were not due to the effects of end restraint. Moreover, before the commencement of any test each cylinder was subjected to increasing hydrostatic pressure until either one or both of the bulk heads began to slide away from the column shell. It was noted that when this separation occurred the actual movement was visibly evenly distributed around the circumference, thereby suggesting that the friction ring used to join the bulkhead to the cylindrical wall (Figure 7.15) was able to evenly distribute the loads applied to the bulkheads around the circumference of the shell.

pressurization, while in other areas tension fields were created. For example, strain gauge V_2 indicates a *4000 psi* stress reduction during pressurization while gauge V_8 indicates an increase in compressive stress of *1000 psi* after internal pressurization to *18 psig*. Similar situations occurred in all columns quite independently, regardless of whether the load was axial or applied with a *0.5 IN* eccentricity.

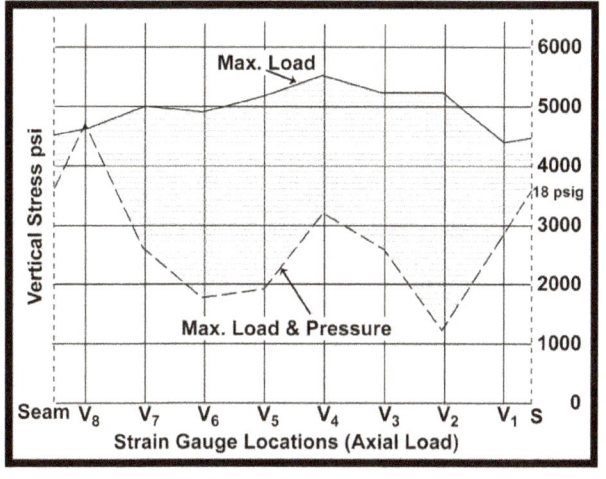 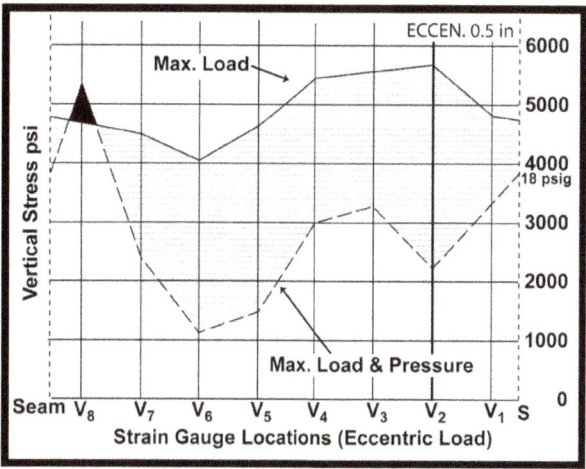

Figure 7.18: Stress contours under axial compression and internal pressure

Figure 7.19: Stress contours under eccentric compression and internal pressure

It was observed during the loading of the test specimen that under the action of small compressive loads the stresses tended to be quite evenly distributed throughout the column envelope. However, as the magnitude of the compressive load increases small stress concentrations begin to develop. At approximately 5000 psi (i.e., about 35% of the critical buckling stress) local stress concentrations become quite pronounced (Tables 7.1 and 7.2).

Table 7.1: Comparison of highest and lowest stresses under axial load

Column Height	Highest Stress (f_{max})	Lowest Stress (f_{min})	((f_{max}- f_{min})/f_{max}) x 100
9 IN	5600 psi	4500 psi	19%
18 IN	5700 psi	3600 psi	37%
30 IN	6900 psi	4800 psi	30%
48 IN	5600 psi	4900 psi	13%
Average:	5950 psi	4450 psi	25%

Table 7.2: Comparison of highest and lowest stresses under eccentric load

Column Height	Highest Stress (f_{max})	Lowest Stress (f_{min})	((f_{max}- f_{min})/f_{max}) x 100
9 IN	5700 psi	4100 psi	28%
18 IN	6100 psi	3600 psi	41%
30 IN	7200 psi	4600 psi	36%
48 IN	5800 psi	4900 psi	16%
Average:	6200 psi	4450 psi	31%

For reasons mentioned previously, these stress concentrations cannot be attributed to the effects of end restraint, although stresses induced by edge support could have played a minor role as reported by Stein (1962). It seems more likely that small imperfections in the form of deviations from perfect curvature, variations in thickness, and so on, which may not be apparent during a visual inspection, are responsible for initiating stress concentrations that will ultimately lead to localized instability of the cylindrical surface. The long thin-walled cylinder subjected to axial compression has been in the past described as the most imperfection sensitive shell structure (Budiansky and Hutchinson 1966). The stress contours represented in Figures 7.18 and 7.19 seem to be a further validation of this supposition.

However, the fact that the stress pattern under combined compression load (*1260 LB*) and internal pressure (*18 psig*) is quite unrelated to the stress pattern under compression load alone merits further discussion. Again, it can be argued that the irregular stress patterns under the action of internal pressure were not due to uneven edge support of the cylindrical shell. The test cylinders were pressurized while being subjected to a maximum compression load of *1260 LB*.[10] The maximum internal pressure was purposely chosen to be equal to the compression load. In the case of a flexible membrane wall this would have led to a zero stress condition in the cylinder wall (see Chapter 2, Section 2.5.1 and Chapter 4, Section 4.2). However, in the case of the rigid membrane wall of the test specimen the actual stress reduction due to internal pressure was found to be much less than would have occurred in the case of a flexible membrane wall. Therefore, the nature of the transfer of tensile forces from the bulkheads to the cylindrical shell is irrelevant to this discussion.

Although the stress pattern induced by internal pressure is apparently quite independent of the developing pattern of stress concentrations observed during compression loading, it was perhaps not surprising to find that each test column had a unique stress pattern. On comparing Figures 7.18 and 7.19, we find that there is basically no difference between the axial and eccentric loading condition, for any one column. Furthermore, stress patterns were repeatable despite the wide range of stresses (Table 7.3) encountered in each column.

Table 7.3: Comparison of stresses with combined axial load and internal pressure

Column Height	Highest Stress (f_{max})	Lowest Stress (f_{min})	((f_{max}- f_{min})/f_{max}) x 100
9 IN	4700 psi	1200 psi	75%
18 IN	5400 psi	1200 psi	78%
30 IN	6700 psi	-30 psi	101%
48 IN	5600 psi	1100 psi	80%
Average:	5600 psi	870 psi	84%

Two possible conclusions may be drawn from these results. First, the initial imperfections in the cylindrical wall provide a convenient explanation of the stress distributions observed in the test cylinders, especially since it was found that a unique stress pattern seemed to exist for each specimen. Second, there was little variation in the average reduction in compressive stress due to internal pressure among the four cylinders of the test specimen. The results obtained for all four cylinders are summarized in Figure 7.20, where the longitudinal stress has been plotted against

---

[10] Maximum internal pressure of *18 psig* acting on the underside of the top bulkhead of the test specimen creates an upward force of approximately *1260 LB* (i.e., *18 x 70.65 = 1271.7*).

the dual loading condition of axial or eccentric compressive load and internal pressure. For convenience these results are further tabulated in Table 7.4, which indicates that the reduction in compressive stress due to an internal pressure that is equal in magnitude to an externally applied compression load is approximately 50% (i.e., mean = 49.6%, standard deviation = 5.4%).

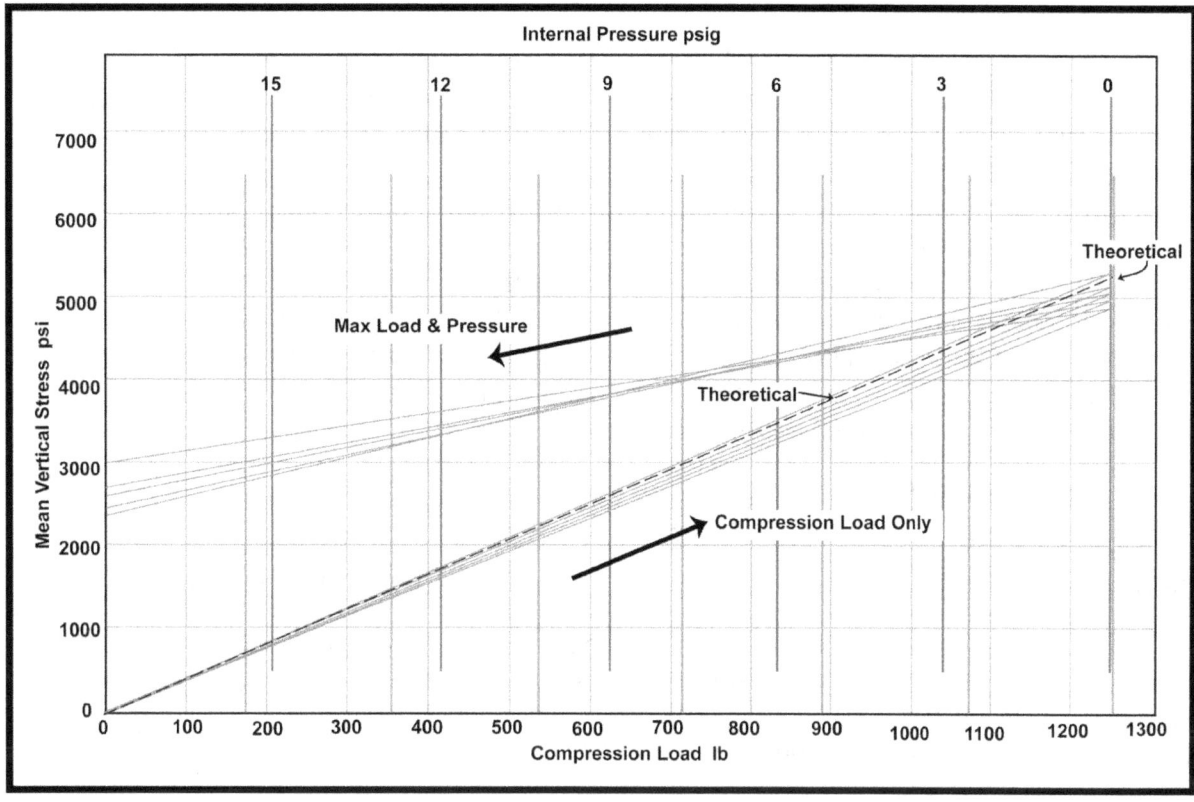

Figure 7.20: Summary of test results for cylinders under vertical load and internal pressure

Table 7.4: Mean compressive stress reduction under internal pressure

Test Cylinder Height	Vertical Load Eccentricity	Mean Stress No Pressure	Mean Stress With Pressure	Stress Reduction Due To Pressure
9 IN	0.0 IN	5100 psi	2600 psi	49%
9 IN	0.5 IN	5000 psi	2700 psi	46%
18 IN	0.0 IN	4900 psi	2800 psi	43%
18 IN	0.5 IN	5000 psi	2900 psi	42%
30 IN	0.0 IN	5400 psi	2300 psi	57%
30 IN	0.5 IN	5400 psi	2400 psi	55%
48 IN	0.0 IN	5200 psi	2500 psi	52%
48 IN	0.5 IN	5100 psi	2400 psi	53%
	Average:	5140 psi	2580 psi	50%

This relatively high correlation between test cylinders was obtained despite a number of minor changes in technique adopted during the fabrication of the cylindrical wall due to the height of each cylinder. It is thus very doubtful whether similar imperfections were initially present in each column shell. In fact, visual examination of columns before testing seemed to indicate slight localized deviations from perfect curvature of the cylindrical wall in some cylinders and not in others. Accordingly it may be suggested that although initial imperfections have a significant effect on the critical buckling stress of thin-walled cylindrical shells, the nature of the imperfections and the individual variations that are bound to occur in different cylinders are less critical.

The second part of this experimental investigation was concerned with the determination of ultimate loads (i.e., critical buckling stresses) of a number of thin-walled cylinders, similar to those used in the first part of the investigation. It was intended to establish whether or not the stress patterns observed previously could be used as a guide for predicting the critical buckling stresses of these cylinders. The experimental results obtained are tabulated in Table 7.5 for test specimen type 1 and in Table 7.6 for test specimen type 2. In all calculations made for the analysis of test data, the actual height of test cylinders was used in preference to the effective height of a normal free-standing column (i.e., $H_E=2H$). It was assumed that in cases where local buckling of the cylindrical shell occurs, the buckling pattern will be independent of the end-fixing conditions of the cylinder (i.e., as distinct from the boundary conditions of the cylindrical shell). The validity of this assumption had been previously recognized by Batterman (1965).

Table 7.5: Ultimate load test results for test specimen type 1 (height = 18 IN)

Internal Pressure	Ultimate Vertical Load	Mean Stress	k_x $[(f_x t H^2)/(D\pi^2)]$	P' $[(P/E)(R/t)^2]$	f_x' $[(f_x/E)(R/t)]$
0 psig	2,675 LB	11,300 psi	1515	(0.00)	(0.19)
5 psig	3,480 LB	14,500 psi	--	0.04	0.24
10 psig	4,180 LB	17,400 psi	--	0.08	0.29
15 psig	4,500 LB	18,000 psi	--	0.12	0.32
20 psig	4,950 LB	20,600 psi	--	0.16	0.35

where: R/t = 475; H/R = 3.79; Z = 6700; D = 2.44; and, R = 4.75

Table 7.6: Ultimate load test results for test specimen type 2 (height = 6.8 IN)

Internal Pressure	Ultimate Vertical Load	Mean Stress	k_x $[(f_x t H^2)/(D\pi^2)]$	P' $[(P/E)(R/t)^2]$	f_x' $[(f_x/E)(R/t)]$
0 psig	2,383 LB	23,800 psi	4500	(0.00)	(0.14)
50 psig	3,050 LB	30,500 psi	--	0.05	0.18
100 psig	3,317 LB	33,200 psi	--	0.09	0.19

where: R/t = 163; H/R = 4.14; Z = 2750; D = 2.44; and, R = 1.62

The occurrence of diamond shaped buckles was unmistakable for all test specimen of type 1, although ring shaped buckles with a rather small wave length appeared whenever the internal pressure was high. In the case of test specimen type 2 the diamond shaped buckling pattern was discernable at close inspection even though these cylinders tended to burst at the longitudinal seam whenever internal pressure was involved in the test.

Results for both specimen types 1 and 2 are plotted in Figure 7.21 based on the dimensionless parameters P' and f_x'. It is clearly indicated that the ultimate load-bearing capacity of these pressurized cylinders ranging in height to diameter ratio from 1 to 5 (i.e., H/D_i) is greatly influenced by internal pressure. In fact, in all of the test cases the presence of internal pressure increased the load-bearing capacity of the cylinders beyond the proportionate increase due to the product of the internal pressure and cross-sectional cylinder area (i.e., 353 LB for 5 psig, 707 LB for 10 psig, 1060 LB for 15 psig, and 1,413 LB for 20 psig).

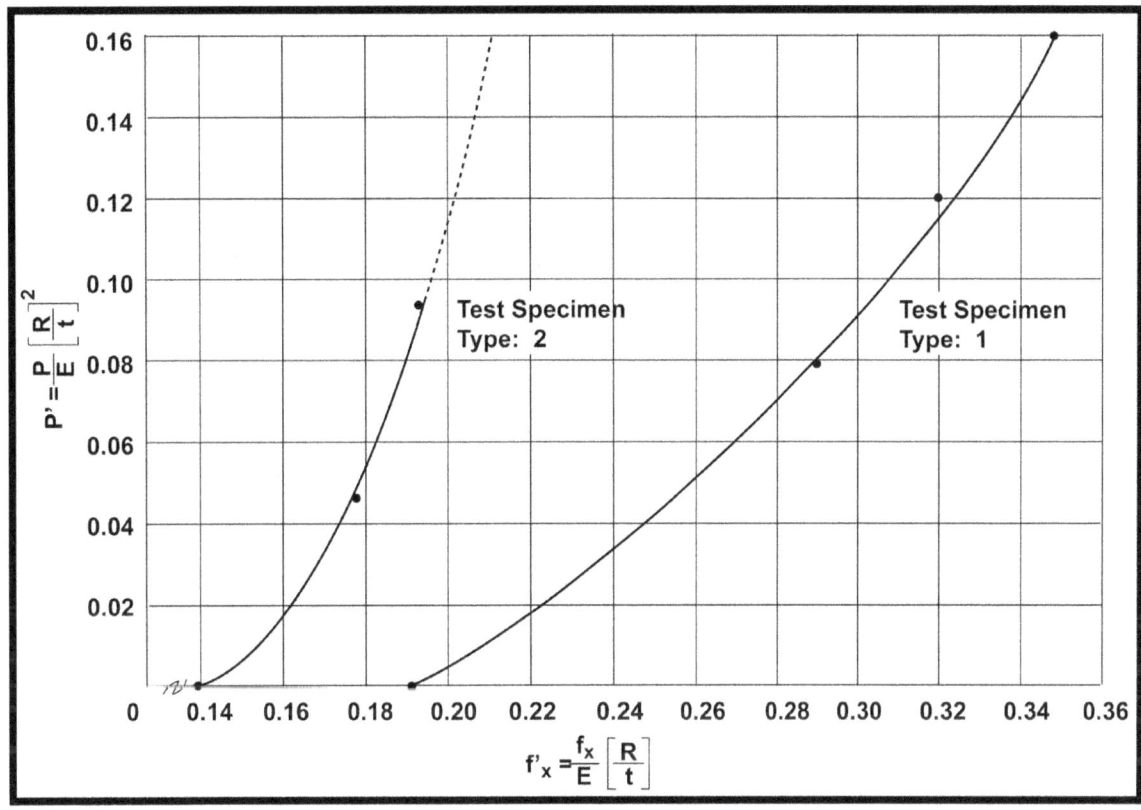

Figure 7.21: Summary of ultimate load results for test specimen type 1 and 2

7.4.4 Conclusions and Design Implications

For thin-walled cylinders, deformation theory combined with the classical stability theory appears to yield results that are generally not in good agreement with the available test data. The limited experimental investigation performed by the author and described in this chapter (Sections 7.4.2 and 7.4.3) indicates severe stress concentrations in the cylinder wall. The measured stresses plotted as contours in Figures 7.18 and 7.19 are representative of the largely unpredictable stress pattern found in the cylinder walls under the action of both axial load and internal pressure.

It can be argued with a reasonable degree of certainty that the irregular stress pattern is greatly influenced by both the condition of the cylinder wall[11] before the axial load is applied and the extent to which the wall material is able to evenly transmit this load from the point of application to the cylinder's supports. The latter is a function of the properties of the wall material; - in

---

[11] In terms of geometric deformations that may be so small that they cannot be visually detected, but yet are sufficient to significantly influence the distribution of stresses within the cylinder wall.

particular its ductility. While the addition of internal pressure reduces the actual compressive stresses it does not appear to change the distribution (i.e., location) of the stress concentrations around the circumference of the cylinder. In other words, the location of the local buckles that will eventually lead to the failure of the cylinder is largely predetermined by the original condition of the cylinder wall before the application of the axial load.

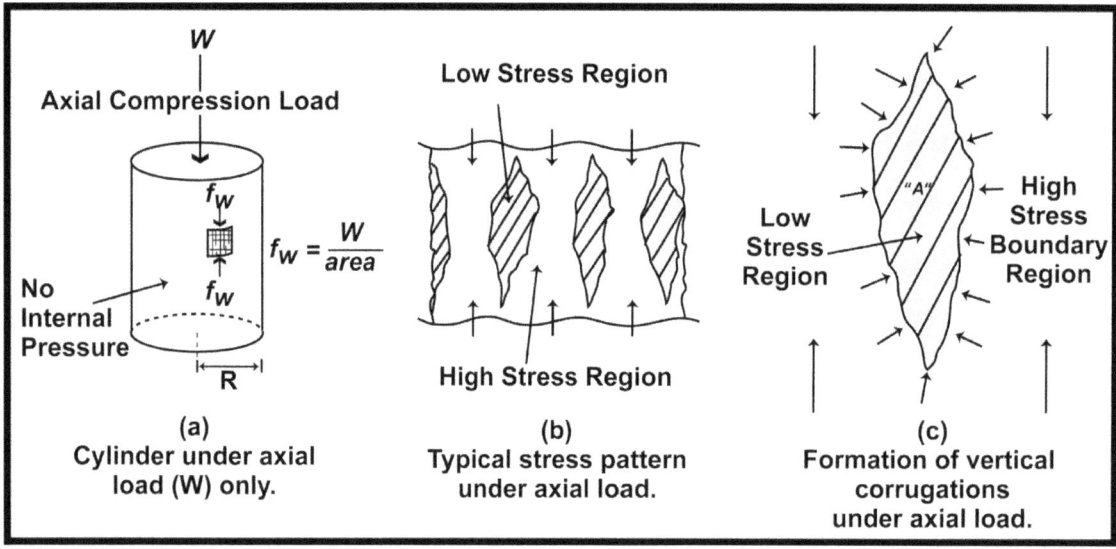

Figure 7.22: Diagrammatic representation of thin-walled cylinder under axial load

The complex failure mechanism of thin-walled cylindrical shells under axial and combined axial with internal pressure loading conditions may be explained in empirical terms by reference to Figures 7.22 and 7.23 (Pohl and Basiulis 1976). Let us consider a section of the rigid membrane wall (Figure 7.22(b) of an axially loaded short thin-walled cylindrical column (Figure 7.22(a)) under unpressurized conditions. Due to material imperfections and slight geometrical deviations the axial compression load (W) is not uniformly transmitted through the column wall to the support at the base. Instead, the rigid membrane wall assumes a corrugated configuration in which regions of low stress are separated by regions of high stress. The formation of corrugations tends to be on an irregular basis (Figure 7.22(c)) and is further facilitated by a tendency for the cylinder to expand under the imposed compression load. Under low stress conditions these geometric distortions are normally of a microscopic nature and therefore not discernable by the human eye. As the compression load is increased, geometric readjustments occur to accommodate the additional stresses until eventually one or more of the low stress regions lose their lateral stability and buckle either inward or outward.

More precisely, the vertical compression load (W) will produce not only vertical stresses, but also horizontal stresses in the rigid membrane (Figure 7.22(c)) due to material expansion. Consequently, the tendency to produce corrugations in the cylinder wall is increased until a point is reached at which the boundary of the low stress region (i.e., region "A" in Figure 7.22(c)) is so severely restricted that this region must bulge inward or outward to accommodate any further expansion of the surrounding material. The resulting *Durchschlag* is always very sudden and this is indicative of the strain energy build-up required to produce adequate plastic hinges around the boundary of the low stress region. While the formation of the first few buckles tends to strengthen the column by relieving stress concentrations, at ultimate load (Figure 7.24(a)) almost the entire membrane wall is distorted into an irregular buckling pattern.

If the same thin-walled cylindrical column is subjected to internal pressure only (Figure 7.23(a)) then three stresses are produced in the column wall: namely, circumferential or hoop stress (f_c), longitudinal stress (f_l) and radial stress (f_r). The radial stress may be neglected for all thin-walled cylindrical shells and of the remaining two stresses the circumferential or hoop stress is by far the greater. Due to the dominance of the hoop stress the cylinder wall is forced to expand. Again, in view of material imperfections and geometrical deviations there is a tendency for the formation of irregular horizontal corrugations (Figure 7.23(b)). This mechanism is easily demonstrated by stretching a wide rectangular rubber strip between two boards, and explains the irregular stress distributions that have been observed during experiments with thin walled cylindrical shells subjected to internal pressure alone. With the simultaneous action of axial compression and internal pressure, the combination of vertical and horizontal corrugations leads to buckling patterns that are more clearly defined and regular (Figure 7.23(c)). Under ultimate load, at low internal pressure, sharply defined diamond shaped buckles occur (Figure 7.24(b)), while at higher pressures the predominance of the horizontal corrugations is verified by the formation of circumferentially elongated buckles or simply horizontal folds (Figure 7.24 (c)).

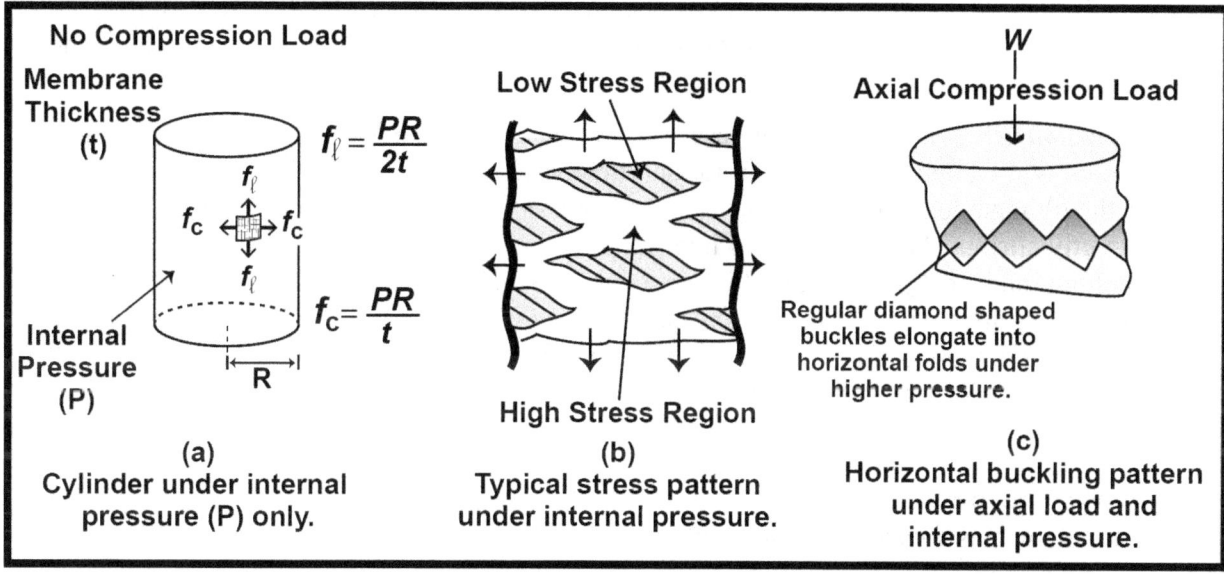

Figure 7.23: Diagrammatic representation of thin-walled cylinder under internal pressure

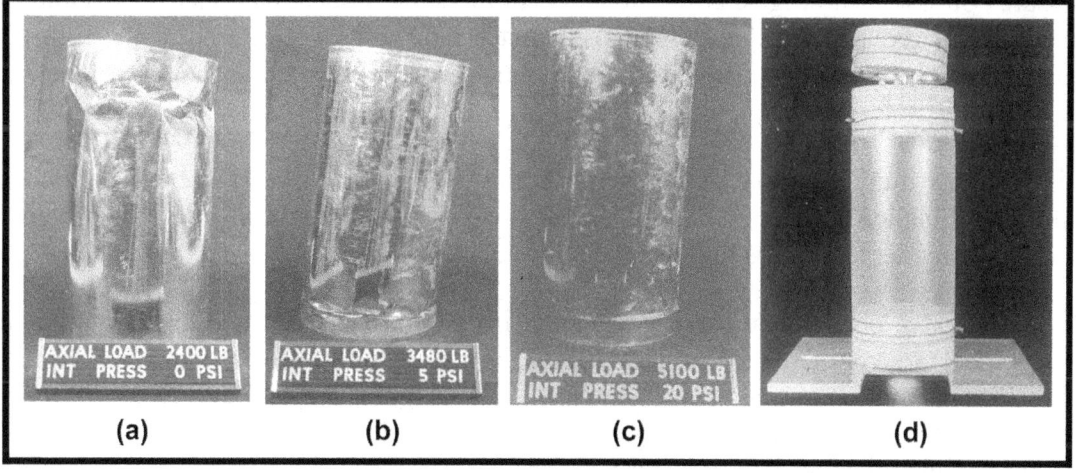

Figure 7.24: Local buckling failure patterns under different load combinations

The ductility of the membrane material will govern the ability of the column wall to form plastic hinges to facilitate the uniform distribution of stresses throughout the membrane. In the extreme case, a flexible plastic membrane (Figure 7.24(d)) will prevent the formation of stress concentrations altogether, with the result that for short columns horizontal folds will occur only when the axial compressive stress is equal to or greater than the longitudinal tensile stress due to internal pressure. In comparison, a rigid membrane has far less ductility and therefore the original geometric state of the cylinder wall becomes a major determinant of both the ultimate axial compression load that causes the cylinder to fail as a column and the local buckling pattern that precipitates the failure. Therefore, the application of internally pressurized rigid membrane structures in building construction must rely almost entirely on empirical data and observations. Based on the published results reviewed in this Chapter and the limited physical tests performed by the author the following observations and design guidelines are offered for consideration:

Observation 1: Internal fluid pressure increases the vertical load-bearing capacity of thin-walled cylindrical shells to a significant degree. However, the mean reduction in compressive stress (Figure 7.20) due to internal pressure is numerically equal to only about 50% of the compressive stress generated by an axial vertical load. Contrary to expectations this moderate relaxation of compressive stresses is not indicative of the ultimate load-bearing capacity of the cylinder acting as a column.

Observation 2: The destruction tests performed by the author (Figure 7.21) on test specimen types 1 and 2 indicate that for short columns (i.e., height to diameter ratio of 5 or less) the ultimate load-bearing capacity in compression increases by slightly more than can be directly attributed to the action of internal pressure acting on the internal surface area of the column end. If W_{ult} *LB* is the ultimate axial load with internal pressure, W_{axial} *LB* is the ultimate axial load without internal pressure, *P psig* is the internal fluid pressure, and *A SI* is the internal cross-sectional area of the column head, then the author's experimental results (Pohl 1970, Appendix 3C) yield the following average expression:

$$W_{ult} = W_{axial} + P A + 13\% \text{ (LB)}$$

However, the percentage margin was reduced to *8%* and *4%* in the case of higher pressures, such as *50 psig* and *100 psig*, respectively.

Recommendation A: For multi-story rigid membrane buildings where the ambient pressure of the building environment is limited to two atmospheres absolute on physiological grounds and the height to diameter ratio does not exceed *5*, the following equation may be used to estimate the ultimate buckling load of the building envelope:

$$W_{ult} = W_{axial} + P A \text{ (LB)} \quad \ldots\ldots\ldots\ldots\ldots\ldots\ldots\ldots\ldots\ldots\ldots 7.20$$

This result is quite contrary to the author's findings in the case of flexible membrane buildings (Chapter 2, Section 2.5.2), where the pressure-utilization efficiency even for very small slenderness ratios falls below *0.95 (95%)*.

The critical stresses obtained in the experimental investigation performed by the author for test specimen type 1 are compared in Table 7.7 with the values projected by Kusmiss (Figures 7.25 and 7.26; Kusmiss 1958) and by Fung and Sechler (Figure 7.12; Fung and Sechler 1956), even though it must be noted that strictly speaking the *H/R* value of *3.8* for test specimen type 1 extends beyond the range of the Fung and Sechler nomogram.

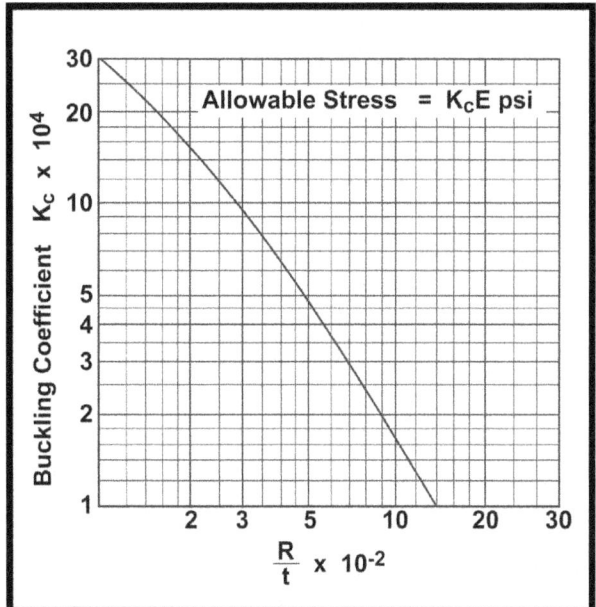

Figure 7.25: Buckling coefficient for unpressurized columns (Kusmiss 1958)

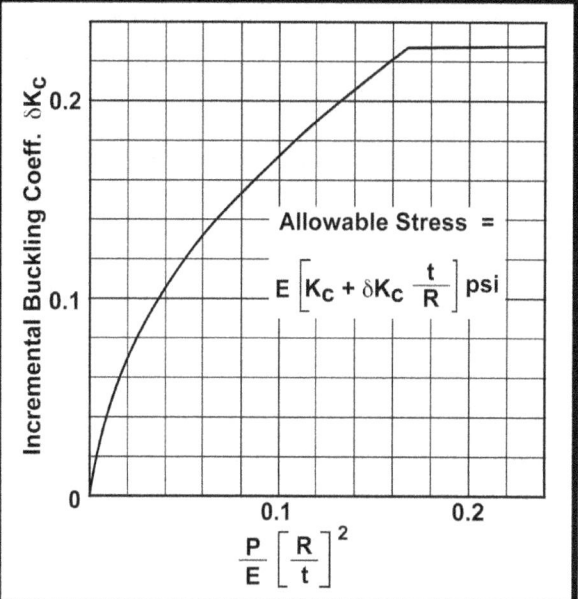

Figure 7.26: Incremental buckling coefficient for pressurized columns (Kusmiss 1958)

Table 7.7: Critical buckling stress comparison of experimental results for specimen type 1 (Pohl 1970, Appendix 2C) of height *18 IN* with Kusmiss (1958) and Fung et al. (1956).

Internal Pressure	Experimental Result (Pohl 1970, Appendix 2C)	Kusmiss Nomogram (Kusmiss 1958)	Fung and Sechler Nomogram (Fung et al. 1956)
0 psig	11,300 psi	13,000 psi (+15%)	14,789 psi (+30%)
5 psig	14,500 psi	18,800 psi (+30%)	15,085 psi (+ 4%)
10 psig	17,400 psi	21,800 psi (+25%)	15,379 psi (-12%)
15 psig	18,800 psi	23,600 psi (+26%)	15,973 psi (-15%)
20 psig	20,600 psi	25,900 psi (+26%)	16,564 psi (-20%)

The ultimate load results for test specimen type 2 are inconclusive because failure always occurred at the seam, suggesting that this did not allow the critical buckling stress to be realized. In any case as shown in Table 7.8 the specimen's *R/t* value of *162* is well below the lowest value of *500* included in the Fung and Sechler nomogram (Figure 7.12).

Table 7.8: Critical buckling stress comparison of experimental results for specimen type 2 (Pohl 1970, Appendix 2C) of height *6.75 IN* with Kusmiss (1958) and Fung et al. (1956).

Internal Pressure	Experimental Result (Pohl 1970, Appendix 2C)	Kusmiss Nomogram (Kusmiss 1958)	Fung and Sechler Nomogram (Fung et al. 1956)
0 psig	23,800 psi	45,000 psi	38,160 psi
50 psig	30,500 psi	64,000 psi	(out of range)
100 psig	33,200 psi	74,300 psi	(out of range)

The percentage differences between the two nomogram predictions and the author's test results for specimen type 1 are shown in parenthesis in Table 7.7. While the critical buckling stress for the pressurized column predicted by Kusmiss is consistently at least 25% higher, the value predicted by Fung and Sechler is at least 15% lower. Both of these nomograms are based on empirical analyses and the considerable differences are most likely indicative of the influence of initial imperfections in the column wall.

Throughout the remainder of this Chapter the author has used the Kusmiss nomogram as a basis for estimating the critical buckling stresses of air-supported and fluid-inflated, rigid membrane building structures. However, it is suggested that a factor of safety of at least *2* should be used for practical construction purposes.

7.5 Potential Rigid Membrane Building Applications

In the past, a clear distinction has generally been drawn between architecture and structure with the contention that whereas architecture is concerned with the provision of spaces, structure may be defined as the mechanical integration of the surfaces or elements that circumscribe these spaces (Howard 1966). Within this subordinate role structure is said to influence the form of a building, although it does not determine it. The concept of a pneumatic construction system in which structure and enclosure are synonymous is clearly at odds with this view of architecture, on the following grounds:

1. Multi-story air-supported structures[12] must be classified as surface structures, for which only a very limited number of shape configurations are feasible.

2. A membrane serving as a pressurized container will assume a form that is compatible with the internal pressure distribution acting on the membrane. Since this pressure distribution is always equal in all directions, the resulting form of the container will be spherical or cylindrical.

Experimental results and observations suggest that pressurized rigid membrane containers could be suitably adapted to multi-story building construction. In fact, the structural variations illustrated schematically in Figures 7.27, 7.28, 7.29, and 7.30 differ only in minor detail from the flexible membrane building types discussed in previous chapters. While similar criteria will apply to the design and integration of mechanical services, vertical transport, and prefabrication methods, there are nevertheless a number of considerations that apply to multi-story air-supported *rigid* membrane construction alone.

1. As shown in Figure 7.27 individual floors may be attached directly to the rigid membrane building envelope. This will allow the design of a built-in floor system that provides structural continuity between floors and building enclosure. The author has given some thought to the incorporation of cable-network floor systems in multi-story pneumatic construction. In these air-inflated disks it is intended to provide the required reaction at the periphery of each floor (where the cables are supported) by means of air pressure, thus obviating the need for a heavy ring beam construction (see Chapter 8).

---

[12] Buildings in which a membrane enclosure (whether rigid or flexible) serves as the container of a pressurized internal building environment.

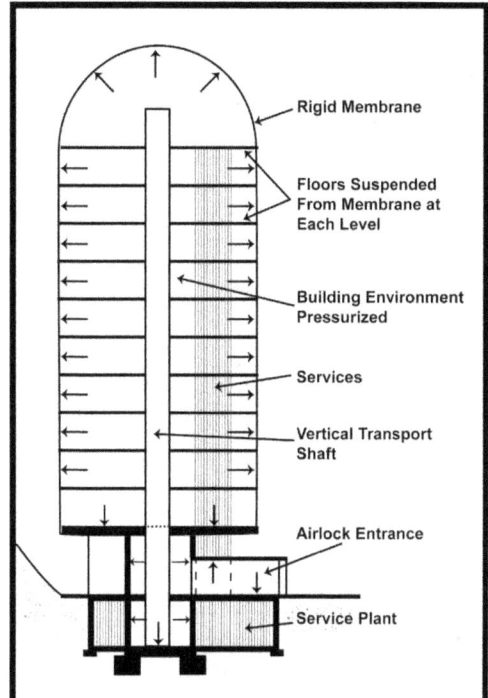 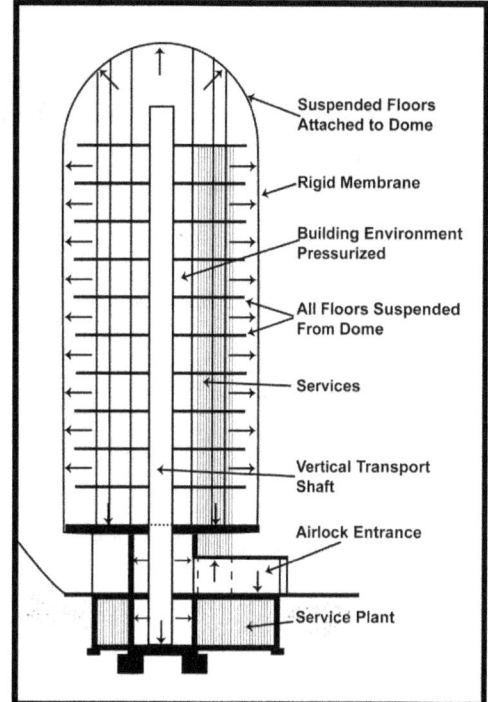

Figure 7.27: Rigid membrane building with built-in floors

Figure 7.28: Rigid membrane building with suspended floors

2. A rigid membrane column can resist lateral fluid pressure that is applied externally to the curved surface. This particular property is of importance in the building type shown in Figure 7.30 where floors are supported by a pressurized annulus, while the habitable building environment remains at ambient atmospheric pressure.

3. With rigid membranes the designer will be able to increase the material thickness well beyond the limits that apply to flexible membranes. Therefore, it will be possible to employ materials that are weaker in tension, but may have other more advantages properties such as transparency or translucency, superior weathering resistance, light weight, and thermal insulation. This leads to a wider choice of materials, including metals, plastics, and composites in general.

4. Whereas in Chapter 4 it is proposed to combine the enclosure of flexible membrane structures with exterior cable-networks, a similar procedure may be adopted in the case of rigid membrane structures using circumferential and longitudinal (i.e., stringers) stiffeners. Although it is unlikely that an optimum solution can be achieved by giving primary structural significance to such stiffeners[13], a reinforced system may be favored where the resistance of stress concentrations (e.g., due to the attachment of floors to the membrane) or the

---

[13] In the case of multi-story, air-supported, flexible membrane buildings the external cable-network serves as the principal structural element, while the membrane acts solely as a non-porous container between cables. In this way a degree of optimization is achieved by transferring the force exerted by the internal pressure via the membrane to the steel cables, which are much stronger in tension than the plastic membrane.

minimization of direct solar heat penetration are major design criteria. In the 1960s there was some interest in the rediscovery of Van der Neut's (1947) early theoretical observations relating to stiffened cylindrical shells under axial compression. His findings were well confirmed by test data, which indicated that external stringers are much more effective than internal stringers in stiffening a cylindrical shell against buckling (Hutchinson and Amazigo 1967).

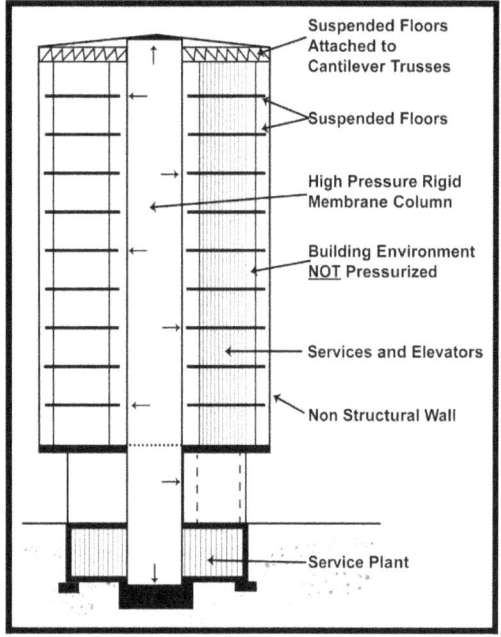
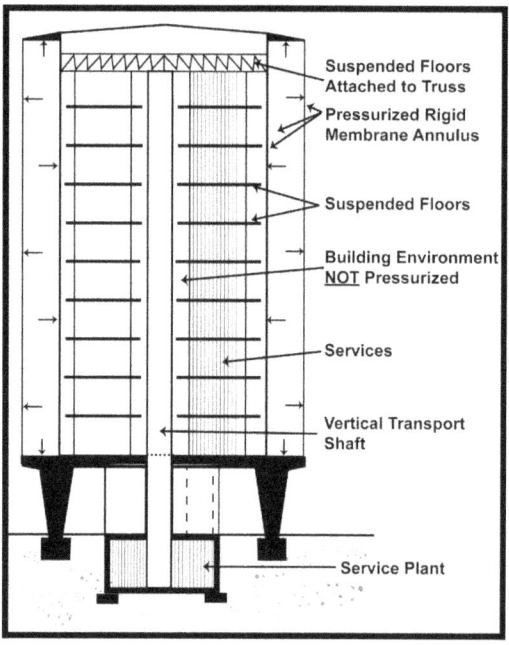

Figure 7.29: High pressure rigid membrane column core

Figure 7.30: Rigid membrane annulus construction

It is not difficult to imagine several aesthetically elegant and functionally useful enclosure configurations for multi-story air-supported *rigid* membrane buildings. In particular, architects would be able to take advantage of the ability to use thicker plastic and composite membrane materials to combine transparent, translucent and opaque sections in the design of the building enclosure. In such combinations external vertical and horizontal stiffeners may be used to advantage as sunshading devices and form delineators in addition to their structural role.

7.5.1 Multi-Story Air-Supported Rigid Membrane Buildings

Multi-story fluid-supported buildings incorporating rigid membrane enclosures fall into two categories; - namely, buildings in which the habitable spaces (i.e., the building environment) are pressurized as shown in Figures 7.27 and 7.28, and buildings in which the habitable spaces are under ambient atmospheric conditions (Figures 7.29 and 7.30). In the latter case the building is typically supported by one or more fluid-inflated columns with floors either attached directly to the columns or more likely suspended from a truss system at roof level.

When the building environment is pressurized the entire building enclosure acts as a short pressurized cylindrical column under axial compression (i.e., the vertical building loads) and lateral wind loads. Using a rigid membrane we are able to calculate the required internal pressure as a function of membrane thickness rather than total building load. Since the cylindrical shell of the building enclosure is rigid and has therefore overall stability, pressurization will serve to extend this range of stability (under increased load) by increasing the critical buckling stress of the whole structure. Whereas flexible membrane buildings discussed in previous chapters derive their form and resistance to buckling, torsion and bending from the internal pressure, rigid membrane buildings are stable in themselves, provided the cylindrical wall is sufficiently thick. Pressure may then be used as a means of decreasing wall-thickness according to economical considerations. The impact of wind loads has not been resolved for rigid membrane buildings and is therefore excluded from examples (1) and (2) below).

Example (1): Consider an air-supported, rigid membrane building of 9 stories (i.e., orthodox load-bearing first floor, 8 suspended floors, and air-supported roof) using a plastic composite material as the cylindrical shell enclosure.

$$
\begin{aligned}
\text{building diameter} &= 100 \text{ FT} \\
\text{radius (R)} &= 50 \text{ FT} \\
\text{building height (H)} &= 100 \text{ FT} \\
\text{floor area} &= 7854 \text{ SF} \\
\text{building circumference} &= 314 \text{ FT} \\
\text{shell thickness (t)} &= 1.5 \text{ IN} \\
\text{weight of composite material} &= 70 \text{ LB/CF} \\
\text{material modulus of elasticity (E)} &= 4{,}000{,}000 \text{ psi} \\
(R/t) &= 400 \\
(H/R) &= 2.0
\end{aligned}
$$

If the dead-load and live-load are taken to be *50 psf* and *100 psf*, respectively then:

$$
\begin{aligned}
\text{load on each floor} &= 1{,}178{,}100 \text{ LB} \\
\text{weight of shell} &= 274{,}750 \text{ LB} \\
\text{total axial building load} &= 12{,}055{,}750 \text{ LB}
\end{aligned}
$$

Therefore the compressive stress in the rigid membrane shell (without internal pressure) is calculated to be *2,133 psi* (i.e., total axial load divided by the cross-sectional material area of the cylindrical shell). According to Kusmiss (Figure 7.25) the critical buckling stress (unpressurized) of the membrane will be approximately *2,200 psi*. In reference to the Fung and Sechler (Figure 7.12) nomogram the estimated increases in the critical buckling stress with internal pressurization are shown in Table 7.9.

Table 7.9: Critical buckling stress according to Kusmiss (unpressurized) and Fung and Sechler (increasingly pressurized)

Internal Pressure	P/E	Coefficient (K)	Critical Buckling Stress
0 psig	---	---	2,200 psi
2 psig	5×10^{-7}	0.25	2,500 psi
4 psig	10×10^{-7}	0.26	2,600 psi
6 psig	15×10^{-7}	0.27	2,700 psi
8 psig	20×10^{-7}	0.28	2,800 psi
10 psig	25×10^{-7}	0.29	2,900 psi
12 psig	30×10^{-7}	0.30	3,000 psi

(The circumferential (hoop) stress at 12 psig internal pressure is 4,800 psi.)

At an internal pressure of *10 psig*[14] the circumferential or hoop stress in the rigid membrane shell is calculated to be *4,000 psi* and the total upward force due to the internal pressure acting on a flat roof area of *7,850 SF* is *11,304,000 LB*. Therefore, in this particular case we are dealing with approximately the same pressure-utilization efficiency (i.e., 94%) as for pressurized, flexible membrane buildings.

On decreasing the wall thickness from *1.5 IN* to *1.0 IN* the critical stress value decreases correspondingly.

$$(R / t) = 600$$
$$(H / R) = 2.0$$

Therefore, the compressive stress in the membrane without internal pressure is now calculated to be *2,680 psi*. According to Kusmiss (Figure 7.25) the critical buckling stress (unpressurized) of the rigid membrane will be approximately *1,400 psi*, while the increase in the critical buckling stress according to the Fung and Sechler nomogram (Figure 7.12) is tabulated in Table 7.10.

Table 7.10: Critical buckling stress according to Kusmiss (unpressurized) and Fung and Sechler (increasingly pressurized)

Internal Pressure	P/E	Coefficient (K)	Critical Buckling Stress
0 psig	---	---	1,400 psi
2 psig	5×10^{-7}	0.25	1,675 psi
4 psig	10×10^{-7}	0.29	1,940 psi
6 psig	15×10^{-7}	0.33	2,210 psi
8 psig	20×10^{-7}	0.37	2,480 psi
10 psig	25×10^{-7}	0.42	2,820 psi
12 psig	30×10^{-7}	0.46	3,080 psi

(The circumferential (hoop) stress at 12 psig internal pressure is 7,200 psi.)

According to Tables 7.9 and 7.10 it is apparent that the effect of the internal pressure is more marked when the *R/t* ratio is large (i.e., as the shell thickness decreases). Indications are that the most economical *R/t* value for plastics and composite materials with a relatively low modulus of elasticity (*E*) is likely to be in the range of *500* to *700*.

Example (2): Consider a pressurized, rigid membrane building of 9 stories (i.e., orthodox load-bearing first floor, 8 suspended floors, and air-supported roof) using rigid steel plate sheeting as the cylindrical building enclosure.

$$\begin{aligned}
\text{building diameter} &= 100 \text{ FT} \\
\text{radius (R)} &= 50 \text{ FT} \\
\text{building height (H)} &= 100 \text{ FT} \\
\text{floor area} &= 7854 \text{ SF} \\
\text{building circumference} &= 314 \text{ FT} \\
\text{shell thickness (t)} &= 0.4 \text{ IN} \\
\text{weight of steel material} &= 490 \text{ LB/CF}
\end{aligned}$$

---

[14] The internal pressure value of 10 psig rather than 12 psig is used for the comparison with flexible membrane buildings that follows, based on the physiological constraints discussed in Chapter 3 (Section 3.2).

material modulus of elasticity (E) = 30,000,000 psi
(R / t) = 1500
(H / R) = 2.0

If the dead-load and live-load are taken to be *50 psf* and *100 psf*, respectively then:

load on each floor = 1,178,100 LB
weight of shell = 512,866 LB
total axial building load = 11,115,766 LB

Therefore the compressive stress in the rigid membrane shell (without internal pressure) is calculated to be *7,375 psi* (i.e., total axial load divided by the cross-sectional material area of the cylindrical shell). According to Kusmiss (Figure 7.25) the critical buckling stress (unpressurized) of the membrane will be approximately *3,000 psi*. In reference to the Fung and Sechler (Figure 7.12) nomogram the estimated increases in the critical buckling stress with internal pressurization are shown in Table 7.11.

Table 7.11: Critical buckling stress according to Kusmiss (unpressurized) and Fung and Sechler (increasingly pressurized)

Internal Pressure	P/E	Coefficient (K)	Critical Buckling Stress
0 psig	---	---	3,000 psi
2 psig	0.7×10^{-7}	0.16	3,200 psi
4 psig	1.3×10^{-7}	0.18	3,600 psi
6 psig	2.0×10^{-7}	0.21	4,200 psi
8 psig	2.7×10^{-7}	0.23	4,600 psi
10 psig	3.3×10^{-7}	0.27	5,200 psi
12 psig	4.0×10^{-7}	0.30	6,000 psi

(The circumferential (hoop) stress at 12 psig internal pressure is 18,000 psi.)

Although the weight of the membrane structure has increased in this example by about 75% (i.e. *300,000 LB* for a *1.5 IN* plastic rigid membrane to *520,000 LB* for a *0.4 IN* steel membrane) it will be difficult to achieve the required stress value with pressurization. It seems likely that plastic materials with a high strength/weight ratio and a relatively low modulus of elasticity are considerably better suited to pressurized rigid membrane construction.

7.5.2 Fluid-Inflated Rigid Membrane Columns

For immediate commercial application, fluid-supported membrane structures that utilize rigid membranes and do not require a hyperbaric building environment have some decided practical advantages. Typically, these structures consist of one or more pressurized columns as shown in Figure 6.3 (b) and (g) of the previous chapter (Chapter 6, Section 6.1). If multiple columns are used then various layouts are possible (Figure 6.4), while in the case of a single column deviation from a central location creates difficulties due to geometric imbalance. The advantages of such fluid-inflated structures are readily apparent. First, they permit the use of orthodox building materials such as steel and aluminum that are of known quality, durability and cost. Second, they afford the designer an opportunity to ensure the safety of the primary building structure even under conditions of mechanical failure, such as the breakdown of the pressurization plant. Third, whereas fluid-supported buildings incorporating flexible membranes derive their form and resistance to buckling, torsion and bending from the internal pressure, rigid membrane buildings are stable in themselves, provided the cylindrical wall is sufficiently thick. Pressure may then be used as a means of decreasing wall thickness according to economical considerations.

The ability of the unpressurized rigid membrane column to support its own weight and a sizeable portion of the superimposed loads very much simplifies the erection procedure for these buildings. Depending on height the column may be fabricated off-site and transported to the building site in one piece, or it may be assembled on-site from prefabricated sections. In either case, provided the slenderness ratio of the column is small its effective load-bearing capacity may be significantly increased by the action of internal fluid pressure. Based on the model analysis tests performed by the author with flexible (Chapter 2) and rigid (Chapter 7) membrane columns it is conservatively recommended that the height to diameter ratio not exceed 10:1 (Chapter 6, Section 6.1.2).

The recommended structural analysis procedure for a fluid-inflated rigid membrane column does not differ in any significant manner from the design process described in the previous section for air-supported rigid membrane buildings. The two nomograms published by Kusmiss (1958) shown in Figures 7.25 and 7.26 (Section 7.4.4) are again used in the example below because they extend into the required height to diameter ratio range. The first curve (Figure 7.25) is used to determine the buckling coefficient (K_C) of the column under axial load without internal pressure and the second curve (Figure 7.26) provides the incremental buckling coefficient (∂K_C) of the column in the pressurized condition.

7.5.3 Example of a Fluid-Inflated Column

The central column of the prototype fluid-inflated experimental building described in Section 6.2 of the previous chapter, pressurized with water, will serve as a convenient example. With a height of *25 FT 3 IN* and diameter of *5 FT* the height to diameter ratio of the column is approximately 5:1 (slenderness ratio of *14*, with $H_E=H$). To simplify the analysis it is assumed that the column is designed to carry vertical loads only. A horizontal wind force of *8,000 LB* at *90 mph* is resisted by three sets of rectangular steel flats (i.e., *1 IN* by *½ IN*) placed diagonally between perimeter cables. A vertical uplift force of *12,000 LB* is resisted by the floor suspension system.

Table 7.12: Axial building load on central column (approximate)

Component	Dimensions	Description	Load
first floor	775 SF	10 psf self-weight 40 psf live-load	7,750 LB 31,000 LB
second floor	775 SF	10 psf self-weight 40 psf live-load	7,750 LB 31,000 LB
roof	850 SF	20 psf self-weight 30 psf live-load	17,000 LB 25,500 LB
column	0.0625 IN 11.78 SI	wall thickness cross-sectional area	

	2.07 CF	steel volume	1,014 LB
	0.27 CF	steel rims (2 IN x ¼ IN)	132 LB
water	736 CF	4,584 gallons	46,000 LB
suspension hangers	1.13 CF	16 of ½ IN diameter	278 LB
prestress	100 LB	for each of 16 hangers	1,600 LB
membrane enclosure	8 CF	double plastic membrane	560 LB
solar collectors	452 SF	single glazed on roof	1,318 LB
miscellaneous	varied	bracing and steel connectors	200 LB
		Total vertical building load[15]:	125,102 LB

Utilizing the nomograms for the design of unpressurized and pressurized thin-walled cylindrical shells published by Kusmiss (1958) and shown in Figures 7.31 and 7.32, the design of the column proceeds in two stages.

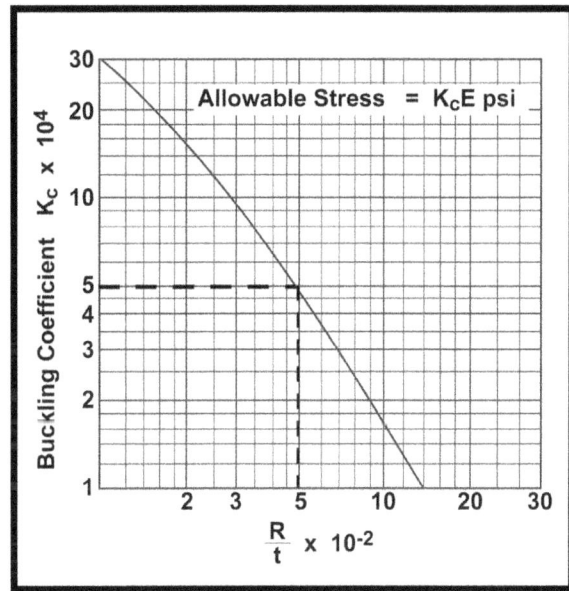

Figure 7.31: Buckling coefficient for unpressurized columns (Kusmiss 1958)

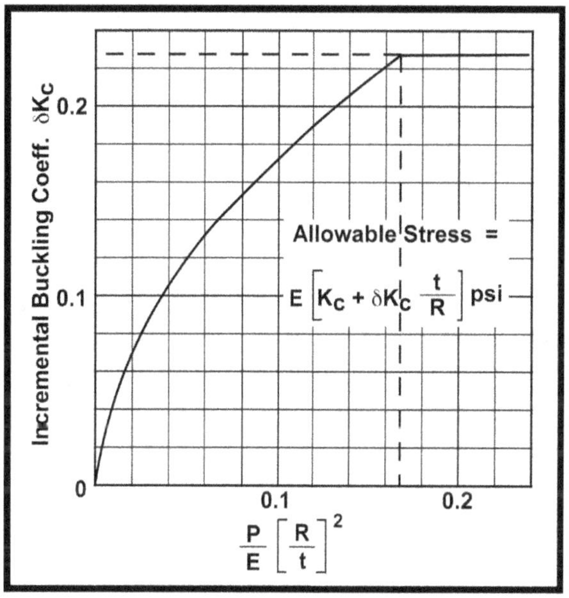

Figure 7.32: Incremental buckling coefficient for pressurized columns (Kusmiss 1958)

(a) Calculation of critical compressive stress of *unpressurized* column:

radius/thickness (R/t) = (2.5 x 12) / 0.0625 = 480

According to the first monograph (Figure 7.31) for an R/t ratio of 480 we obtain:

buckling coefficient (K_C) = 5.0×10^{-4}

allowable stress ($E\,K_C$) = $5.0 \times 10^{-4} \times 30 \times 10^6$ = **15,000 psi**

allowable vertical load = 15,000 x 11.78 = **176,700 LB**

(b) Calculation of critical compressive stress of *pressurized* column:

As shown in the second monograph (Figure 7.32) the incremental buckling coefficient (∂K_C) does not increase beyond:

---

[15] Excludes the weight of the water since it is <u>not</u> imposed as a vertical load on the pressurized central column.

$$(P/E)(R/t)^2 = 0.165$$

Therefore the optimum internal pressure (P_{opt}) is calculated by transposing the above equation:

$$P_{opt} = 0.165 \, E \, t^2 / R^2$$
$$P_{opt} = 21.4 \text{ psig}$$

For this internal pressure we obtain from Figure 7.32:

$$\partial K_C = 0.224$$
$$\text{allowable stress } (f_P) = E(K_c + (\partial K_C \, t / R))$$
$$f_P = E(5.0 \times 10^{-4} + 4.67 \times 10^{-4})$$
$$f_P = \mathbf{29{,}000 \text{ psi}}$$

However, this exceeds the allowable design stress of *24,000 psi* and, therefore, the allowable vertical load must be calculated as the cross-sectional area of the column material times the allowable design stress:

$$\text{allowable vertical load} = 24{,}000 \times 11.78 = \mathbf{282{,}720 \text{ LB}}$$

(c) Check maximum circumferential (hoop) stress in the column wall under internal pressure of *21.4 psig* and static water pressure at bottom of column of *12 psig*:

$$\text{circumferential stress } (f_C) = P_{tot} \, R / t$$
$$f_C = (21.4 + 12)(R / t)$$
$$f_C = \mathbf{16{,}032 \text{ psi}}$$

It can be seen from calculation (a) that the column is capable of comfortably supporting the estimated maximum building loads in the unpressurized state (141%). Under an internal pressure of *21.4 psig* the column incorporates a factor of safety of 2.26, while at all times the column wall is capable of sustaining the circumferential (hoop) stress generated by the internal water pressure plus the maximum static pressure at the bottom of the column due to the weight of the water itself. Accordingly, the building structure will not collapse even if a leak develops in the central column and the entire internal pressure is lost.

7.5.4 Structural Design Procedure for Fluid-Inflated Columns

The designer is faced with choosing among several different starting points and objectives when undertaking the structural design of a rigid fluid-inflated column. While the height of the column is likely to be known in all cases, the column's diameter, the thickness of the rigid membrane shell (i.e., column wall), the internal air pressure, and the axial load to be carried by the column may or may not be known. For example, for a given column height and diameter the designer may wish to determine the maximum axial load that can be carried by the column. In this case either/or the internal pressure and the column wall thickness may be assumed design parameters or optimizable design variables. Alternatively, for a given axial load and column height the designer may wish to determine an acceptable column diameter and/or wall thickness in conjunction with an assumed or optimum internal air pressure.

Several of these different design cases are discussed in some detail below. In all cases the effective height (H_E *FT*) of the column is assumed to be equal to the physical height (*H FT*). Where the presumed safe slenderness ratio of *30* (for a free-standing column) is exceeded the height at which the column needs to be braced to avoid bending is calculated. However, the type and form of the bracing is not discussed in any detail on the assumption that the required lateral restraint of the column at intermediate points can be accomplished by some means. For example, even in the case of a building with a single central column such as the building discussed in Sections 6.2 of Chapter 6 and 7.5.3 of this chapter, some form of bracing will be provided by the truss system at roof level with its tie-downs that are anchored to the footings at ground level[16].

Case 1: What is the maximum vertical load-bearing capacity of a fluid-inflated column with a given height (H FT), diameter (D FT), and wall thickness (t IN), when the internal pressure (P psig) is a variable?

Check for safe slenderness ratio (SR_{safe}) of *30* or less with effective height coefficient (e) equal to unity (*1*):

$$SR_{actual} = e H / (R^2/2)^{0.5}$$

If SR_{actual} is greater than SR_{safe} then determine height (x FT) at which bracing will be required:

$$e = SR_{safe} (R^2/2)^{0.5} / H$$
$$x = e H \; (\text{FT})$$

Calculate the R/t ratio[17] and check that it is in the range of *100* to *1400* for thin-walled columns (also range of Kusmiss nomograms). If R/t is above *1400* then increase t so that R/t is less or equal to *1400* and if R/t is below *100* then decrease t so that R/t is greater or equal to *100*:

$$r = 12 R$$
$$\text{If } R/t > 1400 \text{ then } t = r/1400$$
$$\text{If } R/t < 100 \text{ then } t = r/100$$

Calculate the cross-sectional area (A_m SI) of column wall material:

$$A_m = 12 (\pi D t) \; (\text{SI})$$

Determine the critical buckling coefficient (Kc) and corresponding critical buckling stress of the column wall (f_{Kc} psi) without internal pressure from Figure 7.31 (Kusmiss 1958), for the given modulus of elasticity (E psi) of the column wall material:

$$f_{Kc} = E Kc \; (\text{psi})$$

Determine the critical buckling coefficient (∂Kc) due to internal pressure (P psig) and the corresponding increase in the critical buckling stress of the column wall ($f_{\partial Kc}$ psi) from Figure 7.32 (Kusmiss 1958). As shown in Figure 7.32 the incremental buckling coefficient (∂Kc) does not increase beyond:

$$(P/E)(R/t)^2 = 0.165$$

Therefore the optimum internal pressure (P psig) is calculated by transposing the above equation:

$$r = 12 R$$

---

[16] In this case the end-fixing conditions of the column would be considered to be built-in (totally constrained) at the bottom and hinged at the top (i.e., $H_E = 0.7H$).

[17] The author is using the normal R/t naming convention with an upper case R and lower case t, however in calculating this ratio R must be in inches (IN).

$$P = 0.165 \, E \, t^2 / r^2$$

For this internal pressure we obtain from Figure 7.32:

$$\partial Kc = 0.224$$
$$f_{\partial Kc} = E \, (\partial Kc \, (t/r)) \; (\text{psi})$$

Therefore the total critical buckling stress ($f_{Kc\partial Kc}$ psi) of the internally pressurized column is given by:

$$f_{Kc\partial Kc} = f_{Kc} + f_{\partial Kc} \; (\text{psi})$$

Check that neither the circumferential stress (f_c psi) nor the critical buckling stress of the pressurized column ($f_{Kc\partial Kc}$ psi) exceeds the material design stress (f psi):

$$f_c = P \, r / t \; (\text{psi})$$

The total axial load (W LB) that can be carried by the pressurized column is:

$$W = A_m \, f_{Kc\partial Kc} \; (\text{LB})$$

Example 1: *What is the maximum vertical load-bearing capacity of a fluid-inflated steel column (E=29,000,000 psi, f=60,000 psi) with the following design parameters: 100 FT height; 6 FT diameter; and, 0.0625 IN wall thickness?*

Check for safe slenderness ratio (SR) of 30 or less with effective height coefficient (e) equal to unity (1):

$$SR_{actual} = e \, H / (R^2/2)^{0.5}$$
$$SR_{actual} = (1) \, 100 / (3^2/2)^{0.5}$$
$$SR_{actual} = \underline{\mathbf{47}}$$

Since SR_{actual} is greater than 30 (SR_{safe}) bracing will be necessary at the following height (x FT):

$$e = SR_{safe} \, (R^2/2)^{0.5} / H$$
$$e = 30 \, (3^2/2)^{0.5} / 100$$
$$e = \underline{\mathbf{0.6364}}$$
$$x = e \, H \; (\text{FT})$$
$$x = 0.6364 \, (100)$$
$$x = \underline{\mathbf{63.6 \; FT}}$$

Calculate the R/t ratio and check that it is in the range of 100 to 1400 for thin-walled columns.

$$R/t = 12 \, (3) / 0.0625$$
$$R/t = \underline{\mathbf{576}}$$

Calculate the cross-sectional area (A_m SI) of column wall material:

$$A_m = 12 \, (\pi \, D \, t) \; (\text{SI})$$
$$A_m = 12 \, (\pi \, 6) \, 0.0625$$
$$A_m = \underline{\mathbf{14.1372 \; SI}}$$

Determine the critical buckling coefficient (Kc) and corresponding critical buckling stress of the column wall (f_{Kc} psi) without internal pressure from Figure 7.31 (Kusmiss 1958), for the given modulus of elasticity (29,000,000 psi) of the column wall material:

$$f_{Kc} = E \, Kc \; (\text{psi})$$
$$f_{Kc} = 29000000 \, (0.0005)$$

$$f_{Kc} = \underline{\mathbf{14{,}500\ psi}}$$

Determine the critical buckling coefficient (∂Kc) due to internal pressure (P psig) and the corresponding increase in the critical buckling stress of the column wall ($f_{\partial Kc}$ psi) from Figure 7.32 (Kusmiss 1958). As shown in Figure 7.32 the incremental buckling coefficient (∂Kc) does not increase beyond:

$$(P/E)\,(R/t)^2 = 0.165$$

Therefore the optimum internal pressure (P psig) is calculated by transposing the above equation:

$$P = 0.165\ E\ t^2 / r^2$$
$$P = 0.165\ (29000000)\ 0.0625^2 / (144\,(3^2))$$
$$P = \underline{\mathbf{14.4\ psig}}$$

For this internal pressure we obtain from Figure 7.32:

$$\partial Kc = 0.224$$
$$f_{\partial Kc} = E\,(\partial Kc\,(t/r))\ (psi)$$
$$f_{\partial Kc} = 29000000\,(0.224)\,0.0625 / (12\,(3))$$
$$f_{\partial Kc} = \underline{\mathbf{11{,}278\ psi}}$$

Therefore the total critical buckling stress ($f_{Kc\partial Kc}$ psi) of the internally pressurized column is given by:

$$f_{Kc\partial Kc} = f_{Kc} + f_{\partial Kc}\ (psi)$$
$$f_{Kc\partial Kc} = 14500 + 11278$$
$$f_{Kc\partial Kc} = \underline{\mathbf{25{,}778\ psi}}$$

Check that neither the circumferential stress (f_c psi) nor the critical buckling stress of the pressurized column ($f_{Kc\partial Kc}$ psi) exceeds the material design stress (f psi):

$$f_c = P\,r/t\ (psi)$$
$$f_c = 14.4\,(3)\,12 / 0.0625$$
$$f_c = \underline{\mathbf{8{,}294\ psi}}$$

The total axial load (W LB) that can be carried by the pressurized column is given by:

$$W = A_m\,f_{Kc\partial Kc}\ (LB)$$
$$W = 14.1372\,(25778)$$
$$W = \underline{\mathbf{364{,}429\ LB}}$$

Case 2: What is the maximum vertical load-bearing capacity of a fluid-inflated column with a given height (*H FT*) and diameter (*D FT*), when both the wall thickness (*t IN*) and the internal pressure (*P psig*) are variables? In this case we will optimize the wall thickness by making the value of *t* as small as possible within the upper boundary of *R/t < 1400*.

Check for safe slenderness ratio (SR_{safe}) of *30* or less with effective height coefficient (*e*) equal to unity (*1*):

$$SR_{actual} = e\,H / (R^2/2)^{0.5}$$

If SR_{actual} is greater than SR_{safe} then determine height (*x FT*) at which bracing will be required:

$$e = SR_{safe}\,(R^2/2)^{0.5} / H$$

203

$$x = eH \text{ (FT)}$$

The largest R/t value represented by the nomogram in Figure 7.31 (Kusmiss 1958) is *1400*. Therefore, the thinnest wall thickness of the column and presumably the optimum value of t is given by:

$$r = 12R$$
$$r/t = 1400$$
$$t = r/1400 \text{ (IN)}$$

Calculate the cross-sectional area (A_m *SI*) of column wall material:

$$A_m = 12(\pi D t) \text{ (SI)}$$

Determine the critical buckling coefficient (Kc) and corresponding critical buckling stress of the column wall (f_{Kc} *psi*) without internal pressure from Figure 7.31 (Kusmiss 1958), for the given modulus of elasticity (E *psi*) of the column wall material:

$$f_{Kc} = E\, Kc \text{ (psi)}$$

Determine the critical buckling coefficient (∂Kc) due to internal pressure (P *psig*) and the corresponding increase in the critical buckling stress of the column wall ($f_{\partial Kc}$ *psi*) from Figure 7.32 (Kusmiss 1958). As shown in Figure 7.32 the incremental buckling coefficient (∂Kc) does not increase beyond:

$$(P/E)(R/t)^2 = 0.165$$

Therefore the optimum internal pressure (P *psig*) is calculated by transposing the above equation:

$$r = 12R$$
$$P = 0.165\, E\, t^2 / r^2$$

For this internal pressure we obtain from Figure 7.32:

$$\partial Kc = 0.224$$
$$f_{\partial Kc} = E(\partial Kc\,(t/r)) \text{ (psi)}$$

Therefore the total critical buckling stress ($f_{Kc\partial Kc}$ *psi*) of the internally pressurized column is given by:

$$f_{Kc\partial Kc} = f_{Kc} + f_{\partial Kc} \text{ (psi)}$$

Check that neither the circumferential stress (f_c *psi*) nor the critical buckling stress of the pressurized column ($f_{Kc\partial Kc}$ *psi*) exceeds the material design stress (f *psi*):

$$f_c = Pr/t \text{ (psi)}$$

The total axial load (W *LB*) that can be carried by the pressurized column is:

$$W = A_m\, f_{Kc\partial Kc} \text{ (LB)}$$

Example 2: *For a minimum wall thickness, what is the maximum vertical load-bearing capacity of a fluid-inflated steel column (E=29,000,000 psi, f=60,000 psi) with the following design parameters: 100 FT height and 6 FT diameter?*

Check for safe slenderness ratio (SR) of 30 or less with effective height coefficient (e) equal to unity (1):

$$SR_{actual} = eH/(R^2/2)^{0.5}$$
$$SR_{actual} = (1)100/(3^2/2)^{0.5}$$

$$SR_{actual} = \underline{\mathbf{47}}$$

Since SR_{actual} is greater than 30 (SR_{safe}) bracing will be necessary at the following height (x FT):

$$e = SR_{safe} \, (R^2/2)^{0.5} / H$$
$$e = 30 \, (3^2/2)^{0.5} / 100$$
$$e = \underline{\mathbf{0.6364}}$$
$$x = e \, H \, (FT)$$
$$x = 0.6364 \, (100)$$
$$x = \underline{\mathbf{63.6 \, FT}}$$

For an R/t ratio of 1400 the wall thickness (t IN) of the column is given by:

$$r = 12 \, R$$
$$t = r / 1400$$
$$t = 12 \, (3) / 1400$$
$$t = \underline{\mathbf{0.0257 \, IN}}$$

Calculate the cross-sectional area (A_m SI) of column wall material:

$$A_m = 12 \, (\pi \, D \, t) \, (SI)$$
$$A_m = 12 \, (\pi \, 6) \, 0.0257$$
$$A_m = \underline{\mathbf{5.8132 \, SI}}$$

Determine the critical buckling coefficient (Kc) and corresponding critical buckling stress of the column wall (f_{Kc} psi) without internal pressure from Figure 7.31 (Kusmiss 1958), for the given modulus of elasticity (29,000,000 psi) of the column wall material:

$$f_{Kc} = E \, Kc \, (psi)$$
$$f_{Kc} = 29000000 \, (0.0001)$$
$$f_{Kc} = \underline{\mathbf{2,900 \, psi}}$$

Determine the critical buckling coefficient (∂Kc) due to internal pressure (P psig) and the corresponding increase in the critical buckling stress of the column wall ($f_{\partial Kc}$ psi) from Figure 7.32 (Kusmiss 1958). As shown in Figure 7.32 the incremental buckling coefficient (∂Kc) does not increase beyond:

$$(P/E)(R/t)^2 = 0.165$$

Therefore the optimum internal pressure (P psig) is calculated by transposing the above equation:

$$r = 12 \, R$$
$$P = 0.165 \, E \, t^2 / r^2$$
$$P = 0.165 \, (29000000) \, 0.0257^2 / (144 \, (3^2))$$
$$P = \underline{\mathbf{2.4 \, psig}}$$

For this internal pressure we obtain from Figure 7.32:

$$\partial Kc = 0.224$$
$$f_{\partial Kc} = E \, (\partial Kc \, (t/r)) \, (psi)$$
$$f_{\partial Kc} = 29000000 \, (0.224) \, 0.0257 / (12 \, (3))$$
$$f_{\partial Kc} = \underline{\mathbf{4,637 \, psi}}$$

Therefore the total critical buckling stress ($f_{Kc\partial Kc}$ psi) of the internally pressurized column is given by:

$$f_{Kc\partial Kc} = f_{Kc} + f_{\partial Kc} \text{ (psi)}$$
$$f_{Kc\partial Kc} = 2900 + 4637$$
$$f_{Kc\partial Kc} = \underline{\mathbf{7,537 \text{ psi}}}$$

Check that neither the circumferential stress (f_c psi) nor the critical buckling stress of the pressurized column ($f_{Kc\partial Kc}$ psi) exceeds the material design stress (f psi):

$$f_c = P r / t \text{ (psi)}$$
$$f_c = 2.4 \, (3) \, 12 / 0.0257$$
$$f_c = \underline{\mathbf{3,362 \text{ psi}}}$$

The total axial load (W LB) that can be carried by the pressurized column is given by:

$$W = A_m \, f_{Kc\partial Kc} \text{ (LB)}$$
$$W = 5.8132 \, (7537)$$
$$W = \underline{\mathbf{43,814 \text{ LB}}}$$

Case 3: As in Case 2, what is the maximum vertical load-bearing capacity of a fluid-inflated column with a given height (*H* FT) and diameter (*D* FT), when both the wall thickness (*t* IN) and the internal pressure (*P* psig) are variables? However, in this case we will optimize the internal pressure by making the column wall as thick as possible within the lower boundary of *R/t > 100*.

Check for safe slenderness ratio (SR_{safe}) of *30* or less with effective height coefficient (*e*) equal to unity (*1*):

$$SR_{actual} = e H / (R^2 / 2)^{0.5}$$

If SR_{actual} is greater than SR_{safe} then determine height (*x* FT) at which bracing will be required:

$$e = SR_{safe} \, (R^2 / 2)^{0.5} / H$$
$$x = e H \text{ (FT)}$$

The maximum column wall thickness (*t* IN) is governed by the lowest allowable *R/t* ratio value of *100*, for the column to still qualify as a thin-walled cylindrical shell.

$$r = 12 R$$
$$r/t = 100$$
$$t = r / 100 \text{ (IN)}$$

Calculate the cross-sectional area (A_m SI) of column wall material:

$$A_m = 12 \, (\pi D t) \text{ (SI)}$$

Determine the critical buckling coefficient (*Kc*) and corresponding critical buckling stress of the column wall (f_{Kc} psi) without internal pressure from Figure 7.31 (Kusmiss 1958), for the given modulus of elasticity (*E* psi) of the column wall material:

$$f_{Kc} = E Kc \text{ (psi)}$$

Determine the critical buckling coefficient (∂Kc) due to internal pressure (*P* psig) and the corresponding increase in the critical buckling stress of the column wall

($f_{\partial Kc}$ *psi*) from Figure 7.32 (Kusmiss 1958). As shown in Figure 7.32 the incremental buckling coefficient (∂Kc) does not increase beyond:

$$(P/E)(R/t)^2 = 0.165$$

Therefore the optimum internal pressure (*P psig*) is calculated by transposing the above equation:

$$r = 12 R$$
$$P = 0.165 E t^2 / r^2$$

For this internal pressure we obtain from Figure 7.32:

$$\partial Kc = 0.224$$
$$f_{\partial Kc} = E (\partial Kc (t/r)) \text{ (psi)}$$

Therefore the total critical buckling stress ($f_{Kc\partial Kc}$ *psi*) of the internally pressurized column is given by:

$$f_{Kc\partial Kc} = f_{Kc} + f_{\partial Kc} \text{ (psi)}$$

Check that neither the circumferential stress (f_c *psi*) nor the critical buckling stress of the pressurized column ($f_{Kc\partial Kc}$ *psi*) exceeds the material design stress (*f psi*):

$$f_c = P r / t \text{ (psi)}$$

The total axial load (*W LB*) that can be carried by the pressurized column is:

$$W = A_m f_{Kc\partial Kc} \text{ (LB)}$$

Example 3: *For a maximum allowable wall thickness, what is the maximum vertical load-bearing capacity of a fluid-inflated steel column (E=29,000,000 psi, f=60,000 psi) with the following design parameters: 100 FT height and 6 FT diameter?*

Check for safe slenderness ratio (SR) of 30 or less with effective height coefficient (e) equal to unity (1):

$$SR_{actual} = e H / (R^2/2)^{0.5}$$
$$SR_{actual} = (1)100 / (3^2/2)^{0.5}$$
$$SR_{actual} = \underline{\mathbf{47}}$$

Since SR_{actual} is greater than 30 (SR_{safe}) bracing will be necessary at the following height (*x FT*):

$$e = SR_{safe} (R^2/2)^{0.5} / H$$
$$e = 30 (3^2/2)^{0.5} / 100$$
$$e = \underline{\mathbf{0.6364}}$$
$$x = e H \text{ (FT)}$$
$$x = 0.6364 (100)$$
$$x = \underline{\mathbf{63.6 \text{ FT}}}$$

For an R/t ratio of 100 the wall thickness (t IN) of the column is given by:

$$r = 12 R$$
$$t = r / 100$$
$$t = 12 (3) / 100$$
$$t = \underline{\mathbf{0.3600 \text{ IN}}}$$

Calculate the cross-sectional area (A_m SI) of column wall material:

$$A_m = 12\,(\pi D t) \quad (SI)$$
$$A_m = 12\,(\pi 6)\,0.3600$$
$$A_m = \underline{\mathbf{81.4300\ SI}}$$

Determine the critical buckling coefficient (Kc) and corresponding critical buckling stress of the column wall (f_{Kc} psi) without internal pressure from Figure 7.31 (Kusmiss 1958), for the given modulus of elasticity (29,000,000 psi) of the column wall material:

$$f_{Kc} = E\,Kc \quad (psi)$$
$$f_{Kc} = 29000000\,(0.0030)$$
$$f_{Kc} = \underline{\mathbf{87{,}000\ psi}}$$

Determine the critical buckling coefficient (∂Kc) due to internal pressure (P psig) and the corresponding increase in the critical buckling stress of the column wall ($f_{\partial Kc}$ psi) from Figure 7.32 (Kusmiss 1958). As shown in Figure 7.32 the incremental buckling coefficient (∂Kc) does not increase beyond:

$$(P/E)\,(R/t)^2 = 0.165$$

Therefore the optimum internal pressure (P psig) is calculated by transposing the above equation:

$$r = 12\,R$$
$$P = 0.165\,E\,t^2/r^2$$
$$P = 0.165\,(29000000)\,0.3600^2/(144\,(3^2))$$
$$P = \underline{\mathbf{478.5\ psig}}$$

For this internal pressure we obtain from Figure 7.32:

$$\partial Kc = 0.224$$
$$f_{\partial Kc} = E\,(\partial Kc\,(t/r)) \quad (psi)$$
$$f_{\partial Kc} = 29000000\,(0.224)\,0.3600/(12\,(3))$$
$$f_{\partial Kc} = \underline{\mathbf{64{,}960\ psi}}$$

Therefore the total critical buckling stress ($f_{Kc\partial Kc}$ psi) of the internally pressurized column is given by:

$$f_{Kc\partial Kc} = f_{Kc} + f_{\partial Kc} \quad (psi)$$
$$f_{Kc\partial Kc} = 87000 + 64960$$
$$f_{Kc\partial Kc} = \underline{\mathbf{151{,}960\ psi}}$$

Check that neither the circumferential stress (f_c psi) nor the critical buckling stress of the pressurized column ($f_{Kc\partial Kc}$ psi) exceeds the material design stress (f psi):

$$f_c = P\,r/t \quad (psi)$$
$$f_c = 478.5\,(3)\,12/0.3600$$
$$f_c = \underline{\mathbf{47{,}850\ psi}}$$

The critical buckling stress ($f_{Kc\partial Kc}$ psi) exceeds the material design stress (f psi) by 91,960 psi. Therefore with an allowable material stress of 60,000 psi the total axial load-bearing capacity (W LB) of the column whether pressurized or not must be reduced to:

$$W = A_m\,f \quad (LB)$$

$$W = 81.4300 \ (60,000)$$
$$W = \mathbf{\underline{4,885,800 \ LB}}$$

However, if steel with a yield stress of around 160,000 psi can be used for the column wall then the maximum axial load-bearing capacity (W LB) of the pressurized column would increase to:

$$W = A_m \ f_{Kc\partial Kc} \ (LB)$$
$$W = 81.4300 \ (151960)$$
$$W = \mathbf{\underline{12,374,103 \ LB}}$$

Case 4: What is the required diameter (D FT), wall thickness (t IN) and internal pressure (P psig) of a fluid-inflated column of given height (H FT) that is required to support a specified axial load (W LB)? The load may be the entire multi-floor building load if the column is the central structural support element or a portion of that load if there are multiple columns such as in Figures 6.3(g) and 6.4 (Chapter 6), respectively.

Step 1: Assume column diameter (D FT) based on a safe slenderness ratio (SR_{safe}) of *30* with the effective height coefficient (e) equal to unity (*1*):

$$SR = e \ H / (R^2/2)^{0.5}$$
$$R = 2^{0.5} H / SR$$
$$R = 1.4142 \ H / 30$$
$$R = 0.04714 \ H \ (FT)$$
$$D = 0.09428 \ H \ (FT)$$

Step 2: Assume a column wall thickness (t IN) based on a R/t ratio of *1400*:

$$r = 12 \ R$$
$$r/t = 1400$$
$$t = r / 1400 \ (IN)$$

Step 3: Calculate the cross-sectional area (A_m SI) of column wall material:

$$A_m = 12 \ (\pi \ D \ t) \ (SI)$$

Step 4: Determine the critical buckling coefficient (Kc) and corresponding critical buckling stress of the column wall (f_{Kc} psi) without internal pressure from Figure 7.31 (Kusmiss 1958), for the given modulus of elasticity (E psi) of the column wall material:

$$f_{Kc} = E \ Kc \ (psi)$$

Step 5: Determine the critical buckling coefficient (∂Kc) due to internal pressure (P psig) and the corresponding increase in the critical buckling stress of the column wall ($f_{\partial Kc}$ psi) from Figure 7.32 (Kusmiss 1958). As shown in Figure 7.32 the incremental buckling coefficient (∂Kc) does not increase beyond:

$$(P/E) \ (R/t)^2 = 0.165$$

Therefore the optimum internal pressure (P psig) is calculated by transposing the above equation:

$$r = 12 \ R$$
$$P = 0.165 \ E \ t^2 / r^2$$

For this internal pressure we obtain from Figure 7.32:

$$\partial Kc = 0.224$$

$$f_{\partial Kc} = E\,(\partial Kc\,(t/r))\text{ (psi)}$$

Step 6: Therefore the total critical buckling stress ($f_{Kc\partial Kc}$ *psi*) of the internally pressurized column is given by:

$$f_{Kc\partial Kc} = f_{Kc} + f_{\partial Kc}\text{ (psi)}$$

Step 7: Check that neither the circumferential stress (f_c *psi*) nor the critical buckling stress of the pressurized column ($f_{Kc\partial Kc}$ *psi*) exceeds the material design stress (*f psi*):

$$f_c = P\,r/t\text{ (psi)}$$

Step 8: The total axial load (W_{allow} *LB*) that can be carried by the pressurized column is:

$$W_{allow} = A_m\,f_{Kc\partial Kc}\text{ (LB)}$$

Step 9: If the allowable load (W_{allow}) is less than the specified axial load (*W*) then incrementally increase the wall thickness (*t*) and repeat *Steps 2 to 8* up to a limit of *R/t=100*, checking each time whether the allowable load (W_{allow}) is still less than the specified load (*W*). If either the circumferential (f_c) or critical buckling stress ($f_{Kc\partial Kc}$) exceeds the material design stress (*f*), or W_{allow}< *W* when *R/t=100* then incrementally increase the column diameter (*D*) and repeat *Steps 1 to 9* until W_{allow} is greater or equal to *W*.

While this is a tedious process when performed manually such an iterative process is easily automated with a computer program. In such a computer program the author has found it efficient to increase the wall thickness by increments of *2.5%* and the column diameter in *6 IN increments*.

Example 4: *Determine the required diameter (D FT), wall thickness (t IN), and internal air pressure (P psig) for an 80 FT high (H FT) fluid-supported column that is required to carry an axial load (W LB) of 1,000,000 LB. Assume the column to be made of stainless steel (i.e., E=29,000,000 psi, f=60,000 psi).*

Assume a column radius (R FT) based on a safe slenderness ratio (SR) of 30 with an effective height coefficient (e) equal to 1:

$$SR = e\,H\,/\,(R^2/2)^{0.5}$$
$$R = 2^{0.5}\,H\,/\,SR$$
$$R = 1.4142\,(80)\,/\,30$$
$$R = \underline{\mathbf{3.77\text{ }FT}}$$
$$D = \underline{\mathbf{7.54\text{ }FT}}$$

Assume a column wall thickness (t IN) based on a R/t ratio of 1400:

$$r = 12\,R$$
$$r = \underline{\mathbf{45.24\text{ }IN}}$$
$$r/t = 1400$$
$$t = r/1400$$
$$t = 45.24/1400$$
$$t = \underline{\mathbf{0.0323\text{ }IN}}$$

Calculate the cross-sectional area (A_m SI) of the column wall material:

$$A_m = 12\,(\pi\,D\,t)$$

$$A_m = 12\ (3.14159)\ (7.54)\ (0.0323)$$
$$A_m = \underline{\mathbf{9.1813\ SI}}$$

Determine the critical buckling coefficient (Kc) and corresponding critical buckling stress of the column wall (f_{Kc} psi) without internal pressure from Figure 7.31 (Kusmiss 1958), for the given modulus of elasticity (E psi) of the column wall material:

$$f_{Kc} = E\ Kc$$
$$f_{Kc} = 29000000\ (0.0001)$$
$$f_{Kc} = \underline{\mathbf{2,900\ psi}}$$

Determine the critical buckling coefficient (∂Kc) due to internal pressure (P psig) and the corresponding increase in the critical buckling stress of the column wall ($f_{\partial Kc}$ psi) from Figure 7.32 (Kusmiss 1958). As shown in Figure 7.32 the incremental buckling coefficient (∂Kc) does not increase beyond:

$$(P/E)\ (R/t)^2 = 0.165$$

Therefore the optimum internal pressure (P psig) is calculated by transposing the above equation:

$$r = 12\ R$$
$$P = 0.165\ E\ t^2 / r^2$$
$$P = 0.165\ (29000000)\ (0.0323)^2 / (45.24)^2$$
$$P = \underline{\mathbf{2.44\ psig}}$$

For this internal pressure we obtain from Figure 7.32:

$$\partial Kc = 0.224$$
$$f_{\partial Kc} = E\ (\partial Kc\ (t/r))$$
$$f_{\partial Kc} = 29000000\ (0.224)\ (0.0323 / 45.24)$$
$$f_{\partial Kc} = \underline{\mathbf{4,638\ psi}}$$

Therefore the total critical buckling stress ($f_{Kc\partial Kc}$ psi) of the internally pressurized column is given by:

$$f_{Kc\partial Kc} = f_{Kc} + f_{\partial Kc}$$
$$f_{Kc\partial Kc} = 2900 + 4638$$
$$f_{Kc\partial Kc} = \underline{\mathbf{7,538\ psi}}$$

Check that neither the circumferential stress (f_c psi) nor the critical buckling stress of the pressurized column ($f_{Kc\partial Kc}$ psi) exceeds the material design stress (60,000 psi):

$$f_c = P\ r / t$$
$$f_c = 2.44\ (45.24) / 0.0323$$
$$f_c = \underline{\mathbf{3,418\ psi}}$$

The total axial load (W_{allow} LB) that can be carried by the pressurized column is:

$$W_{allow} = A_m\ f_{Kc\partial Kc}$$
$$W_{allow} = 9.1813\ (7538)$$
$$W_{allow} = \underline{\mathbf{69,209\ LB}}$$

This allowable axial load of 69,209 LB falls far short of the desired load of 1,000,000 LB. We will first explore whether an increase in the wall thickness while *maintaining the same column diameter will increase the allowable axial load to 1,000,000 LB? An increase in the value of t will reduce the R/t ratio proportionally.*

t	IN	0.0323	0.0452	0.0566	0.0754	**0.1131**	0.2262
R/t	ratio	**1400**	**1000**	**800**	**600**	**400**	**200**
A_m	SI	9.1813	12.8481	16.0886	21.4325	**32.1488**	64.2976
K_c	---	0.000100	0.000164	0.000245	0.000366	**0.000640**	0.001530
f_{Kc}	psi	2,900	4,756	7,105	10,614	**18,560**	44,370
P	psig	2.4	4.8	7.5	13.3	**29.9**	119.62
$f_{\partial Kc}$	psi	4,638	6,490	8,127	10,827	**16,240**	32,480
$f_{Kc\partial Kc}$	psi	7,538	11,246	15,232	21,441	**34,800**	76,850
W_{allow}	LB	69,209	144,490	245,062	459,534	**1,118,778**	4,941,271
f_c	psi	3,418	4,784	5,987	7,974	**11,964**	23,924

As can be seen from the above table, with a wall thickness of 0.1131 IN and a corresponding R/t ratio of 400 the 80 FT high column can be loaded with over 1,000,000 LB without the need to increase the column diameter. Also, both the critical buckling stress ($f_{Kc\partial Kc}$=34,800 psi) and the circumferential stress (f_c=11,964 psi) of the pressurized column are well within the yield stress of the column material (60,000 psi).

Let us assume that the designer is satisfied with the wall thickness of 0.1131 IN but would like to reduce the column diameter. Since the safe slenderness ratio value of 30 will be exceeded bracing is recommended at the column height indicated below.

D	FT	7.0	6.5	6.0	5.5	**5.0**	4.5
SR	---	32.3	34.8	37.7	41.1	**45.2**	50.3
Bracing Height		74 FT	69 FT	64 FT	58 FT	**53 FT**	48 FT
t	IN	0.1131	0.1131	0.1131	0.1131	**0.1131**	0.1131
R	FT	3.50	3.25	3.00	2.75	**2.50**	2.25
R/t	ratio	371	345	318	292	**265**	239
A_m	SI	29.85	27.71	25.58	23.45	**21.32**	19.19
K_c	---	0.000730	0.000806	0.000886	0.001000	**0.001125**	0.001266
f_{Kc}	psi	21,170	23,374	25,694	29,000	**32,625**	36,714
P	psig	34.7	40.2	47.2	56.2	**68.0**	84.0
$f_{\partial Kc}$	psi	17,493	18,838	20,408	22,264	**24,490**	27,211
$f_{Kc\partial Kc}$	psi	38,663	42,212	46,102	51,264	**57,115**	63,925
W_{allow}	LB	1,154,091	1,169,695	1,179,289	1,202,141	**1,217,692**	1,226,721
f_c	psi	12,886	13,862	15,024	16,398	**18,037**	20,053

As can be seen in the above table a 5 FT diameter column with the same wall thickness (0.1131 IN) can support a 9% greater axial load (1,217,692 LB) as long as the column is adequately braced at about mid-height (52 FT above ground level for an effective height coefficient of 0.66).

7.6 Summary of Rigid Membrane Analysis Proposals

The purpose of this final section is to compare the critical buckling stress values produced by the various theoretical and empirical approaches described in this Chapter. Three cylindrical shell examples that have some relevance to the *fluid-supported building structures* theme of this book will serve as a basis for the comparison, namely: (a) a short cylindrical shell with a height to diameter ratio of 1:1 equivalent to a 10-story air-supported building (i.e., internal building environment pressurized); (b) a medium cylindrical shell with a height to diameter ratio of 2.5:1 equivalent to a fluid-inflated column for a three to four story building; and, (c) a long cylindrical shell with a height to diameter ratio of 10:1 equivalent to a fluid-inflated column for a 10-story building.

Example A: Represents a 10-story air-supported rigid membrane building in which the internal building environment is pressurized to support nine floors that are either attached directly to the external cylindrical shell, as shown in Figure 7.27, or suspended from the roof, as shown in Figure 7.28. With a height to diameter ratio of 1:1 this structure would be classified as a *short* cylindrical shell with the following structural characteristics:

$$
\begin{aligned}
\text{height (H FT)} &= 100 \\
\text{diameter (D}_i \text{ FT)} &= 100 \\
\text{radius (R FT)} &= 50 \\
\text{wall thickness (t IN)} &= 0.400 \text{ (or 2/5 IN)} \\
\text{modulus of elasticity (E psi)} &= 30{,}000{,}000 \\
\text{Poison's ratio (u)} &= 0.316 \\
\text{height to diameter ratio (H}_E = 100 \text{ FT)} &= 1.0 \\
H/R &= 2.0 \\
R/t &= 1500 \\
(H^2/(Rt))(1-u^2)^{0.5} = Z &= 5693 \\
(Et^3)/(12(1-u^2)) = D &= 177749
\end{aligned}
$$

Example B: Represents a medium height building supported by one or more fluid-inflated rigid membrane columns. The axial building load may be borne by a single central column, as shown in Figures 6.6 and 6.11 (see also Section 7.5.3)[18]. With a height to diameter ratio of 5:1 this structure would be classified as a *medium* or *transition* cylindrical shell with the following pertinent structural characteristics:

$$
\begin{aligned}
\text{height (H FT)} &= 25 \\
\text{diameter (D}_i \text{ FT)} &= 5 \\
\text{radius (R FT)} &= 2.5 \\
\text{wall thickness (t IN)} &= 0.0625 \text{ (or 1/16 IN)} \\
\text{modulus of elasticity (E psi)} &= 30{,}000{,}000 \\
\text{Poison's ratio (u)} &= 0.316 \\
\text{height to diameter ratio (H}_E = 25 \text{ FT)} &= 5.0 \\
H/R &= 10.0 \\
R/t &= 480
\end{aligned}
$$

---

[18] This fluid-inflated rigid membrane column, which served as the principal structural component of the prototype building described in Section 6.2, has a slenderness ratio of 14 for $H_E = H$ (i.e., virtually the same slenderness ratio as the *Example B* column).

$$(H^2 / (R t))(1 - u^2)^{0.5} = Z = 45540$$
$$(E t^3) / (12 (1 - u^2)) = D = 678$$

Table 7.13: Comparison of various analytical and empirical buckling stress projections

Type of Approach (Prominent Researcher(s))	Equation or Nomogram	Critical Buckling Stress Example A	Example B	Example C
Small Deflection Theory $f_x = Et/(R(3(1-u^2))^{0.5})$	equation 7.1 $f_x = 0.608(Et/R)$	12,160 psi	38,000 psi	19,000 psi
Large Deflection Theory $Z=(H^2/(Rt))((1-u^2)^{0.5})$ $D=(Et^3)/(12(1-u^2))$	equation 7.6 $k_x = 0.702\ Z$ $f_x = k_x\ D\ \pi^2/(tH^2)$	12,171 psi	38,035 psi	19,017 psi
Initially Perfect Cylinders (Tsien 1942)	equation 7.6a $f_x = 0.238\ (Et/R)$	4,760 psi	14,875 psi	7,438 psi
Empirical Design Formulas (Ballerstedt & Wagner 1936)	equation 7.10 $f_x = E(3.3(t/H)^2)+(0.2(t/R))$	4,011 psi	12,504 psi	6,250 psi
Empirical Design Formulas (Kanemitsu & Nojima 1939)	equation 7.11 $f_x = E(0.16(t/H)^{1.3})+(9(t/R)^{1.6})$	2,382 psi	13,926 psi	4,581 psi
Empirical Design Formulas (Batdorf et al. 1947)	equation 7.14 $k_x = 1.15\ C\ Z$ $f_x = D\ \pi^2/(tH^2)\ k_x$	2,293 psi (C=0.115)	13,645 psi (C=0.219)	4,953 psi (C=0.159)
Empirical Nomogram (Fung and Sechler 1957)	Figure 7.12	3,198 psi	15,936 psi	5,781 psi
Empirical Nomogram (Kusmiss 1958)	Figures 7.25 & 7.26	3,000 psi	15,000 psi	5,400 psi

Example C: Represents a tall, slender building supported by either a single central fluid-inflated column, as shown in Figure 7.29, or a number of fluid-inflated columns such as the cellular annulus shown in Figure 7.30. With a height to diameter ratio of 10:1 this structure would be classified as a *long* cylindrical shell with the following pertinent structural characteristics:

$$
\begin{aligned}
\text{height (H FT)} &= 100 \\
\text{diameter (D}_i \text{ FT)} &= 10 \\
\text{radius (R FT)} &= 5 \\
\text{wall thickness (t IN)} &= 0.0625 \text{ (or 1/16 IN)} \\
\text{modulus of elasticity (E psi)} &= 30{,}000{,}000 \\
\text{Poisson's ratio (u)} &= 0.316 \\
\text{height to diameter ratio (H}_E = 100 \text{ FT)} &= 10.0 \\
H / R &= 20 \\
R / t &= 960
\end{aligned}
$$

$$(H^2 / (R t)) (1 - u^2)^{0.5} = Z = 364324$$
$$(E t^3) / (12 (1 - u^2)) = D = 678$$

These three examples were selected to cover the principal range of slenderness ratios of cylindrical shell columns that could serve as the primary structural component of a building. With the exception of Example C, they are also within the height to diameter range of thin-walled columns (i.e., 1, 2, 3, and 5) that were tested by the author and discussed earlier in this Chapter (see Section 7.4).

Taking each of these three examples in turn it will be of interest to determine the critical stress predictions under internal pressure based on the Fung and Sechler (Figure 7.12) and the Kusmiss (Figures 7.25 and 7.26) nomograms and then compare these with the author's equation 7.20, as an estimate of the maximum vertical building loads that could be carried by these cylindrical shells in their intended structural applications.

Table 7.14: **Example A** - Critical buckling stress and axial building load capacity (Fung and Sechler (1956) comparison with Kusmiss (1958))

H = 1200 IN; R = 600 IN; t = 0.4 IN; A_{rigid} = 1508 SI; E = 30 x 10^6 psi; A_{roof} = 1130972 SI						
Pressure	P/E	H/R	R/t	$(P/E)(R/t)^2$	Fung and Sechler	Kusmiss
0 psig	0.0	2.0	15 x 10^2	0.00	3,198 psi	3,000 psi
12 psig	4.0 x 10^{-7}	2.0	15 x 10^2	0.90	5,900 psi	7,479 psi
W_N based on critical buckling stress (P = 0 psig)......					4,822,584 LB	4,524,000 LB
W_P based on critical buckling stress (P = 12 psig)..					**8,897,200 LB**	**11,278,332 LB**
Based on equation 7.20 ($W_{ult} = W_N$ + P A_{roof}) and 12 psig internal pressure (P):						
W_P based on cross-sectional area (P A_{roof})...............					13,571,664 LB	13,571,664 LB
W_{ult} based on (W_N + P A_{roof})............................					**18,394,248 LB**	**18,095,664 LB**
Assume a multi-story office building with nine suspended floors and a live-load of 100 psf, a dead-load of 50 psf, and a floor area of 7,543 SF (A_{floor}):						
weight of rigid building envelope (assume steel)					513,126 LB	513,126 LB
dead/live-load of 9 floors plus roof (150 psf)					11,781,000 LB	11,781,000 LB
total vertical building load					**12,294,126 LB**	**12,294,126 LB**
deficit vertical load bearing capacity................					- 3,396,926 LB	- 1,015,794 LB
excess vertical load bearing capacity (equation 7.20).......					**+ 5,801,538 LB (FS = 1.5)[19]**	
hoop stress in building envelope due to pressure					18,000 psi	18,000 psi

Example A assumes a multi-story building that provides public access to offices and retail occupancies with a rather high live-load of *100 psf*. The floor suspension system consisting of

---

[19] The considerable difference between the maximum vertical load bearing capacity estimated by the nomograms (i.e., Fung and Sechler (Figure 7.12) and Kusmiss (Figures 7.25 and 7.26)) and equation 7.20 is noted. Based on the tests described in Section 7.4 the author believes that the nomograms underestimate the vertical load bearing capacity of very short cylindrical shells; - in this case *$H/D_i = 1.0$*.

steel trusses at roof level, supporting vertical steel hangers that reach down to the nine suspended floors, is included in the load of the roof. For this reason the full floor load of *150 psf* is also assumed for the roof, although in the case of the roof the ratio of live-load to dead-load is reversed (i.e., *50 psf* live-load and *100 psf* dead-load). The building envelope is assumed to be solid *0.4 IN* thick steel with a self-weight of *490 LB/CF*. This is somewhat unrealistic, since it ignores the desirability of transparent, or at least translucent, sections of the building envelope for daylighting purposes. It is more likely that a building of this kind would take advantage of the availability of composite materials that are comparable to steel in strength, but much lighter and more versatile. Such synthetic materials can be customized to include the properties that are required for a particular application. Although the desirability of transparency for perhaps 20% of the building enclosure would still constitute a challenge in respect to strength and ultraviolet degradation, it is likely that such barriers will be overcome with advances in technology.

Example B represents a much smaller residential building with only two floors suspended from a roof that is supported by a central fluid-inflated column. It is similar in most respects to the design of the residential building described in Chapter 6 (Section 6.2), a smaller prototype version of which was constructed as a student project on the experimental building site at Cal Poly, San Luis Obispo, California in the mid 1970s.

Table 7.15: **Example B** - Critical buckling stress and axial building load capacity (Fung and Sechler (1956) comparison with Kusmiss (1958))

\multicolumn{7}{c}{$H = 300$ IN; $R = 30$ IN; $t = 0.0625$ IN; $A_{rigid} = 11.78$ SI; $E = 30 \times 10^6$ psi; $A_{col} = 2827$ SI}
Pressure	P/E	H/R	R/t	$(P/E)(R/t)^2$	Fung and Sechler	Kusmiss
0 psig	0.0	10.0	4.8×10^2	0.00	15,936 psi	15,000 psi
60 psig	20.0×10^{-7}	10.0	4.8×10^2	0.46	21,250 psi	28,698 psi
80 psig	26.0×10^{-7}	10.0	4.8×10^2	0.60	22,500 psi	28,698 psi
100 psig	33.0×10^{-7}	10.0	4.8×10^2	0.76	24,375 psi	28,698 psi
W_N based on critical buckling stress (P = 0 psig).........					187,726 LB	176,700 LB
W_P based on critical buckling stress (P = 100 psig)....					**287,138 LB**	**338,062 LB**
Based on equation 7.20 ($W_{ult} = W_N + P A_{col}$) and 100 psig internal pressure (P):						
W_P based on cross-sectional area ($P A_{col}$)..................					282,700 LB	282,700 LB
W_{ult} based on ($W_N + P A_{col}$)..............................					**470,426 LB**	**459,400 LB**
Assume that the column is supporting a 37 FT diameter residential building with two suspended wood floors plus roof and a live-load of 40 psf, a dead-load of 35 psf, a floor area of 1,106 SF (A_{floor}), and a roof area of 1,134 SF (A_{roof}):						
weight of rigid column wall (assume steel)					1,002 LB	1,002 LB
weight of column cap and suspension trusses					11,000 LB	11,000 LB
dead/live-load of 2 floors plus roof (75 psf)					250,950 LB	250,950 LB
total vertical building load					**262,952 LB**	**262,952 LB**
excess vertical load bearing capacity.................					+ 24,186 LB	+ 75,110 LB
excess vertical load bearing capacity (equation 7.20).......					**+ 196,448 LB (FS = 1.7)**	
hoop stress in building envelope due to pressure					48,000 psi	48,000 psi

Example C is not really feasible as a single central column supporting a *100 FT* high multi-story building, unless we are dealing with some kind of an observation tower with no more than two or three floors. In a more practical application of such a very long, internally pressurized, thin-walled cylindrical column, the column would serve only as a typical component of a structural annulus of columns around the external perimeter of a multi-story building in which, contrary to Example A, the internal habitable environment is not pressurized. For a building with a *100 FT* diameter and *314 FT* perimeter the *10 FT* diameter columns would be spaced approximately *16 FT 10½ IN* apart (center to center with a clear space *2 FT* wide between each column and the external building wall). As shown in Table 7.16, 16 such columns with an internal pressure of *40 psig* would be able to support a combined building load of just over *9,270,00 LB* or *118 psf* (based on equation 7.20).

Table 7.16: **Example C** - Critical buckling stress and axial building load capacity
(Fung and Sechler (1956) comparison with Kusmiss (1958))

$H = 1200$ IN; $R = 60$ IN; $t = 0.0625$ IN; $A_{rigid} = 23.56$ SI; $E = 30 \times 10^6$ psi; $A_{col} = 11310$ SI						
Pressure	P/E	H/R	R/t	$(P/E)(R/t)^2$	Fung and Sechler	Kusmiss
0 psig	0.0	20.0	9.6×10^2	0.00	5,781 psi	5,400 psi
20 psig	6.0×10^{-7}	20.0	9.6×10^2	0.55	8,750 psi	12,399 psi
30 psig	10.0×10^{-7}	20.0	9.6×10^2	0.92	10,625 psi	12,399 psi
40 psig	13.0×10^{-7}	20.0	9.6×10^2	1.20	12,344 psi	12,399 psi
W_N based on critical buckling stress (P = 0 psig).........					136,200 LB	127,224 LB
W_P based on critical buckling stress (P = 40 psig).....					**290,825 LB**	**292,120 LB**

Based on equation 7.20 ($W_{ult} = W_N + P \cdot A_{col}$) and 12 psig internal pressure (P):

W_P based on cross-sectional area (P A_{col})..................	452,400 LB	452,400 LB
W_{ult} based on ($W_N + P \cdot A_{col}$).............................	**588,600 LB**	**579,624 LB**

Assume that column is one of 16 columns spaced at 16 FT 10½ IN centers around the perimeter of a 100 FT diameter apartment building, with the following tributary floor and roof areas supported by each column: $A_{floor} = 413$ SF; $A_{roof} = 491$ SF.

weight of rigid column wall (assume steel)	8,018 LB	8,018 LB
weight of column cap (assume 0.5 IN steel)	1,604 LB	1,604 LB
weight of suspension system (per column)	40,000 LB	40,000 LB
total self-weight of column and suspension system	49,622 LB	49,622 LB
dead/live-load of 9 floors plus roof (100 psf)	380,800 LB	380,800 LB
total vertical building load	**430,422 LB**	**430,422 LB**
deficit vertical load-bearing capacity....................	- 139,597 LB	- 138,302 LB
excess vertical load bearing capacity (equation 7.20)....	**+ 149,202 LB (FS = 1.3)**	
hoop stress in column wall due to internal pressure	38,400 psi	38,400 psi

The author's limited experiments with long rigid membrane cylinders up to a height to diameter ratio of *5:1* (slenderness ratio of *14* assuming $H_E=H$) did not indicate any overall buckling tendencies (see Section 7.4). This is in contrast to the author's extensive experimental analysis of flexible membrane columns that showed a marked influence of overall buckling at slenderness ratios exceeding *10*. Therefore, until conclusive tests have been performed to determine the influence of overall buckling tendencies in very long cylinders (i.e., up to at least a height to diameter ratio of *10:1*) it is prudent to assume that the pressure-utilization efficiency is less than 100%.

In the case of Example C, the fluid-inflated column is not free-standing but part of an annular ring of 16 columns that are tied together at the uppermost end (i.e., at roof level of the building) by a system of trusses from which the building floors are suspended. The bracing provided by this truss system should be taken into account in the slenderness ratio determination. With built-in end-fixing conditions at the lower end of the cylinder and significant bracing at the upper end, the effective height (H_E) of the column is likely to be close to the actual height (H). Therefore the slenderness ratio of the column as part of the perimeter structure is approximately *14*, which is half of the slenderness ratio of the same column as a free-standing structure.

Chapter 8
Pressurized Cable Floor and Roof Systems

Multi-story air-supported buildings, particularly those with a flexible membrane enclosure surrounded by a cable-network, are very lightweight structures in comparison with orthodox steel or reinforced concrete building frames. It therefore does not seem appropriate to negate much of this reduction in the self-weight of the building with orthodox concrete floor construction. Even prestressed concrete floor systems are likely to weigh at least *40 LB per square foot (psf)* of floor area. In contemplating this dilemma some years ago the author considered the possibility of applying the concepts of fluid-inflated rigid membrane structures to the design of a lightweight floor system that would be more in character with a multi-story air-supported building.

A second objective of this investigation was to explore the feasibility of a structural system that could span significant horizontal distance with all of its component members in tension. By significant distances the author was hoping for horizontal spans two to five times (i.e., *50 FT* to *150 FT*) those normally considered in orthodox concrete and steel floor construction. The fact that the cross-sectional stress distribution in a beam supported at its two ends varies from maximum compression at the top surface to maximum tension at the bottom surface introduces an inherent degree of structural inefficiency. To reduce this inefficiency rectangular beams such as timber sections are designed to be much deeper than their width (e.g., a *10 IN* (depth) by *2 IN* (width) timber roof joist). However, even with this elongated rectangular cross-section the stress distribution is triangular with a theoretical zero stress condition at the center (i.e., at the neutral axis).

Since steel beams are manufactured from molten iron ore they can be formed into cross-sectional shapes that place most of the material at the top and bottom of the section. Therefore, the typical cross-sectional shape of a steel girder is in the form of an I. The load is essentially carried by the top (compression) and bottom (tension) flanges, while the function of the vertical web is to tie the two flanges together. In fact, the web is made only as thick as is necessary for it not to buckle when the girder is fully loaded and the two flanges are under maximum stress. Open web steel joists in which the solid web of an I section is replaced by a lattice work of steel bars and/or angles (i.e., essentially a truss) is about as far as the structural engineer can go to optimize a beam and still maintain a horizontal floor surface. Thin concrete shell structures that are capable of spanning greater distances due to the rigidity provided by their curvature are not suitable as floors since they cannot provide a flat horizontal surface.

8.1 Circular Pneumatic Cable Floors

The intriguing question that the author wrestled with was whether a combination of cable-network and fluid-supported construction might be feasible. Cable-networks have been used effectively in multiple configurations for large span roof structures. However, while the application of cable structures as floor systems has received some attention in the past, two serious problems were encountered.

1. It was found that the resultant cable reactions at the perimeter of such a floor will require an edge beam or equivalent horizontal support system. Even for the optimum case of a circular floor the required size and weight of such a

compression beam would negate much if not all of the economy gained by the cable structure. Designs that replace the compression ring with a single or double layered truss system (Boom 2012) are only suitable for large span roofs, such as sport stadiums, where the depth of the perimeter ring is not necessarily a disadvantage.

2. The characteristic sag at the centre of any cable structure is directly related to the magnitude of the tensile cable forces. Accordingly, minimum central deflection is accompanied by maximum edge beam weight and therefore much reduced mechanical economy. At the same time, major reductions in cable tension will lead to large central deflections and the requirement of a relatively expensive secondary structural system to provide a level floor surface.

It occurred to the author that it should be possible to construct a circular cable floor as a rigid membrane disk that is pressurized internal with air (Pohl and Sanchez 1986). Cables could be threaded through the cylindrical disk, radiating from a central tension ring like the spokes of a bicycle wheel (Figure 8.1). Depending on the diameter of the floor multiple concentric tension rings might be required to maintain an acceptable spacing of cables at the perimeter.

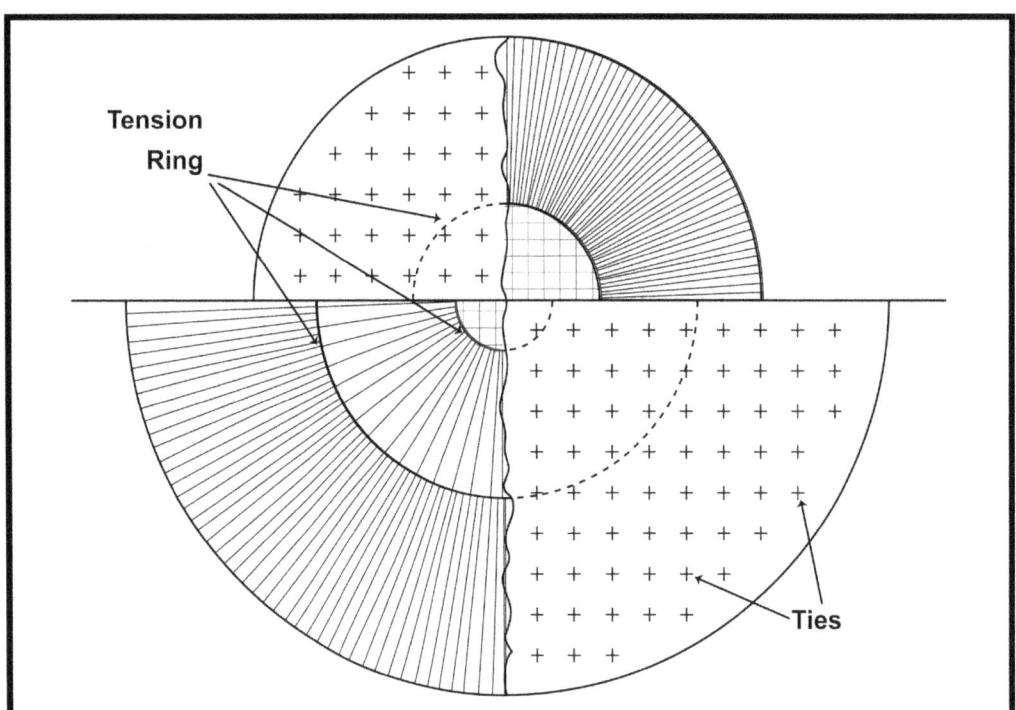

Figure 8.1: Plan views of a smaller and larger pneumatic cable floor

During construction, tensioning of the cables is accompanied by pressurization of the enclosed volume of the disk. The required internal pressure is calculated so that the entire horizontal reaction of the cables at the perimeter of the floor disk is resisted by an equal and opposite force, produced by the action of the air pressure on the surface area of the perimeter rim. For larger diameter floors it would be possible to provide a number of tension rings at varying distances from the center of the floor, so that the spacing of cables can be adjusted to the extent necessary. However, as will be shown later in this Chapter there does not appear to be a compelling need for multiple tension rings in the range of spans (up to *130 FT* for pneumatic cable floors and up to *800*

FT for roofs) investigated by the author.

The design of such a pneumatic cable floor would be essentially similar to a normal cable structure. At least for preliminary design purposes it is adequate to apply the theory of single cables subjected to uniformly distributed loads. For ratios of span to sag greater than 6:1 a reasonable approximation is provided by the parabolic cable, on the assumption that loads are given as functions of the horizontal projections of points on the cable rather than as a function of distances along the cable. Based on these assumptions the horizontal component of cable tension (H_{CA} LB per cable), the maximum cable tension (T_{max} LB), the support area for each cable at the perimeter of the floor on which the air pressure acts (A_P SF), and the required internal air pressure (P_F psig) may be approximated with equations 8.1, 8.2, 8.3, and 8.4, respectively.

$$H_{CA} = w L^2 / (8 d) \text{ LB} \quad \text{... 8.1}$$

$$T_{max} = H_{CA} [1 + (16 d^2 / L^2)]^{0.5} \text{ LB} \quad \text{........................... 8.2}$$

$$A_P = d C_S \text{ SF} \quad \text{.. 8.3}$$

$$P_F = T_{max} / (144 A_P) \text{ psig} \quad \text{................................... 8.4}$$

where: w = load (LB/FT-run)
L = span (FT)
d = sag (FT)
C_S = cable spacing at perimeter (FT)

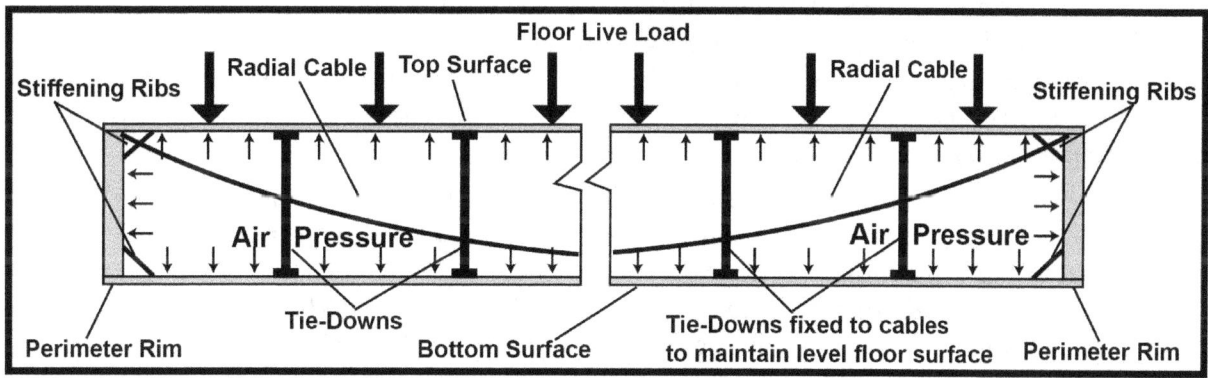

Figure 8.2: Sectional view of floor showing tie-downs to prevent dishing of top and bottom disk surfaces.

The internal air pressure that pushes outwards against the perimeter rim of the floor, thereby opposing the inward forces exerted by the cables on the rim, is equal in all directions and therefore tries to force the top and bottom floor plates to dish outwards. To counteract this tendency these plates are tied together with tie-downs at suitable centers (Figure 8.2). While the tie-downs could be in the form of cables, it may be preferable to design them as solid steel tension rods that are firmly anchored at the top and bottom plates. In this way they could facilitate the assembly of the plates during the construction of the floor. Additionally, it is recommended that the tie-downs be connected to the radial floor cables whenever any of them crosses the path of a cable. Even if the connection between tie-downs and cables is not required for maintaining a level horizontal floor surface, it should contribute to the overall stability of the floor by increasing its structural redundancy.

The proposed pneumatic cable floor is circular and in the shape of a donut, so that central elevators and ducts (e.g., plumbing, air-conditioning) can penetrate vertically through the floors. In a multi-story air-supported or fluid-inflated building the floors would be suspended from roof level hangers located at equal spacing in two concentric circles around the perimeter of the floor and the innermost tension ring, respectively. The center-to-center spacing around the floor perimeter may be equal to the spacing of the radial cables at the perimeter rim, while the spacing at the innermost tension ring is more likely to be a multiple of the radial cable spacing at that internal rim. For example, in the case of a *300 FT* diameter floor in which *94* radial cables are spaced at *1 FT* centers at a *30 FT* diameter innermost tension ring and at *10 FT* centers on the perimeter rim there could be 94 hangers at the perimeter and only 16 at the tension ring.

As shown in Figure 8.2, the proposed pneumatic cable floor consists of seven principal components, namely: radial cables; perimeter rim; innermost rim; tension ring(s); top floor disk plate; bottom floor disk plate; and, tie-downs. Extensive preliminary design explorations by the author of floor diameters ranging from *50 FT* to *400 FT* (equivalent cable spans of *15 FT* to *180 FT*) suggest that intermediate tension rings do not appear to be required. Even in the case of a *400 FT* diameter floor the spacing of the radial cables at the perimeter is unlikely to exceed *20 FT* with a single *40 FT* diameter innermost tension ring.

It is interesting to note that of these seven components only the rim around the innermost tension ring is in compression. Due to its relatively small diameter the weight contributed by this component to the total self-weight of the floor is likely to be less than *2%*, even if its thickness is conservatively assumed to be equal to the thickness of the floor perimeter rim. For example, in the case of a *300 FT* diameter (*4.88 FT* or *58½ IN* depth) all-steel floor with a single *30 FT* diameter innermost tension ring, assuming a design stress of *60,000 psi* for the internal and perimeter rims, top and bottom disk plates, and tie-downs, and *180,000 psi* for the radial cables and tension ring, the self-weight of *40 psf* is made up as follows:

weight of perimeter rim	=	288,495 LB	(10.30%)
weight of inner rim	=	28,850 LB	(1.03%)
weight of top and bottom disk plates	=	2,249,736 LB	(80.36%)
weight of radial cables	=	87,750 LB	(3.13%)
weight of innermost tension ring	=	1,948 LB	(0.07%)
weight of 4,374 tie-downs	=	142,815 LB	(5.10%)
total self-weight of floor	=	2,799,594 LB	(100.00%) or 40.01 psf

The top and bottom disk plates are by far the largest contributors to the self-weight of the floor (i.e., just over *80%* of the total weight). In the above design calculations the allowable deflection of these plates has been set at *1/480th* of the distance between tie-downs. In this case with the tie-downs at *4 FT* center-to-center in both directions, the thickness of the steel plates is *4/10th IN* and the maximum deflection under an internal air pressure of *51 psig* is *1/10th IN*. In a more detailed design it is likely that the thickness of the plates could be further reduced with a secondary structure of steel channels at *2 FT* centers, thereby halving the effective span of the plates. The slight increase in floor depth due to such a secondary structure would need to be compared with the reduction in plate thickness that can be achieved by increasing the number of tie-downs and/or increasing the cable sag with an attendant increase in the depth of the floor.

As might be expected, the self-weight of any pneumatic cable floor is very much dependent on the depth of the floor (i.e., the cable sag). The shallower the floor, the greater the tension in the radial cables and the larger the internal air pressure that is required to resist the inward pull of the cables on the perimeter floor rim. For the same *300 FT* diameter floor (cable span is *135 FT*) with tie-downs at *4 FT* centers in two directions, the following relationships between floor depth and self-weight were calculated by the author:

    3.00 FT (36 IN) floor depth .... Self-weight = 61 psf (2.2% sag)
    3.75 FT (45 IN) floor depth .... Self-weight = 50 psf (2.8% sag)
    4.88 FT (58½ IN) floor depth .... Self-weight = 40 psf (3.6% sag)
    6.75 FT (81 IN) floor depth .... Self-weight = 31 psf (5.0% sag)
   11.63 FT (139½ IN) floor depth .... Self-weight = 20 psf (8.6% sag)

Table 8.1 lists the preliminary design dimensions of a variety of floor diameters and depths assuming a single *20 FT* diameter tension ring, *31* radial cables at *2 FT* centers around the tension ring, tie-downs at *4 FT* centers in both directions, and a live-load of *100 psf*.

Table 8.1: Calculated dimensions of typical circular air-inflated cable floors

Floor Diameter	Cable Span	Floor Depth	Internal Pressure	Self-Weight	Span/Weight Ratio	Span/Depth Ratio	% Sag
50 FT	15 FT	1 FT (12 IN)	17 psig	23 psf	0.66	15	6.7%
100 FT	40 FT	2 FT (24 IN)	27 psig	28 psf	1.43	20	5.0%
150 FT	65 FT	3 FT (36 IN)	30 psig	31 psf	2.13	22	4.6%
200 FT	90 FT	4 FT (48 IN)	32 psig	33 psf	2.75	23	4.4%
250 FT	115 FT	4 FT (48 IN)	55 psig	42 psf	2.75	29	3.5%
300 FT	140 FT	4 FT (48 IN)	87 psig	52 psf	2.67	35	2.9%
350 FT	165 FT	4 FT (48 IN)	129 psig	65 psf	2.55	41	2.4%
400 FT	190 FT	4 FT (48 IN)	185 psig	79 psf	2.39	48	2.1%

It can be seen in Table 8.1 that as the span/depth ratio increases both the internal air pressure that is required to counterbalance the cable forces and the self-weight of the floor increase disproportionally. Both of these non-linear relationships are shown in Figures 8.3 and 8.4 for a *200 FT* diameter floor with a single *30 FT* diameter tension ring and a cable span of *85 FT*. The floor depths range from *1.3 FT (15 IN)* to *7.25 FT (87 IN)* with a corresponding percentage sag range of *1.62%* to *8.53%*.

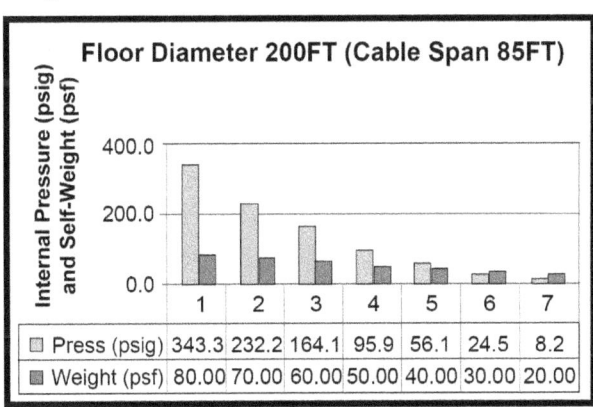

Figure 8.3: Pressure to Weight Relationship

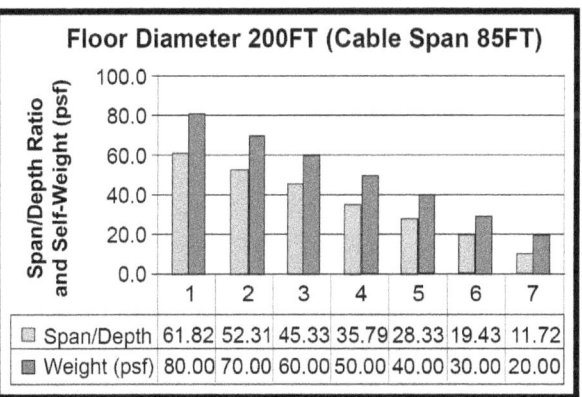

Figure 8.4: Span/Depth to Weight Relationship

Since by far the primary contributors to the self-weight of a pneumatic cable floor are the top and bottom plates the choice of material and the secondary structural design of these plates requires careful consideration. Treating each plate as a constrained two-way slab that is supported at four corners by equidistant tie-downs (Figure 8.13), the limiting factor in optimizing the thickness of the plate (i.e., to minimize self-weight) is deflection. This can be achieved in two ways, by selecting a material with a high modulus of elasticity and by reducing the distance between tie-downs. For example, the difference in self-weight of a *200 FT* diameter, *3 FT deep* floor with a single *30 FT* diameter tension ring (i.e., cable span of *85 FT*) for various center-to-center tie-down spacings is shown in Table 8.2 (for *94* radial cables at *1 FT* spacing around *30 FT* diameter tension ring, maximum allowable deflection of $1/480^{th}$ of span between tie-downs, and modulus of elasticity of steel plate material *29,000,000 psi*).

Table 8.2: Impact of tie-down spacing on self-weight of pneumatic cable floor

Tie-down Spacing FT (IN)	Floor Self-Weight LB/SF (psf)	Plate Thickness IN	Plate Contribution to Floor Weight
1 FT (12 IN)	16.94 psf	0.1517 IN	73%
2 FT (24 IN)	24.96 psf	0.2461 IN	81%
3 FT (36 IN)	31.95 psf	0.3284 IN	84%
4 FT (48 IN)	38.46 psf	0.4047 IN	86%
5 FT (60 IN)	44.54 psf	0.4763 IN	87%
6 FT (72 IN)	50.39 psf	0.5451 IN	88%

While the steel plate material that was used in this analysis (Table 8.2) has a favorably high modulus of elasticity (i.e., *29,000,000 psi*) it also carries with it the disadvantage of a far greater weight per unit volume (i.e., *490 LB/CF*) than all other structural building materials. While fiber reinforced plastic materials are far lighter and of comparable strength, they typically suffer from a lower and non-linear modulus of elasticity. However, the stiffness that they lack in their natural state can be mitigated to some extent by surface configuration. Therefore a high strength fiber reinforced plastic with a shallow folded plate surface configuration in combination with a secondary steel structure (e.g., steel angles or channels on the inside surface of the top and bottom floor plates) could potentially reduce the self-weight of a pneumatic cable floor by another *25%* to *50%*.

8.1.1 Construction and Safety Considerations

The concept of a pneumatic cable floor system is entirely theoretical at this time. To the author's best knowledge no building floors of this type have been constructed to date. While there are no a priori reasons why such a structural system should not be feasible, there are issues that would need to be investigated with a physical model analysis before proceeding with a full scale implementation.

- There is the possibility that the disk could be subject to an unacceptable degree of warping under certain loading conditions. The disk is in reality a very thin prestressed plate that may experience overall buckling, particular under unequal loading conditions. Such conditions may occur in buildings due to variably distributed live-loads.

- The vertical ties inside the floor that prevent the top and bottom surfaces of the disk from dishing outward under the action of the internal air pressure may contribute to the overall buckling danger. The natural dishing of these surfaces would decrease the slenderness ratio of the plate. By preventing this natural deformation the plate not only maintains its thinness, but also embodies a great deal of potential energy. Should one or more of the vertical ties rupture the sudden release of this potential energy could jeopardize the integrity of the entire floor structure.

- The floor disk may be sensitive to stress concentrations that are likely to be unavoidable in post-tensioning operations during the construction stage. While every precaution would of course be taken to carefully control the iterative stressing of individual cables, the sudden rupture of a single cable during this post-tensioning operation could have serious consequences. While experience has shown that strand failures frequently occur during the post-tensioning of prestressed concrete beams, the cables in pneumatic cable floors are of much larger dimensions and therefore not really comparable.

- The fire protection of a pneumatic cable floor is a major concern. While normal active fire protection measures such as automatic fire detectors and sprinkler systems are applicable, the principal concern is related to passive fire protection. The very notion of large open floor spaces uninterrupted by columns, which is the fundamental advantage of the pneumatic cable floor concept, creates a serious fire protection vulnerability. As exemplified by the catastrophic collapse of the World Trade Center Towers in 2001 the light weight, long span, open web, steel bar joists that spanned from the external wall to the central core were a major factor in the ultimate structural failure (Scheuerman 2003, Usmani et al. 2003). Since passive fire protection measures are intended to contain a fire by limiting its spread from the compartment of origin, very large open floor spaces almost ensure the spread of a fire throughout the floor of its origin.

In the case of pneumatic cable floors it is necessary to not only contain the fire within its floor of origin, but there is the additional need to protect the space within the floor disk from the heat generated by the fire. Since there is every incentive to preserve the light weight of the floor the available fire protection measures are currently limited to endothermic[1] materials such as calcium silicate sheeting and intumescents[2], which swell as a result of heat exposure to produce a heat insulating char. Intumescent coatings are normally applied as an intermediate coating between a primer and finish coat with a combined thickness of between *1/100th* and

---

[1] Endothermic materials contain chemically bound water (in solid form) that is turned into steam when exposed to high enough temperature. As long as there is enough steam the temperature of the protected material cannot rise much above the boiling point of water. However, once the endothermic material is spent the temperature of the protected surface will rise rapidly.

[2] Intumescent materials can be divided into two groups; - thin film and thick film. Thin film intumescents are normally applied in buildings where the fire rating requirements are *30 to 90 minutes*, although products with a *2-hour* fire rating are available. Thick film intumescents have a much greater dry film thickness and were originally developed for more extreme fire conditions (e.g., hydrocarbon fires). They are sufficiently tough and durable for external building applications.

3/100th IN.

Finally, there is the impact of unintended reductions in air pressure that needs to be considered. While such unintended reductions or a complete loss of air pressure could occur during construction, it is more likely to occur after the construction phase during the lifespan of the building. The latter case is of course much more serious due to the danger that it poses to the occupants of the building. This safety concern is even more serious than in the case of multi-story air-supported buildings in which the enclosure is a flexible plastic membrane surrounded by a cable-network. The reason is that the required air pressure in the pneumatic floor system is much higher and the volume is much smaller than in the air-supported building[3]. Therefore, additional (i.e., stand-by) pressurization equipment to allow time for the mass evacuation of the building occupants to a basement shelter will not be an acceptable solution.

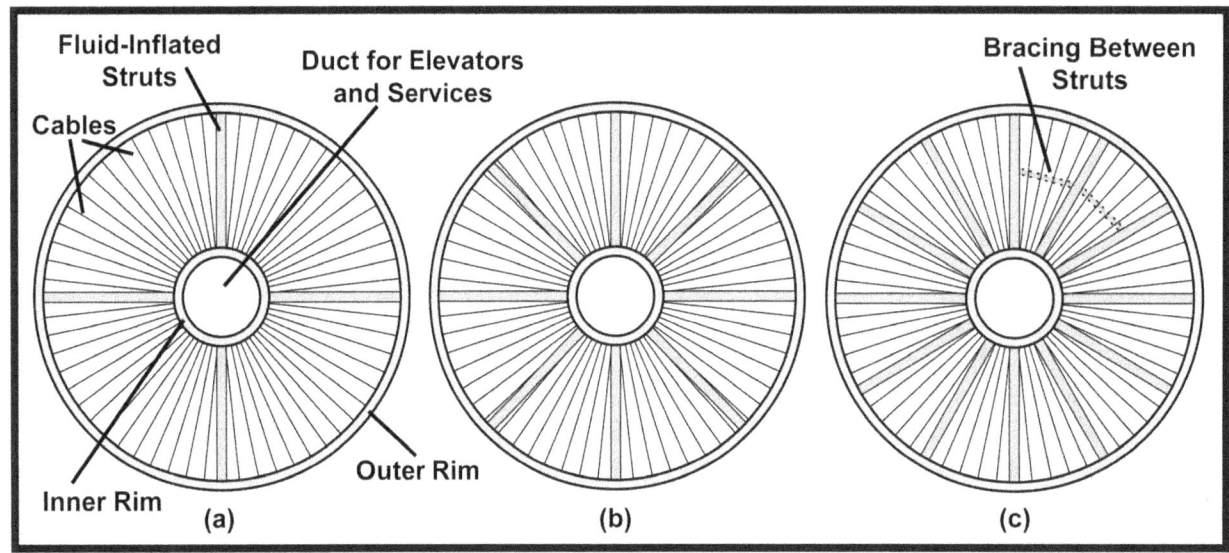

Figure 8.5: Circular cable-floor with horizontal fluid-inflated struts.

A more fruitful approach to the safety problem may be to either replace or supplement the internal air pressure in the pneumatic floor with a framework of high pressure, horizontal columns as shown in Figure 8.5. For an *80 FT* diameter *3 FT* deep doughnut shaped floor with a *12 FT* diameter central hole for vertical transportation and services, the slenderness ratio of such horizontal columns, or better referred to as struts, would be in the range of *20 to 30* depending on the degree of intermediate constraint[4]. Since each fluid-inflated strut is firmly fixed at both ends, as shown in Figure 8.5 (a), it would be classified as a column with *built-in* end-fixing conditions. Although it is common practice in orthodox building construction to consider the effective height (H_E) of such a member to be equal to half the physical length, a conservative factor of *0.65* may be more appropriate since the degree of constraint at the outer rim of the floor may be less than perfect (Lin and Stotesbury 1988, 317). However, if the strut is additionally braced at one or more

---

[3] According to Table 8.1, for a 10-story air-supported building with a diameter of at least 40 FT the air pressure in the pneumatic cable floor is likely to be 4 to 8 times higher and the volume is likely to be 1/50th of that in the building.

[4] Slenderness Ratio (SR) = $H_E / (R^2/2)^{0.5}$, where R is the radius and H_E is the effective height of the strut. With hinged end-supports and intermediate bracing the effective height of such a strut is likely to be equal or less than the actual height.

intermediate points, as shown in Figure 8.5 (c), then the effective length (synonymous with height) would be much less than the physical length with a suggested practical limit of *0.25H* (for pneumatic floors). It should be noted that for orthodox steel columns a slenderness ratio of less than *50* is normally categorized as a *short* column (Timoshenko and Gere 1961).

The combination of air-pressure within the entire floor disk volume and fluid-inflated struts may be the most desirable practical solution from a safety point of view. This would allow the struts to be designed to support the self-weight of the floor and a portion of the live-load. They would serve as a safety factor to maintain the structural integrity of the floor under emergency conditions, such as the sudden loss of air pressure within the disk. While several arrangements of struts are possible, it is likely that a symmetrical plan with at least four struts would be favored (Figure 8.5 (a)). Larger span circular floors would add struts in multiples of four depending on the practical spacing limitations around the perimeter of the inner rim near the center of the floor (Figure 8.5 (b) and (c)).

Regardless of whether pressurized safety struts are employed, as long as the integrity of the floor is wholly or partially dependent on the internal pressurization of the floor disk the maintenance of that air pressure is of paramount importance. Therefore, provision should be made for on-site monitoring and pressurization equipment during the life-span of the building. Both the pressure gauges for monitoring purposes and the stand-by pressurization equipment can be installed centrally for the entire building or as individual units on each floor. Where the proposed pneumatic cable floors became part of the kind of multi-story air-supported or fluid-inflated buildings described in this book, centralized facilities are likely to be preferred. In this case it would appear to make sense to combine the multiple monitoring and active and/or stand-by pressurization facilities in a central mechanical control room.

During the construction of a multi-story building with multiple pneumatic cable floors the assembly of each floor can take place at ground level, similar to the lift-slab construction process described in Chapter 3 (Section 3.9) for multi-story air-supported buildings. As far as possible the floor components would be prefabricated off-site. On-site assembly would start with the bottom surface plate. The prefabricated plate sections complete with tie-down attachments would be joined together, presumably by welding if the sections are made of steel. Next the prefabricated floor perimeter rim sections, with cable attachments already in place, would be assembled at the edge of the circular bottom surface plate. Again, the rim sections would be welded together if they are made of steel.

The radial cables can now be attached to the perimeter rim using a pin connector or similar fastening device (see Section 8.1.2, Figure 8.11(a)). The other ends of the radial cables are connected to solid steel shaft units as shown in Figure 8.6, again with pin connectors or similar fastening devices. Each of these shaft units is threaded to a length that is sufficient to allow for the cable to be stretched from a relaxed state to the final state plus any re-stressing that may have to be applied during the life of the floor to compensate for material creep.

Next, the inner floor rim that serves also as the innermost tension ring is assembled from prefabricated sections (welded if steel). The sections have predrilled holes for the attachment of the remaining ends of the radial cables. After each hole has been fitted with a rubber gasket the cable-end shafts are pushed through the rim and temporarily secured in a relaxed state with double nuts on steel washers and rubber rings (Figure 8.6). This is followed by the assembly of the top surface plate. Again, prefabricated plate sections complete with tie-down attachments are joined together by welding if the sections are made of steel. During this process the tie-downs are installed as each plate section is placed into position and welded to its adjoining sections.

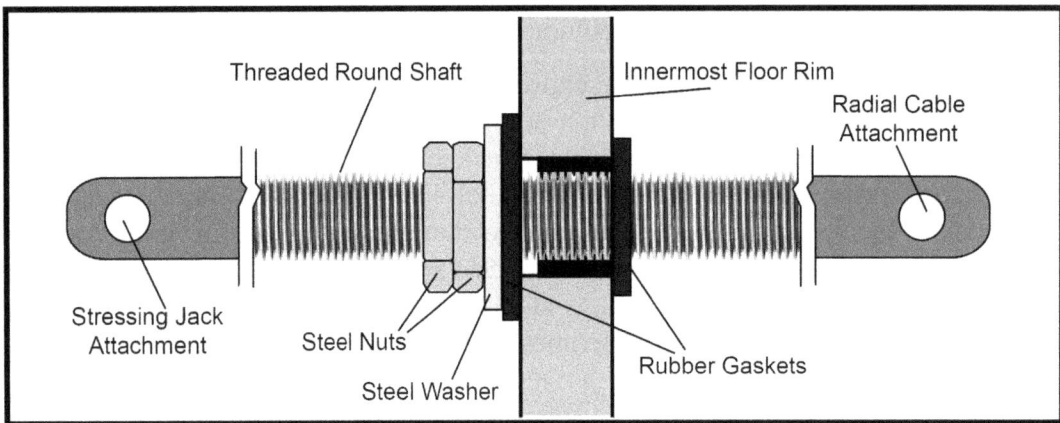

Figure 8.6: Sectional view of the cable-end shaft that attaches to the cable tensioning unit

The floor disk is now fully assembled as a sealed unit. Where the steel shaft ends of the radial cables penetrate the inner rim the provision of rubber gaskets and washers in combination with the screwed joint detail shown in Figure 8.6 should be adequate to prevent the leakage of air once the floor disk has been pressurized. The final operation involves the stretching of the radial cables and the concurrent internal pressurization of the floor disk to counterbalance the inward forces exerted by the cables.

Ideally the cables would be stretched to the desired sag level in unison. What is envisioned is a mobile cable tensioning unit with multiple cable attachments and a central jacking mechanism that is capable of exerting sufficient force to stretch all of the radially attached cables together in a sequence of single actions. With the tensioning unit positioned in the center of the inner rim the cable tensioning operation is ready to commence. After the cable-end shaft of each radial cable has been attached to the corresponding attachment of the cable tensioning unit, the tensioning of the cables can proceed in increments until the desired sag level is reached. However, each cable tensioning increment must be preceded by a commensurate pressurization of the air inside the floor disk so that the cable force acting inward is counterbalanced by the air pressure acting outward on the perimeter rim. As soon as the required cable tension has been reached the double nuts on each cable-end shaft are tightened to ensure a long-term air-tight seal. The cable tensioning unit is then disconnected from the cable-end shafts and hoisted up one floor depth level for the assembly of the next floor on top of the previously assembled floor.

There are two potential concerns that should be addressed. First, during the tensioning operation the radial cables will be totally hidden from view inside the floor disk. Therefore the size of each tensioning increment must be based on the indirect measurement of the tension in each cable rather than the direct measurement of the vertical sag level. While it would certainly be reassuring to be able to visually follow the incremental reduction in sag as the tension in each cable increases, this is not an essential requirement. However, it is most important that care is taken during the assembly of the floor to ensure that all of the cables are free from any actual or potential entanglement with each other and the tie-downs while in a relaxed state.

The second concern relates to the ability of the floor disk to maintain the progressively increasing internal air pressure during the incremental cable tensioning operation. While there may be reasonable confidence in the ability of the cable-end shaft detail shown in Figure 8.6 to provide a reliable long-term air-tight seal after the cables have reached their final tension and the double nuts have been tightened, the ability of the gaskets to remain air-tight during the tensioning operation is less certain. In fact, it should be expected that some air will escape through the cable holes in the inner rim before the double nuts have been tightened. For this reason the pressurization equipment must have the capacity to maintain the required internal air pressure despite the leakage of air through the cable holes in the inner rim. This should be possible in respect to commercially available pressurization equipment, particularly in the cable span to floor depth ratio range of *15* to *25* (i.e., *4.5%* to *6.5%* sag) where the pressure is unlikely to exceed *35 psig*.

If pressurized safety struts are part of the floor design (Figure 8.5) then these are prefabricated and either inflated during prefabrication or on-site before or after they have been placed into position. To ensure adequate access the positioning and bracing (if any) of the struts would normally occur after the assembly of the bottom surface plate and the perimeter and inner rims, but prior to the assembly of the top surface plate.

8.1.2 Cables and Connections

The history of wire rope, referred to in this book as cables, goes back to the mid 19th Century when hand-twisted strands of wrought-iron were used for hoisting material and equipment in German silver mines. Over the ensuing 50 years the machine production of modern steel cables developed progressively with the pioneering work of Andrew Smith and Robert Newell in England and John Roebling, Thomas Seale, Andrew Hallidie[5] and James Stone in the U.S. Even today, Stone's *(filler) 6 by 25 wire rope* and Seale's *equal-lay stranding* concepts form the basis of most modern cables.

Steel cables consist of three principal components, namely steel wire, strands and a core, with the wires and strands twisted around the core (Figure 8.7). The result is not a static structure, but a mechanism composed of several moving parts that are designed and manufactured with precise relationships to each other. These relationships vary depending on the specific purpose of the cable and the characteristics of the application environment. For example, a moving cable used for hoisting loads will be subject to both bending and tensile stresses must have a certain degree of flexibility, while stiffness is more desirable for a stationary cable that is primarily subject to tension. Therefore moving cables are typically composed of a larger number of small wires and cables for structural applications where strength is a major requirement are made up of a smaller number of large wires.

The fundamental material in a steel cable is the steel wire, normally made of high-strength, non-alloy carbon steel with a carbon content of 0.4% to 0.95% also often referred to as Plow Steel, which is a specific grade of steel. The most common steel grades are Improved Plow Steel (IPS), Extra Improved Plow Steel (EIP) and Extra Extra Improved Plow Steel (EEIP), with Stainless Steel and other grades of steel provided for special applications. In the manufacturing process a

---

[5] Actually Andrew H. Smith, the son of Andrew Smith, who eventually moved to San Francisco and changed his name to Andrew Smith Hallidie.

hot-rolled rod of around ½ *IN* diameter is annealed[6] and then drawn through a series of dies that increases the tensile strength of the rod. At the conclusion of this annealing process a round wire intended for structural applications can be expected to have a tensile strength of around *250,000 psi* with sufficient ductility to withstand a number of turns around a shaft that is three times the rod's diameter. For structural applications the wires are normally galvanized to provide some level of corrosion protection. In addition, the cable can be treated with a corrosion resistant lubricant during the manufacture and again after erection or encased in a tough plastic tube with up to a ¼ *IN* thick wall (e.g., high-density polyethylene).

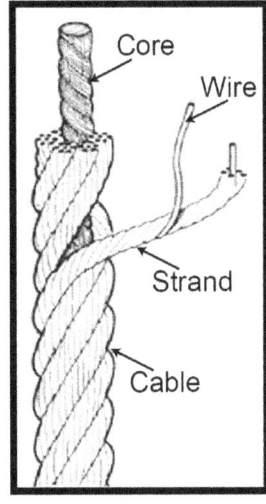
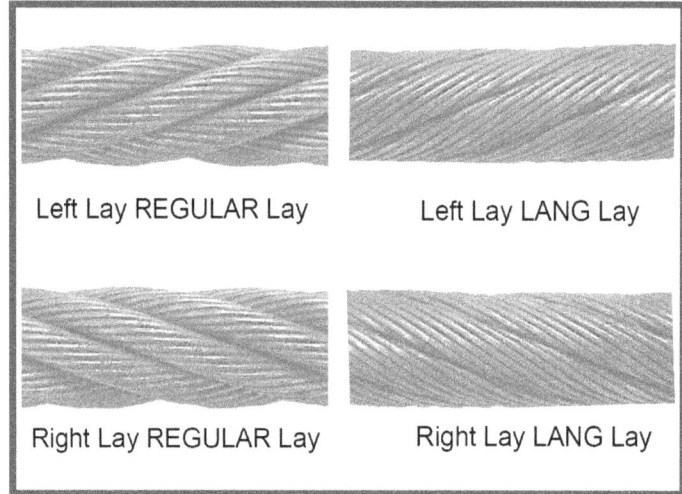

Figure 8.7: Cable components

Figure 8.8: Regular and Lang lays

The *lay* of a cable describes the way in which the wires and strands are twisted. While right lay and left lay refer to the direction of strands, Regular Lay and Lang Lay describe the way the wires are placed within each strand. In Regular lay the direction of the lay of the wires in the strand is in the opposite direction to the lay of the strands in the cable, while in Lang lay the direction of the wires in the strand is the same as the direction of the strands in the cable (Figure 8.8).

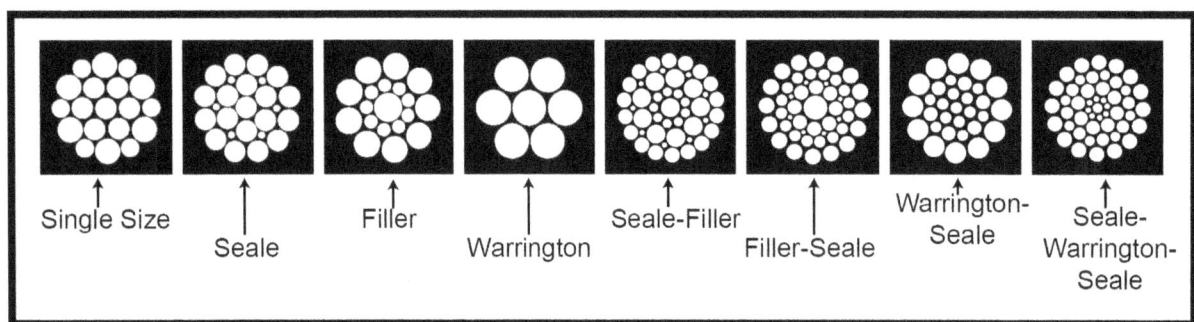

Figure 8.9: Strand construction patterns

According to these lay rules the wires are helically wound around a central wire into anyone of four strand patterns, namely: Single Size, in which wires of the same size are wound around a center wire; Seale, in which large outer wires with the same number of smaller inner wires are

---

[6] In the annealing process the rod is heated to over 1700 deg F and then quenched in a liquid bath to just less than 1000 deg F.

wound around a central wire; Filler, in which small wires fill spaces between large wires; and, Warrington, consisting of alternate large and small wires. As shown in Figure 8.9, the final cable may consist of a combination of these four strand patterns and may be covered with one or more layers of uniform-sized wires.

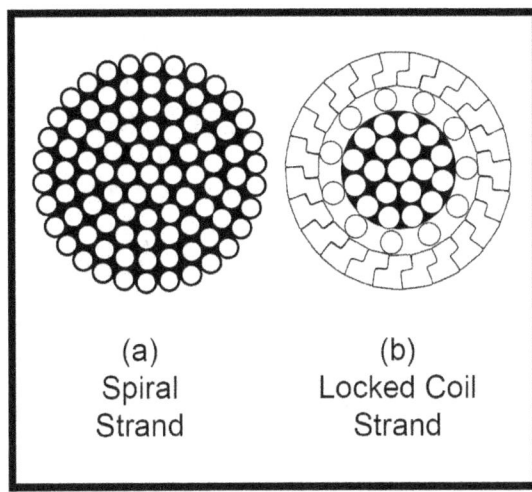

Figure 8.10: Cable strand configurations

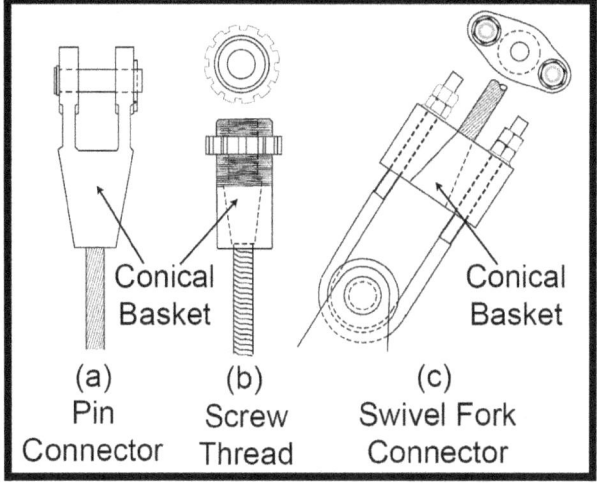

Figure 8.11: Typical socket terminals

Structural cables are most often of the single-strand type, in which layers of wires are twisted around a central wire until the required strength is obtained. If only round wires are used then the cable is referred to as a *spiral-strand* (Figure 8.10 (a)). In an alternative configuration one or more interlocking layers of wires around the perimeter provide the cable with a smooth external finish and a greater resistance to deformation. These are referred to as *locked coil strands* (Figure 8.10 (b)). While it is common practice to use the same tensile strength of wire throughout a spiral-strand, a locked coil cable may have a higher tensile strength for the internal round wires then for the external shaped wires. However, both the spiral-strand and locked coil configurations are satisfactory for structural cables (Table 8.3).

A high modulus of elasticity and a high tensile strength are desirable for all structural cable applications, to minimize the extension under load and the weight of the cable. While the modulus of elasticity of the steel wire is in the order of *27,500,000 psi*, this value will be reduced when the wire is stranded into a cable. The actual reduction depends greatly upon the lay length. Similarly the tensile strength of the cable is governed to a large extent by the lay length. The longer the lay length the closer the modulus of elasticity comes to the value of the steel wire and the higher the breaking load of the cable. For spiral-strands the lay length normally ranges from nine to 12 times the diameter of the cable depending on the size and complexity of the strands. In large, complex spirals the lay length has to be shortened to maintain a tight strand.

The interlocking of the outer layer allows locked coil cables to have longer lays across the entire size range that extends beyond *4 IN* diameter. Thus, while the modulus of elasticity of spiral-strand cables can vary between *21,000,000 psi* and *24,500,000 psi*, the equivalent value for locked coil cables is normally considered to be constant at *23,000,000 psi*. However, even though the locked coil cables have longer lays they do not necessarily offer greater strength because of the lower tensile strength of the external locking wires.

Table 8.3: Typical properties of Spiral-Strand and Locked Coil cables[7]

Diameter (IN)	Max. Load (LB)	Steel Area (SI)	Equiv. Stress (psi)	Weight (LB/FT)	Mod. of Elasticity (psi)
Spiral-Strand Cables:					
0.98	125,264	0.6	216,083	2.0	24,612,949
1.30	204,576	1.1	194,668	3.8	24,612,949
1.65	337,416	1.6	210,733	5.8	24,612,949
1.81	405,780	1.9	211,124	7.0	24,612,949
2.60	842,449	4.0	211,485	14.5	22,901,500
3.40	1,378,371	6.7	205,375	24.6	21,349,594
4.02	1,916,474	9.3	205,388	34.2	21,349,594
4.57	2,357,550	12.2	193,462	45.2	21,349,594
5.00	3,005,921	14.6	205,217	53.7	21,349,594
5.39	3,387,467	17.1	198,408	61.1	21,349,594
Locked Coil Cables:					
0.94	114,428	0.6	197,921	2.1	22,974,019
1.53	295,511	1.5	197,363	5.4	22,974,019
2.03	551,344	2.9	193,318	10.3	22,974,019
3.43	1,473,196	7.8	189,635	28.2	22,974,019
4.00	2,031,149	10.7	189,916	38.5	22,974,019
4.57	2,785,384	14.3	194,252	52.1	22,974,019

Cable weights cannot be calculated by simply multiplying the cross-sectional area of the cable with the weight of steel as is normal practice with structural steel members. The reason is the void space between wires, which is referred to as the fill factor of the cable. In the case of a single spiral-strand the fill factor is about 75%, while for a locked coil strand it is closer to 85%. However, the fill factor decreases further when a cable consists of multiple strands. For example, a six-stranded cable with a wire core may have a fill factor of only 60%. The same cable with a fiber core will have an even lower fill factor of around 50%. For this and other reasons related to greater cable elongation under stress and reduced strength properties, fiber core cables are not recommended for structural applications[8].

The terminals (Figure 8.11) that are used to connect cables to the supporting structure are generally galvanized steel castings that provide a socket for the cable-end. The process of securing a cable within the socket requires the wires at the cable-end to be unraveled and thoroughly cleaned and dried for a distance of about five to six times the cable diameter. The socket basket, with a major diameter that is two to three times the diameter of the cable, is then completely filled with a hot metal fill material such as zinc or a cold-poured polyester resin. The combination of a well designed connector and carefully prepared cable-end that is properly secured in the socket can be confidently expected to achieve the full breaking load of the cable.

---

[7] British Ropes Ltd (see Buchholdt 1985, 109-110); - converted from metric to American units by the author.

[8] Due to the tendency of fiber cores to stretch with an attendant reduction in diameter, increased fill factor, loss of pretension due to lengthening, and decreased modulus of elasticity. A fiber core is particularly susceptible to humid environments.

8.1.3 Design Process for Circular Pneumatic Cable Floors

This section describes a preliminary design process for circular pneumatic cable floors to establish order of magnitude tension member sizes and the approximate self-weight of the floor. The design formulas listed below apply to a circular pneumatic cable floor that is suspended from two concentric sets of equally spaced hangers or other supports located at the perimeter of the floor and along the inner tension ring. Therefore the cable span is less than half of the floor diameter (i.e., floor radius minus inner tension ring radius). Applicable variables are in the following units of measurement:

D = diameter of floor (FT)
d_1 = diameter of innermost tension ring (FT)
S = cable sag and depth of floor (FT)
f_{fl} = design strength in tension of the floor disk material (psi)
E = modulus of elasticity of floor disk material (psi)
w = weight of floor disk material (LB/CF)
f_{ca} = design strength in tension of cable material (psi)
w_{ca} = weight of cable material (LB/CF)
L_L = live-load on floor (psf)
D_L = dead-load (self-weight) of floor (psf)

Step 1: At the beginning the designer would typically specify the overall floor diameter (D FT), the diameter of the innermost tension ring (d_1 FT), the live-load (L_L psf) and dead-load (D_L psf) to be carried by the floor, the cable (f_{ca} psi) and floor disk (f_{fl} psi) material properties, and the depth of the floor (S FT). If the designer does not wish to specify the depth of the floor (i.e., cable sag) then it can be automatically assumed to be between 5% and 6% of the cable span. Since the self-weight (i.e., dead-load) of the floor is not known at the beginning, the designer would normally start with an estimate and then cycle through the design process a second time with a better estimate based on the first result.

Step 2: Determine the usable floor area (A SF) and the total floor load (W LB).

$A = \pi [(D/2)^2 - (d_1/2)^2]$ (SF)
$W = A (L_L + D_L)$ (LB)

Step 3: Assume cable spacing (s_{ca} FT) at innermost tension ring and no additional intermediate tension rings between the innermost tension ring and the outer compression rim. Then determine cable spacing (S_{ca} FT) at floor perimeter (i.e., compression rim), number of cables (n_{ca}), average load per *FT-run* of cable length (W_{run} LB/FT-run), cable span (L FT), horizontal component of cable tension (H_{CA} LB), and maximum cable tension (T_{max} LB).

$n_{ca} = \pi (d_1 / s_{ca})$
$S_{ca} = \pi (D / n_{ca})$ (FT)
$W_{run} = (W/A) [\pi ((D/n_{ca}) + (d_1/n_{ca}))] / 2$ (LB/FT-run)
$L = (D/2) - (d_1/2)$ (FT)
$H_{CA} = (W_{run} L^2) / (8 S)$ (LB) 8.1
$T_{max} = H_{CA} [1 + (16 S^2 / L^2)]^{0.5}$ (LB) 8.2

Step 4: Determine the required internal air pressure (P_F *psig*) to resist the inward cable forces acting on the perimeter rim of the floor. The internal pressure acts on an area (A_P *SF*) that is the product of the cable spacing at the floor perimeter (S_{ca} *FT*) and the floor depth (S *FT*).

$$A_P = S\,(S_{ca})\;(SF) \quad \text{...} \quad 8.3$$
$$P_F = H_{CA} / (144\,A_P)\;(\text{psig}) \quad \text{...} \quad 8.4$$

Step 5: Estimate the minimum cable material area (A_{CA} *SI*), radius (r_{ca} *IN*) and diameter (d_{ca} *IN*), allowing for a fill factor (F_{CA}) of *60%* to *85%*. This is only a rough order of magnitude of the cable size for preliminary design purposes. Manufacturers normally rate cables based on minimum breaking load rather than material stress (f_{ca} *psi*) due to the dependence of strength and modulus of elasticity on strand configuration, core and fill factor. For example, a *4 IN* diameter spiral-strand cable with a fill factor of *75%* may have a maximum breaking load rating of *1,916,000 LB* (*205,200 psi*) with a modulus of elasticity of *21,350,000 psi*, while a *4 IN* diameter locked coil cable with a fill factor of *85%* may have a maximum breaking load rating of *2,030,000 LB* (*190,000 psi*) with a modulus of elasticity of *23,000,000 psi* (Buchholdt 1985, 110). Therefore, the estimated cable diameter determined below must be adjusted for the type of cable and the appropriate factor of safety.

$$A_{CA} = T_{max} / f_{ca}\;(\text{SI})$$
$$r_{ca} = (A_{CA} / \pi)^{0.5}\;(\text{IN})$$
$$d_{ca} = 2\,r_{ca} / F_{CA}\;(\text{IN})$$

Step 6: Determine the thickness of the perimeter rim (t_{orim} *IN*) of the floor that must resist the balancing forces of the cables (H_{CA} *LB*) pulling inward and the internal air pressure (P_F *psig*) pushing outward, based on the material design stress (f_{orim} *psi*).

$$f_{orim} = P_F\,(12\,R) / t_{orim}\;(\text{psi})$$
$$t_{orim} = P_F\,(12\,R) / f_{orim}\;(\text{IN})$$

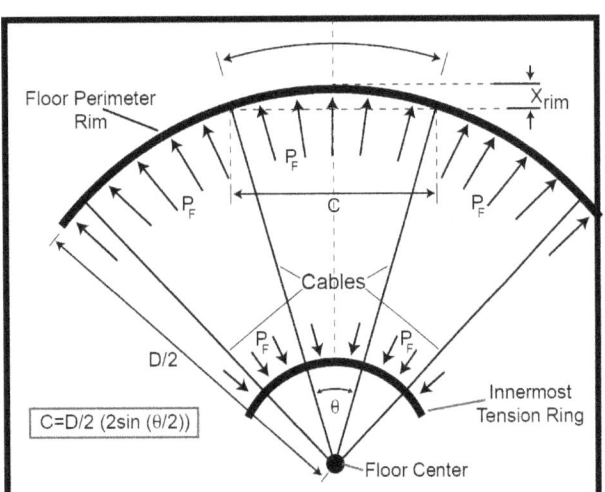
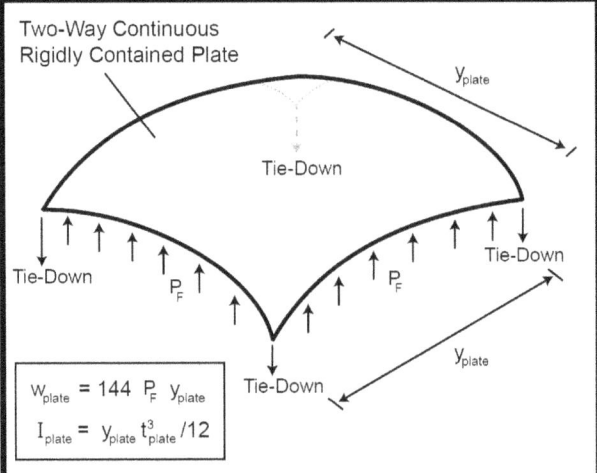

Figure 8.12 : Floor perimeter rim as a cable between two radial cables

Figure 8.13 : Top and bottom surfaces as two-way continuously constrained plates

An alternative method of calculating the thickness of the rim (t_{orim} *IN*) assumes that the rim acts like a cable between any two radial cables pulling inward (Figure 8.12). The angle subtended at the center of the floor (θ) by any two radial cables is equal to *360* divided by the total number of cables (n_{ca}), as follows:

$$\text{angle } \theta = 360 / n_{ca}$$

The span of the perimeter rim acting as a cable (*C FT* in Figure 8.12) between any two radial cables is given by:

$$C = (D/2)(2\sin(\theta/2)) = D\sin(\theta/2) \quad (FT)$$

and the sag of the rim (i.e., distance x_{orim} *FT* in Figure 8ab.1) is calculated as:

$$x_{orim} = (D/2) - [(D^2/4) - (C^2/4)]^{0.5} \quad (FT)$$

The load (L_{orim} *LB/FT-run*), horizontal component of the tension (h_{orim} *LB*), the full tension in the rim (T_{orim} *LB*), and the thickness of the rim (t_{orim} *IN*) are given by:

$$L_{orim} = 144 \, P_F \, (S) \quad (LB/FT\text{-run})$$

$$h_{orim} = L_{orim} \, C^2 / (8 \, x_{orim}) \quad (LB)$$

$$T_{orim} = h_{orim} \, [1 + (16 \, x_{orim}^2 / C^2)]^{0.5} \quad (LB)$$

$$t_{orim} = T_{orim} / (f_{orim} (12 \, S)) \quad (IN)$$

Step 7: Determine the thickness of the top and bottom floor plates with equally spaced (both directions) center-to-center (*y FT*) tension tie-downs between the two plates to resist the dishing effect due to the internal air pressure (P_F *psig*). Treating these plates as rigidly contained two-way slabs under distributed loading (w_{plate} *psf*), deflection (d_{plate} *IN*) rather than material stress in bending is the critical factor (Figure 8.13). Allowing for a maximum deflection of *span/480*, the thickness of each plate (t_{plate} *IN*) for the given material modulus of elasticity (E_{plate} *psi*) is given by:

$$w_{plate} = P_F (12 \, y) \quad (psf)$$

$$d_{plate} = 12 \, y / 480 \quad (IN)$$

$$d_{plate} = (1/384) \, [(w_{plate} \, y^3) / (E_{plate} \, (y \, t_{plate}^3) / 12)] \quad (IN)$$

$$t_{plate} = [(0.0312 \, P_F \, y^3) / (E_{plate} \, d_{plate})]^{0.3333} \quad (IN)$$

Step 8: Determine the cross-sectional area (A_{ties} *SI*), radius (r_{ties} *IN*), and diameter (d_{ties} *IN*) of the tension tie-downs that are needed to resist the dishing of the top and bottom floor plates due to the internal air pressure (L_{ties} *LB*), based on the design stress of the tie-down material (f_{ties} *psi*).

$$L_{ties} = 144 \, P_F \, y^2 \quad (LB)$$

$$A_{ties} = L_{ties} / f_{ties} \quad (SI)$$

$$r_{ties} = [(L_{ties}) / (\pi \, f_{ties})]^{0.5} \quad (IN)$$

$$d_{ties} = 2 \, r_{ties} \quad (IN)$$

and the number of tie-downs (n_{ties}) is given by dividing the total floor area (*A SF*) by the area supported by each tie-down, as follows:

$$n_{ties} = A / y^2$$

Step 9: Determine the total self-weight of the floor disk (W_{fl-LB} *LB*) consisting of the separate weights of the perimeter rim (W_{orim} *LB*), the inner rim (W_{irim} *LB*), the top and bottom floor plates (W_{plate} *LB*), the main (radial) cables (W_{rca} *LB*), and the tie-downs (W_{ties} *LB*) based on the respective material weights (w_{orim}, w_{irim}, w_{plate}, w_{rca}, and w_{ties} *LB/CF*). It seems reasonable to assume the thickness of the innermost tension ring to be the same thickness as the outer perimeter rim ($t_{orim\ IN}$).

$$W_{orim} = w_{orim} \, [(\pi \, D \, S) \, (t_{orim}/12)] \quad (LB)$$
$$W_{irim} = w_{irim} \, [(\pi \, d_1 \, S) \, (t_{orim}/12)] \quad (LB)$$
$$W_{plate} = w_{plate} \, [(2 \, A) \, (t_{plate}/12)] \quad (LB)$$
$$W_{ties} = w_{ties} \, [(n_{ties} \, S) \, (A_{ties}/144)] \quad (LB)$$

Before we can determine the weight of the radial cables we must calculate the length of a typical radial cable (X FT). The radius of curvature of the cable (R_{CA} FT) may be calculated as follows (see Table A-9 in Section A-11.2 of Appendix A):

$$R_{CA} = [((4 \, S^2) + D^2) / (8 \, S)] \quad (FT)$$

and the length of the cable (X_{CA} FT) is given by:

$$X_{CA} = (2 \, R_{CA} \, \arcsin\{((D - d_1)/2) / (2 \, R_{CA})\}) \quad (FT)$$
$$W_{rca} = w_{rca} \, [(n_{ca} \, X_{CA}) \, (A_{CA}/144)] \quad (LB)$$

The total self-weight of the floor (W_{fl-LB} LB) is equal to the sum of the component weights:

$$W_{fl-LB} = [W_{orim} + W_{irim} + W_{plate} + W_{ties} + W_{rca}] \quad (LB)$$

and the pounds per square foot self-weight of the floor (W_{fl-psf}) becomes:

$$W_{fl-psf} = W_{fl-LB} / A \quad (psf)$$

8.1.4 Example Design of Two Pneumatic Cable Floors

Based on the sequential design process outlined in the previous section we will perform the preliminary design of two circular pneumatic cable floors. In each case it will be assumed that the doughnut shaped floors are carrying a live-load of *100 psf* and that they are suspended from hangers at the floor perimeter and at an inner tension ring of some given diameter. The floor material is steel sheeting and steel cables with the following characteristics:

$$\text{yield strength of steel sheeting } (f_{fl}) = 60{,}000 \text{ psi}$$
$$\text{modulus of elasticity of steel sheeting } (E) = 29{,}000{,}000 \text{ psi}$$
$$\text{yield strength of cables } (f_{ca}) = 180{,}000 \text{ psi}$$
$$\text{weight of steel } (w) = 490 \text{ LB/CF}$$

Example 1 (150 FT diameter floor)

Step 1: The diameter (D FT) of the first example floor is *150 FT* with a single inner tension ring of *30 FT* diameter (d_1 FT). Radial cables are spaced at approximately *1 FT* centers around the inner tension ring and the floor has a depth of *3 FT* (i.e., cable sag). The dead-load (i.e., self-weight) of the floor is assumed to be *30 psf* for design purposes (will be verified upon completion).

Step 2: Determine the usable floor area (A SF) and the total floor load (W LB).

$$A = \pi \, [((D/2)^2 - (d_1/2)^2)] \quad (SF)$$
$$A = \pi \, [((75)^2 - (15)^2)]$$
$$A = \mathbf{16{,}964.59} \text{ SF}$$

$$W = A \, (L_L + D_L) \quad (LB)$$
$$W = 16964.59 \, (100 + 30)$$
$$W = \mathbf{2{,}205{,}396} \text{ LB}$$

Step 3: With cable spacing (s_{ca} FT) of *1 FT* at inner tension ring we can determine the cable spacing (S_{ca} FT) at floor perimeter (i.e., compression rim), number of cables (n_{ca}), average load per *FT-run* of cable length (W_{run} LB), cable span (*L* FT), horizontal component of cable tension (H_{CA} LB), and maximum cable tension (T_{max} LB).

$$n_{ca} = \pi\,(d_l/s_{ca})$$
$$n_{ca} = \pi\,(30/1)$$
$$n_{ca} = \mathbf{94\ cables}$$

$$S_{ca} = \pi\,(D/n_{ca})\ (\text{FT})$$
$$S_{ca} = \pi\,(150/94)$$
$$S_{ca} = \mathbf{5\ FT}$$

$$W_{run} = (W/A)\,[\pi\,(\,(D/n_{ca}) + (d_l/n_{ca})\,)]\,/2\ (\text{LB/FT-run})$$
$$W_{run} = 130\,[\pi\,(\,(150/94) + (30/94)\,)]\,/2$$
$$W_{run} = 130\,[\pi\,(\,(1.596) + (0.319)\,)]\,/2$$
$$W_{run} = \mathbf{391\ LB/FT\text{-}run}$$

$$L = (D/2) - (d_l/2)\ (\text{FT})$$
$$L = (75) - (15)$$
$$L = \mathbf{60\ FT}$$

$$H_{CA} = (W_{run}\,L^2)\,/\,(8\,S)\ (\text{LB}) \quad\quad\quad 8.1$$
$$H_{CA} = (1407600)\,/\,(24)$$
$$H_{CA} = \mathbf{58{,}650\ LB}$$

$$T_{max} = H_{CA}\,[1 + (16\,S^2/L^2)]^{0.5}\ (\text{LB}) \quad\quad\quad 8.2$$
$$T_{max} = 58650\,[1 + (0.04)]^{0.5}$$
$$T_{max} = 58650\,[1.0198]$$
$$T_{max} = \mathbf{59{,}811.5\ LB}$$

Step 4: Determine the required internal air pressure (P_F psig) to resist the inward cable forces acting on the perimeter rim of the floor. The internal pressure acts on an area (A_P SF) that is the product of the cable spacing at the floor perimeter (S_{ca} FT) and the floor depth (*S* FT).

$$A_P = S\,(S_{ca})\ (\text{SF}) \quad\quad\quad 8.3$$
$$A_P = 3\,(5)$$
$$A_P = \mathbf{15\ SF}$$

$$P_F = H_{CA}\,/\,(144\,A_P)\ (\text{psig}) \quad\quad\quad 8.4$$
$$P_F = 58650\,/\,(144\,(15))$$
$$P_F = \mathbf{27.15\ psig}$$

Step 5: Determine the minimum cable material area (A_{CA} SI), radius (r_{ca} IN) and diameter (d_{ca} IN), allowing for a fill factor (F_{CA}) of *75%*. This is only a rough order of magnitude of the cable size for preliminary design purposes.

$$A_{CA} = T_{max}\,/\,f_{ca}\ (\text{SI})$$
$$A_{CA} = 59811.5\,/\,180000$$
$$A_{CA} = \mathbf{0.3323\ SI}$$

$$r_{ca} = (A_{CA}\,/\,\pi)^{0.5}\ (\text{IN})$$
$$r_{ca} = (0.3323\,/\,\pi)^{0.5}$$

$$r_{ca} = \mathbf{0.3252} \text{ IN}$$
$$d_{ca} = 2\, r_{ca} / F_{CA} \text{ (IN)}$$
$$d_{ca} = 2\,(0.3252) / 0.75$$
$$d_{ca} = \mathbf{0.8672} \text{ IN}$$

Step 6: Determine the thickness of the perimeter rim (t_{orim} *IN*) of the floor that must resist the balancing forces of the cables (H_{CA} *LB*) pulling inward and the internal air pressure (P_F *psig*) pushing outward, based on the material design stress (f_{fl} *psi*).

$$f_{fl} = P_F\,(12\,R) / t_{orim} \text{ (psi)}$$
$$t_{orim} = P_F\,(12\,R) / f_{fl} \text{ (IN)}$$
$$t_{orim} = 27.15\,(12\,(75)) / 60000 \text{ (IN)}$$
$$t_{orim} = \mathbf{0.41} \text{ IN}$$

An alternative method of calculating the thickness of the rim (t_{orim} *IN*) assumes that the rim acts like a cable between any two radial cables pulling inward (Figure 8.12). The angle subtended at the center of the floor (θ) by any two radial cables is equal to *360* divided by the total number of cables (n_{ca}), as follows:

$$\text{angle } \theta = 360 / n_{ca} \text{ deg}$$
$$\text{angle } \theta = 360 / 94$$
$$\text{angle } \theta = \mathbf{3.8298} \text{ deg} \quad \text{(or 3 deg 50 min)}$$

The span of the perimeter rim acting as a cable (*C FT* in Figure 8.12) between any two radial cables is given by:

$$C = D \sin(\theta/2) \text{ (FT)}$$
$$C = 150 \sin(1.9149)$$
$$C = \mathbf{4.98} \text{ FT}$$

and the sag of the rim (i.e., distance x_{orim} *FT* in Figure 8.12) is calculated as:

$$x_{orim} = (D/2) - [(D^2/4) - (C^2/4)]^{0.5} \text{ (FT)}$$
$$x_{orim} = (75) - [(5625) - (6.2)]^{0.5}$$
$$x_{orim} = (75) - [74.96]$$
$$x_{orim} = \mathbf{0.04} \text{ FT}$$

The load (L_{orim} *LB/FT-run*), horizontal component of the tension (h_{orim} *LB*), the full tension in the rim (T_{orim} *LB*), and the thickness of the rim (t_{orim} *IN*) are given by:

$$L_{orim} = 144\,P_F\,(S) \text{ (LB/FT-run)}$$
$$L_{orim} = 144\,(27.15)\,(3)$$
$$L_{orim} = \mathbf{11{,}728.8} \text{ LB/FT-run}$$

$$h_{orim} = L_{orim}\,C^2 / (8\,x_{orim}) \text{ (LB)}$$
$$h_{orim} = 11728.8\,(24.8) / (0.32)$$
$$h_{orim} = \mathbf{908{,}982} \text{ LB}$$

$$T_{orim} = h_{orim}\,[1 + (16\,x_{orim}^2 / C^2)]^{0.5} \text{ (LB)}$$
$$T_{orim} = 908982\,[1 + (0.0256 / 24.8)]^{0.5}$$
$$T_{orim} = 908982\,[1.0010]^{0.5}$$
$$T_{orim} = \mathbf{909{,}451} \text{ LB}$$

$$t_{orim} = T_{orim} / (f_{fl}\,(12\,S)) \text{ (IN)}$$

$$t_{orim} = 909451 / (60000 (12 (3)))$$
$$t_{orim} = \mathbf{0.42 \text{ IN}}$$

Step 7: Determine the thickness of the top and bottom floor plates with tie-downs spaced at *4 FT* centers (*y FT*) between the two plates to resist the dishing effect due to the internal air pressure (P_F *psig*). Treating these plates as rigidly contained two-way slabs under distributed loading (w_{plate} *psf*), deflection (d_{plate} *IN*) rather than material stress in bending is the critical factor (Figure 8.13). Allowing for a maximum deflection of *span/480*, the thickness of each plate (t_{plate} *IN*) for the given material modulus of elasticity (*E psi*) is given by:

$$w_{plate} = P_F (12 y) \text{ (psf)}$$
$$w_{plate} = 27.15 (12 (4))$$
$$w_{plate} = \mathbf{1{,}303.2 \text{ psf}}$$

$$d_{plate} = 12 y / 480 \text{ (IN)}$$
$$d_{plate} = 48 / 480$$
$$d_{plate} = \mathbf{0.1 \text{ IN}}$$

$$d_{plate} = (1/384) [(w_{plate} \, y^3) / (E_{plate} (y \, t_{plate}^3) / 12)] \text{ (IN)}$$
$$t_{plate} = [(0.0312 \, P_F \, y^3) / (E_{plate} \, d_{plate})]^{0.3333} \text{ (IN)}$$
$$t_{plate} = [(0.0312 (27.15)(110592) / (29000000 (0.1))]^{0.3333}$$
$$t_{plate} = [93680.27 / 2900000]^{0.3333}$$
$$t_{plate} = \mathbf{0.32 \text{ IN}}$$

Step 8: Determine the cross-sectional area (A_{ties} *SI*), radius (r_{ties} *IN*), and diameter (d_{ties} *IN*) of the tension tie-downs that are needed to resist the dishing of the top and bottom floor plates due to the internal air pressure (L_{ties} *LB*), based on the design stress of the tie-down material (f_{fl} *psi*).

$$L_{ties} = 144 \, P_F \, y^2 \text{ (LB)}$$
$$L_{ties} = 144 (27.15)(16)$$
$$L_{ties} = \mathbf{62{,}553.6 \text{ LB}}$$

$$A_{ties} = L_{ties} / f_{fl} \text{ (SI)}$$
$$A_{ties} = 62553.6 / 60000$$
$$A_{ties} = \mathbf{1.0426 \text{ SI}}$$

$$r_{ties} = [(L_{ties}) / (\pi \, f_{fl})]^{0.5} \text{ (IN)}$$
$$r_{ties} = [62553.6 / (\pi (60000))]^{0.5}$$
$$r_{ties} = [0.3319]^{0.5}$$
$$r_{ties} = \mathbf{0.5761 \text{ IN}}$$

$$d_{ties} = 2 \, r_{ties} \text{ (IN)}$$
$$d_{ties} = 2 (0.5761)$$
$$d_{ties} = \mathbf{1.152 \text{ IN}}$$

and the number of tie-downs (n_{ties}) is given by dividing the total floor area (*A SF*) by the area supported by each tie-down, as follows:

$$n_{ties} = A / y^2$$
$$n_{ties} = 16964.59 / 16$$
$$n_{ties} = \mathbf{1{,}061}$$

Step 9: Determine the total self-weight of the floor disk (W_{fl-LB} LB) consisting of the separate weights of the perimeter rim (W_{orim} LB), the inner rim (W_{irim} LB), the top and bottom floor plates (W_{plate} LB), the main (radial) cables (W_{rca} LB), and the tie-downs (W_{ties} LB) based on the respective material weights (w_{orim}, w_{irim}, w_{plate}, w_{rca}, and w_{ties} LB/CF). It seems reasonable to assume the thickness of the innermost tension ring to be the same thickness as the outer perimeter rim (t_{orim} IN).

$$W_{orim} = w_{orim} \,[(\pi \, D \, S)(t_{orim}/12)] \quad (LB)$$
$$W_{orim} = 490 \,[(\pi \,(150)(3))(0.41/12)]$$
$$W_{orim} = \mathbf{23{,}668 \text{ LB}}$$

$$W_{irim} = w_{irim} \,[(\pi \, d_1 \, S)(t_{orim}/12)] \quad (LB)$$
$$W_{irim} = 490 \,[(\pi \,(30)(3))(0.41/12)]$$
$$W_{irim} = \mathbf{4{,}734 \text{ LB}}$$

$$W_{plate} = w_{plate} \,[(2 \, A)(t_{plate}/12)] \quad (LB)$$
$$W_{plate} = 490 \,[(2 \,(16964.59))(0.32/12)]$$
$$W_{plate} = \mathbf{443{,}341 \text{ LB}}$$

$$W_{ties} = w_{ties} \,[(n_{ties} \, S)(A_{ties}/144)] \quad (LB)$$
$$W_{ties} = 490 \,[(1061 \,(3))(1.0426/144)]$$
$$W_{ties} = \mathbf{11{,}292 \text{ LB}}$$

Before we can determine the weight of the radial cables we must calculate the length of a typical radial cable (X FT). The radius of curvature of the cable (R_{CA} FT) may be calculated as follows (see Table A-9 in Section A-11.2 of Appendix A):

$$R_{CA} = [((4 \, S^2) + D^2)/(8 \, S)] \quad (FT)$$
$$R_{CA} = [((4 \,(9)) + 22500)/(8 \,(3))]$$
$$R_{CA} = \mathbf{939 \text{ FT}}$$

and the length of the cable (X_{CA} FT) is given by:

$$X_{CA} = (2 \, R_{CA} \arcsin\{((D - d_1)/2)/(2 \, R_{CA})\}) \quad (FT)$$
$$X_{CA} = (2 \,(939) \arcsin\{0.0319\})$$
$$X_{CA} = (1878 \,(0.0319))$$
$$X_{CA} = \mathbf{59.9 \text{ FT}}$$

$$W_{rca} = w_{rca} \,[(n_{ca} \, X_{CA})(A_{CA}/144)] \quad (LB)$$
$$W_{rca} = 490 \,[(94)(59.9)(0.3323/144)]$$
$$W_{rca} = \mathbf{6{,}367 \text{ LB}}$$

The total self-weight of the floor (W_{fl-LB} LB) is equal to the sum of the component weights:

$$W_{fl-LB} = [W_{orim} + W_{irim} + W_{plate} + W_{ties} + W_{rca}] \quad (LB)$$
$$W_{fl-LB} = [23668 + 4734 + 443341 + 11292 + 6367]$$
$$W_{fl-LB} = \mathbf{513{,}070 \text{ LB}}$$

and the pounds per square foot self-weight of the floor (W_{fl-psf}) becomes:

$$W_{fl-psf} = W_{fl-LB} / A \quad (psf)$$
$$W_{fl-psf} = 513070 / 16964.59$$
$$W_{fl-psf} = \mathbf{30.24 \text{ psf}} \text{ (confirms the assumed self-weight of the floor)}$$

Example 2 (300 FT diameter floor)

For the second example the pneumatic cable floor is much larger with twice the diameter of the floor in the first example. This example will show that such large floor spans are feasible with a commensurate increase in floor depth.

Step 1: The diameter (D FT) of the second example floor is *300 FT* with a single inner tension ring of *30 FT* diameter (d_1 FT). Like the first example radial cables are again spaced at approximately *1 FT* centers around the inner tension ring. However, this time the floor depth has been increased to just under *5 FT* (i.e., *4.88 FT*). The dead-load (i.e., self-weight) of the floor is assumed to be *40 psf* for design purposes and will again be verified upon completion.

Step 2: Determine the usable floor area (A SF) and the total floor load (W LB).

$$A = \pi [(D/2)^2 - (d_1/2)^2] \text{ (SF)}$$
$$A = \pi [(150)^2 - (15)^2]$$
$$A = \mathbf{69{,}978.9 \text{ SF}}$$

$$W = A(L_L + D_L) \text{ (LB)}$$
$$W = 69978.9 \,(100 + 40)$$
$$W = \mathbf{9{,}797{,}046 \text{ LB}}$$

Step 3: With cable spacing (s_{ca} FT) of *1 FT* at inner tension ring we can determine the cable spacing (S_{ca} FT) at floor perimeter (i.e., compression rim), number of cables (n_{ca}), average load per *FT-run* of cable length (W_{run} LB), cable span (L FT), horizontal component of cable tension (H_{CA} LB), and maximum cable tension (T_{max} LB).

$$n_{ca} = \pi (d_1 / s_{ca})$$
$$n_{ca} = \pi (30/1)$$
$$n_{ca} = \mathbf{94 \text{ cables}}$$

$$S_{ca} = \pi (D / n_{ca}) \text{ (FT)}$$
$$S_{ca} = \pi (300/94)$$
$$S_{ca} = \mathbf{10 \text{ FT}}$$

$$W_{run} = (W/A) [\pi((D/n_{ca}) + (d_1/n_{ca}))]/2 \text{ (LB/FT-run)}$$
$$W_{run} = 140 [\pi((300/94) + (30/94))]/2$$
$$W_{run} = 140 [\pi(3.191) + (0.319)]/2$$
$$W_{run} = \mathbf{771.9 \text{ LB/FT-run}}$$

$$L = (D/2) - (d_1/2) \text{ (FT)}$$
$$L = (150) - (15)$$
$$L = \mathbf{135 \text{ FT}}$$

$$H_{CA} = (W_{run} L^2) / (8S) \text{ (LB)} \quad\quad\quad 8.1$$
$$H_{CA} = (14067877) / (39.04)$$
$$H_{CA} = \mathbf{360{,}345 \text{ LB}}$$

$$T_{max} = H_{CA} [1 + (16 S^2 / L^2)]^{0.5} \text{ (LB)} \quad\quad\quad 8.2$$
$$T_{max} = 360345 [1 + (0.0209)]^{0.5}$$
$$T_{max} = 360345 [1.0104]$$
$$T_{max} = \mathbf{364{,}092 \text{ LB}}$$

Step 4: Determine the required internal air pressure (P_F *psig*) to resist the inward cable forces acting on the perimeter rim of the floor. The internal pressure acts on an area (A_P SF) that is the product of the cable spacing at the floor perimeter (S_{ca} FT) and the floor depth (S FT).

$$A_P = S (S_{ca}) (SF) \quad\quad\quad\quad 8.3$$
$$A_P = 4.88 (10)$$
$$A_P = \mathbf{48.8 \text{ SF}}$$

$$P_F = H_{CA} / (144 A_P) \text{ (psig)} \quad\quad\quad\quad 8.4$$
$$P_F = 360345 / (144 (48.8))$$
$$P_F = \mathbf{51.28 \text{ psig}}$$

Step 5: Determine the minimum cable material area (A_{CA} SI), radius (r_{ca} IN) and diameter (d_{ca} IN), allowing for a fill factor (F_{CA}) of *75%*. This is only a rough order of magnitude of the cable size for preliminary design purposes.

$$A_{CA} = T_{max} / f_{ca} \text{ (SI)}$$
$$A_{CA} = 364092 / 180000$$
$$A_{CA} = \mathbf{2.0227 \text{ SI}}$$

$$r_{ca} = (A_{CA} / \pi)^{0.5} \text{ (IN)}$$
$$r_{ca} = (2.0227 / \pi)^{0.5}$$
$$r_{ca} = \mathbf{0.8024 \text{ IN}}$$

$$d_{ca} = 2 r_{ca} / F_{CA} \text{ (IN)}$$
$$d_{ca} = 2 (0.8024) / 0.75$$
$$d_{ca} = \mathbf{2.1397 \text{ IN}}$$

Step 6: Determine the thickness of the perimeter rim (t_{orim} IN) of the floor that must resist the balancing forces of the cables (H_{CA} LB) pulling inward and the internal air pressure (P_F *psig*) pushing outward, based on the material design stress (f_{fl} *psi*).

$$f_{fl} = P_F (12 R) / t_{orim} \text{ (psi)}$$
$$t_{orim} = P_F (12 R) / f_{fl} \text{ (IN)}$$
$$t_{orim} = 51.28 (12 (150)) / 60000 \text{ (IN)}$$
$$t_{orim} = \mathbf{1.5384 \text{ IN}}$$

Step 7: Determine the thickness of the top and bottom floor plates with tie-downs spaced at *4 FT* centers (*y* FT) between the two plates to resist the dishing effect due to the internal air pressure (P_F *psig*). Treating these plates as rigidly contained two-way slabs under distributed loading (w_{plate} *psf*), deflection (d_{plate} IN) rather than material stress in bending is the critical factor (Figure 8.13). Allowing for a maximum deflection of *span/480*, the thickness of each plate (t_{plate} IN) for the given material modulus of elasticity (*E psi*) is given by:

$$w_{plate} = P_F (12 y) \text{ (psf)}$$
$$w_{plate} = 51.28 (12 (4))$$
$$w_{plate} = \mathbf{2{,}461.4 \text{ psf}}$$

$$d_{plate} = 12 y / 480 \text{ (IN)}$$
$$d_{plate} = 48 / 480$$
$$d_{plate} = \mathbf{0.1 \text{ IN}}$$

$$d_{plate} = (1/384) [(w_{plate} \, y^3) / (E_{plate} (y \, t_{plate}^3) / 12)] \text{ (IN)}$$

$$t_{plate} = [(0.0312 \, P_F \, y^3) / (E_{plate} \, d_{plate})]^{0.3333} \quad (IN)$$
$$t_{plate} = [(0.0312 \, (51.28) \, (110592)) / (29000000 \, (0.1))]^{0.3333}$$
$$t_{plate} = [176940.12 / 2900000]^{0.3333}$$
$$t_{plate} = \mathbf{0.3937 \, IN}$$

Step 8: Determine the cross-sectional area (A_{ties} *SI*), radius (r_{ties} *IN*), and diameter (d_{ties} *IN*) of the tension tie-downs that are needed to resist the dishing of the top and bottom floor plates due to the internal air pressure (L_{ties} *LB*), based on the design stress of the tie-down material (f_{fl} *psi*).

$$L_{ties} = 144 \, P_F \, y^2 \quad (LB)$$
$$L_{ties} = 144 \, (51.28) \, (16)$$
$$L_{ties} = \mathbf{118{,}149.1 \, LB}$$

$$A_{ties} = L_{ties} / f_{fl} \quad (SI)$$
$$A_{ties} = 118149.1 / 60000$$
$$A_{ties} = \mathbf{1.9692 \, SI}$$

$$r_{ties} = [(L_{ties}) / (\pi \, f_{fl})]^{0.5} \quad (IN)$$
$$r_{ties} = [118149.1 / (\pi \, (60000))]^{0.5}$$
$$r_{ties} = [0.6268]^{0.5}$$
$$r_{ties} = \mathbf{0.7917 \, IN}$$

$$d_{ties} = 2 \, r_{ties} \quad (IN)$$
$$d_{ties} = 2 \, (0.5761)$$
$$d_{ties} = \mathbf{1.5834 \, IN}$$

and the number of tie-downs (n_{ties}) is given by dividing the total floor area (*A SF*) by the area supported by each tie-down, as follows:

$$n_{ties} = A / y^2$$
$$n_{ties} = 69978.9 / 16$$
$$n_{ties} = \mathbf{4{,}373}$$

Step 9: Determine the total self-weight of the floor disk (W_{fl-LB} *LB*) consisting of the separate weights of the perimeter rim (W_{orim} *LB*), the inner rim (W_{irim} *LB*), the top and bottom floor plates (W_{plate} *LB*), the main (radial) cables (W_{rca} *LB*), and the tie-downs (W_{ties} *LB*) based on the respective material weights (w_{orim}, w_{irim}, w_{plate}, w_{rca}, and w_{ties} *LB/CF*). It seems reasonable to assume the thickness of the innermost tension ring to be the same thickness as the outer perimeter rim (t_{orim} *IN*).

$$W_{orim} = w_{orim} \, [(\pi \, D \, S) \, (t_{orim}/12)] \quad (LB)$$
$$W_{orim} = 490 \, [(\pi \, (300) \, (4.88)) \, (1.5384/12)]$$
$$W_{orim} = \mathbf{288{,}918 \, LB}$$

$$W_{irim} = w_{irim} \, [(\pi \, d_1 \, S) \, (t_{orim}/12)] \quad (LB)$$
$$W_{irim} = 490 \, [(\pi \, (30) \, (4.88)) \, (1.5384/12)]$$
$$W_{irim} = \mathbf{28{,}891.8 \, LB}$$

$$W_{plate} = w_{plate} \, [(2 \, A) \, (t_{plate}/12)] \quad (LB)$$
$$W_{plate} = 490 \, [(2 \, (69978.9)) \, (0.3937/12)]$$
$$W_{plate} = \mathbf{2{,}249{,}973 \, LB}$$

$$W_{ties} = w_{ties} \, [(n_{ties} \, S) \, (A_{ties}/144)] \quad (LB)$$

$$W_{ties} = 490\ [(4373\ (4.88))\ (1.9692/144)]$$
$$W_{ties} = \mathbf{142{,}995.6\ \text{LB}}$$

Before we can determine the weight of the radial cables we must calculate the length of a typical radial cable (X FT). The radius of curvature of the cable (R_{CA} FT) may be calculated as follows (see Table A-9 in Section A-11.2 of Appendix A):

$$R_{CA} = [((4\ S^2) + D^2)/(8\ S)]\ (\text{FT})$$
$$R_{CA} = [((4\ (23.81)) + 90000)/(8\ (4.88))]$$
$$R_{CA} = \mathbf{2{,}307.77\ \text{FT}}$$

and the length of the cable (X_{CA} FT) is given by:

$$X_{CA} = (2\ R_{CA}\ \arcsin\{((D - d_1)/2)/(2\ R_{CA})\})\ (\text{FT})$$
$$X_{CA} = (2\ (2307.77)\ \arcsin\{0.0292\})$$
$$X_{CA} = (4615.54\ (0.0292))$$
$$X_{CA} = \mathbf{134.77\ \text{FT}}$$

$$W_{rca} = w_{rca}\ [(n_{ca}\ X_{CA})\ (A_{CA}/144)]\ (\text{LB})$$
$$W_{rca} = 490\ [(94)(134.77)\ (2.0227/144)]$$
$$W_{rca} = \mathbf{87{,}193.9\ \text{LB}}$$

The total self-weight of the floor ($W_{fl\text{-}LB}$ LB) is equal to the sum of the component weights:

$$W_{fl\text{-}LB} = [W_{orim} + W_{irim} + W_{plate} + W_{ties} + W_{rca}]\ (\text{LB})$$
$$W_{fl\text{-}LB} = [288918 + 28891.8 + 2249973 + 142995.6 + 87193.9]$$
$$W_{fl\text{-}LB} = \mathbf{2{,}797{,}972\ \text{LB}}$$

and the pounds per square foot self-weight of the floor ($W_{fl\text{-}psf}$) becomes:

$$W_{fl\text{-}psf} = W_{fl\text{-}LB}/A\ (\text{psf})$$
$$W_{fl\text{-}psf} = 2797972/69978.9$$
$$W_{fl\text{-}psf} = \mathbf{39.98\ \text{psf}}\ (\text{confirms the assumed self-weight of the floor})$$

Comparison of Examples 1 and 2

It is interesting to note that the comparison of the two example floors (Table 8.4) shows that the increase in the self-weight of a pneumatic cable floor is not linear with increasing cable span.

Table 8.4: Comparison of *150 FT* and *300 FT* diameter pneumatic cable floors

Design Parameters	Example (1)	Example (2)	Difference
floor diameter	150 FT	300 FT	+ 100%
cable span	60 FT	135 FT	+ 125%
floor depth (cable sag)	3.00 FT	4.88 FT	+ 63%
percent sag	5.0%	3.6%	- 28%
internal air pressure	27.15 psig	51.28 psig	+ 89%
diameter of radial cables	0.8672 IN	2.1397 IN	+ 146%
usable floor area	16,968 SF	69,972 SF	+ 312%
self-weight of floor	30.24 psf	39.98 psf	+ 32%
span/depth ratio	20.0	27.7	+ 38%
span/weight ratio	1.97	3.38	+ 72%

With a *125%* increase in cable span (i.e., from *60 FT* to *135 FT*) the self-weight of the floor has increased by only *32%* (i.e., from *30.24 psf* to *39.98 psf*). However, since the cable sag and therefore the depth of the floor have also increased by *63%* one could argue that the span/weight ratio might be a more accurate comparison metric. As shown in the last row of Table 8.4, the span/weight ratio has risen from *1.97* for the *150 FT* diameter floor to *3.38* for the *300 FT* diameter floor; - representing an increase of *72%*. Perhaps even more significant is the *312%* increase in usable floor area in favor of the *300 FT* diameter floor. Finally, it should be noted that these economies for the *300 FT* diameter floor were achieved with only a *38%* increase in the span/depth ratio from *20* to *27.7* and, surprisingly, an attendant reduction of *28%* in the cable sag percentage (from *5.0%* to *3.6%*) indicating that the larger floor is proportionally shallower than the smaller floor.

8.2 Circular Pneumatic Cable Roofs

A circular pneumatic cable roof will differ from a floor in respect to significantly larger span, less restrictive depth (i.e., cable sag), and the likely need to cover the hole in the roof inside the inner tension ring. While in the case of a pneumatic cable floor this hole is convenient for vertical access in a multi-story building (i.e., elevators and staircase) and the provision of a vertical services shaft (i.e., plumbing, electric power, HVAC), these requirements do not apply in the case of a roof.

The structural design of a pneumatic cable roof proceeds in the same steps outlined in Section 8.1.3 for pneumatic cable floors with the following exceptions:

Step 2: The area of the roof is calculated as the total area covered by the roof and the live-load is likely to be much less than *100 psf* unless the roof is openly accessible to the public.

Step 7: The allowable maximum deflection of the top and bottom roof plates is likely to be less stringent than in the case of a floor. Whereas a maximum deflection of *span/480* is recommended for floors, it is suggested by the author that this limit may be reasonably increased to *span/240* in the case of roofs, allowing either an increased spacing of tie-downs or a reduction in the thickness of the plate sheeting with the same center-to-center spacing of the tie-downs used in the design of the two example floors (see Section 8.1.4).

Step 8: The roof area within the inner rim (i.e., innermost tension ring) is not pressurized and will require a secondary structure (e.g., a circular inset of radial open web joists with steel angle bracing at equidistant centers from the center of the roof outward) presumably covered with the same top/bottom plate material employed for the pressurized section of the roof. Therefore, no tie-downs will be required in this unpressurized central section of the roof. Accordingly the roof area requiring tie-downs will be the total roof area less the area of the unpressurized central section.

The self-weight reduction that can be achieved over orthodox steel or concrete construction with the total tension structure of a pneumatic cable roof is significant, even in comparison with a concrete shell structure. For example, as will be seen in Example 2 in the next section (Section 8.2.1), a *400 FT* span pneumatic cable roof with a depth of *20 FT* (*5%* sag) will have a self-weight of just over *28 psf*. Assuming a reasonably shallow concrete shell dome with a central height of *80 FT* the self-weight of the dome including edge beam is likely to be well over *100 psf* per covered floor area[9]. Similar to pneumatic cable floors, the principal self-weight component of a pneumatic cable roof will be the weight of the top and bottom plates. In this regard the discussion at the end of Section 8.1 regarding alternative fiber reinforced plastic materials in combination with a secondary stiffening structure of steel angles or channels, is relevant to pneumatic cable roofs as well.

8.2.1 Example Design of Two Pneumatic Cable Roofs

Based on the sequential design process outlined for pneumatic cable floors in Section 8.1.3 we will perform the preliminary design of two circular pneumatic cable roofs. In each case it will be assumed that the roofs are carrying a live-load of *50 psf* and that they are supported at the perimeter only. The roof material is steel sheeting and steel cables with the following characteristics:

$$\begin{aligned} \text{yield strength of steel sheeting } (f_{fl}) &= 60{,}000 \text{ psi} \\ \text{modulus of elasticity of steel sheeting } (E) &= 29{,}000{,}000 \text{ psi} \\ \text{yield strength of cables } (f_{ca}) &= 180{,}000 \text{ psi} \\ \text{weight of steel } (w) &= 490 \text{ LB/CF} \end{aligned}$$

Example 1 (200 FT diameter roof)

Step 1: The diameter (D *FT*) of the first example roof is *200 FT* with a single inner tension ring of *40 FT* diameter (d_1 *FT*). Radial cables are spaced at approximately *1 FT* centers around the inner tension ring and the roof has a depth of *11.75 FT* (i.e., cable sag). The dead-load (i.e., self-weight) of the roof is assumed to be *20 psf* for design purposes (will be verified upon completion).

Step 2: Determine the roof area (A *SF*) and the total roof load (W *LB*).

$$\begin{aligned} A &= \pi\,[\,(D/2)^2\,] \text{ (SF)} \\ A &= \pi\,[\,(100)^2\,] \\ A &= \mathbf{31{,}415.9 \text{ SF}} \\ W &= A\,(L_L + D_L) \text{ (LB)} \\ W &= 31415.9\,(50 + 20) \\ W &= \mathbf{2{,}199{,}113 \text{ LB}} \end{aligned}$$

Step 3: With cable spacing (s_{ca} *FT*) of *1 FT* at inner tension ring we can determine the cable spacing (S_{ca} *FT*) at roof perimeter (i.e., compression rim), number of cables (n_{ca}), average load per *FT-run* of cable length (W_{run} *LB*), cable span (L *FT*), horizontal component of cable tension (H_{CA} *LB*), and maximum cable tension (T_{max} *LB*).

$$\begin{aligned} n_{ca} &= \pi\,(d_1/s_{ca}) \\ n_{ca} &= \pi\,(40/1) \\ n_{ca} &= \mathbf{125 \text{ cables}} \\ S_{ca} &= \pi\,(D/n_{ca}) \text{ (FT)} \end{aligned}$$

---

[9] For an *80 FT* high low profile concrete dome with a diameter at ground level of *400 FT* (i.e., *125,664 SF* floor area), assuming an average shell thickness of only *2 IN* and an edge beam of *4 SF* cross-section around the perimeter, the self-weight of the dome per covered area is *111 psf* (for applicable equations see Table A-6 in Appendix A).

$$S_{ca} = \pi (200/125)$$
$$S_{ca} = \mathbf{5 \text{ FT}}$$

$$W_{run} = (W/A) [\pi ((D/n_{ca}) + (d_l/n_{ca}))] /2 \text{ (LB/FT-run)}$$
$$W_{run} = (2199113 / 31415.9) [\pi ((200/125) + (40/125))] /2$$
$$W_{run} = 70 [\pi ((1.6) + (0.32))] /2$$
$$W_{run} = 70 [\pi (1.92)] /2$$
$$W_{run} = \mathbf{211.1 \text{ LB/FT-run}}$$

$$L = (D) \text{ (FT)}$$
$$L = \mathbf{200 \text{ FT}}$$

$$H_{CA} = (W_{run} L^2) / (8 S) \text{ (LB)} \quad \dots \quad 8.1$$
$$H_{CA} = (8444000) / (94)$$
$$H_{CA} = \mathbf{89{,}829.8 \text{ LB}}$$

$$T_{max} = H_{CA} [1 + (16 S^2 / L^2)]^{0.5} \text{ (LB)} \quad \dots \quad 8.2$$
$$T_{max} = 89829.8 [1 + (0.0552)]^{0.5}$$
$$T_{max} = 89829.8 [1.0272]$$
$$T_{max} = \mathbf{92{,}276.9 \text{ LB}}$$

Step 4: Determine the required internal air pressure (P_F *psig*) to resist the inward cable forces acting on the perimeter rim of the roof. The internal pressure acts on an area (A_P *SF*) that is the product of the cable spacing at the roof perimeter (S_{ca} *FT*) and the roof depth (*S FT*).

$$A_P = S (S_{ca}) \text{ (SF)} \quad \dots \quad 8.3$$
$$A_P = 11.75 (5)$$
$$A_P = \mathbf{58.75 \text{ SF}}$$

$$P_F = H_{CA} / (144 A_P) \text{ (psig)} \quad \dots \quad 8.4$$
$$P_F = 89829.8 / (144 (58.75))$$
$$P_F = \mathbf{10.6 \text{ psig}}$$

Step 5: Determine the minimum cable material area (A_{CA} *SI*), radius (r_{ca} *IN*) and diameter (d_{ca} *IN*), allowing for a fill factor (F_{CA}) of 75%. This is only a rough order of magnitude of the cable size for preliminary design purposes.

$$A_{CA} = T_{max} / f_{ca} \text{ (SI)}$$
$$A_{CA} = 92276.9 / 180000$$
$$A_{CA} = \mathbf{0.5126 \text{ SI}}$$

$$r_{ca} = (A_{CA} / \pi)^{0.5} \text{ (IN)}$$
$$r_{ca} = (0.5126 / \pi)^{0.5}$$
$$r_{ca} = \mathbf{0.4039 \text{ IN}}$$

$$d_{ca} = 2 r_{ca} / F_{CA} \text{ (IN)}$$
$$d_{ca} = 2 (0.4039) / 0.75$$
$$d_{ca} = \mathbf{1.0772 \text{ IN}}$$

Step 6: Determine the thickness of the perimeter rim (t_{orim} *IN*) of the roof that must resist the balancing forces of the cables (H_{CA} *LB*) pulling inward and the internal air pressure (P_F *psig*) pushing outward, based on the material design stress (f_{fl} *psi*).

$$f_{fl} = P_F(12R)/t_{orim} \text{ (psi)}$$
$$t_{orim} = P_F(12R)/f_{fl} \text{ (IN)}$$
$$t_{orim} = 10.6(12(100))/60000 \text{ (IN)}$$
$$t_{orim} = \mathbf{0.21 \text{ IN}}$$

Step 7: Determine the thickness of the top and bottom roof plates with tie-downs spaced at *4 FT* centers (*y FT*) between the two plates to resist the dishing effect due to the internal air pressure (P_F *psig*). Treating these plates as rigidly contained two-way slabs under distributed loading (w_{plate} *psf*), deflection (d_{plate} *IN*) rather than material stress in bending is the critical factor (Figure 8.13). Allowing for a maximum deflection of *span/240*, the thickness of each plate (t_{plate} *IN*) for the given material modulus of elasticity (*E psi*) is given by:

$$w_{plate} = P_F(12y) \text{ (psf)}$$
$$w_{plate} = 10.6(12(4))$$
$$w_{plate} = \mathbf{508.8 \text{ psf}}$$

$$d_{plate} = 12y/240 \text{ (IN)}$$
$$d_{plate} = 48/240$$
$$d_{plate} = \mathbf{0.2 \text{ IN}}$$

$$d_{plate} = (1/384)[(w_{plate} \, y^3)/(E_{plate}(y \, t_{plate}^3)/12)] \text{ (IN)}$$
$$t_{plate} = [(0.0312 \, P_F \, y^3)/(E_{plate} \, d_{plate})]^{0.3333} \text{ (IN)}$$
$$t_{plate} = [(0.0312(10.6)(110592)/(29000000(0.2))]^{0.3333}$$
$$t_{plate} = [36574.99/5800000]^{0.3333}$$
$$t_{plate} = \mathbf{0.1848 \text{ IN}}$$

Step 8: Determine the cross-sectional area (A_{ties} *SI*), radius (r_{ties} *IN*), and diameter (d_{ties} *IN*) of the tension tie-downs that are needed to resist the dishing of the top and bottom roof plates due to the internal air pressure (L_{ties} *LB*), based on the design stress of the tie-down material (f_{fl} *psi*).

$$L_{ties} = 144 \, P_F \, y^2 \text{ (LB)}$$
$$L_{ties} = 144(10.6)(16)$$
$$L_{ties} = \mathbf{24{,}422.4 \text{ LB}}$$

$$A_{ties} = L_{ties}/f_{fl} \text{ (SI)}$$
$$A_{ties} = 24422.4/60000$$
$$A_{ties} = \mathbf{0.4070 \text{ SI}}$$

$$r_{ties} = [(L_{ties})/(\pi f_{fl})]^{0.5} \text{ (IN)}$$
$$r_{ties} = [24422.4/(\pi(60000))]^{0.5}$$
$$r_{ties} = [0.1296]^{0.5}$$
$$r_{ties} = \mathbf{0.36 \text{ IN}}$$

$$d_{ties} = 2 \, r_{ties} \text{ (IN)}$$
$$d_{ties} = 2(0.36)$$
$$d_{ties} = \mathbf{0.72 \text{ IN}}$$

and the number of tie-downs (n_{ties}) is given by dividing the total roof area (*A SF*) minus the area inside the inner rim (A_R *SF*) by the area supported by each tie-down, as follows:

$$n_{ties} = [(A - A_R)] / y^2$$
$$n_{ties} = [(31415.9 - (\pi (20)^2)) / 16$$
$$n_{ties} = [(31415.9 - 1256.6) / 16$$
$$n_{ties} = \mathbf{1,884}$$

Step 9: Determine the total self-weight of the roof disk ($W_{r\text{-}LB}$ LB) consisting of the separate weights of the perimeter rim (W_{orim} LB), the inner rim (W_{irim} LB), the top and bottom roof plates (W_{plate} LB), the main (radial) cables (W_{rca} LB), and the tie-downs (W_{ties} LB) based on the respective material weights (w_{orim}, w_{irim}, w_{plate}, w_{rca}, and w_{ties} LB/CF). It seems reasonable to assume the thickness of the innermost tension ring to be the same thickness as the outer perimeter rim (t_{orim} IN).

$$W_{orim} = w_{orim} [(\pi D S)(t_{orim}/12)] \text{ (LB)}$$
$$W_{orim} = 490 [(\pi (200)(11.75))(0.21/12)]$$
$$W_{orim} = \mathbf{63,307 \text{ LB}}$$

$$W_{irim} = w_{irim} [(\pi d_1 S)(t_{orim}/12)] \text{ (LB)}$$
$$W_{irim} = 490 [(\pi (40)(11.75))(0.21/12)]$$
$$W_{irim} = \mathbf{12,661 \text{ LB}}$$

$$W_{plate} = w_{plate} [(2 A)(t_{plate}/12)] \text{ (LB)}$$
$$W_{plate} = 490 [(2 (31415.9))(0.1848/12)]$$
$$W_{plate} = \mathbf{474,129 \text{ LB}}$$

$$W_{ties} = w_{ties} [(n_{ties} S)(A_{ties}/144)] \text{ (LB)}$$
$$W_{ties} = 490 [(1884 (11.75))(0.4070/144)]$$
$$W_{ties} = \mathbf{30,658 \text{ LB}}$$

Before we can determine the weight of the radial cables we must calculate the length of a typical radial cable (X FT). The radius of curvature of the cable (R_{CA} FT) may be calculated as follows (see Table A-9 in Section A-11.2 of Appendix A):

$$R_{CA} = [((4 S^2) + D^2) / (8 S)] \text{ (FT)}$$
$$R_{CA} = [((4 (11.75)^2 + 40000) / (8 (11.75))]$$
$$R_{CA} = \mathbf{431.4 \text{ FT}}$$

and the length of the cable (X_{CA} FT) is given by:

$$X_{CA} = (2 R_{CA} \arcsin\{D / (2 R_{CA})\}) \text{ (FT)}$$
$$X_{CA} = (2 (431.4) \arcsin\{0.2318\})$$
$$X_{CA} = (862.8 (0.2339))$$
$$X_{CA} = \mathbf{201.8 \text{ FT}}$$

$$W_{rca} = w_{rca} [(n_{ca} X_{CA})(A_{CA}/144)] \text{ (LB)}$$
$$W_{rca} = 490 [(125)(201.8)(0.5126/144)]$$
$$W_{rca} = \mathbf{43,999 \text{ LB}}$$

The total self-weight of the roof ($W_{r\text{-}LB}$ LB) is equal to the sum of the component weights:

$$W_{r\text{-}LB} = [W_{orim} + W_{irim} + W_{plate} + W_{ties} + W_{rca}] \text{ (LB)}$$
$$W_{r\text{-}LB} = [63307 + 12661 + 474129 + 30658 + 43999]$$
$$W_{r\text{-}LB} = \mathbf{624,754 \text{ LB}}$$

and the pounds per square foot self-weight of the roof ($W_{r\text{-}psf}$) becomes:

$$W_{r\text{-}psf} = W_{r\text{-}LB} / A \text{ (psf)}$$

W_{r-psf} = 624754 / 31415.9
W_{r-psf} = **19.88 psf** (confirms the assumed self-weight of the roof)

Example 2 (400 FT diameter roof)

For the second example the pneumatic cable roof is twice the diameter of the first example. This example will show that such large roof spans are feasible at an acceptable structural roof depth, with a surprisingly low self-weight of less than *30 psf*.

Step 1: The diameter (*D FT*) of the second example roof is *400 FT* with a single inner tension ring of *40 FT* diameter (d_1 *FT*). Like the first example radial cables are again spaced at approximately *1 FT* centers around the inner tension ring. However, this time the roof depth has been increased to *20 FT* (i.e., *5% sag*). The dead-load (i.e., self-weight) of the roof is assumed to be *30 psf* for design purposes and will again be verified upon completion.

Step 2: Determine the roof area (*A SF*) and the total roof load (*W LB*).

A = $\pi [(D/2)^2]$ (SF)
A = $\pi [(200)^2]$
A = **125,663.6 SF**

W = A ($L_L + D_L$) (LB)
W = 125663.6 (50 + 30)
W = **10,053,088 LB**

Step 3: With cable spacing (s_{ca} *FT*) of *1 FT* at inner tension ring we can determine the cable spacing (S_{ca} *FT*) at roof perimeter (i.e., compression rim), number of cables (n_{ca}), average load per *FT-run* of cable length (W_{run} *LB*), cable span (*L FT*), horizontal component of cable tension (H_{CA} *LB*), and maximum cable tension (T_{max} *LB*).

n_{ca} = $\pi (d_1 / s_{ca})$
n_{ca} = $\pi (40 / 1)$
n_{ca} = **125 cables**

S_{ca} = $\pi (D / n_{ca})$ (FT)
S_{ca} = $\pi (400 / 125)$
S_{ca} = **10 FT**

W_{run} = (W/A) $[\pi ((D/n_{ca}) + (d_1/n_{ca}))] / 2$ (LB/FT-run)
W_{run} = (10053088 / 125663.6) $[\pi ((400/125) + (40/125))] / 2$
W_{run} = 80 $[\pi ((3.2) + (0.32))] / 2$
W_{run} = 80 $[\pi (3.52)] / 2$
W_{run} = **442.3 LB/FT-run**

L = (D) (FT)
L = **400 FT**

H_{CA} = ($W_{run} L^2$) / (8 S) (LB) 8.1
H_{CA} = (70773736) / (160)
H_{CA} = **442,335.8 LB**

T_{max} = $H_{CA} [1 + (16 S^2 / L^2)]^{0.5}$ (LB) 8.2
T_{max} = $442335.8 [1 + (0.04)]^{0.5}$

T_{max} = 442335.8 [1.0198]
T_{max} = **451,095.8 LB**

Step 4: Determine the required internal air pressure (P_F *psig*) to resist the inward cable forces acting on the perimeter rim of the roof. The internal pressure acts on an area (A_P SF) that is the product of the cable spacing at the roof perimeter (S_{ca} FT) and the roof depth (S FT).

A_P = S (S_{ca}) (SF) 8.3
A_P = 20 (10)
A_P = **200 SF**

P_F = H_{CA} / (144 A_P) (psig) 8.4
P_F = 442335.8 / (144 (200))
P_F = **15.36 psig**

Step 5: Determine the minimum cable material area (A_{CA} SI), radius (r_{ca} IN) and diameter (d_{ca} IN), allowing for a fill factor (F_{CA}) of *75%*. This is only a rough order of magnitude of the cable size for preliminary design purposes.

A_{CA} = T_{max} / f_{ca} (SI)
A_{CA} = 451095.8 / 180000
A_{CA} = **2.5061 SI**

r_{ca} = (A_{CA} / π)$^{0.5}$ (IN)
r_{ca} = (2.5061 / π)$^{0.5}$
r_{ca} = **0.8931 IN**

d_{ca} = 2 r_{ca} / F_{CA} (IN)
d_{ca} = 2 (0.8931) / 0.75
d_{ca} = **2.38 IN**

Step 6: Determine the thickness of the perimeter rim (t_{orim} IN) of the roof that must resist the balancing forces of the cables (H_{CA} LB) pulling inward and the internal air pressure (P_F *psig*) pushing outward, based on the material design stress (f_{fl} *psi*).

f_{fl} = P_F (12 R) / t_{orim} (psi)
t_{orim} = 15.36 (12 R) / f_{fl} (IN)
t_{orim} = 15.36 (12 (200)) / 60000 (IN)
t_{orim} = **0.61 IN**

Step 7: Determine the thickness of the top and bottom roof plates with tie-downs spaced at *4 FT* centers (*y FT*) between the two plates to resist the dishing effect due to the internal air pressure (P_F *psig*). Treating these plates as rigidly contained two-way slabs under distributed loading (w_{plate} *psf*), deflection (d_{plate} *IN*) rather than material stress in bending is the critical factor (Figure 8.13). Allowing for a maximum deflection of *span/240*, the thickness of each plate (t_{plate} *IN*) for the given material modulus of elasticity (*E psi*) is given by:

w_{plate} = P_F (12 y) (psf)
w_{plate} = 15.36 (12 (4))
w_{plate} = **737.28 psf**

d_{plate} = 12 y / 240 (IN)

d_{plate} = 48 / 240
d_{plate} = **0.2 IN**

d_{plate} = $(1/384) [(w_{plate} \, y^3) / (E_{plate} (y \, t_{plate}^3) / 12)]$ (IN)
t_{plate} = $[(0.0312 \, P_F \, y^3) / (E_{plate} \, d_{plate})]^{0.3333}$ (IN)
t_{plate} = $[(0.0312 \, (15.36) \, (110592)) / (29000000 \, (0.2))]^{0.3333}$
t_{plate} = $[52999.23 / 5800000]^{0.3333}$
t_{plate} = **0.2091 IN**

Step 8: Determine the cross-sectional area (A_{ties} SI), radius (r_{ties} IN), and diameter (d_{ties} IN) of the tension tie-downs that are needed to resist the dishing of the top and bottom roof plates due to the internal air pressure (L_{ties} LB), based on the design stress of the tie-down material (f_{fl} psi).

L_{ties} = $144 \, P_F \, y^2$ (LB)
L_{ties} = $144 \, (15.36) \, (16)$
L_{ties} = **35,389.4 LB**

A_{ties} = L_{ties} / f_{fl} (SI)
A_{ties} = $35389.4 / 60000$
A_{ties} = **0.5898 SI**

r_{ties} = $[(L_{ties}) / (\pi \, f_{fl})]^{0.5}$ (IN)
r_{ties} = $[35389.4 / (\pi \, (60000))]^{0.5}$
r_{ties} = $[0.1877]^{0.5}$
r_{ties} = **0.4333 IN**

d_{ties} = $2 \, r_{ties}$ (IN)
d_{ties} = $2 \, (0.4333)$
d_{ties} = **0.8666 IN**

and the number of tie-downs (n_{ties}) is given by dividing the total roof area (A SF) minus the area inside the inner rim (A_R SF) by the area supported by each tie-down, as follows:

n_{ties} = $[(A - A_R)] / y^2$
n_{ties} = $[(125663.6 - (\pi \, (20)^2)) / 16]$
n_{ties} = $[(125663.6 - 1256.6) / 16]$
n_{ties} = **7,775**

Step 9: Determine the total self-weight of the roof disk (W_{r-LB} LB) consisting of the separate weights of the perimeter rim (W_{orim} LB), the inner rim (W_{irim} LB), the top and bottom roof plates (W_{plate} LB), the main (radial) cables (W_{rca} LB), and the tie-downs (W_{ties} LB) based on the respective material weights (w_{orim}, w_{irim}, w_{plate}, w_{rca}, and w_{ties} LB/CF). It seems reasonable to assume the thickness of the innermost tension ring to be the same thickness as the outer perimeter rim (t_{orim} IN).

W_{orim} = $w_{orim} [(\pi \, D \, S) \, (t_{orim}/12)]$ (LB)
W_{orim} = $490 [(\pi \, (400) \, (20)) \, (0.61 / 12)]$
W_{orim} = **626,014 LB**

W_{irim} = $w_{irim} [(\pi \, d_1 \, S) \, (t_{orim}/12)]$ (LB)
W_{irim} = $490 [(\pi \, (40) \, (20)) \, (0.61 / 12)]$

$$W_{irim} = \mathbf{62{,}601 \text{ LB}}$$

$$W_{plate} = w_{plate}\ [(2\ A)\ (t_{plate}/12)]\ (\text{LB})$$
$$W_{plate} = 490\ [(2\ (125663.6))\ (0.2091/12)]$$
$$W_{plate} = \mathbf{2{,}145{,}894 \text{ LB}}$$

$$W_{ties} = w_{ties}\ [(n_{ties}\ S)\ (A_{ties}/144)]\ (\text{LB})$$
$$W_{ties} = 490\ [(7775\ (20))\ (0.5898/144)]$$
$$W_{ties} = \mathbf{312{,}082 \text{ LB}}$$

Before we can determine the weight of the radial cables we must calculate the length of a typical radial cable (X FT). The radius of curvature of the cable (R_{CA} FT) may be calculated as follows (see Table A-9 in Section A-11.2 of Appendix A):

$$R_{CA} = [((4\ S^2) + D^2)/(8\ S)]\ (\text{FT})$$
$$R_{CA} = [((4\ (20)^2 + 160000)/(8\ (20))]$$
$$R_{CA} = \mathbf{1{,}010 \text{ FT}}$$

and the length of the cable (X_{CA} FT) is given by:

$$X_{CA} = (2\ R_{CA}\ \arcsin\{D/(2\ R_{CA})\})\ (\text{FT})$$
$$X_{CA} = (2\ (1010)\ \arcsin\{0.1980\})$$
$$X_{CA} = (2020\ (0.1993))$$
$$X_{CA} = \mathbf{402.6 \text{ FT}}$$

$$W_{rca} = w_{rca}\ [(n_{ca}\ X_{CA})\ (A_{CA}/144)]\ (\text{LB})$$
$$W_{rca} = 490\ [(125)\ (402.6)\ (2.5061/144)]$$
$$W_{rca} = \mathbf{429{,}156 \text{ LB}}$$

The total self-weight of the roof ($W_{r\text{-}LB}$ LB) is equal to the sum of the component weights:

$$W_{r\text{-}LB} = [W_{orim} + W_{irim} + W_{plate} + W_{ties} + W_{rca}]\ (\text{LB})$$
$$W_{r\text{-}LB} = [626014 + 62601 + 2145894 + 312082 + 429156]$$
$$W_{r\text{-}LB} = \mathbf{3{,}575{,}747 \text{ LB}}$$

and the pounds per square foot self-weight of the roof ($W_{r\text{-}psf}$) becomes:

$$W_{r\text{-}psf} = W_{r\text{-}LB}/A\ (\text{psf})$$
$$W_{r\text{-}psf} = 3575747/125663.6$$
$$W_{r\text{-}psf} = \mathbf{28.45 \text{ psf}}\ (\text{confirms the assumed self-weight of the roof})$$

Comparison of Examples 1 and 2

Similar to the comparison of the two floors in Section 8.1.4 (Table 8.4), true to expectations the increase in self-weight of a pneumatic cable roof is also not linear with increasing cable span. As shown in Table 8.5, with a *100%* increase in cable span (i.e., from *200 FT* to *400 FT*) the self-weight of the roof has increased by only *43%* (i.e., from *19.88 psf* to *28.45 psf*). At the same time the span/weight and span/depth ratios have increased by *40%* and *18%*, respectively. In other words, with a doubling of the span and a *70%* increase in roof depth the span/depth ratio (*40% increase*) has increased less than half as much as the span/weight ratio (only *18%* increase).

Table 8.5: Comparison of *200 FT* and *400 FT* diameter pneumatic cable roofs

Design Parameters	Example (1)	Example (2)	Difference
roof diameter	200 FT	400 FT	+ 100%
cable span	200 FT	400 FT	+ 100%

roof depth (cable sag)	11.75 FT	20.00 FT	+70%
percent sag	5.9%	7.1%	+20%
internal air pressure	10.6 psig	15.36 psig	+45%
diameter of radial cables	1.0772 IN	2.3816 IN	+121%
total roof area	31,416 SF	125,664 SF	+300%
self-weight of roof	19.88 psf	28.45 psf	+43%
span/depth ratio	17.0	20.0	+18%
span/weight ratio	10.06	14.06	+40%

8.3 Rectangular Fluid-Inflated Cable Floors

The ability of internal air pressure to solely counterbalance the inward forces exerted by radial cables in a circular pneumatic cable floor is the structural advantage that is directly responsible for the feasibility of astoundingly light weight, large span floors. At the same time the dependence of the structural integrity of the floor on maintaining the internal air pressure throughout the life cycle of the floor is also its greatest vulnerability. While the use of pressurized struts shown in Figure 8.5 as an additional safety precaution is certainly feasible, it does reduce the structural economy of the pneumatic cable floor concept.

The same applies to multi-story air-supported buildings when we replace the air pressure in the internal building environment (Chapter 6, Figure 6.3(a)) with fluid-inflated columns (Chapter 6, Figure 6.3(g)), thereby allowing the building environment to remain at ambient atmospheric pressure. In each case, whether building or floor, the intrinsic structural economy of ubiquities air-support is significantly downgraded as soon as the air or liquid pressure is restricted to a relatively small component of the entire structure. Yet, even in this downgraded state the structural economy of a fluid-inflated (as opposed to air-supported[10]) structure may still far exceed that of a conventional steel, reinforced concrete or prestressed concrete alternative.

In the case of pneumatic cable floors, apart from safety, there are two additional incentives for not pressurizing the entire volume within the floor disk. First, since in practice most buildings are rectangular the removal of the circular shape restriction would allow cable floors to be used in any building regardless of the shape of the floor. Second, since only the struts are pressurized the space between struts and cables is available for ducts, pipes and electrical wiring. In the case of pneumatic cable floors in which the entire floor disk is internally pressurized all utility services will need to be accommodated below the structural floor, thereby further increasing the effective depth of the floor.

The question then arises: Can the concept of light-weight cable floors be applied to rectangular floors? Before answering this question we will explore in a little more detail the reason why the form of the pressurized disk of a pneumatic cable floor needs to be cylindrical. The preferred circular shape of a pneumatic cable floor is based on two factors. First, the air pressure inside the floor disk acts equally in all directions. This favors a cylindrical form so that stress concentrations can be avoided. Second, multi-story air-supported buildings whether utilizing flexible or rigid enclosures will be cylindrical in form for similar reasons. Therefore, the mandate of a cylindrical

---

[10] See Chapter 6, in particular pages 127-128 and Section 6.1 for a more detailed discussion of pressure utilization efficiency considerations.

shape is tied directly to the pressurization of the entire internal volume of the structure. If this requirement is removed then non-circular shapes, in particular rectangular shapes become possible.

A rectangular version of the pneumatic cable floor structure described so far in this Chapter would need to resist the inward forces exerted by cables at the perimeter of the floor with fluid-inflated struts alone (Figure 8.14). Bracing of the struts at intermediate points will reduce the effective length (H_E FT) of an individual strut to well below its physical length (H FT). In this case a factor of *0.5* (i.e., $H_E=0.5H$) or even less could be acceptable. The depth of such floors would be governed by the optimum relationship between the maximum cable sag, which translates into the axial load that needs to be resisted by the fluid-inflated struts, and the slenderness ratio of the strut, which governs to a large extent its pressure-utilization efficiency.

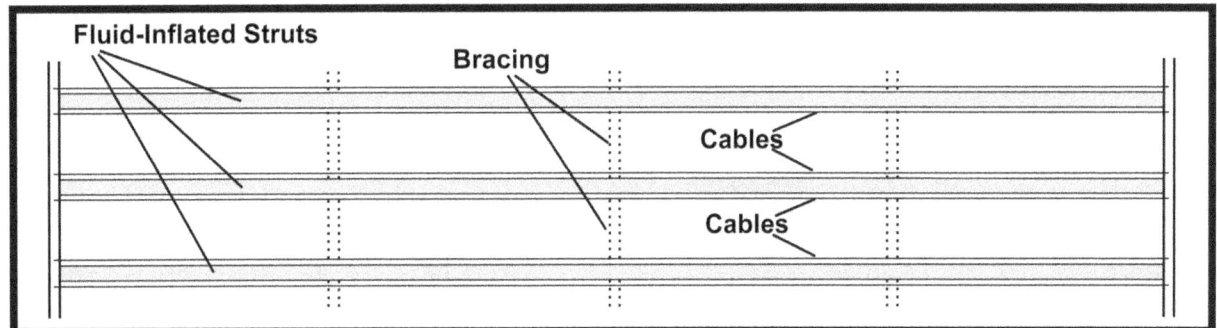

Figure 8.14: Rectangular cable-floor with horizontal fluid-inflated struts.

As shown in Figure 8.14 cables would be located in parallel on either side of each internally pressurized strut, with a clearance of two or three inches between each cable and the strut. In this way the inward forces exerted by the cables are most effectively counterbalanced by the struts. This combination of two cables and one strut is repeated at suitable spacings along the width of the rectangular floor. The actual spacing between struts can be optimized in relationship to the depth of the floor, which in turn governs the cable forces and the size (i.e., diameter) of the strut. A secondary structure will be required to transmit the floor and ceiling loads directly to the cables. It is important that these vertical loads are carried by the cables and not the pressurized struts, since the sole function of the struts is to oppose the axial load due to the tensioned cables. The struts are not intended to act as beams and therefore care should be taken in the design of the floor to ensure that the struts are not subjected to bending actions. Two alternative ways in which this design criterion can be satisfied is discussed in a subsequent section (see Section 8.3.1).

The approximate size of the cable and strut components and the estimated magnitude of the stresses involved can be assessed on the basis of the following hypothetical example:

$$\begin{aligned}
\text{floor span (L)} &= 100 \text{ FT} \\
\text{cable spacing } (C_S) &= 5 \text{ FT} \\
\text{live-load (LL)} &= 100 \text{ psf} \\
\text{assumed dead-load (DL)} &= 20 \text{ psf} \\
\text{maximum cable sag (d)} &= 3.5 \text{ FT} \\
\text{strut wall thickness (t)} &= 0.0625 \text{ IN} \\
\text{strut diameter (D)} &= 3.5 \text{ FT} \\
\text{strut radius (R)} &= 21 \text{ IN}
\end{aligned}$$

strut cross-sectional wall area (A_S) = 8.2467 SI
load on each cable (w) = 600 LB/FT run (w = C_S (LL + DL))

The horizontal component of cable tension (H_{CA} LB per cable) is given by equation 8.1:

$$H_{CA} = w L^2 / (8 d) \text{ LB} \quad\quad\quad 8.1$$

$$H_{CA} = 600 \times 100 \times 100 / (8 \times 3.5) = 214{,}886 \text{ LB}$$

The maximum cable tension (T_{max} LB) is given by equation 8.2:

$$T_{max} = H_{CA} [1 + (16 d^2 / L^2)]^{0.5} \text{ LB} \quad\quad\quad 8.2$$

$$T_{max} = 214286 [1 + (16 \times 3.5 \times 3.5 / (100 \times 100))]^{0.5}$$

$$T_{max} = 214286 [1 + 0.0196]^{0.5} = 216{,}376 \text{ LB}$$

The design of the fluid-inflated strut proceeds as follows with reference to the Kusmiss (1958) nomograms shown in Figures 8.15 and 8.16 (assuming $E=30 \times 10^6$):

radius/thickness (R/t) = 21 / 0.0625 = 336

According to the first nomogram (Figure 8.15) for an *R/t* ratio of 336 we obtain:

buckling coefficient (K_C) = 8.0×10^{-4}

allowable stress ($E K_C$) = $8.0 \times 10^{-4} \times 30 \times 10^6$ = **24,000 psi**

allowable axial load = $24{,}000 \times 8.2467$ = **197,920 LB**

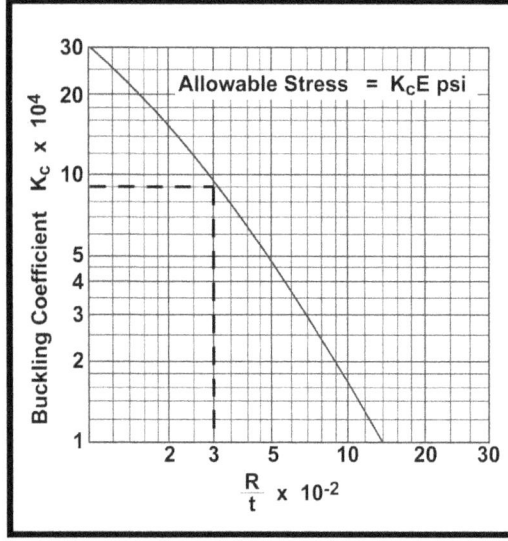 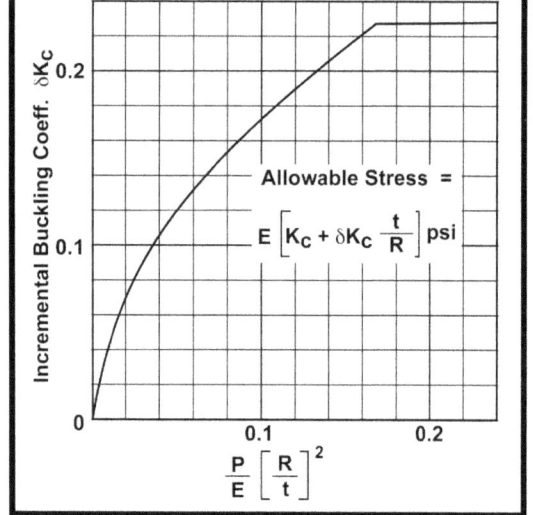

Figure 8.15: Buckling coefficient for unpressurized columns (Kusmiss 1958)

Figure 8.16: Incremental buckling coefficient for pressurized columns (Kusmiss 1958)

Calculation of critical compressive stress of *pressurized* strut:

As shown in the second nomogram (Figure 8.16) the incremental buckling coefficient (∂K_C) does not increase beyond:

$$(P/E) (R/t)^2 = 0.165$$

Therefore the optimum internal pressure (P_{opt}) is calculated by transposing the above equation:

$$P_{opt} = 0.165 \, E \, t^2 / R^2$$
$$P_{opt} = 43.8 \text{ psig}$$

For this internal pressure we obtain from Figure 8.16:

$$\partial K_C = 0.224$$

$$\text{allowable stress } (f_P) = E \, (K_c + (\partial K_C \, t / R))$$
$$f_P = E \, (8.0 \times 10^{-4} + 6.67 \times 10^{-4})$$
$$f_P = \mathbf{44{,}000 \text{ psi}}$$

On the assumption that this stress does not exceed the allowable design stress of the column wall material, the allowable axial load is calculated as the cross-sectional area of the column material times the allowable design stress:

$$\text{allowable axial load} = 44{,}000 \times 8.2467 = \mathbf{362{,}854 \text{ LB}}$$

The allowable axial compression load on the strut (*362,854 LB*) is *1.7* times the horizontal component of the cable tension (i.e., H_{CA} = *214,886 LB*). If we assume H_E = *0.5H* then the slenderness ratio of the strut is about *40*.

Check maximum circumferential (hoop) stress in the strut wall under an internal pressure of *43.8 psig*:

$$\text{circumferential stress } (f_C) = P_{opt} \, R / t$$
$$f_C = 43.8 \, (21 / 0.0625)$$
$$f_C = \mathbf{14{,}717 \text{ psi}}$$

It can be seen from this hypothetical example that fluid-inflated cable floors, like their pneumatic cousins, call for high strength materials both in respect to the cables and the presumably rigid membrane wall of the fluid-inflated struts. With a cable tension of *216,376 LB* per cable a material with an allowable design stress in tension of *180,000 psi* would require a cable diameter of at least *1¾ IN*. In the case of the strut a sheet metal material with an allowable design stress in tension of more than *24,000 psi* is required to be able to take advantage of any internal pressure at all. In the above example the optimum pressure of *43.8 psig* requires an allowable design stress in tension of *44,000 psi*, which is still well below the *60,000 psi* yield stress that has been assumed for the steel floor disk material used in the pneumatic cable floor examples described in Section 8.1.4. As shown in Table 8.6, steel alloys commercially available for both high strength cables and stainless steel sheeting range in yield strength from *16,000 psi* to over *300,000 psi*.

Table 8.6: Overview of mechanical properties of AISI steel categories

Classification	Type/Alloy	Yield Strength	Modulus of Elasticity	Density
AISI T400	stainless steel	23,900-276,000 psi	10,500-46,000 KSI	383-493 LB/CF
AISI T600	stainless steel	6,790-230,000 psi	28,600-29,000 KSI	474-515 LB/CF
AISI 1000	carbon (C) steel	23,900-132,000 psi	29,000-29,700 KSI	490-491 LB/CF
AISI 4000	molybdenum (Mo)	42,900-270,000 psi	28,400-30,900 KSI	484-490 LB/CF
AISI 8000	Ni, Cr, Mo	52,200-194,000 psi	27,100-30,300 KSI	484-490 LB/CF
AISI 9000	Ni, Cr, Mo	63,800-226,000 psi	29,000-30,300 KSI	484-491 LB/CF

8.3.1 Constructional Aspects of Fluid-Inflated Cable Floors

A rectangular fluid-inflated cable floor is suspended (or supported) at opposite ends where the cables are attached, so that the length or span of the floor is also the span of the cables. The primary structural components are the cables and the pressurized struts that counterbalance the inward forces of the cables. Secondary components include the two floor ends that need to accommodate the cable anchorages, the strut attachments, and the floor supports, as well as the secondary structure that allows the cables to support the top floor surface and the ceiling below.

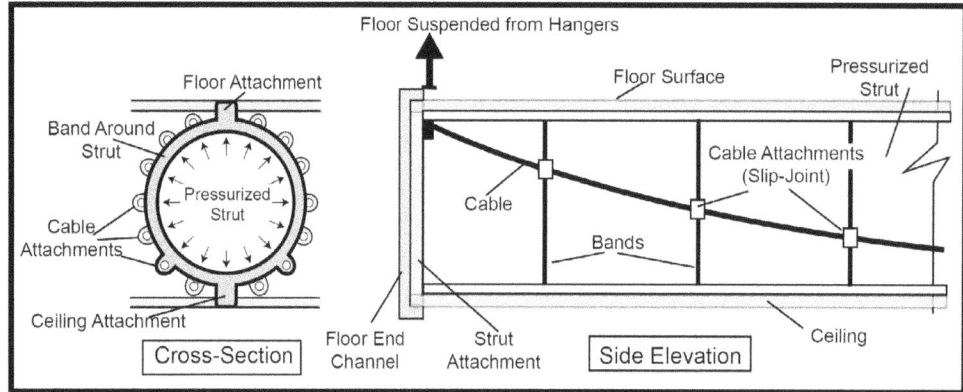

Figure 8.17: Cables support floor surface and ceiling with strut bands

As mentioned previously the need to support both floor and ceiling loads directly on the cables and not on the pressurized struts is an important design criterion. Two alternative approaches for satisfying this requirement with a secondary structure are depicted in Figures 8.17 and 8.18. In the first alternative (Figure 8.17) bands are placed around the perimeter of each strut and spaced equidistantly along the length of the strut. If the strut is made of galvanized steel sheets (e.g., 0.0625 IN thick) that are welded together, then the bands might be made of ¼ IN steel, *3 IN* on edge spaced at *4 FT* centers along the length of the strut. The bands are purposely not welded to the strut wall so that they can freely rotate around the strut. Each band has two ear-like protrusions with holes through which the cables on each side of the strut are threaded. Again, similar to the ability of the bands to rotate freely around the struts, the cables are free to slide through these holes (i.e., in slip-joint fashion). Rectangular ear-like protrusions at the top and bottom of each band provide for the attachment of the floor and ceiling surfaces.

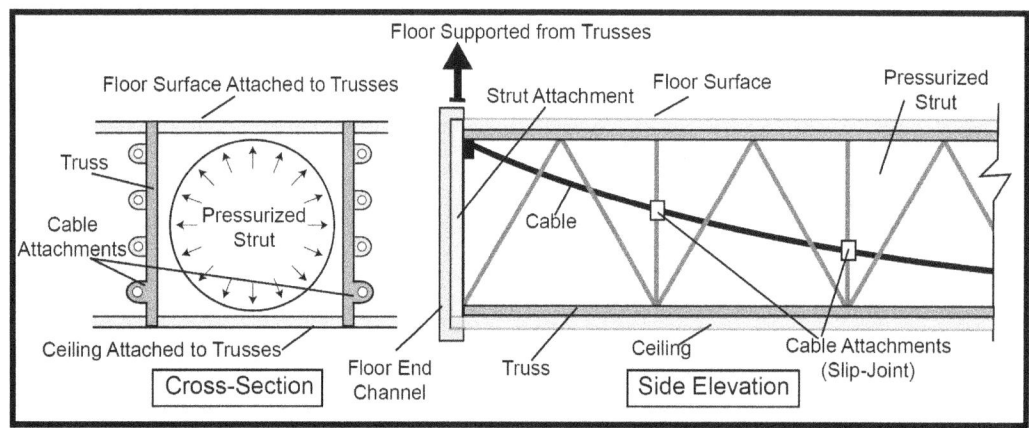

Figure 8.18: Cables support floor surface and ceiling with trusses

In the second alternative trusses made of steel angles are placed on each side of the strut (Figure 8.18), on the outside of the cables. The cables are coupled to the trusses through slip-joints that provide vertical support to the trusses without restraining the cables horizontally. The trusses are firmly attached to the floor end sections that also provide anchorage for the cable ends and the necessary attachments for hangers if the floors are suspended from above. The floor surface and ceiling are attached directly to the top and bottom chords of the trusses, respectively.

The structural advantage of the second alternative (Figure 8.18) is that the top and bottom surfaces of the floor are supported by the cables in total isolation of the pressurized struts. This prevents the secondary structure of trusses from inducing bending stresses onto the struts. While the first alternative in which the floor surface and ceiling are supported by bands around the struts is a more economical and elegant solution, it does not provide a complete physical separation of the secondary structure from the struts. Even though the bands are relatively free to rotate around the strut walls and are supported vertically by the cables, the possibility that the bands may cause some bending in the struts through frictional forces cannot be excluded from the realm of possibilities. In either alternative the connection to the cables must ensure that the required joint does not restrain the cable. As indicated in Figures 8.17 and 8.18 this connection is implemented as a slip-joint that does not prevent the cable from moving horizontally or vertically while supporting the vertical floor load[11].

Similar to pneumatic cable floors, fire protection is of course also a major concern for fluid-inflated cable floors. Again, in addition to the prescribed structural fire rating between floors (i.e., compartments) that applies to multi-story buildings there is the need to protect the struts and cables within the floor. However, the problem is partially mitigated in this case by the *3 IN* layer of concrete on corrugated steel sheeting that is recommended for the top floor surface. This layer will be sufficient to provide the necessary fire protection on the upper floor plate. The only acceptable solution for the lower plate (i.e., ceiling) is likely to be an adequately thick layer of endothermic material such as calcium silicate board, sprayed gypsum plasters lightened with inorganic aggregates (e.g., vermiculite and perlite), and/or intumescent films.

8.3.2 Design Process for Fluid-Inflated Cable Floors

The design process for fluid-inflated cable floors differs in several ways from the design of pneumatic cable floors described previously in this Chapter (see Section 8.1.3). While the relationship between span and floor depth largely governs the design of pneumatic cable floors, the fluid-inflated cable floor introduces the pressurized strut as a third major structural element. The strut is in essence a thin-walled cylindrical column on its side that is subjected to an axial horizontal load. Its principal design parameters are its slenderness ratio, the inward cable force that must be resisted, the wall thickness, and the internal pressure. Combinations of these parameters will determine the critical buckling stress of the strut's thin wall. The design objective is to minimize the depth and the self-weight of the floor for a given span.

The preliminary design process described below is intended to establish order of magnitude cable and strut sizes and the approximate self-weight of the floor. It is assumed that the floor is either suspended from equally spaced hangers or supported from below at the perimeter where the

---

[11] However, both alternative secondary structures do constrain the cables from moving sideways which is not only acceptable but actually desirable.

cables are anchored. Therefore the cable span is equal to the length of the floor. Applicable variables are in the following units of measurement:

L = length of floor and span of cables (FT)
B = width of floor (FT)
S = cable sag (FT)
f_{st} = design strength in tension of the strut wall material (psi)
E = modulus of elasticity of the strut wall material (psi)
f_{ca} = design strength in tension of cable material (psi)
L_L = live-load on floor (psf)
D_L = dead-load (self-weight) of floor (psf)

At the beginning the designer would typically specify the length (L FT) and width (B FT) of the floor, the live-load (L_L psf) and dead-load (D_L psf) to be carried by the floor, the cable (f_{ca} psi) material yield stress, and the strut wall (f_{st} psi) design stress. Since the self-weight (i.e., dead-load) of the floor is not known at the beginning, the designer would normally start with an estimate and then cycle through the design process a second time with a better estimate based on the first result.

Step 1: With the design objective of minimum floor depth (S FT) stipulate the floor length and cable span (L FT), the floor width (B FT), the live-load (L_L psf), and the estimated dead-load (D_L psf). Then calculate the floor area (A SF) and the total estimated floor load (W LB).

A = $L(B)$ (SF)
W = $A(L_L + D_L)$ (LB)

Step 2: Determine the required strut radius (R FT) and diameter (D FT) based on not exceeding a maximum slenderness ratio (SR) of 30 and an effective strut length (H_E FT) of half the actual length ($H_E = 0.5H$ FT) due to adequate bracing between struts and strut end constraints.

SR = $H_E / [R^2/2]^{0.5}$ and for $SR = 30$:
R = $H_E / 21.2132$ (FT)
D = $2R$ (FT)

The actual depth of the floor (D_{floor} FT) is slightly larger than the strut diameter (D FT)[12] to allow for the upper floor surface and the ceiling on the underside. An additional 6 IN will provide a minimum clearance of ½ IN above and below the strut plus thicknesses of 3 IN for the upper floor surface and 2 IN for the ceiling below. Therefore the depth of the floor (D_{floor} FT) is given by:

D_{floor} = $D + 0.5$ (FT)

Step 3: Establish a practical strut wall thickness (t IN) based on the following considerations: (a) $R/t >= 100$ (or $t = 0.1200R$ with R in FT) for strut to be in range of a thin-walled cylindrical shell; (b) The extent to which minimum self-weight of the floor is a design criterion (upper limit is $R/t <= 1400$ or $t = 0.00857R$ with R in FT); and, (c) desirable wall thickness due to material and fabrication constraints. Based on the experience of the author with the prototype central column building described in Chapters 6 and 7 (Sections 6.2 and 7.5.3) a readily available galvanized sheet metal thickness that can be arc welded is *0.0625 IN (1/16 IN)*. In the floor depth range of *1.5*

---

[12] Incidentally, it is reasonable to assume that the diameter of the struts is equal to the maximum cable sag at the center of the floor span.

to *4.5 FT* (equivalent strut radius (*R FT*) range of *0.75* to *2.25 FT*) the *R/t* range is *277* to *432*.

Step 4: Assume the center-to-center spacing of struts (S_{st} *FT*) and determine the number of struts (n_{strut}), the number of cables (n_{ca}), load on cables (W_{run} *LB/FT-run*), horizontal component of cable tension (H_{CA} *LB*), and maximum cable tension (T_{max} *LB*). Since the cables are arranged in pairs with one cable on each side of a strut (Figures 8.17 and 8.18) it may be assumed for purposes of determining the load on each cable pair (W_{run} *LB/FT-run*) that the cable spacing is equal to the spacing between struts (S_{st} *FT*) and that the load is carried equally by two cables.

$$n_{strut} = (B / S_{st})$$
$$n_{ca} = 2 n_{ca}$$
$$W_{run} = S_{st}(W/A) \text{ (LB/FT-run)}$$
$$\mathbf{H = (W_{run} L^2) / (8 S) \text{ (LB)}} \quad \ldots \ldots \text{ 8.1}$$
$$H_{CA} = 0.5 H \text{ (i.e., divided between two cables)}$$
$$\mathbf{T_{max} = H_{CA}[1 + (16 S^2 / L^2)]^{0.5} \text{ (LB)}} \quad \ldots \ldots \text{ 8.2}$$

Step 5: Calculate the cross-sectional material area of the strut wall (A_{strut} *SI*) and determine the allowable stress without internal pressure ($K_C(E)$ *psi*) based on the Kusmiss graph shown in Figure 8.15.

$$A_{strut} = \pi(12 D) t \text{ (SI)}$$
$$K_C = \text{(from Kusmiss graph in Figure 8.15)}$$
$$\text{buckling stress} = K_C(E) \text{ (psi) without internal pressure}$$

Step 6: Determine the strut's optimum internal air pressure (P_{strut} *psig*) to provide the maximum critical buckling stress based on the Kusmiss graph shown in Figure 8.16. The maximum ∂K_C value of *0.224* occurs at *(P/E)[R/t]²* equal to *0.165*. Then calculate the critical buckling stress of the strut wall under pressurized conditions (f_{strut} *psi*).

$$P_{strut} = 0.165 E t^2 / (144 R^2) \text{ (psig)}$$
$$\partial K_C = 0.224$$
$$f_{strut} = E[K_C + (\partial K_C t / (12 R))] \text{ (psi)}$$

Step 7: Calculate stress in strut wall (f_{cable} *psi*) due to cable tension (*H LB*) force in the two cables on either side of the strut and compare with the critical buckling stress of the strut wall under pressurized conditions (f_{strut} *psi*).

$$\text{if: } f_{strut} < f_{cable} \text{ (factor of safety) (psi)}$$
$$\text{then increase the strut wall thickness (} t \text{ IN) until}$$
$$f_{strut} >= f_{cable} \text{ (factor of safety) (psi)}$$

Examination of the Kusmiss graph in Figure 8.15 shows that increases in the wall thickness (*t IN*) decreases the value of *R/t* and therefore increases the value of the critical buckling stress without internal pressure ($K_C(E)$ psi). However, the wall thickness cannot be increased beyond *R/t=100* (i.e., the maximum allowable value of *t* is *12R/100*, where *R* is in *FT*) for the strut to be classified as a thin-walled shell. Thereafter, further increases in the axial load capacity of the strut will require increases in the strut radius (*R FT*). Accordingly it is suggested that if at the given radius (*R FT*) the axial load bearing capacity of the strut is less than the product of the combined force of the two cables on either side of the strut and the factor of safety, even after the strut's wall thickness (*t IN*) has been increased to the maximum value (i.e., *t = 12R/100*), then the designer would incrementally increase the strut radius (e.g., in *0.5 FT* increments) and test for the maximum allowable wall thickness at each increment. If the axial load bearing capacity of the strut now exceeds the required load (i.e., product of cable force and factor of safety) then the wall thickness can be reduced to the required value for that strut radius. On the other hand, if the axial load bearing capacity of the strut is still inadequate then the designer would cycle through the same process at the next incrementally larger strut radius.

Step 8: Estimate the minimum cable material area (A_{CA} *SI*), radius (r_{ca} *IN*) and diameter (d_{ca} *IN*), allowing for a fill factor (F_{CA}) of *60%* to *85%*. This is only a rough order of magnitude of the cable size for preliminary design purposes. As explained previously under circular pneumatic cable floors (Section 8.1.3, *Step 5*) manufacturers normally rate cables based on minimum breaking load rather than material stress due to the dependence of strength and modulus of elasticity on strand configuration, core and fill factor. Therefore, the estimated cable diameter determined below must be adjusted for the type of cable and the appropriate factor of safety.

$$A_{CA} = T_{max} / f_{ca} \quad (SI)$$
$$r_{ca} = (A_{CA} / \pi)^{0.5} \quad (IN)$$
$$d_{ca} = 2 r_{ca} / F_{CA} \quad (IN)$$

Depending on sag the length of each cable (X_{CA} *FT*) is normally only slightly longer than the length of the floor (i.e., span). Based on its radius of curvature (R_{CA} *FT*) the length of the cable is given by:

$$R_{CA} = [((4 S^2) + L^2) / (8 S)] \quad (FT)$$
$$X_{CA} = [2 R_{CA} \arcsin\{(L / (2 R_{CA})\}] \quad (FT)$$

Step 9: Determine the total self-weight of the floor (W_{fl-LB} *LB*) consisting of the separate weights of the cables (W_{CA} *LB*), the struts (W_{STRUT} *LB*), the floor end sections (W_{END} *LB*), the secondary floor surface/ceiling structure (W_{SEC} *LB*), the floor surface (W_{SURF} *LB*), and the ceiling (W_{CEIL} *LB*) based on the respective material weights (w_{ca}, w_{strut}, w_{end}, w_{sec}, w_{surf}, and w_{ceil} *LB/CF*).

Cables: $\quad W_{CA} = w_{ca} [(n_{ca} X_{CA}) (A_{CA} / 144)]$ (LB)

Struts: Assuming two *½ IN* thick circular cap plates serving as the attachments of each strut to the two end sections of the floor:

$$W_{STRUT} = w_{strut} [(n_{strut} L) (A_{strut} / 144) + (2 \pi R^2 (0.5/12))] \quad (LB)$$

End Sections: Assuming *1 IN* thick steel channels with *4 IN* flanges and a width equal to the diameter of the struts for the end sections of the floor to provide anchorage for the struts and attachments for the floor supports (e.g., hangers if suspended):

$$W_{END} = w_{end} [(2 B) ((S + (8/12)) (1/12))] \quad (LB)$$

Secondary (A): For alternative (A) shown in Figure 8.17 we will assume *¼ IN* thick *3 IN* wide on-edge bands around each strut at S_{band} *FT* centers, and adding an extra *1 IN* to the width of each band to allow for the cable ears so that the effective width of the on-edge bands is *4 IN* for calculation purposes. The approximate weight (W_{SEC-A} *LB*) of this secondary structure alternative based on strut bands is a function of the number of bands (n_{band}), the amount of material (A_{band} SI) and the unit weight of the material (w_{band} LB/CF):

$$A_{band} = \pi[((12R)+8)^2 - (12R)^2] \quad (SI)$$

$$n_{band} = n_{strut}(\text{truncate}(L/S_{band}))$$

$$W_{SEC-A} = w_{band}[n_{band}(A_{band}/144)(0.25/12)] \quad (LB)$$

Secondary (B): For alternative (B) shown in Figure 8.18 we will assume that the trusses on each side of each strut (on the outside of the cables) are fabricated from angles with a cross-sectional area of A_a SI and top and bottom channel chords with a cross-sectional area of A_c SI. The approximate weight (W_{SEC-B} LB) of this secondary structure alternative based on trusses is a function of the number of trusses (n_{truss}), the distance between cable attachment points since the trusses are supported by the cables at intermediate points, the spacing between vertical members in the 'V' pattern truss configuration shown in Figure 8.18 (S_v FT), the volume of channel material (A_{chan} CI), the volume of angle material (A_{ang} CI), and the unit weight of the material (w_{truss} LB/CF):

$$n_{truss} = n_{ca}$$

$$A_{chan} = n_{truss}[2(12L(A_c))] \quad (CI)$$

$$A_{ang} = n_{truss}[(L/S_v)A_a(12S + 2((12S)^2 + (12S_v/2)^2)^{0.5})] \quad (CI)$$

$$W_{SEC-B} = w_{truss}[(A_{chan}/12^3) + (A_{ang}/12^3)] \quad (LB)$$

Floor Surface: Assume average of *3 IN* concrete screed with lightweight steel mesh (w_{surf} psf) on corrugated steel decking:

$$W_{SURF} = w_{surf}[L(B)] \quad (LB)$$

Ceiling: Assume 2-hour fire rated ceiling (w_{ceil} psf):

$$W_{CEIL} = w_{ceil}[(L(B))] \quad (LB)$$

The total self-weight of the floor (W_{fl-LB} LB) is equal to the sum of the component weights (including either W_{SEC-A} or W_{SEC-B} as W_{SEC}):

$$W_{fl-LB} = [W_{CA} + W_{STRUT} + W_{END} + W_{SEC} + W_{SURF} + W_{CEIL}] \quad (LB)$$

and the pounds per square foot self-weight of the floor (W_{fl-psf}) becomes:

$$W_{fl-psf} = W_{fl-LB}/A \quad (psf)$$

In the above design process for rectangular fluid-inflated cable floors fire proofing is provided in the floor surface and ceiling components of the floor assembly. As can be seen in the two worked examples in the next section (Section 8.3.3) the concrete floor surface contributes greatly to the self-weight of the floor. When comparing the self-weight of pneumatic cable floors (Section 8.1.4) with fluid-inflated cable floors (Section 8.3.3) it should be taken into consideration that fire proofing measures were not included in the design of the circular pneumatic cable floors described previously in this Chapter (see Sections 8.1.3 and 8.1.4).

8.3.3 Example Design of Two Fluid-Inflated Cable Floors

Based on the sequential design process outlined for rectangular fluid-inflated cable floors in the previous section (Section 8.3.2) we will perform the preliminary design of two rectangular floors. In each case it will be assumed that the floors are carrying a live-load of *100 psf* and that they are supported at the span ends only. The strut material is steel sheeting and the cables are either of the spiral-strand or locked coil type, with the following characteristics:

yield strength of steel sheeting (f_{fl}) = 60,000 psi
modulus of elasticity of steel sheeting (E) = 29,000,000 psi
yield strength of cables (f_{ca}) = 180,000 psi
weight of steel (w) = 490 LB/CF

Example 1 (100 FT span rectangular floor)

Step 1: The span (*L FT*) and width (*B FT*) of the first example floor are *100 FT* and *200 FT*, respectively. Struts are equally spaced at *8 FT* centers with cables on either side. Assuming a live-load (L_L *psf*) of *100 psf* and a dead-load (D_L *psf*) of *50 psf* we are able to calculate the floor area (*A SF*) and the total estimated floor load (*W LB*) as follows:

$$A = L(B) \quad (SF)$$
$$A = 100(200)$$
$$\mathbf{A = 20{,}000 \ SF}$$

$$W = A(L_L + D_L) \quad (LB)$$
$$W = 20000(100 + 50)$$
$$\mathbf{W = 3{,}000{,}000 \ LB}$$

Step 2: Determine the required strut radius (*R FT*) and diameter (*D FT*) based on not exceeding a maximum slenderness ratio (*SR*) of 30 and an effective strut length (H_E *FT*) of half the actual length ($H_E = 0.5H$ *FT*) due to adequate bracing between struts and strut end constraints.

$$SR = H_E / [R^2 / 2]^{0.5} \text{ and for } SR = 30:$$
$$R = H_E / 21.2132 \quad (FT)$$
$$R = 50 / 21.2132$$
$$\mathbf{R = 2.36 \ FT}$$
$$D = 2R \quad (FT)$$
$$D = 2(2.36)$$
$$\mathbf{D = 4.71 \ FT}$$

The actual depth of the floor (D_{floor} *FT*) is slightly larger than the strut diameter (*D FT*) to allow for the upper floor surface and the ceiling on the underside. An additional *6 IN* will provide a minimum clearance of ½ *IN* above and below the strut plus thicknesses of *3 IN* for the upper floor surface and *2 IN* for the ceiling below. Therefore the depth of the floor (D_{floor} *FT*) is given by:

$$D_{floor} = D + 0.5 \quad (FT)$$
$$D_{floor} = 4.71 + 0.5$$
$$\mathbf{D_{floor} = 5.21 \ FT}$$

Step 3: To be able to utilize the Kusmiss graphs (Figures 8.15 and 8.16) the strut wall thickness (t IN) must be in the range $R/t >= 100$ (or $t = 0.1200R$ with R in FT) and $R/t <= 1400$ (or $t = 0.00857R$ with R in FT). For R equal to *2.36 FT* (i.e., *28.32 IN*) the equivalent range for t is *0.2832 IN* to *0.0202 IN*. A readily available galvanized sheet metal thickness that can be arc welded is *0.0625 IN (1/16 IN)*.

$$R/t = 28.32 / 0.0625$$
$$\mathbf{R/t = 453}$$

Step 4: If the struts are spaced at *8 FT* centers (S_{st} FT) then the number of struts (n_{strut}), the number of cables (n_{ca}), the load on each cable (W_{run} LB/FT-run), the horizontal component of cable tension (H_{CA} LB), and the maximum cable tension (T_{max} LB) can be readily calculated. Since the cables are arranged in pairs with one cable on each side of a strut (Figures 8.17 and 8.18) it may be assumed for purposes of determining the load on each cable pair (W_{run} LB/FT-run) that the cable spacing is equal to the spacing between struts (S_{st} FT) and that the load is carried equally by two cables.

$$n_{strut} = (B / S_{st})$$
$$n_{strut} = (200 / 8)$$
$$\mathbf{n_{strut} = 25}$$

$$n_{ca} = 2\, n_{strut}$$
$$n_{ca} = 2\,(25)$$
$$\mathbf{n_{ca} = 50}$$

$$W_{run} = S_{st}\,(W/A) \text{ (LB/FT-run)}$$
$$W_{run} = 8\,(3000000 / 20000)$$
$$\mathbf{W_{run} = 1{,}200 \text{ LB/FT-run}}$$

$$\mathbf{H} = (W_{run} L^2) / (8\,S) \text{ (LB)} \quad\dots\dots\dots\dots\dots\dots\dots\dots\dots\dots\dots\text{ 8.1}$$
$$H = 1200\,(100^2) / (8\,(4.71))$$
$$H = 12000000 / 37.68$$
$$\mathbf{H = 318{,}471 \text{ LB}}$$

$$H_{CA} = 0.5\,H \text{ (i.e., divided between two cables)}$$
$$H_{CA} = 318471 / 2$$
$$\mathbf{H_{CA} = 159{,}236 \text{ LB}}$$

$$\mathbf{T_{max}} = H_{CA}\,[1 + (16\,S^2 / L^2)]^{0.5} \text{ (LB)} \quad\dots\dots\dots\dots\dots\text{ 8.2}$$
$$T_{max} = 159236\,[1 + (16\,(4.71^2)) / 100^2]^{0.5}$$
$$T_{max} = 159236\,[1 + 0.0355]^{0.5}$$
$$T_{max} = 159236\,(1.0176)$$
$$\mathbf{T_{max} = 162{,}037 \text{ LB}}$$

Step 5: We can now calculate the cross-sectional material area of the strut wall (A_{strut} SI) and determine the allowable stress without internal pressure ($K_C(E)$ psi) based on the Kusmiss graph shown in Figure 8.15.

$$A_{strut} = \pi\,(12\,D)\,t \text{ (SI)}$$
$$A_{strut} = 3.14159\,(12)\,(4.71)\,(0.0625)$$
$$\mathbf{A_{strut} = 11.10 \text{ SI}}$$

for R/t of 453 K_C = 0.000550 (from Kusmiss graph in Figure 8.15)
$$K_C(E) = 29000000\,(0.000550)$$

$$K_C(E) = 15{,}950 \text{ psi}$$

Step 6: The strut's optimum internal air pressure (P_{strut} psig) to provide the maximum critical buckling stress based on the Kusmiss graph shown in Figure 8.16 occurs at $(P/E)[R/t]^2$ equal to *0.165* for which the value of ∂K_C is *0.224*.

$$P_{strut} = 0.165 \, E \, t^2 / (144 \, R^2) \text{ (psig)}$$
$$P_{strut} = 0.165 \, (29000000) \, (0.0625^2) / (144 \, (2.36^2))$$
$$\mathbf{P_{strut} = 23.31 \text{ psig}}$$

and $\partial K_C = 0.224$

This allows us to calculate the critical buckling stress of the strut wall under pressurized conditions (f_{strut} *psi*).

$$f_{strut} = E \, [\, K_C + (\partial K_C \, t / (12 \, R) \,] \text{ (psi)}$$
$$f_{strut} = 29000000 \, [0.000550 + (0.224 \, (0.0625) / (12 \, (2.36)))]$$
$$f_{strut} = 29000000 \, [0.000550 + 0.000494]$$
$$\mathbf{f_{strut} = 30{,}285 \text{ psi}}$$

It is also necessary to check that the circumferential stress in the strut wall due to the internal pressure (f_{circ} *psi*) does not exceed the design stress of the column wall material. It is given by:

$$f_{circ} = 12 \, P \, R / t \text{ (psi)}$$
$$f_{circ} = 12 \, (23.31) \, (2.36) / 0.0625$$
$$\mathbf{f_{circ} = 10{,}562 \text{ psi}}$$

Step 7: Calculate stress in strut wall ($f_{s\text{-}ca}$ *psi*) due to cable tension (*H LB*) force in the two cables on either side of the strut and compare with the critical buckling stress of the strut wall under pressurized conditions (f_{strut} *psi*).

$$f_{s\text{-}ca} = H / A_{strut}$$
$$f_{s\text{-}ca} = 318471 / 11.10$$
$$\mathbf{f_{s\text{-}ca} = 28{,}691 \text{ psi}}$$

This compares with the critical buckling stress (f_{strut} *psi*) of *30,285 psi* and a factor of safety of only *1.06*. If we wish to increase the factor of safety to at least *1.5* then we have two options. We can either increase the wall thickness (*t IN*) or the diameter (*D IN*) of the strut. Since the required increase in the load-bearing capacity of the strut is moderate it should be sufficient to increase the thickness of the column strut wall. The process is easily automated with a computer program that incrementally increases the wall thickness until:

$$f_{strut} \geq f_{s\text{-}ca} \text{ (factor of safety) (psi)}[13]$$

In this particular case increasing the wall thickness from *0.0625 IN* to *0.0707 IN*[14] and returning to Step 5 produces the desired result as follows:

$$A_{strut} = \pi \, (12 \, D) \, t \text{ (SI)}$$
$$A_{strut} = 3.14.159 \, (12) \, (4.71) \, (0.0707)$$

---

[13] However, the wall thickness cannot be increased beyond *R/t=100* (i.e., the maximum allowable value of *t* is *12R/100*, where *R* is in *FT*) for the strut to be classified as a thin-walled shell.

[14] With the use of a computer program the designer would increase the wall thickness in small increments (e.g., 2.5%) until the required thickness has been found.

$$A_{strut} = 12.55 \text{ SI}$$

for R/t of 401 K_C = 0.000790 (from Kusmiss graph in Figure 8.15)
$$K_C(E) = 29000000 \,(0.000790)$$
$$\mathbf{K_C(E)} = \mathbf{22{,}910 \text{ psi}}$$

Recalculation of the strut's optimum internal air pressure (P_{strut} psig) to provide the maximum critical buckling stress based on the Kusmiss graph shown in Figure 8.16, yields:

$$P_{strut} = 0.165 \, E \, t^2 / (144 \, R^2) \text{ (psig)}$$
$$P_{strut} = 0.165 \,(29000000)\,(0.0707^2) / (144\,(2.36^2))$$
$$\mathbf{P_{strut}} = \mathbf{29.82 \text{ psig}}$$

and $\partial K_C = 0.224$

This allows us to calculate the critical buckling stress of the strut wall under pressurized conditions (f_{strut} psi).

$$f_{strut} = E\,[\,K_C + (\partial K_C \, t / (12\,R))\,] \text{ (psi)}$$
$$f_{strut} = 29000000\,[0.000790 + (0.224\,(0.0707)) / (12\,(2.36)))$$
$$f_{strut} = 29000000\,[0.000790 + 0.000559]$$
$$\mathbf{f_{strut}} = \mathbf{39{,}124 \text{ psi}}$$

It is also necessary to recalculate the circumferential stress in the strut wall due to the internal pressure (f_{circ} psi), check that it does not exceed the design stress of the column wall material.

$$f_{circ} = 12\,P\,R / t \text{ (psi)}$$
$$f_{circ} = 12\,(29.82)\,(2.36) / 0.0707$$
$$\mathbf{f_{circ}} = \mathbf{11{,}945 \text{ psi}}$$

Since the strut's wall thickness has been increased the stress in the strut wall ($f_{s\text{-}ca}$ psi) due to the cable tension (H LB) force in the two cables on either side of the strut will be decreased:

$$f_{s\text{-}ca} = H / A_{strut}$$
$$f_{s\text{-}ca} = 318471 / 12.55$$
$$\mathbf{f_{s\text{-}ca}} = \mathbf{25{,}376 \text{ psi}}$$

This provides a factor of safety of **_1.54_** (i.e., *39124 / 25376 = 1.54*).

Step 8: We are now ready to determine the minimum required cable material area (A_{CA} SI), as well as estimate the cable radius (r_{ca} IN) and diameter (d_{ca} IN) using a fill factor (F_{CA}) of *75%* and cable material stress of *180,000 psi*.

$$A_{CA} = T_{max} / f_{ca} \text{ (SI)}$$
$$A_{CA} = 162037 / 180000$$
$$\mathbf{A_{CA}} = \mathbf{0.9002 \text{ SI}}$$
$$r_{ca} = (A_{CA} / \pi)^{0.5} \text{ (IN)}$$
$$r_{ca} = (0.9002 / 3.14159)^{0.5}$$
$$\mathbf{r_{ca}} = \mathbf{0.5353 \text{ IN}}$$
$$d_{ca} = 2\,r_{ca} / F_{CA} \text{ (IN)}$$
$$d_{ca} = 2\,(0.5353 / 0.75)$$
$$\mathbf{d_{ca}} = \mathbf{1.4275 \text{ IN}}$$

The calculation of the length of each cable (X_{CA} FT) is based on its sag, expressed geometrically as the radius of curvature (R_{CA} FT) of the cable:

$$R_{CA} = [((4 S^2) + L^2) / (8 S)] \text{ (FT)}$$
$$R_{CA} = [((4 (4.71^2)) + 100^2) / (8 (4.71))]$$
$$\mathbf{R_{CA} = 267.75 \text{ FT}}$$

$$X_{CA} = [2 R_{CA} \arcsin\{(L / (2 R_{CA})\}] \text{ (FT)}$$
$$X_{CA} = [(2 (267.75)) \arcsin\{100 / (2 (267.75))\}]$$
$$X_{CA} = 535.5 \arcsin\{0.1867\}$$
$$X_{CA} = 535.5 (0.1878)$$
$$\mathbf{X_{CA} = 100.57 \text{ FT}}$$

Step 9: The total self-weight of the floor (W_{fl-LB} LB) consisting of the separate weights of the cables (W_{CA} LB), the struts (W_{STRUT} LB), the floor end sections (W_{END} LB), the secondary floor surface/ceiling structure (W_{SEC} LB), the floor surface (W_{SURF} LB), and the ceiling (W_{CEIL} LB) is based on the respective material weights (w_{ca}, w_{strut}, w_{end}, w_{sec}, w_{surf}, and w_{ceil} LB/CF).

Cables: $\quad W_{CA} = w_{ca} [(n_{ca} X_{CA}) (A_{CA} / 144)]$ (LB)

Assuming a cable material weight (w_{ca}) of *490 LB/CF* we obtain:

$$W_{CA} = 490 [50 (100.57) (0.9002 / 144)]$$
$$W_{CA} = 490 [31.4351]$$
$$\mathbf{W_{CA} = 15,403 \text{ LB}}$$

Struts: Assuming two ½ *IN* thick circular steel cap plates serving as the attachments of each strut to the two end sections of the floor and a steel material weight (w_{strut}) of *490 LB/CF* we obtain:

$$W_{STRUT} = w_{strut} [(n_{strut} L) (A_{strut} / 144) + (2 \pi R^2 (0.5/12))] \text{ (LB)}$$
$$W_{STRUT} = 490 [25 (100) (12.55 / 144) + 2 (3.14159) (2.36)^2 (0.5 / 12)]$$
$$W_{STRUT} = 490 [217.88 + 1.458]$$
$$\mathbf{W_{STRUT} = 107,476 \text{ LB}}$$

End Sections: Assuming *1 IN* thick channels with *4 IN* flanges and a width equal to the diameter of the struts for the end sections of the floor to provide anchorage for the struts and attachments for the floor supports (e.g., hangers if suspended). If the material weight (w_{end}) of the steel channels is *490 LB/CF*, then:

$$W_{END} = w_{end} [(2 B) ((S + (8/12)) (1/12))] \text{ (LB)}$$
$$W_{END} = 490 [2 (200) (4.71 + 0.667) (1/12))$$
$$W_{END} = 490 [2150.8 / 12]$$
$$\mathbf{W_{END} = 87,824 \text{ LB}}$$

Secondary (A): For alternative (A) shown in Figure 8.17 we will assume ¼ *IN* thick *3 IN* wide on-edge bands around each strut at *8 FT* (S_{band}) centers, and adding an extra *1 IN* to the width of each band to allow for the cable ears so that the effective width of the on-edge bands is *4 IN* for calculation purposes. The approximate weight (W_{SEC-A} LB) of this secondary structure alternative based on strut bands is a function of the number of bands (n_{band}), the amount of material (A_{band} SI) and the unit weight of the material (w_{band} LB/CF):

$$A_{band} = \pi[((12\,R)+8)^2 - (12\,R)^2]\ (\text{SI})$$
$$A_{band} = 3.14159\,[(12(2.36)+8)^2 - (12(2.36))^2]$$
$$A_{band} = 3.14159\,[1319.14 - 802.02]$$
$$\mathbf{A_{band} = 1{,}624.58\ \text{SI}}$$

$$n_{band} = n_{strut}(\text{truncate}(L/S_{band}))$$
$$n_{band} = 25\,(\text{truncate}(100/8))$$
$$n_{band} = 25\,(12)$$
$$\mathbf{n_{band} = 300}$$

$$W_{SEC\text{-}A} = w_{band}\,[n_{band}\,(A_{band}/144)(0.25/12)]\ (\text{LB})$$
$$W_{SEC\text{-}A} = 490\,[300\,(1624.58/144)(0.25/12)]$$
$$W_{SEC\text{-}A} = 490\,[70.51]$$
$$\mathbf{W_{SEC\text{-}A} = 34{,}550\ \text{LB}}$$

Therefore the total structural weight of the floor with secondary structure option (A) is:

$$W_{STRUC\text{-}A} = [W_{CA} + W_{STRUT} + W_{END} + W_{SEC\text{-}A}]\ (\text{LB})$$
$$W_{STRUC\text{-}A} = [15403 + 107476 + 87824 + 34550]$$
$$\mathbf{W_{STRUC\text{-}A} = \underline{245{,}253\ \text{LB}\ (\text{or 12.3 psf})}}$$

Secondary (B): For alternative (B) shown in Figure 8.18 we will assume that the trusses on each side of each strut (on the outside of the cables) are fabricated from *3 IN* x *3 IN* x *0.25 IN* steel angles with a cross-sectional area of *1.50 SI* (A_a) and *4 IN* x *2 IN* x *0.25 IN* steel top and bottom channel chords with a cross-sectional area of *2.00 SI* (A_c). The approximate weight ($W_{SEC\text{-}B}$ *LB*) of this secondary structure alternative based on trusses is a function of the number of trusses (n_{truss}), the distance between cable attachment points (assumed at *8 FT* centers along the length of the truss) since the trusses are supported by the cables at intermediate points, the spacing between vertical members in the 'V' pattern truss configuration shown in Figure 8.18 (S_v *FT*), the volume of channel material (A_{chan} *CI*), the volume of angle material (A_{ang} *CI*), and the unit weight of the material (w_{truss} *LB/CF*). Assuming that the vertical truss members are spaced *8 FT* apart (S_v) and a material weight (w_{truss} *LB/CF*) of *490 LB/CF*, we obtain:

$$n_{truss} = n_{ca}$$
$$\mathbf{n_{truss} = 50}$$

$$A_{chan} = n_{truss}\,[2\,(12\,L\,(A_c))]\ (\text{CI})$$
$$A_{chan} = 50\,[2\,(12)(100)(2.00)]$$
$$\mathbf{A_{chan} = 240{,}000\ \text{CI}}$$

$$A_{ang} = n_{truss}\,[(L/S_v)\,A_a\,(12S + 2\{(12S)^2 + (12S_v/2)^2\}^{0.5})]\ (\text{CI})$$
$$A_{ang} = 50\,[(100/8)\,1.50\,(12(4.71) + 2\{(12(4.71))^2 + (12(8)/2)^2\}^{0.5})]$$
$$A_{ang} = 50\,[18.75\,(56.52 + 2\{3194.51 + 2304\}^{0.5})]$$
$$A_{ang} = 50\,[18.75\,(56.52 + 148.30)]$$
$$A_{ang} = 50\,[3840.45]$$
$$\mathbf{A_{ang} = 192{,}022\ \text{CI}}$$

$$W_{SEC\text{-}B} = w_{truss}\,[(A_{chan}/12^3) + (A_{ang}/12^3)]\ (\text{LB})$$
$$W_{SEC\text{-}B} = 490\,[240000/(12(144)) + 192022/(12(144))]$$

$$W_{SEC-B} = 490\,[\,138.89 + 111.12\,]$$
$$W_{SEC-B} = 490\,[\,250.01\,]$$
$$\mathbf{W_{SEC-B} = 122{,}507 \text{ LB}}$$

Therefore the total structural weight of the floor with secondary structure option (B) is:

$$W_{STRUC-B} = [\,W_{CA} + W_{STRUT} + W_{END} + W_{SEC-B}\,]\ (LB)$$
$$W_{STRUC-B} = [\,15403 + 107476 + 87824 + 122507\,]$$
$$\mathbf{W_{STRUC-B} = \underline{333{,}210 \text{ LB (or 16.7 psf)}}}$$

Floor Surface: Assuming a *3 IN* concrete screed with lightweight steel mesh on corrugated steel decking, weighing approximately *30 psf* (w_{surf}):

$$W_{SURF} = w_{surf}\,[\,L\,(B)\,]\ (LB)$$
$$W_{SURF} = 30\,[\,100\,(200)\,]$$
$$\mathbf{W_{SURF} = 600{,}000 \text{ LB}}$$

Ceiling: Assume 2-hour fire rated lightweight ceiling with sprayed fire proofing applied directly to struts, cables and secondary structure (A) or (B), weighing approximately *10 psf* (w_{ceil}):

$$W_{CEIL} = w_{ceil}\,[(\,L\,(B))\,]\ (LB)$$
$$W_{CEIL} = 10\,[\,100\,(200)\,]$$
$$\mathbf{W_{CEIL} = 200{,}000 \text{ LB}}$$

The total self-weight of the floor ($W_{FLOOR-A}$ LB) with secondary structure option (A) is equal to the sum of the component weights:

$$W_{FLOOR-A} = [\,W_{CA} + W_{STRUT} + W_{END} + W_{SEC-A} + W_{SURF} + W_{CEIL}\,]\ (LB)$$
$$W_{FLOOR-A} = [\,15403 + 107476 + 87824 + 34550 + 600000 + 200000\,]$$
$$\mathbf{W_{FLOOR-A} = \underline{1{,}045{,}253 \text{ LB (or 52.3 psf)}}}$$

… and the total self-weight of the floor ($W_{FLOOR-B}$ LB) with secondary structure option (B) is equal to the sum of the component weights:

$$W_{FLOOR-A} = [\,W_{CA} + W_{STRUT} + W_{END} + W_{SEC-B} + W_{SURF} + W_{CEIL}\,]\ (LB)$$
$$W_{FLOOR-A} = [\,15403 + 107476 + 87824 + 122539 + 600000 + 200000\,]$$
$$\mathbf{W_{FLOOR-A} = \underline{1{,}133{,}242 \text{ LB (or 56.7 psf)}}}$$

Example 2 (200 FT span rectangular floor)

Step 1: The span (*L FT*) and width (*B FT*) of the second example floor are *200 FT* and *400 FT*, respectively. Struts are equally spaced at *8 FT* centers with cables on either side. Assuming a live-load (L_L *psf*) of *100 psf* and a dead-load (D_L *psf*) of *50 psf* we are able to calculate the floor area (*A SF*) and the total estimated floor load (*W LB*) as follows:

$$A = L\,(B)\ (SF)$$
$$A = 200\,(400)$$
$$\mathbf{A = 80{,}000 \text{ SF}}$$

$$W = A\,(L_L + D_L)\ (LB)$$
$$W = 80000\,(100 + 50)$$
$$\mathbf{W = 12{,}000{,}000 \text{ LB}}$$

Step 2: We will assume the same the same strut radius (R FT) and diameter (D FT) as in Example (1) even though this will increase the slenderness ratio (SR) of the strut beyond the recommended value (*30*) to *60*. The justification is based on horizontal bracing between struts at frequent intervals (e.g., at *10 FT* centers along the length of each strut) reducing the effective strut length (H_E FT) to one quarter of the actual length ($H_E = 0.25H$ FT) due to adequate bracing between struts and strut end constraints.

$$SR = H_E / [R^2 / 2]^{0.5} \text{ and for } SR = 60:$$
$$R = H_E / 21.2132 \text{ (FT)}$$
$$R = 200 (0.25) / 21.2132$$
$$\mathbf{R = 2.36 \text{ FT}}$$
$$D = 2R \text{ (FT)}$$
$$D = 2 (2.36)$$
$$\mathbf{D = 4.71 \text{ FT}}$$

The actual depth of the floor (D_{floor} FT) is slightly larger than the strut diameter (D FT) to allow for the upper floor surface and the ceiling on the underside. An additional *6 IN* will provide a minimum clearance of ½ *IN* above and below the strut plus thicknesses of *3 IN* for the upper floor surface and *2 IN* for the ceiling below. Therefore the depth of the floor (D_{floor} FT) is given by:

$$D_{floor} = D + 0.5 \text{ (FT)}$$
$$D_{floor} = 4.71 + 0.5$$
$$\mathbf{D_{floor} = 5.21 \text{ FT}}$$

Step 3: To be able to utilize the Kusmiss graphs (Figures 8.15 and 8.16) the strut wall thickness (t IN) must be in the range $R/t >= 100$ (or $t = 0.1200R$ with R in FT) and $R/t <= 1400$ (or $t = 0.00857R$ with R in FT). For R equal to *2.36 FT* (i.e., *28.32 IN*) the equivalent range for t is *0.2832 IN* to *0.0202 IN*. As in Example (1) we will start off with the readily available galvanized sheet metal thickness of *0.0625 IN (1/16 IN)*.

$$R/t = 28.32 / 0.0625$$
$$\mathbf{R/t = 453}$$

Step 4: Spacing the struts at *8 FT* centers (S_{st} FT) the number of struts (n_{strut}), the number of cables (n_{ca}), the load on each cable (W_{run} LB/FT-run), the horizontal component of cable tension (H_{CA} LB), and the maximum cable tension (T_{max} LB) can be calculated. With the cables are arranged in pairs with one cable on each side of a strut (Figures 8.17 and 8.18) we will again assume for purposes of determining the load on each cable pair (W_{run} LB/FT-run) that the cable spacing is equal to the spacing between struts (S_{st} FT) and that the load is carried equally by two cables.

$$n_{strut} = (B / S_{st})$$
$$n_{strut} = (400 / 8)$$
$$\mathbf{n_{strut} = 50}$$

$$n_{ca} = 2 n_{strut}$$
$$n_{ca} = 2 (50)$$
$$\mathbf{n_{ca} = 100}$$

$$W_{run} = S_{st}(W/A) \text{ (LB/FT-run)}$$
$$W_{run} = 8 (12000000 / 80000)$$
$$\mathbf{W_{run} = 1{,}200 \text{ LB/FT-run}}$$

$$H = (W_{run} L^2) / (8 S) \quad (LB) \quad \text{.. 8.1}$$
$$H = 1200 (200^2) / (8 (4.71))$$
$$H = 48000000 / 37.68$$
$$H = 1{,}273{,}885 \text{ LB}$$
$$H_{CA} = 0.5 H \quad \text{(i.e., divided between two cables)}$$
$$H_{CA} = 1273885 / 2$$
$$H_{CA} = 636{,}943 \text{ LB}$$

$$T_{max} = H_{CA} [1 + (16 S^2 / L^2)]^{0.5} \quad (LB) \quad \text{...................................... 8.2}$$
$$T_{max} = 636943 [1 + (16 (4.71^2) / 200^2)]^{0.5}$$
$$T_{max} = 626943 [1 + 0.0089]^{0.5}$$
$$T_{max} = 636943 (1.0044)$$
$$T_{max} = 639{,}763 \text{ LB}$$

Step 5: We can now calculate the cross-sectional material area of the strut wall (A_{strut} *SI*) and determine the allowable stress without internal pressure ($K_C(E)$ *psi*) based on the Kusmiss graph shown in Figure 8.15.

$$A_{strut} = \pi (12 D) t \quad (SI)$$
$$A_{strut} = 3.14.159 (12) (4.71) (0.0625)$$
$$A_{strut} = 11.10 \text{ SI}$$

for R/t of 453 K_C = 0.000550 (from Kusmiss graph in Figure 8.15)
$$K_C(E) = 29000000 (0.000550)$$
$$K_C(E) = 15{,}950 \text{ psi}$$

Step 6: The strut's optimum internal air pressure (P_{strut} *psig*) to provide the maximum critical buckling stress based on the Kusmiss graph shown in Figure 8.16 occurs at $(P/E)[R/t]^2$ equal to *0.165* for which the value of ∂K_C is *0.224*.

$$P_{strut} = 0.165 E t^2 / (144 R^2) \quad (psig)$$
$$P_{strut} = 0.165 (29000000) (0.0625^2) / (144 (2.36^2))$$
$$P_{strut} = 23.31 \text{ psig}$$

and ∂K_C = 0.224

This allows us to calculate the critical buckling stress of the strut wall under pressurized conditions (f_{strut} *psi*).

$$f_{strut} = E [K_C + (\partial K_C t / (12 R))] \quad (psi)$$
$$f_{strut} = 29000000 [0.000550 + (0.224 (0.0625) / (12 (2.36)))]$$
$$f_{strut} = 29000000 [0.000550 + 0.000494]$$
$$f_{strut} = 30{,}285 \text{ psi}$$

It is also necessary to check that the circumferential stress in the strut wall due to the internal pressure (f_{circ} *psi*) does not exceed the design stress of the column wall material. It is given by:

$$f_{circ} = 12 P R / t \quad (psi)$$
$$f_{circ} = 12 (23.31) (2.36) / 0.0625$$
$$f_{circ} = 10{,}562 \text{ psi}$$

Step 7: Calculate stress in strut wall ($f_{s\text{-}ca}$ *psi*) due to cable tension (*H LB*) force in the two cables on either side of the strut and compare with the critical buckling stress of the strut wall under pressurized conditions (f_{strut} psi).

$$f_{s\text{-}ca} = H / A_{strut}$$
$$f_{s\text{-}ca} = 1273885 / 11.10$$
$$\mathbf{f_{s\text{-}ca} = 114{,}764 \text{ psi}}$$

This is almost four times greater than the critical buckling stress (f_{strut} psi) of *30,285 psi*, with an unacceptable strut load to capacity ratio of only *0.26*. In fact we should apply a reasonable factor of safety of around *1.5* as well. Again, as in Example (1), we can either increase the wall thickness (*t IN*) or the diameter (*D IN*) of the strut. Since the required increase in the load-bearing capacity of the strut is significant an increase in the diameter of the strut is indicated. However, let us assume that for non-structural reasons we do not wish to increase the depth of the floor but increase the thickness of the column strut wall instead. As mentioned previously the process is easily automated with a computer program that incrementally increases the wall thickness until:

$$f_{strut} >= f_{s\text{-}ca} \text{ (factor of safety) (psi)}$$

In this particular case increasing the wall thickness from *0.0625 IN* to *0.1412 IN* and returning to Step 5 produces the desired result as follows:

$$A_{strut} = \pi(12\,D)\,t \text{ (SI)}$$
$$A_{strut} = 3.14159\,(12)\,(4.71)\,(0.1412)$$
$$\mathbf{A_{strut} = 25.07 \text{ SI}}$$

for R/t of 200 K_C = 0.001530 (from Kusmiss graph in Figure 8.15)
$$K_C(E) = 29000000\,(0.001530)$$
$$\mathbf{K_C(E) = 44{,}370 \text{ psi}}$$

Recalculation of the strut's optimum internal air pressure (P_{strut} psig) to provide the maximum critical buckling stress based on the Kusmiss graph shown in Figure 8.16, yields:

$$P_{strut} = 0.165\,E\,t^2 / (144\,R^2) \text{ (psig)}$$
$$P_{strut} = 0.165\,(29000000)\,(0.1412^2) / (144\,(2.36^2))$$
$$\mathbf{P_{strut} = 118.95 \text{ psig}}$$

and $\partial K_C = 0.224$

This allows us to calculate the critical buckling stress of the strut wall under pressurized conditions (f_{strut} psi).

$$f_{strut} = E\,[\,K_C + (\partial K_C\,t / (12\,R))\,] \text{ (psi)}$$
$$f_{strut} = 29000000\,[0.001530 + (0.224\,(0.1412) / (12\,(2.36)))]$$
$$f_{strut} = 29000000\,[0.001530 + 0.001117]$$
$$\mathbf{f_{strut} = 76{,}763 \text{ psi}}$$

It is also necessary to recalculate the circumferential stress in the strut wall due to the internal pressure (f_{circ} psi), check that it does not exceed the design stress of the column wall material.

$$f_{circ} = 12\,P\,R / t \text{ (psi)}$$
$$f_{circ} = 12\,(118.95)\,(2.36) / 0.1412$$
$$\mathbf{f_{circ} = 23{,}857 \text{ psi}}$$

Since the strut's wall thickness has been increased the stress in the strut wall ($f_{s\text{-}ca}$ psi) due to the cable tension (*H LB*) force in the two cables on either side of the strut will be decreased:

$$f_{s\text{-}ca} = H / A_{strut}$$
$$f_{s\text{-}ca} = 1273885 / 25.07$$
$$\mathbf{f_{s\text{-}ca} = 50{,}813 \text{ psi}}$$

This provides a factor of safety of **_1.51_** (i.e., *76763 / 50813 = 1.51*) on the assumption that the yield strength of the strut material is at least *76,763 psi*.

Step 8: We are now ready to determine the minimum required cable material area (A_{CA} *SI*), as well as estimate the cable radius (r_{ca} *IN*) and diameter (d_{ca} *IN*) using a fill factor (F_{CA}) of *75%* and cable material stress of *180,000 psi*.

$$A_{CA} = T_{max} / f_{ca} \quad (SI)$$
$$A_{CA} = 639763 / 180000$$
$$\mathbf{A_{CA} = 3.5542 \text{ SI}}$$

$$r_{ca} = (A_{CA} / \pi)^{0.5} \quad (IN)$$
$$r_{ca} = (3.5542 / 3.14159)^{0.5}$$
$$\mathbf{r_{ca} = 1.0636 \text{ IN}}$$

$$d_{ca} = 2 \, r_{ca} / F_{CA} \quad (IN)$$
$$d_{ca} = 2 \, (1.0636 / 0.75)$$
$$\mathbf{d_{ca} = 2.8364 \text{ IN}}$$

The calculation of the length of each cable (X_{CA} *FT*) is based on its sag, expressed geometrically as the radius of curvature (R_{CA} *FT*) of the cable:

$$R_{CA} = [\,((4 \, S^2) + L^2) / (8 \, S)\,] \quad (FT)$$
$$R_{CA} = [\,((4 \, (4.71^2)) + 200^2) / (8 \, (4.71))\,]$$
$$\mathbf{R_{CA} = 1{,}063.93 \text{ FT}}$$

$$X_{CA} = [\,2 \, R_{CA} \arcsin\{(L / (2 \, R_{CA})\}\,] \quad (FT)$$
$$X_{CA} = [\,(2 \, (1063.93)) \arcsin\{200 / (2 \, (1063.93))\}\,]$$
$$X_{CA} = 2127.85 \arcsin \{0.0940\}$$
$$X_{CA} = 2127.85 \, (0.0941)$$
$$\mathbf{X_{CA} = 200.23 \text{ FT}}$$

Step 9: The total self-weight of the floor ($W_{fl\text{-}LB}$ *LB*) consisting of the separate weights of the cables (W_{CA} *LB*), the struts (W_{STRUT} *LB*), the floor end sections (W_{END} *LB*), the secondary floor surface/ceiling structure (W_{SEC} *LB*), the floor surface (W_{SURF} *LB*), and the ceiling (W_{CEIL} *LB*) is based on the respective material weights (w_{ca}, w_{strut}, w_{end}, w_{sec}, w_{surf}, and w_{ceil} *LB/CF*).

Cables: $\quad W_{CA} = w_{ca} \, [(n_{ca} \, X_{CA}) \, (A_{CA} / 144)] \quad (LB)$

Assuming a cable material weight (w_{ca}) of *490 LB/CF* we obtain:

$$W_{CA} = 490 \, [\, 100 \, (200.23) \, (3.5542 / 144) \,]$$
$$W_{CA} = 490 \, [494.2066]$$
$$\mathbf{W_{CA} = 242{,}161 \text{ LB}}$$

Struts: Assuming two ½ *IN* thick circular steel cap plates serving as the attachments of each strut to the two end sections of the floor and a steel material weight (w_{strut}) of *490 LB/CF* we obtain:

$$W_{STRUT} = w_{strut} \, [(n_{strut} \, L) \, (A_{strut} / 144) + (2 \, \pi \, R^2 \, (0.5/12))] \quad (LB)$$
$$W_{STRUT} = 490 \, [\, 50 \, (200) \, (25.07 / 144) + 2 \, (3.14159) \, (2.36)^2 \, (0.5 / 12)]$$

	W_{STRUT}	=	490 [1740.97 + 1.458]
	W_{STRUT}	=	**853,790 LB**

End Sections: Assuming *1 IN* thick channels with *4 IN* flanges and a width equal to the diameter of the struts for the end sections of the floor to provide anchorage for the struts and attachments for the floor supports (e.g., hangers if suspended). If the material weight (w_{end}) of the steel channels is *490 LB/CF*, then:

W_{END} = w_{end} [(2 B) ((S + (8/12)) (1/12))] (LB)
W_{END} = 490 [2 (400) (4.71 + 0.667) (1/12))
W_{END} = 490 [4301.6 / 12]
W_{END} = **175,649 LB**

Secondary (A): For alternative (A) shown in Figure 8.17 we will assume ¼ *IN* thick *3 IN* wide on-edge bands around each strut at *8 FT* (S_{band}) centers, and adding an extra *1 IN* to the width of each band to allow for the cable ears so that the effective width of the on-edge bands is *4 IN* for calculation purposes. The approximate weight (W_{SEC-A} *LB*) of this secondary structure alternative based on strut bands is a function of the number of bands (n_{band}), the amount of material (A_{band} *SI*) and the unit weight of the material (w_{band} *LB/CF*):

A_{band} = $\pi [((12 R) + 8)^2 - (12 R)^2]$ (SI)
A_{band} = $3.14159 [(12 (2.36) + 8)^2 - (12 (2.36))^2]$
A_{band} = 3.14159 [1319.14 – 802.02]
A_{band} = **1,624.58 SI**

n_{band} = n_{strut} (truncate (L / S_{band}))
n_{band} = 50 (truncate (200 / 8))
n_{band} = 50 (25)
n_{band} = **1,250**

W_{SEC-A} = w_{band} [n_{band} (A_{band}/144) (0.25/12)] (LB)
W_{SEC-A} = 490 [1250 (1624.58 / 144) (0.25 / 12)]
W_{SEC-A} = 490 [293.80]
W_{SEC-A} = **143,961 LB**

Therefore the total structural weight of the floor with secondary structure option (A) is:

$W_{STRUC-A}$ = [W_{CA} + W_{STRUT} + W_{END} + W_{SEC-A}] (LB)
$W_{STRUC-A}$ = [242161 + 853790 + 175649 + 143961]
$W_{STRUC-A}$ = **1,415,561 LB (or 17.7 psf)**

Secondary (B): For alternative (B) shown in Figure 8.18 we will assume that the trusses on each side of each strut (on the outside of the cables) are fabricated from *3 IN* x *3 IN* x *0.25 IN* steel angles with a cross-sectional area of *1.50 SI* (A_a) and *4 IN* x *2 IN* x *0.25 IN* steel top and bottom channel chords with a cross-sectional area of *2.00 SI* (A_c). The approximate weight (W_{SEC-B} *LB*) of this secondary structure alternative based on trusses is a function of the number of trusses (n_{truss}), the distance between cable attachment points (assumed at *8 FT* centers along the length of the truss) since the trusses are supported by the cables at intermediate points, the spacing between vertical members in the 'V' pattern truss configuration shown in Figure 8.18 (S_v FT), the volume of channel material (A_{chan} CI), the volume of angle material (A_{ang} CI), and the unit weight of the material (w_{truss} LB/CF). Assuming that the vertical truss members are spaced *8 FT* apart (S_v) and a material weight (w_{truss} LB/CF) of *490 LB/CF*, we obtain:

$$n_{truss} = n_{ca}$$
$$\mathbf{n_{truss} = 100}$$
$$A_{chan} = n_{truss} [\, 2\, (12\, L\, (A_c)\,] \text{ (CI)}$$
$$A_{chan} = 100\, [\, 2\, (12)\, (200)\, (2.00)\,]$$
$$\mathbf{A_{chan} = 960{,}000 \text{ CI}}$$
$$A_{ang} = n_{truss} [(L/S_v)\, A_a\, (12S + 2\{(12S)^2 + (12S_v/2)^2\}^{0.5})] \text{ (CI)}$$
$$A_{ang} = 100\, [\, (200/8)\, 1.50\, (12\, (4.71) + 2\{(12\, (4.71))^2 + (12(8)/2)^2\}^{0.5})]$$
$$A_{ang} = 100\, [\, 37.5\, (56.52 + 2\{3194.51 + 2304\}^{0.5})]$$
$$A_{ang} = 100\, [\, 37.5\, (56.52 + 148.30)]$$
$$A_{ang} = 100\, [\, 7680.75\,]$$
$$\mathbf{A_{ang} = 768{,}075 \text{ CI}}$$
$$W_{SEC-B} = w_{truss}\, [(A_{chan}/12^3) + (A_{ang}/12^3)] \text{ (LB)}$$
$$W_{SEC-B} = 490\, [\, 960000/(12(144)) + 768075/(12(144))\,]$$
$$W_{SEC-B} = 490\, [\, 555.56 + 444.49\,]$$
$$W_{SEC-B} = 490\, [\, 1000.05\,]$$
$$\mathbf{W_{SEC-B} = 490{,}023 \text{ LB}}$$

Therefore the total structural weight of the floor with secondary structure option (B) is:

$$W_{STRUC-B} = [\, W_{CA} + W_{STRUT} + W_{END} + W_{SEC-B}\,] \text{ (LB)}$$
$$W_{STRUC-B} = [\, 242161 + 853790 + 175649 + 490023\,]$$
$$\mathbf{W_{STRUC-B} = \underline{1{,}761{,}623 \text{ LB (or 22.0 psf)}}}$$

Floor Surface: Assuming a *3 IN* concrete screed with lightweight steel mesh on corrugated steel decking, weighing approximately *30 psf* (w_{surf}):

$$W_{SURF} = w_{surf}\, [\, L\, (B)\,] \text{ (LB)}$$
$$W_{SURF} = 30\, [\, 200\, (400)\,]$$
$$\mathbf{W_{SURF} = 2{,}400{,}000 \text{ LB}}$$

Ceiling: Assume 2-hour fire rated lightweight ceiling with sprayed fire proofing applied directly to struts, cables and secondary structure (A) or (B), weighing approximately *10 psf* (w_{ceil}):

$$W_{CEIL} = w_{ceil}\, [(\, L\, (B))\,] \text{ (LB)}$$
$$W_{CEIL} = 10\, [\, 200\, (400)\,]$$
$$\mathbf{W_{CEIL} = 800{,}000 \text{ LB}}$$

The total self-weight of the floor ($W_{FLOOR-A}$ LB) with secondary structure option (A) is equal to the sum of the component weights:

$$W_{FLOOR-A} = [\, W_{CA} + W_{STRUT} + W_{END} + W_{SEC-A} + W_{SURF} + W_{CEIL}\,] \text{ (LB)}$$
$$W_{FLOOR-A} = [\, 242161 + 853790 + 175649 + 143961 + 2400000 + 800000\,]$$
$$\mathbf{W_{FLOOR-A} = \underline{4{,}615{,}561 \text{ LB (or 57.7 psf)}}}$$

... and the total self-weight of the floor ($W_{FLOOR-B}$ LB) with secondary structure option (B) is equal to the sum of the component weights:

$$W_{FLOOR-B} = [\ W_{CA} + W_{STRUT} + W_{END} + W_{SEC-B} + W_{SURF} + W_{CEIL}\ ]\ (LB)$$
$$W_{FLOOR-B} = [\ 242161 + 853790 + 175649 + 490023 + 2400000 + 800000\ ]$$
$$\mathbf{W_{FLOOR-B} = \underline{4{,}961{,}623\ LB\ (or\ 62.0\ psf)}}$$

Comparison of Examples 1 and 2

Comparison of the results obtained for the two example rectangular floors (Table 8.7) leads to some somewhat surprising conclusions. Even though the span has doubled in Example 2 while maintaining the same floor depth as in Example 1, the structural self-weight and the span to self-weight ratio have increased by only 44% and 40%, respectively. Also, even though the internal air pressure of each strut has increased by 300% from *29.91 psig* to *119.42 psig* the strut's wall thickness has increased by only 100% from *0.0707 IN* to *0.1412 IN*. Of course the significant increase in the required air pressure is due to the much lower cable sag percentage in the case of the *200 FT* span floor, leading to a much higher cable tension of *639,763 LB* as compared with *162,037 LB* for the *100 FT* span in Example 1 (i.e., *295%* difference).

Table 8.7: Comparison of *100 FT* and *200 FT* span fluid-inflated cable floors

Design Parameters	Example (1)	Example (2)	Difference
floor (cable) span	100 FT	200 FT	+ 100%
floor depth	5.21 FT	5.21 FT	0%
cable sag and strut diameter	4.71 FT	4.71 FT	0%
percent cable sag	4.7%	2.4%	- 100%
diameter of cables	1.43 IN	2.84 IN	+ 100%
strut internal air pressure	29.91 psig	119.42 psig	+ 300%
tension in each cable	161,903 LB	639,762 LB	+ 295%
strut wall thickness	0.0707 IN	0.1412 IN	+ 100%
strut critical buckling stress	39,151 psi	76,822 psi	+ 96%
factor of safety	1.5	1.5	+ 0%
structural self-weight of floor	12.3 psf	17.7 psf	+ 44%
span to cable sag ratio	20.0	40.0	+ 100%
span to self-weight ratio	8.1	11.3	+ 40%
slenderness ratio (L/D)	30 (21.2)	60 (42.4)	+ 100%

The feasibility of a *200 FT* span floor with the same depth as a *100 FT* span floor depends on the ability to reduce the slenderness ratio of the strut, so that the failure mechanism of the strut remains in the local buckling range of a short column. The argument presented previously in Step 2 of Example 2 relies on the ability to provide adequate horizontal bracing between struts at certain intervals along the length of each strut. The required *effective length coefficient* to reduce the slenderness ratio of a *200 FT* long strut with a diameter of *4.71 FT* to *30* is *0.25* (i.e., *0.25* x *200 = 50 FT* and the slenderness ratio $(SR) = 50 / (2.36^2/2) = 30$). The secondary structure (Option A) for supporting the upper floor surface and the ceiling on the underside of the floor that is assumed in Examples 1 and 2 utilizes strut bands (Figure 8.17). For the *200 FT* span floor these bands are spaced at *8 FT* centers along the length of each strut. It would seem plausible to utilize these bands as attachments for bracing the struts horizontally. To achieve an effective strut length of one quarter (*50 FT*) of the actual length (*200 FT*) such horizontal braces could be spaced at *24 FT* to *32 FT* centers attached to every third or fourth strut band along the length of the strut. It follows that greater floor spans than *200 FT* are feasible with strut length to diameter ratios in excess of *60* with closer spacings of the horizontal bracing.

The questions then arises; what is the maximum span for a given floor depth? There are three structural factors that are relevant to this question. The first factor is related to the effectiveness of the horizontal bracing in reducing the *effective length* of a strut? Theoretically, if the bracing is 100% effective then it should reduce the *effective length* of the strut to one half the spacing between braces. In other words, the braces would be equivalent to built-in ends that prevent the ends of the strut from rotating in any direction. Since it is unlikely that this ideal condition can be achieved in practice, the author would suggest that the distance between braces serve as the *effective length* of the strut[15].

The second factor pertains to the thickness of the strut wall. As discussed earlier in Section 8.3.2 (Step 3), if we assume the maximum strut radius to wall thickness ratio (*R/t*) to be *100* then the maximum wall thickness (*t IN*) is equal to *0.12R* (where *R* is in *FT*). In the case of Example 2, for a strut length of *200 FT* and diameter of *4.71 FT* the maximum wall thickness would be *0.2826 IN*. The third factor is the material strength of the strut wall. As the *R/t* ratio of the strut decreases the allowable (i.e., critical) buckling stress under pressurized conditions increases and can easily exceed the maximum yield stress of the wall material. Even though the internal air pressure in the strut also increases with larger floor span to depth ratios the circumferential stress produced by the pressure in the strut wall increases at a much lower rate and is therefore unlikely to exceed the material yield strength.

Table 8.8: Comparison of increased floor spans at a fixed strut diameter of *4.71 FT* and bracing between struts at *50 FT* centers to maintain a constant slenderness ratio below *30*.

Strut Length (Floor Span)	Effect. Length Coefficient	Structural Self-Weight	Strut Wall Thickness	Strut Wall Critical Stress	Internal Pressure	R/t Ratio
100 FT	0.50	11.5 psf	0.0800 IN	41,300 psi	38 psig	353
150 FT	0.33	13.1 psf	0.1130 IN	70,355 psi	77 psig	250
200 FT	0.25	16.3 psf	0.1558 IN	85,121 psi	146 psig	149
250 FT	0.20	19.7 psf	0.1899 IN	110,924 psi	216 psig	149
300 FT	0.17	24.0 psf	0.2750 IN	127,996 psi	321 psig	122
350 FT	0.14	28.9 psf	0.2371 IN	150,210 psi	453 psig	103

The relationship among these three factors is shown in Table 8.8, where the length (i.e., floor span) of a fixed diameter strut is increased from *100 FT* to *350 FT* in *50 FT* increments, with the following constant parameters: *100 psf* live-load; *50 psf* dead-load; *4.71 FT* strut diameter; *9.71 FT* spacing between parallel struts (i.e., strut diameter plus *5 FT*); and a factor of safety of *1.5* for the strut wall material stress. The spacing between the horizontal braces is *50 FT* to maintain the slenderness ratio of the strut at a constant value of *30* regardless of the actual length of the strut (i.e., the floor span). The effective length of the strut is assumed to be the spacing between braces

---

[15] Therefore in Tables 8.8 and 8.9 the actual slenderness ratio is *15* since due to practical considerations the effective length of the struts is assumed to be the distance between braces on the assumption that the braces will allow some rotational moments.

on the basis that neither the braces nor the floor ends will provide complete rotational constraint. This is a conservative design recommendation that the author believes to be warranted from a practical construction point of view.

As indicated in Table 8.8 the critical buckling stress of the strut wall increases significantly (although at a decreasing rate) with increasing floor span. A material with a yield stress of *140,000 psi* would be desirable for floor span to depth ratios above *60*. The largest span for a *4.71 FT* strut diameter is just over *360 FT* (i.e., *361 FT* with a strut wall thickness of *0.2819 IN*, critical buckling stress of *151,790 psi*, air pressure of *476 psig*, and self-weight of *29.9 psf*).

Table 8.9 examines the effect of increasing depth on a floor with a *200 FT* span. The floor depth includes an additional *6 IN* for the top floor surface and the ceiling on the underside (i.e., floor depth = strut diameter + *6 IN*). Therefore, the equivalent strut diameter range shown is *3.5 FT* to *9.5 FT* with equivalent cable sag percentages of *1.8%* to *4.8%*.

Table 8.9: Comparison of increased floor depth at a fixed span of *200 FT* and bracing between struts at *50 FT* centers to maintain a slenderness ratio below *30*.

Floor Depth	Strut Diameter	Structural Self-Weight	Strut Wall Thickness	Strut Wall Critical Stress	Internal Pressure	R/t Ratio
4.0 FT	3.5 FT	15.9 psf	0.1678 IN	126,731 psi	306 psig	125
5.0 FT	4.5 FT	15.9 psf	0.1520 IN	92,258 psi	152 psig	178
6.0 FT	5.5 FT	16.4 psf	0.1447 IN	72,855 psi	92 psig	228
7.0 FT	6.5 FT	16.7 psf	0.1412 IN	58,315 psi	63 psig	276
8.0 FT	7.5 FT	17.9 psf	0.1412 IN	47,930 psi	47 psig	318
9.0 FT	8.5 FT	18.4 psf	0.1412 IN	40,892 psi	37 psig	361
10.0 FT	9.5 FT	19.1 psf	0.1412 IN	34,649 psi	29 psig	404

Comparison of the critical buckling stress in the strut wall with the structural self-weight of the *200 FT* span floor for different floor depths, shown in Table 8.9, indicates that the self-weight actually increases with greater depth. The increase is fairly constant at an average of *3%* for each additional *1 FT* of floor depth. Also, as expected, the required internal air pressure in the struts decreases by a much larger percentage non-linearly between *102%* and *28%* with increased floor depth. All of the design values shown in Table 8.9 are based on a *1.5* factor of safety.

Although the strut wall thickness decreases with increasing depth the self-weight of the floor increases. The reason for this is shown in Table 8.10, where the percentage contributions of the individual structural components to the self-weight of the floor are itemized for the same *200 FT* span floor. The only structural component that is omitted is the horizontal bracing between struts. In the case of a *200 FT* span there would be a maximum of three braces between struts across the width of the floor (i.e., at *50 FT* centers as discussed previously in this Section), with a negligible weight contribution (i.e., less than *1%*).

It can be seen in Table 8.10 that the major contributions to the structural self-weight of the floor come from the cables and the struts; - over *75%* at floor depths up to *6.0 FT* (span to strut diameter ratio of *36*) and over *65%* for greater floor depths. However, the proportional contributions of the cables and struts change with greater floor depth. While the contribution of the cables decreases the contribution of the struts increases, although beyond a span to strut diameter ratio of *26* the contribution of the struts remains fairly constant at over *60%*.

Table 8.10: Comparison of the contributions of the principal structural components to the self-weight of a *200 FT* span floor for a range of floor depths.

Floor Depth	Strut Diameter	Structural Self-Weight	Supporting Cables	Pressurized Struts	End Sections	Secondary Structure (A)
4.0 FT	3.5 FT	15.9 psf	25.5%	55.6%	10.7%	8.2%
5.0 FT	4.5 FT	15.9 psf	19.8%	57.9%	13.2%	9.1%
6.0 FT	5.5 FT	16.4 psf	15.8%	59.2%	15.4%	9.6%
7.0 FT	6.5 FT	16.7 psf	12.9%	59.9%	17.5%	9.7%
8.0 FT	7.5 FT	17.9 psf	10.7%	60.9%	18.6%	9.8%
9.0 FT	8.5 FT	18.4 psf	9.1%	60.9%	20.3%	9.7%
10.0 FT	9.5 FT	19.1 psf	7.8%	60.9%	21.7%	9.6%

8.4 Comparison of Pneumatic and Fluid-Inflated Cable Floors

Perhaps the most surprising observation in comparing the preliminary design results of circular pneumatic cable floors (Section 8.1.4) with rectangular fluid-inflated cable floors (Section 8.3.3) is that for a given span the self-weight of the circular floors decreases with increasing depth while the self-weight of the rectangular floors increases with increasing depth. Due to the slenderness considerations that pertain to the struts one would have expected the relatively small diameter pressurized struts of a rectangular floor to be structurally less efficient than the large diameter pressurized cylinder of a circular pneumatic cable floor.

A direct comparison of the performance of these two types of pressurized structural floor systems in respect to self-weight is not possible due to certain constructional differences.

1. The circular pneumatic cable floors include a tension ring at the center and are designed to be supported at both the perimeter and the tension ring. Therefore, the cable span of these floors is less than half the diameter of the floor. For example, the actual cable span of a *100 FT* diameter pneumatic cable floor with a single *10 FT* diameter tension ring at the center is only *45 FT*. On the other hand, the cable span of the rectangular fluid-inflated cable floor is equal to the floor span.

2. While neither of the two types of floors includes fire-protection as an integral component of its structural configuration, the circular floors include both floor and ceiling (steel) surfaces that are necessary to contain the internal air pressure and are therefore part of the self-weight of the floor. The rectangular floors do not include such surfaces because the internal pressure is contained within the struts and therefore require a secondary structure to support these surfaces. Two alternatives for such a secondary structure have been discussed in Section 8.3.1 (Figures 8.17 and 8.18).

3. Since pneumatic cable roofs are supported at the perimeter only their diameter is equal to the cable span. This assumes that even though the cables are fixed at the perimeter and at the inner tension ring, they can be considered to span the full diameter of the roof from a structural point of view.

An indirect comparison of circular pneumatic cable roofs and floors with rectangular fluid-inflated cable floors is provided in Table 8.11 for a *100 FT* diameter and span, respectively. For all three of these horizontal structures the live-load is assumed to be *100 psf* and the dead-load is taken to be equal to the structural self-weight of the roof/floor. The circular pneumatic cable structures include a *10 FT* diameter tension ring in the center, so that the radial cables are connected to both the floor perimeter and the inner tension ring. All of the components of these cylindrical structures are assumed to be made of steel in alignment with the worked examples of Sections 8.1.4 and 8.2.1.

In the case of the rectangular fluid-supported floor the Option A secondary structure described in Section 8.3.1 and shown in Figure 8.17 is used to support the floor surface. While the self-weight of the secondary structure has been included in the design calculations, *10 psf* has been added to the calculated structural self-weight to allow for the floor surface material. In addition, *3 IN* has been added to the depth of the floor (i.e., to the diameter of the strut) to allow for the attachment and thickness of the floor surface material.

Table 8.11: Comparison of *100 FT* diameter circular pneumatic cable roofs/floors with *100 FT* span rectangular fluid-inflated cable floors over varying floor depths.

Floor Depth	Pneumatic Cable Roof			Pneumatic Cable Floor			Fluid-Inflated Cable Floor		
	Cable Span	Self-Weight	Strut Press.	Cable Span	Self-Weight	Strut Press.	Cable Span	Self-Weight	Strut Press.
2 FT	100 FT	53 psf	182 psig	45 FT	29 psf	31 psig	100 FT	18 psf	374 psig
3 FT	100 FT	37 psf	73 psig	45 FT	22 psf	13 psig	100 FT	19 psf	118 psig
4 FT	100 FT	29 psf	39 psig	45 FT	18 psf	7 psig	100 FT	20 psf	55 psig
5 FT	100 FT	24 psf	24 psig	45 FT	15 psf	4 psig	100 FT	21 psf	31 psig

For a diameter (circular roof/floor) or span (rectangular floor) of *100 FT* Table 8.11 lists the calculated internal air pressure and structural self-weight for four floor depths (i.e., *2, 3, 4, 5 FT*). At higher diameter to depth ratios of *33* and above the weight advantage of the rectangular floor is clearly apparent. Even though the self-weight of the rectangular floor gradually increases with increasing floor depth it is still significantly less than the circular roof at a depth of *5 FT* (diameter to depth ratio of *20*). The lower self-weight of the circular floor at larger floor depths is due to the fact that these floors are supported both at the perimeter and the inner tension ring, thereby greatly reducing the actual span of the supporting radial cables.

Unless the requirement of a cylindrical building shape is dictated by other considerations such as an air-supported multi-story structure of the type described in previous chapters, the rectangular fluid-inflated cable floor is likely to be a superior structural solution. It is intrinsically modular and can therefore be configured to satisfy any floor area requirements. The circular floor/roof structures are not only limited to cylindrical buildings but also restricted in usable floor area. For example, the floor area provided by a *100 FT* diameter floor is only *7,854 SF*, while the floor area provided by a *100 FT* long fluid-inflated cable module is essentially unlimited.

From a more general point of view this chapter validates that horizontal structures of significant span, in which the structural components are entirely in tension, are feasible. Surprisingly the rectangular configuration in which thin-walled pressurized struts counteract the tensile forces exerted by the cables have a lower self-weight than the cylindrical floors in which the entire floor volume is pressurized. This is contrary to the vertical multi-story air-supported and fluid-inflated building designs discussed in Chapters 6 and 7, respectively. In the case of rigid pressurized columns (Chapter 7) the height to diameter ratio is the limiting factor that favors the air-supported multi-story building design in which the entire building environment is pressurized. As a result, in all but tall towers the height to diameter ratio of the multi-story air-supported building is structurally of less concern.

One would expect the same to apply to pressurized horizontal cable structures. In other words, the ability to apply the counterbalancing air pressure to the entire volume of the cylindrical floor or roof would be expected to produce greater structural economy in terms of a minimum weight criterion than the pressurized struts of the rectangular floor design. The reason that this is not the case lies in the ability to brace the struts in the horizontal plane and securely anchor the ends to the end sections of the floor. In this way the formation of rotational moments in the struts is effectively restricted. The horizontal braces can be conveniently spaced along the length of the struts with the distance between braces governed by the length to diameter ratio of the strut that the structural designer is willing to accept.

References and Bibliography

Acton F. (1966); 'Analysis of Straight Line Data'; Dover Publications, New York, New York.

Allinikov S. (1960); 'Exploratory Evaluation of a Polyurethane Material Capable of Foaming at Reduced Atmospheric Pressure'; Aeronautical Systems Division, Technical Memo 604, June (pp. 1-4).

Allison D. (1959); 'Those Ballooning Air Buildings'; Architectural Forum, July (pp. 134-139).

Allison D. (1960); 'A Great Balloon for Peaceful Atoms (Architect: Lundy V.)'; Architectural Forum; November (pp. 143-6).

Almroth B. (1963); 'Postbuckling Behavior of Axially Compressed Circular Cylinders'; AIAA Journal, 1(3), March (pp. 630-633).

Angerer F. (1961); 'Surface Structure in Building'; Norman Press, London, UK (pp. 63-65).

Arbocz J., J. Starnes and M. Nemeth (1999); 'A Hierarchical Approach to Buckling Load Calculation'; 40th AIAA/ASCE/AHS/ASC Structures, Structural Dynamics, and Material Conference, AIAA Paper No. 99-1232, St Louis, Missouri, April 12-15.

Arbocz J. (1983); 'Shell Stability Analysis: Theory and Practice'; in Thompson J. and G. Hunt (eds.) *Collapse*, Cambridge University Press, Cambridge, UK (pp. 43-74).

Arnold K. and E. Amir (1992); 'Screen Updating and Cursor Movement Optimization: A Library Package'; http://www.mirbsd.org/cman/manPSD/19.curses.htm.

Ashton L. (1965); 'Fire Regulations and Plastics'; Plastics in Building Structures; Proceedings of a Conference; Pergamon Press, London.

Axelrad D. (1965); 'Strength of Materials for Engineers'; Pitman Press, UK.

Bailey G. (1915); 'Vertical Farming'; Nabu Press (BiblioBazaar), Charleston, South Carolina.

Ballerstedt W. and H. Wagner (1936); 'Versuche über die Festigkeit Dünner Unversteifter Zylinder unter Schub- und Längskräften'; Luftfahrtforschung, 13(9), September (pp. 309-312).

Batdorf S., M. Schildcrout and M. Stein (1947); 'Critical Stress of Thin-Walled Cylinders in Axial Compression'; NACA Report No. 887, March (pp 543-550).

Batdorf S. (1947); 'A Simplified Method of Elastic Stability Analysis for Thin Cylindrical Shells'; 33rd Annual Report, NACA Report No. 874, March (pp 285-309).

Batdorf S. and B. Budiansky (1949); 'A Mathematical Theory of Plasticity Based on the Concept of Slip'; NAGA TN 1871, April.

Batterman S. (1965); 'Plastic Buckling of Axially Compressed Cylindrical Shells'; AIAA Journal (pp. 316).

Benham P. (1965); 'Elementary Mechanics of Solids'; Commonwealth and International Library; Pergamon Press (pp. 13-18).

Benham P. (1965); 'Elementary Mechanics of Solids'; Pergamon Press, U.K., 1965.

Berger Bros. (1958); 'Pneumatic Geodesic Dome'; Architectural Forum, July (pp. 177).

Bethlehem Steel Corporation (1967); 'Excerpts from Hanging Roofs'; Booklet 2319, U.S.A.

Bijlaard P. (1949); 'Theory and Tests on the Plastic Stability of Plates and Shells'; Journal of the Aeronautical Sciences, Vol, 16, No. 9, Sept (pp. 529-541).

Bijlaard P. (1938); 'A Theory of Plastic Stability and its Application to Thin Plates of Structural Steel'; Proc. Koninkl. Ned. Adad. Metenschap. 41 (pp. 731-743).

Bijlaard P. ((1947); 'On the Plastic Stability of Thin Plattes and Shells'; Proc. Koninkl. Ned. Adad. Wetenschap. 50 (pp. 765-775).

Bijlaard P. (1949); 'Theory and Tests on the Plastic Stability of Plates and Shells'; Journal of Aeronautical Sciences 16 (pp. 529-541).

Blanjean L. (1961); 'Wind Action on Buildings'; Dept. of Scientific and Industrial Research, Building Research Station, Library Communication 1048; Garston, Wattford, Herts, UK, May.

Blanjean L. (1961); 'Wind Action on Buildings'; Library Communication No. 1048, Building Research Station, U.K., Hertfordshire.

Bodner S. and W. Berks (1952); 'The Effect of Imperfections on the Stresses in a Circular Cylindrical Shell Under Hydrostatic Pressure'; Polytechnic Institute of Brooklyn, Report No. 210.

Boom I. (2012); 'Tensile-Compression Ring: A Study for Football Stadia Roof Structures'; Master Thesis, Department of Building Engineering, University of Technology Delft, Delft, The Netherlands.

Born J. (1964); 'Rippenkuppeln, Faltwerke, Hangedacher'; Werner-Verlag, Germany (pp. 41-70).

Boys C. (1959); 'Soap-Bubbles, Their Colours and the Forces Which Mold Them'; Dover Publications, New York.

BRS (1963); 'Plastics in Building'; Overseas Building Notes (No. 86, March), Dept. of Scientific and Industrial Research; Building Research Station, Garston, Watford, Hertfordshire, UK.

BRS (1965); 'Basic Sanitary Requirements for Buildings with no Windows or Skylights'; Library Communication No. 1264, Building Research Station, Garston, Watford, Hertfordshire, UK.

Brush D. and B. Almroth (1976); 'Buckling of Bars, Plates, and Shells'; McGraw-Hill, New York, New York.

Buchholdt H. (1985); 'An Introduction to Cable Roof Structures'; Cambridge University Press, Cambridge, London, UK.

Budiansky B. and J. Hutchinson (1966); 'A Survey of Some Buckling Problems'; AIAA Journal (pp. 1505).

Budiansky B. (1959); 'A Reassessment of Defomration Theories of Plasticity'; Journal of Appl. Mech., Vol. 26, Series E., No.2 June (pp. 259-264).

Bushnell D. (1985); 'Computerized Buckling Analysis of Shells'; Martimus Nijhaff, Dordrecht, The Netherlands.

Bushnell D. (1967); 'Buckling of Spherical Shells Ring Supported at the Edges'; AIAA Journal (pp. 2041).

Calladine C. (1983); 'Theory of Shell Structures'; Cambridge University Press, Cambridge, UK.

Cavallo T. (1785); London: Printed for the Author, and sold by C. Dilly, in the Poultry; P. Elmsly, in the Strand; and J. Stockdale, in Piccadilly.

Cicala P. (1951); 'The Effect of Initial Deformations on the Behavior of a Cylindrical Shell under Axial Compression'; Quarterly of Applied Mathematics, Vol. 9 (pp. 273-293).

Cicala, P (1944); 'Il Cilindro in Parete Sottile Compresso Assialmente. Nuovo Orentamanto Dell'indagine Tulla Stabilite Elastics'; L'Aerotecnica, Vol. 24 (p. 3-18).

Como M. and A. Grimaldi (1995); 'Theory of Stability of Continuous Elastic Structures'; CRC Press, Boca Raton, Florida.

Cooley W. (1959); 'Buckling in Hydraulic Tubing'; Product Engineering, May.

Corkill P., H. Puderbaugh and H. Sawyers (1965); 'Structure and Architectural Design'; Sernoll Inc., Iowa City, Iowa.

Courant R. and H. Robbins (1961); 'What is Mathematics?'; Oxford University Press, Oxford, UK (pp. 386-7).

Cowan H. and J. Pohl (1967); 'A Preliminary Investigation into the Load-Bearing Capacity of Open-Ended Cylindrical Columns Subjected to Internal Fluid Pressure'; Proceedings 1st International Colloquium on Pneumatic Structures, Stuttgart, Germany, May 11-12 (pp. 154-8).

Cowan H. (1977); 'An Historical Outline of Architectural Science'; Applied Science Publishers, London, UK (pp. 102).

CRCJ (1971); 'Handbook of Structural Stability'; Column Research Council of Japan, Corona, Tokyo, Japan.

Crowder J. (1964); 4th Reinforced Plastics Conference; B.P.F., 25 November.

Cui S., H. Cheong and H. Hao (2000); 'Experimental Study of Dynamic Post-Buckling Characteristics of Columns under Fluid-Solid Slamming'; Engineering Structures, Vol 22 (pp. 647-656).

D.I.S.R. (1959); 'Principles of Modern Building Research'; Vol. 1, U.K., Building Research Station; (pp. 4-6).

Davies W. (1962); Medical Hazards of Underwater Swimming'; Practitioner 188, May (pp. 656-660).

Davies A. (1967); 'Solid Geometry in 3-D for Technical Drawing'; Chatto and Windus, London, UK (pp. 94-5).

Davy M. (1950); 'Aeronautics, Lighter-Than-Air Craft'; Ministry of Education - Science Museum; HMSO, London (pp. 7-15).

Dean W. (1925); 'On the Theory of Elastic Stability'; Proc. Roy. Soc. London, Series A, 107(744), April (pp. 734-760).

Dent R. (1971); 'Principles of Pneumatic Architecture'; Architectural Press, London, UK.

Despommier D. (2010); 'The Vertical Farm: Feeding the World in the 21st Century'; Thomas Dunne Books, New York, New York.

Despommier D. (2009); 'The Rise of Vertical Farms'; Scientific American, November (pp. 80-87).

Devore J. (1987); 'Probability and Statistics for Engineering and the Sciences'; 2nd Edition, Brooks/Cole, Monterey, California (pp. 456-467).

Dewey A. (1962); 'Decompression Sickness, an Emerging Recreational Hazard'; The New England Journal of Medicine, 267(15 and 16).

Dietz A. (1955); 'Physical and Engineering Properties of Plastics'; Plastics in Building, Conference conducted by the Building Research Institute, National Academy of Sciences, National Research Council; Washington, April.

Donnell L. and C. Wan (1950); 'Effect of Imperfections on the Buckling of Thin Cylinders and Columns Under Axial Compression'; Journal of Applied Mechanics, 17(1), March (pp. 73-83).

Donnell L. (1934); 'A New Theory for the Buckling of Thin Cylinders Under Axial Compression and Bending'; ASME Trans. Vol. 56, No. 11, November (pp. 795-806).

Donnell L. (1933); 'Stability of Thin-Walled Tubes Under Torsion'; NACA Report No. 479.

Drexler A. (1960); 'Ludwig Mies van der Rohe'; Masters of World Architecture; George Braziller, New York, New York (pp. 14).

Drucker D. (1960); 'Plasticity, Structural Mechanics'; Goodier J. and N. Hoff (eds.), Pergamon Press, New York, New York.

Drucker D. and E. Onat (1954); 'On the Concept of Stability of Inelastic Systems'; Journal of Aeronautical Sciences 21 (pp. 543-9).

Drucker D. (1951); 'A More Fundamental Approach to Plastic Stress Strain Relations'; Proceedings of the First U.S. National Congress of Applied Mechanics, ASME (pp. 487-491).

Editorial (1957); 'Pneumatic Structures'; Vol. 106, Architectural Forum, April.

Editorial (1964); 'Two Air-Supported Structures for Athletics'; Architectural Record; March (pp. 209-210).

Editorial (1965); 'Traglufthallen (Neuheiten)'; Werk - Chronik Nr.1.; January (pp.3).

Editorial (1966); 'Modern Plastics Encyclopedia, 1967'; McGraw-Hill, New York, September (pp. 48).

Editorial (1961); 'New Studies of Decompression Sickness'; British Medical Journal 5218, 7 January (pp. 45-6).

Editorial (1964); 'Flame Retardance - Key to New Plastics Markets'; Modern Plastics, October (pp. 84).

Euler L. (1759); 'On the Strength of Columns'; Academie Royale des Sciences et Belle Lettres Memoires, Vol 13 (pp 252). English translation: Van den Broek A. (1947); 'Euler's Classic Paper - On the Strength of Columns'; American Journal of Physics, 15(4), July-August (pp 309-318).

Engesser F. (1898); Zeitung, Verein Deutscher Ingeneure (VDI), Vol. 42 (pp. 927).

Everard H. (1965); 'The Properties of Plastics in Relation to Building Structures'; Plastics in Building Structures Conference, Pergamon Press, London, UK, 14 June.

Fischer G (1965); Influence of Boundary Conditions on Stability of Thin-Walled Cylindrical Shells Under Axial Load and Internal Pressure'; AIAA Journal (pp. 736).

Fisher D. (2010a); [www.dynamicarchitecture.net/home.html].

Fisher D. (2010b); [www.dynamicarchitecture.net/_PREFABRICATION.html].

Fitch J. (1960); 'Walter Gropius'; Masters of World Architecture, George Braziller, Inc., New York, New York.

Flook V. (1987); ‚Physics and Physiology in the Hyperbaric Environment'; Clin. Phys. Physiol. Meas., 8(3) (pp. 197-230).

Flügge W. (1973); 'Stresses in Shells'; Springer Verlag, New York, New York.

Flügge W. (1934); 'Statik und Dynamik der Schalen'; Julius Springer, Berlin (pp. 189-199).

Flügge W. (1932); 'Die Stabilität der Kreiszylinderschale'; Ingenieur Archiv, Vol 3, Dec (pp. 463-506).

Forbes F. and A. Vasiloff (1963); 'Current Aerospace Research in Expandable Structures'; IEEE Transactions on Aerospace - Support Conference Procedures, 1(2), August (pp. 507-521).

Forbes F. (1962); 'Expandable Structures for Aerospace Applications'; American Rocket Society, November (pp. 1).

Forgy C. (1979); 'On the Efficient Implementation of Production Systems'; Ph.D. Thesis, Computer Science Department, Carnegie-Mellon University, Pittsburgh, Pennsylvania.

Forgy C. (1982); 'Rete: A Fast Algorithm for the Many Pattern/Many Object Pattern Match Problem", Artificial Intelligence, Vol.19 (pp. 17–37).

Friedrichs K. (1941); 'On the Minimum Buckling Load for Spherical Shells'; Theodore von Karman Anniversary Volume, California Institute of Technology, Pasadena, California, 11 May (pp 258-272).

Frischmann W. and S. Prabhu (1967); 'Planning Concepts Using Shear Walls'; Proceedings of a Symposium on Tall Buildings, University of Southampton, Pergamon Press, London, UK (pp. 49-79).

Fuller R. Buckminster (1968); 'An Extraordinary Conversation'; Building Research, July-Sept (pp. 9-17).

Fung Y. and E. Sechler (Eds.) (1974); 'Thin-Shell Structures: Theory, Experiment, and Design'; Prentice-Hall, Englewood Cliffs, New Jersey.

Fung Y. and E. Sechler (1957); 'Buckling of thin-Walled Circular Cylinders Under Axial Compression and Internal Pressure'; Journal of Aeronautical Sciences, May (pp 351-356).

Gaume J. (1958); 'Lunar Housing Simulator'; Martin Co., Denver M-M- (pp. 58-62).

General Electric (1960); 'Building on the Moon'; Architectural Forum; March.

Gerard G. (1967); 'Comparative Efficiencies of Aerospace Pressure Vessel Design Concepts'; AIAA Journal, U.S., December (pp. 2083).

Gerard G. (1957); 'Plastic Stability Theory of Thin Shells'; Journal of the Aeronautical Sciences; April (pp. 269-274).

Gerard G. (1956); 'Compressive and Torsional Buckling of Thin-Walled Cylinders in Yield Region'; NACA TN 3726, August.

Gero J. (1966); 'The Analysis of Suspension Cable Roofs Used in Architecture'; Master of Building Science Thesis; University of Sydney, Dept. of Architectural Science (pp. 4-10).

Gero J. (1967); 'Pneumatic Structures Constrained by Networks'; Proceedings 1st International Colloquium on Pneumatic Structures, Stuttgart, Germany, May 11-12.

Gero J. (1967); 'The Analysis of Cable-Networks Using An Iteration Technique', Architectural Science Review, 10(1), March.

Gero J., G. Ding and H. Cowan (1967); in Davies R. (ed.) *Research in Space Structures*, Blackwell Scientific Publications, UK.

Giarratano J. and G. Riley (1994); 'Expert Systems: Principles and Programming'; PWS Publishing Company, Boston, Massachusetts (pp. 363-596).

Grassie J. (1958); 'Elementary Theory of Structures'; Longmans, Green and Co.

Grassie, J. (1960); 'Applied Mechanics for Engineers'; Longmans, UK (pp. 579-580).

Guenschel G. (1960); Europäisches Bauforum, 12.

Hall A. (1957); 'Some Comments on Current Aviation Topics'; Journal of the Aeronautical Sciences, March (pp. 171).

Handelman G., C. Lin, and W. Prager (1947); 'On the Mechanical Behavior of Metals in the Strain Hardening Range'; Quarterly Appl. Math, Vol. 4; January (pp. 397-407).

Handelman G. and W. Warner (1954); 'Loading Paths and the Incremental Stress Law'; Journal Math. and Phys. Vol. 33, July (pp. 157-164).

Handelman G. and W. Prager (1949); 'Plastic Buckling of a Rectangular Plate Under Edge Thrust'; NACA Report 946.

Harris L., H. Suer, W. Skene and R. Benjamin (1957); 'The Stability of Thin-Walled Unstiffened Circular Cylinders Under Axial Compression Including the Effects of Internal Pressure'; Journal of the Aeronautical Sciences, August.

Hartog D. (1949); 'Strength of Materials'; McGraw-Hill, New York, New York.

Hay H. (1973); 'Energy Technology and Solarchitecture'; Mechanical Engineering, Vol 94 (pp. 18).

Heine E. (1963); 'They Like it Hot'; Dupont Magazine, 57(2), March (pp. 26).

Hencky H. (1925); 'Uber Langsame Stationäre Stromungen in Plastischen Massen mit Rücksicht auf die Vorgänge beim Walzen, Pressen und Zehen von Metallen'; Z. angewandte Math. und Mech., 5(2) (pp. 115).

Herzog T. (1976); 'Pneumatische Konstruktionen: Bauten aus Membranen und Luft'; Hatje, Stuttgart, Germany.

Higdon A., E. Ohlsen, W. Stiles and J. Weese (1967); 'Mechanics of Materials'; Wiley, New York, New York (pp 429-431).

Hillier M. (1965); 'Tensile Plastic Instability of Thin Tubes'; Int. J. Mech. Sci., Pergamon Press, Vol 7 (pp. 531-549).

Hoff N. (1966); 'The Perplexing Behavior of Thin Circular Cylindrical Shells in Axial Compression'; Second Theodore von Karman Memorial Lecture of the Israel Society of Aeronautical Sciences, SUDAAR No. 256, Department of Aeronautics and Astronautics, Stanford University, Stanford, California, February.

Hoff N. (1954); 'Buckling and Stability'; The Forty-First Wilbur Wright Memorial Lecture, Fourth Anglo-American Aeronautical Conference, London, 14 September 1953: Journal of the Royal Aeronautical Society, 58(517), January (pp 3-52).

Holland M., M. Lalor and J. Walsh (1974); 'Principal Displacements in a Pressurized Elliptical Cylinder: Theoretical Predictions with Experimental Verification by Laser Interferometry'; Journal of Strain Analysis, 9(3) (pp. 159-165).

Hottinger H. (1962); 'Concepts for the Design of Structures using Tensional Cable Systems'; Proceedings of the IASS Colloquium on Hanging Roofs, Continuous Metallic Shell Roofs and Superficial Lattice Roofs; Paris, 9-11 July (Wiley, Interscience Publication).

Howard H. (1966); 'Structure an Architect's Approach'; McGraw-Hill, New York, New York (pp. 8-12, 270-286).

Howard S. (1966); 'Structure an Architect's Approach'; McGraw-Hill, New York, New York (pp. 8-12).

Howatson A., P. Lund and J. Todd (1972); 'Engineering Tables and Data'; Chapman and Hall, London, UK.

Hutchinson J. and J. Amazigo (1967); 'Imperfection-Sensitivity of Eccentrically Stiffened Cylindrical Shells'; AIAA Journal, 5(3), March (pp 392-401).

Hutchinson J. and W. Koiter (1970); 'Postbuckling Theory'; Applied Mechanics Reviews, 23(12), December (pp 1353-1356).

IASS (1972); 'Proceedings International Symposium on Pneumatic Structures, Vol. 1 and 2; Delft University of Technology, Stichting PDOB, Delft, The Netherlands.

Jennings S. (1963); 'Sanitation in High Buildings'; Royal Society of Health Journal, UK, March-April (pp. 77-86).

Joedicke J. (1962); 'Office Buildings'; Crosby Lockwood and Sons, London, UK (pp. 44-7).

Joedicke J. (1959); 'A History of Modern Architecture'; Architectural Press, London, UK.

Jones R. (2007); 'Buckling of Bars, Plates and Shells'; CRC Press, Boca Raton, Florida.

Jones R. (1966); 'Toward a New Snap-Through Buckling Criterion for Axially Compressed Circular Cylindrical Shells'; AIAA Journal, 4(9) (pp. 1526-1530).

Kanemitsu S. and N. Nojima (1939); 'Axial Compression Test of Thin Circular Cylinders'; Thesis, California Institute of Technology, Pasadena, California.

Kappus R. (1939); 'Zur Elastizitätstheorie Endlicher Verschiebung'; ZAMM, Vol. 19 (pp. 271-285).

Kemper J (1953); 'Analysis of the Post-Buckling Behavior of an Axially Compressed Cylindrical Shell'; Polytechnic Institute of Brooklyn; Report No. 212.

Kingsford P. (1960); "F. W. Lanchester, a Life of an Engineer'; Edward Arnold Publishers, London (pp. 223-4).

Koiter W. (1963); 'Elastic Stability and Post-Buckling Behavior'; in Langer R. (ed.) *Non-Linear Problems*, Proceedings of a Symposium Conducted by the Mathematics Research Center, 30 April – 2 May 1962, Publication Number 8, Mathematics Research Center, United States Army, University of Wisconsin Press, Madison, Wisconsin.

Kromm A. (1939); 'The Limit of Stability of a Curved Plate Strip Under Shear and Axial Stresses'; NACA-TM Report No. 898.

Kuranishi M. (1950); 'The Buckling Stress of Thin Cylindrical Shell Under Axial Compression Load, Forming Axial-Symmetrical Deformation'; Journal Soc. Appl. Mech. Japan 3 (pp. 139-144).

Kusmiss I (1958); 'Compression Strength of Thin-Walled Cylinders'; Product Engineering, July (pp. 77-79).

Lanchester F. (1938); 'Span'; Lecture presented to the Manchester Association of Engineers, Butterly and Wood, Manchester, UK (pp. 84-95).

Landau L. and E. Lifshitz (1986); 'Theory of Elasticity'; Course of Theoretical Physics, Vol 7, Third Edition, Butterworth-Heinemann, Oxford, UK.

Lanthier E. (1964); 'Man in High Pressures'; in Dill B. (ed.) *Handbook of Physiology*, Section 4, American Physiological Society, Washington, DC.

Le Ricolais R. (1962); 'Tension Structures and Related Research'; New Building Research, Spring, 1961, National Academy of Sciences - National Research Council, Washington, DC (pp. 58-79).

Lee L. H. (1962); 'Inelastic Buckling of Initially Imperfect Cylindrical Shells Subject to Axial Compression'; Journal of Aerospace Sciences 29 (pp. 87-95).

Legget D. (1946); 'The Buckling of Thin Cylindrical Shells Under Axial Compression'; 6th International Congress of Applied Mechanics, Paris, France, September (pp 47-60).

Legget D. (1942); 'The Buckling of a Long Curved Panel Under Axial Compression'; R. and M. Report No. 1899, British ARC.

Legget D. and R. Jones (1942); 'The Behaviour of a Cylindrical Shell Under Axial Compression when the Buckling Load has been Exceeded'; A.R.C., R and M, Report No. 2190, August.

Lever A. and J. Rhys (1962); 'The Properties and Testing of Plastic Materials'; Temple Press Books, London, UK.

Lim C. and E. Lui (2010); 'Smartcities and Eco-Warriors'; Rutledge, New York, New York.

Lin T. (1954); 'A Proposed Theory of Plasticity Based on Slips'; Proceedings of the Second U.S. National Congress of Applied Mechanics; ASME (pp. 461-8).

Lin T. and S. Stotesbury (1988); 'Structural Concepts and Systems for Architects and Engineers'; 2nd ed., Van Nostrand Reinhold, New York, New York (pp. 317, 411-3, 422-2).

Lo H., H. Crate and E. Schwarz (1951); 'Buckling of Thin-Walled Cylinders Under Axial Compression and Internal Pressure'; NACA Report No. 1027 (pp 647-655).

Lorenz R. (1908); 'Achsensymmetrische Verzerrungen in Dünnwandigen Hohlzylinder'; Zeitschrift des Vereines Deutscher Ingenieure (VDI), Vol 52 (pp. 1706-1713).

Lorenz R. (1911); 'Die nicht Achsensymmetrische Knickung Dünnwandiger Hohlzylinder'; Physikalische Zeitschrift; Vol. 13 (pp. 241-260).

Lundquist E. (1933); 'Strength Tests of Tin-Walled Drualimin Cylinders in Compression'; NACA Report No. 473.

MacPherson R. (1965); 'Physiological Aspects of Thermal Comfort'; Third Conference of the ANZ Architectural Science Association on Climate, Comfort and Environment, Architectural Science Review, Department of Architectural Science, University of Sydney, Sydney, Australia, December.

Makowski Z. (1964); 'The Structural Applications of Plastics'; in Davies R. (ed.) *Proceedings Plastics in Building Construction Conference*, Battersea College of Technology, UK, September.

Makowski Z. (1967); 'Space Structures, A Short Review of their Development'; Space Structures, ed., Davies, R.M.; Blackwell Scientific Publication (pp. 5-8).

Makowski Z. (1966); 'Structural Plastics'; The Institute of Structural Engineers, Conference on Industrialized Building and the Structural Engineer; SFB HN6, VDC 69.057:678.5, Battersea College of Technology, UK, May.

Marguerre K. (1938); 'On the Application of the Energy Method to Stability Problems'; (translated from German), National Advisory Committee for Aeronautics (NACA), Technical Memorandum 1138, October 1947

Marguerre K. (1938); 'Die Dürchschlagskraft Eines Schwach Gekrümmten Balkens'; Sitzungsberichte der Berliner Mathematischen Gesellschaft, Vol. 37 (pp. 22-40).

Mark R. (1960); 'The Dymaxion World of Buckminster Fuller'; Reinhold, New York.

McHale J. (1962); 'R. Buckminster Fuller'; Braziller Publishers, New York, New York.

Michielsen H. (1948); 'The Behaviour of Thin Cylindrical Shells After Buckling Under Axial Compression'; Journal of the Aeronautical Sciences, Vol. 15, No. 12, December (pp. 738-744).

Mills B. (1960); 'The Fluid Column'; American Journal of Physics, 28(4), April (pp. 353-356).

Mohacsy L. (1966); Contemporary Forming Methods'; Akademaia Kaido, Publishing House of the Hungarian Academy of Sciences, Budapest.

Monsanto Research Corporation (1962); 'Gelatine as a Possible Structural Material for Space Use'; Report No. 6, USA, October (pp. 1-50).

Montero J. (1973); 'Multi-Cellular, Multi-Enclosure Air-Building'; Master of Science (Architecture) thesis; College of Architecture and Environmental Design, California Polytechnic State University, San Luis Obispo, California.

Montero J. and J. Pohl (1976); 'The Multi-Enclosure Air-Supported Dwelling'; Proceedings WCOS-76, IIASS World Congress on Space Enclosures, Building Research Centre, Concordia University, Montreal, Canada, July 4-9 (pp. 691-705).

Mooney J. (1983); 'Cost Effective Building Design'; New South Wales University Press, Kensington, New South Wales, Australia (pp. 30-42).

Moreland J. (ed.) (1974); 'Practical Applications of Air-Supported Structures: Proceedings International Conference, Canvas Products Association International (CPAI), Las Vegas, Nevada (28-29 October).

Murata Y. (1972); 'Pneumatic in Pneumatic'; IASS, Proceedings International Symposium on Pneumatic Structures, Delft, Netherlands (Paper 1.3).

Nadai A. (1950); 'Theory of Flow and Fracture of Solids'; McGraw-Hill, New York, New York (pp. 229, 379).

Nash W. (1957); 'Schaum's Outline of Theory and Problems of Strength of Materials'; Schaum, New York, New York.

Nash W. (1957); 'Strength of Materials'; Schaum, New York, New York (pp. 257-9).

Nash W. (1955); 'Effect of Large Deflections and Initial Imperfections on the Buckling of Cylindrical Shells Subject to Hydrostatic Pressure'; Journal of the Aeronautical Sciences, April.

Neville A. and J. Kennedy (1964); 'Basic Statistical Methods for Engineers and Scientists'; International Text Book Co.

Nix M. and V. van Aardt (1964); 'Some New Building Materials with Particular Reference to Plastics'; South African Council for Scientific and Industrial Research, No. R/Bou 139; Pretoria, South Africa, July (pp. 7-9).

Novozhilov V. (1958); 'Thin Shell Theory'; Second Edition, Translated from Russian by P. Lowe and J. Radok (eds.) in 1964, Noordhoff, Groningen, The Netherlands.

NRC (1955); 'Plastics in Building'; Building Research Institute, National Research Council, Division of Engineering and Industrial Research, Washington, DC.

Oberdick W. (1965); 'Application of Minimum Structure To Cellular Plastics'; Plastics in Building Structures, Plastics Conference; London, June; Pergamon Press.

Oemac (1966); Trade Literature, Technical Bulletin No. 5, Mascot, N.S.W., Australia.

Onat E. and D. Drucker (1953); 'Inelastic Instability and Incremental Theories of Plasticity'; Journal of Aeronautical Sciences 20 (pp. 181-6).

Osgood W. and W. Graustein (1946); 'Plane and Solid Analytic Geometry'; Macmillan, New York, New York (pp. 101-123).

Otto F. and R. Trostel (1962); 'Zugbeanspruchte Konstruktionen'; Ullstein GmBH, Germany.

Otto F. (1961); 'Spannweiten'; Ullstein GmBH, Germany.

Otto F. and P. Stromeyer (1961); 'Pneumatic Structures' (transl.); Deutsche Bauzeitung, July (pp. 519-527).

Otto F. (1963); "Development of Lightweight Construction and Use of Plastic In Construction of Multi-Form Buildings'; Arts and Architecture, October (pp. 18-20).

Otto F. (ed.) (1973); 'Tensile Structures'; MIT Press, Cambridge, Massachusetts.

Otto F and R. Trostel (1967); 'Tensile Structures: Design, Structure, and Calculations of Buildings of Cables, Nets and Membranes'; MIT Press, Cambridge, Massachusetts.

Pannell J. (1964); 'An Illustrated History of Civil Engineering; Thames and Hudson, London (pp. 257-80).

Petroski H. (2004); 'Pushing the Limits: New Adventures in Engineering'; Knopf, New York, New York (pp. 8-11).

Petroski H. (2002); 'The Fall of Skyscrapers'; American Scientist, 90(1), January-February (pp. 16-20).

Plastic Study Group (1957); Building Research Institute, National Research Council, Division of Engineering and Industrial Research, Washington DC.

Platts R. (1964); 'The Role of Plastics in House Structure'; Division of Building Research, National Research Council, Canada.

Pohl J. (2010); 'The Emergence of Building Science: Historical Roots, Concepts, and Applications'; 2nd edition, Collaborative Agent Design Research Center (CADRC), Cal Poly, San Luis Obispo, California, ISBN 0-9763512-0-X (pp. 293-331)

Pohl J. and R. Sanchez (1986); 'Fluid-Supported Building Systems'; IABSE Colloquium on Thin-Walled Metal Structures in Buildings, Poster Sessions, Stockholm, Sweden, June 9-12, (pp. 22-23)

Pohl J. and A. Basiulis (1976); 'Fluid-Supported Structures and Environmental Control'; IASS World Congress on Space Enclosures, Building Research Centre, Concordia University, Montreal, Canada, July (pp. 189-205).

Pohl J. and J. Montero (1975); 'The Multi-Storey Air-Supported Greenhouse: A Feasibility Study'; Architectural Science Review, 18(3), September (pp. 50-59).

Pohl J. (1973); 'Multi-Storey Air-Supported Buildings'; Asian Building & Construction, Hong Kong, September (pp. 14-19).

Pohl J. and J. Montero (1973); 'The Construction of Two Prototype Multi-Storey Air-Supported Buildings'; Build International, 6(6), November-December (pp. 545-580).

Pohl J. (1971); 'The Reinforcement and Bracing of Multi-Story Pneumatic Buildings'; Architectural Science Review, 14(1), March (pp. 11-18)

Pohl J. (1970); 'Pneumatic Structures: Architectural Application with Special Reference to Multi-Storey Buildings'; Doctor of Philosophy Thesis in Architectural Science, University of Sydney, Sydney, Australia.

Pohl J. (1970); 'The Structural Pressurized Flexible Membrane Column'; Architectural Science Review, September.

Pohl J. (1968); 'Pneumatic Structures'; Architecture in Australia, Journal of the Royal Australian Institute of Architects, July (pp. 635-9).

Pohl J. (1967); 'Multi-Storey Pneumatic Buildings as a Challenge to the Plastics Industry'; Australian Building Science and Technology, Journal of the Building Science Forum of Australia, June (pp. 5-8).

Pohl J. (1966); 'The Load-Bearing Capacity of Open-Ended Cylindrical Tubes Under Internal Pressure'; Master of Building Science Thesis in Architectural Science, University of Sydney, Sydney, Australia.

Prescott J. (1946); 'Applied Elasticity'; Reprinted by Dover Publications, New York (originally published 1924).

Pugsley A. (1957); 'The Theory of Suspension Bridges'; Edward Arnold Publishers Ltd, U.K., London (pp. 11-20).

Quarmby A. (1967); 'The Redevelopment of the Building Industry'; Space Structures, ed. Davies, R.M.; Blackwell Scientific Publications (pp. 1153-8).

Ramm E. (ed.) (1982); 'Buckling of Shells'; Proceedings State-of-the-Art Colloquium, University of Stuttgart, Germany, May 6-7, Springer Verlag, Berlin.

Randerson H. Y. (1964); 'Australian Sanitary Engineering Practice'; Angus and Robertson, Australia (pp. 360-370).

Raviv M. and H. Lieth (eds.) (2008); 'Soilless Culture: Theory and Practice'; Elsevier, London, UK.

Rawlings B. (1967); 'Inflated Ductile Metal Structures'; Architectural Science Review, 10(2), June, Australia (pp. 44-48).

Redshaw S. (1938); 'The Elastic Stability of a Curved Plate Under Axial Thrust'; Journal RAS, XLI(330), June (pp. 536-553).

Richardson H. and R. Mayo (1941); 'Practical Tunnel Driving'; McGraw-Hill, New York, New York (pp. 286-299).

Robertson A. (1928); 'The Strength of Tubular Struts'; Proc. Royal Society of London, Series A. Vol. 121 (pp. 558-585).

Roland C. (1963); 'Multi-Storey Suspension Structures'; Architectural Design, November (pp. 530-5).

Rotter J. (2004); 'Cylindrical Shells Under Axial Compression'; in Teng J. and J. Rotter (eds.) *Buckling of Thin Metal Shells*, Spoon Press, London, UK (pp. 47-87).

Roubal J., L. Oppl and B. Berounski (1963); 'Basic Sanitary Requirements for Buildings with no Windows or Skylights'; Ceskoslovenska Hygiena, 8 (8), (pp. 481-490).

Rugger G. (1965); 'Weathering of Plastics'; Plastics in Building Structures; Proceedings of a Conference; Pergamon Press, London.

SAA Int. (1961); Minimum Design Loads on Buildings'; Standards Association of Australia, Sydney (pp. 16).

Samuelson L. and S. Eggwertz (1992); 'Shell Stability Handbook'; Elsevier Applied Science, London, UK.

Scheuerman A. (2003); 'The Towers, Fire-Induced Collapse, and the Building Codes'; unedited version provided to Structure Magazine, 10 October (pp 84) www.structuremag.org/downloads/WTC-Scheuermann.pdf

Schriever W. (1960); 'Loads and Load Factors'; NRC 5995, National Research Council, Canada, Division of Building Research, October; also: Transactions of the Engineering Institute of Canada, 4(2), 1960 (pp.72-81).

Schultze H. (1964); 'Die Traglufthalle'; Industrielle Technik, (1).

Seide P. and V. Weingarten (1968); 'Buckling of Thin-Walled Truncated Cones'; NASA SP-8019, NASA Space Vehicle Design Criteria (Structures), September.

Sergev S. (1961); 'On Column Behavior'; Journal of the Aerospace Sciences, 28(4), April.

Sergev S. and D. Walton (1962); 'Strength of Pressurized Columns'; The Trend in Engineering at the University of Washington, April (pp. 13-16).

Shanley F. (1947); 'Inelastic Column Theory'; Journal of Aeronautical Sciences, 14 (pp 261-268).

Siegel C. (1962); Structure and Form in Modern Architecture'; Lockwood, London, UK.

Simitses G. (1986); 'Buckling and Postbuckling of Imperfect Cylindrical Shells: A Review'; Applied Mechanical Review, ASME, 39(10), October (pp. 1517-1524).

Singer J., J. Arbocz and T. Weller (2002); 'Buckling Experiments: Experimental Methods in Buckling of Thin-Walled Structures'; Volume 2, *Shells, Built-up Structures, Composites, and Additional Topics*, Wiley, New York, New York.

Singer J. (1982); 'The Status of Experimental Buckling Investigations of Shells'; in Ramm E. (ed.) *Buckling of Shells*, Proceedings State-of-the-Art Colloquium, University of Stuttgart, Germany, May 6-7, Springer Verlag, Berlin (pp 501-533).

Smiles S. (1966); 'Lives of the Engineers'; MIT Press, Cambridge, Massachusetts (pp. 378-393).

Smith W. and J. Hashemi (2006); 'Foundations of Material Science and Engineering'; Fourth Edition, McGraw-Hill, New York, New York.

Smith A. (1958); 'A Plastic Shelter For House Building in Winter'; National Builder, Canada, Nov.-Dec.

Smith P. and J. Pohl (1970); 'Pneumatic Construction Applied to Multistory Buildings'; Progressive Architecture, 11(9), September (pp. 100-117).

Sokolnikoff I. and R. Redheffer (1958); 'Mathematics of Physics and Modern Engineering'; McGraw-Hill, New York, New York.

Sokolnikoff I. (1956); 'Mathematical Theory of Elasticity'; Second Edition, McGraw-Hill, New York, New York.

Southwell R. (1914); 'On the General Theory of Elastic Stability'; Phil.Trans. Royal Society, London, Series A, Vol. 213 (pp. 187-244).

Soutas-Little R. (1973); 'Elasticity'; Dover Publications, Mineola, New York.

Spiegel M. (1961); 'Theory and Problems of Statistics'; Schaum, New York, New York (pp. 247-265).

Standards Association of Australia (1961); 'SAA Int. 351, Structural Steel in Building'; Published by the Standards Association of Australia, Sydney (pp. 9).

Stein M. (1962); 'The Effect on the Buckling of Perfect Cylinders of Prebuckling Deformations and Stresses Induced by Edge Support'; NASA TN D-1510.

Steinhaus H. (1960); 'Mathematical Snapshots'; Oxford University Press, Oxford, UK (pp. 270-1).

Stevens P. (1974); 'Patterns in Nature'; Little Brown and Company, Boston, Massachusetts.

Stowell E. (1948); 'A Unified Theory of Plastic Buckling of Columns and Plates'; NACA Report 898.

Sturm R. (1941); 'A Study of the Collapsing Pressure of Thin-Walled Cylinders'; University of Illinois Engineering Experiment Station Bulletin No. 329.

Szilard R. (1967); 'Pneumatic Structures for Lunar Bases'; Proceedings of the 1st International Colloquium on Pneumatic Structures, Germany (pp. 34-5).

Szilard R. (1959); "Structures for the Moon'; Civil Engineering, USA, October.

Taunton J., E. Banister, T. Patrick, P. Oforsagd and W. Duncan (1970); 'Physical Work Capacity in Hyperbaric Environments and Conditions of Hyperoxia'; Journal of Applied Physiology, 28(4), April.

Teng J. (1996); 'Buckling of Thin Shells: Recent Advances and Trends'; Applied Mechanics Review, ASME 49(4) (pp. 263-274).

Teng J. and Y. Hu (2007); 'Behaviour of FRP-Jacketed Circular Steel Tubes and Cylindrical Shells under Axial Compression'; Construction and Building Materials, Vol 21 (pp. 827-838).

Teng J. and J. Rotter (Eds.) (2004); 'Buckling of Thin Metal Shells'; Spoon Press, London, UK.

Tennyson R. (1969); 'Buckling Modes of Circular Cylindrical Shells under Axial Compression'; AIAA Journal, 7(8), August (pp. 1481-1487).

Thompson D. (1942); 'On Growth and Form'; Cambridge University Press, London, UK.

Thompson J. and G. Hunt (eds.) (1983); 'Collapse'; Cambridge University Press, Cambridge, UK.

Timoshenko S. (1983); 'History of Strength of Materials'; Dover Publications, New York, New York.

Timoshenko S. and G. MacCullough (1949); 'Elements of Strength of Materials'; D. Van Nostrand Company, New York, New York (pp. 317-8).

Timoshenko S. (1936); 'Theory of Elastic Stability'; McGraw-Hill, New York, New York (Chapter 36), also United Engineering Trustees Inc., New York, New York.

Timoshenko S. (1910); 'Einige Stabilitäts Probleme der Elastizitätstheorie'; Zeitschrift für Mathematik und Physik; Vol. 58 (pp. 337-385).

Timoshenko S. and J. Gere (1961); 'Theory of Elastic Stability'; Second Edition, Dover Publications, Mineola, New York.

Tsai-Chen Soong (1967); 'Buckling of cylindrical Shell Under Pressure by Using Sander's Theory'; Technical Note, AIAA Journal (pp. 1049).

Tsien H. (1942); 'A Theory for the Buckling of Thin Shells'; Journal of the Aeronautical Sciences, 9(10), August (pp. 373-384).

Turki A. (1974); 'The Pneumatic Home: Concept, Evaluation and Computer Program'; Master of Science (Architecture) thesis; College of Architecture and Environmental Design, California Polytechnic State University, San Luis Obispo, California.

University of Michigan (1965); 'Architectural Research on Structural Potential of Foam Plastics for Housing in Underdeveloped Areas'; Architectural Research Laboratory, The University of Michigan, Ann Arbor, USA, November (Section 6).

Usmani A., Y. Chung and J. Torero (2003); 'How Did the WTC Towers Collapse: A New Theory'; Fire Safety Journal, Number 38 (pp. 501-533).

Van den Broek A. (1947); English Translation of 'Euler's Classic Paper - On the Strength of Columns'; American Journal of Physics, 15(4), July-August (pp 309-318).

Van der Neut A. (1962); 'General Instability of Orthogonally Stiffened Cylindrical Shells'; NASA TN- D-1510 (pp. 309-321).

Van der Neut A. (1947); 'General Instability of Stiffened Cylindrical Shells Under Axial Compression'; Nat. Luchtraartlab, 13 Repr. S. 314.

Van Patten G. (2012); 'Hydrofarm BKHB Hydroponic Basics, 0.2 Pounds'; Hydrofarm, Petaluma, California.

Von Karman T. and H. Tsien (1939); 'The Buckling of Spherical Shells by External Pressure'; Journal of the Aeronautical Sciences, 7(2), December (pp. 43).

Von Karman T., L. Dunn and H. Tsien (1940); 'The Influence of Curvature on the Buckling Characteristic of Structures'; Journal of the Aeronautical Sciences, 7(7), May (pp. 276).

Von Karman T. and H. Tsien (1941); 'The Buckling of Thin Cylindrical Shells Under Axial Compression'; Journal of the Aeronautical Sciences, 8(8), June (pp. 303-312).

Wang L. (1967); 'Discrepancy of Experimental Buckling Pressures of Spherical Shells'; Technical Note, AIAA Journal (pp. 357).

Weidlinger P. (1964); 'Review of Zugbeanspruchte Konstruktionen by Frei Otto and Rudolf Trostel (Ulstein, Frankfurt 1962)'; Progressive Architecture; June (pp. 226-234).

Weingarten V., P. Seide and J. Peterson (1968); 'Buckling of Thin-Walled Circular Cylinders'; NASA SP-8007, NASA Space Vehicle Design Criteria (Structures), August.

Welham R. (1963); 'Plastics in Building'; Plastics (J), 28(303); January (pp. 97).

WCLA (1958); 'Douglas Fir Use Book - Structural Data and Design Tables'; West Coast Lumbermen's Association, Daily Journal of Commerce, Portland, Oregon (pp. 156-7)

Wilson E. and N. Newmark (1933); 'The Strength of Thin Cylindrical Shells as Columns'; Eng. Exp. Sta. Bull. No. 255, University of Illinois, February.

Wright F. (1960); 'Airhouse'; Domus; March (pp. 17-18).

Wu T., L. Goodman and N. Newmark (1953); 'Effect of Small Initial Irregularities on the Stresses in Cylindrical Shells'; Civil Engineering Studies, Structural Research Series No. 50, University of Illinois.

Yamaki N. (1984); 'Elastic Stability of Circular Cylindrical Shells'; North-Holland, Amsterdam, The Netherlands.

Yoshimura Y. (1951); 'On the Mechanism of Buckling of a Circular Cylindrical Shell Under Axial Compression' (in Japanese); Report of the Institute of Science and Technology, University of Tokyo, Vol. 5 (pp. 179-198).

Yoshimura Y and J. Nisawa (1957); 'Lower Buckling Stress of Circular Cylindrical Shells Subjected to Torsion'; Journal of the Aeronautical Sciences, March (pp. 211).

Appendix A
Single-Story Air-Supported and Air-Inflated Structures

The air-supported dome became a commercial proposition in 1956 with the formation of Birdair Structures Inc. by Walter Bird, the pioneer developer of air-supported membrane buildings. Bird and his associates had concluded that the commercial possibilities of pneumatic structures were of sufficient scope to justify the financial gamble undertaken. Although Birdair's first major contract involved the design and fabrication of an air-supported *Radome* (i.e., weather protection for military radar installations in the Arctic region), the main objective of the company from the beginning was to create a commercial market. The intent was to produce shelters for swimming pools, tennis courts, athletic fields, and sporting arenas in general, as well as temporary warehouses for food, crop, and machinery storage. The prospects in fact, were so attractive that within two years some 40 firms leaped into competition with Birdair, coming from fields involving the manufacture of awnings, tents, tarpaulins, and parachutes. The popularity of air-buildings grew rapidly during the later part of the 1950s and early 1960s. Birdair's turnover approximately doubled every year from 1956 onward to reach peak revenues of over one million U.S. dollars in 1961. Table A-1 traces the historical development and commercialization of air-building technology from the earliest beginnings of Lanchester's innovative ideas and patents in 1917 to the early 1970s when the air-building market collapsed almost as suddenly as it had appeared (Kingsford 1960, Dent 1971, Cowan 1977).

Table A-1: The historical evolution and demise of the commercial air-building market

1917	Lanchester F.	First two patents covering the basic principles of single-skin air-supported buildings (U.K.).
1925	Lanchester F.	Conceptual design of an air-supported exhibition building (U.K.).
1932	Lanchester F.	Public lecture presented to the Manchester Association of Engineers at the University of Manchester (U.K.), in which Lanchester described the fundamental principles of single-skin air-supported construction.
1932-5	Stevens H.	Concerted efforts to promote the basic concepts of air-buildings in the U.S. by Stevens who designed a number of air-supported factory projects.
1946-8	Cornell University	The U.S. Air Force supported research in the Cornell Aeronautical Laboratory to devise a method of enclosing large radar antennae planned for the Arctic. The beginnings of the *Radome* development (U.S.).
1948	Bird W.	Significant breakthrough in the U.S. with the erection and successful testing of the first *Radome* in the U.S.

1950-5	Neff W.	Use of inflated balloons for formwork for concrete shells (U.S.).
1950-5	Birdair Inc, U.S. Rubber Company, Irving, Krupp GmBH, Texair, Schjedahl	Considerable number of companies began to design, manufacture and promote air-buildings in U.S. and Europe.
1958-62	Otto F.	Studied the stiffening of pneumatically tensioned skins by means of an applied layer of plastic with and without cables and cable-networks (Germany).
1958 c.	Koch C. and Weidlinger P.	Boston Arts Center Theater Project, incorporating an air-supported roof spanning 145 feet (U.S.).
1958 c.	Berger Brothers	Double-skin pneumatic *geodome* based on Buckminster Fuller's patent (U.S.).
1959	Lundy V.	Double-skin air-inflated exhibition building for the U.S. Atomic Energy Commission enclosing 22,000 square feet (U.S.).
1959 c.	Irving	Air-supported pavilion for Pan American Airways at the Brussels World Fair (U.S.).
1959 c.	Buckminster Fuller	Inflated balloons used as auxiliary rigging elements in rib-shell domes (U.S.).
1958-60	Otto F.	Fundamental work on the theory of pneumatic construction at Washington University of St. Louis, Yale University and Hochschule für Gestaltung at Ulm (U.S. and Germany).
1960	Wright F. and Irvin Airchute Co.	Air-supported home exhibited at the New York International Home Exhibition (U.S.).
1962	Otto F. and Trostel R.	Book: " Zugbeanspruchte Konstruktionen " (Ulstein GmBH). First comprehensive publication about single-story pneumatic construction (Germany).
1962-4	Otto F., Trostel, R., Koch C., Miles F., Roland K. et al.	Integrated team research into pneumatic construction sponsored by Stromeyer and Company at the Entwicklungsstätte für den Leichtbau, Berlin (Germany).

1963	Architects' Collaborative	Air-supported gymnasium and swimming pool complex, at Forman School, Litchfield, Connecticut (U.S.).
1967	IASS	First Colloquium on Pneumatic Structures held at Stuttgart, Germany and organized by the International Association for Shell and Spatial Structures (IASS).
1970	EXPO'70	World Fair in Osaka, Japan, (often referred to as *EXPO PNEU*) featured many air-building exhibition pavilions; - notably the air-inflated tubular structure of the Fuji Group.
1972	IASS	International Symposium on Pneumatic Structures hosted by the University of Delft, Netherlands and organized by the International Association for Shell and Spatial Structures (IASS).
1976	IASS	WCOSE-76: IASS World Congress on Space Enclosures hosted by the Building Research Centre, Concordia University, Montreal, Canada (4-9 July), still included several papers on pneumatic structures.
1977	CIB/IASS	International Symposium on Air Supported Structures sponsored by the International Council for Building Research Studies and Documentation (CIB) and the IASS, and hosted by ICITE-CNR in Milan, Italy (13-18 June). Discussed structural, constructional, membrane material, fire protection, energy conservation, and failure issues. However, this appears to be the last international conference in which pneumatic structures featured prominently.

The applications of air-supported buildings have been varied, although generally of a temporary nature. For example, it has been considered practical in countries where building operations are often substantially retarded by inclement weather conditions to cover critical sections of building sites (Figure A-1) with these extremely light shelters (Smith 1958, Makowski 1964, Pohl 1968). More mainstream building types included theaters, mobile storage warehouses, field hospitals, sport arenas (Figure A-2), hermetically sealed tropical food-stores, and portable housing for civil and mineralogical engineering survey exploration. Perhaps one of the most remarkable features about the history of air-supported buildings has been their relatively quick rise in popularity and their almost equally rapid exodus from the construction industry. In comparison, it took the best part of 20 years before Buckminster Fuller's geodesic domes won real commercial recognition (Allison 1959). The air-building, unlike many geodesic dome structures, was never considered as a permanent structure and has therefore not been forced to compete with conventional building construction. However, despite this advantage and its low cost, which allowed it to be discarded or replaced after a life-span of seven to nine years, the air-building phenomenon faded away in less than 20 years.

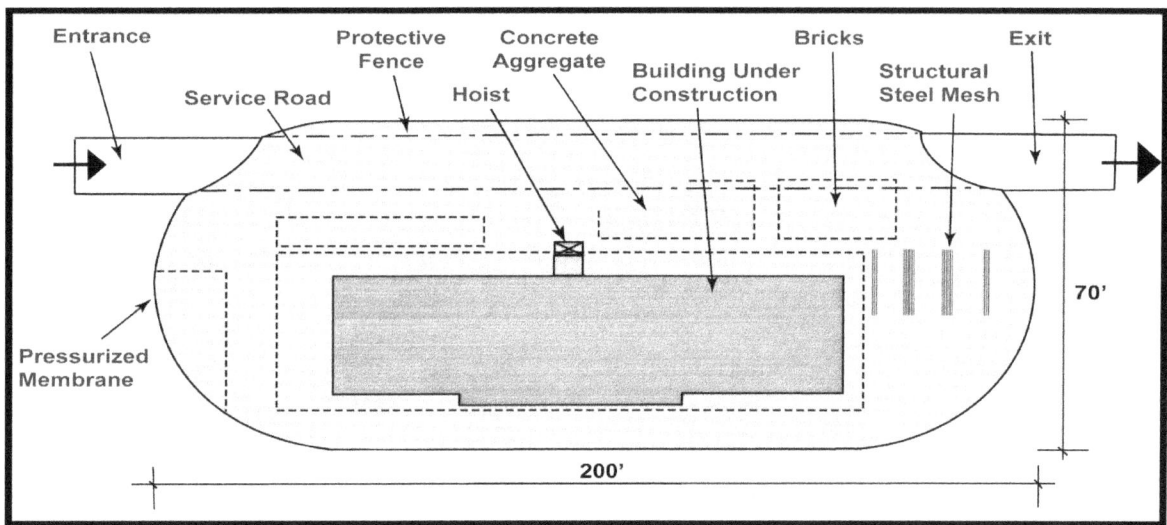

Figure A-1: Construction site sheltered within an air-supported enclosure

Figure A-2: In-door tennis courts within an air-supported enclosure

A-1 Air-Building Types

Air-supported membrane buildings in their temporary capacity are known to give satisfactory weather protection and be capable of withstanding substantial wind velocities (Allison 1959, Otto and Trostel 1962 and 1967, Born 1964). For example, the *Radome* with a diameter of about 50 feet and an internal pressure of less than 0.05 pounds per square inch maintained its stability when subjected to wind speeds in excess of 140 miles per hour (Dent 1971 [35])[1]. Many of those built have featured quite remarkable spans and large dimensions, with lengths and widths in excess of 300 feet and 200 feet, respectively (Figure A-3). Such dimensions are possible due to the fact that span is not limited in structures where a membrane cover is supported by air pressure at every point over its entire surface. The air acts as a cushion and as long as the upward and outward force of its pressure is at least equal to the inward and downward force of the containing envelope, the building will retain its form. Typically, the internal air is held at a higher pressure to ensure stability under windy conditions and maintain an acceptable factor of safety.

Figure A-3: Typical large span air-supported pavilion

From this fundamental solution of a single-skin air-supported membrane have come two related building types that do not require the internal building environment to be pressurized. In these buildings the air pressure is contained within structural components that support the building enclosure. The three basic types of single-story air-supported structures can be described as follows:

1. **Single-skin systems:** Normally shaped as half-cylinders with quarter-spherical ends, or domes (Figure A-4). Shallower designs with a greater radius of curvature are better suited aerodynamically, but have intrinsically higher membrane stresses at a given internal pressure. The outer coating of the membrane skin can be made reflecting for regions with much sunlight. To provide daylight, the top of the half-cylinder is usually made transparent in parts.

2. **Double-skin systems:** Typically consisting of cellular, inflated panels interconnected to form vaults of various shapes as shown in Figure A-5. As an example of this form of air-inflated construction, the Geodome based on Buckminster Fuller's geodesic principle and marketed in the 1960s by Berger

---

[1] For additional details of wind tunnel tests on pneumatic structures see Cornell University, Ithaca, New York, U.S., Cornell Aeronautical Laboratory Reports: UB-909-D-1; UB-909-D-2; UB-512-J-1; UB-664-D-1; and, UB-747-D-19.

Bros. Company, consists of pneumatic panels of neoprene coated nylon fabric. To erect the Geodome these panels are simply pumped up simultaneously, like an air mattress. Once the dome has been inflated the compressor can be disconnected, and windows as well as doors can be left open, since each air-filled panel maintains its pressure individually. In addition, the pneumatic method of stiffening the panels provides an insulating air-cavity space of three inches or more, while in the deflated state the entire dome can be folded to fit comfortably into the back of a hatchback car or small pickup truck.

Figure A-4: Typical single-skin air-supported building shapes

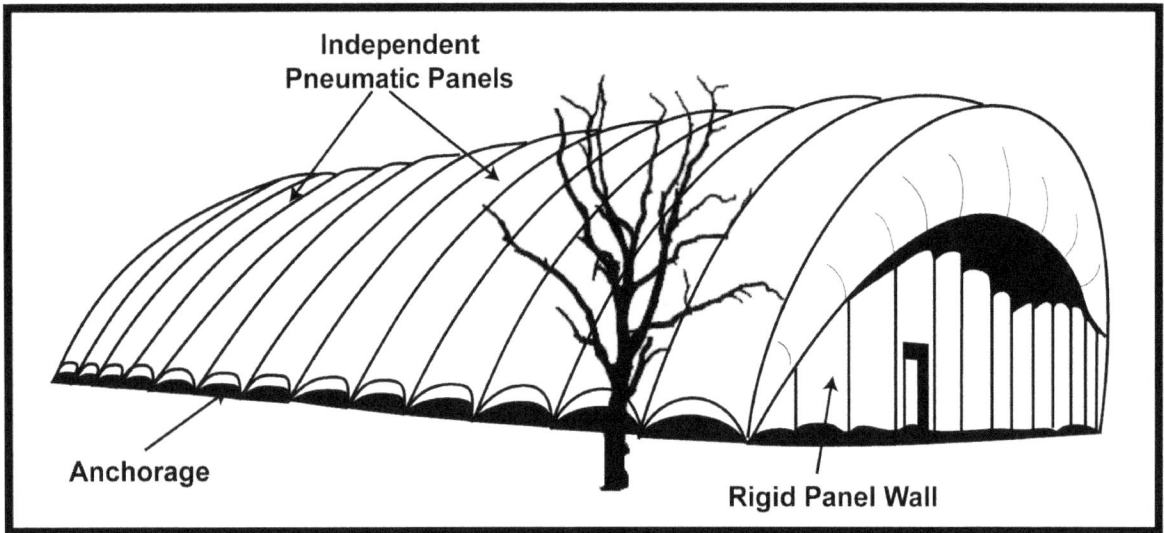

Figure A-5: Typical double-skin air-inflated building shape

3. **Tubular systems:** Systems in which the weather-resisting skin is supported by a framework of inflated, high pressure tubing (Figure A-6). When in normal use, the thin ribs alone carry the lightweight skin. However, when excessive loads are anticipated (e.g., snow or wind) the building may be closed and pressurized internally for added stability. This type of air-inflated structure is suitable for relatively small buildings, where large span is not a design criterion. The *Igloo* inflatable poleless tent shown in Figure A-7 has overall dimensions 7 feet 6 inches by 6 feet (height) and requires an air pressure of 16 pounds per square inch. It may be erected in a few minutes with the aid of a normal car tire pump. The complete

Igloo weighs only 24 pounds and packs into a bag 24 inches by 18 inches.

The single-skin air-supported building (i.e., Lanchester's original idea) certainly has the greatest potential for large span building structures. While it is the simplest form and the least expensive implementation, it is also the most interesting from a structural point of view because it requires such a minute internal pressure. A typical single-skin enclosure regardless of size can be supported by raising the internal pressure only 0.04 pounds per square inch (or 0.3%) above the ambient atmospheric pressure of approximately 14.5 pounds per square inch.

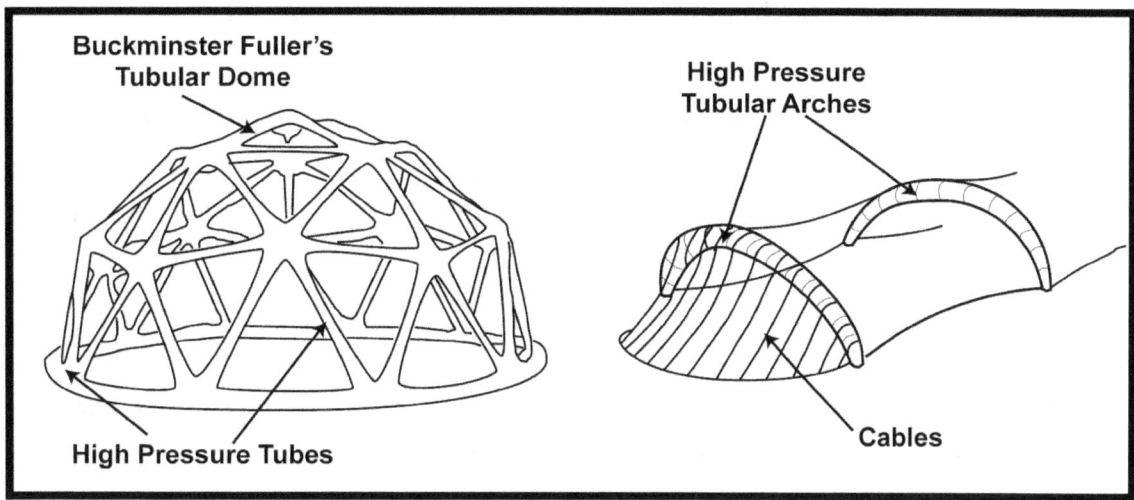

Figure A-6: Tubular air-inflated structures

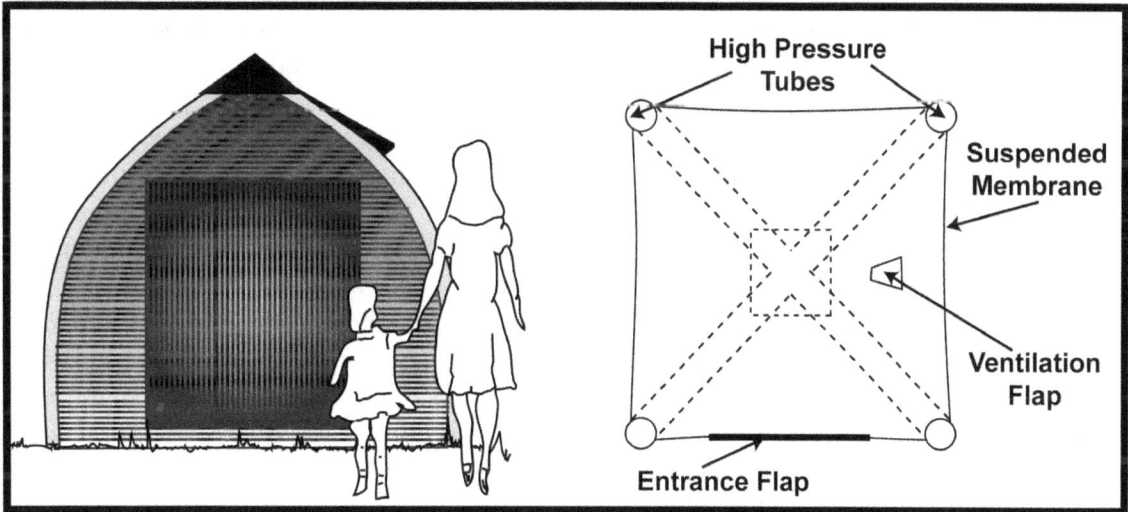

Figure A-7: The *Igloo* inflatable poleless tent

A-2 Intrinsic Structural Morphology

Air-supported structures are basically prestressed membrane shells in which the post-tensioning force is provided by internal air-pressure of sufficient intensity to ensure that the membrane remains under tension for all foreseeable loading conditions (Weidlinger 1964). Consequently, for this type of pneumatic construction the possibility of overall buckling of the surface is eliminated, although local flutter due to dynamic wind loading may still occur. The sphere and cylinder are natural forms of air-supported membranes since a uniform internal pressure will produce these forms in the absence of any other external restraint. Other more complex forms may be achieved by the suitable placement of primary cables or networks (Otto and Trostel 1962 and 1967).

Most forms of building construction can be readily traced to one of three broad classifications, namely: post and beam construction; shell construction; and, suspension construction. Pneumatic construction as a tension system is strongly related to suspension structures and yet displays some fundamental differences. On the basis of being air-supported, the membrane building is normally devoid of compression members and efficient in its ability to fully utilize the material strength in tension of the enclosure.

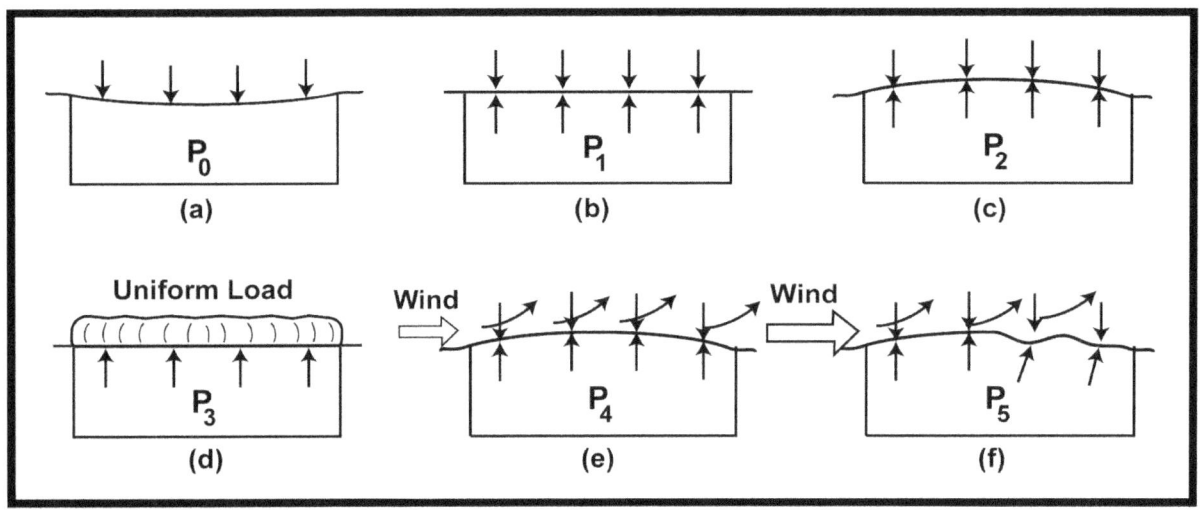

Figure A-8: Membrane under different loading conditions

In the absence of internal pressure (Figure A-8(a)) the membrane will act as a suspended mat and experience only tensile stresses in proportion to its self-weight. The self-weight can be balanced by internal pressure so that the membrane experiences no stresses at all (Figure A-8(b)). Progressive increases in internal pressure will again produce tensile stresses in the membrane, in direct proportion to the internal pressure and the radius of curvature of the outward bulging membrane (Figure A-8(c)). The superimposition of a uniformly distributed load will lead to a reduction in these tensile stresses until a stage is reached where the internal pressure is again counterbalanced by an equal and opposite load pressure, resulting in a *zero-stress* condition of the membrane (Figure A-8(d)). Theoretically, we are faced with the extraordinary structural condition that under ultimate load conditions the structure experiences no stresses (i.e., the load is supported by the air pressure). Of course in practice, to add a factor of safety and allow for uncontrollable changes in load conditions (e.g., wind forces and internal pressure variations) the membrane would be prestressed in tension by an internal pressure that exceeds all foreseeable load increases by a predefined margin.

However, taking the *zero-stress* condition of the membrane as an arbitrary criterion we may further illustrate the fundamental characteristics of single-skin air-supported construction, as follows:

> If the membrane material has a normal weight of 0.2 pounds per square foot then an internal pressure of one inch water gauge (i.e., 0.035 psi) will suffice to support this

material load. With a uniformly distributed load of 5 pounds per square foot acting on the membrane, we now require an internal pressure of 0.94 inch water gauge (i.e., 0.035 psi) to support the superimposed load and the membrane (Figure A-8(d)).

In practice snow and earth loads are fairly evenly distributed over plane surfaces, while wind loads are generally unevenly distributed. Wind acting on an air-supported membrane will induce an upward force (Figure A-8(e)). If we assume that this suction is fairly uniformly distributed and of magnitude 8 pounds per square foot, then the pressure within the building must be increased by 1.46 inches water gauge (i.e., 0.054 psig) above normal atmospheric pressure[2]. Instability conditions that may accompany the generally uneven pressure patterns of wind forces are referred to as *flutter* (Figure A-8(f)) and will be discussed in more detail in a later section of Appendix A.

A-3 Comparison of Air-Building Types

Early implementations of single-skin air-supported buildings were required to be fairly airtight (Allison 1959). However, this concern was soon alleviated by the availability of larger centrifugal air blowers with much greater capacities. In fact, it became common practice for manufacturers to claim as part of their promotional campaign that even relatively large doors (i.e., for vehicles) could be left open permanently. The double-skin and tubular framework air-building types were initially developed to overcome the air tightness requirement. During the 30-year period (approximately 1950 to 1980) that constituted the heyday of air-buildings most of the major manufacturers experimented with various double-skin systems and air-inflated beams and arches (Editorial 1957). All of these air-inflated systems require much higher pressures, often in excess of 15 pounds per square inch, because they do not share the intrinsic structural efficiency of the single-skin air-building type in which the entire building environment is pressurized. Furthermore, at these pressures a simple blower unit is no longer adequate and must be replaced by a compressor, normally leading to higher operating costs and susceptibility to leakage.

The tubular pneumatic structure has in itself given rise to a number of prototypes, combining to various degrees air-support with metal ribs and other auxiliary rigid support elements. Where metal ribbing is designed to carry normal working loads, internal pressurization is considered an adjunct to be used at will for special circumstances, such as high winds during storms. An example of this type of air-inflated building was a summer arts theater in Boston (Massachusetts, U.S.), which opened in 1959. Due to lack of funding for a permanent theater, this project started out to be nothing more than a tent. However, no tent could be found to span the required distances and at the same time provide an unobstructed view for an audience of 2,000 persons. Therefore, the designers, Kock (architect) and Weidlinger (engineer), chose a disc-shaped, air-filled roof with a clear span diameter of 1,435 feet. The roof disc, fabricated by Birdair Inc., tapered from 20 feet in depth at the center to half an inch at the circumference. Its two skins were zippered together and rested on a column-supported steel frame ring (Allison 1959). Two compressors kept the roof inflated and one additional compressor continually fed cool air into the envelope, thus keeping the roof at a moderate temperature. The roof was tilted for acoustical reasons. During the winter months the roof could be detached from the frame, deflated, and stored away.

---

[2] The addition of *g* in *psig* indicates pressure above ambient atmospheric pressure. All internal pressures referred to in this Appendix, whether indicated as *psi* or *psig* are internal pressures above atmospheric pressure.

Table A-2 provides a comparison of the advantages, disadvantages, and limitations of the single-skin and double-skin air-building types.

Table A-2: Comparison of single-skin and double-skin air-buildings

Single-Skin Air-Supported Buildings

Advantages	Limitations
Large spans without intermediate supports or compression members are possible.	Maximum possible span is proportional to membrane material strength in tension.
Full realization of material strength in tension. Incorporates most of the properties of a *minimal structure*.	Durability, heat, and acoustical insulation are directly related to the properties of a single layer of the membrane material.
Inherent advantage of being able to consider *structure* and *enclosure* as one integrated entity.	Continuous entry and exit has been solved in recent years, but the number and size of openings is limited.
Extremely light-weight structure that is portable and highly suitable for the application of prefabrication techniques.	The potential for local instability (flutter) under wind loads increases with the size of the structure.
Possible future application as a large scale town-planning structure spanning a number of miles may be feasible.	Pressurization equipment (i.e., air blower) is required on a continuous basis.

Double-Skin Air-Inflated Buildings

Advantages	Limitations
Better thermal insulation than single-skin air-supported building due to air cavity and second membrane skin.	Span much more limited than single-skin air-supported buildings due to reduced rigidity of interconnected air-inflated panels.
Building environment not pressurized, therefore virtually no limitation on number and size of openings.	Much reduced structural efficiency, since the stability of individual inflated components is a major design criterion.
Pressurization equipment (i.e., compressors) required for erection purposes only.	Increased self-weight of structure due to double wall.
Suitable for portability and the application of prefabrication techniques.	Compressors required and therefore higher operating costs initially.

One of the most prominent and certainly by all accounts in the media of the times the most spectacular tubular pneumatic structure was the Fuji Group Pavilion at Expo'70 in Osaka, Japan (Dent 1971, 215-9). Designed by architect Yutaka Murata and engineer Mamoru Kawaguchi, it featured 16 air-inflated tubes that were arched over a circular plan of about 165 feet diameter (Figure A-9). Each tube was approximately 13 feet in diameter, pressurized from 1.5 to 3.5

pounds per square inch (i.e., approximately 10% to 25% above atmospheric pressure) depending on wind conditions. The tubes were made of a multi-layered plastic fabric that consisted of a polyvinyl alcoholic (PVA) core with an internal coating of polyvinyl chloride (PVC) for airtightness and an external coating of hypalon for weatherproofing. The fabric was quite heavy weighing about ¾ pound per square foot and had a tensile strength of around 1,120 pounds per inch (Herzog 1976, 76-8). The base of each tube was clamped to a metal cylinder that was anchored to a concrete slab floor. Although spectacular both in size and its internal revolving audio-visual platform, it was by no means an elegant structure. The large diameter of its arched tubes evidenced the inherent structural inefficiency of a pneumatic tubular structure in comparison to its single-skin cousin.

Figure A-9: The Fuji Pavilion at Expo'70, Osaka, Japan (1970)
(Source: Herzog (1976); 'Pneumatische Konstruktionen'; Verlag Gerd Hatje, Stuttgart, Germany (pp. 76-77))

Table A-3: Advantages and limitations of tubular air-inflated building structures

Tubular Air-Inflated Building Structures	
Advantages	**Limitations**
Building environment need not be pressurized, although under certain circumstances it may be pressurized for added stability. Internal pressure when required need be no higher than with a single-skin building, while in normal usage the pressurized tubing carries all of the load.	Span severely limited by the instability of pressurized tubular frames, which act as closed pressurized membrane columns. It has been found that even for moderate slenderness ratios (i.e., 80-100) the pressure-utilization efficiency of these columns may fall below 60% (Pohl 1966).
Tubes may be pressurized to high pressures (e.g., 100 pounds per square inch or more) without affecting the building environment.	High pressure tubes require more elaborate pressurization equipment such as compressors, and are susceptible to leakage.
The tubular air-building will tend to be more costly than its counterparts, not only because it uses more material, but also because the type of material used for the high pressure tubes will need to be of high quality, high strength, and non-porous.	Less suitable for the application of prefabrication techniques than single and double-skin air-buildings, due to the difficulties encountered in the joining of high pressure tubes. However, from a general point of view, it must be considered an advantage that prefabrication is at all possible.

During the 1960s, when single-story air-supported structures were hailed as an inexpensive and exciting new building type, there were also some disappointments and even failures. First, it was not immediately understood that there are some serious constraints hidden beneath the apparent resilience and structural simplicity of an air-supported membrane. It was soon learned that care was in order to ensure that the design, erection and maintenance of these novel buildings did not violate the intrinsic characteristics of the underlying technology. The number of failures was relatively small and in virtually all cases due to an inexperienced builder or occupant ignoring one or more aspects of this technology. For example, it was not always realized that the stability of an air-supported building is derived entirely from the internal air pressure. Therefore, under gale force winds the internal pressure has to be increased. Unfortunately, in a few cases the building maintenance personnel made the decision to deflate the building during high winds, based on the ill-conceived notion that this would save the membrane. Instead, the membrane was severely damaged or totally destroyed.

Second, very early air-supported structures sometimes ruptured as a result of poorly designed membrane joints. Material manufacturers such as ICI, DuPont, Wellington Sears, Sawyer-Tower, U.S. Rubber, and others made major contributions to the development of the air-building through their research into improved fabrics and durable coatings such as polyvinyl chloride (PVC) and polyvinyl fluoride (PVF). However, misuse of these materials in terms of over-designed working stresses, could lead to failure. In addition, the life-span of an air-supported building is directly proportional to the durability of the membrane material. As will be discussed in a later section, particularly transparent and translucent plastic materials are subject to ultraviolet light degradation.

Third, there was the problem of compliance with existing building codes. From a general point of view air-buildings are inherently quite safe structures. The membrane material does not support combustion and there is no heavy roof structure overhead. In case of power failure and in the absence of alternative stand-by equipment the building settles down very slowly, normally taking several hours to collapse completely. Certainly very few new methods of construction have come to the building industry with a background of field testing and the trials of such severe exposure as demanded by the Arctic *Radomes*.

Finally, there remained the problem of gauging the market capacity for air-buildings. Lanchester was conscious of the limited commercial market for large span structures in 1938, when he predicted their use for entertainment centers and sports arenas alone (Lanchester 1938). During the 20 years that marked the heyday of air-buildings (1955-75 c.) some further applications, such as convention halls, exhibition pavilions, and warehouses were added to this short list. In the future there may again be some interest in very large air-supported structures covering entire communities. At the time that such mega-structures were proposed by Buckminster Fuller (1962) to cover the city of New York and by Frei Otto in collaboration with Ewald Bubner (1970) for the Arctic region, neither the necessary membrane materials nor the knowledge of how to deal with the micro-climatic and pollution aspects of a large-scale biosphere were available (Figure A-21). Even today there would need to be extenuating circumstances due to some imminent threat, before a construction project of such an enormous scale could be considered.

Apart from some totally unexpected circumstances the need for large span structures is unlikely to significantly increase in the foreseeable future and therefore at least the exploitation of single-skin air-buildings will continue to be severely limited. On the other hand, it is rather surprising that double-skin and tubular air-buildings have not gained in popularity. One would have thought that they would have gained a more permanent foothold as an economical proposition for a host of building applications, including temporary disaster relief and residential construction (Wright 1960).

A-4 Air-Building Technology

Air-buildings incorporate various facets of the science of hydraulics and as such are governed by a technology not normally considered in building construction. For example, the shape of air-buildings will be dictated rigorously by symmetry if the ideal condition of equal stress distribution throughout the enclosing membrane is to be achieved. Even though the internal hyperbaric building environment in single-skin air-supported structures is only at a slightly higher pressure than the external atmosphere, the provision of openings for pedestrian and vehicular traffic requires special attention. It has been necessary to devise door systems based on design criteria quite foreign to normal building practice. Nevertheless, exhibition pavilions and sport centers with high volume entry and exit requirements have been popular applications.

Similar deviations from normal construction technology apply to lighting, acoustics, thermal insulation, foundation engineering, and stability under high wind conditions. Some of these aspects of air-building technology are discussed below, while anchorage considerations are treated in some depth in Section A-8.

A-4.1 Basic Shapes

Fundamentally, single-skin air-supported buildings are most economically designed in the form of symmetrical shapes, such as domes and cylindrical shells. Internal pressure acting equally in all directions will naturally dictate the shape of the container. Therefore, if stresses in any direction are to be similar in magnitude throughout the container, a symmetrical shape will automatically evolve. In the case of double-skin air-buildings, where the building environment is normally not pressurized, the stability required of the interconnected inflated panels will often also demand a symmetrical layout. A departure from the symmetrical solution may be achieved by using single cables or cable-networks. This is discussed in more detail in Sections A-4.3 and A-5.

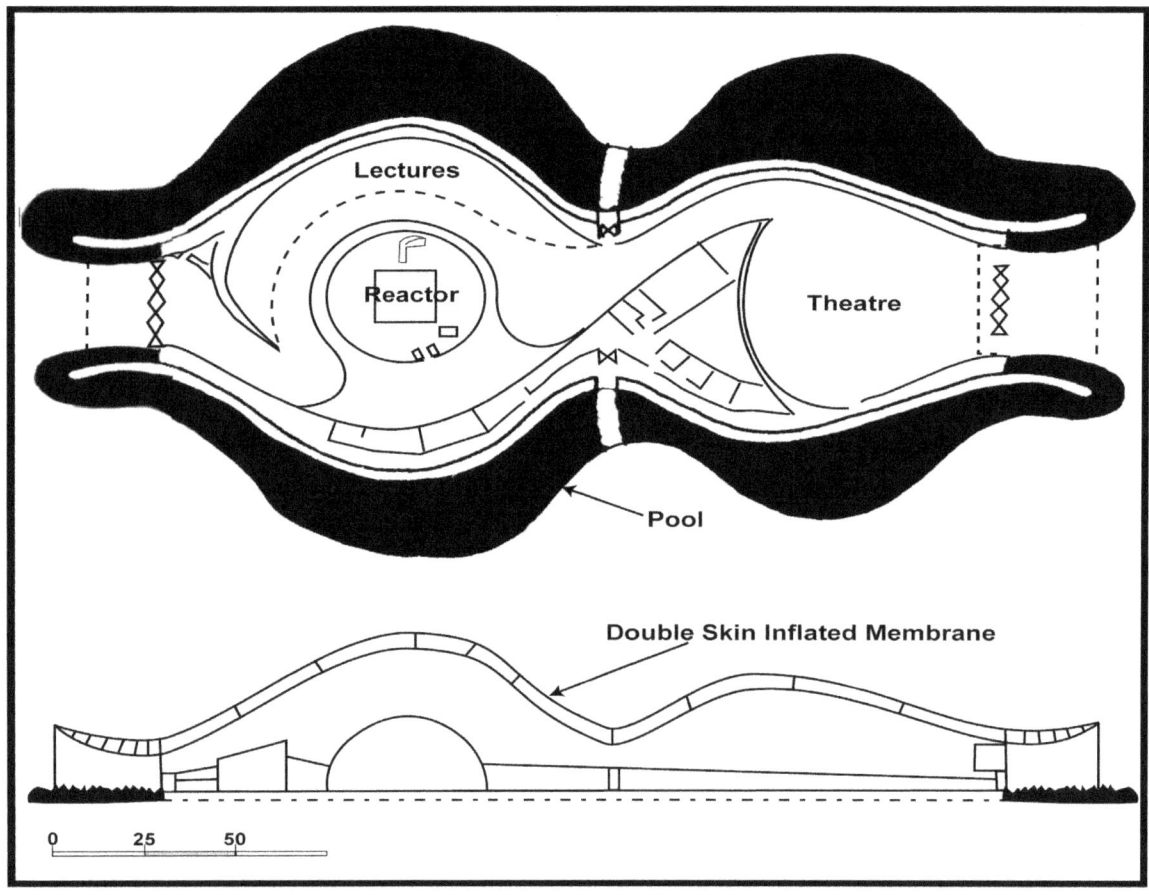

Figure A-10: Double-skin air-building for the U.S. Atomic Energy Commission

A departure from the normal shape of air-buildings was proposed by architect Victor Lundy in 1960, when he designed and executed an exhibition building for the U.S. Atomic Energy Commission (Allison 1960). He enclosed a space of about 20,000 square feet, comprising a theater and a technical center that included a working nuclear reactor, within a double-skin inflated membrane shaped similar to an hour-glass (Figure A-10). The structure basically consisted of two skins of vinyl-coated nylon, separated by a 4 feet wide air space. Independent pressure sources were provided for each. The inner skin was pressurized to 0.07 pounds per square inch and the outer skin to 0.054 pounds per square inch (i.e., approximately 2 inches and 1.5 inches water gauge, respectively).

Manufactured by Birdair with Severud in the role of consulting engineer, Lundy's design was a hybrid structural solution that combined an air-inflated double-skin external envelope with the internal air pressure of a normal single-skin air-supported structure. The latter was provided to resist wind speeds of up to 90 miles per hour. In fact, it is claimed that the building withstood winds of over 125 miles per hour during a storm in Santiago, Chile (Dent 1971, 42). The four-foot wide space between the inner and outer skins was divided into eight compartments so that if either skin should rupture, this damage would remain localized and not affect the overall stability of the building. It typically took less than three to four days for the building to be erected by a team of 12 laborers under expert supervision[3].

For high pressure tubular frames the symmetrical shape may not necessarily result in the most efficient solution. This class of air-buildings has characteristics very similar to those normally encountered in three-dimensional *space frame* structures. One of the drawbacks of such structures has always been the need to join multiple members at each node. Several proprietary solutions have been devised and patented in the past, adding to the cost of space frames. However, apart from their ability to span over large areas without intermediate vertical supports, these structures also have an inherent structural advantage. Due to the interconnection of members, concentrated loads acting upon a certain part of a space frame are carried not only by the directly loaded member, but also by other members that may be situated remotely from the point of application of the load (Makowski 1967, 5-8).

The duplication of these and similar space frame systems by means of pneumatic construction was apparently never seriously explored. Whether or not practical solutions can be found will depend largely on two factors. First, there is the fabrication issue. Is it possible to devise a low cost method of joining multiple flexible membrane tubes at a node and produce a joint that will perform reliably under fairly high internal pressure? The required seams at each node will be intricate. Second, even if the fabrication problem can be solved, will the pressurized tubular members be able to transmit their stiffness through the node joint to other members? In other words, can a pressurized node joining multiple pressurized tubular members serve to translate the rigidity of the individual members into a stable structural framework?

There are essentially two alternative design approaches for such a high pressure tubular frame. Each member could be treated as a pressurized tube that is sealed at both ends, or the framework could be inflated as a whole with the continuous passage of air through each node to the structural members that are joined at the node. Apart from the structural implications that are currently unknown and therefore subject to speculation only, there are serious constructional implications. If each member is a self-contained pressurized unit then the joint at the node is greatly simplified, however, the pressurization of the entire frame would be a tedious and time consuming undertaking requiring each member to be pressurized separately. If the pressurized air is continuous throughout the entire structure then the frame can be easily inflated, but the joints at each node will be difficult to fabricate and the entire structure can fail if only one of its members ruptures.

---

[3] For transportation purposes the total weight of the building (including fans) was held to about 30 tons (66,000 pounds) and packed into a volume of a little less than 5,500 cubic feet. (For comparison the volume of a standard 8 feet by 8 feet by 20 feet MILVAN shipping container is 1,280 cubic feet. Therefore, the equivalent of five standard MILVAN containers would have been required to transport the dissembled building from one location to another.

A-4.2 Access and Exit Facilities

In the case of single-skin air-supported construction, where the entire building environment is pressurized, special entry facilities are required. The systems that have been used to date generally fall into one of the following three categories:

1. Airlocks in the form of a double-door tunnel system of sufficient size to comfortably accommodate a semi-trailer truck. These do not necessarily require separate air-blower equipment or ducts.

2. Partially leak proof revolving doors (Figure A-11, lower left side) have in the past been favored for exhibition pavilions and convention halls, where pedestrian movement is a major design criterion.

3. Double swinging-type forklift truck doors are often standard items incorporated in air-supported warehouses (Figure A-11, lower right side).

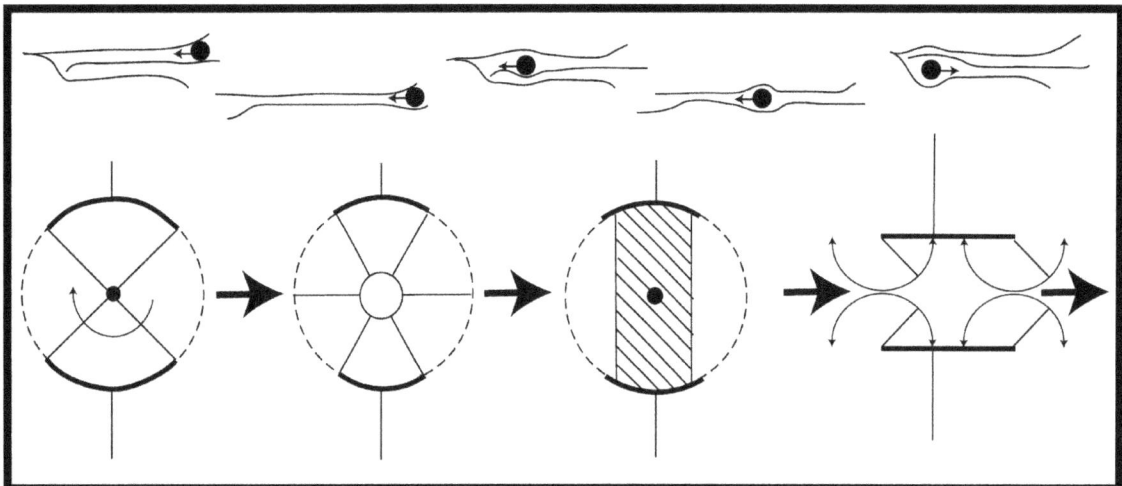

Figure A-11: Common entry-exit systems for single-skin air-supported buildings

Some manufacturers of air-supported buildings advised their customers that in the case of exhibition pavilions, where the continuous and uninhibited movement of pedestrians is essential, moderately sized openings could be left open for extended periods. Fundamentally, it is simply a matter of balancing total air leakage with air-input. Since the internal operating pressure of these air-supported buildings is normally very low (i.e., 0.02 to 0.08 pounds per square inch) the additional expense is more of an energy utilization rather than a capital equipment cost burden.

For relatively small air-buildings, or in the case of infrequently used personal entrances, a satisfactory and quite ingenious means of access may be provided by the *lap-pocket* system depicted as the upper sequence of diagrams in Figure A-11. Two or three membrane layers are lapped so that the interior layer is pressed against the exterior membrane by virtue of the slightly higher internal air-pressure.

A-4.3 Physical Dimensions and Stresses

Apart from the functional requirements of the occupancy the overall dimensions of single-skin air-supported membrane buildings are governed by two structural considerations, namely: the tensile strength of the membrane material; and, the propensity for local instability of the membrane (i.e., flutter) due to dynamic wind loads. The tensile stresses induced in the membrane material by the internal air pressure are a direct function of the radius of curvature of the membrane. Thus for this type of air-building span is limited largely by material strength in tension. As shown in Figure A-12, the spherical membrane stress (f_s pounds per inch) in the case of a dome is equal to half of the product of the internal pressure (P_i pounds per square inch above atmospheric pressure) and the radius of curvature (R_{cv} inches), and this applies equally to the quarter spherical ends of a cylindrical air-building. However, the circumferential stress (f_c pounds per inch) in the half-cylinder section of a cylindrical air-building is equal to twice the longitudinal (f_l) or spherical stress (f_s), namely the product of the internal pressure and the radius of curvature.

Figure A-12: Membrane stresses in air-supported buildings

$$f_s = f_l = [\,P_i \;\; x \;\; R_{cv}\,] / 2 \;\; \textbf{pounds/inch} \; \ldots\ldots\ldots\ldots\ldots\ldots \; \textbf{A-1}$$

$$f_c = [\,P_i \;\; x \;\; R_{cv}\,] \;\; \textbf{pounds/inch} \; \ldots\ldots\ldots\ldots\ldots\ldots \; \textbf{A-2}$$

Alternatively, the corresponding membrane stresses in *pounds per square inch* (i.e., *psi*) are obtained by dividing equations A-1 and A-2 by the thickness (t inches) of the membrane material.

$$f_s = f_l = [\,P_i \;\; x \;\; R_{cv}\,] / (2\,t) \;\; \textbf{psi} \; \ldots\ldots\ldots\ldots\ldots\ldots \; \textbf{A-3}$$

$$f_c = [\,P_i \;\; x \;\; R_{cv}\,] / t \;\; \textbf{psi} \; \ldots\ldots\ldots\ldots\ldots\ldots \; \textbf{A-4}$$

If we assume an internal pressure of 0.08 psi (i.e., equivalent to about 2¼ inches water gauge) then membrane stresses for spans[4] of 100 ft, 250 ft, 500 ft, 750 ft, and 1000 ft will be as follows:

Span/Diameter	**Radius (R_{cv})**	**Pressure (P_i)**	**Stress (f_s or f_l)**	**Stress (f_c)**
100 ft	50 ft	0.08 psi	2 lb/in	4 lb/in
250 ft	125 ft	0.08 psi	5 lb/in	10 lb/in
500 ft	250 ft	0.08 psi	10 lb/in	20 lb/in
750 ft	375 ft	0.08 psi	15 lb/in	30 lb/in
1000 ft	500 ft	0.08 psi	20 lb/in	40 lb/in

[4] Span in these examples refers to the diameter of a cylindrical single-skin air-supported building with quarter spherical ends. It should be noted that the internal pressure remains the same regardless of span.

In view of the somewhat limited tensile strength of available membrane materials and to increase the stability of single-skin air-supported buildings under wind loads it is often advisable to utilize some form of cable-network to reinforce buildings of larger spans (i.e., in excess of 200 ft.). External cables are also useful for counteracting the local instability that can occur in sections of the membrane due to dynamically fluctuating wind loads, referred to as *flutter*. In this case the membrane is provided with a positive reaction, while the loading on the cable-network is opposite to gravity. Since the shape is *anticlastic*[5] it will be self-damping and this will tend to eliminate flutter (Figure A-13 (left side)).

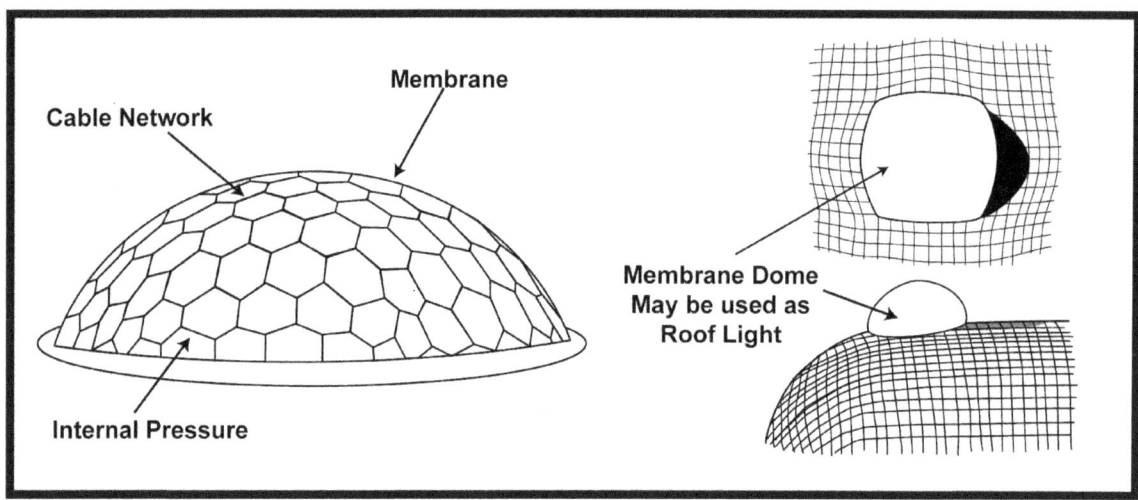

Figure A-13: Air-supported membrane restrained by an external cable-network

However, the implementation of cable-networks as a means of stabilizing single-skin air-buildings is subject to an economic penalty since the increased air pressure required to prestress the cables will negate some of the benefits derived from increased local stability. In the case of double-skin systems, where stability is derived from the stiffness of a cellular wall, very large spans (i.e., exceeding 200 feet) tend to become uneconomical and structurally untenable, while medium spans (i.e., 50 to 150 feet) are achieved at the expense of proportionally larger panel thicknesses. For example, in the case of Victor Lundy's U.S. Atomic Energy Commission exhibition pavilion (Figure A-10) a panel thickness of 4 feet was required for a span of approximately 100 feet.

Little research has been carried out in regard to the economical dimensions of pneumatic systems employing tubular frameworks. The author's own investigations in this field have been confined to a cursory empirical study of closed, flexible, plastic tubes under internal pressure. Thirty tubes with height to diameter ratios of 14, 18 and 24 were tested as simply hinged columns pressurized internally to 4 psig and 6 psig, respectively. A summary of results obtained is expressed graphically in Figure A-14.

Under low internal pressure conditions (i.e., less than 1 psig) the failure mechanism was found to be local buckling near the point of application of the load, while under conditions of medium pressure (i.e., 4 and 6 psig) the columns tended to fail due to overall buckling (Figure A-15, column on right side). The graphs shown in Figure A-14 compare the experimental results

---

[5] Anticlastic refers to a double-curvature shape in which the two dominant curves at any point run in opposite directions to each other (e.g., hyperbolic paraboloid).

(bottom graph) with the theoretical calculations of the product of the *area* and the *internal pressure* (middle graph) and the load predicted by the Euler formula on the assumption that the membrane is rigid and not flexible (upper graph). For example, for a column diameter of 1 inch and internal pressure of 6 psig the maximum load recorded during the experiment was 1.5 pounds, while the product of the *cross-sectional area* and *internal pressure* is approximately 4.5 pounds and the predicted Euler load (assuming a rigid membrane is approximately 15.5 pounds (i.e., a ratio of 1:3:10). It is interesting to note that while none of the graphs are linear the shapes of the curves, in particular the shapes of the curves representing the experimental results and the theoretical *cross-sectional area* and *internal pressure* calculation, are quite similar.

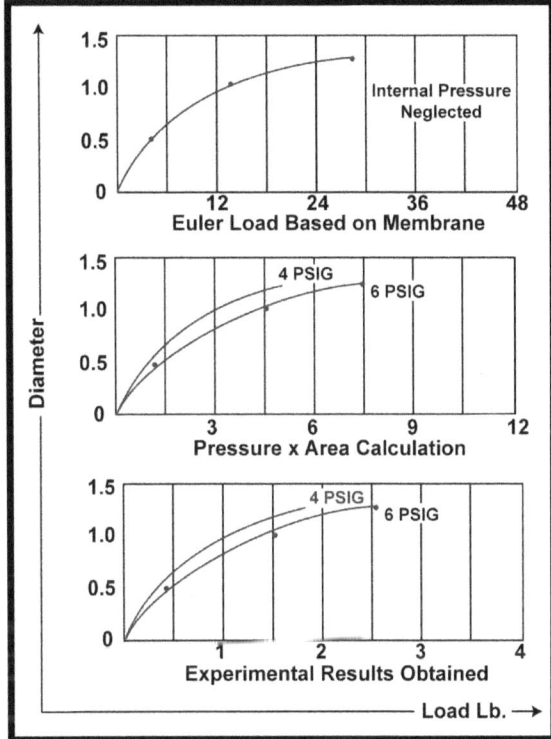
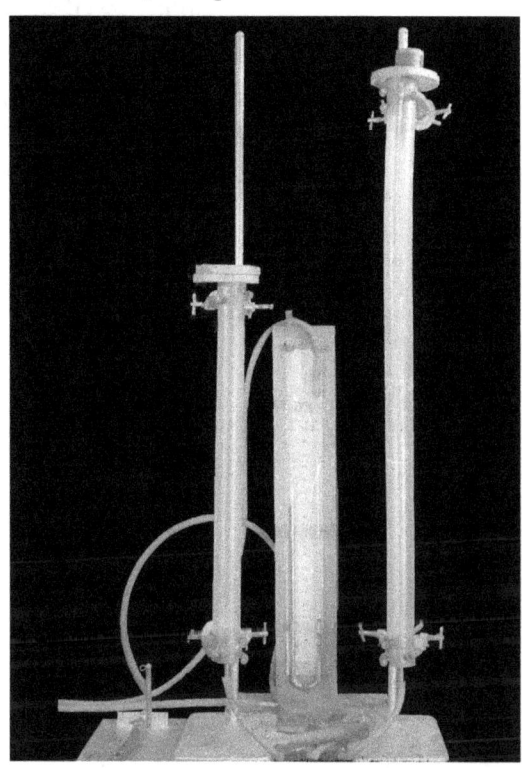

Figure A-14: Experimental results of flexible membrane columns under internal pressure and maximum axial load.

Figure A-15: Simple apparatus for testing the load-bearing capacity of pressurized flexible membrane columns.

Additional experiments with column clusters presented some interesting results. The author compared the load-bearing capacity of a cluster of three columns tied together top and bottom only with a single column of identical height and diameter (i.e., height to diameter ratio of 24). While one would not have predicted a strict relationship between the number of columns tied together and the load capacity of a single column of identical dimensions, the actual results obtained favored the column cluster more than expected, as shown in Table A-4.

Table A-4: Comparison of single column and cluster of 3 columns

Test Column Type	Height	Diameter	Load at 6 psig	Ratio
Single column	12 inches	½ inch	0.4 pounds	1.0
Cluster of 3 columns	12 inches	(each) ½ inch	1.8 pounds	4.8

In summary the experimental results seem to suggest that slender, flexible, plastic columns closed at both ends and subjected to internal pressure display properties that are partly related to the Euler theory and partly to the theoretically obtained product of the *internal pressure* and the *cross-sectional column area*. Although certainly inconclusive for extrapolation purposes, a relationship of 1:3:10 was observed for the limited number of tests conducted.

i.e.,   experimental results $= (P \times A) / 3 = (\pi^2 \times E \times I) / (10 \times H^2)$

where: P =   internal pressure (psig)
         A =   cross-sectional area of column (sqin)
         E =   modulus of elasticity of membrane material (psi)
         I =   moment of inertia (i.e., second moment of area)
         H =   height of the column (in)

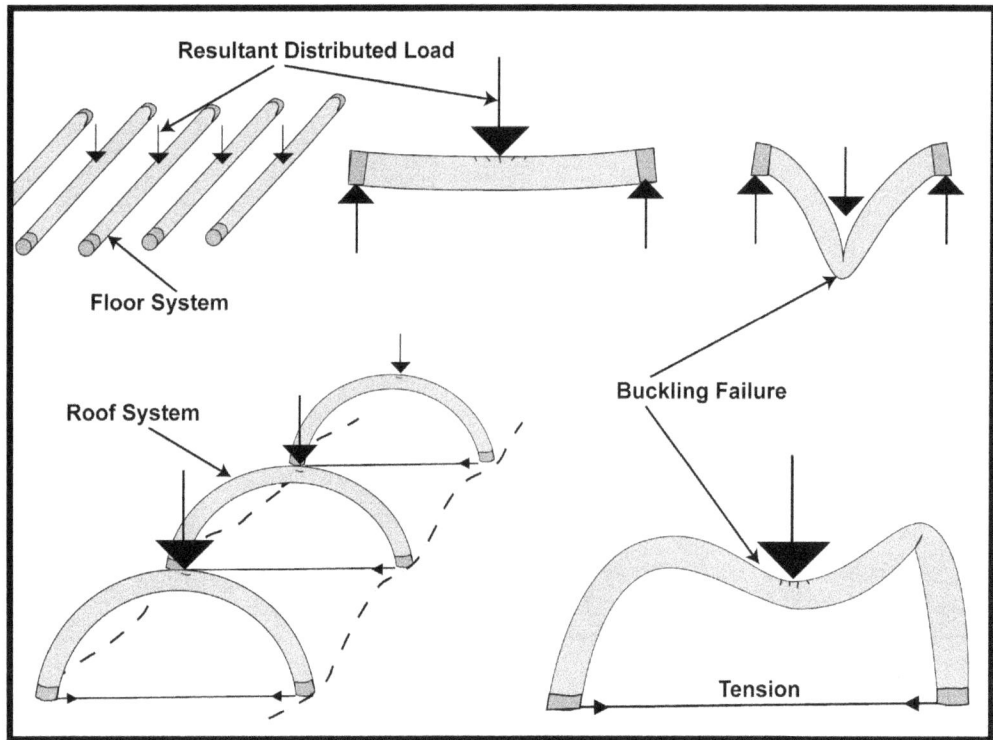

Figure A-16: Air-inflated tubular beam and arch systems

In whichever form air-inflated tubular systems (Figure A-16) are applied they suffer from the basic disadvantage of buckling failure. This failure mechanism has been confirmed experimentally for single beams, arches and column clusters. It is apparent that the air-inflated tubular system is neither a true tension structure nor a minimal structure and does not appear to present the same advantages that make the single and double-skin air-supported buildings an attractive proposition.

A-4.4 Lighting, Thermal Insulation, and Ventilation

In his lecture on *span* to the Manchester Association of Engineers, Lanchester commented that the concept of an inflated roof structure had met with certain objections (Lanchester 1938). He explained that each of these objections denoted some definite problem and spoke briefly on the questions of ventilation, lighting and fire protection. It is of interest to briefly reiterate his thoughts as a starting point in this discussion.

Ventilation: Lanchester calculated the pressure within his proposed air-building to be 2.75 in water gauge (i.e., 0.1 psig), supplied by blowers or wind cowlings. He suggested that the only regular provision for air ventilation be by percolation through the canvas envelope, regulated by the nature of the weave of the material.

Daylighting: In view of the limitations of membrane materials available at that time, Lanchester admitted that daylight solely derived from the limited translucency of the material would be unsatisfactory. He therefore suggested the incorporation of a central skylight of up to 100 feet in diameter, supported by a suspension system similar to a gigantic wire wheel, so that its weight could be distributed throughout the dome and thus remain below 10 pounds per square foot. Supplementary to this, he envisaged a number of circular glass panels in the canvas envelope, to provide adequate lighting in the peripheral regions.

Fire protection: On the question of fire protection and mass egress Lanchester was able to point out some of the inherent advantages of the air-supported roof. He suggested that the canvas may be treated as being non-combustible. Therefore, during a fire there would be no tendency for the roof to cave in, since it would be sustained by the heated air alone (i.e., like a hot-air balloon). In regards to emergency exits he proposed the provision of airlocks into which people could crowd, before escaping en mass.

Due to the development of superior quality plastic membrane materials after World War II the lighting of air-buildings was able to be achieved without resorting to the extravagance of a large central skylight proposed by Lanchester in 1938.

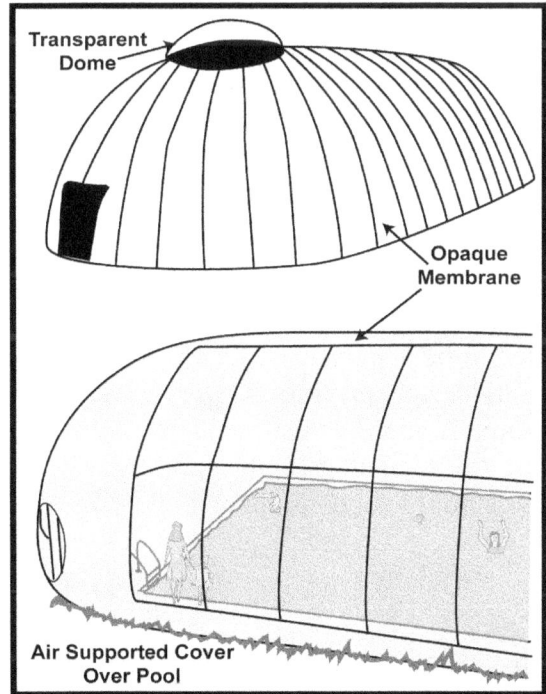 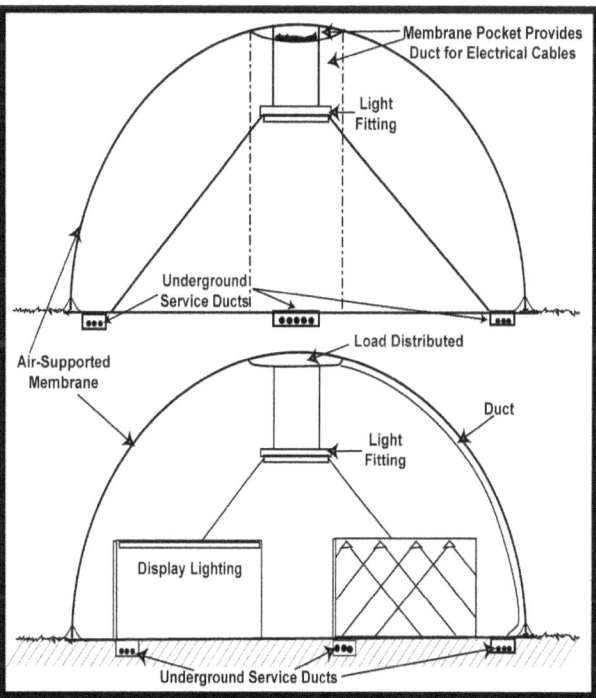

Figure A-17: Daylighting options   Figure A-18: Artificial lighting options

While daylight may be provided by using transparent or translucent membrane sections (Figure A-17), the problem of heat transmission both into the building due to direct solar radiation and out of the building due to inadequate thermal insulation remains a concern that will be discussed later in this section. Such daylight transmitting panels, serving as fixed windows, can be placed in optimum positions within an otherwise opaque membrane. However, to avoid stress concentrations the number of seams should be kept to a minimum and as far as possible the same membrane material should be used throughout the one air-building. In this respect an argument can be made to rely on artificial lighting in conjunction with the use of a cellular membrane material to improve the thermal insulation of the building envelope. Artificial light fittings may be suspended from the membrane, as long as their weight is distributed, or attached to free-standing space dividers (Figure A-18).

The problem of heat insulation, on the other hand, cannot be resolved quite as easily. Simple membranes of the type normally used in single-skin air-supported buildings will afford little heat insulation. During the heyday of air-buildings in the 1960s and 1970s there was some interest in exploring the use of cellular membrane materials (Oberdick 1965). The challenge was to produce a material with good thermal insulation and structural properties. Factors influencing the structural characteristics of candidate materials were investigated through scale models representing minimum surfaces. It was concluded that it might be feasible to use cellular plastics as a structural membrane. However, with the fairly sudden demise of the air-building market from the late 1970s onward there remained little incentive for further investigation of this promising solution. If the interest in air-buildings had continued it is likely that a plastic membrane material with balanced structural and thermal properties would have been developed and mass-produced at a reasonable cost.

Lanchester's suggestion to control the ventilation rate in air-buildings by regulating the natural percolation through the membrane by virtue of the mesh size of the weave, although a novel approach, is nevertheless impractical for a number of reasons. First, it would be very difficult to predict with any accuracy the percolation rate of a whole structure, in the light of material irregularities, wind suction and pressure, dust settlement, and so on. Second, with the invention of plastics very few, if any, air-buildings were ever constructed with canvass membranes. The plastic membranes were essentially airtight. Finally, the whole issue of ventilation became a mute point because the ventilation rate could be so easily controlled by simply providing one or more very small openings in the membrane.

The total volume of single-skin air-supported buildings is proportionally much larger than in orthodox unpressurized buildings. Therefore, since the air volume available to each occupant is quite large, ventilation rates are not normally considered to be a significant factor. It is assumed that the unavoidable air-losses due to leakages through airlocks, membrane and anchorage provide more than the required number of air-changes per hour. A more scientific approach may be followed by calculating or measuring the air-input at the blower assembly and providing a manometer operated safety-valve, so that the internal pressure is kept constant at all times.

A-4.5 Wind Loads

The action of wind on a building is one of the most complex problems that arise in civil engineering. Wind forces depend not only on the prevailing winds, freak storms, and the site topography, but also on the specific shape and size of the building itself. The overall wind effect on a building is not the sum of the wind effects of each of the component parts taken separately. The parts will interact and the total effect is mainly a question of air flow around the obstacle presented by the structure. The pattern of the flow and all the resulting effects will thus depend primarily on the shape of the building and any specific details in the outline of this shape. The distribution of high and low pressures over a free-standing and air-tight sphere follows the pattern shown in Figure A-19 (Blanjean 1961).

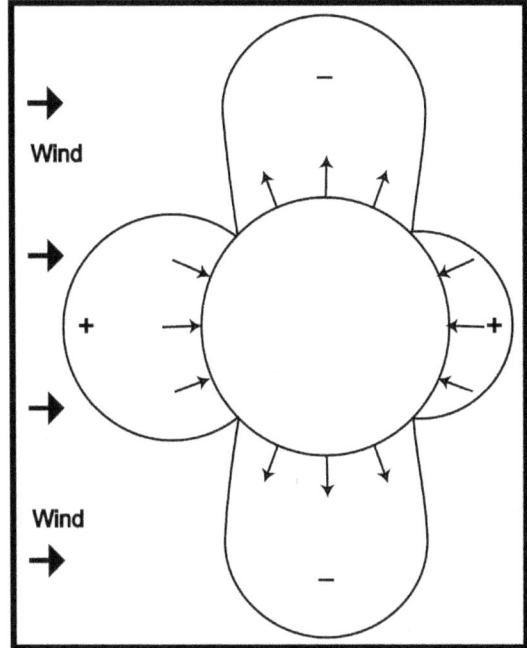

Figure A-19: Positive and negative pressure distribution for wind acting on a sphere

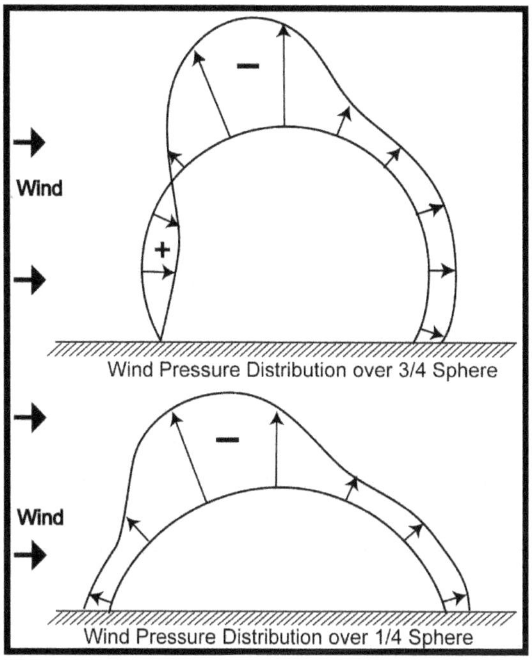

Figure A-20: Positive and negative pressure distributions for partial spheres

Wind pressure acting on a three-quarter sphere will experience a small positive pressure region on the windward side (Figure A-20 upper diagram). When there is insufficient internal pressure a single-skin air-supported building will be indented at this point[6]. All other regions of the three-quarter sphere will experience suction. In the case of a shallow dome (Figure A-19 lower diagram) we are generally concerned with suction only. The low profile air-building is a more favorable shape in respect to wind forces, however, at the expense of increased material stress due to the increased radius of curvature[7].

Although the aerodynamic properties of spheres have been studied by a number of researchers in considerable detail, much less is known regarding domes and spherical sections generally. This is particularly true for large structures. Wind tunnel experiments are convenient but not always a satisfactory basis for structural design. Similarly, little is known of the microscopic structure of naturally occurring wind. The latter may rapidly change, both in strength and direction without any apparent harmony. It is for this reason that the designer is forced to treat wind forces as dynamic loads of non-symmetrical character.

---

[6] However, this external wind pressure load will be at least partially counteracted by the formation of dynamic pressure due to the slight reduction in volume of the air-building.

[7] In reference to equations A-1 and A-3 (see Section 4.3) the membrane stress due to internal pressure is directly proportional to the radius of curvature of the membrane.

The action of wind forces on single-skin, air-supported buildings will influence basic design considerations in regard to at least two aspects:

1. Temporary instability of the structure as a whole due to wind gusts. In this case a tension net may be superimposed on the membrane. Since the final shape is *anticlastic* it will be self-damping and *flutter* will be less likely to occur (Gero 1967).

2. Calculation of the required anchorage forces in relation to the vertical pressure component and wind suction.

Both of these aspects will be discussed in more detail in subsequent sections (see Sections 5 and 8, respectively).

A-5 Tension Cables and Nets

One of the major problems associated with the design and construction of suspension structures has been the costly procedure of fabricating the waterproof covering material. While joints must be waterproof, they must also allow sufficient movement to accommodate loading and temperature deflections. In combining pressurized, continuous membranes with external cables or nets it may be possible to achieve a more efficient structure, in which each of the two component parts compensates for a particular weakness of the other (Figure A-21).

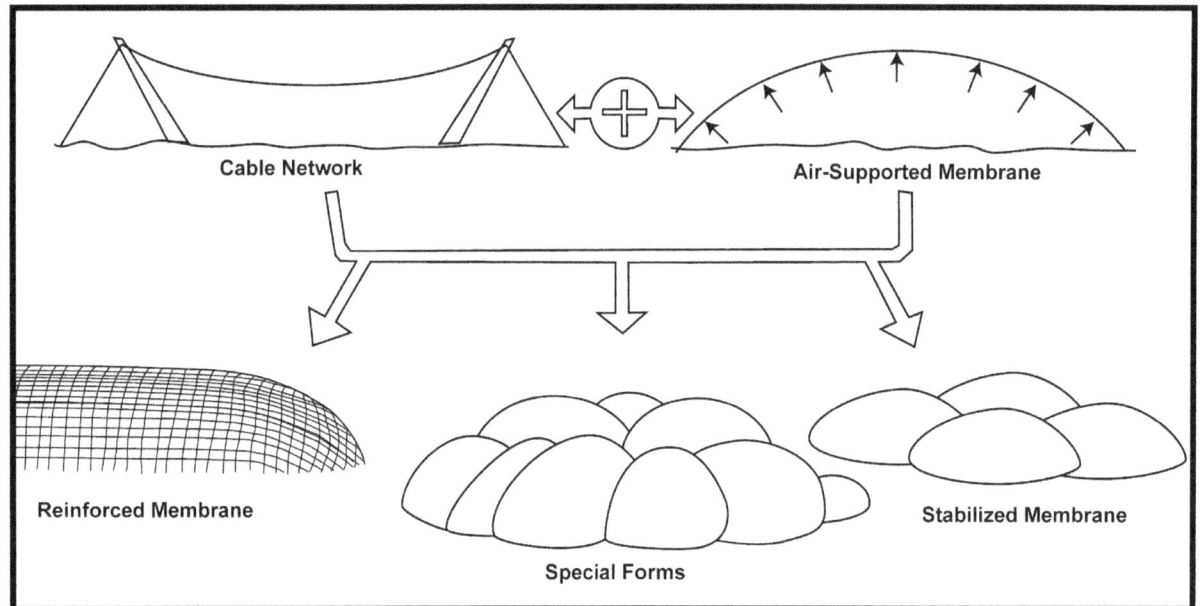

Figure A-21: Functions of networks and cables in combination with air-supported structures

The largest single-skin air-supported buildings that have been constructed to date are probably the 200 feet diameter wheat stores, marketed by the Schjeldahl Company in Norway. An approximate calculation of relevant membrane stresses will indicate that the required membrane strength in tension for these stores would need to be in the vicinity of 300 pounds per inch-wide strip of membrane material. If a plastic-coated fabric with natural synthetic or mineral fibers were to be used it would be difficult to achieve a tensile strength of more than 400 pounds per inch, with one layer of fabric. With an acceptable safety factor, such a membrane material would be satisfactory for domes up to about 300 feet diameter.

Material strength is even more critical when we consider air-supported mega-structures for entire communities, as proposed by Buckminster Fuller in 1962 (Figure A-22 (left)). Assuming a dome with a shallow profile spanning one mile with a radius of curvature (R_{cv}) of two miles (i.e., 10,560 feet) the material stress (f_s) under an internal pressure (P_i) of 0.04 psig (i.e., 1.14 inch water gauge) can be calculated by application of equation A-1:

$$f_s = [P_i \ \times \ R_{cv}] / 2 \ \text{pounds/inch} \quad \ldots\ldots\ldots\ldots\ldots\ldots \quad \text{A-1}$$

material stress = [0.04 x 10560 x 12] / 2

material stress = <u>2534.4 pounds/inch</u>

For very large structures it is therefore absolutely necessary to employ external cables. Since the membrane material due to its much lower modulus of elasticity will bulge out between the steel cables most of the material stress will be resisted by the cables. For example, with a cable spacing of 100 feet the effective radius of curvature of the membrane in the above mega-structure could be reduced to about 400 feet. By application of equation A-1 the corresponding stress in the membrane would then become:

$$f_s = [P_i \ \times \ R_{cv}] / 2 \ \text{pounds/inch} \quad \ldots\ldots\ldots\ldots\ldots\ldots \quad \text{A-1}$$

material stress = [0.04 x 400 x 12] / 2

material stress = <u>96 pounds/inch</u>

However, at a spacing of 100 feet the stress in 1½ inch diameter steel cables would still be over 600,000 pounds per square inch. Even without allowing for a factor of safety a stress of that magnitude is well above the design strength in tension of high tensile steel.

Figure A-22: Mega-structures proposed by Buckminster Fuller (left) and Frei Otto (right)
[Source: Herzog (1976); 'Pneumatische Konstruktionen'; Verlag Gerd Hatje, Stuttgart, Germany (pp. 107 and 115)]

A combination of tension net and membrane is particularly efficient when the mesh-size is reasonably constant and the radius of curvature of the resulting membrane sections is similar (Figure A-23). It can be seen in Figure A-23 that a dome or cylindrical shell with spherical ends is easily contained within a network of suitable mesh-size. Networks that are composed of square mesh configurations are unsuitable due to very marked differences in mesh-size when wrapped around a double curvature form (Figure A-24).

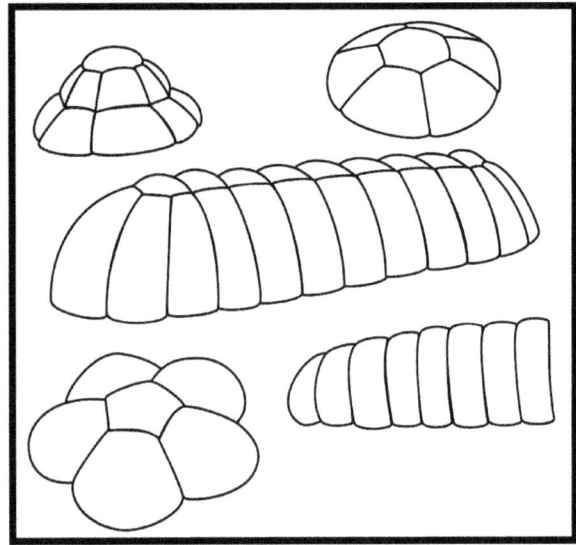
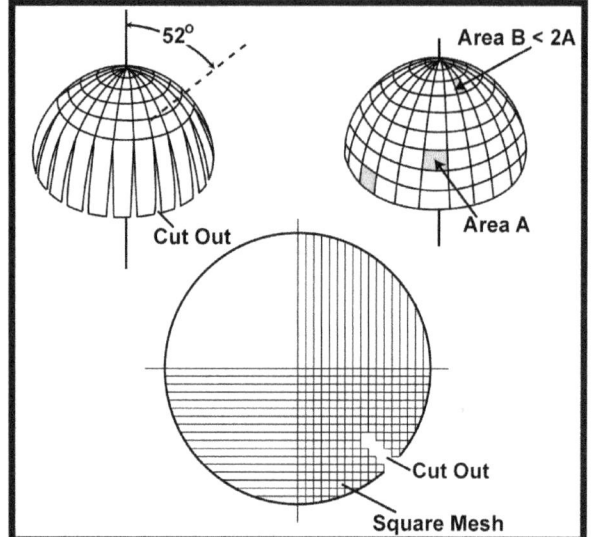

Figure A-23: Typical cable configurations   Figure A-24: Network difficulties in domes

For example, a square mesh network placed over a dome will lead to skew sectional areas at four points. However, this fault may be partly eliminated with specially cut nets as shown in Figure A-24. A section through a typical membrane with tension-net stabilization shows that cables between nodes are almost straight lines while the radius of curvature of the membrane is only slightly increased between the cable boundaries. Thus water pools will not develop since the surface of the dome will be sloping sufficiently for the natural drainage of rainwater to occur.

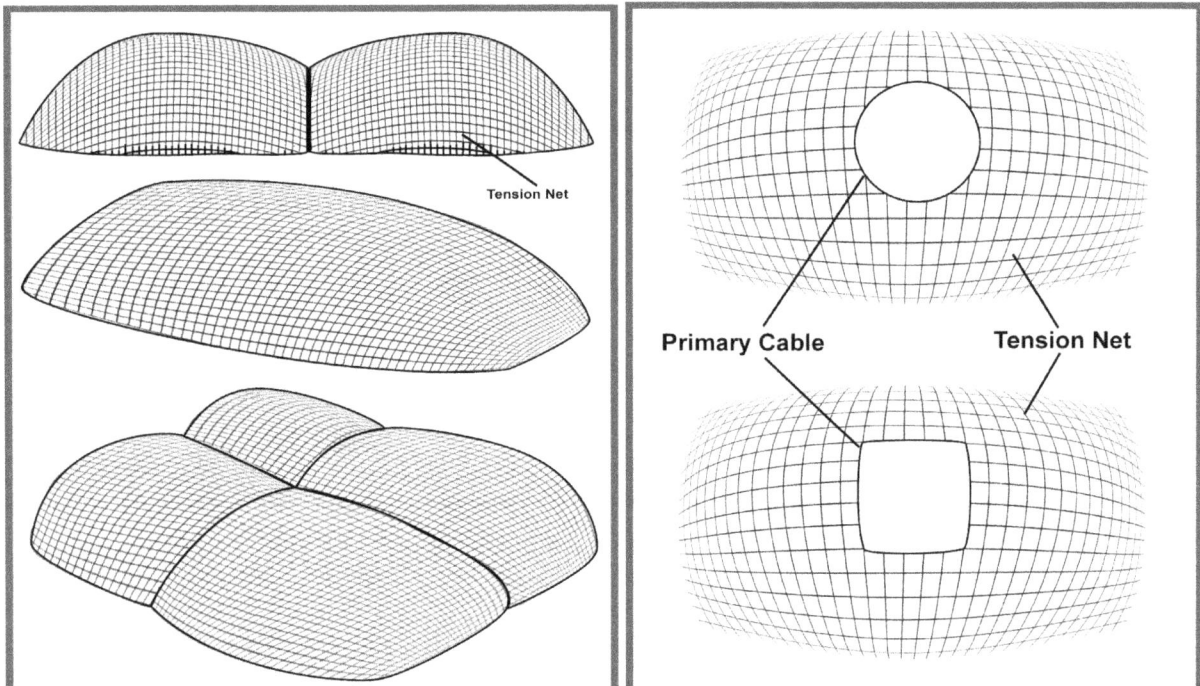

Figure A-25: Network on rectangular plan   Figure A-26: Effect of network openings

The wide variety of forms over any particular plan that can be created when air-supported membranes are combined with tension nets or primary cables was comprehensively explored by

Frei Otto and his group of student researchers at the University of Stuttgart (Germany) during the 1950s and 1960s (Otto and Trostel 1962). The combination of an air-supported membrane and an external tension net on a rectangular plan will form a symmetrical cushion as shown in Figure A-25. If we tie a single primary cable across the cushion at the centre, we obtain a form that approximates a minimum surface and may be altered to correspond to different cable tensions. Similarly, we may study the behavior of membrane forms, when a hole is cut in the exterior tension net (Figure A-26). If the hole is a square then the opening will assume a relatively circular shape after the membrane has penetrated. However, if we form the opening by threading a primary cable through an octagon then the final shape will be circular and the resulting membrane shape a dome. Such secondary domes are particularly functional for providing daylight in large span structures when the main building membrane is opaque.

A-6 Soap Bubbles

The study of soap bubbles is of considerable help in understanding the fundamental characteristics of single-skin air-supported construction[8]. Neglecting the small stress concentrations due to self-weight of the film it is correct to assume that for every individual soap bubble the membrane stresses are equal in every direction at any point. The same holds for conglomerates of bubbles. Stress concentrations cannot occur, since they would be immediately eliminated by liquid flow. Similarly, if three or more bubbles of dissimilar membrane tensions combine, instantaneous stress equalization must take place.

Unfortunately, the dimensions of soap bubbles are limited and surface measurements with instruments are hardly possible since the bubbles tend to burst due to the physical contact required for such a procedure. Generally speaking, a photographic shape-analysis remains the most promising approach[9]. Of particular interest are soap bubble shapes that will naturally occur in non-gravitational space, where the basic membrane forms are not influenced by self-weight. Under normal gravitational conditions, despite the thinness of the film (i.e., between 0.000001 and 0.00005 inch according to Boys (1959)), the self-weight of the membrane will influence the shape of the bubble. A soap film contained within a horizontal wire loop, sags minutely at the center thereby clearly indicating that the film has weight.

Bubbles that are blown from heated glass are very stable, yet they seldom represent *minimum surfaces*[10]. This is due to the fact that it is almost impossible to maintain the same stresses throughout the glass membrane when these are a function of thickness, temperature and self-weight. The same criticism applies to bubbles blown from plastic solutions that are self-hardening, since minute deformations will occur during the setting process (Boys 1959). Various self-drying synthetic solutions were studied by General Electric (1960), Günschel (1960) and others in the late 1950s for the possible construction of mega-structures in regions where

---

[8] Bubbles blown from a soap solution containing a small amount of glycerin, and prepared in absolutely dust free conditions, will remain intact over a considerable period of time if they are stored in a hermetically sealed container (Otto and Trostel 1962). Additionally, there are a number of synthetic aqueous, froth producing solutions commercially available that are well suited to the preparation of bubbles (Boys 1959).

[9] It is however possible to insert pipes into bubbles, and this simple method has been used by the author to measure the internal pressure in floating bubbles of various sizes and combinations.

[10] A *minimum surface* has a minimum area within a given boundary and all stresses lie within the surface.

prevailing weather conditions are singularly unsuitable for efficient urbanization.

Soap bubbles naturally assume *minimum surfaces*. Moreover, any soap bubble shape may be reproduced as a pneumatic structure. We may magnify in strict geometric proportion any particular bubble form and reconstruct it using membrane materials. Assuming negligible self-weight, the large scale structure will experience proportional membrane stresses at every point under pressurized conditions. However, even though the membrane enclosure of an air-supported structure is very light, it does have some weight. Therefore, strictly speaking equation A-1 (see Section 4.3) for the design of air-supported buildings should be modified to take into account the weight of the membrane. This is typically neglected in practice because the analysis is considered too complex for the small adjustment to membrane stresses that would result. In any case, the factor of safety normally applied by air-building designers far exceeds the stress increase due to the self-weight of the membrane.

Identical twin-bubbles will be separated by a perfectly plane membrane partition indicating that the internal pressures of the two joined bubbles are the same. On the other hand, if bubbles of dissimilar radii combine then the membrane partition will be slightly curved in favor of the smaller bubble. Since the membrane stresses are identical, the internal pressure must be slightly higher for the smaller bubble. For all cases of compound soap bubbles we may establish the following relationship between internal pressure (P) and radius (R), since the membrane stress (F_s) must be constant throughout the conglomerate:

$$F_s = [P_1 \times R_1]/2 = [P_2 \times R_2]/2 = [P_3 \times R_3]/2$$

This series is normally not extended further since only three membrane partitions can join at one common edge. However, the fourth and fifth terms may be added in three-dimensional space (i.e., rather than floating on a water surface) with the addition of a bubble above and below the conglomerate (Figure A-26).

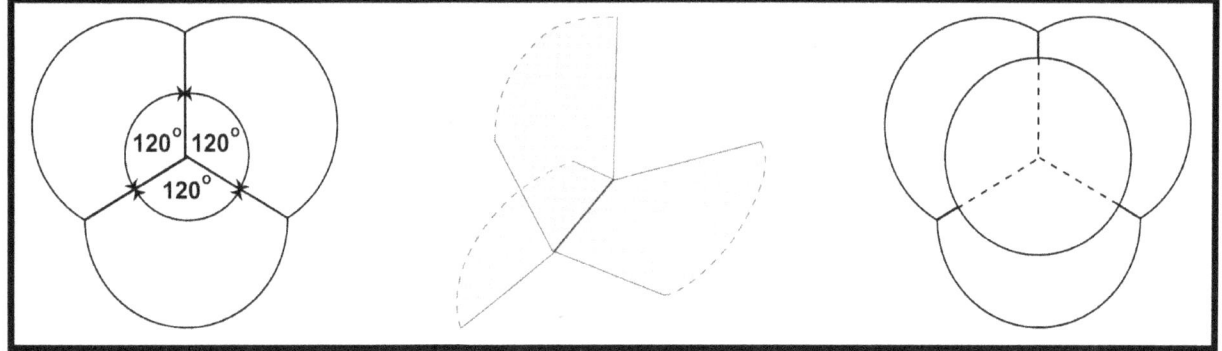

Figure A-27: A conglomerate of five bubbles in three-dimensional space

The simplest floating bubble is a dome, within which the water level is a little lower than the external level and slightly curved (Figure A-28). Since smaller bubbles with approximately the same membrane thickness will have a slightly higher internal pressure the curvature of the internal water level will be more pronounced. The extreme case is a very small floating air globule.

When a floating bubble is touched with a flat horizontal surface at the apex a cylindrical form will result. This confirms that under the action of internal pressure a cylinder is also a *minimum surface*. Even if we raise the horizontal surface by a few inches, we will preserve the basic cylindrical shape, until finally the cylinder separates into two separate dome-shaped bubbles. This experiment can be fairly easily repeated for two or three attached cylinders, where the common membrane partition is however curved in accordance to the pressure differences.

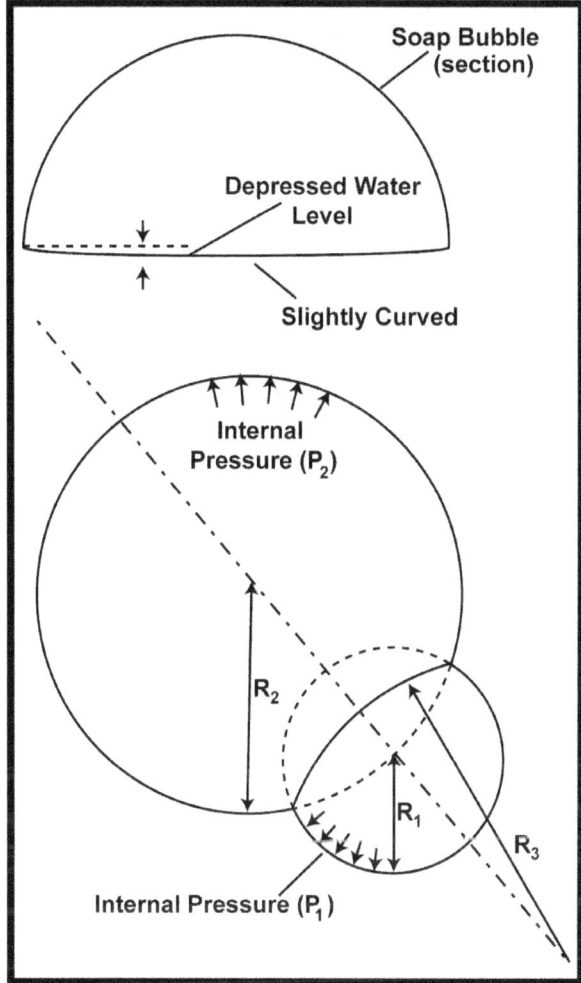

Figure A-28: Soap bubble characteristics - curved internal water level and curved partition between attached bubbles

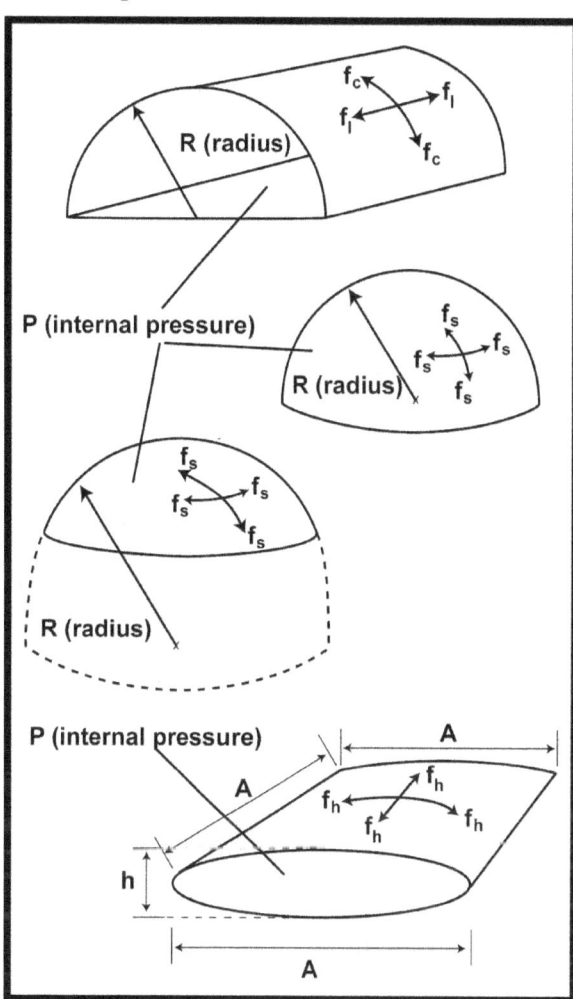

Figure A-29: Membrane stresses in air-supported cylindrical shell, sphere and cushion structures

A-7 Mathematical Analysis

In principle the structural design of single-skin, air-supported structures will require the separate solution of three primary conditions, namely:

1. Determination of the required internal air pressure under static working loads.
2. Calculation of the maximum membrane stress, which is largely determined by the overall dimensions of the structure.
3. Allowance for dynamic wind loads in relation to flutter and anchorage.

As a basic criterion it is normally assumed that in the pressurized condition all parts of the membrane must be under tension. This assumption eliminates the presence of folds, which would be accompanied by uneven material stresses and localized instabilities. If we further assume that the membrane is essentially undeformed and that the working loads will therefore act on an undeformed membrane shape, then we have the idealized condition that adheres to the Membrane Theory analysis procedure, which is commonly applied to the design of concrete shells. This theory assumes that no bending stresses exist in the shell and that therefore all the stresses in the membrane are statically determinate. To be able to apply this theory to curved structures the designer is forced to make the following assumptions that are often difficult to support in the case of concrete shells, but much more easily sustained in air-supported membrane structures.

- *The curvature of the membrane should be continuous:* The curvature of an air-supported membrane is continuous above ground and discontinuous at the footings.
- *The thickness of the membrane must be reasonably constant:* The thickness of the membrane material is constant throughout.
- *The membrane should be very thin in relation to its span:* The membrane is about one 50th of the thickness of a two-inch thick concrete shell.
- *The load should be distributed as uniformly as possible:* This assumption applies under normal operating conditions, but may be intermittently violated by both snow and wind loads.
- *The supports at the edge of the membrane should be designed to compensate for the lack of continuity at that point:* The air-supported membrane must be secured firmly to the footings to minimize air leakage.

In reference to Figure A-29, application of equations A-1 and A-2 (see Section 4.3) provides us with the following membrane stresses for the cylindrical shell and the two spheres:

$$f_s = f_l = [\,P\ \times\ R\,]\,/\,2 \quad \text{pounds/inch} \quad \ldots\ldots\ldots\ldots\ldots\ldots \text{A-1}$$

$$f_c = [\,P\ \times\ R\,] \quad \text{pounds/inch} \quad \ldots\ldots\ldots\ldots\ldots\ldots \text{A-2}$$

The spherical stress (f_s) in the membrane of a shallow sphere is of course much greater than in the membrane of the full hemisphere since the radius of curvature (R) is much larger. In the case of a cushion the membrane stress (f_h) equates to approximately:

$$\mathbf{f_h = [\,P\ \times\ h\,]} \quad \text{pounds/inch} \quad \ldots\ldots\ldots\ldots\ldots\ldots \text{A-5}$$

A-8 Anchorage Forces and Methods

The footings of orthodox buildings that are primarily subject to compression forces are designed to support the dead-load of the building and the live-load of its contents, by equating the size of the footing with the bearing capacity of the foundations. However, allowances must be made for the unstableness of the foundations (i.e., soil movement in the form of shrinkage, expansion, and settlement) resulting in shear and bending forces that must also be resisted by the footings.

Air-supported structures by virtue of internal pressure and their lightness require relatively simple footings capable of withstanding only direct tension (i.e., tension anchors). The additional requirement of containing the small internal air pressure at the junction between the ground and the membrane is easily accommodated by a wrap-around detail at the perimeter. The attendant reduction in construction cost are due to material savings, less excavations and a high potential for the efficient application of prefabricated components (e.g., metal anchors and pipes serving concurrently as an edge beam and air seal).

Apart from the internal pressure acting on the membrane, the suction forces generated by wind will add to the tensile forces that must be resisted by the perimeter anchorage. According to geographical region, microclimatic site conditions, and the height and shape of the building this suction force is normally assumed to vary between 8 and 24 pounds per square foot., but may increase to 40 pounds per square foot under extreme conditions. However, wind forces are not constant in magnitude nor direction and will thus impose dynamic loads on footings. Maximum speed values are immediately followed by minimum values, which may be less than 25% of the wind gust. These wide variations in wind velocity will result in larger loads being applied instantaneously, only to be completely dissolved within seconds. This suggests that the variations in perimeter loads that must be assumed for the anchorage of an air-supported structure are potentially much greater than those for compression footings.

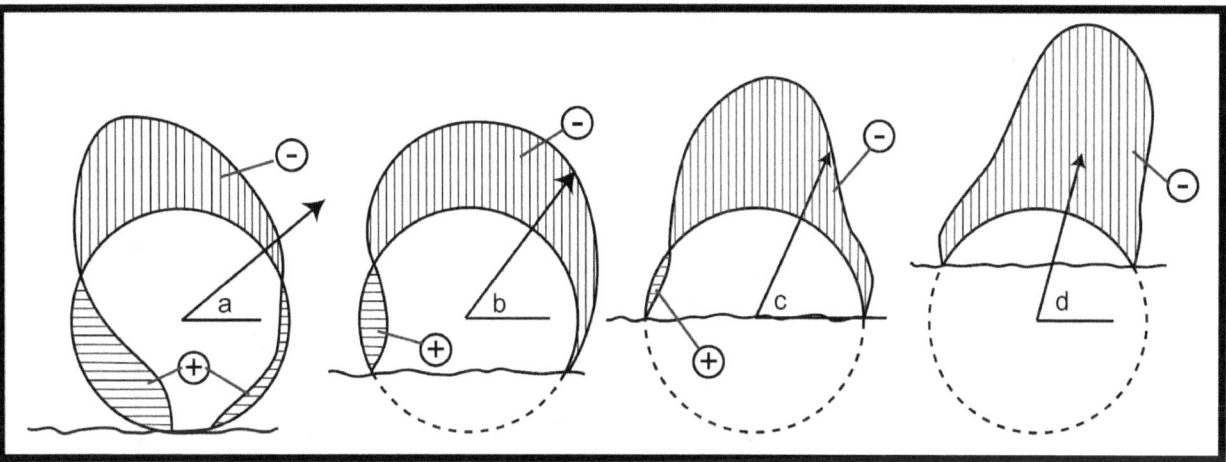

Figure A-30: Resultant wind suction forces as a function of air-building profile

In summary, the anchorage system of an air-supported building must be designed to perform two main functions:

- Transmit to the foundations all forces due to internal pressure and wind loading.
- Provide an effective air seal that can be maintained with minimum maintenance during the life-cycle of the building.

These functional requirements are met by a number of anchorage systems that can be broadly classified into four groups, namely: self-weight anchors; auger anchors; split anchors; and, pavement anchors.

Self-weight anchors: The simplest form of anchorage that satisfies both requirements is the provision of a perimeter tube as an integral part of the membrane, which is filled with sand, gravel or water (Figure A-31 (left)). The weight and friction of the filled tube must be at least as great as the anchorage forces that may arise. The necessary air-seal is obtained when the tube is sufficiently full so that it settles on the ground where small irregularities may be allowed for. A typical calculation will however demonstrate that this type of anchorage is only applicable to small air-supported buildings. In general an internal pressure of 0.04 psig or 6.25 pounds per square foot (i.e., 1.14 inch water gauge) is sufficient to stabilize an air-supported building subjected to a wind speed of up to 80 miles per hour (mph).

As a function of the radius of curvature (R ft) of the membrane, the following formula for estimating anchorage forces was proposed by a German engineer during the 1960s (Schultze 1964):

overall anchorage force = 0.44 R   pounds per foot A-6

Thus for a full profile 100 ft diameter air-building, allowing for a safety factor of 2, a perimeter anchorage load of 44 lb/ft run would be required. This equates to an 11½ in diameter tube filled with water or sand.

Alternatively, weights that rest on the ground are capable of supporting vertical tension loads of at least equal value (Figure A-31 (right)). A flexible connection between two anchor weights will allow for some structural movement. Such refinements, while costly in terms of components and labor, may be considered in cases where substantial thermal and/or moisture movement is expected.

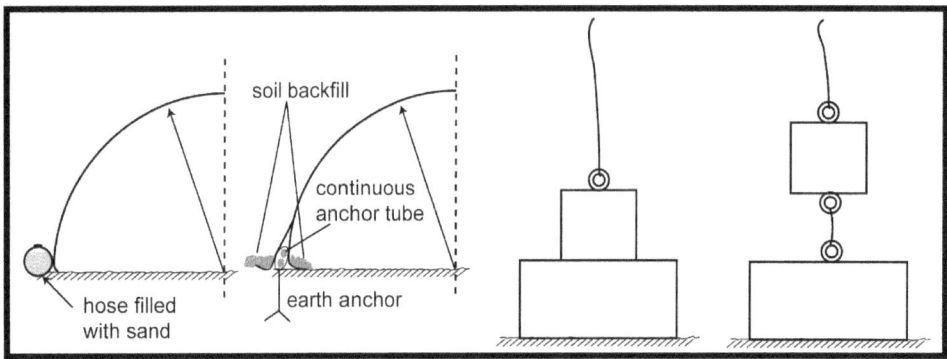

Figure A-31: Typical self-weight anchors

Auger anchors: The screw or auger anchor was originally used to drill holes in soft soil, in which case it would be retrieved after a few turns to allow waste soil to spill out. However, there is historical evidence that even during the 19th Century auger implements were employed as permanent ground anchors. This type of anchor is normally attached to a highly torsion-resistant handle and is screwed into the earth manually (Figure A-32 (left)). Generally, a horizontal lever arm is provided at the upper end of the handle to reduce the required operational power.

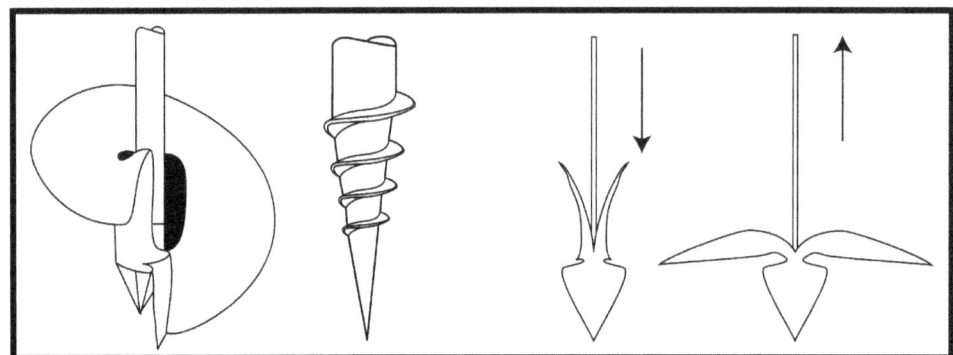

Figure A-32: Auger and split anchors

It is of interest to note that if a self-weight anchor rests on flat ground the allowable tension load may increase beyond the self-weight of the anchor. If the air-space between the weight and the foundation is minimized a further advantage may be derived from atmospheric pressure acting on the upper surface of the weight. The most efficient anchor in this respect is a relatively thin plate partially immersed in the top soil and attached to cables centrally (not at the ends), so that tilting is less likely to occur. Particularly, when a structure is acted upon by wind gusts of short duration, atmospheric equilibrium through the soil is less likely to occur.

Split anchors: These are designed according to the harpoon principle. While they are driven into the ground they are completely free of projections, yet automatically open up when jerked up after the final position has been reached (Figure A-32 (right)). The non-reversible thorns may be attached at the pointed end or at the side of the shaft, which is particularly effective when the surface area of the thorns is small.

Pavement anchors: Larger air-supported buildings are best anchored with concrete foundations. In this case special care must be taken to ensure that the anchorage force corresponding to the force system prevailing in the building membrane is transmitted uniformly to the footings. Anchorage by attachment to pre-laid strips of concrete in the form of paths or roadways is ideal if air-supported covers are considered at the design stage of an orthodox building as a means of protecting new construction work against inclement weather. In this case it is particularly useful to provide a cement path or service track on one or more sides of the building.

A-9 Ancillary Plant

Air at the required pressure is pushed into an air-supported building by way of air ducts from one or more blowers located external to the membrane (Figure A-33). The blower assembly is designed to produce an internal air-pressure of up to 0.04 psig or 6.25 psfg (i.e., about 1¼ inch water gauge), which experience has shown to be sufficient to hold the membrane in its prescribed shape without stabilizers. Largely unavoidable leakage through doorways and under anchorages will ensure three to four air changes per hour. In large air-supported buildings several blowers are normally used simultaneously, although at times when the internal pressure may be safely reduced, a roster system can be instituted. The energy requirement for such blowers is comparatively small. A building with an internal volume of 100,000 cubic feet will require a blower with a 3 horse power motor. It is possible and often desirable to modify the blowers, so that the injected air can be heated or cooled. The blower assembly, although incapable of controlling humidity, then virtually provides an air-conditioned building environment.

Membrane weights vary from 0.1 to 0.2 pound per square foot, requiring only about 0.04 inch water gauge internal pressure for self-support. In absolutely calm conditions single-skin air-buildings can be erected with an internal pressure of ⅛ to ¼ inch water gauge, and in normal calm weather, the 1¼ inch water gauge operating pressure may be safely reduced to ½ inch water gauge. This excess pressure is so slight that it cannot be perceived by a person walking about in the building. For comparison it may be of interest to note that at middle altitude levels the proportional drop in atmospheric pressure relative to a change of 30 feet in altitude is also approximately ½ inch water gauge.

To prevent excessive air-leakage, entrances to the air-building are normally arranged with simple airlocks or air-excluding rotating doors (Figure A-11). The larger the air-building, the less significant the loss of air through entrances becomes and, therefore, in very large air-supported buildings doors may be left open for extended periods.

Typical air-blower sizes (rated in horse powers (HP)) for various sizes of single-skin air-supported buildings (i.e., shaped as cylindrical shells with quarter spherical ends (see Figure A-4, left side)) are shown in Table A-5.

Table A-5: Recommended air-blower ratings (HP) for various air-supported building sizes

Span	Length	Area	Volume	Air-Blower (HP)
40 ft	80 ft	3,000 sqft	60,000 cubft	
		(up to)		2 of 3.0 HP
50 ft	120 ft	5,600 sqft	108,000 cubft	
60 ft	100 ft	5,300 sqft	113,000 cubft	
		(up to)		2 of 5.0 HP
60 ft	180 ft	10,000 sqft	280,000 cubft	
60 ft	200 ft	11,100 sqft	320,000 cubft	
		(up to)		2 of 7.5 HP
60 ft	250 ft	14,100 sqft	500,000 cubft	

While the material cost rises fairly linearly with the overall dimensions of single-skin air-buildings, the same does not necessarily apply to the mechanical pressurization equipment. For small air-buildings the cost of air-blowers will form an appreciable portion of the total cost, while in the case of larger structures this cost is overshadowed by the greater material cost.

A-10 Membrane Materials

It is undoubtedly the development of a considerable number of high quality plastic membrane materials that made the air-building a feasible and economically attractive proposition in the 1960s. Both nylon and terylene fabrics coated with polyvinyl chloride (PVC) were used extensively, the strength depending in each case on filler, lamination, and thickness. These materials combine considerable tear resistance and durability with high tensile strength and lightness.

Plastics possess their own inherent advantages and limitations that distinctly separate them from other materials. Among the factors favoring their use for air-buildings can in include:

Flexibility: The ability to produce simple and complex forms under the action of internal pressure and various systems of boundary restraint (e.g., cables).

Durability: The comparatively stable and permanent character of plastics.

Clarity: The ability to control light transmittance, from transparency to opacity.

Tensile Strength: In combination with fiberglass reinforcement it is possible to produce plastic materials of higher strength-weight ratio than may be attained by any other combination of materials.

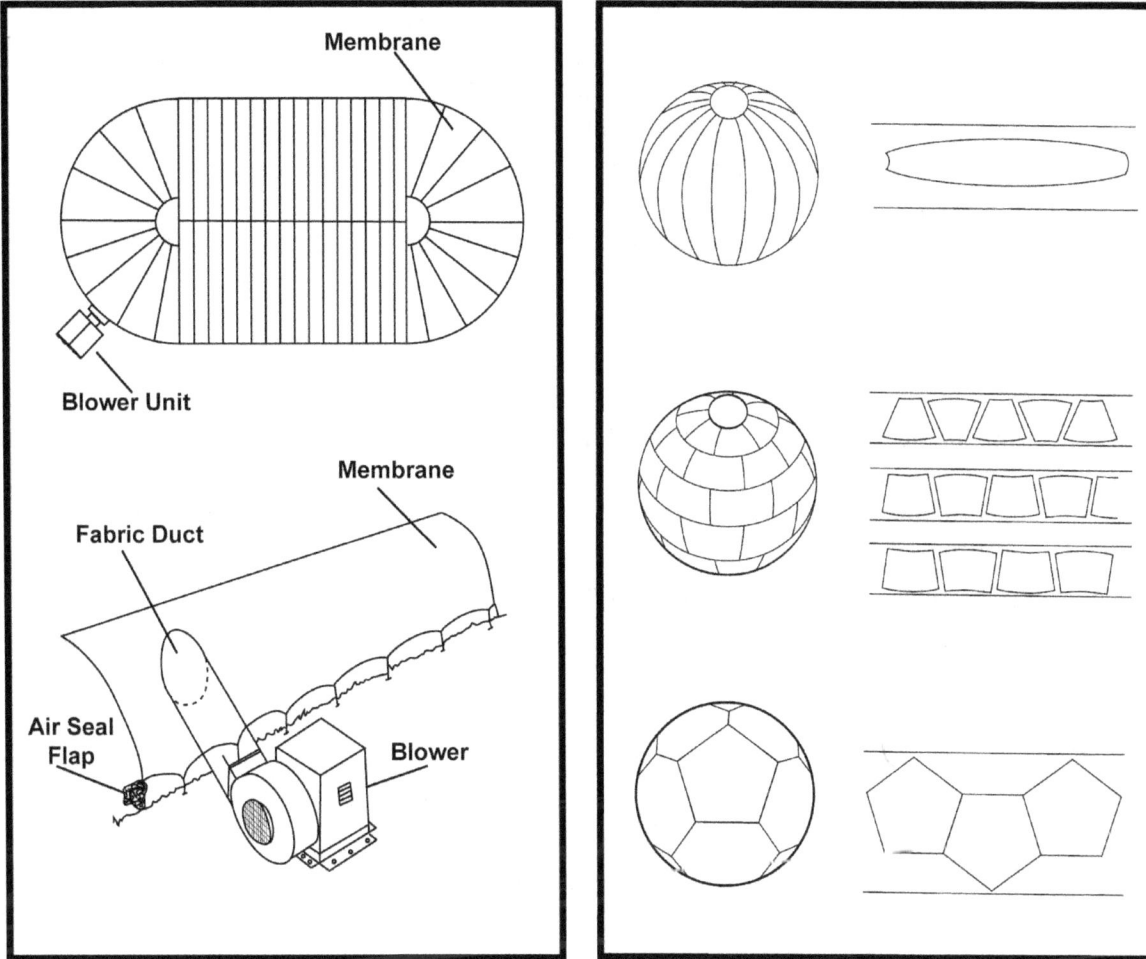

Figure A-33: Typical air-blower arrangement   Figure A-34: Membrane fabrication patterns

However, the following limiting properties must be also considered:

Plasticity: Especially the thermoplastic type of plastic materials exhibit time-dependent plastic behavior (i.e., creep) under load. In the absence of a defined yield point working stresses will be more dependent on the degree of creep.

Heat Tolerance: All plastic materials can be destroyed by fire. They may burn easily or they may be self-extinguishing. Maximum temperatures to which plastics may be exposed are below 500°F and in some cases even below 200°F. Thermosetting plastics are generally superior to thermoplastics in respect to heat resistance.

Weathering: While plastics are resistant to corrosion their life-span is generally shorter than traditional building materials. Therefore, from the time of their first introduction in the 1950s air-buildings were considered to be temporary structures, with a life-span of only 10 to 20 years. Transparent plastics have a much shorter useful life of two to 4 years due to their susceptibility to ultraviolet radiation. Available fillers that are commonly used in plastic materials to inhibit ultraviolet degradation are unfortunately opaque.

More specifically, the three most important properties sought for the membrane envelope of a single-skin air-supported building are: high tensile strength and tear resistance (i.e., in the vicinity of 20,000 pounds per square inch ultimate strength; flame resistance and spark proofness; and, a medium useful service life of at least 20 years in terms of weather resistance. During the 1960s a variety of plastic membrane materials that combined these necessary physical properties at a reasonable cost, became commercially available. In particular, both nylon and terylene fabrics coated with PVC became popular air-building materials due to their tear-resistance, durability, and light weight. The surface coating of PVC lends the fabric a relatively high resistance to abrasion and an acceptable combination of flame-resistance and spark proofness (Makowski 1964, Pohl 1967).

A-10.1 Fire Hazard

During the 1960s it was already well known that in a building constructed of orthodox materials a fire will progress according to a pattern whose general characteristics may be largely predetermined. Two main phases in which the behavior of materials is determined by different criteria occur in the course of a fire (Ashton 1965).

> Phase (1) is the period of development of a fire, from ignition time to full involvement of a compartment. It is the critical stage for occupants, since the nature and arrangements of the materials present will determine the rate of development.

In the case of a fire occurring in an air-supported building we are primarily concerned with the safety of the occupants, while economic loss is relegated to secondary importance. The membrane envelope will have considerable influence on the duration of this first phase. The material properties that are particularly relevant include ignitability, tendency to propagate flames, and the rate at which heat is generated. Ashton (1965) recognized that it is not necessarily the total heat generation potential of a material that is the determining factor, but rather the rate of temperature increase to the point of *flash-over*.

> Phase (2) is the period of time from full involvement of all of the materials in a compartment until the fire is either brought under control by fire services or extinguished due to depletion of fuel.

In the case of an air-supported building, if a fire is permitted to enter this second phase then complete destruction of the building will take place in a matter of minutes. It is therefore imperative that all occupants have been evacuated from an air-building during the first phase of a fire. Accordingly, this initial development stage of the fire must be prolonged as much as possible. The best way to meet this objective is to control the spread of flames, which is promoted mostly by radiation, through the provision of smoke and heat sensors (i.e., alarms), fire extinguishers, and sprinkler systems.

A-10.2 Fabrication

The surfaces of all spherical shapes are basically anticlastic. To fabricate such membrane surfaces it is necessary to join panels that have curved boundaries. It is interesting to note that in practice the higher the modulus of elasticity of a material (i.e., the more rigid the material) the more sections are required to make up a complete form. Markedly fewer sections are necessary with a rubber membrane than with a fiberglass scrim-based material.

Buckminster Fuller's work with geodesic domes has furnished much information about the economical sub-division of spherical surfaces (Mark 1960). In the case of the membrane envelope of an air-building we are concerned not only with the fabrication of the membrane by heat-sealing or sewing individual small panels together (Figure A-34), but also the on-site erection of the structure. The weight of large membranes is considerable requiring further sub-division into panels that may be handled by conventional fabrication techniques. Experience has shown that large membrane sections in excess of 7,000 square feet are too heavy to handle without the assistance of special hoisting equipment (Otto and Trostel 1962).

The separate panels shown in Figure A-34 may be sewn, glued or welded together, or joined by a combination of these techniques. If the sections are sewn together, the seam can be hermetically sealed by means of an adhesive strip. The fabrication of large sections of the membrane is typically undertaken in a factory environment and these sections are then transported to the site and joined prior to erection with continuous zippers. In this way the seam between the quarter-spherical ends and cylindrical shell of an air-building can be designed in such a manner that it is airtight and yet may be dismantled if the building is required to be relocated in the future.

A-11 Geometry of Single-Story Air-Buildings

There are several reasons why a low profile is preferred for large-span air-supported buildings. First, as discussed previously in Section 4.5, high profile air-inflated domes are subject to positive wind pressures on the windward side and negative wind pressures over all other parts of their curved surface (see Figure A-20). Since wind velocities and directions are variable, the forces that are generated are dynamic in nature and can lead to undesirable *flutter* conditions[11]. While this *flutter* condition can also occur in low profile domes due to sudden wind pressure changes, it is more easily managed by increasing the internal air pressure[12]. Experience has shown that the complete elimination of positive wind pressure regions increases the stability of an air-building.

Second, in larger air-supported buildings with spans in excess of 100 feet the height of the internal space becomes excessive. For example, a high profile air-supported dome spanning 150 feet would have an internal height of 75 feet at the center[13]. Since in most cases such a head height would have no practical value, the additional material cost may not be justified.

---

[11] *Flutter* is a potentially destructive vibration caused by aerodynamic forces (e.g., fluctuating wind forces) acting on a structure in unison with the structure's natural mode of vibration to produce rapid motion. Particularly lightweight structures such as air-supported buildings and cable-networks can experience localized flutter conditions when subjected to wind gusts. Stiffening the structure by increasing the internal air pressure and/or providing an external cable-network are proven ways of reducing the risks associated with flutter conditions.

[12] Alternatively or in addition, as discussed in Section 5, large-span air-supported structures are normally combined with an external cable-network. The function of the cables is to stabilize the building under severe and/or fluctuating (i.e., to avoid flutter) wind loads and to reduce the stresses due to the internal air pressure in the membrane material. The material stresses are reduced because the modulus of elasticity of the plastic membrane material is much lower than the modulus of elasticity of steel. Consequently the membrane tends to bulge out between the restraining cables, thereby reducing the radius of curvature.

[13] A full profile dome spanning 150 feet (i.e., diameter) has a radius of 75 feet and therefore the head height at the center of the dome will also be 75 feet.

A-11.1 Full Profile and Low Profile Domes

Since a low profile dome is the top part of a full profile dome its geometry, as shown in Figures A35 and A-36, can be derived from the geometry of the full profile dome. The distances (i.e., *R, D, H, h, d,* and *x*) shown in Figures A-35 and A-36 are all measured in feet (FT) and therefore areas and volumes are in square feet (SF) and cubic feet (CF), respectively (Table A-6).

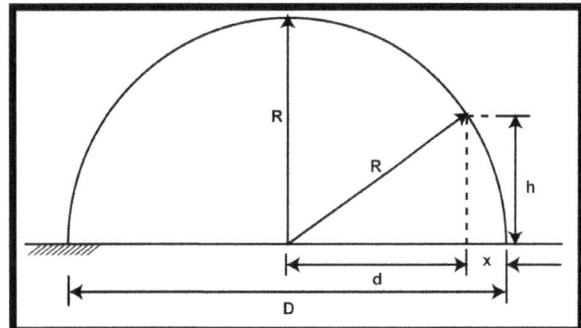
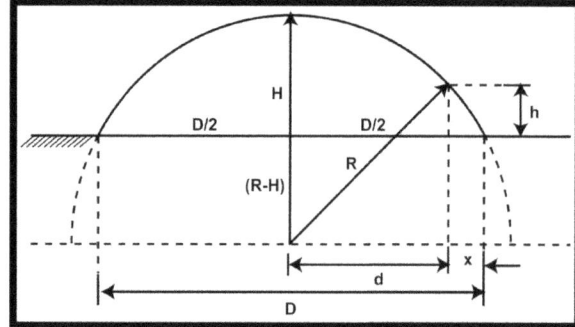

Figure A-35: Full profile dome   Figure A-36: Low profile dome

Table A-6: Geometry of full profile and low profile air-supported domes

Floor Area (A SF)	
$A = \pi R^2$	$A = \pi D^2 / 4$
Perimeter at Ground level (C FT)	
$C = 2 \pi R$	$C = \pi D$
Radius of Full Profile Dome (R FT)	
$R = R$	$R = (4 H^2 + D^2) / (8 H)$
Head Height at Distance (d FT) from Center	
$h = (R^2 - d^2)^{0.5}$	$h = (H - R) + (R^2 - d^2)^{0.5}$
Head Height at Distance (x FT) from Perimeter	
$h = (2 R x - x^2)^{0.5}$	$h = (H - R) + [R^2 - (D/2 - x)^2]^{0.5}$
Distance from Center (d FT) of a Given Head Height (h FT)	
$d = (R^2 - h^2)^{0.5}$	$d = [R^2 - (R - H + h)^2]^{0.5}$
Curved Surface Area of Membrane Enclosure (S SF)	
$S = 2 \pi R^2$	$S = \pi (4 H^2 + D^2)^2 / (32 H^2)$
Internal Volume of Enclosed Space (V CF)	
$V = 2 \pi R^3 / 3$	$V = \pi (4 H^2 + D^2)^3 / (768 H^3)$

As discussed previously in Section 10.2, for fabrication purposes the enclosing membrane of an air-supported building is typically divided into a number of equal-sized panels. The number of panels determines the size of the individual panel and depends on the fabrication facilities of the manufacturing plant available to the air-building contractor. The determination of the exact shape (i.e., the width at, for example, 1 foot intervals from the top of the dome to the ground) is a somewhat more complicated calculation. The two sides of the triangular membrane panel are slightly curved, while the bottom that touches the ground is straight. The required calculations are shown in Table A-7 with reference to Figure A-37. Again all distances in Figure A-37 (i.e., R, D, and ℓ) are measured in feet (FT) and the angle α is in degrees.

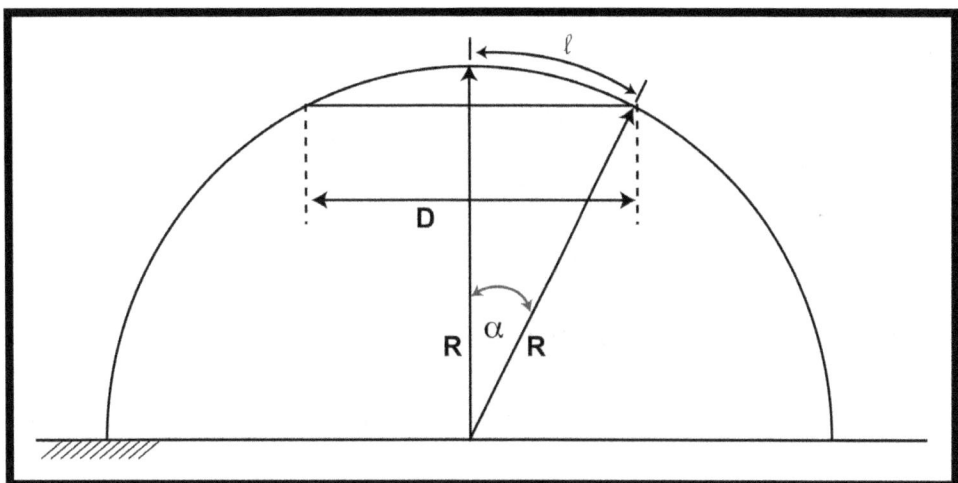

Figure A-37: Determination of the shape of a panel of the curved surface of a dome

Table A-7: Determination of the shape of N equal-sized membrane panels
(Each panel extends from the top of the dome to the ground)

Step 1: Calculate angle α from the top of the dome to the point at which the width of the panel is to be determined (i.e., ℓ FT from top of dome).

$$\alpha = 360\,(\ell)/(2\pi R)$$

Step 2: Calculate the diameter of the dome (D FT) at a distance of (ℓ FT) along the curved surface from the top of the dome.

$$D = 2R\sin(\alpha)$$

Step 3: Calculate the perimeter (L FT) of the dome at a distance of (ℓ FT) along the curved surface from the top of the dome.

$$L = \pi D$$

Step 4: Calculate the width of the panel (W FT) at a distance of (ℓ FT) along the curved surface from the top of the dome.

$$W = L/N$$

A-11.1.1 Design of Low Profile Dome

As an example we will apply the equations provided in Tables A-6 and A-7 in reference to Figure A-36 to a low profile air-supported dome that spans *200 FT* and has a maximum head height of *40 FT* at the center.

$$\begin{aligned}
\text{floor area} &= (\pi D^2)/4 \\
&= (3.14159 \times 200 \times 200)/4 \\
&= \underline{\mathbf{31{,}416 \text{ SF}}}
\end{aligned}$$

$$\begin{aligned}
\text{perimeter at ground level} &= (\pi D) \\
&= (3.14.159 \times 200) \\
&= \underline{\mathbf{628.32 \text{ FT}}}
\end{aligned}$$

$$\begin{aligned}
\text{radius of full profile dome} &= (4H^2 + D^2)/(8H) \\
&= [(4 \times 40 \times 40) + (200 \times 200)]/(8 \times 40) \\
&= \underline{\mathbf{145.0 \text{ FT}}}
\end{aligned}$$

$$\begin{aligned}
\text{head height 80 ft from center} &= (H - R) + (R^2 - d^2)^{1/2} \\
&= (40 - 145) + [(145 \times 145) - (80 \times 80)]^{1/2} \\
&= (-105) + [21025 - 6400]^{1/2} \\
&= (-105 + 121) \\
&= \underline{\mathbf{16 \text{ FT}}}
\end{aligned}$$

$$\begin{aligned}
\text{head height 10 ft from side} &= (H - R) + [(R^2 - (D/2 - x)^2]^{1/2} \\
&= (40 - 145) + [(145 \times 145) - (200/2 - 10)^2]^{1/2} \\
&= (-105) + [21025 - (100 - 10)^2]^{1/2} \\
&= (-105 + 114) \\
&= \underline{\mathbf{9 \text{ FT}}}
\end{aligned}$$

$$\begin{aligned}
\text{7 ft head height from center} &= [R^2 - (R - H + h)^2]^{1/2} \\
&= [(145 \times 145) - ((145 - 40 + 7) \times (145 - 40 + 7))]^{1/2} \\
&= [21025 - 12544]^{1/2} \\
&= \underline{\mathbf{92 \text{ FT}}} \text{ (or 8 FT from side)}
\end{aligned}$$

$$\begin{aligned}
\text{external curved surface area} &= \pi(4H^2 + D^2)^2/(32H^2) \\
&= (3.14159)[(4 \times 40 \times 40) + (200 \times 200)]^2/(32 \times 40 \times 40) \\
&= (3.14159 \times 46400 \times 46400)/51200 \\
&= \underline{\mathbf{132{,}104 \text{ SF}}}
\end{aligned}$$

$$\begin{aligned}
\text{internal volume} &= \pi(4H^2 + D^2)^3/(768 H^3) \\
&= (3.14159)[(4 \times 40 \times 40) + (200 \times 200)]^3/(768 \times [40]^3) \\
&= (3.14159)[46400]^3/(768 \times 64000) \\
&= \underline{\mathbf{6{,}385{,}019 \text{ CF}}}
\end{aligned}$$

If the external membrane enclosure is divided into 20 equal-sized panels (i.e., $N = 20$) then the widths of each panel at the indicated distances along the curved surface from the top of the dome are as follows:

at 5 FT from top of dome:
- $\alpha = (360 \times \ell)/(2\pi R) = (360 \times 5)/(2 \times 3.14159 \times 145) =$ **1° 59'**
- $D = 2R\sin(\alpha) = (2 \times 145 \times 0.0346) =$ **10.03 FT**
- $L = \pi D = (3.14159 \times 10.03) =$ **31.51 FT**
- $W = L/N = 31.51/20 =$ **1 FT 7 IN**

at 10 FT from top of dome:
- $\alpha = (360 \times \ell)/(2\pi R) = (360 \times 10)/(2 \times 3.14159 \times 145) =$ **3° 57'**
- $D = 2R\sin(\alpha) = (2 \times 145 \times 0.0689) =$ **19.98 FT**
- $L = \pi D = (3.14159 \times 19.98) =$ **62.77 FT**
- $W = L/N = 62.77/20 =$ **3 FT 2 IN**

at 20 FT from top of dome:
- $\alpha = (360 \times \ell)/(2\pi R) = (360 \times 20)/(2 \times 3.14159 \times 145) =$ **7° 54'**
- $D = 2R\sin(\alpha) = (2 \times 145 \times 0.1374) =$ **39.85 FT**
- $L = \pi D = (3.14159 \times 39.85) =$ **125.19 FT**
- $W = L/N = 125.19/20 =$ **6 FT 3 IN**

at 30 FT from top of dome:
- $\alpha = (360 \times \ell)/(2\pi R) = (360 \times 30)/(2 \times 3.14159 \times 145) =$ **11° 51'**
- $D = 2R\sin(\alpha) = (2 \times 145 \times 0.2053) =$ **59.54 FT**
- $L = \pi D = (3.14159 \times 59.54) =$ **187.05 FT**
- $W = L/N = 187.05/20 =$ **9 FT 4 IN**

at 40 FT from top of dome:
- $\alpha = (360 \times \ell)/(2\pi R) = (360 \times 40)/(2 \times 3.14159 \times 145) =$ **15° 48'**
- $D = 2R\sin(\alpha) = (2 \times 145 \times 0.2723) =$ **78.97 FT**
- $L = \pi D = (3.14159 \times 78.97) =$ **248.09 FT**
- $W = L/N = 248.09/20 =$ **12 FT 5 IN**

at 60 FT from top of dome:
- $\alpha = (360 \times \ell)/(2\pi R) = (360 \times 60)/(2 \times 3.14159 \times 145) =$ **23° 43'**
- $D = 2R\sin(\alpha) = (2 \times 145 \times 0.4025) =$ **116.73 FT**
- $L = \pi D = (3.14159 \times 116.73) =$ **366.72 FT**
- $W = L/N = 366.72/20 =$ **18 FT 4 IN**

at 90 FT from top of dome:
- $\alpha = (360 \times \ell)/(2\pi R) = (360 \times 90)/(2 \times 3.14159 \times 145) =$ **35° 34'**
- $D = 2R\sin(\alpha) = (2 \times 145 \times 0.5812) =$ **168.55 FT**
- $L = \pi D = (3.14159 \times 168.55) =$ **529.51 FT**
- $W = L/N = 529.51/20 =$ **26 FT 6 IN**

At ground level (i.e., $D = 200$ *FT* and the perimeter length $L = 628$ *FT*) the width of each panel will be *31 FT 5 IN*. At ground level for the sake of completeness $\alpha = 43° 36'$ and $\ell = 110$ *FT 4 IN*.)

Panel width for given material roll width: In practical air-building fabrication situations the membrane material normally comes in rolls of fixed width. Under these circumstances the number of panels must be calculated and there is likely to be an odd panel that is less than one roll width wide at ground level.

Let us assume in the above example that the membrane material is provided by the manufacturer with a roll width of *150 IN*. Allowing for a seam width between panels of *2 IN*, the effective width of the panels at ground level will be *148 IN* (i.e., *150 IN* less *2 IN*). We previously calculated the perimeter of the low profile dome to be *628.32 FT*.

number of panels = (perimeter / panel width)
        = (628.32 / (148/12))
        = **50.94**

In other words, there will be *50* panels with a maximum width at ground level of *148 IN* plus one panel that is only *139 IN* (i.e., *148 x 0.94 = 139*) wide at ground level. Proceeding in steps with the equations listed in Table A-7, the widths of each of the *50* equal-sized panels and the odd-sized panel at the indicated distance along the curved surface from the top of the dome are determined as follows:

at 5 FT from top of dome: α = (360 x ℓ)/(2 π R) = (360 x 5)/(2 x 3.14159 x 145) = **1° 59'**
           D = 2 R sin(α) = (2 x 145 x 0.0346) = **10.03 FT**
           L = π D = (3.14159 x 10.03) = **31.51 FT**
           W = L / N = 31.51 / 50.94 = **0 FT 7½ IN** (or 0.62 FT)

          The width of the odd-sized panel is given by:
           W = 31.51 – (50 x 0.62) = **0 FT 6⅞ IN**

at 10 FT from top of dome: α = (360 x ℓ)/(2 π R) = (360 x 10)/(2 x 3.14159 x 145) = **3° 57'**
           D = 2 R sin(α) = (2 x 145 x 0.0689) = **19.98 FT**
           L = π D = (3.14159 x 19.98) = **62.77 FT**
           W = L / N = 62.77 / 50.94 = **1 FT 2¾ IN** (or 1.23 FT)

          The width of the odd-sized panel is given by:
           W = 62.77 – (50 x 1.23) = **1 FT 1½ IN**

at 20 FT from top of dome: α = (360 x ℓ)/(2 π R) = (360 x 20)/(2 x 3.14159 x 145) = **7° 54'**
           D = 2 R sin(α) = (2 x 145 x 0.1374) = **39.85 FT**
           L = π D = (3.14159 x 39.85) = **125.18 FT**
           W = L / N = 125.18 / 50.94 = **2 FT 5½ IN** (or 2.46 FT)

          The width of the odd-sized panel is given by:
           W = 125.18 – (50 x 2.46) = **2 FT 2 IN**

at 40 FT from top of dome: α = (360 x ℓ)/(2 π R) = (360 x 40)/(2 x 3.14159 x 145) = **15° 48'**
           D = 2 R sin(α) = (2 x 145 x 0.2723) = **78.97 FT**
           L = π D = (3.14159 x 78.97) = **248.08 FT**
           W = L / N = 248.08 / 50.94 = **4 FT 10½ IN** (or 4.87 FT)

          The width of the odd-sized panel is given by:
           W = 248.08 – (50 x 4.87) = **4 FT 7 IN**

at 60 FT from top of dome: α = (360 x ℓ)/(2 π R) = (360 x 60)/(2 x 3.14159 x 145) = **23° 52'**
           D = 2 R sin(α) = (2 x 145 x 0.4046) = **117.33 FT**
           L = π D = (3.14159 x 117.33) = **368.62 FT**
           W = L / N = 368.62 / 50.94 = **7 FT 3 IN** (or 7.24 FT)

          The width of the odd-sized panel is given by:
           W = 368.62 – (50 x 7.24) = **6 FT 7½ IN**

at ground level: α = arcsin(D/(2 R)) = arcsin(0.6897) = 0.7611 radians = **43° 36'**
         ℓ = (2 π R α)/360 = (2 x 3.14159 x 145 x 43.6)/360 = **110.34 FT**
         D = 2 R sin(α) = (2 x 145 x 0.6896) = **200 FT**

$$L = \pi D = (3.14159 \times 200) = \mathbf{628.32 \text{ FT}}$$
$$W = L/N = 628.32/50.94 = \underline{\mathbf{12 \text{ FT } 4 \text{ IN}}} \text{ (or } 12.33 \text{ FT or } 148 \text{ IN)}$$

The width of the odd-sized panel is given by: $628.32 - (50 \times 12.33) = \underline{\mathbf{11 \text{ FT } 7 \text{ IN}}}$ (or 139 IN).

Quantity of membrane material required: The total quantity of membrane material will be given by the product of the length of the panels (*110.34 FT* or *1,324 IN*) and the number of panels required (*51*). However, the length of the panels should be adjusted for the anchorage mechanism at ground level. Typically, this will require an extension of the length of the panel to provide a sleeve for a perimeter pipe or a doubling of the thickness of the membrane at the ground end for added strength in the case of a bolted connection to a concrete footing.

Let us assume an additional *8 IN* for providing a sleeve for a pipe anchor[14], so that the total length of each panel is approximately *1,332 IN* (i.e., *1324 + 8 = 1332*) or *111 FT*. Since there are *51* panels the total quantity of membrane material is given by:

$$Q_m = 51 \times 111 = \underline{\mathbf{5,661 \text{ FT}}}$$

Membrane weight: If the weight of the membrane is *0.25 LB/SF* (for thickness of *0.04 IN*) then the total roll weight of the membrane material before shaping and fabrication is:

$$W_m = 5661 \times 0.25 \times (150/12)$$
$$= \underline{\mathbf{17,691 \text{ LB}}}$$

Membrane stress without external cables: Assuming an internal pressure of 0.04 psig (i.e., equivalent to about 1⅛ IN water gauge) then the material stress in the enclosing membrane (without cables) is the spherical stress, which can be calculated with equation A-1 (see Section 4.3) as follows:

$$f_s = [P_i \times R_{cv}]/2 \text{ LB/IN} \quad \ldots\ldots\ldots\ldots\ldots\ldots\ldots\ldots \text{ A-1}$$

In equation A-1 the internal pressure (P_i) is in pounds per square inch (psig) and the radius of curvature of the shallow dome (R_{cv}) is in inches. If we prefer to measure the radius of the dome in feet then equation A-1 can be rewritten as:

$$\mathbf{f_s = 6[P_i \times R_{cv}]} \text{ LB/IN} \quad \ldots\ldots\ldots\ldots\ldots\ldots \text{ A-7}$$

For the shallow dome that we are considering here, the radius of curvature (R_{cv}) can be expressed in terms of the head height (*H*) at the center of the dome and the diameter of the dome at ground level (*D*), as shown in Table A-6:

$$R_{cv} = (4H^2 + D^2)/(8H)$$

Therefore, substituting for R_{cv} in equation A-7 we obtain:

$$\mathbf{f_s = 6P_i(4H^2 + D^2)/(8H)} \text{ LB/IN} \quad \ldots\ldots\ldots\ldots \text{ A-8}$$

Solving for f_s with *H* and *D* in FT:

$$f_s = 6 \times 0.04 [(4 \times 40 \times 40) + (200 \times 200)]/(8 \times 40)$$
$$= 0.48[6400 + 40000]/320$$
$$= \underline{\mathbf{34.8 \text{ LB/IN}}}$$

---

[14] Typically a steel or plastic pipe that is anchored to the ground at regular intervals (e.g., 4-foot centers) with steel spikes or auger anchors.

Membrane stress with external cables: While a material stress of *34.8 LB/IN* may be within the range of commercially available scrim-based plastic membrane materials, the application of a factor of safety (e.g., *2*) could easily result in a material strength requirement (i.e., *69.6 LB/IN*) that is outside of that range. Under these circumstances an external cable-network can be used to transfer a substantial amount of the membrane stress to the cables. The simplest cable arrangement would consist of an external horizontal cable one to five feet (ℓ_1 in Figures A-38 and A-39) below the top of the dome from which vertical cables at equal spacing radiate to the ground level where they are firmly anchored.

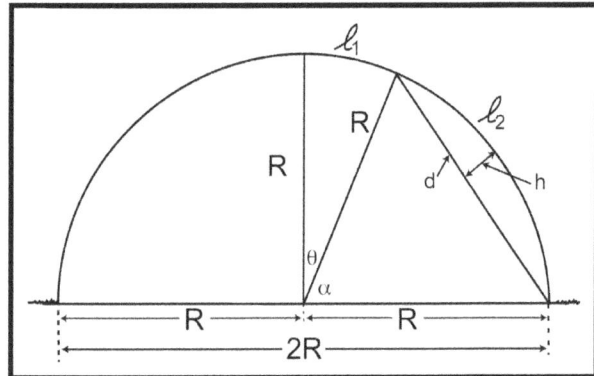
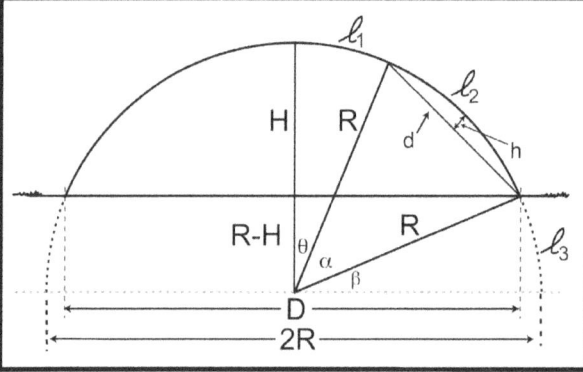

Figure A-38: Full profile dome with external cables

Figure A-39: Low profile dome with external cables

Table A-8: Geometry of vertical cables for full profile and low profile air-supported domes

Angle θ Subtended by Horizontal Cable Near Top of Dome	
$\theta = 360 (\ell_1) / (2 \pi R)$ (Therefore: angle $\alpha = 90 - \theta$)	$\theta = 360 (\ell_1) / (2 \pi R)$ (Therefore: angle $\alpha = 90 - (\theta + \beta)$) (Where: angle $\beta = \arcsin((R-H)/R)$)
Length of Vertical Cables (ℓ_2 FT)	
$\ell_2 = (\alpha / 180) \pi R$	
Chord Length (d FT) for Vertical Cables	
$d = 2 R \sin(\alpha/2)$	
Segment Height (h FT) for Vertical Cables	
$h = R - [R^2 - (d^2/4)]^{0.5}$	
Maximum Tension (T_{max} LB) in Vertical Cables	
$T_{max} = H_{CA} [1 + (16 h^2 / d)]^{0.5}$	
(Where the horizontal cable tension component (H_{CA}) = $w d^2/(8 h)$ and w LB/FT-run is the load on the cable)	

Let us assume that the cables are made of steel with a modulus of elasticity of 29,000,000 psi and the membrane is made of plastic with a modulus of elasticity of 500,000 psi. With a modulus ratio of 1:58 in favor of the steel cables the membrane will bulge out appreciably between cables. The perimeter of the dome was previously calculated to be *628.32 FT*. If we arbitrarily divide the perimeter into say *30* equal sections then the maximum distance between cables at ground level is:

cable spacing (ground) = 628.32 / 30 = **20.9 FT** (or 20 FT 11½ IN)

If we assume the horizontal cable near the top of the dome to be *3 FT* below the apex of the dome then the length of the cable can be determined in three steps by reference to Table A-7 as follows:

$$\theta = 360 (\ell_1) / (2 \pi R)$$
$$= 360 \times 3 / (2 \times 3.14159 \times 145)$$
$$= \mathbf{1.19°} \text{ (or 1° 11')}$$

The diameter (*D FT*) of the horizontal cable is given by:

$$D = 2 R \sin(\theta)$$
$$= 2 \times 145 \times 0.0207$$
$$= \mathbf{6.0 \text{ FT}}$$

Therefore, the perimeter (*C FT*) of the horizontal cable is:

$$C = \pi D$$
$$= 3.14159 \times 6$$
$$= \mathbf{18.85 \text{ FT}}$$

Again, if we divide the perimeter of the horizontal cable into *30* equal sections then the minimum distance between cables at the level of the horizontal cable near the top of the dome is:

cable spacing (top) = 18.85 / 30 = **0.63 FT** (or 7½ IN)

Even a very conservatively estimated maximum membrane deflection of *9 IN* between cables at the ground level will reduce the radius of curvature of the membrane surface appreciably. Applying equation A-8 with *H=0.75 FT* and *D=20.9 FT*, we determine the maximum membrane stress (f_s) to be:

$$f_s = 6 P_i (4 H^2 + D^2) / (8 H) \text{ LB/IN}$$
$$f_s = 6 \times 0.04 [(4 \times 0.75 \times 0.75) + (20.9 \times 20.9)] / (8 \times 0.75)$$
$$= 0.24 [2.25 + 436.8] / 6$$
$$= \mathbf{17.6 \text{ LB/IN}}$$

Cable stress (dome): We will treat each vertical cable as an inverted suspension cable between the horizontal cable near the top of the dome and ground. Based on Table A-8 and in reference to Figures A-38 and A-39, the span (*d FT*) and sag (*h FT*) at the center of the vertical cable can be calculated as follows:

$$\text{angle } \beta = \arcsin((R-H)/R)$$
$$= \arcsin((145-40)/145)$$
$$= \arcsin(0.7241)$$
$$= 0.8097 \text{ radians}$$
$$= \mathbf{46° 24'} \text{ (or 46.40°)}$$

$$\text{angle } \alpha = 90 - (\theta + \beta)$$
$$= 90 - (1.19 + 46.40)$$
$$= 90 - 47.59$$
$$= \mathbf{42.41°} \text{ (or 42° 25')}$$

$$d = 2 R \sin(\alpha/2)$$

$$
\begin{aligned}
&= 2 \times 145 \times \sin(21° \, 12') \\
&= 2 \times 145 \times 0.3616 \\
&= \mathbf{104.9 \; FT}
\end{aligned}
$$

$$
\begin{aligned}
h &= R - [\, R^2 - (d^2/4) \,]^{0.5} \\
&= 145 - [\, (145 \times 145) - (104.9 \times 104.9)/4 \,]^{0.5} \\
&= 145 - [21025 - 2749]^{0.5} \\
&= 145 - 135.2 \\
&= \mathbf{9.8 \; FT}
\end{aligned}
$$

To determine the cable tension we need to establish the load on the cable. With the horizontal cable located *3 FT* down along the curved surface (ℓ_1 *FT*) from the apex of the dome the cable spacing at the top level was calculated previously to be *0.63 FT*. Similarly the cable spacing at ground level was calculated to be *20.9 FT*. Accordingly the average load per foot-run (*w LB/FT-run*) on the cable will be the product of the pressure inside the building (P_i *psig*) and the average length of a one foot wide membrane strip supported by the vertical cable:

$$
\begin{aligned}
w &= 144 \, P_i \, (0.63 + 20.9)/2 \\
&= 144 \times 0.04 \times 10.77 \\
&= \mathbf{62 \; LB/FT\text{-}run}
\end{aligned}
$$

In reference to Table A-8 the horizontal cable tension component (H_{CA} *LB*) and the maximum cable tension (T_{max} *LB*) are determined as follows:

$$
\begin{aligned}
H_{CA} &= w \, d^2 / (8 \, h) \\
&= 62 \times 104.9 \times 104.9 / (8 \times 9.8) \\
&= 682248.6 / 78.4 \\
&= \mathbf{8{,}702.2 \; LB}
\end{aligned}
$$

$$
\begin{aligned}
T_{max} &= H_{CA} \, [\, 1 + (16 \, h^2/d) \,]^{0.5} \\
&= 8702.2 \, [\, 1 + (16 \times 9.8 \times 9.8)/104.9 \,]^{0.5} \\
&= 8702.2 \, [\, 1 + 14.65 \,]^{0.5} \\
&= 8702.2 \times 3.96 \\
&= \underline{\mathbf{34{,}424.5 \; LB}}
\end{aligned}
$$

Assuming a cable design strength of *60,000 psi* the required cross-sectional area (A_{CA} *SI*) and diameter (A_D *IN*) of the cable can be calculated as follows:

$$
\begin{aligned}
A_{CA} &= T_{max} / 60000 \\
&= 34424.5 / 60000 \\
&= \mathbf{0.574 \; SI}
\end{aligned}
$$

$$
\begin{aligned}
A_D &= [\, 4 \, A_{CA} / \pi \,]^{0.5} \\
&= [\, 4 \times 0.574 / 3.14159 \,]^{0.5} \\
&= [\, 0.73 \,]^{0.5} \\
&= \underline{\mathbf{0.85 \; IN}} \; \text{(or approximately 7/8 IN diameter)}
\end{aligned}
$$

Anchorage forces: If the air-building is anchored at ground level with a steel pipe that fits into a membrane sleeve and is anchored to the ground at *4-foot* (*48 IN*) centers then according to equation A-6 the anchorage force per foot-run of perimeter is given by:

anchorage force = 0.44 R LB/FT-run = 4 (0.44 R) LB/anchor point

Since the radius of curvature (*R FT*) of the dome is *145 FT* the anchorage force per anchor point is:

$$\text{anchorage force} = 4 (0.44 \times 145)$$
$$= \underline{\mathbf{255.2} \text{ LB/anchor}}$$

A-11.1.2 Design of Full Profile Dome

As a second example we will apply the equations provided in Tables A-6 and A-7 in reference to Figure A-35 to a full profile air-supported dome that has a diameter at ground level of *120 FT* and therefore the radius of curvature (*R*) is *60 FT*.

$$\text{floor area} = (\pi R^2)$$
$$= (3.14159 \times 60 \times 60)$$
$$= \underline{\mathbf{11,310} \text{ SF}}$$

$$\text{perimeter at ground level} = (2 \pi R)$$
$$= (2 \times 3.14159 \times 60)$$
$$= \underline{\mathbf{377} \text{ FT}}$$

$$\text{head height 40 FT from center} = [R^2 - d^2]^{0.5}$$
$$= [(60 \times 60) - (40 \times 40)]^{0.5}$$
$$= [3600 - 1600]^{0.5}$$
$$= \underline{\mathbf{45} \text{ FT}}$$

$$\text{head height 10 FT from side} = [(2 R x) - x^2]^{0.5}$$
$$= [(2 \times 60 \times 10) - (10 \times 10)]^{0.5}$$
$$= [1200 - 100]^{0.5}$$
$$= \underline{\mathbf{33} \text{ FT}}$$

$$\text{7 FT head height from center} = [R^2 - h^2]^{0.5}$$
$$= [(60 \times 60) - (7 \times 7)]^{0.5}$$
$$= [3600 - 49]^{0.5}$$
$$= \underline{\mathbf{59.6} \text{ FT}} \text{ (or 5 IN from side)}$$

$$\text{external curved surface area} = 2 \pi R^2$$
$$= 2 \times 3.14159 \times 60 \times 60$$
$$= \underline{\mathbf{22,619} \text{ SF}}$$

$$\text{internal volume} = (2 \pi R^3)/3$$
$$= (2 \times 3.14159 \times 60 \times 60 \times 60)/3$$
$$= (1357166.8/3)$$
$$= \underline{\mathbf{452,389} \text{ CF}}$$

Panel width for given material roll width: If the membrane material is provided by the manufacturer with a roll width of *150 IN* and we allow a seam width between panels of *2 IN*, then the effective width of the panels at ground level will be *148 IN* (i.e., *150 IN* less *2 IN*). We previously calculated the perimeter of the low profile dome to be *377 FT*.

$$\text{number of panels} = (\text{perimeter} / \text{panel width})$$
$$= (377 / (148/12))$$
$$= \underline{\mathbf{30.57}}$$

In other words, there will be *30* panels with a maximum width at ground level of *148 IN* plus one panel that is only *84.4 IN* (i.e., *148 x 0.57 = 84.36*) wide at ground level. Proceeding in steps with the equations listed in Table A-7, the widths of each of the *30* equal-sized panels and the odd-sized panel at the indicated distance along the curved surface from the top of the dome are determined as follows:

at 5 FT from top of dome: $\alpha = (360 \times \ell)/(2 \pi R) = (360 \times 5)/(2 \times 3.14159 \times 60) = $ **4° 46'**
$D = 2 R \sin(\alpha) = (2 \times 60 \times 0.0831) = $ **9.97 FT**
$L = \pi D = (3.14159 \times 9.97) = $ **31.33 FT**
$W = L / N = 31.33 / 30.57 = $ **1 FT 0¼ IN** (or 1.02 FT)

The width of the odd-sized panel is given by: $W = 31.33 - (30 \times 1.02) = $ **0 FT 8¾ IN**

at 10 FT from top of dome: $\alpha = (360 \times \ell)/(2 \pi R) = (360 \times 10)/(2 \times 3.14159 \times 60) = $ **9° 33'**
$D = 2 R \sin(\alpha) = (2 \times 60 \times 0.1659) = $ **19.91 FT**
$L = \pi D = (3.14159 \times 19.91) = $ **62.54 FT**
$W = L / N = 62.54 / 30.57 = $ **2 FT 0½ IN** (or 2.05 FT)

The width of the odd-sized panel is given by: $W = 62.54 - (30 \times 2.05) = $ **1 FT 0½ IN**

at 20 FT from top of dome: $\alpha = (360 \times \ell)/(2 \pi R) = (360 \times 20)/(2 \times 3.14159 \times 60) = $ **19° 6'**
$D = 2 R \sin(\alpha) = (2 \times 60 \times 0.3272) = $ **39.26 FT**
$L = \pi D = (3.14159 \times 39.26) = $ **123.35 FT**
$W = L / N = 123.35 / 30.57 = $ **4 FT 0½ IN** (or 4.04 FT)

The width of the odd-sized panel is given by: $W = 123.35 - (30 \times 4.04) = $ **2 FT 2 IN**

at 40 FT from top of dome: $\alpha = (360 \times \ell)/(2 \pi R) = (360 \times 40)/(2 \times 3.14159 \times 60) = $ **38° 12'**
$D = 2 R \sin(\alpha) = (2 \times 60 \times 0.6184) = $ **74.21 FT**
$L = \pi D = (3.14159 \times 74.21) = $ **233.13 FT**
$W = L / N = 233.13 / 30.57 = $ **7 FT 7½ IN** (or 7.63 FT)

The width of the odd-sized panel is given by: $W = 233.13 - (30 \times 7.63) = $ **4 FT 2¾ IN**

at ground level: $\alpha = $ **90°**
$\ell = (2 \pi R \alpha)/360 = (2 \times 3.14159 \times 60 \times 90)/360 = $ **94.25 FT**
$D = 2 R = $ **120 FT** and $L = $ **377 FT**
$W = L / N = 377 / 30.57 = $ **12 FT 4 IN** (or 12.33 FT or 148 IN)

The width of the odd-sized panel is given by: $W = 377 - (30 \times 12.33) = $ **7 FT 1 IN** (or 85 IN)

Quantity of membrane material required: The total quantity of membrane material will be given by the product of the length of the panels (*94.25 FT* or *1,131 IN*) and the number of panels required (*31*). However, the length of the panels should be adjusted for the anchorage mechanism at ground level. Let us assume an additional *8 IN* for providing a sleeve for a pipe anchor, so that the total length of each panel is approximately *1,139 IN* (i.e., *1131 + 8 = 1139*) or *94.92 FT*. Since there are *31* panels the total quantity of membrane material is given by:

$$Q_m = 31 \times 94.92 = \underline{\mathbf{2,942 \text{ FT}}}$$

Membrane weight: If the weight of the membrane is *0.25 LB/SF* (for thickness of *0.04 IN*) then the total roll weight of the membrane material before shaping and fabrication is:

$$W_m = 2942 \times 0.25 \times (150/12)$$
$$= \underline{\mathbf{9,194\ LB}}$$

Membrane stress without external cables: Assuming an internal pressure of 0.04 psig (i.e., equivalent to about 1⅛ IN water gauge) then the material stress in the enclosing membrane (without cables) is the spherical stress, which can be calculated with equation A-7 as follows:

$$f_s = 6\,[\,P_i \times R_{cv}\,]\ \text{LB/IN} \quad \text{................................} \quad \text{A-7}$$
$$= 6 \times 0.04 \times 60$$
$$= \underline{\mathbf{14.4\ LB/IN}}$$

Even with a factor of safety of 100% (i.e., *28.8 LB/IN*) the material stress is unlikely to exceed the design stress of commercially available scrim-based plastic membrane materials and therefore external cables will not be required.

Anchorage forces: If the air-building is anchored at ground level with a steel pipe that fits into a membrane sleeve and the pipe is fixed to the ground at *4-foot* (*48 IN*) centers then according to equation A-6 the anchorage force per foot-run of perimeter is given by:

$$\text{anchorage force} = 0.44\,R\ \text{LB/FT-run} = 4\,(0.44\,R)\ \text{LB/anchor point}$$

Since the radius of curvature (*R FT*) of the dome is *60 FT* the anchorage force per anchor point is:

$$\text{anchorage force} = 4\,(0.44 \times 60)$$
$$= \underline{\mathbf{105.6\ LB/anchor}}$$

A-11.2 Full Profile and Low Profile Elongated Air-Buildings

The barrel vault air-building with quarter spherical ends is more common than the dome since it provides a more usable internal space for storage and sporting facilities.

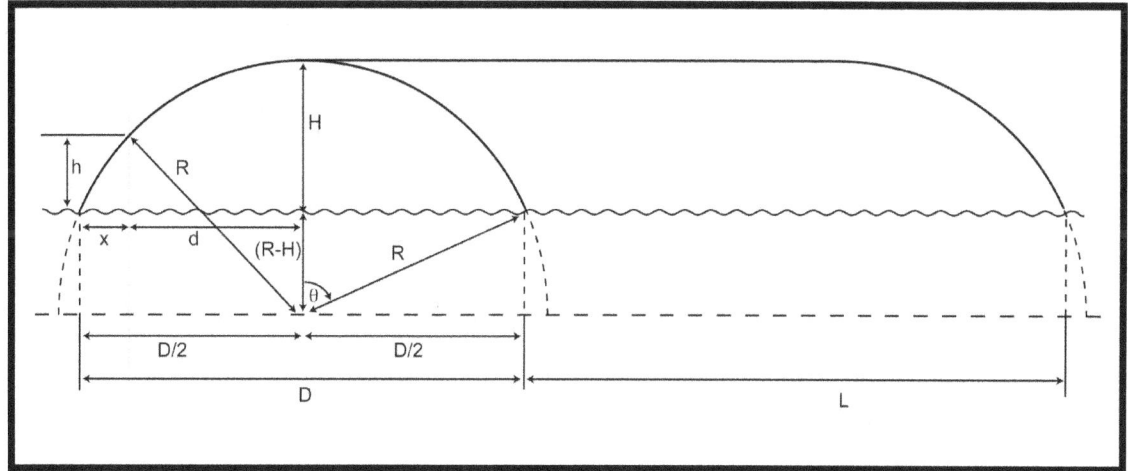

Figure A-40: Low profile cylindrical barrel vault with quarter spherical dome ends

The low profile cylindrical barrel vault with quarter spherical dome ends (Figure A-40) is more commonly seen as an air-supported structure than the full profile counterpart, because of the excessive height of the latter. The complete design analysis of the barrel vault portion of that structure involves some of the same geometric equations that are included in Table A-6, as well as a few additional equations.

Table A-9: Geometry of full profile and low profile cylindrical vault of *L FT* length
with and without quarter spherical ends

Floor Area (A SF)

$A = 2 R L$ (without ends) $\qquad$ $A = D L$ (without ends)
$A = \pi R^2 + (2 R L)$ (with ends) $\qquad$ $A = (\pi D^2/4) + (D L)$ (with ends)

Perimeter at Ground level (C FT)

$C = 2 L$ (without ends) $\qquad$ $C = 2 L$ (without ends)
$C = (2 \pi R) + (2 L)$ (with ends) $\qquad$ $C = (\pi D) + (2 L)$ (with ends)

Radius of Full Profile Barrel Vault (R FT)

$R = R$ $\qquad$ $R = (4 H^2 + D^2) / (8 H)$

Head Height at Distance (d FT) from Center

$h = (R^2 - d^2)^{0.5}$ $\qquad$ $h = (H - R) + (R^2 - d^2)^{0.5}$

Head Height at Distance (x FT) from Perimeter

$h = [(2 R x) - x^2]^{0.5}$ $\qquad$ $h = (H - R) + [(R^2 - (D/2 - x)^2]^{0.5}$

Distance from Center (d FT) of a Given Head Height (h FT)

$d = (R^2 - h^2)^{0.5}$ $\qquad$ $d = [R^2 - (R - H + h)^2]^{0.5}$

Curved Surface Area of Barrel Vault (S sqft) only

$S = \pi R L$ $\qquad$ $S = [4 \pi R L \arcsin(D/(2 R))] / 360$
$\qquad\qquad\qquad\qquad\qquad$ (arcsin(D/(2R)) in degrees)

$\qquad\qquad\qquad\qquad\qquad$ $S = 2 R L \arcsin(D/(2 R))$
$\qquad\qquad\qquad\qquad\qquad$ (arcsin(D/(2R)) in radians)

Internal Volume of Barrel Vault (V CF) only

$V = (\pi R^2 L) / 2$ $\qquad$ $V = [(\pi R^2 \arcsin(D/(2R))) / 180 - (D R)/2 + (D H)/2] L$
$\qquad\qquad\qquad\qquad\qquad$ (arcsin(D/(2R)) in degrees)

$\qquad\qquad\qquad\qquad\qquad$ $V = [(R^2 \arcsin(D/(2R))) - (D R)/2 + (D H)/2] L$
$\qquad\qquad\qquad\qquad\qquad$ (arcsin(D/(2R)) in radians)

A-11.2.1 Design of Low Profile Elongated Air-Building

As an example we will apply the equations provided in Tables A-9, A-8, A-7 and A-6 to a low profile air-supported barrel vault with quarter spherical ends, with a width of *250 FT* (i.e., *D=250*), a total length of *450 FT* (i.e., *L=(450-125-125)=200*), and a maximum head height of *30*

FT (i.e., $H=30$) at the center.

$$\begin{aligned}
\text{floor area} &= ((\pi D^2)/4) + (DL) \\
&= ((3.14159 \times 250 \times 250)/4) + (250 \times 200) \\
&= 49087 + 50000 \\
&= \underline{\mathbf{99{,}087 \text{ SF}}}
\end{aligned}$$

$$\begin{aligned}
\text{perimeter at ground level} &= (\pi D) + (2L) \\
&= (3.14.159 \times 250) + (2 \times 200) \\
&= 785.4 + 400 \\
&= \underline{\mathbf{1{,}185 \text{ FT}}}
\end{aligned}$$

$$\begin{aligned}
\text{radius of full profile dome} &= (4H^2 + D^2)/(8H) \\
&= [(4 \times 30 \times 30) + (250 \times 250)]/(8 \times 30) \\
&= \underline{\mathbf{275.4 \text{ FT}}}
\end{aligned}$$

$$\begin{aligned}
\text{head height 80 FT from center} &= (H - R) + (R^2 - d^2)^{0.5} \\
&= (30 - 275.4) + [(275.4 \times 275.4) - (80 \times 80)]^{0.5} \\
&= (-245.4) + [75845 - 6400]^{0.5} \\
&= (-245.4 + 263.5) \\
&= \underline{\mathbf{18.1 \text{ FT}}}
\end{aligned}$$

$$\begin{aligned}
\text{head height 10 FT from side} &= (H - R) + [(R^2 - (D/2 - x)^2]^{0.5} \\
&= (30 - 275.4) + [(275.4 \times 275.4) - (250/2 - 10)^2]^{0.5} \\
&= (-245.4) + [75845 - (125 - 10)^2]^{0.5} \\
&= (-245.4 + 250.2) \\
&= \underline{\mathbf{4.8 \text{ FT}}}
\end{aligned}$$

$$\begin{aligned}
\text{7 FT head height from center} &= [R^2 - (R - H + h)^2]^{0.5} \\
&= [(275.4 \times 275.4) - ((275.4 - 30 + 7) \times (275.4 - 30 + 7))]^{0.5} \\
&= [75845 - 63706]^{0.5} \\
&= \underline{\mathbf{110.1 \text{ FT}}} \text{ (or 14.9 FT from side)}
\end{aligned}$$

$$\begin{aligned}
\text{external curved surface area} &= \pi(4H^2 + D^2)^2/(32H^2) + [4\pi R L \arcsin(D/(2R))]/360° \\
&= (3.14159)[(4 \times 30 \times 30) + (250 \times 250)]^2/(32 \times 30 \times 30) \\
&\quad + [4 \times 3.14159 \times 275.4 \times 200 \times 27°]/360° \\
&= 476606 + 51912 \\
&= \underline{\mathbf{528{,}518 \text{ SF}}}
\end{aligned}$$

$$\begin{aligned}
\text{internal volume} &= \pi(4H^2 + D^2)^3/(768 H^3) \\
&\quad + [(R^2 \arcsin(D/(2R))) - (DR)/2 + (DH)/2] L \\
&= (3.14159)[(4 \times 30 \times 30) + (250 \times 250)]^3/(768 \times [30]^3) \\
&\quad + [(275.4 \times 275.4 \times 0.4711^{\text{rad}}) - (250 \times 275.4)/2 + (250 \times 30)/2] \times 200
\end{aligned}$$

$$= (3.14159) [66100 \times 66100 \times 66100] / (768 \times 27000)$$
$$+ [(35731) - (34425) + (3750)] \times 200$$
$$= (43,755,116) + (1,011,200)$$
$$= \underline{\mathbf{44,766,316\ CF}}$$

Panel width for given material roll width: Let us assume in the above example that the membrane material provided by the manufacturer has a roll width of only *70 IN*. Allowing a seam width between panels of *2 IN*, the effective width of the panels at ground level will be *68 IN* (i.e., *70 IN* less *2 IN*). Previously in this Section we calculated the perimeter of the low profile dome portion (i.e., without the barrel vault portion) to be *785.4 FT*.

number of dome panels = (perimeter / panel width)
$$= (785.4 / (68/12))$$
$$= \underline{\mathbf{138.6}}\ \text{(or 69.3 panels for each end dome section)}$$

Therefore, for the two dome-shaped ends of the air-building will each require *69* equal-sized panels and one odd-sized panel with a width at ground level of *20.5 IN*. In addition, the *200 FT* long barrel vault section between the two quarter spherical ends will require:

number of barrel vault panels = (200 / panel width)
$$= (200 / (68/12))$$
$$= \underline{\mathbf{35.29}}$$

Using the equations in Table A-8 in reference to Figure A-39, the angle (β) subtended from the center of the radius of curvature of the dome to where the dome meets the ground is given by:

$$\beta = \arcsin((R-H)/R)$$
$$= \arcsin((275.4-30)/275.4)$$
$$= \arcsin(0.8911)$$
$$= 1.0997\ \text{radians}$$
$$= \mathbf{63°}$$

The length of a dome panel (ℓ) can then be calculated by transposing the following equation:

$$\theta = 360\,(\ell) / (2\pi R)$$
$$\ell = 2\pi R\theta / 360 \quad \text{where } \theta = (90 - \beta)\ \text{or}\ 27°$$
$$= 2 \times 3.14159 \times 275.4 \times 27 / 360$$
$$= \underline{\mathbf{129.78\ FT}}\ \text{(or 129 FT 9½ IN)}$$

Since these panels do not vary in width from the top of the building to the ground they can be continuous from one side of the barrel vault to the other. Therefore, since the dome panels are *129.78 FT* (or *129 FT 9½ IN*) long, the barrel vault panels will be twice as long (i.e., *259.56 FT or 259 FT 7 IN*).

Proceeding in steps with the equations listed in Table A-7, the widths of each of the *69* equal-sized panels and the odd-sized panel at the indicated distance along the curved surface from the top of the dome are determined for the quarter spherical ends of the building as follows:

at 5 FT from top of dome: $\alpha = (360 \times \ell)/(2\pi R) = (360 \times 5)/(2 \times 3.14159 \times 275.4) = \mathbf{1°\ 2'}$
$$D = 2R\sin(\alpha) = (2 \times 275.4 \times 0.0182) = \mathbf{10.02\ FT}$$
$$L = \pi D / 2 = (3.14159 \times 10.02 / 2) = \mathbf{15.75\ FT}$$

$$W = L / N = 15.75 / 69.3 = \underline{\textbf{0 FT 2¾ IN}} \text{ (or 0.227 FT)}$$

The width of the odd-sized panel is given by: $W = 15.75 - (69 \times 0.227) = \underline{\textbf{0 FT 1 IN}}$

at 10 FT from top of dome:
$$\alpha = (360 \times \ell)/(2 \pi R) = (360 \times 10)/(2 \times \pi \times 275.4) = \textbf{2° 5'}$$
$$D = 2 R \sin(\alpha) = (2 \times 275.4 \times 0.0363) = \textbf{19.99 FT}$$
$$L = \pi D / 2 = (3.14159 \times 19.99 / 2) = \textbf{31.41 FT}$$
$$W = L / N = 31.41 / 69.3 = \underline{\textbf{0 FT 5½ IN}} \text{ (or 0.453 FT)}$$

The width of the odd-sized panel is given by: $W = 31.41 - (69 \times 0.453) = \underline{\textbf{0 FT 1⅔ IN}}$

at 20 FT from top of dome:
$$\alpha = (360 \times \ell)/(2 \pi R) = (360 \times 20)/(2 \times \pi \times 145) = \textbf{4° 7'}$$
$$D = 2 R \sin(\alpha) = (2 \times 275.4 \times 0.0725) = \textbf{39.93 FT}$$
$$L = \pi D / 2 = (3.14159 \times 39.93 / 2) = \textbf{62.73 FT}$$
$$W = L / N = 62.73 / 69.3 = \underline{\textbf{0 FT 10¾ IN}} \text{ (or 0.905 FT)}$$

The width of the odd-sized panel is given by: $W = 62.73 - (69 \times 0.905) = \underline{\textbf{0 FT 3¼ IN}}$

at 40 FT from top of dome:
$$\alpha = (360 \times \ell)/(2 \pi R) = (360 \times 40)/(2 \times \pi \times 275.4) = \textbf{8° 19'}$$
$$D = 2 R \sin(\alpha) = (2 \times 275.4 \times 0.1447) = \textbf{79.70 FT}$$
$$L = \pi D / 2 = (3.14159 \times 79.70 / 2) = \textbf{125.19 FT}$$
$$W = L / N = 125.19 / 69.3 = \underline{\textbf{1 FT 9¾ IN}} \text{ (or 1.81 FT)}$$

The width of the odd-sized panel is given by: $W = 125.19 - (69 \times 1.81) = \underline{\textbf{0 FT 6½ IN}}$

at 60 FT from top of dome:
$$\alpha = (360 \times \ell)/(2 \pi R) = (360 \times 60)/(2 \times \pi \times 275.4) = \textbf{12° 30'}$$
$$D = 2 R \sin(\alpha) = (2 \times 275.4 \times 0.2161) = \textbf{119.03 FT}$$
$$L = \pi D / 2 = (3.14159 \times 119.03 / 2) = \textbf{186.97 FT}$$
$$W = L / N = 186.97 / 69.3 = \underline{\textbf{2 FT 8½ IN}} \text{ (or 2.70 FT)}$$

The width of the odd-sized panel is given by: $W = 186.97 - (69 \times 2.70) = \underline{\textbf{0 FT 9¾ IN}}$

at 120 FT from top of dome:
$$\alpha = (360 \times \ell)/(2 \pi R) = (360 \times 120)/(2 \times \pi \times 275.4) = \textbf{24° 58'}$$
$$D = 2 R \sin(\alpha) = (2 \times 275.4 \times 0.4221) = \textbf{232.49 FT}$$
$$L = \pi D / 2 = (3.14159 \times 232.49 / 2) = \textbf{365.20 FT}$$
$$W = L / N = 365.20 / 69.3 = \underline{\textbf{5 FT 3¼ IN}} \text{ (or 5.27 FT)}$$

The width of the odd-sized panel is given by: $W = 365.20 - (69 \times 5.27) = \underline{\textbf{1 FT 7 IN}}$

at ground level:
$$\alpha = \arcsin(D/(2 R)) = \arcsin(0.4539) = 0.4711 \text{ radians} = \textbf{27° 0'}$$
$$\ell = (2 \pi R \alpha)/360 = 2 \times 3.14159 \times 275.4 \times 27)/360 = \textbf{129.78 FT}$$
$$D = 2 R \sin(\alpha) = (2 \times 275.4 \times 0.4540) = \textbf{250 FT}$$
$$L = \pi D / 2 = (3.14159 \times 250 / 2) = \textbf{392.70 FT}$$
$$W = L / N = 392.70 / 69.3 = \underline{\textbf{5 FT 8 IN}} \text{ (or 5.67 FT or 68 IN)}$$

The width of the odd-sized panel is given by: $392.70 - (69 \times 5.67) = \underline{\textbf{1 FT 8½ IN}}$ (or 20.5 IN)

Quantity of membrane material required: Allowing for an *8 inches* return loop at ground level for anchorage the total length of membrane material required for the air-building is calculated as follows:

for the quarter spherical ends = 140 x (129 FT 9½ IN + 8 IN) = 140 x 130.45 = 18,263 FT
for the barrel vault section = 36 x (259 FT 7 IN + 16 IN) = 36 x 260.89 = 9,392 FT
total = **27,655 FT** (or 9,218 YD)

Membrane weight: If the weight of the membrane is *0.25 LB/SF* (for thickness of *0.04 IN*) then the total roll weight of the membrane material before shaping and fabrication is:

$$W_m = 27655 \times 0.25 \times (70/12)$$
$$= \underline{\mathbf{40{,}330 \text{ LB}}}$$

Membrane stress without external cables: Assuming an internal pressure of 0.04 psig (i.e., equivalent to about 1⅛ IN water gauge) then the material stress in the enclosing membrane (without cables) is the circumferential stress, which can be calculated with equation A-2 (see Section 4.3)[15] as follows:

$$f_s = [\, P_i \times R_{cv} \,] \quad \text{LB/IN} \quad \ldots\ldots\ldots\ldots\ldots\ldots\ldots\ldots\ldots \text{A-2}$$

In equation A-2 the internal pressure (P_i) is in pounds per square inch (psig) and the radius of curvature of the shallow dome (R_{cv}) is in inches. If we prefer to measure the radius of the dome in feet then equation A-2 can be rewritten as:

$$\mathbf{f_s = 12\,[\, P_i \times R_{cv} \,]} \quad \text{LB/IN} \quad \ldots\ldots\ldots\ldots\ldots\ldots\ldots\ldots \text{A-9}$$

For the low profile air-building that we are considering here, the radius of curvature (R_{cv}) can be expressed in terms of the head height (H) at the center of the dome and the diameter of the dome at ground level (D), as shown in Tables A-6 and A-9:

$$R_{cv} = (4H^2 + D^2)/(8H)$$

Therefore, substituting for R_{cv} in equation A-9 we obtain:

$$\mathbf{f_s = 12\,P_i\,(4H^2 + D^2)/(8H)} \quad \text{LB/IN} \quad \ldots\ldots\ldots\ldots\ldots\ldots \text{A-10}$$

Solving for f_s with H and D in feet:

$$f_s = 12 \times 0.04\,[(4 \times 30 \times 30) + (250 \times 250)]/(8 \times 30)$$
$$= 0.48\,[3600 + 62500]/240$$
$$= \underline{\mathbf{132.2 \text{ LB/IN}}}$$

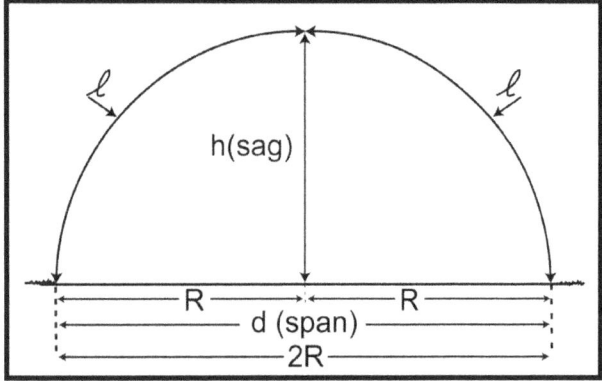

Figure A-41: Full profile barrel vault with external cables

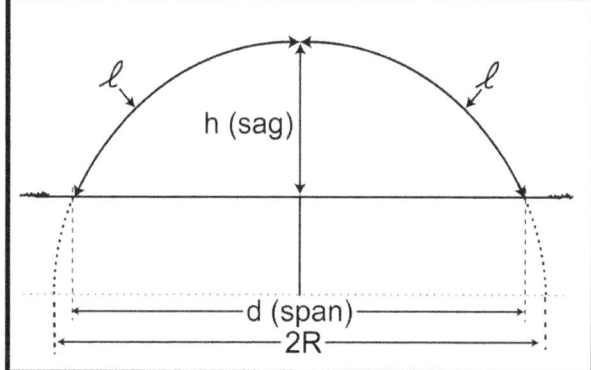

Figure A-42: Low profile barrel vault with external cables

---

[15] As shown in Figure A-12 (right side) of Section 4.3), for a barrel vaulted air-building with quarter spherical ends (i.e., dome-shaped ends) the maximum membrane stress is the circumferential stress in the barrel vault section, which is equal to twice the stress in the dome-shaped end sections.

Membrane stress with external cables: The application of a factor of safety (e.g., *2*) will result in a material strength requirement (i.e., *264.4 LB/IN*) that is well outside the strength range of commercially available membrane materials. Under these circumstances, as discussed previously in Section A-11.1.1, an external cable-network can be used to transfer a substantial amount of the membrane stress to the cables. Since the membrane stress in the barrel vault section is twice the stress in the dome sections we will design the cables for the barrel vault section only. The simplest arrangement will consist of external cables extending from one side of the building to the other across the barrel vault as shown for a low profile barrel vault in Figure A-42.

Let us assume that the cables are made of steel with a modulus of elasticity of 29,000,000 psi and the membrane is made of plastic with a modulus of elasticity of 500,000 psi. With a modulus ratio of 1:58 in favor of the steel cables the membrane will bulge out appreciably between cables. If we arbitrarily divide the *200 FT* length of the barrel vault into say *20* equal sections then the maximum distance between cables at ground level is:

$$\text{cable spacing (ground)} = 200 / 20 = \textbf{10 FT}$$

Even a very conservatively estimated maximum membrane deflection of *6 IN* between cables will reduce the radius of curvature of the membrane surface appreciably. Applying equation A-10 with $H=0.5$ *FT* and $D=10$ *FT*, we determine the maximum membrane stress (f_s) to be:

$$f_s = 12\, P_i\,(\,4\,H^2 + D^2\,)/(\,8\,H\,) \quad \text{LB/IN}$$
$$f_s = 12 \times 0.04\,[(4 \times 0.5 \times 0.5) + (10 \times 10)] / (8 \times 0.5)$$
$$= 0.48\,[1 + 100] / 4$$
$$= \textbf{12.1 LB/IN}$$

Cable stress (barrel vault): We will treat each cable as an inverted suspension cable between the two opposite sides of the barrel vault, anchored at ground level on each side. As shown in Figure A-42 the span (*d FT*) and the sag (*h FT*) at the center of the cable are simply equal to the width (*250 FT*) and the height (*30 FT*) of the barrel vault, respectively. The load per foot-run (*w LB/FT-run*) on the cable will be the product of the pressure inside the building (P_i *psig*) and the length of a one foot wide membrane strip supported by the cable:

$$w = 144\, P_i\,(10)$$
$$= 144 \times 0.04 \times 10$$
$$= \textbf{58 LB/FT-run}$$

In reference to Table A-8 the horizontal cable tension component (H_{CA} *LB*) and the maximum cable tension (T_{max} *LB*) are determined as follows:

$$H_{CA} = w\,d^2 / (8\,h)$$
$$= 58 \times 250 \times 250 / (8 \times 30)$$
$$= 3625000 / 240$$
$$= \textbf{15,104.2 LB}$$

$$T_{max} = H_{CA}\,[\,1 + (16\,h^2/d)\,]^{0.5}$$
$$= 15104.2\,[\,1 + (16 \times 30 \times 30)/250\,]^{0.5}$$
$$= 15104.2\,[\,1 + 57.6\,]^{0.5}$$
$$= 15104.2 \times 7.66$$
$$= \textbf{115,624 LB}$$

Assuming a cable design strength of *60,000 psi* the required cross-sectional area (A_{CA} *SI*) and diameter (A_D *IN*) of the cable can be calculated as follows:

$$A_{CA} = T_{max} / 60000$$
$$= 115624 / 60000$$
$$= \mathbf{1.93 \text{ SI}}$$

$$A_D = [4 A_{CA} / \pi]^{0.5}$$
$$= [4 \times 1.93 / 3.14159]^{0.5}$$
$$= [2.46]^{0.5}$$
$$= \mathbf{1.57 \text{ IN}} \text{ (or approximately 1¾ IN diameter)}$$

Membrane and cable stress (dome ends): Since the quarter-spherical ends of the elongated air-building are not complete domes it will not be possible to use the cable arrangement described previously for a low profile dome (see Section A-11.1.1). The external horizontal cable near the top of the dome will need to be replaced by some other device to which the radial vertical cables can be attached. As shown in Figure A-43, a small steel plate positioned at the apex of each of the dome-shaped ends of the air-building may serve this purpose. The two plates are tied together along the length of the building by means of a single cable that counterbalances the forces exerted by the vertical radial cables that embrace each quarter-spherical end sections[16].

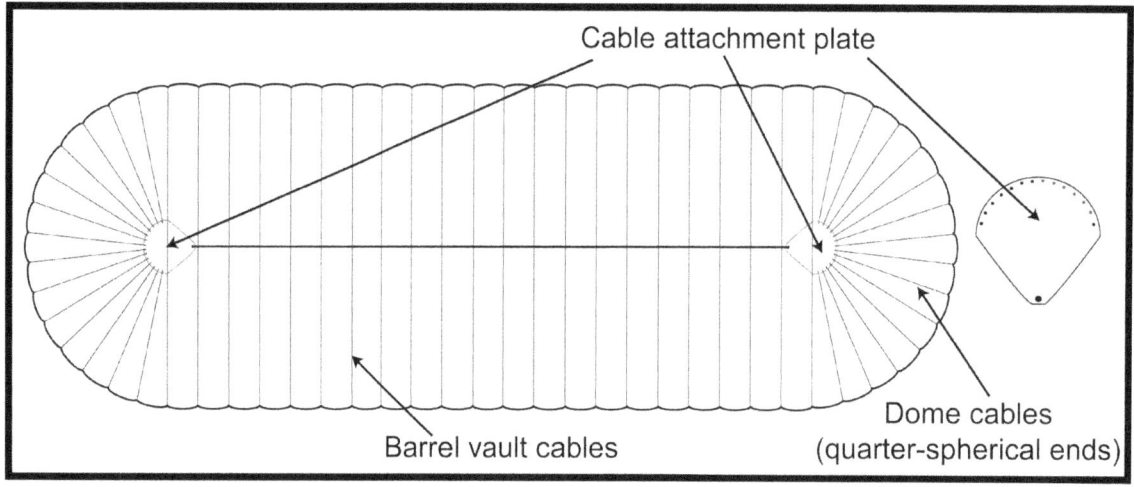

Figure A-43: Cable arrangement for elongated air-building with quarter-spherical ends

Let us assume that the cables are made of steel with a modulus of elasticity of 29,000,000 psi and the membrane is made of plastic with a modulus of elasticity of 500,000 psi. With a modulus ratio of 1:58 in favor of the steel cables the membrane will bulge out appreciably between cables. If the perimeter of the quarter-spherical end sections is *785.4 FT* then the perimeter of one end section is *392.7 FT* (i.e., *785.4 / 2 = 392.7*). If we arbitrarily divide the perimeter of each end section into *20* equal sections then the maximum distance between cables at ground level is:

cable spacing (ground) = 392.7 / 20 = **19.6 FT** (or 19 FT 7½ IN)

---

[16] The cable attachment plate could be made of some other material, such as plastic, as long as it is strong enough to resist the forces exerted by the vertical radial cables that reach down to the ground and the opposing force of the horizontal cable between the two plates along the apex of the barrel vault section. In either case, a slightly oversized rubber or plastic mat should be placed under each plate to protect the membrane enclosure of the air-building.

The plate would typically be no more than two feet in width so that the value of ℓ_1 in Figure A-39 would be *1 FT*. Therefore, if the cable attachment (i.e., plate) at the apex of the end sections is *1 FT* below the apex of the dome then the length of the cable can be determined in three steps by reference to Table A-7 as follows:

$$\begin{aligned} \theta &= 360\,(\ell_1)\,/\,(2\pi R) \\ &= 360 \times 1\,/\,(2 \times 3.14159 \times 275.4) \\ &= \mathbf{0.21°} \text{ (or 0° 12')} \end{aligned}$$

Assuming that the plate has been fabricated to have the same radius of curvature as the membrane enclosure then the diameter (*D FT*) of the plate is given by:

$$\begin{aligned} D &= 2R\sin(\theta) \\ &= 2 \times 275.4 \times 0.0035 \\ &= \mathbf{1.9 \text{ FT}} \end{aligned}$$

Therefore, the half-perimeter (*C/2 FT*) of each plate to which the vertical cables in an end section are attached to is given by:

$$\begin{aligned} C/2 &= \pi D\,/\,2 \\ &= 3.14159 \times 1.9\,/\,2 \\ &= \mathbf{2.98 \text{ FT}} \end{aligned}$$

If we divide the half-perimeter of the plate into *20* equal sections then the minimum distance between cable attachments to the plate at the top of the end sections is:

$$\text{cable spacing (top)} = 2.98\,/\,20 = \mathbf{0.15 \text{ FT}} \text{ (or 1¾ IN)}$$

Even a very conservatively estimated maximum membrane deflection of *9 IN* between cables at the ground level will reduce the radius of curvature of the membrane surface appreciably. Applying equation A-8 with *H=0.75 FT* and *D=19.6 FT*, we determine the maximum membrane stress (f_s) to be:

$$\begin{aligned} f_s &= 6\,P_i\,(4H^2 + D^2)\,/\,(8H) \quad \text{LB/IN} \\ f_s &= 6 \times 0.04\,[(4 \times 0.75 \times 0.75) + (19.6 \times 19.6)]\,/\,(8 \times 0.75) \\ &= 0.24\,[2.25 + 384.2]\,/\,6 \\ &= \mathbf{15.5 \text{ LB/IN}} \end{aligned}$$

We will treat each vertical cable as an inverted suspension cable between the plate at the top of the end sections and ground. Based on Table A-8 and in reference to Figure A-39, the span (*d FT*) and sag (*h FT*) at the center of the vertical cable can be calculated as follows:

$$\begin{aligned} \text{angle } \beta &= \arcsin((R-H)/R) \\ &= \arcsin((275.4-30)/275.4) \\ &= \arcsin(0.8911) \\ &= 1.0997 \text{ radians} \\ &= \mathbf{63° \, 0'} \end{aligned}$$

$$\begin{aligned} \text{angle } \alpha &= 90 - (\theta + \beta) \\ &= 90 - (0.21 + 63) \\ &= 90 - 63.21 \\ &= \mathbf{26.79°} \text{ (or 26° 47')} \end{aligned}$$

$$d = 2 R \sin(\alpha/2)$$
$$= 2 \times 275.4 \times \sin(13.4)$$
$$= 2 \times 275.4 \times 0.2317$$
$$= \mathbf{127.6 \text{ FT}}$$

$$h = R - [R^2 - (d^2/4)]^{0.5}$$
$$= 275.4 - [(275.4 \times 275.4) - (127.6 \times 127.6)/4]^{0.5}$$
$$= 275.4 - [75845.2 - 4070.4]^{0.5}$$
$$= 275.4 - 267.9$$
$$= \mathbf{7.5 \text{ FT}}$$

To determine the cable tension we need to establish the load on the cable. With the top cable attachment (i.e., at the plate) located *1 FT* down along the curved surface (ℓ_1 *FT*) from the apex of the end sections the cable spacing at the top level was calculated previously to be *0.15 FT*. Similarly the cable spacing at ground level was calculated to be *19.6 FT*. Accordingly the average load per foot-run (*w LB/FT-run*) on the cable will be the product of the pressure inside the building (P_i *psig*) and the average length of a one foot wide membrane strip supported by the vertical cable:

$$w = 144 P_i (0.15 + 19.6)/2$$
$$= 144 \times 0.04 \times 9.88$$
$$= \mathbf{57 \text{ LB/FT-run}}$$

In reference to Table A-8 the horizontal cable tension component (H_{CA} *LB*) and the maximum cable tension (T_{max} *LB*) are determined as follows:

$$H_{CA} = w d^2 / (8 h)$$
$$= 57 \times 127.6 \times 127.6 / (8 \times 7.5)$$
$$= 928060.3 / 60$$
$$= \mathbf{15{,}467.7 \text{ LB}}$$

$$T_{max} = H_{CA} [1 + (16 h^2/d)]^{0.5}$$
$$= 15467.7 [1 + (16 \times 7.5 \times 7.5)/127.6]^{0.5}$$
$$= 15467.7 [1 + 7.05]^{0.5}$$
$$= 15467.7 \times 2.84$$
$$= \mathbf{43{,}895 \text{ LB}}$$

Assuming a cable design strength of *60,000 psi* the required cross-sectional area (A_{CA} *SI*) and diameter (A_D *IN*) of the cable can be calculated as follows:

$$A_{CA} = T_{max} / 60000$$
$$= 43895 / 60000$$
$$= \mathbf{0.73 \text{ SI}}$$

$$A_D = [4 A_{CA} / \pi]^{0.5}$$
$$= [4 \times 0.73 / 3.14159]^{0.5}$$
$$= [0.93]^{0.5}$$
$$= \mathbf{0.97 \text{ IN}} \text{ (or approximately 1 IN diameter)}$$

Anchorage forces: If the air-building is anchored at ground level with a steel pipe that fits into a membrane sleeve and is anchored to the ground at *4-foot* (*48 IN*) centers then according to equation A-6 the anchorage force per foot-run of perimeter is given by:

anchorage force = 0.44 R LB/FT-run = 4 (0.44 R) LB/anchor point

Since the radius of curvature (R FT) of the dome is *275.4 FT* the anchorage force per anchor point is:

anchorage force = 4 (0.44 x 275.4)
= **484.7 LB/anchor**

A-11.2.2 Design of Full Profile Elongated Air-Building

As a final example in Section A-11 we will apply the equations provided in Tables A-9, A-8, A-7 and A-6 to a full profile air-supported barrel vault with quarter spherical ends, with a width of *200 FT* and a total length of *600 FT* (i.e., *L=(600-100-100)=400*).

$$\begin{aligned}
\textbf{floor area} &= (\pi R^2) + (2RL) \\
&= (3.14159 \times 100 \times 100) + (2 \times 100 \times 400) \\
&= 31415.9 + 80000.0 \\
&= \underline{\textbf{111,416 SF}}
\end{aligned}$$

$$\begin{aligned}
\textbf{perimeter at ground level} &= (2\pi R) + (2L) \\
&= (2 \times 3.14159 \times 100) + (2 \times 400) \\
&= 628.3 + 800 \\
&= \underline{\textbf{1,428 FT}}
\end{aligned}$$

$$\begin{aligned}
\textbf{head height 80 FT from center} &= [R^2 - d^2]^{0.5} \\
&= [(100 \times 100) - (80 \times 80)]^{0.5} \\
&= [10000 - 6400]^{0.5} \\
&= \underline{\textbf{60 FT}}
\end{aligned}$$

$$\begin{aligned}
\textbf{10 FT head height from side} &= [(2Rx) - x^2]^{0.5} \\
&= [(2 \times 100 \times 10) - (10 \times 10)]^{0.5} \\
&= [2000 - 100]^{0.5} \\
&= \underline{\textbf{43.6 FT}}
\end{aligned}$$

$$\begin{aligned}
\textbf{7 FT head height from center} &= [R^2 - h^2]^{0.5} \\
&= [(100 \times 100) - (7 \times 7)]^{0.5} \\
&= [10000 - 49]^{0.5} \\
&= \underline{\textbf{99.75 FT}} \text{ (or 9 IN from side)}
\end{aligned}$$

$$\begin{aligned}
\textbf{external curved surface area} &= (2\pi R^2) + (\pi R L) \\
&= (2 \times 3.14159 \times 100 \times 100) + (3.14159 \times 100 \times 400) \\
&= 62831.8 + 125663.6 \\
&= \underline{\textbf{188,495 SF}}
\end{aligned}$$

$$\begin{aligned}
\textbf{internal volume} &= (2\pi R^3 / 3) + (\pi R^2 L / 2) \\
&= [(2 \times \pi \times 100 \times 100 \times 100) / 3] + [(\pi \times 100 \times 100 \times 400) / 2]
\end{aligned}$$

$$= [(2094393.3) + (6283180.0)]$$
$$= \underline{\mathbf{8{,}377{,}573 \; \text{CF}}}$$

Panel width for given material roll width: Let us assume in the above example that the membrane material provided by the manufacturer has a roll width of only *70 IN*. Allowing a seam width between panels of *2 IN*, the effective width of the panels at ground level will be *68 IN* (i.e., *70 IN* less *2 IN*). Previously in this Section we calculated the perimeter of the full profile dome portion (i.e., without the barrel vault portion) to be *628.3 FT*.

number of dome panels = (perimeter / panel width)
$$= (628.3 / (68/12))$$
$$= \underline{\mathbf{110.9}} \text{ (or 55.45 panels for each end dome section)}$$

Therefore, for the two dome-shaped ends of the air-building will each require *55* equal-sized panels and one odd-sized panel with a width at ground level of *29.8 IN*. In addition, the *400 FT* long barrel vault section between the two quarter spherical ends will require:

number of barrel vault panels = (400 / panel width)
$$= (400 / (68/12))$$
$$= \underline{\mathbf{70.59}}$$

Since these panels do not vary in width from the top of the building to the ground they can be continuous from one side of the barrel vault to the other. Therefore, since the dome panels are *157.1 FT* (or *157 FT 1 IN*) long, the barrel vault panels will be twice as long (i.e., *314.2 FT* or *314 FT 2 IN*).

Proceeding in steps with the equations listed in Table A-7, the widths of each of the *70* equal-sized panels and the odd-sized panel at the indicated distance along the curved surface from the top of the dome are determined for the quarter spherical ends of the building as follows:

at 5 FT from top of dome: α = (360 x ℓ)/(2 π R) = (360 x 5)/(2 x 3.14159 x 100) = **2° 52'**
$\qquad\qquad\qquad\qquad\quad$ D = 2 R sin(α) = (2 x 100 x 0.0500) = **10 FT**
$\qquad\qquad\qquad\qquad\quad$ L = π D / 2 = (3.14159 x 10 / 2) = **15.71 FT**
$\qquad\qquad\qquad\qquad\quad$ W = L / N = 15.71 / 55.45 = **$\underline{\mathbf{0 \; \text{FT} \; 3\frac{1}{2} \; \text{IN}}}$** (or 0.283 FT)

The width of the odd-sized panel is given by: W = 15.71 − (55 x 0.283) = $\underline{\mathbf{0 \; \text{FT} \; 1\frac{3}{4} \; \text{IN}}}$

at 10 FT from top of dome: α = (360 x ℓ)/(2 π R) = (360 x 10)/(2 x 3.14159 x 100) = **5° 44'**
$\qquad\qquad\qquad\qquad\quad$ D = 2 R sin(α) = (2 x 100 x 0.0999) = **19.98 FT**
$\qquad\qquad\qquad\qquad\quad$ L = π D / 2 = (3.14159 x 19.98 / 2) = **31.38 FT**
$\qquad\qquad\qquad\qquad\quad$ W = L / N = 31.38 / 55.45 = **$\underline{\mathbf{0 \; \text{FT} \; 6\frac{3}{4} \; \text{IN}}}$** (or 0.566 FT)

The width of the odd-sized panel is given by: W = 62.77 − (55 x 1.132) = $\underline{\mathbf{0 \; \text{FT} \; 1\frac{2}{3} \; \text{IN}}}$

at 20 FT from top of dome: α = (360 x ℓ)/(2 π R) = (360 x 20)/(2 x 3.14159 x 100) = **11° 28'**
$\qquad\qquad\qquad\qquad\quad$ D = 2 R sin(α) = (2 x 100 x 0.1989) = **39.78 FT**
$\qquad\qquad\qquad\qquad\quad$ L = π D / 2 = (3.14159 x 39.78 / 2) = **62.49 FT**
$\qquad\qquad\qquad\qquad\quad$ W = L / N = 62.49 / 55.45 = **$\underline{\mathbf{1 \; \text{FT} \; 1\frac{1}{2} \; \text{IN}}}$** (or 1.126 FT)

The width of the odd-sized panel is given by: W = 62.49 − (55 x 1.126) = $\underline{\mathbf{0 \; \text{FT} \; 6\frac{3}{4} \; \text{IN}}}$

at 40 FT from top of dome: α = (360 x ℓ)/(2 π R) = (360 x 40)/(2 x 3.14159 x 100) = **22° 55'**
$\qquad\qquad\qquad\qquad\quad$ D = 2 R sin(α) = (2 x 100 x 0.3894) = **77.88 FT**

$$L = \pi D / 2 = (3.14159 \times 77.88 / 2) = \textbf{122.33 FT}$$
$$W = L / N = 122.33 / 55.45 = \textbf{2 FT 2½ IN} \text{ (or 2.21 FT)}$$

The width of the odd-sized panel is given by: $W = 122.33 - (55 \times 2.21) = \textbf{0 FT 9¼ IN}$

at 60 FT from top of dome:
$$\alpha = (360 \times \ell)/(2 \pi R) = (360 \times 60)/(2 \times 3.14159 \times 100) = \textbf{34° 23'}$$
$$D = 2 R \sin(\alpha) = (2 \times 100 \times 0.5648) = \textbf{112.96 FT}$$
$$L = \pi D / 2 = (3.14159 \times 112.96 / 2) = \textbf{177.44 FT}$$
$$W = L / N = 177.44 / 55.45 = \textbf{3 FT 2½ IN} \text{ (or 3.2 FT)}$$

The width of the odd-sized panel is given by: $W = 177.44 - (55 \times 3.2) = \textbf{1 FT 5 IN}$

at 120 FT from top of dome:
$$\alpha = (360 \times \ell)/(2 \pi R) = (360 \times 120)/(2 \times (\pi) \times 100) = \textbf{68° 45'}$$
$$D = 2 R \sin(\alpha) = (2 \times 100 \times 0.9320) = \textbf{186.4 FT}$$
$$L = \pi D / 2 = (3.14159 \times 186.4 / 2) = \textbf{292.8 FT}$$
$$W = L / N = 292.8 / 55.45 = \textbf{5 FT 3¼ IN} \text{ (or 5.28 FT)}$$

The width of the odd-sized panel is given by: $W = 365.20 - (55 \times 5.27) = \textbf{1 FT 7 IN}$

at ground level:
$$\alpha = \textbf{90° 0'}$$
$$\ell = (\pi R)/2 = (3.14159 \times 100)/2 = \textbf{157.1 FT}$$
$$D = 2 R = \textbf{200 FT}$$
$$L = \pi R = (3.14159 \times 100) = \textbf{314.16 FT}$$
$$W = L / N = 314.16 / 55.45 = \textbf{5 FT 8 IN} \text{ (or 5.67 FT or 68 IN)}$$

The width of the odd-sized panel is given by: $314.16 - (55 \times 5.67) = \textbf{2 FT 3¾ IN}$ (or 27.7 IN)

Quantity of membrane material required: Allowing for an *8 IN* return loop at ground level for anchorage the total length of membrane material required for the air-building is calculated as follows:

for the quarter spherical ends = $112 \times (157 \text{ FT } 1 \text{ IN} + 8 \text{ IN}) = 112 \times 157.77 = 17,670$ FT
for the barrel vault section = $71 \times (314 \text{ FT } 2 \text{ IN} + 16 \text{ IN}) = 71 \times 315.5 = 22,403$ FT
total = **40,073 FT** (or 13,358 YD)

Membrane weight: If the weight of the membrane is *0.25 LB/SF* (for thickness of *0.04 IN*) then the total roll weight of the membrane material before shaping and fabrication is:

$$W_m = 40073 \times 0.25 \times (70 / 12)$$
$$= \textbf{58,440 LB}$$

Membrane stress without external cables: Assuming an internal pressure of 0.04 psi (i.e., equivalent to about 1⅛ IN water gauge) then the material stress in the enclosing membrane (without cables) is the circumferential stress, which can be calculated with equation A-9 as follows:

$$f_s = 12 [P_i \times R_{cv}] \text{ LB/IN} \quad\quad\quad\quad\quad\quad \text{A-9}$$
$$= 12 \times 0.04 \times 100$$
$$= \textbf{48 LB/IN}$$

Membrane stress with external cables: The application of a factor of safety (e.g., *2*) will result in a material strength requirement (i.e., *96 LB/IN*) that is likely to be outside of the strength range of commercially available membrane materials. Under these circumstances, as discussed previously in Section A-11.2.1, an external cable-network can be used to transfer a substantial amount of the membrane stress to the cables. Since the membrane stress in the barrel vault section is twice the stress in the dome sections we will design the cables for the barrel vault section only. The simplest arrangement will consist of external cables extending from one side of the building to the other across the barrel vault as shown for a full profile barrel vault in Figure A-41.

Let us assume that the cables are made of steel with a modulus of elasticity of 29,000,000 psi and the membrane is made of plastic with a modulus of elasticity of 500,000 psi. With a modulus ratio of 1:58 in favor of the steel cables the membrane will bulge out appreciably between cables. If we arbitrarily divide the *400 FT* length of the barrel vault into say *20* equal sections then the maximum distance between cables at ground level is:

cable spacing (ground) = 400 / 20 = **20 FT**

Even a very conservatively estimated maximum membrane deflection of *12 IN* between cables will reduce the radius of curvature of the membrane surface appreciably. Applying equation A-10 with *H=1 FT* and *D=20 FT*, we determine the maximum membrane stress (f_s) to be:

$$f_s = 12\, P_i\, (4\,H^2 + D^2)\, / \,(8\,H) \quad \text{LB/IN}$$

$$f_s = 12 \times 0.04\, [(4 \times 1 \times 1) + (20 \times 20)]\, /\, (8 \times 1)$$
$$= 0.48\, [4 + 400]\, /\, 8$$
$$= \mathbf{24.24 \text{ LB/IN}}$$

Cable stress (barrel vault): We will treat each cable as an inverted suspension cable between the two opposite sides of the barrel vault, anchored at ground level on each side. As shown in Figure A-41 the span (*d FT*) and the sag (*h FT*) at the center of the cable are simply equal to the diameter (*200 FT*) and the radius (*100 FT*) of the barrel vault, respectively. The load per foot-run (*w LB/FT-run*) on the cable will be the product of the pressure inside the building (P_i *psig*) and the length of a one foot wide membrane strip supported by the cable:

$$w = 144\, P_i\, (20)$$
$$= 144 \times 0.04 \times 20$$
$$= \mathbf{115.2 \text{ LB/FT-run}}$$

In reference to Table A-8 the horizontal cable tension component (H_{CA} *LB*) and the maximum cable tension (T_{max} *LB*) are determined as follows:

$$H_{CA} = w\, d^2\, /\, (8\,h)$$
$$= 115.2 \times 200 \times 200 \,/\, (8 \times 100)$$
$$= 4608000 \,/\, 800$$
$$= \mathbf{5{,}760 \text{ LB}}$$

$$T_{max} = H_{CA}\, [\, 1 + (16\, h^2/d)\,]^{0.5}$$
$$= 5760\, [\, 1 + (16 \times 100 \times 100)/200\,]^{0.5}$$
$$= 5760\, [\, 1 + 800\,]^{0.5}$$
$$= 5760 \times 28.3$$
$$= \mathbf{163{,}019 \text{ LB}}$$

Assuming a cable design strength of *60,000 psi* the required cross-sectional area (A_{CA} *SI*) and diameter (A_D *IN*) of the cable can be calculated as follows:

$$A_{CA} = T_{max}\, /\, 60000$$
$$= 115624\, /\, 60000$$

$$= \mathbf{2.72 \text{ SI}}$$
$$A_D = [4 A_{CA} / \pi]^{0.5}$$
$$= [4 \times 2.72 / 3.14159]^{0.5}$$
$$= [3.46]^{0.5}$$
$$= \underline{\mathbf{1.86 \text{ IN}}} \text{ (or approximately 2 IN)}$$

Membrane and cable stress (dome ends): As discussed previously in Section A-11.2.1 for the low profile case, the quarter-spherical ends of the elongated air-building are not complete domes. Therefore it will not be possible to use the cable arrangement described previously for a low profile dome (see Section A-11.1.1). Instead, as shown in Figure A-43, a small steel plate positioned at the apex of each of the dome-shaped ends of the air-building can be used to attach the vertical radial cables. The two plates are tied together along the length of the building by means of a single cable that counterbalances the forces exerted by the vertical radial cables at each end of the air-building.

Again, as in the previous examples, we will assume the cables to be made of steel with a modulus of elasticity of 29,000,000 psi surrounding a plastic membrane enclosure with a modulus of elasticity of 500,000 psi. Due to its much lower modulus of elasticity the membrane will bulge out appreciably between cables. If the perimeter of the quarter-spherical end sections is *628.3 FT* then the perimeter of one end section is *314.2 FT* (i.e., *628.3 / 2 = 314.2*). If we arbitrarily divide the perimeter of each end section into *12* equal sections then the maximum distance between cables at ground level is:

cable spacing (ground) = 314.2 / 12 = **26.2 FT** (or 26 FT 2 IN)

The plate would typically be no more than two feet in width so that the value of ℓ_1 in Figure A-38 would be *1 FT*. Therefore, if the cable attachment (i.e., plate) at the apex of the end sections is *1 FT* below the apex of the dome then the length of the cable can be determined in three steps by reference to Table A-7 as follows:

$$\theta = 360 (\ell_1) / (2 \pi R)$$
$$= 360 \times 1 / (2 \times 3.14159 \times 100)$$
$$= \mathbf{0.57°} \text{ (or 0° 34')}$$

Assuming that the plate has been fabricated to have the same radius of curvature as the membrane enclosure then the diameter (*D FT*) of the plate is given by:

$$D = 2 R \sin(\theta)$$
$$= 2 \times 100 \times 0.0166$$
$$= \mathbf{3.3 \text{ FT}}$$

Therefore, the half-perimeter (*C/2 FT*) of each plate to which the vertical cables in an end section are attached to is given by:

$$C/2 = \pi D / 2$$
$$= 3.14159 \times 3.3 / 2$$
$$= \mathbf{5.22 \text{ FT}}$$

If we divide the half-perimeter of the plate into *12* equal sections then the minimum distance between cable attachments to the plate at the top of the end sections is:

cable spacing (top) = 5.22 / 12 = **0.43 FT** (or 5¼ IN)

Even a very conservatively estimated maximum membrane deflection of *9 IN* between cables at the ground level will reduce the radius of curvature of the membrane surface appreciably. Applying equation A-7 with *H=0.75 FT* and *D=26.2 FT*, we determine the maximum membrane stress (f_s) to be:

$$f_s = 6 (P_i \times R_{cv}) \text{ LB/IN}$$
$$f_s = 6 \times 0.04 \times 100$$
$$= \mathbf{24 \text{ LB/IN}}$$

We will treat each vertical cable as an inverted suspension cable between the plate at the top of the end sections and ground. Based on Table A-8 and in reference to Figure A-38, the span (*d FT*) and sag (*h FT*) at the center of the vertical cable can be calculated as follows:

$$\text{angle } \alpha = 90 - \theta$$
$$= 90 - 0.57$$
$$= \mathbf{89.43°} \text{ (or 89° 26')}$$

$$d = 2 R \sin(\alpha/2)$$
$$= 2 \times 100 \times \sin(44.7)$$
$$= 2 \times 100 \times 0.7036$$
$$= \mathbf{140.7 \text{ FT}}$$

$$h = R - [R^2 - (d^2/4)]^{0.5}$$
$$= 100 - [(100 \times 100) - (140.7 \times 140.7)/4]^{0.5}$$
$$= 100 - [10000 - 4950.5]^{0.5}$$
$$= 100 - 71.1$$
$$= \mathbf{28.9 \text{ FT}}$$

To determine the cable tension we need to establish the load on the cable. With the top cable attachment (i.e., at the plate) located *1 FT* down along the curved surface (ℓ_1 *FT*) from the apex of the end sections the cable spacing at the top level was calculated previously to be *0.43 FT*. Similarly the cable spacing at ground level was calculated to be *26.2 FT*. Accordingly the average load per foot-run (*w LB/FT-run*) on the cable will be the product of the pressure inside the building (P_i *psig*) and the average length of a one foot wide membrane strip supported by the vertical cable:

$$w = 144 P_i (0.43 + 26.2)/2$$
$$= 144 \times 0.04 \times 13.32$$
$$= \mathbf{77 \text{ LB/FT-run}}$$

In reference to Table A-8 the horizontal cable tension component (H_{CA} *LB*) and the maximum cable tension (T_{max} *LB*) are determined as follows:

$$H_{CA} = w d^2 / (8 h)$$
$$= 77 \times 140.7 \times 140.7 / (8 \times 28.9)$$
$$= 1524329.7 / 231.2$$
$$= \mathbf{6{,}593.1 \text{ LB}}$$

$$T_{max} = H_{CA} [1 + (16 h^2/d)]^{0.5}$$
$$= 6593.1 [1 + (16 \times 28.9 \times 28.9)/140.7]^{0.5}$$
$$= 6593.1 [1 + 94.98]^{0.5}$$
$$= 6593.1 \times 9.8$$

$$= \underline{\mathbf{64{,}591 \text{ LB}}}$$

Assuming a cable design strength of *60,000 psi* the required cross-sectional area (A_{CA} *SI*) and diameter (A_D *IN*) of the cable can be calculated as follows:

$$\begin{aligned}
A_{CA} &= T_{max} / 60000 \\
&= 64591 / 60000 \\
&= \mathbf{1.08} \text{ SI} \\
A_D &= [\, 4\, A_{CA} / \pi \,]^{0.5} \\
&= [\, 4 \times 1.08 / 3.14159 \,]^{0.5} \\
&= [\, 1.38 \,]^{0.5} \\
&= \underline{\mathbf{1.17 \text{ IN}}} \text{ (or approximately 1¼ IN diameter)}
\end{aligned}$$

Anchorage forces: If the air-building is anchored at ground level with a steel pipe that fits into a membrane sleeve and is anchored to the ground at *4-foot* (*48 IN*) centers then according to equation A-6 the anchorage force per foot-run of perimeter is given by:

anchorage force = 0.44 R LB/FT-run = 4 (0.44 R) LB/anchor point

Since the radius of curvature (*R FT*) of the dome is *100 FT* the anchorage force per anchor point is:

anchorage force = 4 (0.44 × 100)
$$= \underline{\mathbf{176 \text{ LB/anchor}}}$$

Appendix B
Pneumatic-Within-Pneumatic Dwellings

Almost without exception air-supported and air-inflated construction has been applied to large span buildings spanning anywhere from 100 to 500 feet. This may be one of the reasons why such a promising system of construction from a structural point of view, could not sustain its popularity beyond a 20-year life-span. Since the need for large-span buildings is rather small, it follows that the commercial market for air-supported structures was likewise limited. Certainly, to capture an appreciable portion of the building market a constructional system must be adaptable to a wider range of applications. Ideally, this range should extend into one or more sectors of greater demand, such as housing.

In the early 1970s the author together with one of his graduate architecture students (James Montero) in the School of Architecture and Environmental Design at the California Polytechnic State University (San Luis Obispo), explored the feasibility of a pneumatic-within-pneumatic *air-home* that utilizes both air-supported and air-inflated components. The impetus for Montero's Master degree thesis (Montero 1972) was his unwillingness to accept at face value the assumption that the pneumatic concept of construction is unsuitable for small-span shelters, such as single-family dwellings. At the outset of his thesis research he recognized that while from a structural point of view the single skin air-supported dome or cylindrical form with square or spherical ends is a feasible structural solution even for very small spans, there are a number of non-structural factors that appear to present formidable obstacles to the realization of a commercially viable, mass-produced air-home.

- Air-structures are dynamic, not static structures. While they naturally form double curvature synclastic forms, such as domes, they resist being distorted and forced into non-conforming shapes. This leads to difficulties in the subdivision of internal spaces for architectural planning purposes. Obviously, the space enclosed by a dome cannot be subdivided into rigid, rectangular box-like rooms, without considerable constructional difficulties, excessive cost due to structural duplication, and at least partial sacrifice of the intrinsically favorable characteristics of the pneumatically enclosed space.

- The enclosing membrane of an air-supported building is very thin and, therefore, offers virtually no thermal insulation to the building interior. To make matters worse, under daytime insolation the typical plastic membrane behaves similar to glass and is subject to the *greenhouse* effect. The membrane material admits incident solar radiation but resists the passage of the characteristically long wavelength radiation which is emitted internally by the objects within the enclosed space. During a 24-hour period this can lead to severe overheating during the day and significant heat losses at night.

- Air-supported membranes are unable to sustain concentrated loads. Therefore, all building support services, such as lighting fixtures, electric cables, air ducts and water pipes are required to be either self-supporting or directly attached to secondary structural systems (i.e., partitions or frames).

The results of this research project, which were presented at an international symposium in Montreal, Canada in 1976 (Montero and Pohl 1976) and a subsequent thesis (Turki 1974) form the basis of this appendix. It is not intended to be suggested that the approach described in this appendix for the design of air-supported single-family dwellings overcomes all of the problems that may have hindered such efforts in the past. However, the research results do indicate that skillful application of the pneumatic-within-pneumatic concept (Murata 1972) can lead to some novel and interesting design solutions for small span structures such as homes.

B-1 The Pneumatic-Within-Pneumatic Approach

In the pneumatic-within-pneumatic concept a single-skin air-supported membrane encloses a space containing one or more smaller air-supported or air-inflated structures (Figure B-1). The outer membrane functions as the principal structural support system of the building by resisting wind forces and all forms of precipitation, such as rain, snow, hail, dust, and pollution. The internal structures serve purely as self-supporting spatial definers, by subdividing the building into architecturally and functionally useful spaces.

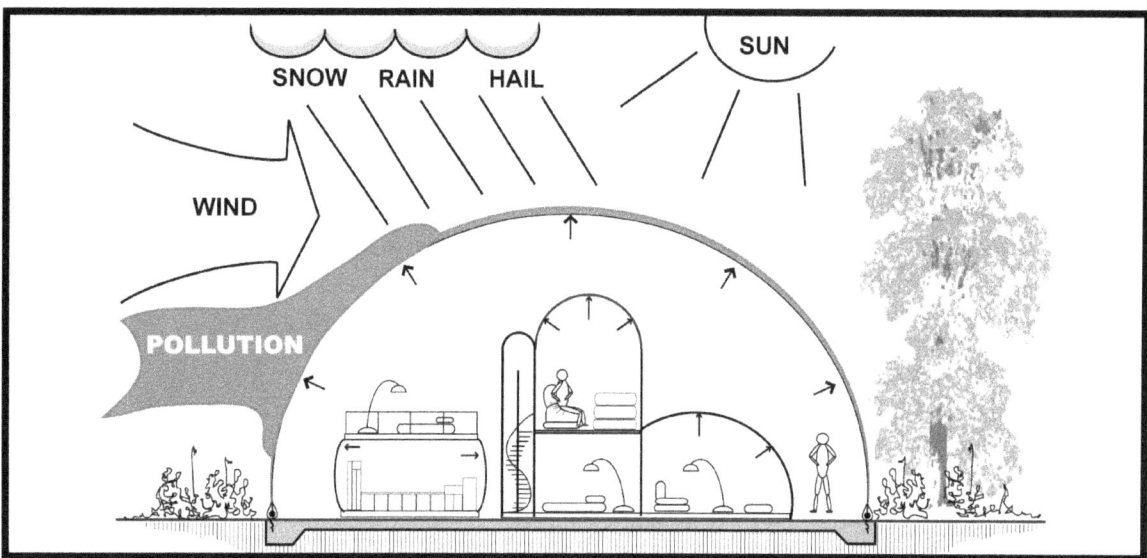

Figure B-1: The pneumatic-within-pneumatic concept applied to a dwelling

At the commencement of the investigation a number of design criteria were established to serve as a performance specification in the development of a pneumatic-within-pneumatic single-family dwelling.

1. Despite the characteristically low thermal resistivity provided by a thin plastic film, the dwelling should provide a reasonable degree of thermal insulation. In this respect, the exclusion from the interior spaces of direct solar radiation during the warmest period of the day in combination with an average thermal transmittance value (i.e., U-value) of 0.5 BTU per °F-hour-square foot was established as an acceptable upper limit for mild coastal climates.

2. The fabrication of the components of the constructional system should be amenable to low cost mass-production techniques. At the same time, the relatively unskilled building owner should be able to accomplish the final on-site assembly and installation of the components.

3. For the subdivision of internal spaces the building system should draw upon the full range of air-supported and air-inflated single-story and multi-story building types that were known at that time, regardless of whether they had already been tested in the commercial market or were still mere research proposals (Figure B-2).

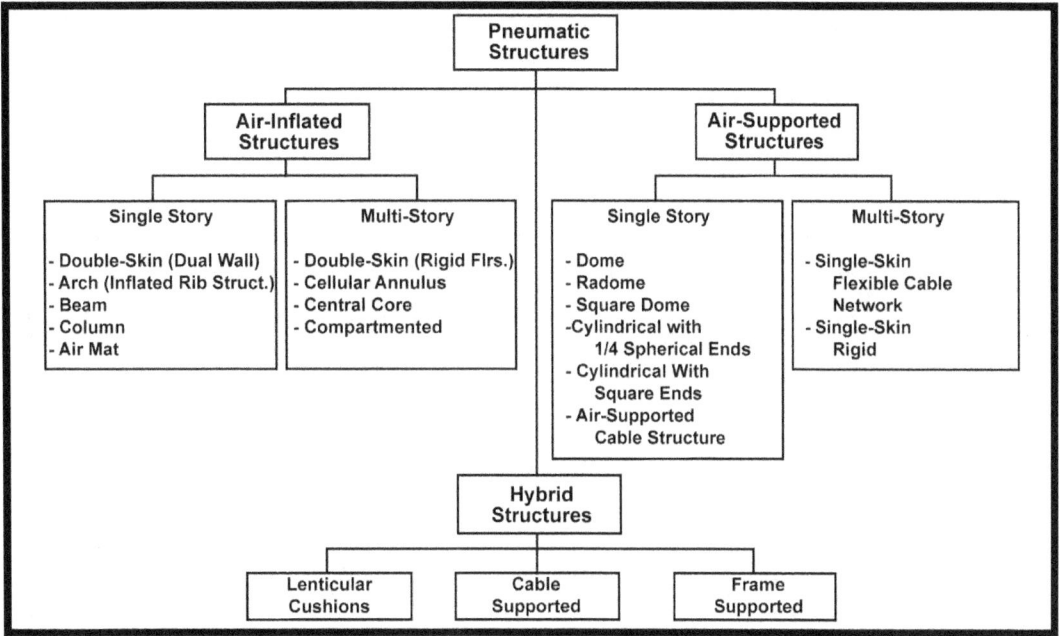

Figure B-2: Classification of pneumatic building types

4. The completed dwelling should offer the building owner a high degree of flexibility in space planning, throughout the life-span of the building. At short notice and without undue effort or cost, the building owner should be able to rearrange the spaces within the building to accommodate temporary and permanent changes in function.

5. The total cost, to the owner, of the completed dwelling should be less than the cost of a mobile home serving an equivalent function.

Finally, to simplify the investigation, it was agreed that the building site could be assumed to be level. This decision was considered in recognizing a fundamental limitation of all types of air-supported structures. Although a small number of air-buildings extending over multi-level footings have been constructed in the past, they have necessitated the development of unique anchorage details and fabrication patterns.

B-2 The Conceptual Design

To satisfy the above criteria the pneumatic-within-pneumatic constructional system was conceived, ideally, as an integrated conglomeration of air-supported and air-inflated space enclosures in which all but the external weather and wind resisting membrane could be rearranged, added to, deleted, or replaced during the life-span of the dwelling. The practical realization of this ideal required the detailed analysis of a number of structural, environmental, and architectural design determinants.

B-2.1 Structural Considerations

The exterior air-supported enclosure, which is assumed to be in the shape of a shallow dome, is required to resist two principal forces. A uniform vertical upward force due to an internal pressure of approximately 1 inch water gauge and horizontal wind drag and uplift forces based on an assumed maximum design velocity. These forces will generate tensile material stresses as well as anchorage forces that need to be resisted by means of ties or footing anchors positioned around the perimeter of the building. Typical numerical values for these anchorage forces and resultant, material stresses for a design wind velocity of 90 mph are listed in Table B-1.

Table B-1: Material stresses and anchorage forces for the exterior dome shaped enclosure

Exterior Dome		Max. Material Stress lb./in.	Anchorage Force lb./ft.	Covered Area	
Diameter ft.	Height ft.			Total sq.ft.	Min. 6 ft. Stand. Ht. sq.ft.
40	20	35	203	1257	1144
40	15	31	212	1257	924
50	25	44	254	1964	1850
50	20	40	260	1964	1638
50	15	38	288	1964	1348
60	30	52	305	2827	2714
60	25	48	310	2827	2705
60	20	46	330	2827	2243
60	15	46	381	2827	1866

In most cases it will be desirable to reinforce the exterior membrane with cables to allow a wider choice of plastic materials. The typical polyester scrim-based material coated with polyvinyl chloride (PVC), which became a worldwide standard for air-buildings, provides neither the range of finishes nor the degree of transparency likely to be desired by home owners. Instead, it is anticipated that ultraviolet stabilized clear, translucent and colored PVC and polyethylene films in the thickness range of 10 to 24 mil[1] would be preferred. However, due to excessive elongation under load (i.e., relatively low modulus of elasticity) the tensile working strength of these materials is only about 15 pounds per inch, which is well below the required material stresses shown in Table B-1.

The ability to use such materials for the exterior dome of an *air-home* therefore depends on the existence of an exterior reinforcing cable-network. As long as the cable material has a significantly higher modulus of elasticity than the membrane material, the latter will bulge out between adjacent cables thereby transferring a considerable portion of the structural forces to the cables. More precisely, this transfer is achieved by the resultant increase in the radius of curvature of the membrane between adjacent cables. Since the tensile stresses experienced by a membrane container under internal pressure are directly proportional to the radius of curvature of the container surface, the smaller the radius of curvature (or the more curved the surface) the smaller

---

[1] One *mil* is equal to one thousands of an inch.

will be the stresses required to be resisted by the membrane enclosure. For practical purposes, utilizing cables in this manner, it is possible to reduce the tensile stresses in an air~ supported dome by a factor of two or more.

As shown in Figure B-3, a wide range of both single-story and multi-story air-supported and air-inflated configurations are available for consideration as interior space enclosures. For these structures, only the forces due to self-weight, superimposed live-load (in the case of multi-story structures) and internal pressure need to be considered for design purposes.

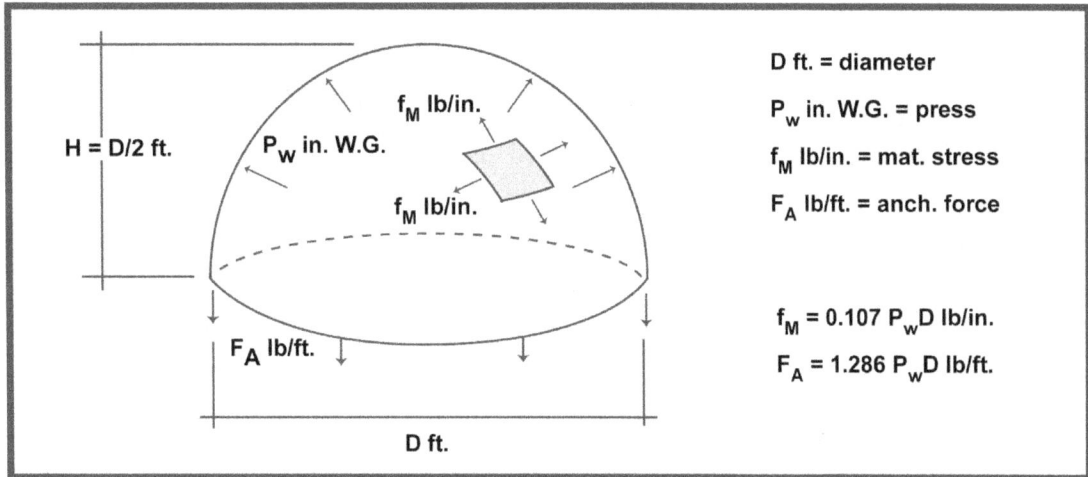

Figure B-3: Material stresses and anchorage forces in a high profile dome

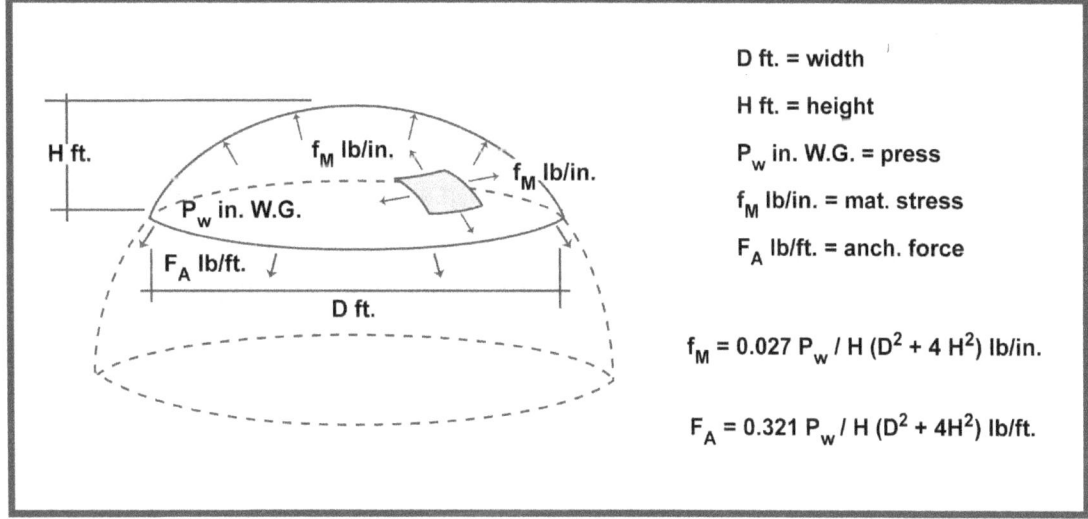

Figure B-4: Material stresses and anchorage forces in a low profile dome

For all single-story configurations (Figures B-3 to B-14) the self-weight of the membrane material should be less than 1 lb/sqft, requiring a supporting air pressure of around 0.2 inch water gauge above the ambient pressure of 1 inch water gauge that is assumed to be required to stabilize the external membrane enclosure. It is recommended that these internal structures be provided with a light edge beam, such as a ¾ inch diameter plastic conduit pipe, to serve as a self-weight anchorage system. If considered necessary the anchorage beam may be tied to the building floor by means of small metal hooks. Such hooks should allow for some upward movement of the perimeter beam, thereby acting as a convenient relief valve in case of over-pressurization.

Figures B-3 to B-18 indicate the expected internal pressures, material stresses, anchorage forces, and load-bearing capacities (where appropriate) for a wide range of air-supported and air-inflated space enclosures. The single-skin air-supported structures shown in Figures B-3 to B-8, as well as the donut-shaped air-building shown in Figure B-11, are prime candidates for the external enclosure of a pneumatic-within-pneumatic constructional system. While the tubular air-inflated structures (Figures B-9 and B-10) and double-skin air-inflated structures (Figures B-12 to B-14) are good candidates for defining internal spaces, they may of course be used also as the external enclosure of a pneumatic-within-pneumatic constructional system. In this case only the innermost living space may be pressurized. However, even the internal spaces could be defined by air-inflated structures thereby obviating the need for any of the habitable spaces to be pressurized. On the other hand, any combination of air-supported and air-inflated can be used to define the internal spaces within the external enclosure.

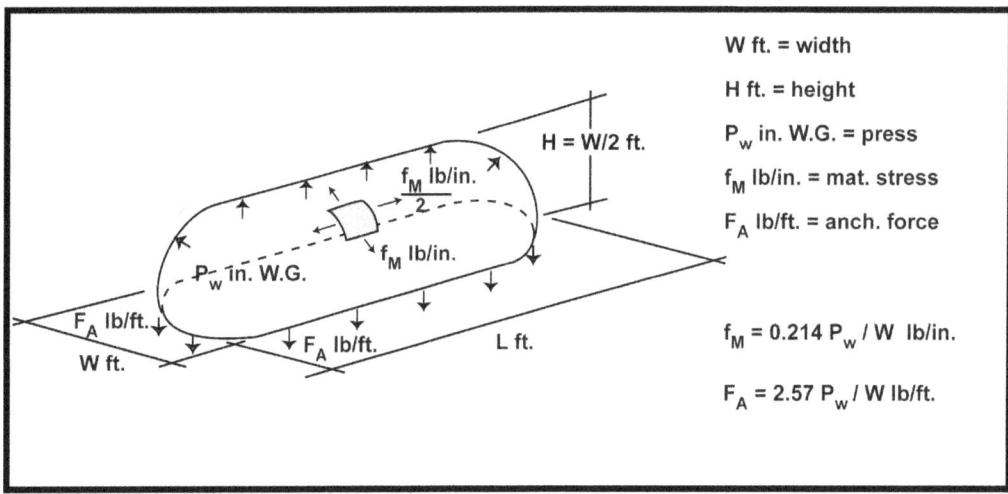

Figure B-5: Material stresses and anchorage forces in a high profile elongated air-building

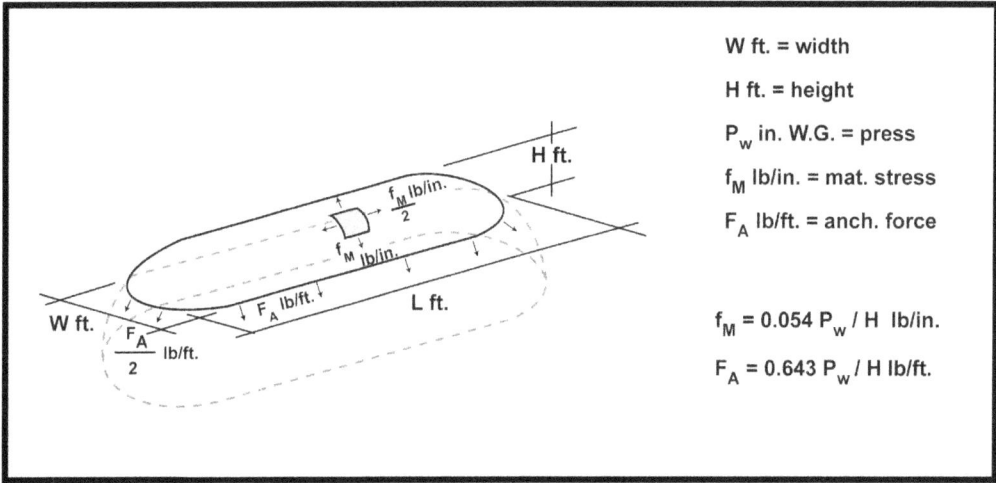

Figure B-6: Material stresses and anchorage forces in a low profile elongated air-building

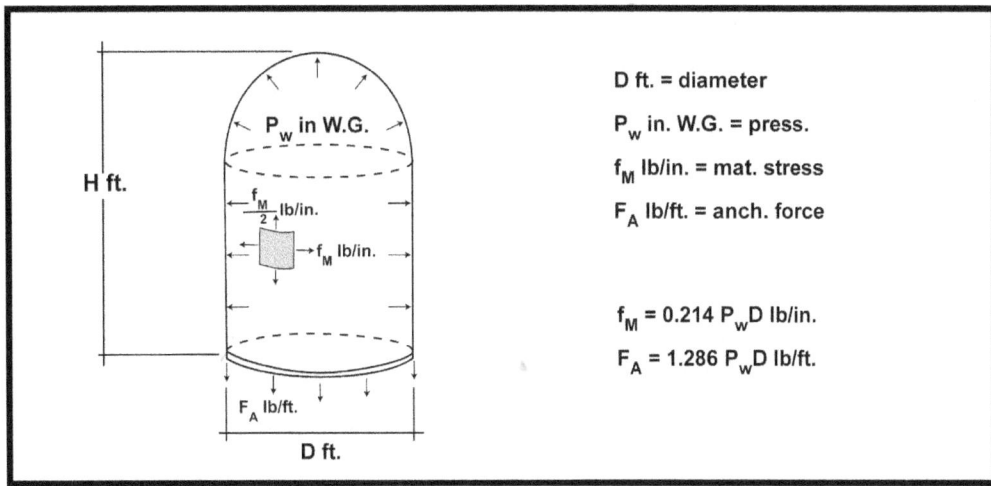

Figure B-7: Material stresses and anchorage forces in a vertical air-supported cylinder

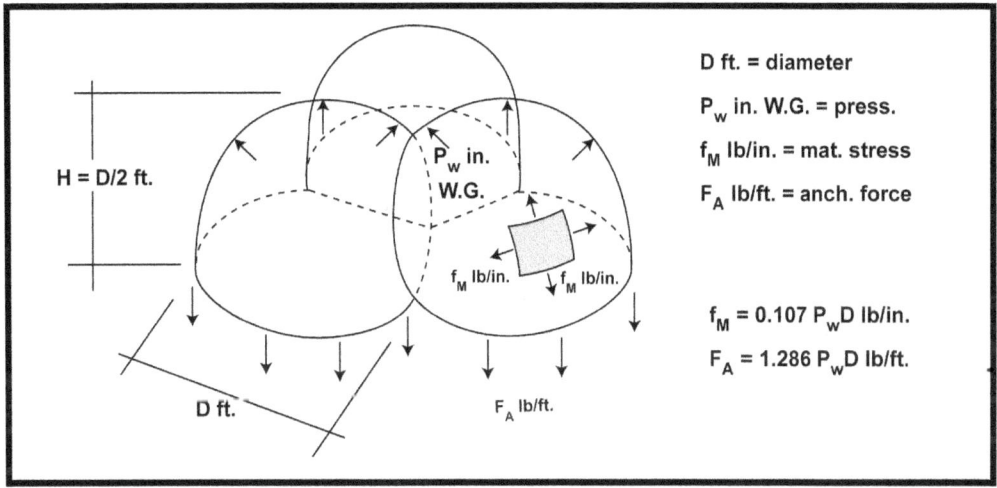

Figure B-8: Material stresses and anchorage forces in a high profile air-supported conglomerate

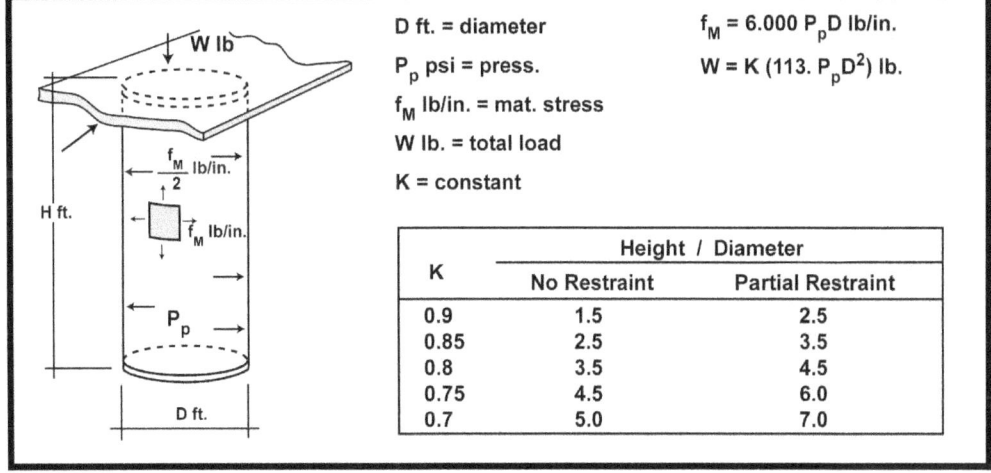

Figure B-9: Material stresses and anchorage forces in a vertical air-supported column

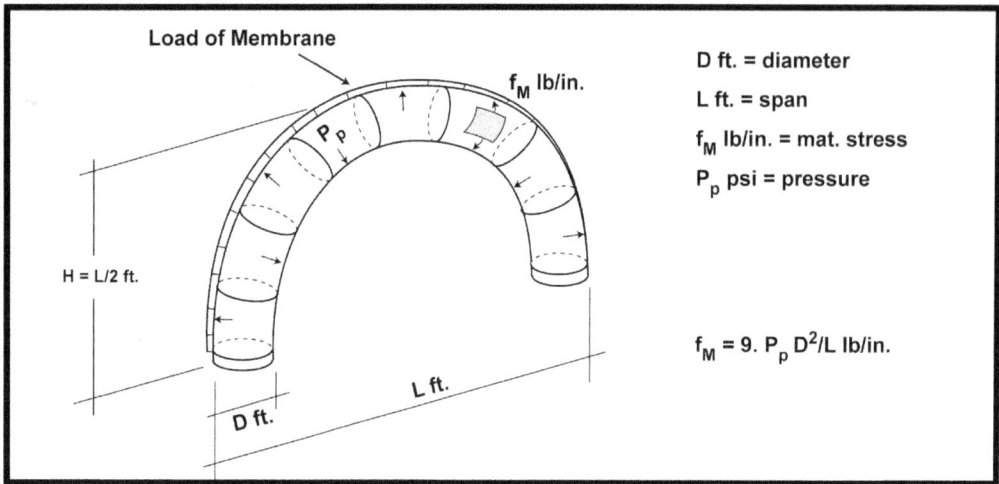

Figure B-10: Material stresses in a high profile air-inflated arch

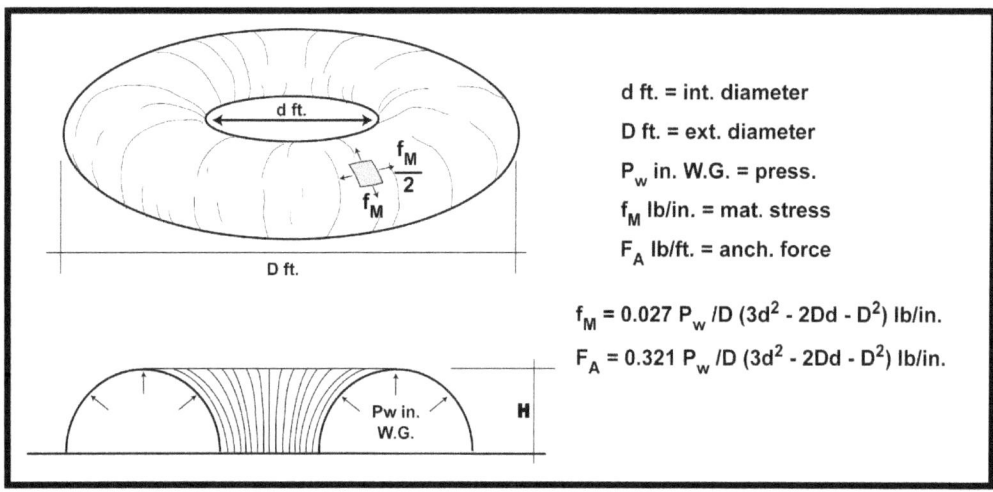

Figure B-11: Material stresses and anchorage forces in a high profile donut-shaped air-building

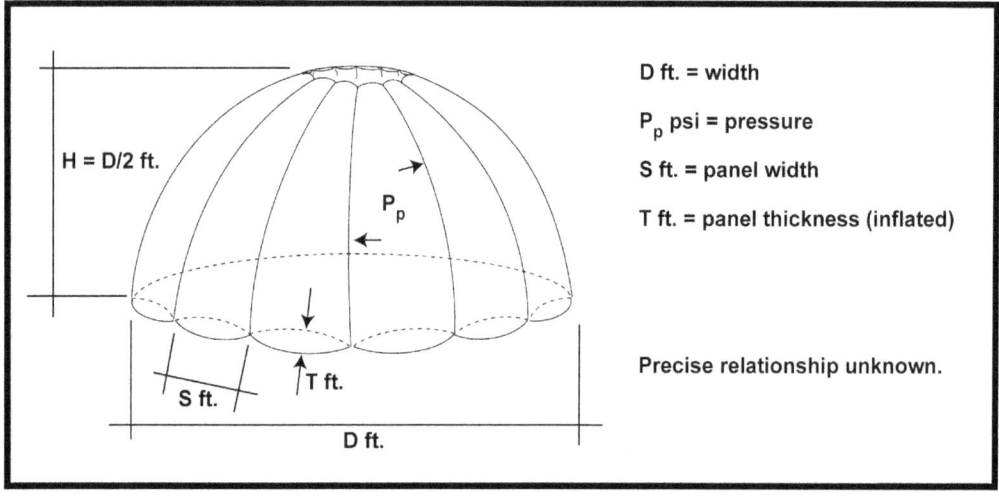

Figure B-12: Approximate material stresses in a high profile in a double-skin air-inflated dome

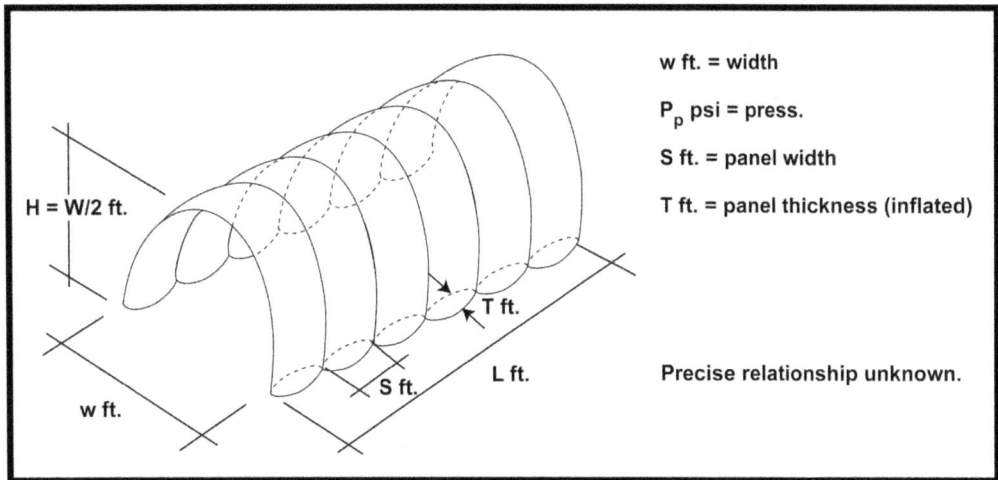

Figure B-13: Approximate material stresses in an elongated high profile, double-skin air-building

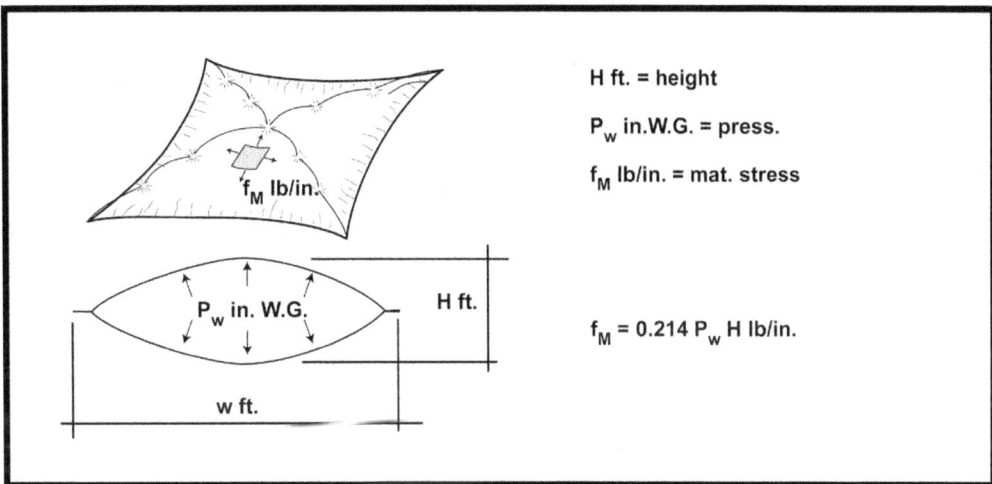

Figure B-14: Material stresses in an air-inflated cushion

In the case of the multi-level air-supported and air-inflated configurations shown in Figures B-15 to B-18, the required internal pressure is a function of the superimposed live-load and the height to diameter ratio (H/D) of the particular structural configuration. For the air-supported configurations (Figures B-15 and B-18) an internal pressure of at least 6 inches water gauge (0.21 psig) above ambient pressure atmospheric pressure is likely to be required for each supported floor level. This type of enclosure may be considered as a self-contained, completely sealed pressure vessel, which would normally require no anchorage to the building floor. Multi-level air-inflated enclosures, on the other hand, will require considerably higher pressures depending on the relationship between the effective cross-sectional pressure support area and the total floor area, as well as the H/D ratio of the structural elements[2].

---

[2] The required internal air pressures in multi-level air-inflated enclosures (Figures B-9 and B-15 to B-18) are typically measured in pounds per square inch (psig) rather than inches of water gauge. For purposes of conversion the following approximate relationships may be assumed: 0.035 psig is equal to 1 inch water gauge; 1 psig is equal to 28 inches water gauge; and, 1 atmosphere is equal to 14.5 psi or 406 inches water gauge (which for all practical purposes is close enough to 400 inches (or 33 feet) water gauge).

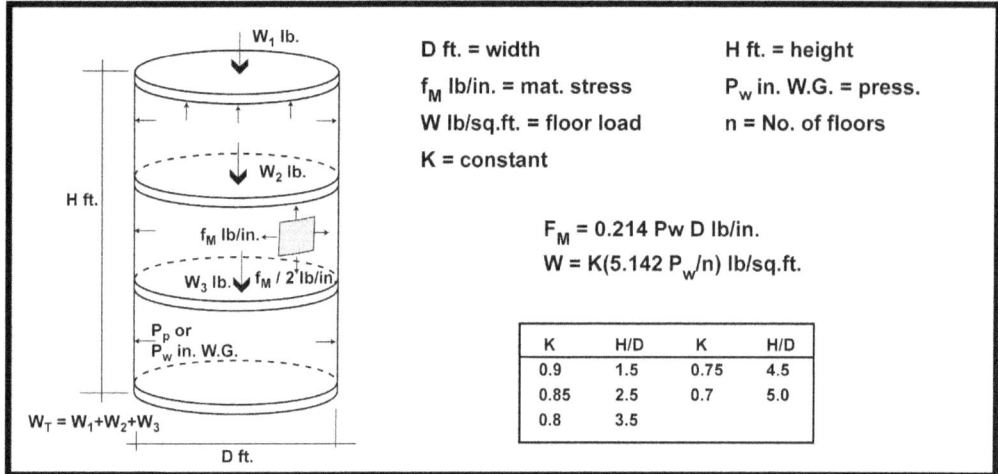

Figure B-15: Material stresses and load-bearing capacity of a multi-level air-supported cylinder

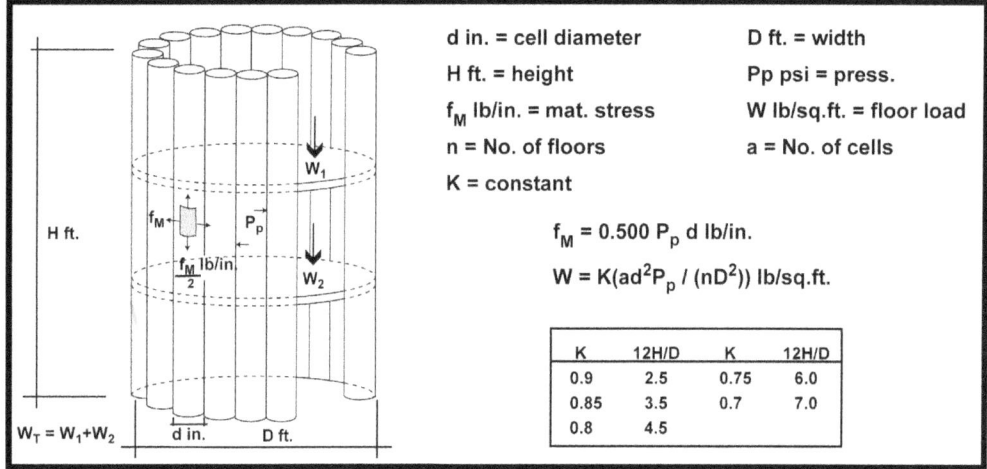

Figure B-16: Material stresses and load-bearing capacity of a cellular air-inflated cylinder

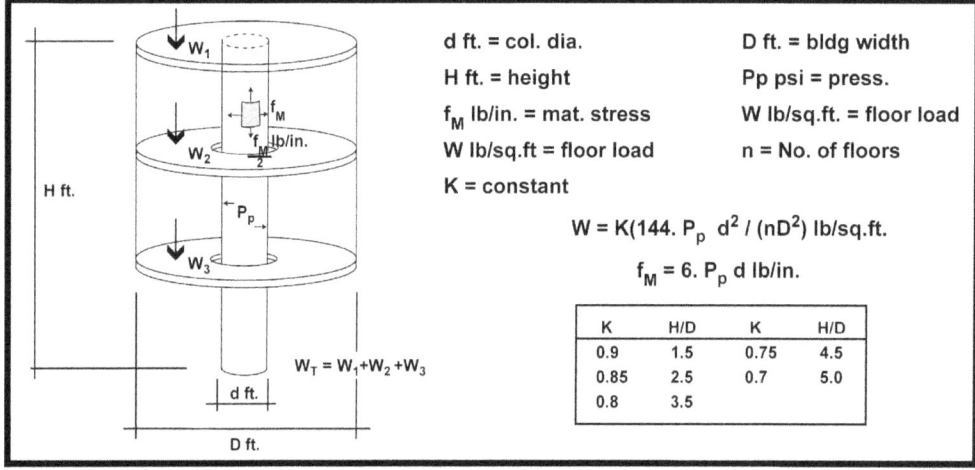

Figure B-17: Material stresses and load-bearing capacity of an air-inflated central column

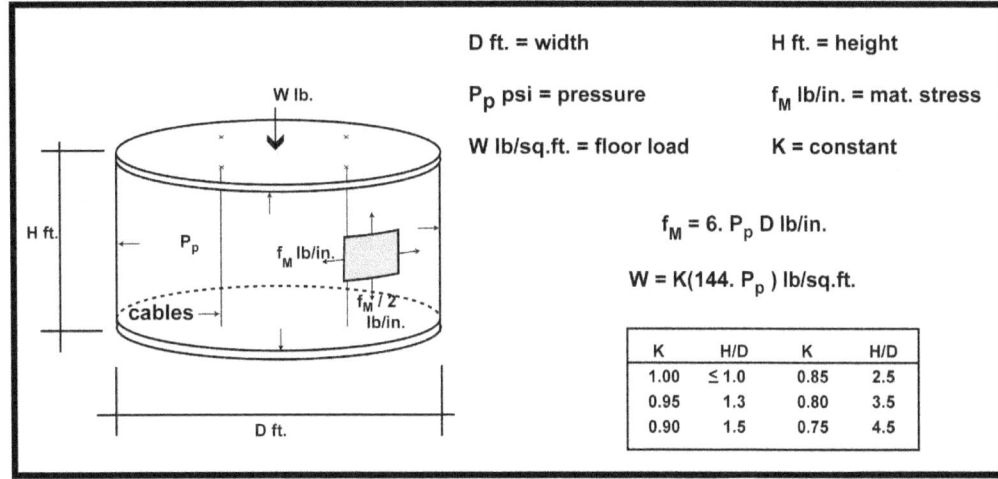

Figure B-18: Material stresses and load-carrying capacity of an air-inflated disc

B-2.2 Thermal Considerations

Plastic membrane materials have thermal characteristics that are very similar to glass. They display high transmittance in the visible region of the electromagnetic spectrum (Figure B-19) and variable transmittance in the infra-red region. Beyond wavelengths of 2500 millimicrons, plastics are virtually opaque giving rise to the well known *greenhouse* condition[3].

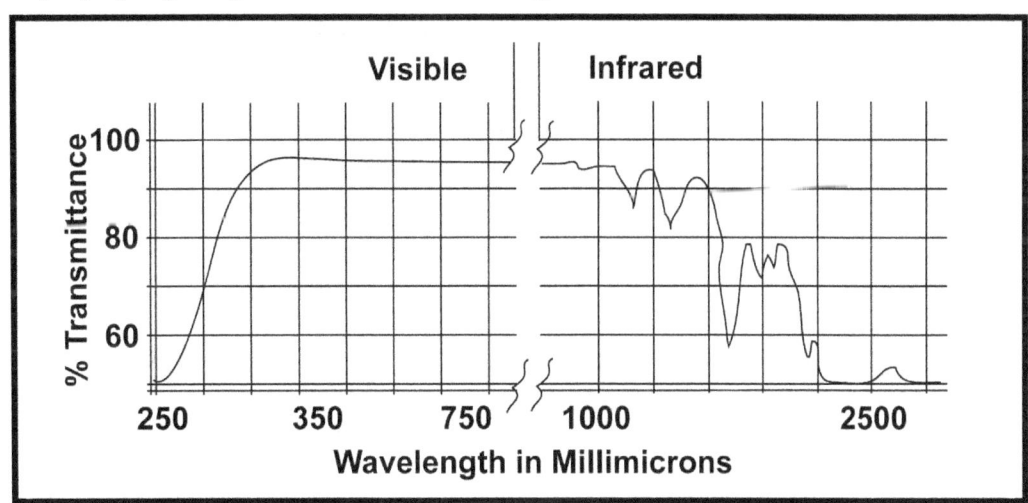

Figure B-19: Typical transmittance spectrum of a transparent plastic membrane material

At night or in winter under clouded conditions the loss of heat from the enclosed space is governed principally by the thermal resistivity of the thin plastic membrane, which is extremely low. In Europe, during the 1970s, air-building manufacturers explored the possibility of spraying the exterior surface of the air-supported membrane with water. The results, however, were disappointing and led to the conclusion that this type of artificially induced evaporative cooling is

---

[3] After solar radiation has entered a building space through a window it heats up the materials inside the space (e.g., floor, walls, and furniture). When the temperature of these materials increases above ambient temperatures they become radiators themselves. However, most of the radiation emitted is of a longer wavelength that cannot pass through the glass window and is therefore trapped in the building space.

not very useful. A different approach would be the application of an insulative foam coating that is sprayed directly onto the inside membrane surface. However, there are several potential disadvantages of this approach that would need to be addressed either through material advances or innovative air-building design and construction solutions. First, such coatings could not be used where transparency or translucency of the membrane is required. Second, the thickness of the coating and therefore the degree of thermal insulation provided is likely to be limited, since the coating is bound to adversely affect the flexibility of the membrane enclosure.

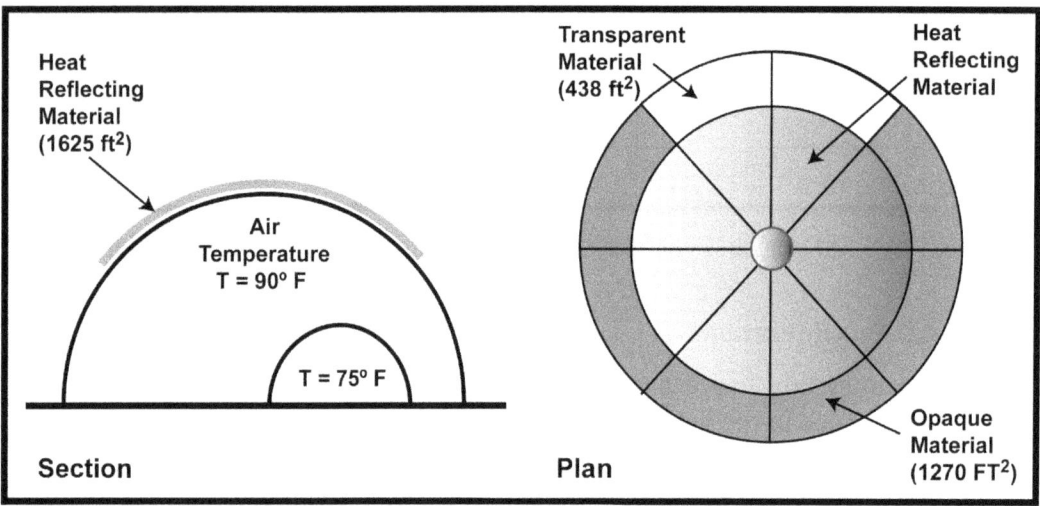

Figure B-20: Subdivision of the enclosure into transparent, heat reflecting, and opaque sections

The pneumatic-within-pneumatic concept considerably improves the thermal performance of an air-supported building by providing a wide interstitial air cavity between the external membrane and the internal space dividers. In this manner, a thermal transmittance value in the vicinity of 0.55 BTU/°F-hr-sqft may be achieved for the internal building spaces. Although this is a considerable improvement over the thermal transmittances that are characteristic of single layers of clear and opaque plastic membranes (i.e., 1.0 BTU/°F-hr-sqft and 0.71 BTU/°F-hr-sqft, respectively), it still falls far short of an acceptable level of thermal insulation such as might be provided by a two-inch thick layer of polystyrene (i.e., U-value of 0.13 BTU/°F-hr-sqft)[4].

Additional relief from overheating can be provided by treating those sections of the external membrane enclosure that are exposed to direct solar radiation and not required to be transparent with a highly reflective shield. In other words, as shown in Figure B-20, it is suggested that the external membrane of a pneumatic-within-pneumatic dwelling should be divided into heat reflecting, opaque, and transparent sections. This strategy will allow the designer to adjust the relative proportion and location of each of these sections based on thermal and architectural criteria. Typical summer heat gains and winter losses for a high profile (i.e., 50-foot diameter) pneumatic-within-pneumatic dwelling, featuring various external membrane configurations are shown in Table B-2. These values are based on the relatively mild climatic conditions of the California Central Coast region (e.g., San Luis Obispo, latitude 36° N) for which the average

---

[4] Polystyrene has a thermal resistance value of 3.57 sqft-°F-hr/BTU per inch thickness. The thermal transmittance or U-Value of a construction assembly is the reciprocal of the total thermal resistance. Adding the external and internal surface resistances of 0.17 and 0.61 sqft-°F-hr/BTU to the thermal resistance of two inches of polystyrene provides a total thermal resistance of 7.92 sqft-°F-hr/BTU, which is equivalent to a U-Value of 0.126 BTU/ °F-hr-sqft.

summer cooling and winter heating Degree Days rarely exceed 60 (July, August, and September) and 400 (December, January, and February), respectively.

Table B-2: Estimated energy costs for heating and cooling a pneumatic-within-pneumatic home in a mild climate (San Luis Obispo, California Central Coast)

Exterior Membrane Configuration			Assumed Annual Cooling or Heating Hrs.*	Maximum Cooling or Heating Load BTU/HR.	Max. Expected Cooling or Heating Cost (Elec.-U.S. $ (2009))
Transparent	Opaque	Reflecting			
30%	20%	50%	512	+66,571	$ 975
50%	10%	40%	512	+81,365	1,190
40%	30%	30%	512	+85,251	1,247
30%	50%	20%	512	+89,137	1,304
30%	20%	50%	720	-22,383	$ 460
50%	10%	40%	720	-23,955	492
40%	30%	30%	720	-25,525	525
30%	50%	20%	720	-27,096	557
*Assumed hours = 2 x average hours, based on utility company statistics.					

As shown in Table B-2, the distribution of heat reflecting foil over 50% of the external membrane enclosure has a considerable impact on reducing the heat gain under direct solar radiation. Maximum hourly cooling and heating loads are based on allowable maximum and minimum temperatures within the internal space enclosures of 78°F in summer and 65°F in winter.

While it is not suggested that the thermal insulation provided by a pneumatic-within-pneumatic dwelling is adequate for very hot or cold climates, it would appear that by the careful allocation of clear, opaque and reflective sections within the exterior membrane it is possible to achieve an acceptable thermal balance for exposure to mild climatic conditions. It is of interest to note, however, that if air-inflated double-skin or tubular structures are employed as internal space dividers then a thermal transmittance value of less than 0.35 BTU/°F-hr-sqft may be obtained for the innermost habitable spaces. Taking this approach to the extreme case, it is feasible to reduce the overall thermal transmittance to 0.25 BTU/°F-hr-sqft by using air-inflated, double-skin structural configurations for both the exterior enclosure and the interior space dividers. Under these circumstances the pneumatic-within-pneumatic dwelling could be considered a viable shelter solution even for moderately warmer and colder climates.

B-2.3 Architectural Planning

The difficulties that the designer encounters when faced with the subdivision of the space enclosed by an air-supported structure have severely hindered the development of a mass produced air-home. The internal curved surface of a dome simply does not lend itself to the subdivision of the space it encloses, by standard architectural means. Typical full-height self-supporting timber or masonry partitions will tend to destroy the form of the enclosed space. Half-height partitions, on the other hand, are less than satisfactory from the point of view of visual and acoustic privacy. Plastic curtains are difficult to suspend or support due to the inability of the air-supported membrane to carry concentrated loads. Inflated walls tend to be unstable unless they are very wide, in which case they take up an inordinate amount of floor space.

A more useful approach is to build complete self-contained space enclosures within the external air-supported membrane. The most inexpensive type of self-supporting enclosure is of course another air-supported or air-inflated structure, which leads directly to the pneumatic-within-pneumatic concept.

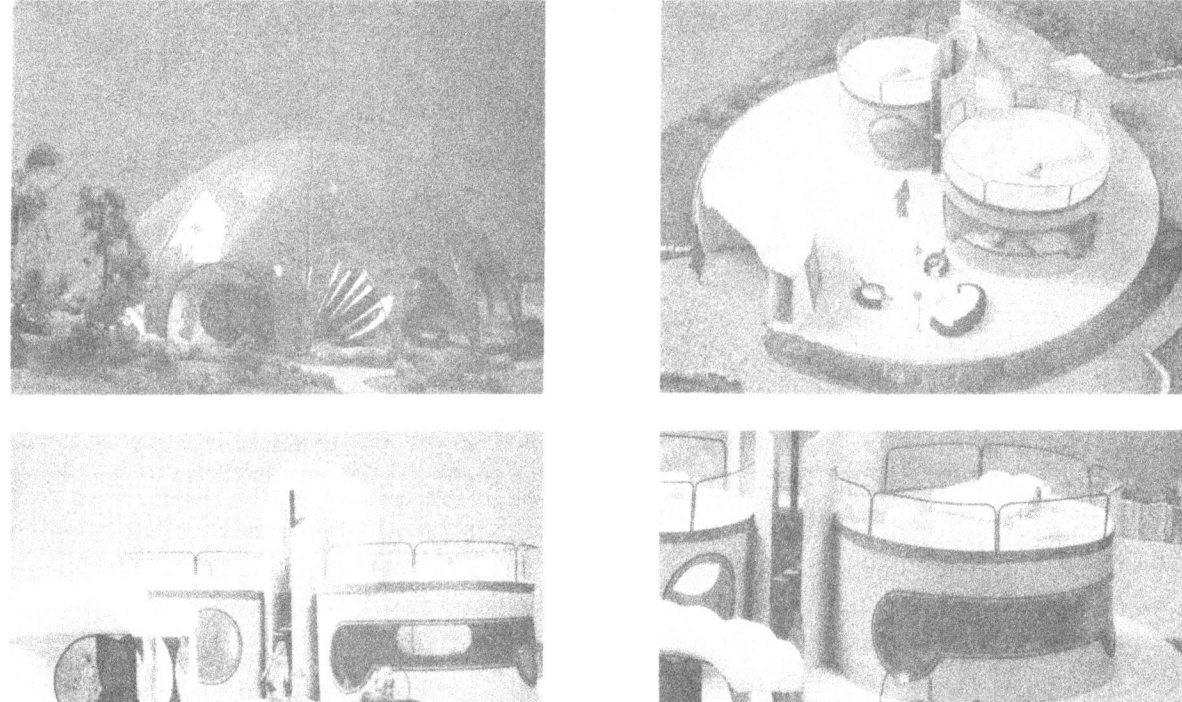

Figure B-21: Typical internal space divisions in a pneumatic-within-pneumatic home

As shown in Figures B-7 to B-9 and B-15 to B-18, a wide range of pneumatic enclosures ranging from simple single-skin, air-supported domes to multi-story, air-inflated systems are available to the designer. While all of these are relatively inexpensive and readily lend themselves to the design of pleasant and compatible internal space enclosures (Figure B-21), they nevertheless carry with them some disadvantages. First, all air-supported enclosures (in contrast to air-inflated enclosures) require some form of airlock entrance and exit system. Second, household tradition calls for certain types of devices (e.g., kitchen and bathroom appliances and fittings) and storage facilities (e.g., cupboards) that are traditionally of a rigid nature and therefore perhaps less acceptable in an intrinsically more flexible pneumatic form.

Various airlock systems suitable for a wide range of pressure differentials are shown in Figures B-22 to B-24. For pressures below 0.4 inches water gauge (0.014 psig) very simple devices such as plastic streamers or curtains, friction joints, zips, overlaps, and even air curtains may suffice. The majority of single-story air supported enclosures, in which the internal air pressure is only required to support the self-weight of the plastic membrane fall into this category. In the case of medium pressures (0.5 to 1.4 inches water gauge or 0.018 to 0.049 psig) and higher pressures (1.5 to 10 inches water gauge or 0.05 to 0.35 psig) that are applicable to multi-level air-supported enclosures, more substantial airlock systems ranging from revolving doors to vertical or horizontal airlock tubes are required (Figures B-22 to B-24).

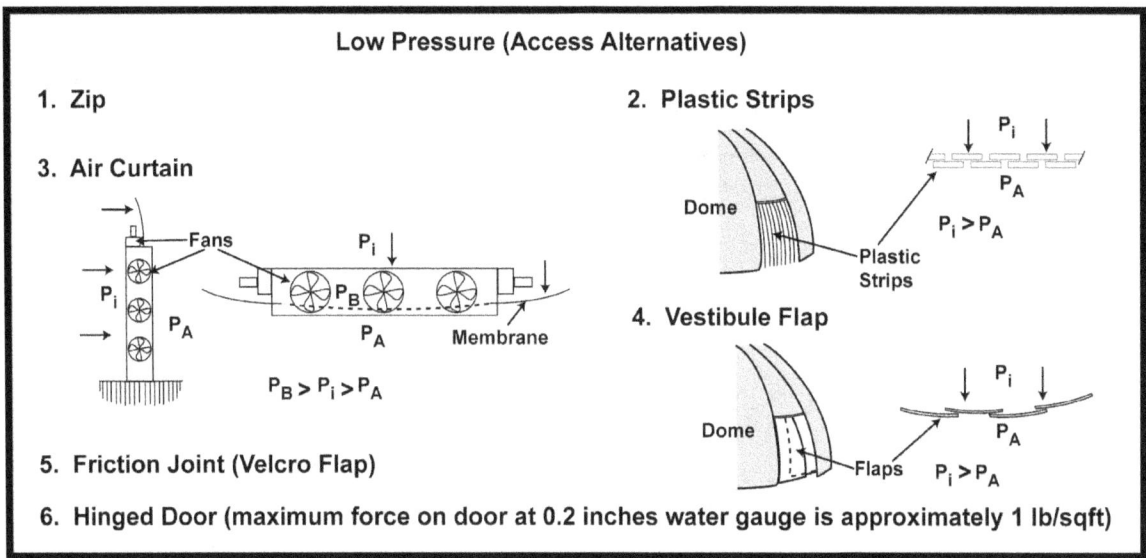

Figure B-22: Low internal pressure access alternatives for air-buildings

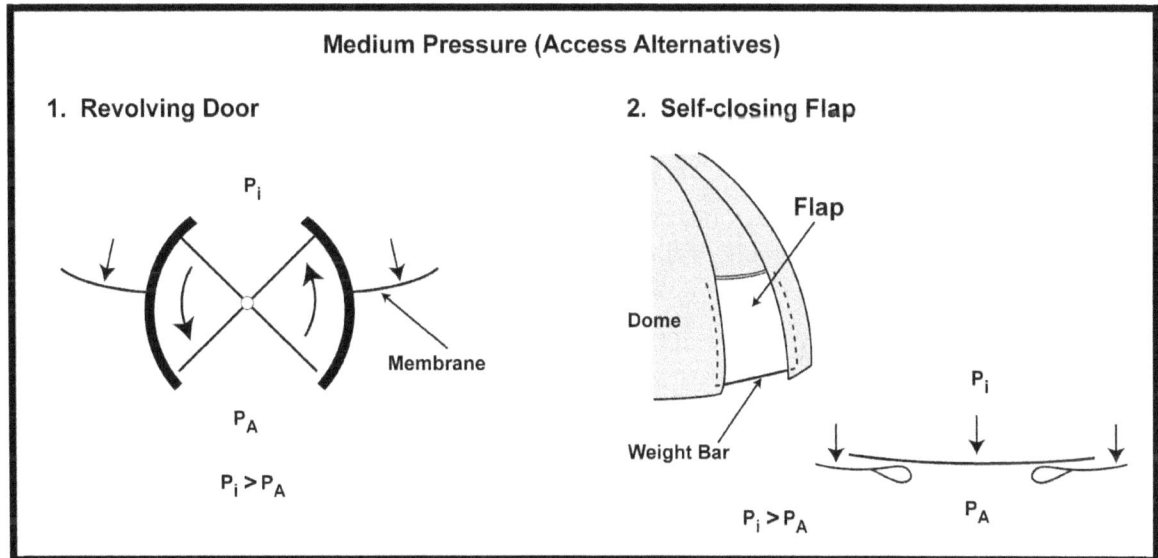

Figure B-23: Medium internal pressure access alternatives for air-buildings

Experience with two prototype multi-story air-supported buildings (Pohl and Montero 1973) suggests that a modified form of the revolving door system may be suitable for the type of multi-level internal space enclosure that it being proposed in Figures B-15 to B-17 and Figure B-21 for pneumatic-within-pneumatic homes. As shown in Figure B-24 (see diagram on right side), the standard revolving door may be modified by the addition of a floor and perimeter plastic membrane walls for two of the four compartments. Each plastic wall is provided with a vertical zipper, to enable the compartment to be used as a self-contained airlock entrance. A person may leave a high-pressure space enclosure by opening the zipper in the revolving door compartment facing the high-pressure space, enter the compartment, close the zipper, rotate the revolving door mechanically through 180°, open the zipper and enter the adjacent low-pressure space. For pressure differences exceeding 5 inches water gauge (0.18 psig) it is recommended that a pressure relief valve be provided either in the plastic wall or the roof of the revolving door compartment to facilitate the gradual equalization of the pressure within the compartment and the adjacent space. Such a valve will avoid the difficulties that may be experienced in opening zippers in enclosures that are severely stressed by higher internal pressures.

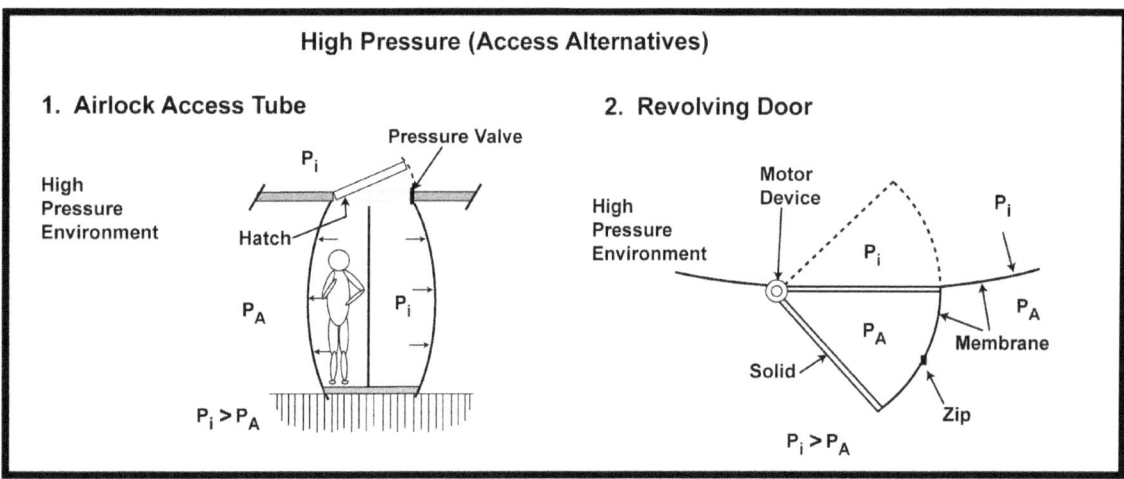

Figure B-24: Higher internal pressure access alternatives for air-buildings

It is unlikely that inflatable service cores incorporating normal kitchen and bathroom fixtures will become commercially available or even be technically feasible in the foreseeable future. Therefore, rigid all-plastic service cores of the type now commercially produced in the U.S., Europe and other countries will provide the most acceptable alternative solution. Where appropriate from an architectural or constructional point of view such rigid components may also provide a convenient entry point (i.e., airlock) to one or more internal space enclosures at one or more levels (Figure B-21).

All ducts, pipes and electric cables should be integrated in the building floor system, which may be prefabricated or constructed on site. While the principal blower, required to pressurize the external enclosure would normally be located outside the building, any secondary blowers responsible for the inflation of internal air-supported space enclosures should obtain their air supply from the interstitial space between the exterior and interior enclosures. Consideration should be given to the inflation of low-pressure spaces by utilizing the air discharge from higher pressure enclosures. In this way a skilled designer would be able to minimize the required number of air pressurization devices and optimize the operational efficiency of the dwelling.

Pneumatic furniture in the form of inflatable chairs, tables and beds have been commercially available since the 1960s. While this type of furniture has by no means replaced conventional forms, it has been found acceptable as a novelty by many and as a functional necessity by some. However, when the designer is confronted with the creation of a total pneumatic environment in which as far as possible all components are preferably to be air-supported or air-inflated, some difficulties are encountered. In particular, there appear to be no natural pneumatic forms suitable for storage facilities, such as cupboards and shelves. Faced with this dilemma, the author was persuaded to undertake a cursory investigation of pneumatic furniture solutions for the storage of clothes on hangers. The results of this exploration are shown in Figures B-25 and B-26.

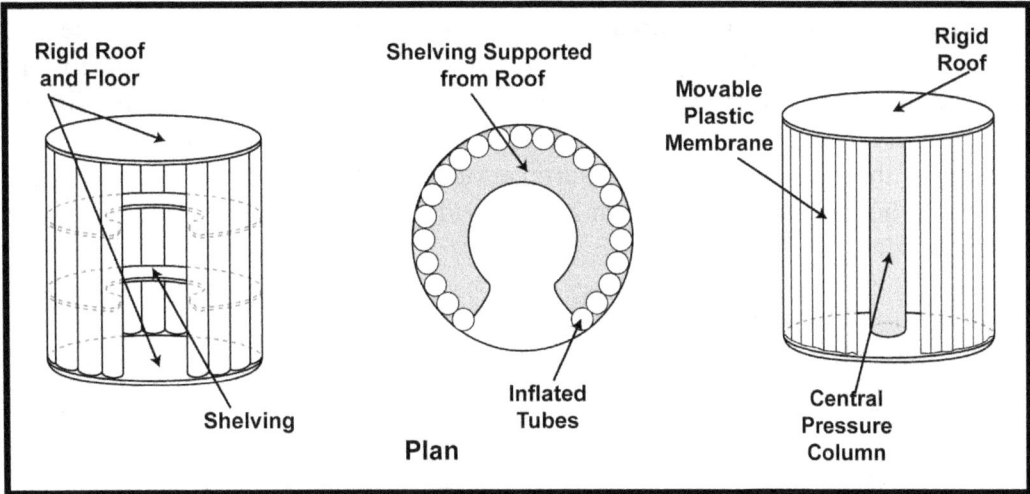

Figure B-25: Cellular air-inflated wardrobes for hanging clothes

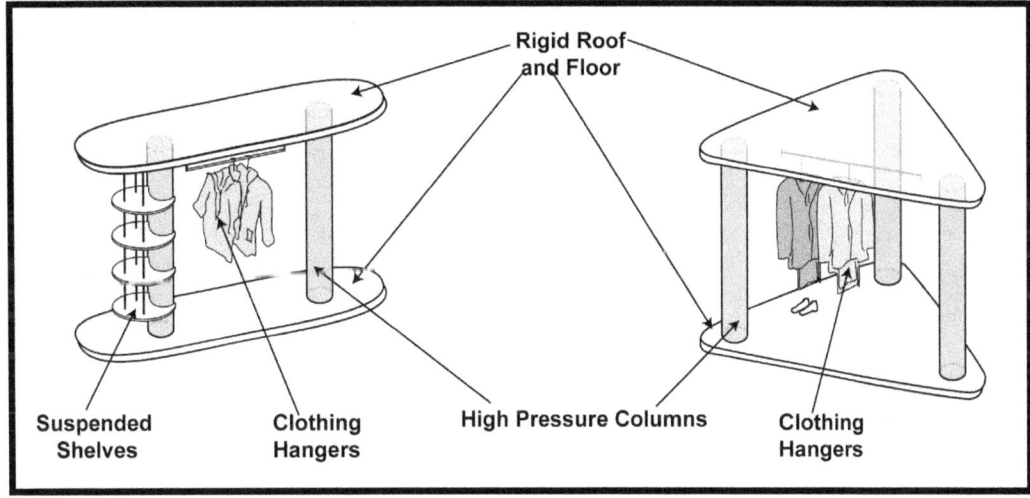

Figure B-26: Wardrobes for hanging clothes supported by air-inflated columns

The requirement for hanging clothes calls for some type of suspension capability within the pneumatic configuration. This consideration, together with the need for easy access, favors an air-inflated rather than air-supported solution. However, all pneumatic structures whether air-supported or air-inflated are susceptible to concentrated loads. Therefore, the requirement to suspend loads suggests that the air-inflated structure should be designed to support a rigid plate at some convenient height above floor level. From this plate, which may be supported by pressurized columns or double-skin air-inflated cellular walls, rigid shelves, conventional coat hangers and any other articles may be conveniently suspended by conventional means. In the case of light loads the rigid roof plate may be fabricated from plastic foam, honeycomb paper or any type of lightweight sandwich panel.

B-3 Postscript

It would be presumptuous to propose the pneumatic-within-pneumatic dwelling as an alternative approach for satisfying the worldwide need for affordable industrialized housing, at this time. Even on the assumption that all functional requirements can be satisfied by this type of dwelling, there is likely to be considerable opposition on aesthetic grounds from the majority of potential home owners. Although pneumatic structures in some form or another have been utilized for more than half a century, this unconventional structural form may never be considered as anything more than a novelty in the housing field. The purpose of this Appendix is to show that pneumatic-within-pneumatic homes are feasible from a structural, functional, and even environmental (i.e., thermal) point of view.

Figure B-27: The pneumatic-within-pneumatic home lends itself to modular design, mass-production, and relocation

There is no doubt that the concepts that have been explored may be practically implemented on a mass-production basis, today. In comparison with the commercially available mobile home, which can be relocated and is relatively inexpensive, the pneumatic-within-pneumatic dwelling is a highly competitive novelty. It lends itself to prefabrication, mass-production and may be easily erected, dismantled, and transported to another site (Figure B-27). However, as can be clearly seen in Figure B-27, the pneumatic-within-pneumatic home is intrinsically spacious and does not lend itself at all to the dimensional site restrictions of a typical suburban residential subdivision. Nevertheless, preliminary cost estimates based principally on material quantities and labor indicate an ownership cost that is barely half of the cost of a mobile home consisting largely of factory produced components.

Definition of Symbols

Chapter 1 (Historical Roots)

Chapter 2 (Slender Column Challenges)

A	=	area (general)	SF
A_m	=	cross-sectional area of membrane	SI
B	=	horizontal force on column	LB
D	=	diameter of column	IN
d	=	maximum deflection of rod attached to column cap	IN
E	=	modulus of elasticity of column material	psi
e	=	eccentricity of axial load	IN
H	=	actual height of column	IN
H_E	=	effective height of column	IN
I	=	moment of inertia of column cross-section	IN^4
I_m	=	moment of inertia of column membrane	IN^4
k	=	recommended pressure-utilization factor	
L	=	axial load per unit area	psi
P	=	internal fluid pressure	psig
P_{UE}	=	pressure-utilization efficiency	%
R	=	radius of column	IN
S	=	strength utilization factor for steel columns under axial load	
t	=	thickness of membrane material (column wall)	IN
SR	=	slenderness ratio of column	
W	=	axial buckling load of column	LB
X	=	effective eccentricity of axial load	IN
Z_m	=	modulus of section of membrane	IN^3

Chapter 3 (Multi-Story Air-Supported Buildings)

A	=	area (general)	SF, SI
A_{CA}	=	cross-sectional area of one vertical (diagonal) cable	SI
A_E	=	total cross-sectional area of vertical (diagonal) cables	SI
A_M	=	cross-sectional area (membrane)	SI
D_H	=	horizontal force (wind drag force)	LB
E_{CA}	=	modulus of elasticity of cable material	psi
e	=	eccentricity of axial load	IN
f_c	=	circumferential (hoop) stress in membrane	psi, LB/IN
f_L	=	compressive force due to vertical axial load	LB
f_M	=	stress in membrane (with cable-network in place)	psi

f_P	=	tensile force due to internal fluid pressure	LB
H	=	height (general)	FT, IN
H_E	=	effective height depending on end-fixing conditions	FT, IN
H_F	=	total circumferential force resisted by horizontal cables	LB
H_S	=	horizontal component of tension in vertical cable	psi
I_{CA}	=	moment of inertia of cable-network	IN^4
k	=	pressure-utilization factor for flexible membrane columns	
k	=	number of vertical (diagonal) cables	
L	=	load-bearing capacity per unit area	psi
n	=	number of horizontal cables	
P	=	internal pressure	psig
P_E	=	additional internal pressure to resist horizontal forces	psig
R	=	radius	IN, FT
R_M	=	vertical cable spacing (mesh size of cable-network)	IN
r	=	radius of each vertical (diagonal) cable	IN
θ	=	optimum angle to vertical of diagonal vertical cables	degrees
T_{CA}	=	tension in each vertical (diagonal) cable	LB
T_{CAH}	=	horizontal component of cable tension	LB
T_{CAV}	=	vertical component of cable tension	LB
T_H	=	tension in each horizontal cable	LB
t	=	thickness of membrane	IN
t_{CA}	=	cross-sectional area of vertical (diagonal) cables spread around external membrane perimeter	SI
V_S	=	vertical component of tension in vertical cable	psi
W	=	axial load	LB
W_{ULT}	=	ultimate axial load	LB
Z_{CA}	=	modulus of section of cable-network	IN^3

Chapter 4 (Bracing of Multi-Story Air-Supported Buildings)

A	=	area (general)	SF
A_m	=	cross-sectional area of membrane	SI
a	=	increased area on the convex side of deflected column	SI
A_{CA}	=	total cross-sectional material area of cable-network	SI
A_{HP}	=	projected area on horizontal plane	SF
A_{VP}	=	projected area on vertical plane	SF
b	=	decreased area on the concave side of deflected column	SI
C_H	=	total aerodynamic drag coefficient (horizontal)	
C_V	=	overall aerodynamic coefficient in vertical direction	
D	=	diameter	FT

d	=	deflection	IN
d_{CA}	=	diameter of cable	IN
D_H	=	wind drag force component (drag)	LB
E	=	modulus of elasticity	psi
E_{CA}	=	modulus of elasticity of cable material	psi
E_m	=	modulus of elasticity of membrane material	psi
e	=	axial load eccentricity	IN
F	=	force in each vertical (diagonal) cable	LB
F_H	=	stress due to horizontal force	psi
f_c	=	circumferential (hoop) stress in membrane	psi
f_{CA}	=	stress in cable	psi
f_l	=	stress due to internal pressure P on tension side of column	psi
$f_{m(allow)}$	=	allowable membrane stress in tension	psi
H	=	height	FT, IN
∂H	=	increased/decreased height on convex/concave sides of deflected column	IN
H_E	=	effective height depending on end-fixing conditions	IN
I	=	moment of inertia	IN^4
I_{CA}	=	moment of inertia of cable-network	IN^4
I_m	=	moment of inertia of membrane	IN^4
k	=	number of vertical (diagonal) cables	
n	=	number of horizontal cables	
P	=	internal pressure	psig
P_E	=	additional internal pressure required to resist horizontal loads	psig
P_H	=	horizontal component of internal pressure P	psig
P_{HC}	=	restoring force acting on area $(a + b)$ due to P	LB
P_{HS}	=	restoring force acting on inclined column head due to P	LB
P_V	=	vertical component of internal pressure P	psig
q	=	wind pressure as a function of wind speed	psf
R	=	radius	FT, IN
r	=	radius of each vertical (diagonal) cable	IN
R_{xn}	=	component of internal pressure P along X-axis	psig
R_{yn}	=	component of internal pressure P along Y-axis	psig
S_{max}	=	principal maximum stress	psi
S_{min}	=	principal minimum stress	psi
S_x	=	stress along X-axis	psi
S_y	=	stress along y-axis	psi
S_{xy}	=	shear stress	psi

SR	=	slenderness ratio	
θ	=	optimum angle to vertical of diagonal vertical cables	degrees
T_{CA}	=	tension in each vertical (diagonal) cable	LB
T_H	=	tension in each horizontal cable	LB
$T_{H(allow)}$	=	allowable tension in each horizontal cable	LB
t	=	thickness of column wall	IN
t_{CA}	=	equivalent thickness of cable-network if spread continuously around perimeter of column	SI
t_m	=	thickness of membrane	IN
U_V	=	wind lift force component (vertical)	LB
V	=	wind speed	mph
W	=	vertical axial compression load	LB
W_H	=	horizontal force	LB
W_{zero}	=	zero compression load condition	LB
Y_n	=	distance of cable from horizontal axis of column	IN
Z	=	modulus of section	IN^3
Z_{CA}	=	modulus of section of cable-network	IN^3
Z_m	=	modulus of section of membrane	IN^3

Chapter 5 (Two Prototype Multi-Story Air-Supported Buildings)

Chapter 6 (Multi-Story Air-Supported and Fluid-Inflated Building Types)

A_W	=	cross-sectional area of column wall	SI
D	=	diameter of fluid-inflated column	FT
D_p	=	diameter of inflated floor (pneumatic greenhouse)	IN
d_p	=	diameter of inflated cells (wedges) at perimeter	IN
D_U	=	diameter of floor before inflation (pneumatic greenhouse)	IN
f	=	stress in wall of access column (pneumatic greenhouse)	LB/IN
H	=	height of fluid-inflated column	FT
H_E	=	effective height of column dependent on end-fixing conditions	IN
I	=	moment of inertia	IN^4
n	=	number of cells (wedges) at perimeter	
P	=	fluid pressure	psig
p	=	air pressure inside access column (pneumatic greenhouse)	psig
∂P_c	=	capillary pumping head (heat pipe)	psi
∂P_g	=	gravity head (heat pipe)	psi
∂P_l	=	pressure drop in the liquid (heat pipe)	psi
∂P_S	=	additional fluid pressure due to weight of sand	psig
∂P_v	=	pressure drop in the vapor (heat pipe)	psi

∂P_W	=	additional fluid pressure due to weight of water	psig
R	=	radius of column	IN
r	=	radius of access column (pneumatic greenhouse)	FT
s	=	width of seam between cells (wedges) at perimeter	IN
SR	=	slenderness ratio	
t	=	thickness of column wall	IN
TP	=	total fluid pressure	psig
W	=	allowable vertical load	psf
w	=	total vertical load (pneumatic greenhouse)	LB
X	=	number of suspended floors	

Chapter 7 (Air-Supported and Fluid-Inflated Rigid Membrane Structures)

A	=	area (general)	SF
A_{col}	=	inside area at top of column	SI
A_{floor}	=	floor area	SF
A_{rigid}	=	cross-sectional area of cylinder wall	SI
A_{roof}	=	inside area at top of cylinder	SI, SF
A_S	=	cross-sectional area of cylinder wall	SI
a	=	parameter	
b	=	parameter	
β	=	cylinder height (H) divided by half wavelength in measured in circumferential direction (λ)	
c	=	parameter	
C	=	buckling coefficient	
d	=	parameter	
D	=	flexural stiffness per unit length	LB/IN
D	=	diameter (general)	FT
D_{build}	=	diameter of building	FT
DL	=	dead-load	psf
e	=	shortening of the cylinder	IN
E	=	modulus of elasticity	psi
ε_c	=	strain in circumferential direction	
ε_l	=	strain in longitudinal direction	
f	=	applied shear stress (also average stress)	psi
f_c	=	circumferential (hoop) stress	psi
f_l	=	longitudinal stress	psi
f_{max}	=	maximum stress measured with strain gauge	psi
f_{min}	=	minimum stress measured with strain gauge	psi

f_r	=	radial stress	psi
f_x	=	critical buckling stress or applied axial stress	psi
f_x'	=	dimensionless parameter (stress coefficient)	
f_y	=	applied circumferential stress	psi
H	=	actual height of cylinder (or column)	IN
H_E	=	effective height of cylinder (or column) dependent on end-fixing conditions	IN
k_x	=	dimensionless parameter (compressive stress coefficient)	
K_c	=	buckling coefficient without internal pressure	
∂K_c	=	buckling coefficient due to internal pressure only	
l_x	=	half the wavelength of w in the axial direction	IN
l_y	=	half the wavelength of w in the circumferential direction	IN
LL	=	live-load	psf
λ	=	half wavelength of buckles in circumferential direction	IN
m	=	wave shape factor (integer)	
n	=	number of circumferential waves	
P	=	lateral pressure applied to cylinder wall (internal pressure)	psig
P'	=	dimensionless parameter (pressure coefficient)	
P_{opt}	=	optimum internal pressure	psig
R	=	radius of cylinder (or column)	IN
SR	=	slenderness ratio	
t	=	thickness of cylinder wall	IN
u	=	Poisson's ratio	
U	=	unevenness coefficient	
w	=	displacement in radial direction of point on shell median surface	IN
W	=	axial compression load	LB
W_{axial}	=	ultimate axial load without internal pressure	LB
W_{press}	=	upward force due to internal pressure acting on inside area at top of cylinder (or column)	LB
W_{ult}	=	ultimate axial load with internal pressure	LB
x	=	axial coordinate	
y	=	circumferential coordinate	
Z	=	dimensionless parameter	

Chapter 8 (Pressurized Cable Floor and Roof Systems)

A	=	floor area	SF
A_a	=	material area of angles of secondary structure (Option B) of rectangular cable floor	SI

A_{ang}	=	volume of angle material in trusses of secondary structure (Option B) of rectangular cable floor	CI
A_{band}	=	material area of one band in secondary structure (Option A) of rectangular cable floor	SI
A_c	=	material area of channels of secondary structure (Option B) of rectangular cable floor	SI
A_{chan}	=	volume of channel material in trusses of secondary structure (Option B) of rectangular cable floor	CI
A_{CA}	=	cable steel material area	SI
A_P	=	support area of cable at perimeter of circular cable floor	SF
A_S	=	cross-sectional area of strut wall	SI
A_{strut}	=	cross-sectional material area of strut wall	SI
A_{ties}	=	cross-sectional area of tie-downs	SI
B	=	width of rectangular cable floor	FT
C	=	span of perimeter rim acting as a cable between radial cables	FT
C_S	=	cable spacing at perimeter of floor	FT
D	=	diameter of circular pneumatic cable floors and roofs	FT
D	=	diameter of strut in rectangular cable floors	FT
D_{floor}	=	depth of rectangular cable floor	FT
DL	=	dead-load	psf
D_L	=	dead-load (self-weight) of floor	psf
d	=	sag of cable at center of span	FT
d_1	=	diameter of innermost tension ring	FT
d_{ca}	=	cable diameter	IN
d_{plate}	=	deflection of top/bottom disk plates in circular cable floors	IN
d_{ties}	=	diameter of tie-downs	IN
E	=	modulus of elasticity	psi
E_{plate}	=	modulus of elasticity of disk plate material in circular cable floors	psi
F_{CA}	=	cable fill factor	%
f_C	=	circumferential (hoop) stress in strut wall	psi
f_{circ}	=	circumferential (hoop) stress in strut wall	psi
f_{ca}	=	design strength in tension of cable material	psi
f_{cable}	=	stress in strut wall due to two cables	psi
f_{fl}	=	design strength in tension of the floor disk material	psi
f_{orim}	=	design stress of perimeter rim material for circular cable floors	psi
f_P	=	critical buckling stress of pressurized strut	psi
f_{s-ca}	=	stress in strut wall due to axial force of two cables	psi
f_{st}	=	design strength in tension of strut wall material	psi

f_{strut} =	critical buckling stress of pressurized strut	psi
f_{ties} =	design stress of tie-down material	psi
H =	actual length of strut	FT
H =	axial force exerted by two cable on one strut	LB
H_{CA} =	horizontal component of cable tension	LB
H_E =	effective length of strut dependent on end-fixing conditions	FT
h_{orim} =	horizontal component of tension in perimeter rim acting as a cable between radial cables	LB
K_c =	buckling coefficient without internal pressure	
∂K_c =	buckling coefficient due to internal pressure only	
L =	span	FT
LL =	live-load	psf
L_L =	live-load on floor	psf
L_{orim} =	load per foot run on perimeter rim acting as a cable between radial cables	LB/FT-run
L_{ties} =	load on top/bottom plate segments between tie-downs	LB
n_{band} =	number of bands on each strut in secondary structure (Option A) of rectangular cable floor	
n_{ca} =	number of cables	
n_{strut} =	number of struts	
n_{ties} =	number of tie-downs	
n_{truss} =	number of trusses in secondary structure (Option B) of rectangular cable floor	
P =	internal pressure	psig
P_F =	internal pressure of floor disc for circular cable floors	psig
P_{opt} =	optimum internal pressure	psig
P_{strut} =	optimum internal pressure of strut	psig
R =	radius of circular floor	FT
R =	radius of strut in rectangular cable floors	FT
R_{CA} =	radius of curvature of cable	FT
r_{ca} =	cable radius	IN
r_{ties} =	radius of tie-downs	IN
S =	cable sag (and depth of floor for circular cable floors)	FT
S_{band} =	center-to-center spacing of bands around strut in secondary structure (Option A) of rectangular cable floors	FT
S_{ca} =	cable spacing at floor perimeter	FT
SR =	slenderness ratio	
S_{st} =	center-to-center spacing of struts in rectangular cable floors	FT
S_v =	distance between vertical truss members in secondary structure	

		(Option B) of rectangular cable floor	FT
S_{ca}	=	cable spacing at innermost tension ring	FT
T_{max}	=	maximum cable tension	LB
T_{orim}	=	full tension in perimeter rim acting as a cable between radial cables	LB
t	=	thickness of strut wall	IN
t_{orim}	=	thickness of perimeter rim for circular cable floors	IN
t_{plate}	=	thickness of top/bottom disk plates in circular cable floors	IN
W	=	total load on floor (live-load and dead-load)	LB
W_{CA}	=	weight of cables in rectangular cable floor	LB
W_{CEIL}	=	weight of ceiling in rectangular cable floor	LB
W_{END}	=	weight of end sections in rectangular cable floor	LB
W_{fl-LB}	=	self-weight of floor	LB
$W_{FLOOR-A}$	=	total self-weight of rectangular cable floor with secondary structure (Option A) and floor surface and ceiling	LB
$W_{FLOOR-B}$	=	total self-weight of rectangular cable floor with secondary structure (Option B) and floor surface and ceiling	LB
W_{fl-psf}	=	self-weight of floor per unit floor area	psf
W_{irim}	=	weight of inner rim for circular cable floor	LB
W_{plate}	=	weight of top/bottom disk plates in circular cable floor	LB
W_{orim}	=	weight of perimeter rim for circular cable floor	LB
W_{r-LB}	=	self-weight of roof	LB
W_{r-psf}	=	self-weight of roof per unit roof area	psf
W_{rca}	=	weight of radial cables in circular cable floor	LB
W_{run}	=	average load per foot run on cable for circular cable floor	LB/FT-run
W_{SEC-A}	=	weight of secondary structure for rectangular cable floors (Option A)	LB
W_{SEC-B}	=	weight of secondary structure for rectangular cable floors (Option B)	LB
$W_{STRUC-A}$	=	total structural weight of rectangular cable floor with secondary structure (Option A)	LB
$W_{STRUC-B}$	=	total structural weight of rectangular cable floor with secondary structure (Option B)	LB
W_{STRUT}	=	weight of struts in rectangular cable floor	LB
W_{SURF}	=	weight of floor surface for rectangular cable floor	LB
W_{ties}	=	weight of tie-downs in circular cable floor	LB
w	=	load per foot run on cable for rectangular cable floors	LB/FT-run
w	=	weight of floor disk material for circular cable floors	LB/CF
w	=	weight of steel	LB/CF
w_{band}	=	weight of band material in secondary structure (Option A) of	

		rectangular cable floor	LB/CF
w_{ca}	=	weight of cable material	LB/CF
w_{ceil}	=	weight of ceiling material in rectangular cable floor	LB/CF
w_{end}	=	weight of end section material in rectangular cable floor	LB/CF
w_{irim}	=	weight of inner rim material in circular cable floor	LB/CF
w_{orim}	=	weight of perimeter rim material in circular cable floor	LB/CF
w_{plate}	=	weight of top/bottom plate material in circular cable floor	LB/CF
w_{plate}	=	distributed load on top/bottom disk plates of circular floors	psf
w_{rca}	=	weight of cable material	LB/CF
w_{sec}	=	weight of secondary structure material in rectangular cable floor	LB/CF
w_{strut}	=	weight of strut wall material	LB/CF
w_{surf}	=	weight floor surface material in rectangular cable floor	LB/CF
w_{ties}	=	weight of tie-down material in circular cable floor	LB/CF
w_{truss}	=	weight of truss material in secondary structure (Option B) of rectangular cable floor	LB/CF
X_{CA}	=	actual length of cable	FT
x_{orim}	=	sag of perimeter rim acting as a cable between radial cables	FT
y	=	spacing between tie-downs in circular cable floors	FT

Appendix A (Single-Story Air-Supported Structures)

A	=	area (general)	SI, SF
C	=	perimeter at ground level	FT
D	=	width of shallow dome at ground level and diameter of full dome or full cylindrical shell	FT
d	=	distance from center to minimum head height	FT
E	=	modulus of elasticity of membrane material	psi
F_s	=	stress in soap bubble film	LB/IN
f_c	=	circumferential membrane tension	LB/IN, psi
f_h	=	membrane tension in air-inflated cushion	LB/IN, psi
f_l	=	longitudinal membrane tension	LB/IN, psi
f_s	=	spherical membrane tension	LB/IN, psi
H	=	height of column	IN
H	=	head height at center of building	FT
h	=	thickness of air-inflated cushion	LB/IN
h	=	head height or minimum standing room height	FT
I	=	moment of inertia of column cross-section	IN^4
L	=	perimeter at distance of ℓ FT from apex	FT
ℓ	=	distance from apex along curved surface	FT

N	=	number of equal width building envelope panels	
P	=	internal pressure	psig
P_i	=	internal air pressure	psig
R	=	radius	IN, FT
R_{cv}	=	radius of curvature of air-supported building	IN
S	=	curved surface area of building envelope	SF
t	=	thickness of membrane (building envelope)	IN
V	=	internal volume of building	CF
W	=	width of building envelope panel at ℓ FT from apex	FT
x	=	distance from perimeter along building diameter	FT

Appendix B (Pneumatic-Within-Pneumatic Dwellings)

A	=	area (general)	SF
a	=	number of cells in air-inflated cellular annulus	
D	=	diameter of dome or column at ground level	FT
D	=	diameter of double-skin air-building at ground level	FT
D	=	external diameter of donut-shaped air-supported building	FT
d	=	internal diameter of donut-shaped air-supported building	FT
d	=	diameter of cells in air-inflated cellular annulus	IN
F_A	=	anchorage force	LB/FT
f_M	=	maximum material stress	LB/IN
H	=	height from ground to roof level	FT
H	=	thickness of air-inflated cushion	FT
K	=	pressure-utilization factor	
L	=	length of building at ground level	FT
L	=	external span of air-inflated arch	FT
n	=	number of floors (including roof)	
P_A	=	external atmospheric pressure	IN W.G.
P_B	=	internal air curtain pressure	IN W.G.
P_i	=	internal air pressure	IN W.G.
P_P	=	internal air pressure	psig
P_W	=	internal air pressure	IN W.G.
S	=	inflated width of air-inflated panel at ground level	FT
T	=	inflated thickness of air-inflated panel at ground level	FT
T	=	air temperature	°F
w	=	width of building or air-inflated cushion at ground level	FT
W	=	vertical (axial) load	LB, LB/SF
W_T	=	total vertical building load	LB

Keyword Index

A

acoustics 125
aeroponic 55,146,148,158
aesthetics 9,194,370
air-conditioning 59
  fan-coil 60
  high-pressure circuit 60
air-cushions 23,132,313,316
aircraft 159,164
air-home 353-370
air-inflated structures 45,159-198
  cellular floor 144-156
  solar collector 142-144
  structure types 127-131,297
    double rigid-flexible cylinders 130-131
    double-skin cellular 128-130,193
    high pressure central core 131,192-194
      prototype 135-138
  rigid membrane structures 159-198
air-jets 47
air-lock 59,69,108-113,118,120,124-125,
  146,366-368
air-supported structures 9,23,47-80
  building types 127-131
    greenhouse 144-158
    multi-cellular multi-enclosure 118-126,130
    single-skin compartmentalized 130
    single-skin rigid membrane 130
    single-skin with cable-network 128-129
  multi-story design equations 40-42,94-97
  multi-story design with cables 92-94,97-105
  multi-story design without cables 91-92
  multi-story prototype 107-126, 135-138
  construction 113-115
    erection 114
Antwerpen 91
anticlastic 246
Architects Collaborative 289
Architectural Science (Department) 27
Arctic 299
Arizona Veterans Memorial Coliseum 18
aromatic imide 54
Ashton 322
atmospheric pressure 91,163,293,319
Australia 107,119,137
Australian Plastics Industry 107
Australian Structural Steel Code 39
auxiliary heat source 139-140
awnings 287
axial fan 122,152

B

Bakema 19
Ballerstedt 165,171,175
balloon 22,107,288
balls 23
basins 61
Batdorf 166,171,172,177,181
Batterman 173,176,186
beam 148-150,160,193,208,295
bends syndrome 52
Berger Brothers 288,291
Bessemer process 14
bicycle pump 47
Bijlaard 172
Bird 24,287
Birdair 24,288,295,301
black body 48
blackwater 61
Blanjean 81
Boom 208
Boston Arts Center 288,295
Bourdon pressure gauge 31
Boys 313
bracing 81-93,243,265-266
bridges
  Brooklyn Bridge 14

Menai Bridge 17
Mersey River Bridge 17
suspension bridges 17
Broek 19
Brooklyn Bridge 14
Brussels World Fair 288
Bubner 299
buckling
  classical stability theory 187
  deformation theories 178,187
  Durchschlag 164,168
  incremental coefficient 198
  incremental theories 178
  Large Deflection Theory 166-170,173
  local 11,12,139,163-164,167,168,182,186, 304
    comparison of design formulas 200-206
  overall 10,20,27-45,163,167,182,213,304
  Plastic Buckling Theory 172-173,178
  post-buckling 178
  slip theories 178
  Small Deflection Theory 165,168,173
  stress waves 164,165,172,186,189,190
  Tangent Modulus Theory 172
Buckminster Fuller 19,21,288,290,291,299, 311,323
Budiansky 178
building regulations 9
building sites 289,290

C

cable-end shaft 215-217
cable-network 12,54-55,59,61,62-66,75-76,
  81,87,88-91,92-94,120,146,152,163,193,
  294,300,310-313
cable-network floors 207-270
cable 62-66,207-270,310-313
  components 217-220
  core 217-220
  diagonal vertical 73,84,88-90,109,116

fill factor 220,250
Filler 218-219
floors 207-270
  horizontal 73,89,108,116
  lay 218-219
  locked coil strand 219-220
  modulus of elasticity 219-220
  slip-joint 246-247
  spiral-strand 219-220
  strand 217-220
  terminals 219
  Warrington 218-219
  weight 220
  wire 217-220
calcium silicate 213
Cal Poly (San Luis Obispo) 11,119,135,353, 364
caissons 52,61
car jack 47
caustic curve 143-144
cellular floor 144-156
centrifugal fan 122,124,295,319-320
change 9
chrome-nickel steel 14
CIB 289
civil disturbance 67
climate control 142
coefficient of correlation 39
coefficient of friction 132
column 9,36
  cluster 305-306
  end-fixing conditions 36
  short columns 40,42,49,57,200-206
  slender columns 10,20,27-45
compressed-air illness 52
compressors
  centrifugal blowers 59, 122,124,295,319-320
  reciprocating 59
  rotary vane 59
concentrating solar collector 12,139,142-144
Concordia University 289
condensation 59
construction 68-75,116-118,122-124,212-216,246-247

jacking mechanism 216
liftslab 68-74,76
planning 113-115
sequence 51,69-71,115,123
service ducts 71
sliding panels 71
slip-joint 246-247
staircase 71
tie-downs 209-241
Cornell Aeronautical Laboratory 24,287,291
cost 75-80,316,355
  electrical 78,157
  external wall 78
  floors above grade 78
  floors below grade 78
  foundations 78
  greenhouse 157
  HVAC 78
  membrane enclosure 78
  plumbing 78
  roofing 78
  superstructure 77
  wall finishes 78
crane 72-75
creep 36,91,321
critical buckling stress 164,165,166,168,178
curtain wall 75
cylindrical shells 10,163-192
  imperfections 168,172-192
  long 172,176-177,200-206
  medium 200-206
  monocoque 173-192
  perfect 168
  probability approach 175-176
  short 170,172,176-177,188,190,200-206
  thick-walled 173
  thin-walled 173-192
  unevenness coefficient 170

D

Da Vinci Rotating Tower 47-49
daylight 145
deconstructability 80
deep pressing 161
deflection 35,85,86,89-90,121,210,222-223
  indicator 35
  Large Deflection Theory 166-170,173
  Small Deflection Theory 165,168,173
Degree Days 365
density 133
design
  architectural planning 365-370
  barrel vault (full profile) 333-352,358
  barrel vault (low profile) 324-332,358
  arch 360
  cellular 360,361,362
  column 359,362
  conglomerate 359
  cushion 23,361
  cylinder 359,362
  disc 363
  dome (full profile) 324-333,357
  dome (low profile) 324-325,333-335,357
  donut-shaped 360
De Saussure 22
developable limit 161
dinghies 23
dishing 209
diurnal temperature change 59
diving 52
Donnell 165,166-170
Dorton Arena 17
drainage 312
Drucker 173
Dubai 47-48
ductility 134,188,190
Dulles International Airport 18
Dunn 165
Du Pont 54,298
Durchschlag 164,168,181,188
DVD 12

E

earthquakes 50-51,68
ecological design 48
electrical 71
electric motor 110
elevator 47,71,210
endothermic 213

energy conservation 9
energy storage 141
Engesser 172
entrainment 140
entrance 366-368
Entwicklungsstätte für den Leichtbau 25,288
environmental control 133
environmental impact 9
Euler formula 29-31,40,305
evacuation 58
evaporative cooling 363-364
example design 60-61
exit 366-368
experience 9
Experimental Research Laboratory 107
explosions 51
EXPO'70 World Fair 25,289,296
extraterrestrial structures 11,20,32,45,49,55,
   62,159,161-162

F

fabrication 322-323
factor of safety 80,137,198,202
fan-coil 60
field hospital 23,289
Filler 218-219
fire protection 51,57-58,83,112,213,247,
   251,268,307,322
Fisher 47-49,177
flash-over 322
floor systems 193, 207-270
  cables 217-220
  circular pneumatic 207-233
    design 221-224
  connectors 217-220
  rectangular fluid-inflated 242-268
    bracing 243,265-266
    design 247-251
    secondary structure 246-247
Flügge 165,173
fluid-supported construction 10,135-140,
   142,197-200, 242-268
folded plates 90-91,161

forces
  horizontal 33,81-83
  wind 51,81-83
Forman School 289
foundations
  cost 78
  footings 111,136
  settlement 50
Fung 172-178,190-192,195-197
Fuji Group Pavilion 25,289,295
FOC 75

G

gasometers 23,32
gauge 136
General Electric 313
geodesic dome 290,291,323
Geodome 291
geometric imperfections 134
Gere 172,215
Gerard 173
glass 145-146,
global warming 49
Goldsmith 19
graywater 61
Greeks 21
greenhouse 11,144-158
greenhouse effect 145,147,353,363
Günschel 313

H

Hallidie 217
Handelman 178
Harris 175-176
Hay 47
harvest 147,157
heat gain 59-61
heat pipe 138-139,140-142
heat sensor 83
heat sink 140
heat store 136,138-139,141
heat tolerance 321
Hochschule für Gestaltung 25,288
housing (portable) 289
humidity 59
hydraulic advantage 22

hydraulic jack 32,47,136,181
hydraulics 21,22
hydrodynamics 140
hydroponics 55,146,148,155,158
hyperbaric environment 45,51,62,69,79,125, 150,197
   nitrogen bubble formation 52
   physiological aspects 52-53
   rate of decompression 52
   threshold pressure-gradient 52-53
hyperbolic paraboloid 18,304

I

IASS 25,289
ICI 298
Igloo tent 292
imperfections 168
inert gas 141
inflatable furniture 23
infra-red 146,363
intumescents 213
IOC 75
Irving 288
Irvin Airchute Company 288
Irwin 25
isothermal 140

J

jacking mechanism 215-217
Jawerth 17
joints 323
Jones 169

K

Kanemitsu 171,175
Kappus 168
Kawaguchi 296-297
Kempner 169
Koch 25,288,295
Kromm 166
Krupp 25,288
Kusmiss 171,190-192,195-197,201,203-205

L

Lanchester (Frederick) 9,23,24,287,293,299, 306,307,308
Lanchester (Henry) 23
Lang 218
Large Deflection Theory 166-170,173
latent heat of vaporization 141
leakage 138,140
Least Squares Method 38-39
Lee 173,178
Legget 166,169
Leonidow 19
Le Ricolais 17,27
Lever 54
life-span 9,79,141,144,146,290,321,353,355
lighting 306-308,313
Lin International 18
Liudkovsky 17
Lo 173-174,177
loads
   dead-loads 50,55,68,82,137,144,148,316, 357
   eccentricity 35-45,85,170,182-185
   live-loads 50,55,57,67-68,137,144,148, 316,357
   load-factor principles 80
   loading conditions 64-65
   snow 295
   wind 24,55,65-66,81-83,91,125,144,194-195,295,308-310
Lorenz 165
lunar base 49,62
Lundquist 165,171
Lundy 288,300-301,304

M

MacCullough 42
maintenance trench 108
Manchester Association of Engineers 23
manometer 181,308
Mars 49
material failure 10
materials
   aluminum 197
   canvas 24
   chrome-nickel steel 14
   concrete 75,77-80,82,86,90

shell 159
consumption 9
imperfections 40
plastics 14,24,51,53-54,63,320
  aromatic imide 54
  fiberglass 146,323
  fillers 53
  gelatin 162
  heat-sealer 108,147,151-153
  hypalon 297
  neoprene 292
  nylon 53,146,292,300,320,322
  pigments 53
  plasticizers 53
  polycarbonate 146
  polyester 146,151,356
  polystyrene 364
  polythene 356
  PVA 297
  PVC 54,108,120,146,151,163,297,298, 320,322,356
  PVF 54,298
  terylene 320,322
  thermoplastic 53-54,321
  thermosetting 53-54,321
reeds 13
steel 14,163,197,217,245
  annealing 218
  EEIP 217
  EEP 217
  IPS 217
  Plow steel 217
  stainless 217,245
stone 13
strength 13,53-54,108,321
tin plate 179-182
wood fibers 13
mean (average) 185
mechanical systems 71
mechanical economy 21
median surface 165
mega-structures 47,299,310,313
membrane 320-322
  abrasion 112
  coatings 54
  enclosure 51,78,86,163
  fire resistance 54-55
  flexible 47-80,107-126,159,163,193
  reflecting surface 59-61,142-143
  rigid 136,159-196
  strength 53-54,60
  tear resistance 53
  thermal insulation 59-61
  tubes 30-45,49
  weatherability 54
  weight 72
Membrane Theory 159
metatarsal bone 21
mica 54
Michielsen 169
Mies van der Rohe 50-51
mil 54,120,356
Miles 25,288
Miller 142
minimal structure 21
minimum surface 32-33,308,313-314
minimum weight 9,20,79-80
missiles 159,164
modulus of elasticity 29,34,43,55,56,63,65, 86-87,91,116,146,165,166,171,176,180, 196,197,219-220
Montero 119,353-370
Montevideo 91
Montgolfier 22
Moon 49,62
Murata 296-297

N

National Science Foundation 120
Neff 288
Newell 217
Newmark 165,171
New York Home Exhibition 288
Nijny-Novgorod Industrial Fair 17
nitrogen bubble formation 52
Nix 54
noise level 59
Nojima 171,175
Nowicki 17

O

occupancy 134
Onat 173
optimum angle 64-65,89
Otto 17,19,21,25,288,299,310,313
oxygen-poisoning 52

P

Pan American Airways 288
parabolic 143-144
parachutes 229
partial pressures law 52
patent 142
Pascal's Law 22
passive solar
  roof ponds 47-48
  SkyTherm, 47-48
  solar ponds 47-48
perimeter rim 209,222-223
physiological impact 45,51,52-53,61,190, 195
piles 133
Plateau's problem 33
plastics 14,24,51,67,90,108,139,143,146
plates 210-212,222-223,227
plumbing 71
pneumatics 21
  access (exit) 302
  air leakage 110-111,154
  airlock 302,308,320
  anchorage 310,315,316-319,357-363
    auger anchor 318
    pavement anchor 319
    screw anchor 318
    self-weight anchor 317
    split anchor 319
  ancillary plant 319-320
  balloons 22,107
  Bourdon pressure gauge 31
  buildings 23
    prototype 107-126, 135-138
  columns (slender) 28-45
  cushion 23,361
  design 257-258, 265-293
    arch 360
    architectural planning 365-370
    barrel vault (full profile) 335-336,345-351,358
    barrel vault (low profile) 335-345,358
    cellular 360,361,3362
    column 359,362
    conglomerate 359
    cushion 23,361
    cylinder 359,362
    disc 363
    dome (full profile) 324-325,333-335,357
    dome (low profile) 324-333,357
    donut-shaped 360
  double-skin 290,295-296,300,304
  floor system 191,207-270
  furniture 368-370
  gasometers 23,32
  hydraulic jack 32
  inflatable furniture 23
  internal pressure 55,59,81,90,142-43,173-192,292
  loading conditions 64-65
  membrane tubes 30-45
  nylon scrim base 67
  physiological impact 45, 51,52-53,61,90
  polyethylene 146,152
  polyurethane 67,121
  pressure controls 58-59,181,215-217
  pressure release valve 111
  pressure valve 111,113,216-217
  pressure-utilization 34-45,55-57,127,134, 196,210
  pressure vessels 23,32
  pressurization equipment 110,122,152
  pressurization medium 127,131-133,136, 138-139
  proof-of-concept 75
  prototype 75,107-126,135-138,
  roof system 233-242
  rubber dinghies 23
  safety-valve 308
  sealing system 24
  single-skin 291,296
  tear-resistance 67
  tire 107
  tubular 292-293,296-298,301,304-306
pneumatic-within-pneumatic 353-370

Pohl 208
Poisson's Ratio 34,165,176-177
Prescott 177
press-stud fastener 152-155
pressure vessels 23,32
pressurization medium 127,131-133,138-
   139,198
pressurized slender columns 28-45
pressure-utilization 34-45, 55-57,148,151,
   298
probability approach 175-176

Q

R

Radome 287,290,299
rate of decompression 52
Rawlings 161
recycling 80
Redshaw 166
reeds (strength) 13
rentability 134
rheostat 110
Rhys 54
right cylinder 64
rigid membrane 127-158
rim 209,222-223
Robertson 165
rocket fuselage 32,159,164
Roebling (John) 14,217
Roebling (Washington) 14
Roland 290
Romans 21
roof ponds 47-48
roof structures 233-242
  pneumatic 233-242
    design 233-238
Roots blower 124
rotating floors 47-49
rubber dinghies 22

S

Saarinen 18,
safety 53,66-68,80,86,113,137,197,212-216,301,308
sag 199-205
sail 22
Sampling Theory of Regression 39
Sanchez 208
sanitary fittings 61-62
Sawyer-Tower 298
Schjedahl 25,288,310
Schwarzer 19
Seal 217
sealed environment 9,59
sealing system 24
Sechler 172-178,190-192,195-197
self-weight 210-211,267-269
services (building) 51,58-59,86
  air-lock 59,69,108-113,118,120,124-125,
    145,150-151
  basins 61
  electrical 71
  elevators 71,86,90,193
  fire protection 57-58
  mechanical system 71,193,197
  plumbing 71
  sanitary fittings 61-62
  service ducts 71,82,86,90
  sewerage system 62
  showers 61
  storage tanks 61-62
  waste disposal 62,71
  water closets 61
  water seal 61
  water supply, 61-62
Severud 301
sewage 51,62
shading devices 194
Shanley 173
shear walls 82,90-91
Shookov 17
showers 61
silicon resin 143
Similar Triangles method 35
skylight 307
SkyTherm 47-48
slenderness ratio 10,29,35-45,55-57,127,
   133-135,148,151,176,182,187,190,200-
   206,214-215,298,305

sliding panels 57-58,67,71
Small Deflection Theory 164,165,173-174
Smith 217
soap bubbles 313-315
solar energy 135-140
solar panels 48,135,138,140
solar ponds 47-48
Southwell 165
space-net 50
span 199-205
specific heat 133
sports arenas 287,299
stability failure 10
staircase 71
Standard Deviation 185
steel 217
  annealing 218
  EEIP 217
  EEP 217
  IPS 217
  Plow steel 217
  stainless 217,245
Stein 184
Stevens 24,287
stiffeners 193-194
Stone 217
stone (strength) 13
storage tanks 61-62
strain bridge 181
strain gauges 178-182
stress
  axial coefficient 167
  bending 160,194,197
  circumferential 53-54,63,87,120,132,163,182,189,195-197,198,245,303
  coefficient (k_x) 166-167,170-172,176-177
  coefficient (Z) 166-167,171-172,176-177
  contours 182-184
  critical 164,165,166,168-171,173,175,176,186,194-197,200-206
    comparison 200-206
  hoop stress 53-54,63,87,120,132,163,182,189,195-197,198,245,303
  loading conditions 64-65
  longitudinal 87,182,189,303
  plastic hinge 190
  radial 189
  shear 139
  spherical 303,316
  torsion 176,194,197
  waves 164,165,172,186,189,190
  zero stress condition 35-36,40-41,85,184
Stromeyer 25,288
structural economy 9
structural efficiency 9,127
structural testing 156
structural morphology 293-295
structures
  air-cushions 23
  air-inflated 45,161,207-270
  air-supported 23,47-80
  balloons 22,107
  balls 23
  compression 13,14,293
  cross linking 162
  economy, 9
  efficiency 9
  extraterrestrial 11,20,32,45,161-162
  factor of safety 80,137
  field hospital 23
  gasometers 23,32
  honeycomb 161-162
  inflatable furniture 23
  mechanical economy 21,199
  mega-structures 47,299,311,313
  metatarsal bone 21
  minimal structure 21
  minimum weight 9,20
  plasticizer boil-off 162
  plates 161,172,222-223
  pressure vessels 23,32,79-80
  proof-of-concept 75
  prototype 75, 107-126,135-138
  reeds 13
  reinforced concrete 77-80,82,86,90,198
  rocket fuselage 32
  rubber dinghies 23

self-forming 161
self-rigidizing 161-162
shell (concrete) 293
space frame 301
steel 14,77-80,82,86,139,198
stone 13
tires 23
vapor catalysis 162
wood fibers 13
yield metallic foil 162
struts 214,242-268
submarine 159
sunshading devices 59-61
suspended floors 18,27,34,50,68,75-76,127,
   136,138,192-196,210
   4D Tower Garage 19
   Beach Hotel 19
   BMW Tower 19
   B.P. Petrol Headquarters 91
   Buenos Aires office building 19
   clearance 112
   El Pilar Apartment Building 91
   Moscow Lenin Library 19
   Rotterdam Observation Tower 19
surface structure 192
surface tension 141
suspension structures 294,310
   Arizona Veterans Memorial Coliseum 18
   Bary Boilerworks 17
   Brooklyn Bridge 14
   Dorton Arena 17
   Dulles International Airport 18
   hyperbolic paraboloid cable-network 18
   Menai Bridge 17
   Mersey River Bridge 17
   Raleigh Arena 17
   sail 22
   suspended floors 18,91
   turnbuckles 69-70
sustainable architecture 48
swimming pools 287
Sydney 107,119,137
synclastic 353

T
tarpaulins 287
Tedlar 139
Telford 17
Teflon 54
tennis courts 287
tension ring 210-241
tents 287
terrorism 67
testing 178-187
Texair 25,288
thermal conductivity 141
thermal expansion 138
thermal insulation 59-61,124,127,193,292,
   296,306-308,353,363-365
threshold pressure-gradient 52-53
tie-downs 209-241
Timoshenko 42,165,172,215
tires 23,133
torsion 176
Trostel 25,288
Tsai-Chen 177
Tsien 165,168-170,173,177
turnbuckles 69-70,139

U
U-value 354,364-365
ultra violet radiation 48,146,299,321
United Arab Emirates 47-48
University of Delft 289
University of New South Wales 11,27,107
University of Pennsylvania 27
University of Sydney 27,39
U.S. Air Force 24,287
U.S. Atomic Energy Commission 288,300, 304
U.S. Rubber 25,288,298
U-tube manometer 34,113,124

V
vacuum cleaner 152
valve 111,113,368
Van Aardt 54
Van der Neut 193
vapor 140

vehicle suspension system 47
ventilation 306-308
vertical farming 55,158
Von Karman 165,168-170,173

W

Wagner 165,171,175
Wan 167-170
warehouses 287,299
Warner 178
Warrington 218-219
Washington University 25,288
waste disposal 62,71
water closets 61
Water Gauge 110,112,114,120,122,125,143,
 148,151-152,294,307
water seal 61
water supply, 61-62
WCOSE-76 231
weatherability 54,193,321
Weidlinger 288,295
welding 136
Wellington Sears 298
West Coast Lumberman's Association 38
wick 140-141
Williams 19
Wilson 165,171
wind loads 24,50,65-66,81-83,91,125,144
   drag force 81-82
   flutter 293,295,303-304,310,315,323
   lift force 81-83
wind tunnel tests 291
wind turbines 48
wire rope 217-220
wood fibers (strength) 13
World War I 14
World War II 14,24,307

X

Y

Yale University 25,288
Yochimura 169

Z

zero-stress condition 294
zero-stress criterion 35-36,40-41,85,184

www.ingramcontent.com/pod-product-compliance
Lightning Source LLC
Chambersburg PA
CBHW081214170426
43198CB00017B/2608